HENRY FONDA
HE DID IT HIS WAY

VOLUME ONE OF A TWO-PART BIOGRAPHY

This is Part One of a Two-Part biography about one of the most respected and revered actors of the 20th Century.

Henry Fonda was an American Original,
voted the sixth most renowned actor in the history of Hollywood
by the American Film Institute.

Released in September of 2022, this book is available
through Amazon.com and other booksellers worldwide.

Volume Two gets released in 2023

Henry

Fonda

WHAT IS BLOOD MOON PRODUCTIONS?

"Blood Moon, in case you don't know, is a small publishing house on Staten Island that cranks out Hollywood gossip books, about two or three a year, usually of five-, six-, or 700-page length, chocked with stories and pictures about people who used to consume the imaginations of the American public, back when we actually had a public imagination. That is, when people were really interested in each other, rather than in Apple 'devices.' In other words, back when we had vices, not devices."

—The Huffington Post

HENRY FONDA
HE DID IT HIS WAY

VOLUME ONE (1905-1960)
OF A TWO-PART BIOGRAPHY BY
DARWIN PORTER & DANFORTH PRINCE

HENRY FONDA
HE DID IT HIS WAY

VOLUME ONE (1905-1960)
OF A TWO-PART BIOGRAPHY

Darwin Porter and Danforth Prince

www.BloodMoonProductions.com

ISBN 978-936003-84-6

Manufactured in the USA
Covers and Book Design by Danforth Prince

Thanks to Mike Sevick, Assistant Professor of Art at the University of Michigan, Flint,
for permission to use a replica of his celebrated painting,
The Dust Storm, as a background for this book's front cover

This book is distributed worldwide through
Ingram, Amazon.com, and internet vendors everywhere.

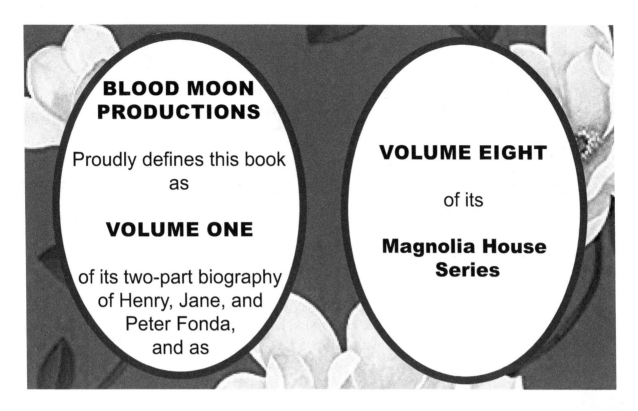

BLOOD MOON PRODUCTIONS

Proudly defines this book as

VOLUME ONE

of its two-part biography of Henry, Jane, and Peter Fonda, and as

VOLUME EIGHT

of its

Magnolia House Series

CONTENTS

CHAPTER ONE   PAGE 1
    FOUNDATIONS OF THE FONDAS
    Henry, a Son of Nebraska, Embarks on a Brutalizing Road
    to Stardom; Brouhahas with the Bourgeoisie; Summer Stock
    with the Sea Monsters of Cape Cod

CHAPTER TWO   PAGE 17
    SURVIVING MARGARET SULLAVAN & THE GREAT DEPRESSION
    Henry Gets Dramatic, Onstage and off, sometimes with players who became
    independently famous in their own right. The Twentieth Century Roars

CHAPTER THREE   PAGE 35
    YOUNG HENRY FACES THE PERILS AND DEBAUCHERIES
    OF THE GREAT WHITE WAY and THE PEOPLE WHO LABOR WITHIN

CHAPTER FOUR   PAGE 51
    REACTING TO HOLLYWOOD—Henry becomes a working movie star

CHAPTER FIVE   PAGE 71
      LOVE, POLITICS, & SHOW BIZ
      Between "Play Dates" with the Natives of La-La Land,
      Henry Meets, Seduces, and Marries FRANCES BROKAW SEYMOUR,
      and celebrates more or less "parallel career success" with JAMES STEWART

CHAPTER SIX   PAGE 89
      HOW, ONCE UPON A TIME IN HOLLYWOOD, HENRY FONDA
      DID IT HIS WAY WITH: Frances Seymour Brokaw, Bette Davis,
      Margaret Sullavan, Joan Bennett, and at least a dozen other pre-eminent
      "Supernovas and Starlettes" of the late 1930s and early 40s.

CHAPTER SEVEN   PAGE 111
      STARTING A DYSFUNCTIONAL FAMILY; BECOMING A
      MOVIE STAR; and Coping with Bette Davis (Jezebel!), Loretta Young
      Dorothy Lamour, "Bloody Babs" Stanwyck, half-truths about
      Abraham Lincoln, and a film with Dolores Del Rio about a haunted
      refugee priest.

CHAPTER EIGHT   PAGE 131
      WAR IN EUROPE, THE GRAPES OF WRATH, a competitive
      "Bromance" with James Stewart, a Flirtation with David Selznick
      about a possible role in Gone With the Wind, and Henry's escape from a
      "Slave Contract" with "Fuck-it-All" (Henry's words) Darryl Zanuck.

CHAPTER NINE   PAGE 155
      MORE ABOUT ZANUCK, LILLIAN ("The Queen of Broadway') RUSSELL,
      LOVING LUCY ("Lucille Ball was the love of my father's life," said his daughter
      Jane), TALES OF MANHATTAN, and that grim but memorable
      classic, THE OX-BOW INCIDENT

CHAPTER TEN   PAGE 183
      A MATURE & DOMESTICATED FATHER OF THREE JOINS THE NAVY
      How Henry Fonda, a low-ranking "Quartermaster, Third Grade"
      Got Drenched in the Blood Baths of the South Pacific, and the obstacles
      he faced, after the war, back in Hollywood.

CHAPTER ELEVEN   PAGE 205
      ONSTAGE WITH MR. ROBERTS, BATTLING COCHISE & THE
      INDIANS WITH JOHN FORD, and the stupid, pointless suicide of Frances
      Seymour Fonda. Daisy Kenyon with volatile Joan Crawford. Introducing Susan
      Blanchard, "Almost Losing" Peter Fonda after a prep school gunshot accident, and
      Stage and Film Offers that didn't always work.

CHAPTER TWELVE PAGE 227
HENRY RETURNS TO BROADWAY. More about Joan Crawford,
Rita Hayworth, John Wayne, Gary Cooper, Dick Powell, June Allyson,
and a sometimes unsavoury Charles Laughton, "Tedium at Sea"
(a Cinematic adaptation of Mr. Roberts, and Dino De Laurentiis'
big-budget blockbuster rendering of Leo Tolstoy's WAR AND PEACE

CHAPTER THIRTEEN PAGE 251
HOLLYWOOD ON THE TIBER: THE FONDAS INVADE ROME
Henry's Divorce from Susan Blanchard and his marriage to the
"socially voracious vampire," Afdera Franchetti, and How Things
Went with Anthony ("Psycho") Perkins when father Henry and daughter
Jane each co-starred with him in separate movies.

CHAPTER FOURTEEN PAGE 269
PLAYTIME ON THE FRENCH RIVIERA, and MORE ABOUT
AFDERA FRANCHETTI. Susan Strasberg, gilded, well-connected *wunderkind* of
Method acting, appears with Henry in *Stage Struck*. Henry's co-starring gig with Anne
Bancroft on Broadway launches her as a superstar. Henry picks some bad scripts as
Afdera is suspected of "inaugural intimacies" with JFK.

CHAPTER FIFTEEN PAGE 289
JANE: Sleeping around Paris with the New Wave; Warren Beatty, and
Anthony Perkins. Arguments with Shelley Winters and Andreas Voutsinas,
and what happened when she inherited a chunk of her late mother's estate.

CHAPTER SIXTEEN PAGE 311
HENRY DIVORCES HIS BARONESS and marries the woman of his
dreams, then forcefully portrays Olivia de Havilland's cancer-ridden husband, onstage.
WHO's AFRAID OF VIRGINIA WOOLF? rocks movie audiences nationwide,
and Jane's bordello flick, *WALK ON THE WILD SIDE,* raises paternal (and
censorship) concerns.

AUTHORS' BIOS PAGE 327

BLOOD
MOON
Productions, Ltd.

PREVIOUS WORKS BY DARWIN PORTER
PRODUCED IN COLLABORATION WITH BLOOD MOON

BIOGRAPHIES FROM BLOOD MOON'S
MAGNOLIA HOUSE SERIES

Lucille Ball & Desi Arnaz: They Weren't Lucy & Ricky Ricardo
(Volume One—1911-1960) of a Two-Part Biography

The Sad & Tragic Ending of Lucille Ball
(Volume Two-1961-1989) of a Two-Part Biography

Marilyn: Don't Even Dream About Tomorrow
(a 2021 revised version of the best-selling
Marilyn at Rainbow's End: Sex, Lies, Murder, &
the Great Cover-Up (2012)

The Seductive Sapphic Exploits of Mercedes de Acosta
Hollywood's Greatest Lover

Jacqueline Kennedy Onassis, Her Tumultuous Life & Her Love Affairs

Judy Garland & Liza Minnelli, Too Many Damn Rainbows

Historic Magnolia House: Celebrity & The Ironies of Fame

Glamour, Glitz, & Gossip at Historic Magnolia House

***

BIOGRAPHIES FROM BLOOD MOON
NOT ASSOCIATED WITH ITS MAGNOLIA HOUSE SERIES

Burt Reynolds, Put the Pedal to the Metal

Kirk Douglas, More Is Never Enough

Playboy's Hugh Hefner, Empire of Skin

Carrie Fisher & Debbie Reynolds,
Princess Leia & Unsinkable Tammy in Hell

Rock Hudson Erotic Fire

Lana Turner, Hearts & Diamonds Take All

Donald Trump, The Man Who Would Be King

James Dean, Tomorrow Never Comes

Bill and Hillary, So This Is That Thing Called Love

Peter O'Toole, Hellraiser, Sexual Outlaw, Irish Rebel

Love Triangle, Ronald Reagan, Jane Wyman, & Nancy Davis

Pink Triangle, The Feuds and Private Lives of Tennessee Williams, Gore Vidal,
Truman Capote, and Famous Members of their Entourages.

Those Glamorous Gabors, Bombshells from Budapest

Inside Linda Lovelace's Deep Throat,
Degradation, Porno Chic, and the Rise of Feminism

Elizabeth Taylor, There is Nothing Like a Dame

J. Edgar Hoover and Clyde Tolson
Investigating the Sexual Secrets of America's Most Famous Men and Women

Frank Sinatra, The Boudoir Singer. All the Gossip Unfit to Print

The Kennedys, All the Gossip Unfit to Print

The Secret Life of Humphrey Bogart (2003), and
Humphrey Bogart, The Making of a Legend (2010)

Howard Hughes, Hell's Angel

Steve McQueen, King of Cool, Tales of a Lurid Life

Paul Newman, The Man Behind the Baby Blues

Merv Griffin, A Life in the Closet

Brando Unzipped

Katharine the Great, Hepburn, Secrets of a Lifetime Revealed

Jacko, His Rise and Fall, The Social and Sexual History of Michael Jackson

Damn You, Scarlett O'Hara,
The Private Lives of Vivien Leigh and Laurence Olivier

FILM CRITICISM
Blood Moon's 2005 Guide to the Glitter Awards
Blood Moon's 2006 Guide to Film
Blood Moon's 2007 Guide to Film, and
50 Years of Queer Cinema, 500 of the Best GLBTQ Films Ever Made

NON-FICTION
Hollywood Babylon, It's Back! and Hollywood Babylon Strikes Again!

NOVELS

Blood Moon,
Hollywood's Silent Closet,
Rhinestone Country,
Razzle Dazzle
Midnight in Savannah

OTHER PUBLICATIONS BY DARWIN PORTER
NOT DIRECTLY ASSOCIATED WITH BLOOD MOON

NOVELS

The Delinquent Heart
The Taste of Steak Tartare
Butterflies in Heat
Marika (a roman à clef based on the life of Marlene Dietrich)
Venus (a roman à clef based on the life of Anaïs Nin)
Sister Rose

TRAVEL GUIDES

Many Editions and Many Variations of The Frommer Guides,
The American Express Guides, and/or TWA Guides, et alia to:

Andalusia, Andorra, Anguilla, Aruba, Atlanta, Austria, the Azores, The Bahamas, Barbados, the Bavarian Alps, Berlin, Bermuda, Bonaire and Curaçao, Boston, the British Virgin Islands, Budapest, Bulgaria, California, the Canary Islands, the Caribbean and its "Ports of Call," the Cayman Islands, Ceuta, the Channel Islands (UK), Charleston (SC), Corsica, Costa del Sol (Spain), Denmark, Dominica, the Dominican Republic, Edinburgh, England, Estonia, Europe, "Europe by Rail," the Faroe Islands, Finland, Florence, France, Frankfurt, the French Riviera, Geneva, Georgia (USA), Germany, Gibraltar, Glasgow, Granada (Spain), Great Britain, Greenland, Grenada (West Indies), Haiti, Hungary, Iceland, Ireland, Isle of Man, Italy, Jamaica, Key West & the Florida Keys, Las Vegas, Liechtenstein, Lisbon, London, Los Angeles, Madrid, Maine, Malta, Martinique & Guadeloupe, Massachusetts, Melilla, Morocco, Munich, New England, New Orleans, North Carolina, Norway, Paris, Poland, Portugal, Provence, Puerto Rico, Romania, Rome, Salzburg, San Diego, San Francisco, San Marino, Sardinia, Savannah, Scandinavia, Scotland, Seville, the Shetland Islands, Sicily, St. Martin & Sint Maarten, St. Vincent & the Grenadines, South Carolina, Spain, St. Kitts & Nevis, Sweden, Switzerland, the Turks & Caicos, the U.S.A., the U.S. Virgin Islands, Venice, Vienna and the Danube, Wales, and Zurich.

BIOGRAPHIES

From Diaghilev to Balanchine, The Saga of Ballerina Tamara Geva

Greta Keller, Germany's Other Lili Marlene

Sophie Tucker, The Last of the Red Hot Mamas

Anne Bancroft, Where Have You Gone, Mrs. Robinson?
(co-authored with Stanley Mills Haggart)

Veronica Lake, The Peek-a-Boo Girl

Running Wild in Babylon, Confessions of a Hollywood Press Agent

HISTORIES

Thurlow Weed, Whig Kingpin

Chester A. Arthur, Gilded Age Coxcomb in the White House

Discover Old America, What's Left of It

This Book Is Dedicated to the unsung heroes of the American Century, the unlucky, hardworking men and women, some of them pawns of fate, as Henry Fonda portrayed so poignantly in so many of his films.

Biographies
from Blood Moon Productions

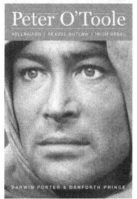

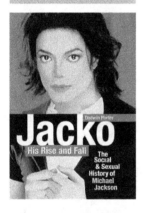

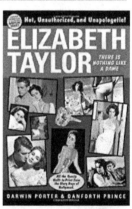

More Biographies
from Blood Moon Productions

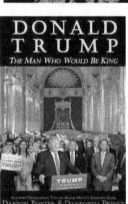

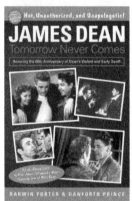

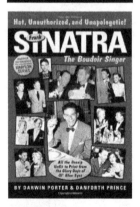

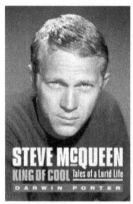

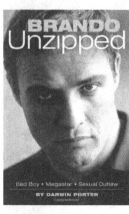

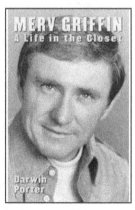

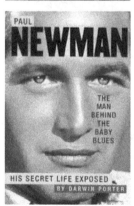

New, Hot, and Next from Blood Moon Productions:

More, MUCH more, about the Fabulous Fondas as they navigated their
ways, beginning in 1961, through New York, Europe, and Hollywood

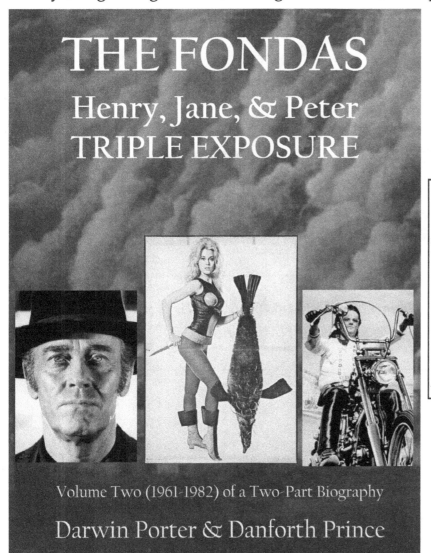

Throughout his forty-five year career, Henry Fonda—a stable, reassuring archetype of the American male—never gave a bad performance. Personal dramas included five wives (two of whom committed suicide) and affairs which starred such mega-divas as Lucille Ball, Joan Crawford, and Bette Davis.

Volume Two of Blood Moon's "FONDA" project turns kleig lights on three emotionally intertwined stars, two of them Oscar winners: The lanky and boyish American hero, **Henry**; his beautiful daughter **Jane**, a political activist and superstar beloved by millions despite her formerly poisonous reputation as "Hanoi Jane;" and the "eternal rebel," **Peter**, a preppy looking thrill-seeker indelibly intertwined with the "bad boy on a bike" narrative of the 60s.

Unlike any other published, this book reflects the private agonies of a father, daughter, and son engulfed by the divisions of their respective generations and the ironies of the American Experience.

BLOOD MOON
Productions, Ltd.

*Challenging the Status Quo's Beliefs
about Classic Hollywood*

FOUNDATIONS OF THE FONDAS

FROM GENOA DURING THE ITALIAN RENAISSANCE;
THEN THROUGH THE PORT OF NIEUW AMSTERDAM
TO THE INDIAN WARS; FEROCIOUS BLIZZARDS
AND DROUGHTS OF THE MIDWESTERN PLAINS; THE FONDAS EMERGE
AS THE QUINTESSENCE OF THE AMERICAN NATION

HENRY, A SON OF NEBRASKA
EMBARKS ON A TRAUMATIC, BRUTALIZING ROAD TO STARDOM

"My first movie role was in child porn."

—Henry Fonda

HIS CHILDHOOD SIGHTING OF HALEY'S COMET:
WAS IT A FAVORABLE OMEN FOR HENRY?

THE ICEMAN COMETH
AS A PAINFULLY SHY, "LOST" TEENAGER MIRED IN
LOW SELF-ESTEEM AND THANKLESS JOBS,
HENRY IS UNEXPECTEDLY ENCOURAGED BY A FLIRTATIOUS
LOCAL DUENNA OF THE THEATER, **DODIE**
(AKA MARLON BRANDO'S MOTHER)
TO GET OUT OF TOWN

BROUHAHAS WITH THE BOURGEOISIE
AMBITIOUS BUT DESTITUTE, HENRY IS UNEXPECTEDLY DESIGNATED AS THE
SALARIED "CHAPERONE" OF THE NAUGHTY HEIR TO A LOCAL FORTUNE

HENRY MAKES OUT IN THE BACK SEAT OF HIS FRIEND'S PACKARD
WITH AN OUT-OF-CONTROL TEENAGED VIXEN, **BETTE DAVIS**

OMENS OF HISTORICAL DRAMAS TO COME
HENRY TOURS THE MIDDLE WEST PORTRAYING
THE PERSONAL ASSISTANT OF A FREQUENTLY INTOXICATED
ABRAHAM LINCOLN

STRUTTING HIS STUFF WITH MARGARET SULLAVAN
HIS VERY SMALL STAGE ROLE CALLED FOR HIM TO RECEIVE FROM HER, EVERY NIGHT,
AT EVERY PERFORMANCE, A FULL-FRONTAL ASSAULT TO HIS FACE.

WAS IT S&M? WAS IT LOVE?

SUMMER STOCK WITH THE
SEA MONSTERS OF CAPE CODE

UNDERNOURISHED AND CHRONICALLY UNDERPAID, HENRY STOICALLY PAINTS SCENERY, INVENTORIES STAGE PROPS, AND SPONGES ACTING TIPS FROM STALWARTS FAMOUS AS "NAUGHTY MARIETTA," AND "AUNT PITTYPAT."

AN "ANGELIC HEIR" TO THE LEATHERBEE FORTUNE INTRODUCES HENRY TO AN EXTROVERTED HOMOSEXUAL, AMERICA'S FUTURE "MOST FAMOUS" BROADWAY PRODUCER. THEY BECOME ROOMMATES

"Henry Fonda showed up so many times at the offices of producers and casting agents that he became the best-known unknown actor in Manhattan."

—Joshua Logan

Following the Japanese attack on Pearl Harbor on December 7, 1941, thousands of young men from Nebraska either volunteered or were drafted into America's rapidly growing fighting forces. One doctor told the press, "These men were the toughest in America, survivors of all those scalding summers and harsh winters in their home state."

Once, where buffalo roamed across the Great Plains, the Nebraska Territory had been occupied by the Sioux, Ioway, Otne, and Pawnee semi-nomadic Native American tribes. Their populations were decimated in the 19th Century, either slaughtered by white settlers or else as victims of smallpox, cholera, and tuberculosis.

During the California Gold Rush, between 1841 and 1866, an estimated 350,000 people passed through the Nebraska Territory. Some 30,000 of them died *en route,*, their corpses often abandoned by the side of the trails.

Hundreds of squatters and claim jumpers remained behind to establish the settlement of Omaha in 1854. Known as "the vortex of vice" or "the crossroads of corruption," the town soon became a densely populated outpost of the Wild West. All kinds of bordellos popped up, usually at their busiest on Saturday nights when cowpokes were willing to shell out two dollars to get laid. Lottie McKee, a prostitute imported from Kansas City, boasted that she could take on twenty-five men a night.

Stern, and ravaged by depression, bad crops, and brutal weather, the residents of Nebraska were tough survivors of conflicts from other places.

These **homesteaders**, photographed in the early 1890s, convey the no-nonsense frugality of the Fonda forebears. Many of their neighbors became so discouraged that they sold or gave up their property and left the state.

Sometimes locals were chased by packs of ravenous, sometimes rabid wild dogs. Otherwise, they endured dust storms in summer. During the rainy seasons, the main streets were clogged with mud and manure, and in winter, the landscapes were frigid.

It was into this stern and forbidding landscape that the patriarch of a family of famous 20th-Century actors was born. His offspring would eventually include his daughter Jane, his son, Peter; his granddaughter Bridget Fonda, and his grandson Troy Garity.

In 1999, the American Film Institute designated Henry Fonda as the "Sixth Greatest Male Star of All Time."

Nebraska would also become the home of two other great actors, Montgomery Clift (born in 1920) and Marlon Brando Jr. (born in 1924). Ironically, Brando's mother, Dodie, an acting coach, would later play an essential role in launching Henry Fonda's career.

The Fondas had originated in the Republic of Genoa in the early 15th Century. One of their Renaissance-era ancestors had been the Marquis de Fonda. During Europe's Wars of Religion, their family landed on the side of the Protestant Reformation, conflicts from which contributed to their flight north to the Protestant-dominated Netherlands.

There, the Fondas lived and flourished for 150 years, intermarrying with the sons and daughters of Dutch burghers.

Eventually, Henry Fonda's ancestors decided to emigrate, via sailing ship, to the burgeoning Port of Nieuw Amsterdam in the New World, settling there before Pieter Stuyvesant capitulated Manhattan to the British.

Packing their possessions into canoes, the Fondas navigated their way up the Hudson River to the Indian village of Caughnawaga. In time, after butchering or chasing away members of the native Iroquois and Mohawk tribes, they renamed their settlement "Fonda."

The village of Fonda, New York (which has a population today of some 800 people) was named for one of Henry Fonda's ancestors, Douw Fonda. In 1780, Douw was killed and scalped by the warlike Mohawks.

During the American Revolution, the Fondas were allied with the British.

The grandfather of Henry Fonda, Ten Eyuck Hilton Fonda, born in 1838, fought with the Union Army during America's Civil War. After the Battle of Gettysburg, General Ulysses S. Grant made him a lieutenant.

After the war, he returned for a while to his namesake settlement in New York State, but when the Burlington & Missouri River Railroad linked Chicago to Omaha, he took off, with his wife, for Nebraska. There, he took a telegraph operator's job in Omaha.

Every night, as he walked home, he encountered squaws with papooses begging for money. Carriages filled with local prostitutes passed by *en route* to any of Omaha's sixty bordellos.

It was here that he and his frontier wife gave birth to their fourth child, William Brace Fonda, born in 1879.

In 1903, after the boy matured, he met and married a local girl, Herberta Lamphear Jaynes. The young married couple left Omaha and settled into a six-room clapboard house at Grand Island, 150 miles to the southwest of Omaha.

It was here, on May 16, 1905, that their first born, Henry Jaynes Fonda, later to become a famous actor, entered the world. "He arrived so early in the morning, the roosters hadn't crowed," the happy father claimed.

At the time, Grand Island was known as the home of Jake Eaton, the champion gum chewer of the world. Amazingly, he could fit into his mouth and chew 300 sticks of gum at the same time.

The birth year of the new boy was also the birth year of the Nickelodeon which, of course, led to the development of the film industry, a venue that would forever change young Henry's life.

Known to French traders as *La Grande Isle*, the settlement where Henry was born dated from 1857. Some three dozen German settlers formed a little village at the intersection of the Wood and Platte Rivers. Grand Island was the last stopover where migrants could obtain tools, supplies, and staples

FONDA, NY, site of scalpings, blood-lettings, and the territorial expensions of the British during the French and Indian Wars (1754-1763).

Henry's ancestral stamping grounds evoke his performance with Claudette Colbert in *Drums Along the Mohawk* (1939).

Mind-bendingly rural to many residents of the East Coast, **the Nebraska Territory**, depicted here on a map from 1854, was a region that many prospectors on their way to California traversed across as quickly as they could.

Some of the hardiest of them, including the Fondas, remained to nurture the "Heartland of America" image that it inexorably retains today.

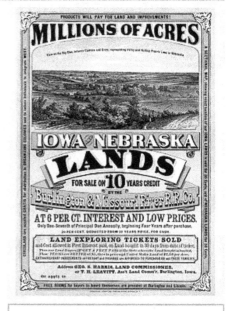

Westward Ho! Land, sometimes cheap but frequently contested, was the only commodity in plentiful supply. Fonda, in some of his movies, personified the danger, hardship, and drama of those early days of "Home on the Range."

before crossing the foreboding plains. Ferocious blizzards and blood-soaked Indian wars became benchmarks in their early struggles.

When Henry was six months old, his father and mother re-located to Dundee, Nebraska, a staid community on the outskirts of "the vile city of Omaha," a cattle town known for its meat-packing industry and slaughterhouses.

Although Henry grew up shy and retiring like his father, his mother was extroverted, singing and frequently playing the piano. "My mother was angelic," Hank, as he was nicknamed, claimed. "My father was stern but loving, although he later opposed my becoming an actor. He predicted, 'No good will come from that reckless decision.'"

It was at Dundee that the Fonda family was enlarged by the birth of two sisters, Harriet, born in 1907, and Herberta (named after her mother) in 1909.

The Fonda children were reared as Christian Scientists. When Hank became ill, even seriously ill, his mother did not summon a doctor, but read to him from the teachings of Mary Baker Eddy, the religious leader and founder of the "Church of Christ, Scientist," in New England in 1879. The "bible" of the sect was her *Science and Health with Key to the Scriptures.* In time, it would sell nine million copies. His mother would die five years after Hank was born. Despite the rigorous religious training she passed on to him, Hank, in time, would lose his faith and become an agnostic.

"My family was so upright and pure that we could have posed for a Norman Rockwell cover for the old *Saturday Evening Post,*" Hank said.

One of the young boy's earliest memories involved being awakened one night in 1910 by his mother. She wanted him to watch Halley's Comet streak across the nighttime sky. Sightings of that comet had appeared in recorded history since 240 B.C., She told her son that the comet would not appear again for another 75 or 76 years. Young Hank hoped that, as an old man, he'd be alive to see its return.

[Halley's Comet last appeared in the inner Solar System in 1986. After streaking by Jupiter, Saturn, Uranus, and Neptune, it will be visible once again to spectators on Earth in 2061.

Another of Hank's earliest memories involved Sunday picnics along the banks of the Missouri River in the family's newly acquired "Hupmobile." It had been mass-produced in Detroit by the Hupp Motor Company in 1909. In various models, the company would turn out automobiles until 1940.

At the age of twelve, Hank's willowy frame had grown to its peak of 6 feet, 1 inch. Still a pre-teen, his father hired him to work at his print shop, located in Omaha across the street from the newly installed Nickelodeon., On his salary of two dollars a week, Hank often invested a nickel to witness the antics of an English actor, Charlie Chaplin, or else William S. Hart fighting off Indians and taming the Wild West.

Sometimes, the Fondas splurged on tickets to the Orpheum, a vaudeville theater where they were likely to be entertained by the magic and escape artistry of Houdini, or by Fred Astaire, a native son of Omaha, dancing with his sister Adele.

Hank's 12th year marked a turning point in his life when he appeared on the silver screen in his first film. "It was a porno flick," he later recalled. A local newsreel cameraman, a rumored pedophile, got twelve pre-teen boys, including Hank, to pose in skimpy loincloths that barely concealed their genitals. "Our butts were completely exposed except for a string. As I watched the screening in horror, I vowed never to appear in another film as long as I lived."

"Instead of showing my ass to the world, I decided to pursue a career in journalism," he said. "When I was only ten, I won a short

Henry Fonda was reared in a strict, serious environment with strong matriarchal influences from the likes of **Mary Baker Eddy** (1821-1910), founder and chief apostle of the Church of Christ, Scientist.

Insiders within the Fonda clan noted the irony of such conservative influences upon an actor later noted for his affairs with women very unlike his family's "spectacularly unfrivolous' role model.

A Child of the Midwest: **Henry** (marked with an oval) appears here as a gregarious boy scout.

An American Family, sheltered within an arbor behind their Omaha house.

Left to right, Henry's father, **William, sister Harriet, Henry** (enclosed in an oval), **Jayne,** and **Henrietta**

story contest for my authorship of *The Mouse*. For a while, I envisioned a writing career for myself. I was also good at painting and drawing. Monet, watch out! Here comes Hank Fonda."

When he turned fourteen, young Hank endured two traumatic events. The most shocking was when he and his father witnessed a lynching. Their printshop stood near Omaha's courthouse and county jail. On the night of September 28, 1919, a black man, Will Brown, had been imprisoned on a charge of raping a white woman.

An angry group of gun-toting, torch-carrying white men raided the jail. They ripped off Brown's clothes, castrated him with a butcher knife, and then dragged him outside for execution. After it was tied to a lamppost, his body was riddled with bullets. Then it was tied to an automobile, dragged through the streets, and tossed into a raging bonfire. The crowd roared its approval.

Young Henry and his father watched with horror. Henry ended up crying. From that day on, and for the rest of his life, he became an advocate of human rights.

The next horror that descended on him was during his fourteenth year, when he joined some of his fellow schoolmates for a visit to one of the local bordellos. "That was the night I lost my virginity, if you want to call it that. It was the most disgusting experience of my life, a quick *wham-bang*. The old whore had a strong vaginal odor. She was a fright, and I was repulsed by her. After that dreadful night, I swore off women for the rest of my life."

Of course, as time went by, he would not honor that adolescent pledge.

In a speech to his high school's graduating class, Hank said, "The early homesteaders to our state had a refrain: 'Nebraska, land of the bedbug, the grasshopper, the flea. I'll tell you of our fame while starving to death on my government claim.'"

"That lament, however, is no longer true. We, the sons and daughters of Nebraska today, are on the rise. We'll go forth from this day and make our mark in the world. Our home state will be proud of us."

"That boy Hank, a son of Nebraska, owes the people of our state a debt of gratitude," a former mayor of Omaha recalled. "We gave him his loping, cornhusker walk, that spare range-riding body, the tonelessness of his speaking voice, and the values and attitudes of the plainsman. Growing up here paved the way for him to create those roles of sheriff, sodbuster, farmer, and rancher."

Hank attributed his looks to his father: "Every time I pass a mirror, I see my father staring back at me. His smoky blue eyes, his hollow cheeks, his strong teeth, everything imbued with a Midwestern melancholy."

Young Henry, as a teenager, witnessed Omaha's bloodthirsty insurrection of 1919, wherein mobs of disgruntled white settlers broke into Omaha's city courthouse to shoot, lynch, and burn the body of 40-year-old **Will Brown** for allegedly (and without proof) raping a white woman

The left side of the photo depicts Will Brown, alive. The right photo shows his mangled body after being dragged through the streets, riddled with bullets, doused with gasoline, and set on fire.

In later years, Henry defined his witnessing this atrocity as one of the factors that made him a life-long liberal.

Left photo, **young Henry, aged five**, with an unidenfied contemporary at one of Omaha's Junior League social functions, and (right) as a cognitively alert 14-year old, horrified by the lynching of Will Brown, described in this chapter and in photos at the top of this page.

Photo above depicts "not necessarily willing," but **"working" prostitutes** in one of the River Towns of the American Midwest during the early 20th century.

Young Henry was maneuvered, at a young age, into a "Wham Bang," interlude with one of them, an experience that he remembered with horror for decades after.

***

With high hopes of becoming a newspaper reporter, perhaps in Chicago, Henry enrolled at the University of Minnesota. He arrived during the peak of the Jazz Age in New York and Hollywood. Young women, "flappers" with bobbed hair and short dresses, were maniacally dancing the Charleston and shocking many of their elders.

During Prohibition, "bootleg hootch" flowed liberally.

But the "flaming youth" movement then in vogue did not set a flame under Henry, at least partly because he was too busy. In addition to keeping up his grade-point average, he held down two jobs to pay his tuition

When he wasn't attending class, he worked as a "trouble shooter" for the Northwestern Bell Telephone Company. After that, he rode trolley cars for six miles to reach a Settlement House, where he was employed as staff director of physical education. For a salary of thirty dollars a month, he was assigned a dreary bedroom, which he shared with another young man. Many nights, Henry fell asleep studying.

The end of his sophomore year found him making a C average, or worse. He opted to drop out of college and return to Omaha, looking for better wages.

During the summer of 1925, he accepted whatever jobs he could find, beginning as an iceman delivering blocks of ice to the overheated residents of Omaha. That didn't work out—"The ice melted too fast." He moved on to a two-week stint as a "grease monkey" in a garage. He decided he didn't know enough about mechanics, and his boss agreed.

Flappers and their beaux: Henry, as a destitute young actor in search of a role, quickly realized that in this strange new world of urbanopolis, he was a long long way from home.

He ended up getting hired as a dresser at the local department store on Omaha's main street. "I took the dresses off female mannequins and put new gowns on them. This did nothing for me, although one of my colleagues sometimes retreated to the toilet to masturbate, obviously because working with these dummies turned him on."

Finally, he was entrusted with a good-paying job—thirty dollars a week—at a local credit company. "I'd never made such big bucks before, and felt on top of the world."

Little did he know at the time, but an older woman was about to enter his life and change it forever.

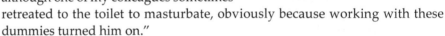

***

A married friend of Henry's mother, she was Julia Pennebacker Brando, born in 1897 at Henry's own birthplace of Grand Island, Nebraska. That made her eight years Henry's senior. In 1918, she had married Marlon Brando Sr., and had given birth to two daughters, Jocelyn and Frances Elizabeth. The couple also produced a very famous son, Marlon Brando Jr.

"Dodie," as she was nicknamed, was a producer and occasional actress at the then newly established Omaha Community Playhouse.

She phoned Mrs. Fonda, telling her that the juvenile lead had dropped out of the latest play the theater was producing. She'd seen Mrs. Fonda's twenty-year-old son on several occasions and felt that he'd be ideal as a replacement for the character of Ricky.

Hank's mother proposed the idea to her son one evening after his return from work. The suggestion seemed to terrify him. "I felt I'd be tongue-tied facing an audience. I could remember lines, but that's about it. I can't act worth a damn."

His father agreed with him, but his mother remained persistent.

The following night, Hank went to the theater, where Dodie graciously welcomed and encouraged him. The director, Gregory Foley, whom Henry likened to an Irish leprechaun, seemed to have the hots for me. Even without rehearsal, he gave me the role. Dad had warned me that the theater attracted

Memories of Omaha's Arts Scene, Long Ago and Far Away

Photos above depict **Julie (aka "Dodie" Pennepacker Brando)** with her eventually very famous son, **Marlon Brando,** at different ages of their lives.

Today, Henry Fonda and Marlon Brando, both of whom were trained and mentored, as young actors, by Dodie, are unrivaled (except by perhaps Fred Astaire) as the most famous entertainers to ever come out of Omaha.

hordes of homosexuals, and Foley insisted that I was one of the most beautiful young men in Omaha."

"During rehearsals, he continued to appraise me like a slab of meat. Not only that, but I felt Dodie also fancied me. I had never felt desired as a man before—not in high school, not in college—but those two seemed to think I was some Golden Boy discovery."

He also likened Dodie to a stage mother, a tradition that dated back in silent films to the mother of Mary Pickford, America's sweetheart. That tradition was followed in the 1930s by the mother of box office champ Shirley Temple, and in the 1940s by the mother of Elizabeth Taylor.

The Philip Barry play, *You and I,* was the first work of the playwright to open on Broadway. It launched his career and would be followed by other big hits, notably the stage and film version of *The Philadelphia Story,* which revived the acting career of Katharine Hepburn, pairing her memorably with James Stewart, Fonda's best friend, and Cary Grant.

You and I was the drama of a father and son trying to choose between commercial success and the pursuit of their artistic goals.

"Years later, I had no memory of playing Ricky," Henry said. "I exhibited myself on the stage where people could stare at me. It seemed insane. All I remembered was the smell of greasepaint and all those eyes staring at me, judging me. I walked on that stage to exhibit myself. Otherwise, that long-ago night in Omaha has faded."

Henry was well received in the role. Dodie, he later reported, "restored my confidence in my manhood after the debacle I'd had in that whorehouse when I was only fourteen."

She revealed the failures of her marriage to Brando Sr., citing his heavy drinking and womanizing. One night, she asked young Henry to remain behind after the theater had closed. She seduced him in a dressing room.

"She had nothing but praise for me, and even cited how well-equipped I was for lovemaking," he later confessed. "At the beginning, she was real patient with me, and made me feel great. I decided that sex wasn't all that bad after all."

Unfortunately, she was falling in love with him, and he didn't feel the same way about her. He was taken aback when she proposed that she might divorce Brando Sr. and marry him.

"I wasn't ready for marriage," he said. "I hadn't decided who I was...the smell of greasepaint had gotten to me. Even after my role was over, I stayed on at the playhouse, doing odd jobs like painting scenery and securing props. I even cleaned the lone shithouse backstage."

One afternoon, Henry got a call from the director, Foley. "I thought he wanted a date with me. Perhaps he did. But what he told me was that he wanted me for the lead in their next play, *Merton of the Movies.*

Originally conceived as a comic novel, it had been adapted into a Broadway play in 1922, the work of George S. Kaufman and Marc Connelly. It had even been made into a silent film.

The lead role offered to Henry was a characterization of Merton Gill, a small town bumpkin who fantasizes about becoming a star of silent pictures. Once in Hollywood, he is disillusioned by the foibles of his screen idols. He turns out to be such a bad actor that directors view him as a screen comedian, assigning him lines which the actor mistakenly interprets as romantic drama.

"I made a self-discovery playing Merton," Henry said. "I didn't have to reveal myself. I could play somebody else and speak their lines, keeping myself hidden behind the makeup and costume. The audience would never know *me*...only my character. Henry Fonda would remain a mystery."

At the climactic end of the play, Henry, as Merton, kneels on the floor. He raises his hands in prayer as he says, "Oh, God, make me a good movie actor! Make me one of the best! For Jesus' sake, Amen."

"God, or someone, must have been listening. My prayer was answered."

His entire family attended opening night. Henry's performance was met with a standing ovation.

Originally, actor Glenn Hunter had starred in both the stage and screen version of Merton. The next morning, a review of the play appeared in an Omaha newspaper: "Who needs Glenn Hunter? Omaha has Henry Fonda!"

The Fondas had gathered in their living room, where all the talk was about Henry's performance. His sister, Harriet, had one criticism. "There is one scene that needs work..."

One of young Henry's most expansive experiences as a newbie actor involved stepping into a role already essayed by the silent screen star **Glenn Hunter,** depicted above in this publicity still for *Merton at the Movies* (1925).

Some casting directors noted Henry's physical similarities to Hunter: Tall, thin, unpretentious, and very much a replica of "the young all-American next door."

But before she could complete her critique, her father rose from his armchair: "Shut up! Hank was perfect!"

***

Mrs. Hunter Scott Sr. was a rich dowager, a queen of Omaha Society, living lavishly on the vast real estate fortune her late husband had left her. The deceased mogul had also left her with Hunter Jr., known as "a wayward boy."

For college, his mother had sent him east to Princeton, where he had already suffered through two years and was ready to bolt. Henry had attended high school in Omaha with her son. At this point, Mrs. Scott had become uncomfortable with the idea of allowing her son to drive from Omaha back to Princeton alone.

Arriving in her sedan at the Fonda home, she filled the air with the scent of lavender. In a meeting with Mrs. Fonda and with Henry, she proposed a deal: Henry would be a driving companion to her son during his upcoming transit to Omaha from Princeton, via Miami and New Orleans. Her proposal included payment of all expenses and a free week "living it up" in Manhattan.

"New Orleans!" Henry said. "I hear that's a wild place!"

"So is my errant son," his mother said. "He needs someone to keep him out of trouble and bring him back here alive."

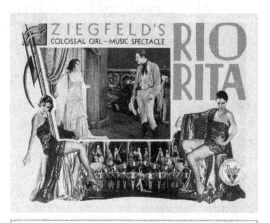

Reserved, taciturn, and obviously a new arrival from the dour Middle West, young Henry on the verge of an acting career felt like a fish out of water when confronted with some of the stage entertainments then in vogue on pre-Depression, flapper-era Broadway.

Here's the ad for a show then in rapturous vogue at the time of Henry's arrival in the very bad, very Big Apple in 1929, Florenz Ziegfeld's "girls as cheesecake" revue, the spectacularly successful **Rio Rita**.

Henry accepted the challenge, giving notice to the Retail Credit Company that he intended to quit. "The business world is not for me. I think I'll become an actor. A stage actor."

The year was 1927.

He later described Hunter Scott as "a young man who had emerged straight from the pages of an F. Scott Fitzgerald novel. He seemed to make it with every gal he dated. They gave in to his insatiable sexual demands, or so he claimed."

Arriving in Manhattan two years before the Great Wall Street Crash of '29, Henry faced a bewildering choice of plays to see, an astounding 275 productions tempting him. He wanted to attend all of them, but eventually settled for Ethel Barrymore in *The Constant Wife;* Helen Hayes in *Coquette;* and Otis Skinner in *The Front Page.* He also went to see Glenn Hunter in *Tommy,* remembering that the Omaha theater critic had compared him favorably to that actor when Henry had starred in a revival of the actor's Broadway triumph, *Merton in the Movies.*

Henry also saw a young actor, Humphrey Bogart, perform in *Saturday's Children.*

[Coincidentally, Henry, in 1955, would be co-starring with Bogie and his wife, Lauren Bacall, in a "Made for TV version" of The Petrified Forest.*]*

As previously agreed, Hunter, in his new Packard convertible, drove up (an hour late) to find Henry waiting for him in front of Manhattan's Ziegfeld Theatre. He had just sat through a performance of Florenz Ziegfeld's *Rio Rita.*

With the top of his convertible down, Hunter had three passengers: A stern-faced mother (Ruth Davis) and her daughters, Bobby and Bette. Not a particularly pretty girl, Bette Davis, age seventeen, invited Henry to sit beside her.

The first words from Bette to her future co-star in *Jezebel* were "Hunter told me you're an actor. I'm an actress. I'm here to audition for Eva Le Gallienne."

[One of the first ladies of the American theater, Miss Le Gallienne would reject Bette in September of 1927, telling her, "My dear, you'll never make it as an actress."]

From there, with Hunter driving, they headed to Princeton with the intention of attending a football game scheduled for the following afternoon. Hunter stashed his three female passengers at the Nassau Inn and invited Henry to share his bedroom at the campus dormitory.

The next day, Hunter challenged Henry to a kissing contest to see which man could tally up the greatest number of kisses from a girl. Henry foolishly entered

Despite her spectacular later successes in entertainment, no one at the beginning, least of all Henry Fonda, could believe that **Bette Davis** would ever emerge from the bratty and somewhat demanding adolescent he "made out with" in the back seat of his friend's Packard.

the contest, realizing in advance that he was destined to lose.

Henry later wrote in a memoir, "Mrs. Davis was a stern New England lady, but she trusted Hunter to let him drive her daughters to the football stadium."

After the game, Hunter drove to a secluded park and disappeared into the bushes with Bobby. From the sounds emanating from those bushes, Henry knew that Hunter was kissing Bobby.

"I was sitting there with Bette, a girl I didn't even know. I knew I'd never win the kissing contest, but I didn't want to disgrace myself by not scoring even one point. I sat there thinking, 'I've got to kiss her. I've got to.' She looked at me with those saucer-like eyes and, what the hell. Well, I sort of leaned over and gave her a peck on the lips. Not a real kiss, but what a relief to me. One point! I felt like Casanova."

The next day, Henry and Hunter said goodbye to the Davis daughters, who boarded a train to Boston.

Within a few days, Henry received a letter from Bette. "I've told my mother about our lovely time in the moonlight. She will soon announce our engagement."

"Holy shit!" he said to Hunter as they headed to Florida in his convertible. "One kiss and I'm engaged. That's how naïve I was. What a devil that Bette Davis is at seventeen. I'm giving the bitch wide berth."

Of course, he never married Davis, his future co-star in films, but he would have an affair with her. Later, he admitted, "I've been close to Bette Davis for thirty-eight years, and I've got the cigarette burns to prove it."

[Ironically, as the years rolled by, Henry became the father of a daughter, Jane, who in the early 1970s would be hailed by the press as "the next Bette Davis."]

***

Back home in Omaha, Henry faced his 22nd birthday out of work. He lived with his family and ate with his parents and two sisters at the dining table. To earn his keep, he did chores around the house, making repairs and mowing the lawn.

On certain nights, he slipped out of the house and met with Dodie Brando at the home of an unmarried friend of hers. There, they spent no more than two hours together, making love, since her husband, Marlon Brando Sr., no longer visited her bed. She told Henry that her infant son, Marlon Jr., was "no longer shitting his diapers."

"I was eating too much licorice, to which I was addicted, and it was blackening my teeth," Henry said. In his spare time, he listened to the family's hand-cranked Victrola, or else read whatever plays he could check out at the small local library. He envisioned what roles he might play one day.

One night, Dodie told him that the director of the community theater, Gregory Foley, wanted to meet with him the following afternoon to offer him a job.

"I hope the job doesn't involve his getting in my underwear," he told her. Nonetheless, he met with Foley to learn that he wanted to hire him as his assistant, doing odd jobs backstage. He promised that he would also offer him any roles that might be suitable for him. The gig paid $500 for the fall season.

The director kept his word, casting Henry in such plays as *The School for Scandal*, *The Enemy*, *Rip Van Winkle*, *Seventeen*, *Secrets*, and *The Potters*.

His breakthrough role came when Foley cast him as the lead opposite Dodie in Eugene O'Neill's *Beyond the Horizon*. When it had premiered on Broadway in 1920, it won the Pulitzer Prize for Drama. New York critics hailed it as "the first Native American tragedy."

The plot centered on two brothers, Robert, who prefers the seafaring life, and Andrew, who wants to marry his sweetheart, Ruth, and settle down on a farm.

"I'm a big frog in a little pond who wants to be a little frog in a big pond," Henry told his mother.

One afternoon, Henry encountered a reporter from the *Omaha World Herald* who told him that the actor, George A. Billings, had checked into Omaha's Fontenell Hotel as part of a stage tour through the Middle West impersonating Abraham Lincoln.

In an interview with the *World Herald*, Billings said he wanted to expand his show and was looking for a young actor to play Major John Hay, Lincoln's presidential secretary.

Within two hours, Henry was in the lobby of the Fontenell, asking for the room number of Billings. Knocking on his door, he was invited into Billings' bedroom,

Early in Henry Fonda's stage career, he toured through the Middle West in a two-man play with the widely respected **George Billings**, depicted above.

Billings closely resembled "Honest Abe" himself, and as such, built a dramatic legacy around his life and accomplishments.

Here's Billings as he appeared in a Silent Film entitled *The Dramatic Life of Abraham Lincoln*, released in 1924, three years before Henry (briefly) joined forces with him.

where he found him intoxicated.

The actor revealed to him that in 1924, he'd been working in Hollywood as a carpenter on the film set of *The Dramatic Life of Abraham Lincoln*. The actor playing the President had had a fight with the director and had stormed off the set. Within the hour, the director noticed that his carpenter bore an uncanny resemblance to Lincoln, complete with beard.

He cast Billings in the role, ordering his wardrobe mistress to give him a Prince Albert jacket and a stovepipe hat.

The film was a surprise hit, but Billings realized that years would pass before Hollywood made another movie about Lincoln. Billings therefore devised a crowd-pleasing stage play about Lincoln and made it the focal point of a tour through the Middle West.

Billings told Henry that physically, he'd look like John Hay, if he grew a pencil-thin mustache. Henry offered to audition for the role of Hay, but was told that there was no script. Consequently, Henry immediately volunteered to write a fifteen-minute scene focused on an encounter between Lincoln and Hay.

After referring to some material about Hay from the library, Henry stayed up all night working on the sketch. When he read it to a sobered-up Billings over breakfast the next morning, he was hired to tour through the Middle West with Billings at a salary of one-hundred dollars a week. He'd never made that kind of money before.

About a week later, with Billings and clad in an outfit inspired by the Union Army, young Henry Fonda headed for Des Moines to try out the new act.

The highlight of the performance was when Henry, cast as Hay, read a touching letter from the wife of a Union soldier sentenced for execution in front of a firing squad because of his desertion from the Army. Billings always shed tears as he tore up the paper ordering the execution.

Henry, as "second fiddle" to Billings, toured the Middle West. As the tour lengthened, the older actor, born in 1870, began to drink more heavily. On some nights, he didn't even show up in time for the curtain. Sometimes, desperately attempting to compensate, Henry stood on stage reading the Gettysburg Address and Lincoln's Second Inaugural Address. Finally, he dropped out of the show, taking the train back to Omaha.

Ironically, in 1939, director John Ford would cast Henry in the title role of *Young Mr. Lincoln,* which critics would hail as one of his finest performances.

***

At the end of the theatrical season in Omaha, and with a bleak, unscheduled summer staring back at him, Henry was in a dilemma. Then an unexpected invitation came in from Millicent Burns, a rich local widow, flush with cash from her late husband's stock brokerage firm of Burns, Brinker, & Co. Millicent wanted to hire him as a driver who'd transport her across the country for a holiday on Cape Cod, where she maintained a large summer cottage. Hoping that one of the theaters there would hire him as an actor, Henry agreed.

During their trek together across the country, Mrs. Burns paid for Henry's food and lodgings, but dropped him fast once they reached Cape Cod. He had managed to save a hundred dollars, which was all the money he had. He had hoped that she might add another hundred dollars to his cache, but she did not.

In Provincetown, he headed, with his only suitcase, for the local playhouse. At the box office, he was told that the cast for every play in the upcoming season had already been selected by the theater's office in Manhattan. There were no other roles available.

He learned there was another theater in Dennis down the coast, and the next train wouldn't depart for another two hours. With time to spare, he asked directions to the summer home of Eugene O'Neill. Henry had previously appeared in O'Neill's *Beyond the Horizon*. But instead of a face-to-face encounter with the playwright, Henry had to settle instead for a look at the exterior of his home. It stood on a mound called "Pecked Hill Bar." As he gazed at it, he wondered if America's greatest playwright was inside, working, perhaps, on his next drama…Preferably one with a role in it for him.

Descending from the train in Dennis, again with his suitcase in hand, Fonda headed for the Cape Playhouse. One of the oldest summer stock the-

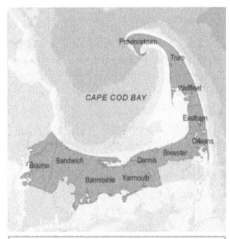

Deeply immersed in the East Coast's arts scene, **Cape Cod** in midsummer was loaded with playgoers who appreciated neophyte actors like Henry Fonda in their early experimentations with stage drama and its craft.

aters in America, it was known for "Bringing the Best of Broadway to Cape Cod every summer."

He found no one at the box office, so he wandered into the theater, finding a seat near the rear, where he watched the company actors rehearsing their next production.

He sat there for about an hour. Eventually, he was approached by Gordon Tannen, an assistant director. Once again, Henry was told that the season's casting had already been arranged by an office in New York. "In spite of that," Henry said, "this guy seemed to be sizing me up, and I knew what role he had in mind. He kept looking at me with a raised eyebrow. I was meat on the market."

When Henry started to leave, Tannen said, "Stick around. We might find something for you this summer. You look hungry. I've rented a small summer cottage overlooking the water. You're welcome to share it with me. I'm a good cook. Lobster twice a week."

Rising from his chair, Henry told the young man, "I'm not that hungry." Then he picked up his suitcase and headed out.

It was twilight when he spotted a large clapboard boarding house advertising rooms for rent. He went inside, and was offered a small, closet-sized room on the top floor for $1.50 a night. He decided to take it. Later that night, as a means of sustaining life, he ordered a lone hamburger, opting not to go for the French fries, although he could have devoured them.

Later, as he fell asleep on his cot, he asked himself, "What will tomorrow bring?"

He woke up the next morning to the sound of seagulls and the smell of frying bacon. His rent included breakfast. After a quick shower, he headed down the steps to the breakfast table, where he discovered that the building housed the actors from the community theater.

At a huge table sat both established stars from Broadway and various juveniles and *ingénues* hoping to break into the theater.

He was the last to arrive at the breakfast table, taking the sole empty chair between two established actresses. On his right sat Peggy Wood, with Laura Hope Crews occupying the chair on his left. Brooklyn-born Wood had made her stage debut in 1910 in the chorus line of *Naughty Marietta*. She was on the dawn of a long and distinguished career, soon to return to Broadway to star as Portia in *The Merchant of Venice*. From there, she starred in musicals on Broadway and in London's West End. Among her roles, she would star in Noël Coward's operetta *Bitter Sweet*.

Whereas Wood had been born in 1892, Crews was older, emerging in San Francisco in 1879. Noël Coward had played a part in her career, too. In 1925, he cast her in *Hay Fever*.

Greater fame was on Crews' horizon too. Soon, she'd be teaching the 1920s silent screen vamp, Gloria Swanson, how to "talk in the Talkies." Director George Cukor would cast her in *Camille* (1936), starring Greta Garbo. In 1939, when Billie Burke turned down the role of Aunt Pittypat in *Gone With the Wind,* it went to Crews, who immortalized herself in a zany Billie Burke-ish kind of way. Who could forget how she handled the burning of Atlanta?

After breakfast, having rejected his homosexual invitation of the previous day, Henry was surprised to see Gordon Tannen from the Playhouse again. With the intention of driving Wood and Crews to the theater, he invited Henry to join them. "I've talked to our director. I think we've found a spot for you as third assistant stage manager, mostly handling props."

With a certain reluctance, Henry agreed to go along for the ride. Later that day, and with even more reluctance, he agreed to accept Tannen's invitation to live free at his summer cottage. -

He immediately went to work on organizing props for the play *The Barker*. It had

Henry ate bacon and eggs with two legends, (left) **Peggy Wood** and (right) **Laura Hope Crews** as they appeared in 1917 and 1910, respectively.

These major-league actresses appeared in the dining room of young Henry Fonda's boarding house on Cape Cod on the first day of his sojourn there.

Even as young Henry Fonda was fine-tuning his stage performance on Cape Cod in **The Barker,** it was being adapted in Hollywood into a film, released in 1927, depicted in the poster above.

Young and intensely ambitious, young Henry paid avid attention.

opened on Broadway in January of 1927, starring Walter Huston and a relatively unknown (at the time) French actress, Claudette Colbert.

In the era that the Playhouse was presenting it, it was being adapted into a pre-Code romantic drama in Hollywood, starring Dorothy Mackail, Milton Sills, and—in the juvenile role—Douglas Fairbanks Jr.

Henry's lucky break came when the young actor cast as the juvenile dropped out. Since he'd already memorized all his lines, Henry went on in his place. He played the estranged son, in love with a dancing girl, of a carnival barker.

In that role, he did reasonably well, or so it seemed at the time. Out of curiosity, he later went to see the play's film adaptation, (entitled *The Barker*). and within the next few years, he attended two of its remakes, *Hoop-La* (1931) starring Clara Bow, and *Diamond Horseshoe* (1945) with Betty Grable.

Before the month was out, this handsome, young, and lanky juvenile from Omaha captured the romantic fantasies of a pretty young actress from New Haven. Although he never mentioned her name in his memoirs, it was probably an eighteen-year-old beauty named Jane Sayer.

One night, she invited Henry to a tavern, where he got drunk on four beers. Later, she asked him to go for a ride in her car along the sand dunes. At one point, he had to get out "and water the sands."

After zipping up and staggering back to the car, he thought at first that Sayer had disappeared. Quickly, however, he surmised that she was completely nude and lying in the back seat. "Come and get it, big boy!" was her aggressive invitation.

He not only accepted her offer, but moved in with her the following night, much to the disappointment of Tannen. Then one afternoon, she left Dennis with no goodbye or farewell note.

Around this time, Henry welcomed a surprise visitor, Bernard Hanighen, a friend when they'd attended high school together in Omaha. By now, Henry's stage role in *The Barker* had ended, and he had returned to working with props and sweeping the stage after every show.

Hanighen convinced Henry that he might get a better break if he migrated with him to West Falmouth, also on Cape Cod. It was there, in 1928, that undergraduates from Harvard, Princeton, and Vassar, had collectively organized a summer stock company known as the University Players.

Its chief founder was Charles Crane Leatherbee, a grandson of the American diplomat and philanthropist, Charles Ricard Crane. Leatherbee would play a key role in launching the careers not only of Henry Fonda, but of Kent Smith, Mildred Natwick, Margaret Sullavan, James Stewart, and Joshua Logan, among others.

Leatherbee's purpose in launching the company involved providing a forum where aspirant actors could continue their theatrical training during the summer months. Well bankrolled, he made a deal with the Elizabeth Movie House. Positioned on the outskirts of Falmouth, it agreed to rent its premises to the theatrical troupe every Monday and Tuesday night, when it had, otherwise, almost no audiences.

Another founder of the troupe was Paris born and England educated Bretaigne Winddust. At Princeton, he'd been president of the Intime Theatre Group.

Winddust directed more frequently than he acted. In 1932, he directed Eugene O'Neill's *Strange Interlude* on Broadway, and around the same time, he helmed the then-very-prestigious Alfred Lunt and Lynn Fontanne in *The Taming of the Shrew*. His biggest hit was *Life With Father*, which became one of the longest-running plays on Broadway. Eventually, he moved to Hollywood, directing Bette Davis in *Winter Greeting* and *June Bride*, both released in 1948.

In the theater at Falmouth, Henry got a front-row seat to watch the George Kelly comedy, *The Torch Bearers*, starring Joshua Logan. He found himself seated next to society matrons attired in *haute couture*, some of them accompanied by their summer gigolos.

He could hardly have known at the time what a major role Logan would play in his future. A son of Texarkana, Texas, Logan had been born in 1908. His father had committed suicide when he was three years old.

His mother remarried and moved to Louisiana. His stepfather taunted the little boy, calling him a sissy, and mocking him every day, claiming, "You walk and act like

Henry landed on his feet and in good company when he joined the avant-garde and quasi-experimental **University Players,** a summer stock theater company that flourished in West Falmouth on Cape Cod for four frenetic years (1928-1932) between the World Wars.

It was established and funded by 18 college undergraduates from Vassar, Princeton, and Harvard, some of whom injected massive amounts of cash into it from their private trusts.

Historians view the troupe today as a major philanthropic asset to the era's arts and drama community that later helped to define the American Experience itself.

After its dissolution in the early 1930s, several of its alumnae emerged as major players in the theater and movie industry: James Stewart, Joshua Logan, Margaret Sullavan, Mildred Natwich, and Henry Fonda are among the most visible.

a girl."

Logan was enrolled at the Culver Military Academy in Culver, Indiana "to toughen him up." Later, he attended Princeton, where he became a key member of the University Players.

On the night that Henry first saw Logan perform, he was playing the comedic role of Huxley Hossefrosse in *The Torch Bearers.*

At first, he didn't seem to be going over with the audience. Then he heard (and felt rescued by) the laughter of a young man, Henry Fonda: "What a laugh the boy had!" Logan claimed. "It started with a strangled sob, then soared into a screech played at the wrong speed. You hear it not with your ears, but in your bones, the most beautiful sound I had ever heard." The audience picked up on Henry's laugh, and soon the whole theater was in stitches.

Backstage, Hanighen introduced Henry to Logan. The director would forever remember his first sight of the aspiring young actor and even described Fonda as "a lanky youth with a concave chest and a protruding abdomen. He wore skinny white linen knickerbockers and had this beautiful face. From the

Joshua Logan (center) on the set of *Bus Stop* with **Marilyn Monroe** and her then-agent, **Milton Greene** in 1956.

moment I gazed into Henry's face, I fell in love with him. Those huge innocent eyes of his drew me in, as well as that rough-hewn physique. Over dinner that night, I invited him to move in with me, and, to my surprise, he accepted my offer. Maybe he wasn't as innocent as I assumed."

The Harvard students in the cast slept aboard the *Brae Burn,* a 110-foot submarine chaser from World War I. The vessel was on loan from the Leatherbee family, owners of the Crane Plumbing Company, and bankrollers of the University Players.

Aboard this overcrowded "tin can," Henry was invited to share Logan's bunk bed. "By now, I was calling him Hank, and the two of us virtually had to sleep on top of each other. Let me rephrase that. Hank was always the top."

That summer, "Josh and Hank," as the University Players collectively tabbed them, became close friends of Johnny Swope. A senior at Princeton and the son of the president of General Electric Corp., he had been reared and educated in Paris. His father had acquired a sailboat for him. Anchored in Falmouth Harbor, it often took Hank and Josh for waterborne excursions along the coast of Cape Cod.

After members of the University Players witnessed Swope's early attempts at acting, they collectively discouraged him from ever attempting it again. He would, however, succeed at another profession. All summer, he took pictures with one of his six cameras, gifts from his father. After World War II, Swope became one of the most famous photographers in America, his pictures appearing frequently in *Time* and *Life* magazines. After graduation, Swope shared his apartment with James Stewart, Henry Fonda, and Josh Logan.

Henry would later introduce Swope to actress Dorothy McGuire. She later became his wife. Mr. and Mrs. Swope, in time, would join with Gregory Peck and Mel Ferrer to found the La Jolla Playhouse in California.

As the University Players soon realized, Logan had "fallen madly in love" with Hank, even though it was a one-sided relationship. Before he met Henry, Logan had been rehearsing a double role in Sem Benelli's comedy, *The Jest.* It had been a minor hit on Broadway when it starred two actor brothers, John and Lionel Barrymore.

Logan relinquished one of his parts to Henry, that of Tornaquinci, an eighty-five-year-old Italian nobleman with a white beard and a cascading wig.

Lionel had been brilliant in that role on Broadway, but Henry was horribly miscast. In his own review he said, "I was an unmitigated catastrophe."

Even Logan, his biggest supporter, was horrified at how bad he was. "Hank's Nebraska drawl in that Florentine setting made the poetic Italianate speeches sound like some midwestern cowpokes gathered around a cracker barrel."

"Although wrong for the role of a Florentine aristocrat, I was a great devotee of Hank's voice," Logan said. "He was never an actor for the rounded phrase or the pear-shaped tone, yet he developed a way of speaking that was the pure essence of America: Mark Twain, Bret Harte, James Fenimore Cooper, Hawthorne, Poe, Washington Irving."

John Swope with this wife, **Dorothy McGuire**, a few years after their wedding in 1943.

After Winddust saw Henry perform in *The Jest,* he said, "Why don't you plan to become a scenic designer? You're actually good at it. If I were you, I'd abandon this acting crap."

"But you're not me," Henry said. "I'm gonna become an actor, hell or high water."

The Jest should have ended Henry's acting stint with the University Players. Likewise, John Swope's acting debut should have led to his banishment from the stage. However, for reasons not known, both of them were cast in yet another play, this time as brainless boxers in a sporting comedy entitled *Is Zat So?.*

Critics reviewed the 1930 Pre-Code movie adaptation of **Outward Bound** as "high class on the high seas." Long before Leslie Howard and Douglas Fairbanks Jr., Henry had stormed a summer stock theater on Cape Cod with a stageplay version.

A silent film had previously been based on it, starring George O'Brien (who was fond of posing in the nude) and the gay actor, Edmund Lowe, with minor roles going to Douglas Fairbanks Jr. and child actor Philippe de Lacy.

In the plot, Hap, a fight manager, promotes an amateur boxer named "Chick," a punchy prizefighter. His friend, Johnny Swope, was his opponent in the ring.

Neither of the two actors, Henry nor Swope, knew anything about boxing. Once, while rehearsing, they bloodied each other's noses. During another rehearsal for a boxing scene set in an alley behind the theater, local Falmouth police officers were summoned to break up the fight.

When the play opened, a local critic wrote, "Jack Dempsey has nothing to fear from these two amateurs. One punch from the champ and either of them would be down for the count."

How did Logan review Henry's performance as an actor in *Is Zat So?* "He wiped us all off the floor simply by seeming to do nothing."

Henry got better notices when he starred in Sutton Vane's *Outward Bound,* which had originally premiered in London in 1923. When it migrated to Broadway in January of 1924, Alfred Lunt and Leslie Howard were cast in key roles.

In the plot, seven passengers meet in the lounge of an ocean liner at sea. Each of them suddenly discovers that they are dead, and they have to face judgment from an Examiner who will determine where to ship them: Heaven or Hell.

A Falmouth critic wrote, "When Alfred Lunt found himself aboard a ghost ship outward bound for Heaven or Hell, he cast over his audience an eerie spell which we thought could never be repeated. But Henry Fonda repeated that experience for us in his excellent interpretation of the same role in the same play."

Outward Bound did not die that summer in Falmouth. In 1930, Warner Brothers made it into a film starring Leslie Howard in the Lunt role.

Laurette Taylor and Vincent Price revived it on Broadway in 1938, and in 1944, it was remade as *Between Two Worlds,* a film starring John Garfield, Paul Henreid, Sydney Greenstreet, and Eleanor Parker.

When Cape Cod's summer season ended, Henry, with very little money in his pocket, caught a train that eventually landed him at Grand Central Station in Manhattan. His future as an actor was uncertain.

An even bigger problem faced him, too: How to survive.

***

New to Manhattan, Henry had to find a place to sleep…something other than a bench in Central Park. In a decaying building on West 114th Street, he rented a former linen closet for ten dollars a week. Its (shared) bathroom was accessible from the hall.

Even such a low rent was more than he could afford. He already knew that a package of rice could go a long way in staving off starvation.

Once, he went for a week without food, filling up his stomach with water. "I spent a lot of time in the latrine, and got some offers from other men, but I wasn't that desperate…at least not yet."

Sometimes, carrying an empty paper bag with him, he'd go into a café and order only a five-cent cup of coffee. When the waitress went to the kitchen to pick up an order, he often stuffed leftover rolls into that bag. Once, someone left two strips of bacon on a plate. "That was a real treat, since meat was a rarity in my diet."

When he wasn't pounding the pavement looking for work, he often nursed a Coke and smoked a Camel cigarette ("my only luxury") in the basement café of Walgreen's Drugstore.

Joshua Logan later said, "Henry showed up so many times at the offices of producers and casting agents that he became the best-known unknown actor in Manhattan."

During one of his auditions, he ran into actor Kent Smith, who had been one of the University Players. He told Henry that since the previous summer, he'd been kicked out of Harvard for not attending classes. "They bored hell out of me."

Years later, to Henry's amazement, this less-than-charismatic actor became a movie star. He'd made his Broadway debut in 1932. When Hollywood beckoned, he appeared in such "B-Picture Trash" (his words) as *Cat People* (1942) and *Hitler's Children* (1943). As time went by, he was cast in minor roles in A-list films, including *My Foolish Heart* (1949) with Susan Hayward, *The Fountainhead* (1949) with Gary Cooper, *The Damned Don't Cry* (1950) with Joan Crawford, and *Sayonara* (1957) with Marlon Brando.

Although Henry, on a personal level, liked Kent, he did agree with a latter-day film critic who wrote: "Because Kent Smith's method was soft and cerebral and unobtrusive, it would be safe to say that he was not a name that caused ripples of excitement at its mere mention."

One day, Kent and Henry were studying a bulletin board posted with Broadway auditions when two elderly ladies approached them. "Are you boys actors?" the older woman asked.

"Indeed we are," Henry responded.

"I'll get to the point," the woman said. "We're from the National Junior Theatre in Washington. A children's theater. The pay is five dollars a week, with room and board. Naturally, we'll include train fare to the capital."

Two views of **Kent Smith**. *Upper photo*: publicity still from 1953. *Lower photo*, with **Joan Crawford** in *The Damned Don't Cry* (1950).

"I'm game," Henry said. "How about you, Kent?"

Although neither of them was thrilled by the salary, he answered, "We're on our way."

Henry's first role in the U.S. capital was that of the doddering Sir Andrew Aguecheek in Shakespeare's *Twelfth Night*. One critic later wrote, "Henry Fonda is the most unlikely Shakespearean actor ever to appear on stage."

In spite of that put-down, the producers asked both Kent and Henry to stay on for the rest of the season. They became roommates, occasionally going out on double dates, during which they could hardly afford the cost of a movie ticket and a hamburger. The two actors remained in Washington until the season ended in April of 1929.

With no prospects other than returning to New York, Henry got a welcome phone call from his friend, Bernard Hanighen, who offered him an acting job.

At Harvard, Hanighen and his theater-industry colleague, and Harold Adamson, had not found a suitable undergraduate for a small but key role in their upcoming musical, *Close Up*. Bernie thought the part would be ideal for Henry.

A train ticket arrived the next day to transport Henry to Boston. There, he had a reunion with his well-heeled friend, Charles Leatherbee, who introduced him to his girlfriend, whom he called "Peggy." [*A Southern belle from Virginia making her debut as an actress, her name was Margaret Sullavan.*]

"She was so short, she barely came up to my shoulder," Henry said. "When not rehearsing her for the play, she made her living working at "The Coop," a leading bookstore for Harvard undergraduates.

Their stage business called for him to walk onstage, notice the attractive girl, and try to pick her up for the night. She was then to give him a stinging slap.

Henry later said, "From that first day, she slapped the hell out of me, not holding back. The left side of my face was left rosy red and stinging. She had this deep-throated laughter as she threw back her head."

"Day after day, I looked forward to that damn slap," he said. "Does that make me a masochist? The brazen little Southern hussy delivered, too. Before *Close Up* opened, I knew I had to tell my buddy Charlie that he was going to have to get another gal. I'd staked this little wench out for myself."

He later said, "Margaret Mitchell had not yet published *Gone With the Wind,* but perhaps she was already plotting its characters. Margaret Sullavan could certainly have provided the inspiration for the creation of that scheming bitch, Scarlett O'Hara."

Backstage Dramas
Behind the Onstage Dramas
at a Summer Theater
in New England
circa 1930

Margaret Sullavan: "There was so much prissy propriety and sexual prudery and emotional repression among the people who inhabited my early life that I suppose I went in the other extreme."

Henry Fonda: "It was never my goal to go to Hollywood. A team of wild horses could not drag me there...No way!"

CHAPTER TWO

STRUGGLING UP THE ROCKY ROAD TO STARDOM,
HENRY SLOGS HIS WAY THROUGH A MARITAL DISASTER:

MARGARET SULLAVAN

*—Being wed to her is a bed of roses where I got only the thorns.
She castrates men, making them feel like two cents—and two inches."*
—Henry Fonda

SURVIVING THE GREAT DEPRESSION

WHILE "TREADING THE BOARDS"
OF THE SUMMER STOCK AND CHILDREN'S THEATER WORLDS
HENRY GETS DRAMATIC
BOTH ONSTAGE AND OFF, SOMETIMES WITH PLAYERS
WHO BECAME INDEPENDENTLY FAMOUS IN THEIR OWN RIGHT
AS "THE AMERICAN CENTURY" ROARS TOWARD

ANOTHER WORLD WAR

Margaret Brooke Sullavan emerged into the world on the windy morning of May 16, 1909 in Norfolk, Virginia. Four years before, on that same date (May 16), an infant, Henry Fonda had emerged from a womb in Omaha.

Sullivan's father was a wealthy stockbroker, and her mother, the former Garland Council, had numbered many Confederate soldiers among her ancestors, notably General Robert E. Lee. She had a younger brother named after his father, but called "Sonny," and a half-sister, Louise Gregory, nicknamed "Weedie."

Although born into a privileged world, Sullivan knew nothing but pain until she was nearly six years old. She suffered from an enduring muscular weakness in her legs, preventing her from walking and sometimes shooting sharp waves of pain throughout both legs, forcing her to scream.

Finally, she gained use of her legs and struggled to walk. Her improvement was quick, and, in fact, she became a bit of a tomboy, climbing trees and running away with a gang of kids from "the wrong side of the tracks." Her socially conscious parents chastised her for not "playing with your own crowd."

From the beginning, Margaret sent signals to her snobbish parents that they had given birth to a rebellious daughter. She was eventually sent to exclusive private schools "to teach you how to be a lady."

"In that," she later said, "they would not succeed. I was born an anarchist."

Years later, she confided to friends, "I became interested in the male anatomy when I was a pre-teen and walked into the bathroom, where Sonny was standing naked, drying himself off. I noticed that his little piece of equipment was different from mine. After that, I became interested in what made boys tick. They were certainly different from the silly girls in my class."

"Sex entered my life right before I turned fourteen," she recalled. "His name was Greg Randall. His equipment was seven times bigger than little Sonny's, and he sure put it to use. It was painful at first, but he delivered the goods. Greg made me a sex addict for life."

"There were plenty of handsome beaux in high school. They turned to ever-faithful me because most of their girlfriends wouldn't put out."

In Hollywood in the years to come, Sullavan told Ruth Waterbury, a reporter, what her early life had been like: "Girls were infused with this sexual prudity and a prissy outlook on life. All of them were emotionally repressed, growing up in a stifling Southern environment, unlike me, who sought adventure. Perhaps I went to the extreme throwing off convention."

The autumn of 1928 found her at Sullins College,

Robbing The Cradle For Stars

Margaret Sullavan was used to being gossipped about. At the center of attention virtually since birth, thanks in part to her wealthy, society-conscious Southern parents, she was a household name earlier than Fonda, James Stewart, or any of the other wannabees she met and interacted with (and sometimes slept with) on Henry's summer stock circuit.

She appears here on the covers of both *Screen Play* and *Photoplay* in 1934, a year after her divorce from a (very young and inexperienced) Henry Fonda, shortly before tying the knot with the very influential director, William Wilder.

which she proclaimed was the best in Virginia. "I was voted most popular, especially among the boys, since many of the girls were jealous of me. I had a big problem. I fell in and out of love too easily. I soon learned that men come in all sizes. God had been very generous to Greg, who was the first to deflower me. His Lordship was a bit of a miser when he come to creating other boys."

"I soon got over this habit of mine of falling in love," she claimed. "Love leads to heartburn. It's better for a gal like me to stick to physical attraction. That way, your male partner can deliver satisfaction, but not break your heart."

A former classmate later told a reporter, "Some guys called her 'Maggie,' others labeling her 'Peggy.' Whatever in hell you called her, she was known in college as an easy piece. All a guy had to do was ask."

After college, Margaret decided she could no longer stand "the smothering air of Norfolk," and she relocated to Boston to study dance and acting. For a brief period, her half-sister, "Weedie," went along as her roommate.

Weedie later reported to their parents, "Maggie is man mad. A handsome guy comes along, and she's a goner. The fat, pudgy, and ugly don't stand a chance with her."

"Those beaner boys in Boston were only too eager to deflower a Southern gal," Weedie claimed.

Soon, in Manhattan, Sullavan enrolled at the Denishawn Studio founded by Ruth St. Denis, sometimes called the Mother of Modern Dance, and her gay husband, Ted Shawn. Their dance company and school would train such modern dancers as Martha Graham.

"Miss Ruth was already a legend," Sullavan said. "She'd danced for King Edward VII in London and been sketched by Rodin. One afternoon, Shawn showed up with two of the most beautiful boy dancers I have ever seen or would see in the future. How I envied him."

"I was a good dancer, but I knew my limitations," Sullavan said. "I would never be a great dancer. I figured I had a better chance becoming an actress, instead, so I enrolled in E.E. Clive's Copley Theater. *[Clive later became a well-known character actor in films.]*

Clive recalled: "Maggie had an instinctive grace, a throaty voice that promised depths to be explored, and a desire to learn that was surprising in such a little Southern girl. Those rangy Harvard boys were only too eager to make her the belle of their ball...or is it 'their balls?'"

After Sullavan joined the University Players in Falmouth, on Cape Cod, and became emotionally involved with Henry, he recalled the dilemmas all those romantic attachments involved: "My friend, Charlie Leatherbee, was madly in love with Maggie, although she seemed rather indifferent to him. Josh (Logan) still had this mad crush on me but must have known I was just hanging in there for room and board. It beat starving to death."

"Josh was better at directing than acting," Henry continued. "He helped me a lot with getting my footing on stage. As time went by, it became clear that Charlie was going to have to give up his love for Maggie, and Josh was going to have to develop a crush on another handsome young actor."

After *Close Up* shut down, Sullavan and Henry were cast as the leads in a badly named play, *The Devil in the Cheese.*

A self-styled "fantastic comedy" in three acts, its plot centered on Greek bandits who capture an American family who have acquired a magical piece of cheese. Consumption of a small piece of it transmits the power to read another person's mind.

"Before opening night, everything went wrong," Logan said. "The scenery, the costumes. Maggie was the only sparkle. I loved Henry dearly, but he wasn't pulling it off. Finally, opening night came. The audience laughed at Henry, even when his lines were tragic, not funny. The play was a surprise hit. During its short run, every seat in the theater was filled."

"What a disaster that cheesy play was for me," Henry said. "On opening night, a vicious sea robin flew in through the large, ocean-fronting window and attacked me. I thought it was going to claw me to death. The audience laughed, thinking it was part of the plot."

Everything presented by Henry and Margaret Sullavan's summer stock theater troupe in Falmouth, on Cape Cod, had been previously tested and improved by other, more seasoned actors, usually on Broadway.

The photo above shows **Fredric March** in 1926 with an unknown actress. Clad in grass skirts and loincloths, they were bringing to life *The Devil in the Cheese* in a production more "professional" than the neophyte, sometimes bumbling, summer stock actors in Falmouth who included Henry Fonda.

Henry's seduction of Sullavan occurred two nights later. After the curtain came down, he invited her to the moonlit beach nearby. Putting on their bathing trunks they ran hand-in-hand toward the beach.

"There was some kissing, actually a lot of kissing," he said. "Then off came those bathing trunks. We raced jaybird naked to the cold waters, where we cuddled for warmth. Back on the beach, we did the dirty deed. Frankly, I think it was more satisfying for me than it was for her. After all, from what I'd heard, she was a hell of lot more experienced than I was."

"We fell asleep on the beach and woke up with the morning sun," he said. "Before going back to our quarters, I taught her to walk on her hands on the sands. There was nothing about sex that I could teach that gal."

According to Sullavan, "That very week, Henry talked about us getting married, but it was a ridiculous idea. Our combined salaries came to ten dollars a week. There were a lot of good-looking guys running around, and I didn't want to be tied down to just one man. I knew I'd never be faithful as a wife. It just wasn't in my nature."

Henry got his first big break just before the close out of the summer season at Falmouth. Cast as the lead in *The Constant Nymph,* which ran for seven performances in September of 1929, Sullavan joined him in the cast, along with his friends, Josh Logan, Bretaigne Winddust, and Kent Smith. *[The Constant Nymph had originated as a novel by Margaret Kenney in 1924. Two years later, it was adapted into a play.]*

Henry played Lewis Dodd, a charming but self-centered Belgian composer whose latest symphony had flopped. To escape his critics, he flees to Switzerland to a rundown mountain villa. The owner has four young daughters, all of whom develop a crush on the composer.

In 1943, *The Constant Nymph* was adapted into a film, a romantic drama starring Charles Boyer and Joan Fontaine.

***

At the end of the summer season on Cape Cod, Sullavan—in a move which her family had adamantly opposed—followed Henry to New York City. Each of them hoped to be cast in a Broadway play.

Henry had learned that one of the city's top theatrical booking agents was Leland Hayward, a fellow Nebraskan. Henry hoped that Hayward would agree to sign himself and Sullavan as clients.

Although his greatest fame would come a decade in the future, Hayward was already a powerhouse on Broadway. By 1940, he represented 150 stars. *[One of them was the novelist, Ernest Hemingway, who had appointed Hayward as the sales agent for the movie rights to his novels. Katharine Hepburn had refused to marry him, although he still represented her.]* In the moments before Henry's first scheduled interview, he witnessed Hayward saying goodbye to one of his clients, Greta Garbo, who had just announced that she was abandoning films forever.

Hayward's future clients would include Ginger Rogers, Boris Karloff, Judy Garland, and Henry's future best friend, James Stewart. Perhaps because of that Nebraska link, a very busy Hayward did grant a ten-minute joint interview with both Henry and Sullavan. It did not go well for either of them. Hayward was not impressed with their slim *resumés.*

Ironically, by 1936, Sullavan would become Hayward's third wife— that is, if you counted the marriage vows he made twice to debutante Lola Gibbs. *[He married Gibbs in 1921, divorced her a year later, then married her again in 1930, divorcing her four years later. In 1948, Hayward produced the hit Broadway play,* Mr. Roberts, *starring Henry Fonda.]*

Rejected by Hayward, both Henry and Sullavan began wearing out their shoe leather on the sidewalks of Manhattan, haunting casting agents' offices and turning up nothing. Finally, Sullavan announced, "I've had it. My parents are sending me a train ticket to Norfolk. I suggest you go back to Omaha."

He begged her to stay, holding out the vague promise that "something good is gonna happen...and soon...for us. I just know it."

"Dream on," were her final words to him as he saw her off at Grand Central Station.

Only five days after her departure, Henry's friend, Charlie Leatherbee, phoned him with a job offer. He had fallen in love with another young woman and had forgiven Henry for stealing Sullavan from him.

Claude Rains and Alice Brady were opening together on Broadway in a play entitled *The Game of Life and Death.* "Rains is a big name, so I think the play will run for at least a year," Leatherbee predicted.

Henry's role as "a soldier citizen" was only a walk-on at a salary of fifteen dollars a week. A production of the Theatre Guild, and formatted as a period piece, it was directed by Rouben Mamoulian. It opened in the drawing room of the De Courvoisier House in Paris during the spring of 1794.

Whereas their friends defined the marriage of **Leland Hayward** to **Margaret Sullavan** as love; their gossipy enemies attributed it to ego reinforcemen, career advantage, and manic infatuation.

Regardless, their union ended in bitterness, suicide (by Margaret, and after her death, by two of their three children), and "tsunamis of despair."

Henry, who had been "dumped" by Sullavan early in her marital adventures, watched it all with horror, bittersweet memories, a sense of amazement, and perhaps just a touch of *Schadenfreude.*

Very soon after it opened, a worldwide economic disaster struck. The Wall Street crash of 1929 shut down the lights of the Great White Way. Notices were posted the following day, announcing the closing of *The Game of Life and Death.*

A then-famous theatrical star born in London who became adept at portraying "cultured villains," Rains would have a career that spanned six decades. He had made his American film debut in *The Invisible Man* in 1933. In time, he would co-star in many Hollywood film classics, including *Mr. Smith Goes to Washington* (1939) opposite James Stewart; and *Casablanca* (1942) with Humphrey Bogart. Even his relentlessly skeptical future co-star, Bette Davis, defined him as "Hollywood's finest actor."

Claude Rains in his most famous role, as the corrupt representative of France's Vichy governmwent soliciting bribes from desperate refugees in the 1942 classic, *Casablanca.*

Filled with pain about losing his acting gig, Henry found himself walking through the streets of the theater district. Everything seemed hopeless.

During his greatest despair, he received a surprise offer from a theatrical group specializing in shows for children and teenagers, the National Junior Theatre in Washington. Apparently, it already had the financing it needed, as it was successfully riding out the Depression. Henry had already gone over so well there that he was invited to return, his former salary of $5 a week raised to $25. He gladly accepted the new offer. Once again operating out of Washington, D.C., he was cast as "The Cowardly Lion" in *The Wizard of Oz.*

At the end of the season, and out of work again, he was rescued by an offer from the Omaha Community Playhouse. "Back where I started from," he said, ruefully. "Back to living with Mom and Dad."

At his homecoming in Omaha, Henry was welcomed with open arms. Over the dinner table, a bit short on meat, he exaggerated his accomplishments in the theater. His father told him he was still keeping a job for him at his print shop open. Ironically, throughout the Depression, that job had consisted for the most part of printing foreclosure notices for many of the farms on the outskirts of town.

The play that had been selected for a week-long presentation, beginning on the night of April 28, 1930, was *A Kiss for Cinderella* by Sir James M. Barrie. In this tender-hearted comedy, Henry would portray a loving policeman.

The Barrie plot centered on "Miss Thing," a poor London girl who cares for a group of refugee children during World War I. In quiet moments, she dreams of becoming Cinderella.

Henry himself was allowed to cast the lead, selecting a fourteen-year-old from among a dozen other applicants. She was Dorothy McGuire, a native daughter of Omaha.

A Kiss for Cinderella had been tested many times since it had first been presented on a stage in London in 1916. Its cast had included the fabled actor Gerald du Maurier. That same year, it had opened on Broadway with the formidable Maude Adams. In 1925, it had been adapted into a feature-length silent film starring Betty Bronson.

After its Omaha production closed, Henry delivered his appraisal of McGuire: "Shy but stagestruck. I don't think she has the balls to make it big as an actress."

He was wrong in his assessment. By 1941, McGuire had achieved success on Broadway in the domestic comedy, *Claudia*, and by 1947, she'd be nominated for a Best Actress Oscar for *Gentleman's Agreement* starring Gregory Peck and John Garfield.

A Kiss
for Cinderella

WHERE CINDERELLA DREAMED
Falling asleep in the snow outside her poor little house, she dreams about going to a ball, beautiful as Venus.

In his early career as a Depression-era trouper in summer stock, Henry Fonda portrayed a kind-hearted police officer in a re-enactment of a "designed for children" play, **A Kiss for Cinderella**, that had been wildly successful in London and New York beginning in 1916.

As he ruefully said about the type of roles and the sometimes prissy plots he was featured in at the time, "A guy and an actor's gotta do what a guy and an actor's gotta do."

***

Despite the ravages of the Depression, in 1930, the grandfather of Charlie Leatherbee provided financing that kept the University Players alive for another season.

Henry—now back in Falmouth—was surprised that the first thing offered to him was a role in *A Kiss for Cinderella*, which he had just performed in Omaha. He had already memorized all his lines. For him, at least, the main difference was that his leading lady, playing Cinderella, would not be cast with Dorothy McGuire but with Margaret Sullavan.

Their reunion was filled with a certain passion, at least on his part. After their separation, he had told Kent Smith, "I guess I'm still in love with the bitch. Yet I'm afraid of her at the same time. Does that make sense? Every time I take two steps toward marrying her, I fall back three."

The University Players next production, *Murray Hill*, had opened on Broadway in September of 1927, as written by the English actor, Leslie Howard. As the title suggests, the action takes place in the Murray Hill section on the east side Manhattan.

Henry's friend, Myron McCormick, had been cast as Vane, one of the leading roles ("The Tweedle Butler") with smaller parts going to Kent Smith and Henry.

Although Henry would have preferred to play the lead, he supported its star, McCormick, and their friendship grew closer that summer.

Henry, later in his life, referred to McCormick as "the smartest of all of us, a Phi Beta Kappa at Princeton. Like the rest of us, he longed for real stardom, which eluded him, although he found work acting." [On Broadway, McCormick was a minor but durable player in the hit musical, *South Pacific*. Ironically, he was the only cast member left from the original when the curtain went down after a staggering 1,925 performances.]

Henry also renewed his friendship with Mildred Natwick, who became one of the most enduring character actresses of her era. Natwick would later work with such stars as Katharine Cornell and Helen Hayes. She also became a favorite actress of Directors Joshua Logan and John Ford. Ironically, in one of her most successful movies, *Barefoot in the Park* (1967), she would co-star with Henry's daughter, Jane.

Also in the cast of *Murray Hill* was the actress, Aleta Freel. Freel had arrived at Falmouth with her boyfriend, Alexander Ross, a fellow actor.

She dreamed of success as a stage actress or perhaps in films. She would later find roles on Broadway, including a big one in *Three Times the Hour* (1931).

Alexander was a genuine charmer, and his fellow actors tended to like him. Freel and Alexander seemed to be in love. They would not marry until 1936, and because they preferred to live apart from each other, Henry invited Alexander to share his bedroom in a cheap boarding house.

Young and *ingénue*: **Mildred Natwick** from the era when she was a summer stock trouper, with Henry Fonda, on Cape Cod at Falmouth in the 1930s.

Alexander seemed to have access to a bit of money, and Henry welcomed having his room rent cut in half. In fact, after the first week, Alexander agreed to pay all the rent.

At first, Henry didn't seem aware of it, but, as Freel later pointed out to him, "I think Ross in falling in love with you."

"You've got to be kidding," Henry said. "He's your boyfriend."

"Oh, Hank, you can be *naïve* about such things."

Indeed, she was right. After a month, Alexander admitted his sexual attraction to Henry, who did not reciprocate. He did, however, remain on site as his roommate.

After the theater season ended in Falmouth, Henry remained friends with both members of the couple, functioning as Alexander's Best Man at his wedding to Freel.

During the first week of July, Henry was cast in *The Wooden Kimono*, in which three of his best friends *[Bretaigne Winddust, Myron McCormick, and Kent Smith]* had bigger roles than he did. Henry had the minor role of Richard Halstead, an author of mystery stories.

The action takes place at the Red Owl Tavern, a hostelry where three unsolved murders had been committed.

At one point of the unfolding drama, Henry was supposed to emulate a corpse lying on the stage floor. Prior to his performance, he'd consumed three beers and an anchovy pizza.

Newspaper announcing **Aleta Freel**'s suicide with **Ross Alexander** inset. Murky with frustration and unexpressed emotion, with dark overtones of repressed homosexuality, these "supposedly in love and married actors," friends and confidants of Henry, each committed suicide within a few months of each other, using the same gun.

Suicide by friends, lovers, and business associates of Henry Fonda was a horrifying phenomenon that repeated itself with alarming frequency throughout the rest of his life.

During his death scene, and obvious to the audience, he developed the hiccups. Everyone watching began to laugh hilariously.

Redefined as a comedy instead of a murder thriller, the play ran for seven nights to a packed house. From that point on, Winddust, who not only acted in the play, but was its director, insisted that Henry repeat the hiccup *schtick* every night.

***

Despite ferocious arguments every day with Sullavan, Henry's affair with her continued. He later recalled that era:

"(Sullivan) was very cruel, abrasive, harsh with men at times, but she was more vulnerable to them than most women. She was a strange combination of feminine wistfulness and masculine directness. 'Always get your objective in love, in anything,' she used to say, but I always felt she was just as much swept along by her feelings as [she was] consciously directing them. And I think it all brought her a great deal of inner heartache and confusion."

Winddust directed *The Watched Pot,* a play that followed *The Wooden Kimono* that July. First produced in 1924, it was a drama set in a country mansion where a family is searching for a suitable bride for their young scion, Trevor Bavvel, played by Charlie Weatherbee.

Henry had only a minor part as William, the best roles going to actress Nancy Sullivan, with Kent Smith cast as her leading man. Aleta Freel had the second female lead, and her not-very-trustworthy boyfriend, Ross Alexander, donated his free time as a prop man, perhaps paying too much attention to one of the studly stagehands from Boston.

Although Henry consistently hoped for better roles, he sometimes expanded his horizons with other crafts associated with theater productions. For a subsequent production that summer, *Thunder to the East,* adapted from a novel by Christopher Morley, he also designed the sets.

For presentation in early August, Winddust directed *The Masque of Venice*. He angered a jealous Henry for assigning its male lead to Kent Smith, and then by casting two other actors (Josh Logan and Charlie Leatherbee) into larger roles than the one assigned to him.

Despite his relatively minor roles, Henry stole one of the scenes when he stepped onstage as Jack Cazenove in *The Moral Complex*. Structured in three acts, that play takes place in a *palazzo* along the Grand Canal in Venice.

That same August, Henry was at first thrilled when director Elizabeth Fenner cast Margaret Sullavan (as Emilia) and himself (as Lasconia) into the respective lead roles of *The Firebrand*. Set in Renaissance Florence in 1535, its plot centers around the rakish sculptor, Benvenuto Cellini, cast with Kent Smith. Cellini (Smith) is sentenced to hang for the attempted murder of Count Maffio.

"Working with Maggie wasn't the dream casting I had envisioned," Henry recalled. "There were times I wanted to bust my fist into her face. The damn bitch criticized everything I did. She felt she was the director. In front of cast and crew, she told me that I didn't have the talent to be an actor. She also claimed that if she ever married me, she would end up supporting me."

"It's obvious that I'll be the only one with any talent in this family," she said, publicly. "I'll give you money to buy groceries, and I bet you'll be good carrying out the garbage."

Cast members, including Winddust, listened in appalled silence. He later urged Henry to drop Sullivan ASAP. "She might be a psycho. Watch out!"

For reasons known only to himself, Henry told Winddust, "I've got to have this wonderful gal as my wife. I know she's a bit detached from me, but I think I can make her love me. In fact, I know I can. Right now, when we have sex, she's on top. But in time, I can change that. She'll learn soon enough who has the balls in this family. I've even taken out a marriage license."

That same August, Henry was designated as director for the latest offering from the University Players, a play entitled *Hell Bent Fer Heaven*. A drama by Hatcher Hughes, it had opened on Broadway in 1924 with George Abbott as its lead. That year, it won the Pulitzer Prize for Drama.

Set in the Blue Ridge Mountains of Kentucky, the play centers on clan rivalries between the Hunts and Lowry families. Henry cast Myron McCormick in the lead, with key roles going to Winddust, Kent Smith, and even Josh Logan, who would probably have made a better director.

Having tucked their marriage license far away and out of sight, Henry and Sullavan continued their affair, despite her frequent complaints: "You must have masturbated a lot as a boy. I read that that's often the cause of a premature ejaculator like you. You're twenty-six years old, and still don't know how to make love to a woman. I have to warn you that I've got to get my rocks off somehow, if not with you then with someone else. There are a lot of good-looking, studly men on Cape Cod. Sometimes, I go to the beach just to look at their well-muscled bodies. I love it when they wear bathing suits that reveal their pouch."

"If you want to find a man to satisfy you, I suggest you not talk to him the way you do to me," he said. "Such talk makes a limp softie out of a hard-on. Another thing: I didn't know that women used the expression, 'get your rocks off.'"

In late August, the University Players presented Noël Coward's *The Marquise*, as directed by Winddust. He assigned the male leads to Kent Smith and Josh Logan, with minor roles going to Sullavan and Charlie Leatherbee.

With Alexander Ross waiting in the wings, Aleta Freel went on as La Marquise Eloise de Kestournel, and Henry was cast in the minor role of Jacques Rijar.

Having opened in London in 1927, the play was set in 18th Century France. The plot depicts the complications arising from the romantic affairs of two generations of aristocratic families.

That night, after the premiere, Sullavan delivered her critique: "I didn't think anything could be as inept as you in bed. But there's one thing that tops your inadequate sexual performance: That's your performance on the stage. You are one lousy actor."

At the end of the 1930 summer, audiences attending performances by the University Players had dwindled as the effects of the Depression had deepened across the land. President Herbert Hoover was doing nothing to handle either joblessness or the country's widespread starvation.

Henry got a taste of that starvation after his return to New York, where he couldn't even afford salt to flavor his skimpy "one bag per week" of rice. The Great White Way remained in partial darkness, its heyday a fading mem-

Henry's roles in summer stock were always "borrowed" from the performances of other actors who had executed them in front of wider audiences.

Here's **John Harron** and **Patsy Ruth Miller,** the doomed lovers in *Hell Bent Fer Heaven,* a 1926 silent film that Henry, in a rare excursion into theater administration, later directed on Cape Cod with other amateur actors.

Despite her bitter tirade of insults, **Margaret Sullavan** continued to play convincingly opposite **Henry Fonda** in romantic plots that continued, off and on, for years after their separation and divorce.

Here she is with Henry, by then her docile ex-husband, in a love scene from *The Moon's Our Home* (1936), a comedy "about marriage and everything related to it."

Neither of the protagonists thought the dilemmas it raised were particularly funny,.

ory.

***

In Manhattan, Henry's living arrangements were temporarily solved when Charlie Leatherbee turned over his apartment at Tudor City to him rent-free. Tudor City, the first residential skyscraper complex in the world, stood on the southern edge of Turtle Bay, east of Second Avenue between 40th and 43rd Streets in Manhattan.

***

Along with Josh Logan, Leatherbee— financed by his grandfather— decided to visit Moscow to study acting under Konstantin Stanislavski, one of the leading theater directors of his generation. Born in 1863, at the age of 33, Stanislavski had founded the renowned Moscow Art Theatre.

The year was 1931 and times were by now especially hard. Although Henry had a comfortable place to live, he didn't have enough money for food except for that bag of rice. "Rice kept me from starving the way it did for so many of the Chinese."

Many Broadway theaters had closed. For performances in the few that remained open, although he had no money for a ticket, he sometimes managed to slip into a theater after the box office closed, providing he could take a seat when the usher wasn't looking.

With that ruse, he was able to see such plays as *Private Lives* with Noël Coward and Gertrude Lawrence, or Alfred Lunt and Lynn Fontanne in *Reunion in Vienna*.

Henry always welcomed overnight visits from Erik Barnow, one of the founders of the University Players. "He always arrived at my doorstep with big, thick steaks, even a bag of potatoes, with some carrots and mushrooms thrown in. Also there were heads of lettuce and a big apple pie for dessert. I was in heaven."

Most weekdays, he walked to Times Square. "Who could afford that nickel subway ride?" he asked. "Apples were being sold by vendors on every corner, but who in hell had the money to crunch into one?"

He missed Sullavan, who'd been configured as an understudy in an out-of-town road show tour of *Strictly Dishonorable*. A romantic comedy by Preston Sturges, it had first been produced on Broadway in 1929 and was being adapted for a 1931 film adaptation in Hollywood.

One night at a performance in Philadelphia, when the leading lady took sick, Sullavan had to go on in her place. There was a problem: She had developed a bad case of laryngitis, giving her a deep, throaty voice like Tallulah Bankhead's.

As a coincidence, Lee Shubert, the famous theater impresario, was in the audience that night, and he liked the sound of her raspy voice.

Within a week, he contacted her and asked her to play the lead in his Broadway Production of *A Modern Virgin*, a comedy by Elmer Harris. Sullavan made her Broadway debut in that play in 1931, and her parents showed up, later coming backstage to praise her skill as an actress. "At last, I had proven myself, and I didn't have to take any more of their damn yapping."

Although Sullavan got good notices in the press, Shubert had to shut down the play after 45 nights because of poor attendance. Humiliated, she phoned the University Players and asked if she could join them at Falmouth for the rest of the summer. That led

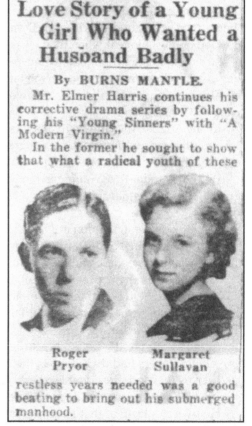

Here's one of the then-very-saucy ads that NYC's Schubert Theater used to promote **Margaret Sullavan** as a "modern virgin" in its 1931 Broadway production with the tag line "Here is one way of taming a modern daughter."

Its plot? Teddy Simpson is rebellious, female, 17, and an heiress obsessed with learning the facts of life. As a means of working things out, she has telephone conversations with strange men, stages wild parties, and reads sexy novels before settling down in marriage with an eligible bachelor friend of her family.

The play closed early, but not before elevating Sullavan's career into that of a sought-after actress, in part because of news stories like the one inserted below.

Love Story of a Young Girl Who Wanted a Husband Badly

By BURNS MANTLE.

Mr. Elmer Harris continues his corrective drama series by following his "Young Sinners" with "A Modern Virgin."

In the former he sought to show that what a radical youth of these

Roger Pryor | Margaret Sullavan

restless years needed was a good beating to bring out his submerged manhood.

24

to a reunion with lovesick Henry, who was back in residence there, too.

On Cape Cod, the players had their dullest, most lackluster summer, even reducing a ticket price to only one dollar. The season's only highlight was *The Straw Hat*. Set in Paris in 1851, it was being directed by Josh Logan.

It had been adapted into a silent film in 1927 and been translated into several languages. It revolved around a secret that, if revealed, would change the lives of all the characters.

Henry had been cast into a relatively minor supporting role as Emile. Others of his colleagues portrayed "a dodderer, a philanderer, a pretty girl, a jealous husband, and a peppery soldier."

From 1915 until it was demolished in the 1950s, the **Maryland Theater,** on West Franklin Street in Baltimore, was a mainstay of that city's vaudeville, theater, and movie scene.

Early in 1932, Henry Fonda appeared here, onstage with Margaret Sullavan, a few hours after their lackluster but real-life wedding at **the Kernan Hotel,** which is visible in the photo, immediately next door to the Maryland Theater.

On stage, they portrayed newlyweds, something that Sullavan, semi-privately, to her friends and fellow actors, reacted to with mordant sarcasm.

Whereas the theater itself no longer exists, the Kernan Hotel was converted into condominiums, the only architectural reminder, decades later, of the ill-fated marriage of Henry Fonda to his ambitious and eventually suicidal first wife, Margaret Sullavan.

***

The Maryland Theatre in Baltimore must have had "an angel" putting up the money for it to operate during the depths of the Great Depression. Its manager made a deal with the University Players to appear there during the early months of 1932.

Fresh from her debut on Broadway, Sullavan was allowed to join Henry, who was already in Baltimore with his fellow players. Eager for a reunion with her, he had booked them a small room at the Kernan Hotel. Its marble pillars and fancy plasterwork were in need of renovation.

A rumor spread that this "Broadway star," as Sullavan billed herself, was going to marry one of the University Players.

When a reporter in Baltimore asked her about that, she snapped back at him, "Are you out of your fucking mind? Who in hell would marry Henry Fonda?"

Despite her insulting denial, their wedding took place at 11AM on Christmas morning in the dining room of the Kernan Hotel. Kent Smith was the Best Man, and Bretaigne Winddust played the decrepit, out-of-tune piano. As its musical theme, he selected, "Ah, Say Not So" from the play *The Constant Nymph*.

That afternoon, a few hours after their real-life wedding ceremony, Sullavan and Henry appeared onstage as newlyweds in the matinée of *The Ghost Train*. A few hours before, Henry had gathered up some of the rice that had been thrown at him and his bride after their "real-life" marriage ceremony. Having gathered it loosely into a handkerchief, he deliberately spilled "prop rice" all over the floor of the stage. The cast and ushers laughed, fully aware of the gesture's irony.

On the final night of the play, a reporter asked Henry what it was like being married to Margaret Sullavan.

"It's like cream and sugar on a bed of hot ashes," he replied.

***

Before their honeymoon, Henry had to finish the short run of a drama called *Death Takes a Holiday*. It had originated in 1924 in Italy as *La Morte in Vacanza* by Alberto Casella. In 1929, Walter Ferris adapted it into English for a premiere on Broadway. By 1934, Hollywood would turn it into a Pre-Code romantic drama starring Fredric March.

After years of questioning why people feared him, Death takes the form of Prince Sirki for three days, hoping that by mingling among mortals, he might find the answer.

When the moment was right, the volatile newlyweds set out on their honeymoon, planning to stop for a sojourn in Norfolk so that Henry could be introduced to Sullavan's parents. Her father was enraged that she'd married an actor and not a member of the local Virginia gentry.

Henry had managed to save $75, which he used to purchase a broken-down Stutz Bearcat, a pre-World War I sports car with a "dog house hood" and open bucket seats.

After a few hours, the car "died" and sputtered out its last breath. Repairing it would cost more than it was worth, so he and Sullavan abandoned it, taking a bus back to Baltimore.

When they got there, Henry and Sullavan reconnected with the University Players to star in *The Ghost Train* at the Maryland Theatre.

In this play by Arnold Ridley, the plot centered on a group of train passengers trapped in remote railway station overnight. The play had first opened in London in 1923.

***

Josh Logan was assigned to direct Henry and Sullavan in *Mary Rose,* a play by Sir J.M. Barrie, best known for his authorship of *Peter Pan*. It was first produced in 1920 at London's Haymarket Theatre, re-opening the following year on Broadway.

The plot focuses on a mystery associated with Mary Rose, who vanished twice. As a child, during an excursion to a remote Scottish island, she vanishes. Although a frantic search turns up nothing, she reappears in three weeks, with absolutely no memory of where she'd been.

Years later, now as a young wife and mother, she persuades her husband to take her back to this same island. Once again, she vanishes, this time for decades, but later re-appears without any awareness of the passage of time. Physically, her body has not changed, and by now, her son is actually older than she is.

Mary Rose a Play in Three Acts

J. M. Barrie

It had been a long day, everyone was tired, and then this horrible fight broke out. Its poisonous after-effects lasted for years

Its players included (left to right) **a script by J.M. Barrie,** its director, **Joshua Logan, Henry Fonda,** and his acting partner/ex-wife, and perhaps lover at the time, **Margaret Sullavan.** Sullavan was particularly scathing, and Logan, it's believed, never forgave or forgot the argument that ensued.

Up until then, Logan had been one of Henry's best friends, and his relationship with Sullavan had been relatively amicable. But suddenly, Logan's relationship with Sullavan turned rancorous and bitter. *[Rumors persist that Sullavan had discovered that Logan had been sexually intimate with her husband, and that she had reacted with scathing fury. In the bitter and embarrassing arguments that evolved, she managed to turn Henry against his former friend.]*

Josh was shocked one afternoon when Henry threw the script of *Mary Rose* in his face. "I'm tired of you and your so-called direction. If you're the best director that the University Players can come up with, I'm out of here. And I'm taking Maggie with me. You're incompetent. If you want to direct, why not go back to Texarkana where you came from? I'm sure you'll go over big with the hicks down there."

Then Sullavan chimed in with: "If you'd spend more time trying to give me some guidance instead of staring at Henry's crotch all the time, we might actually be able to put on a play. Let's hope that you're a better cocksucker than you are as a director!"

Sullavan continued with her temper tantrums and harangues until two nights before the play's opening. Finally, Logan told her, "If you don't shut your trap, I'm firing you and giving the role to your understudy."

Although that seemed to shut her up, Henry continued to be antagonistic. He informed Logan that he was leaving the University Players after *Mary Rose* closed, and that he wouldn't return for the next season. "I don't plan to speak to you again."

In spite of those attacks, Logan valiantly carried on, later telling the local press that "Mr. Fonda and Miss Sullavan gave the best performances of their careers in *Mary Rose.*"

Members of the local press agreed, reviewing Henry as "spellbinding in this meditation on death and loss." Another critic predicted major stardom on Broadway for Sullavan.

Logan recalled, "True to his word, after *Mary Rose,* Henry bolted from the University Players, and so did Miss Sullavan. Together, they headed for Manhattan for the "official" debut of their married life together.

[By now, Henry's labors had affected every aspect of the University Players, and with his departure looming, they desperately needed a replacement.]

"Luck was on my side," Logan later said, "I found an even better actor than Henry at Princeton. He was lanky like Henry, and he still had a midwestern accent. Who would have thought at the time that this tall actor would become one of the most famous on the planet? His name was James Stewart, but I called him Jimmy."

***

With both of them jobless, and with no cash to spare, Mr. and Mrs. Henry Fonda moved into a $30-a-month garden apartment in Manhattan's Greenwich Village, a neighborhood described at the time as "bohemian."

Their married life began in a dingy two-room apartment with a small, beat-up kitchen gerrymandered into the corner of a cramped living room. Almost immediately, their union began to disintegrate. In Henry's words, "Marriage to Margaret Sullavan was like living with lightning."

Every day, the couple staged epic battles whose arguments were overheard by their neighbors. If their screaming denunciations had been delivered from the stage of a Broadway theater, they'd have been clearly heard in the balcony.

During their second week in residence, Kent Smith, their friend and a former member of the University Players, came to visit. Sullavan had gone out to buy food. The first thing Kent noticed was Henry's livid-looking bruises, bad injuries, the result of Sullavan throwing an iron skillet at his face.

Gossiping about his new wife, Henry confessed, "Maggie hates everything about our life—our skimpy diet, my love-making—especially that—our lack of work, our cramped apartment, our shabby wardrobes. But I'm no longer a milquetoast: Every bitchy attack she delivers is met with my counter-attack. Although I resist violence, I let her have it verbally. We have only one butcher knife. She even threw that at me one night."

When Sullavan returned with some groceries, she ordered Henry to prepare dinner while she sat alone with Smith in the garden, sharing her views of her marriage.

"I think he's a homosexual," she said. "He refuses to admit it to himself. You'd better keep it zipped up when you're around him. As a lover, he can't control his orgasm, shooting off almost at the point of entry. There's no satisfaction for me. I like a man who takes his time…at least forty minutes."

To Henry, later that evening, after Smith had left, Sullavan delivered a *coup de grâce* to their marriage. "I'm heading for stardom, bigtime. And you're on the fast track to failure. You're a terrible actor, mumbling in that Nebraska drawl of yours, putting absolutely no conviction behind your lines. You're soppy on the stage, a skinny stack of bones that comes across like a faggot. Perhaps you can find work as a dishwasher, although I doubt if you can turn out a clean plate. You're almost thirty, yet you come across as an inexperienced boy. You're hopeless. I'm not going to let a loser like you stand in the way of my future success. I want to see Leland Hayward again. I already know Lee Shubert. And I hear Jed Harris is a star-maker."

The next morning, after Sullavan left their apartment, Henry packed his meager belongings into his battered suitcase and left the premises without leaving a note. To prove that she'd been wrong about the dishes, he washed the breakfast plates.

He left with his entire life savings, less than twenty dollars. By noon, he'd found himself in a rented room in a decaying hotel on Manhattan's West Side, south of 42nd Street. "I shared it with a colony of cockroaches. A long bulb hung down from the ceiling. The sheets were yellow from years of semen and urine. The communal bathroom had a long, exposed shower—no curtain—exposing you to all the homosexuals who come in to proposition you."

"The hotel was filled with druggies, drunks, female impersonators, and prostitutes. When the Navy was in port, a lot of our sailor boys were entertained in the rooms. The walls were paper thin. You could hear everything."

Unknown to Henry (perhaps he never found out), Kent Smith had long harbored a crush on Sullavan. During his next visit to the apartment that she now occupied alone, Smith took her to a restaurant in Greenwich Village. When it was over, she invited him in for a sleepover, later defining him as "a proficient lover, but uninspired."

After that, Smith visited her apartment when she was not otherwise engaged.

Sullavan had far bigger game in sight than Smith. When she phoned the office of Jed Harris, the producer had vaguely heard of her. He asked her to come by at 6PM the following evening, scheduling her arrival for after the departure of his office staff.

The perceived desirability of **Margaret Sulla-van** began early in her career and continued all the way to its wretched, suicidal conclusion.

Sullavan became, to some degree, a symbol of American femininity itself, as shown in how frequently she was hired to endorse commercial products such as skin cream.

Born Jacob Hirsch Horowitz in Vienna when the 20th Century was only two months old, the one-year-old infant and his parents, the following year, were aboard a ship sailing to the Port of New York, there to begin another life.

By the age of seventeen, the precocious boy, Jacob, was enrolled in Yale. Later, dropping out. He told a professor, "I'm neither rich enough nor dull-witted enough to endure this awful place."

On Broadway, he was to find great success as a producer. After four consecutive Broadway hits, he appeared on the cover of *Time* magazine. *The New York Times* described him as "a flamboyant man of intermittent charm."

But to his co-workers, including his actors, he became "the most hated man on Broadway." Biographer Martin Gottfried wrote of Harris' "arrogance, egotism, cruelty, and Machiavellianism."

Harris' first hit was *Broadway* (1926), followed by *Coquette* (1927), which in a road show later starred Henry Fonda and Sullavan; *The Royal Family* (1927); and *Uncle Vanya* (1930).

At the time of his after-hours office meeting with Sullavan, he was involved in a long-term relationship with the actress, Ruth Gordon. Born the daughter of a New England sea captain, she later became a screenwriter and film star. She had made her Broadway debut in *Peter Pan* (1915) and her silent film debut that same year in *Camille*.

No great beauty, Gordon, in time, became more famous than Harris. Her nasal voice and distinctive personality led to her involvements in a series of notable films, including *Rosemary's Baby* (1968). In addition to her acting career, she wrote numerous plays, film scripts, and books, usually in collaboration with her playwright husband, Garson Kanin, turning out such scripts as *Adam's Rib* (1949), starring their best friends, Katharine Hepburn and Spencer Tracy.

When Sullavan walked into Harris' office, she was surprised to find him sitting in an armchair fully naked. He beckoned her to sit opposite him.

[Sullavan was not the first to receive a nude welcome from Harris. The nude interviews he orchestrated with both actors and actresses became something of a trademark for him, foreplay for eventually maneuvering many of them onto his casting couch. It's unknown how much his mistress, Ruth Gordon, knew of these sexual entanglements. Their romance had begun in 1929 when she starred in Serena Blandish. *That same year she became pregnant. Their son, Jones Harris, was born nine months later in Paris.]*

Before escorting Sullavan to dinner, she accepted his invitation to lie down on his casting couch. In most cases, he would never have sex again with a young actress, but in the case of Sullavan, it marked the beginning of a months-long affair.

As she would tell Myron McCormick, who worked with Henry and her at the University Players, "Jed is a wonderful lover, unlike Henry. He satisfies me deeply, if you get my drift. Henry offers a dog-like kind of love, whereas Jed comes on like the love of a cobra. Not only that…He's going to make me the biggest star on Broadway."

Very soon after it began, Henry learned of his wife's affair with Harris, even though at first, he denied it to himself. He still loved her, later recalling the pain: "I'd wait until night, and then I'd go and stand in front of the garden apartment in the Village where I had lived with her. I'd lean against the fence and stare up at the lights of our living room on the second floor. I would often stand there for more than an hour, watching the light go out. I knew that awful Jed Harris was inside with her, and I also knew that they'd be making love. After the lights in our former living room were turned off, Harris would obviously be screwing her. On more nights than I care to remember, I'd stand outside the building, looking up at my former love nest with Maggie. I'd cry my eyes out."

"Later, I'd take a handkerchief and wipe my face. After all, I didn't want to look like some broken-down wino taking the subway back to my flea-bitten room."

"Once in my room again, I would not turn on that lone electric light bulb. I'd sit on the edge of my bed filled with the utmost despair. I hated that son of a bitch Jed Harris. But in spite of this love for Maggie, I also hated her guts for what she was doing to me. She nearly destroyed me. Never in my life have I felt so betrayed, so rejected, so

The spectacularly successful Broadway producer **Jed Harris,** depicted here on the cover of the September 3, 1928 edition of *Time*, was probably the most loathed figurehead in the entertainment industry.

He was despised by Katharine Hepburn and Margaret Sullavan alike for his roaming hands, rushing fingers, and extreme manipulative cruelties.

Ruth Gordon, as she appeared in Roman Polanski's *Rosemary's Baby* (1968).

alone."

***

The actress, Barbara Barondess, became a footnote in Henry's life. When introduced to her by Joshua Logan, he was surprised at how aggressive she was in pursuing him, even asking him out on a date. "That would be great," he said, "but the truth is, I'm broke. I can't even afford a dinner for myself."

"No problem," Barondess accused him. "I have a few thousand stashed away in the bank."

The following night, wearing a suit borrowed from Myron McCormick, Henry escorted her into Sardi's, a place he had longed to frequent. They passed table after table filled with stars he recognized from their screen performances. "I felt like a gigolo," he claimed.

After Sardi's, Barondess invited Henry back to her apartment, where he made love to her. "After Maggie, she rebuilt my male ego," he later confessed to Logan. "She said I was a great lover."

"Don't let it go to your head," Logan warned. "After all, she's an actress. No man can ever believe what an actress tells him in bed."

Although Henry and Barondess would retain a friendship for many years, he soon became disillusioned with her as a lover. He learned that she was dating him only as a means to make Jed Harris jealous. She was, in effect, Harris' mistress—that is, when he wasn't seducing Ruth Gordon or Margaret Sullavan. "Three mistresses and a bevy of starlets," Henry said to Logan. "How does he keep up?"

"You mean, 'How does he keep it up?'" Logan interjected.

[During the time Henry dated Barondess, he learned about her early life. She'd been born two years after his birth to a Russian Jewish family in Brooklyn. In 1908, the family returned to their native Russia, where they remained until the Russian Revolution of 1917. Fleeing to Poland, both she and her father were wounded by Russian bullets but survived. They returned to New York, where Barondess, as a young woman, sought acting roles in the theater.]

Hollywood would soon beckon to both Henry and to Barondess, too. In 1933 and 1934, she appeared in a number of pictures, including *Hold Your Man, Soldiers in the Storm,* and *Change of Heart.* Her most noted role came when she was cast in Greta Garbo's *Queen Christina,* the film that once again united Garbo with John Gilbert, the former silent screen heartthrob who had been her lover in the 1920s.

Ironically, when James Stewart and Henry Fonda migrated to Hollywood and shared a rented house together, they once again found themselves living near Garbo. By then, Barondess had evolved into a frequent "sleepover" at Garbo's home, and on occasion, Stewart and Henry Fonda invited the two women to their shared home for dinner.

Weeks later, Henry, to his surprise, learned that Barondess didn't really like Garbo, and that she was only pretending. "Garbo is the dullest woman I've ever met," Barondess confessed to Henry.

It was obvious to Henry that the Russian *émigrée* was only hanging out with Garbo because she was the most famous actress in Hollywood. One night, Barondess told Henry that she'd attended a prestigious art auction with the clear instructions that she should bid for and purchase, at Garbo's request, a pair of paintings by Renoir. "She is the most miserly figure who ever lived. She paid for the paintings but didn't even give me a commission. Such a tightwad! She just uses people, then discards them."

During her stint as the mistress of Harris and perhaps of Garbo, too, and during her brief fling with Henry, he learned that Barondess had been married (1929-1934) to someone called Irving Jacobs. "He must have been a very understanding husband," Henry said.

During the years to come, Henry sometimes would encounter Barondess at Hollywood parties. As her screen career faded, she became an interior decorator to upscale movie stars. Her clients eventually included Norma Shearer, Errol Flynn, Gary Cooper, Ronald Reagan, and Reagan's Oscar-winning wife, actress, Jane Wyman.

The last time Henry Fonda ever saw Barondess was at Chasen's Restaurant in Los Angeles. "My god," he later said. "I couldn't believe it. Barbara was dining alone with Marilyn Monroe."

Scion of a wealthy Russian Jewish family, **Barbara Barondess** became legally entrapped among the Soviet Union, Poland, and the United States early in her youth. Flamboyantly self-promotional, she became a B-list actress; a stylist (some said lover) of Greta Garbo; and an interior decorator, details of which were laid out in her autobiography, *One Life is Not Enough.* (For years, copies of it were prominently displayed in the window of Sardi's, a watering hole and "temple" to the *oooh-la-la* of Broadway.

In Barondess's later years, before her death in 2000, she became a hardened member of the social circles of Lucille Lortel.

Lortel, a noted heiress, was the financial backer of dozens of then-experimental off-Broadway plays; a gossipy "go-to" source for information about the inner workings of the theater world, and an intimate friend of the senior co-author of this biography, Darwin Porter.

***

In Manhattan on an empty stomach, Henry faced the bleak summer of 1932, a time when the Depression seemed to affect every aspect of life in America, especially the theater. If a family had any money, they preferred to spend it on food instead of entertainment.

"At one point, I decided to mend fences with Josh Logan and return for a final season at Falmouth," Henry said. But when he got through to Logan's assistant on Cape Cod, he was informed that Logan had already hired a student of architecture from Princeton, James Stewart, as his replacement.

"Let's face it," Henry later claimed. "I had hit rock bottom, but I wasn't going to write home begging for money. Actually, Mom and Dad barely managed to eke out a living for themselves, If I couldn't survive that summer, I was going to give up my dream of becoming an actor and go back to Omaha to find a job of some sort."

As he recalled, he must have been turned away from every talent agent office in New York before he came up with one last hope. He had once met agent Sara Enright, who ran a small talent agency upstairs from Sardi's, within a tiny office lost within a warren of other small, dingy offices.

He climbed the steps to Enright's office for his interview.

She seemed most sympathetic, referring to him as "you poor kid. I don't have any acting jobs for the summer, but there's one opening I heard about. It's in Surry, Maine, outside Bal Harbor. The job is that of a handyman who does everything—drive a station wagon, be a repairman, a plumber who unstops the toilet, an errand boy, an assistant with props."

She smiled before making her final summation: "It also calls for a stud who can drop trou to satisfy a homo director or star actor."

"I'll take it. Room, board, and the twenty dollars a week you mentioned. And as you promised, lobster every Saturday night."

Train fare was included, and he arrived as part of his first-ever visit to Maine. To him, it seemed something akin to Canada. "I was housed in a sort of barracks with rows of Army cots and a communal shower. Rough living, but what the hell! The food was generous. Clam chowder every day."

In show biz parlance, his job in Maine was known as "stooging," which covered almost any task, even driving a young actress north into Canada if and when she needed an abortion.

"I was the company driver in a battered old Ford station wagon," he said. "My first job was to pick up the season's star actor, with his trunk, a guy named Joseph Cotten. I hauled him into Surry, finding out that he was this Southern boy from Virginia."

As time went by, Henry learned a lot more about Cotten. "He was a decent-looking guy with a distinctive voice that would serve him well," Henry said.

In the years to come, Cotten rose high on Hollywood's ladder, especially after appearing in plays such as *Jezebel*. Ironically, *Jezebel*, in its 1938 incarnation as a movie, would become one of Henry's most celebrated films. In it, he was cast opposite "the Southern vixen," Bette Davis.

Three years later, the bisexual actor, Orson Welles, developed "the hots" for Cotten and cast him in his first film role, *Citizen Kane* (1941) as "The Great Man's" friend, a drama critic named Jed Leland.

[Coincidentally, for a while, Cotten had been a drama critic for The Miami Herald *before resigning to become an actor. And in one of those hard-to-predict lucky breaks,* Citizen Kane *became widely hailed as the greatest movie ever made.]*

In Maine, Henry's only chance to appear on stage came when one of the minor actors got sick at the last minute. Henry knew his lines, and went on in the bit role of Inspector Enderby in A.A. Milne's play, *Michael and Mary*.

Its plot involves a young bride who finds joy with a new lover after being cruelly abandoned by her young husband. When she discovers that her new love has made her pregnant, they enter into a bigamous marriage for the sake of their "born out of wedlock" child. It's then that the shameless, bona-fide husband shows up and starts blackmailing them.

Michael and Mary was later adapted into a British film directed by Victor Saville and co-starring Herbert Marshall, Elizabeth Allen, and Frank Lawton. Later it was voted as the third-best British Movie of the Year.

Joseph Cotten, who for a brief period worked as a drama critic for the *Miami Herald*, appears here in *Citizen Kane* (1941)

[In 1947, after both Fonda and Cotten had evolved into leading stars of Tinseltown, they were each invited, separately, to a party at the home of Loretta Young. At the elegant party, Cotten approached Fonda: "Forgive me. I don't remember your name. But weren't

you that errand boy who hauled my trunk from the railway station in Maine!

"Thanks for the memory, you dirty shit," Fonda said, gently and facetiously, smiling to soften the hostility.]

During that long-ago summer in Maine when Henry was smoothing the way for bigger stars like Cotten, the crew's set designer had thrown a temper fit, stalked off, and quit. Henry approached the director, citing his previous work with props and sets on Cape Cod, and was almost immediately hired as the set designer's replacement. It carried a five-dollar weekly raise. "I spent the rest of the summer designing scenery. Then the cold winds blew down from Canada, and it was back to pounding the streets of Manhattan, trying to find something to fill my gut."

One afternoon, perhaps with a sense of remembered embarrassment, he obtained Josh Logan's new phone number and called him, apologizing for the difficulties which he and Margaret Sullavan had catalyzed during his direction of them in *Mary Rose.* "I was under her spell and, as you know, she's a real harridan. I didn't mean all those things I said about you. You're a wonderful director, and I predict you'll become the finest on Broadway."

"So, you're sucking up," Logan said. "You must want something."

"You're sure right about that," Henry said. "I need both a job and a place to live. I don't want to be selling apples on a street corner and sleeping in Central Park."

Later that day, the actor and the director met amicably for a hamburger and a Coke. According to Logan, "Hank and I signed a peace treaty. I even invited him to come and live with me in an apartment I rented on West 64th Street. The building was dubbed *Casa Gangrene* and it was filled with prostitutes who charged from $5 to $10 a night, depending on their age. Many of their customers, shady characters, lurked in the hallways."

Mugshot, taken by the Philadelphia police in 1929, of **Legs (Jack) Diamond.**

Before his gangland killing in 1931, he had been a frequent visitor to the brothel that operated within the building occupied by Henry Fonda during his residency of a low-rent apartment the building contained.

[The most frequent visitor to their building had been the notorious gangster "Legs" Diamond, who had sampled most (or perhaps all) of the prostitutes. But on December 18, 1931, he was shot down in a gangland slaying, having survived multiple attempts on his life since 1916. In reference to the many previous attempts ("shooting practices") on his life, Diamond had become known as "the clay pigeon of the Underworld."]

"The clients of our in-house whores looked like refugees from a James Cagney movie," Henry later recalled. "Chesterfield coats and Borsalino hats, their eyes hidden behind dark glasses. All of them arrived heavily armed. We were told that one of the prostitutes—the fourteen-year-old—was the most desired. One night, again as we heard later, she was gang-raped. During her siege she was killed. Her body just disappeared. There was one thing these hoods knew how to do and that was how to dispose of a corpse."

Sharing the seedy apartment with Logan and Henry would be Myron McCormick, an actor who'd been Henry's friend when he was part of the University Players. "We have a fourth roommate, Jimmy Stewart, this architect student from Princeton," Logan said. "I hired him on Cape Cod as your replacement this past summer. He's a great guy. You'll love him."

"I'm sure I'll be mad about the boy," Henry said sarcastically, his jealousy showing.

[Despite his sarcasm, Henry, in time, would come to truly love Jimmy Stewart. Together, they'd forge one of the great male bondings in the history of Hollywood. Even before the term came into vogue, theirs became one of the most noted instances of a "bromance" in the history of Hollywood.]

When Henry arrived with his battered suitcase for his introduction to James Stewart, it was the beginning of a devoted friendship that endured for half a century.

***

In time, **James Stewart** and Henry Fonda formed the greatest example of male bonding in the history of Hollywood.

"We shared everything from a single bed in a cramped apartmengt to (much later) some of the greatest stars in Hollywood, like Greta Garbo. Even my former wife, Margaret Sullavan."

A son of Indiana, Pennsylvania, and four years younger than Henry, James ("Jimmy") Maitland Stewart became known for his distinctive drawl and "everyman screen persona" in a career that spanned 80 movies produced between 1935 and 1991. The American Film Institute ranked him as third on its list of greatest actors.

Of Scottish and Irish ancestry, Stewart was born to a deeply religious family. His mother was a pianist; his father, Alexander, ran the local hardware store. The smell of linseed oil was one of the boy's earliest memories.

Once, when a customer could not pay his bill with cash, he forfeited to Alexander an accordion instead. His young son learned to play it and proudly carried it around with him for many years.

At the age of thirteen, James discovered "the flickers" and got a job working at The Strand, a local movie house. There, he thrilled to screen vamps like Pola Negri and Gloria Swanson; to Western heroes like William S. Hart; and to "the Little Tramp," Charlie Chaplin, though he preferred Buster Keaton.

As he grew older, James attended Mercersburg Prep School, one of the most prestigious in the Northeast. By then, he had grown tall and lanky. During the summer, he took such jobs as a brick loader and later, a magician's assistant.

When Charles Lindbergh completed history's first solo flight across the Atlantic, Stewart decided he wanted to be a pilot. [*Ironically, in 1957, he'd be cast as Lindbergh in the film* The Spirit of St. Louis.]

Princeton was James' college of choice and, once there, he studied architecture, dreaming one day of designing landmark buildings. On an impulse, with the belief that he might try acting on the side, he joined the Princeton Triangle Club. That led to him replacing Henry during the summer of 1932 at West Falmouth as a member of the University Players.

At Princeton, Stewart had fallen in love (his first time) with the young actress, Margaret Sullavan, who had arrived for an appearance in *The Artist and the Lady*. "I wanted her the first time she looked at me with eyes that danced," Stewart recalled. To his regret, he learned that she was married to another young actor, Henry Fonda.

When Stewart ultimately met Henry, he concealed from him that he harbored a crush on Sullavan.

[*Actually, Logan had tricked Stewart into joining the University Players. He had falsely told Stewart that Sullavan would be appearing in some of the company's plays. Actually, she had other offers and other plans. Ironically, by the time Stewart came to live with Logan and Henry in Manhattan, Henry was headed for the divorce courts.*]

At this point, when Henry spoke to Stewart about his wife, he referred to her as a "ball-breaker."

"Actually, I was aware that Sullavan played the field," Stewart said. "After that time she visited Princeton, I learned that she'd seduced two of the good-looking guys on the football team. She wasn't your typical Jean Harlow beauty. She had her own kind of sex appeal—that of a *femme fatale*, a real heartbreaker. I'd heard she demolished that Fonda guy. The joke among the University Players was that their marriage did not survive the first night, as he struggled to satisfy this sexy vixen. I felt I could handle her in spite of my shyness."

Sullavan had become aware of Stewart's fascination with her. She told Logan, "Jimmy is like a little lost lamb who can't find his mother. If I had started screwing him that summer, I knew I would have broken his heart. I didn't want to hurt him—he's is too sweet a guy. We did have one session of heavy petting. I felt his crotch. I seemed ample enough, but he's just not my type. Too hesitant. Too nervous around a woman. For me, getting involved with him would be like Act Two of my Henry Fonda saga."

By the time Stewart actually moved into that dowdy Manhattan apartment with Fonda, Logan, and McCormick, he no longer seemed to resent Henry for marrying "the girl of my dreams."

According to Logan, "Although they were quite different men, they became the best of pals almost from the beginning. One night when I entered the apartment, the lights were out. In the far corner of the room, I spotted Jimmy playing the accordion for Hank. My god, I thought they might be falling in love."

"I felt that after his break with Sullavan, Hank was worried about his sexual identity," Logan continued. "It was a period he was going through. His masculinity had been wounded. For all I knew, Sullavan had left Hank impotent."

"Jimmy and I talked endlessly about our lives as teenagers," Henry said. "I brought up my limited sexual experience and learned about his. As a boy, he had never participated in a circle jerk like so many boys do. I thought that if Jimmy didn't wank his pecker, he was either a saint or a eunuch. I soon got over the notion that he was either one."

"In almost no time at all," Henry continued, "Jimmy landed in Hollywood, where he became a notorious ladies' man. He told me that his favorite actress was Norma Shearer. She became just one of the stars he seduced, although he didn't neglect starlets, chorus girls, burlesque queens, campus beauties—and the beat goes on."

Amazingly, because Jimmy and I hung out together, almost a daily occurrence, some jealous actors called us 'just a couple of fags.' In Hollywood, gossip can get it oh, so wrong."

***

The rent of $35 a month was past due, and Henry, Logan, Stewart, and McCormick had no money. "At one point, Jimmy and I were so broke, he took his accordion and we found a vacant corner where he gave a concert," Henry said. "I passed the hat. We got five dimes, two nickels, and eight pennies. It felt like a fortune to us at the time."

The men were rescued by the arrival in town of Arthur Beckhard, a Broadway producer who had taken control of the University Players. In Manhattan, casting for his new Broadway play, *Carry [sometimes spelled "Carrie"] Nation*.

It was named for the radical, sour-faced head of the Pre-Prohibition Temperance Movement. Claiming a divine ordination to promote temperance by destroying bars, and strenuously opposing the consumption of alcohol, she became infamous for attacking taverns with a hatchet. In her namesake play, she was described as "the Anti-Souse Queen…a bulldog running along at the feet of Jesus, barking at what he doesn't like."

The female lead in *Carry Nation* was awarded to Esther Dale, who was married to Beckhard. Logan managed to get himself designated as assistant to the producer, with key acting roles going to Stewart and McCormick. The only apartment occupant who didn't get a role was Henry himself. "I felt like an orphan left in the cold without a winter coat."

Carry Nation received mixed reviews, closing in three weeks. Its final performance attracted an audience of only eighteen patrons.

Beckhard didn't give up easily. He rebounded with another show, *Goodbye Again,* a 1932 play by George Haight Allan Scott. Its plot? During a visit to Cleveland, a famous author, Kenneth Bixby, decides to re-ignite a romance with his ex-sweetheart, Julie.

In 1933, it was adapted into a Pre-Code romantic comedy directed by Michael Curtiz and starring Warren William and Joan Blondell.

"Once again, all three of my roommates were hired for *Goodbye Again,*" Henry said. "I was beginning to feel that Beckhard didn't like me."

Receiving respectable reviews, *Goodbye Again* ran for a few months.

Finally, an acting job opened for Henry in East Orange, New Jersey. He went alone there to star in some run-of-the-mill theatrical staples."

Arriving two days early, he walked the lonely streets of East Orange, a town on the Passaic River known at the time for its big shade trees and as the site of Upsala College, a private liberal arts school. *[Founded in Brooklyn in 1893 in association with the Swedish Lutheran Evangelical Church, it had moved to East Orange in 1924. Financial difficulties, urban blight, and declining enrollments forced the school to close in 1995.]*

As the leading man in those stock productions, Henry was entitled to ten percent of the box office gross, which came to "seven lousy bucks a week" (his words).

Fortunately, the producer owned a nearby orchard, apples from which Henry mashed and distilled into applejack. Before the summer ended, Henry was able to export many bottles of it back to the Manhattan apartment he shared with Logan and Stewart to "fight off winter's cold." *[The owner of the building they occupied supplied almost no heat.]*

When he returned to Manhattan from East Orange, his final divorce papers from Margaret Sullavan were waiting for him. He later reported, "I was filled with the deepest despair. I decided then and there that I was not husband material. I vowed never to marry again."

His luck changed when Logan, through a contact, got Henry a small role as a bar patron in a Broadway play, *I Loved You Wednesday.* Written by Molly Ricardel and William DuBois, it ran for sixty-three performances. In addition to his small role as a bar patron, he was also the understudy in that same play to a young actor named Humphrey Bogart.

He also worked with an aspiring actress named Arlene Francis, who was two years younger than he was. Born in Boston, she was of Armenian descent and later studied in Paris. In time, she became a household name during her long-running gig as a panelist on *What's My Line?*, a television game show.

Henry dated her twice. "I ended up with a peck on the cheek," Francis jokingly recalled. "Bogie tried to get to the honeypot, too, but all he succeeded at was fingering it. He also admired my breasts." *[She made these revelations at a drunken party hosted by the producer, Mark Goodson, of* What's My Line? *Its first telecast was hosted by John Charles Daly, who was a guest alongside columnist Dorothy Kilgallen and Steve Allen. Francis was escorted to that party by Cesar Romero, who earlier that night had been* What's My Line?'s *mystery guest.]*

In Hollywood, in 1933, Fox adapted *I Loved You Wednesday* into a film. It starred Warner Baxter, Elissa Landi, and two future character actors from *Gone With the Wind,* Victor Jory and Laura Hope Crews.

Upper photo: **Arlene Francis**, from her early days in the entertainment industry, around the time Henry Fonda started dating her, and

Lower photo, **What's My Line,** the board game based on the long-running CBS-TV game show (1950-1967) in which Francis thrived and became a "daytime TV cult figure" in her own right.

Over Christmas, the four apartment dwellers celebrated with the applejack that Henry had saved for the occasion. "I had enough applejack to bring in the New Year of 1933, too."

"That new year started off with a piece of luck," Henry said. "Finally, in February, Arthur Beckhard got around to giving me a job. He was directing a Broadway drama, *Forsaking All Others,* starring the formidable Tallulah Bankhead.

In this stage-play comedy of errors, three friends (two men and a woman) become involved in a love triangle lasting many years. *[In its film adaptation of 1934, Bankhead lost her role to Joan Crawford, who co-starred with Robert Montgomery and a fast-rising actor named Clark Gable.]*

As is the theatrical custom, It was clearly understood that Henry, the understudy, would not appear in any performances unless its leading man, the Canada-born actor Fred Keating, got sick. Only when (and only if) that happened, Henry would strut his stuff onstage, interacting with and reacting to Tallulah.

Before meeting her, Henry asked Beckhard "Are all of those scandalous rumors about Bankhead true?"

"They're all true, and there are even more scandalous things going on with her that the public hasn't heard about," Beckhard answered.

He then looked Henry up and down before asking, "Are you cut or uncut? Obviously, I'm referring to your penis."

"I'm uncut," he answered, somewhat reluctantly. "Why? Do I have to show my dick on stage for this gig?"

"No, I was just asking," he answered. "Tallulah prefers men uncut."

The formidable **Tallulah Bankhead**, that belle from Alabama, was the most scandal-soaked actress of her day. "I had a brief fling with a young Henry Fonda, but I chew up men like that and spit them out over my breakfast coffee."

"My best sexual partners were Sir Winston Churchill and Hattie McDaniel...you know, Mammy in *Gone With the Wind.*"

Young Henry Fonda, methodically working things out.

CHAPTER THREE

YOUNG HENRY

Faces the Perils and Debaucheries of the Great White Way

"Well, Toto, I guess we're not in Nebraska or Kansas any more."
—**Dorothy**, after arriving with her dog in Oz

"Tallulah Bankhead put me on the casting couch."

—**Henry Fonda**

That afternoon in February of 1933, when Henry was ushered into the dressing room of Tallulah Bankhead, would be forever etched on his brain. "My knees were shaking as she gave me the once-over," he said. "It was more than a once-over. She seemed to have eyes that stripped me bare. I was being inspected like a slab of beef. She delayed speaking for a while, just looking."

She finally said, "So, you're Henry Fonda. Just how old are you, kid?"

He told the truth, informing her that he was 28.

"You're a damn liar," she shot back. "I don't think you're even twenty. That doesn't matter. I'm telling Arthur Beckhard to give you a walk-on and also to let you be the understudy to Fred Keating, my leading man. I'm staying in a suite at the Gotham Hotel. I want you there tonight at nine."

"I'll be there," he said, just before being dismissed by a wave of her hand. He feared what was in store for him.

Before going to the Gotham, he read the play, *Foresaking All Others*, by Edward Barry Roberts and Frank Morgan Cavett. It was a comedy of errors, the saga of three friends (two men and a woman), who are involved in a love triangle that spans many years.

He'd have to learn the lines of Fred Keating in case at the last minute he'd be called onstage in his place. Otherwise, his role was so small that the character he'd play didn't even have a name. In the script it was referred to only as "A Gentleman."

Although Keating had been born in Ohio, most of the cast thought he was from Canada, site of most of his public achievements. In the years to come, he would spend decades there hosting government events, earning him the sobriquet of "Canada's Massacre of Ceremonies."

"Learn my lines, boy!" he'd say to Henry. "Perhaps I'll pretend to be sick for two or three nights, allowing you to go on and strut your stuff. I just hope you have some stuff to strut."

Keating was an odd choice as Tallulah's leading man. At the time, he was down on his luck, working as a magician who specialized in making birds vanish. Before reporting to work, he had declared bankruptcy, including in the inventory of his assets a canary worth one dollar and a canary cage valued at one thousand.

Tallulah also promoted the assignment of a minor role in the play to Anderson Lawler, who soon became her "sidekick." She invited him to live in her suite at the Gotham. "We're not lovers—he doesn't swing that way, *dahling*—but he makes a charming companion and drinking buddy. He's the lover of Gary Cooper."

After having a bite to eat, Henry arrived exactly at nine o'clock at the Gotham. When Tallulah opened the door, he was shocked that she was nude. He was unfamiliar with her legend. If he had been, he would know that she even opened her door nude when hosting a party. In London, she'd been known for turning cartwheels at parties

A tragic figure in show business, **Fred Keating** went from magician (he could make a birdcage disappear) to actor. Between 1936 and 1940, he made 14 films in Hollywood, including starring with Lili Damita (wife of Errol Flynn) in *Devil on Horseback* (1936).. Alcoholism and severe depression hampered his career, which ended in brief stints at seedy dives in Manhattan.

Death from a heart attack came in 1961.

minus her panties.

Emerging from her bedroom carrying a silk robe for the star, Anderson Lawler came into the living room and managed to "wrap" Tallulah. He lectured her, telling her, "Mr. Fonda here will have enough time later tonight to review your honeypot."

A son of Alabama, the state of Tallulah's origins, Lawler was about thirty years old with a pronounced Southern accent. At first, Henry thought he was Tallulah's lover, although she referred to him as "my caddy."

As they talked, Henry was surprised "that his potty mouth matched hers." He later described Lawler as "tall, thin, with a choirboy's face, and red hair beginning to thin."

After drinks were served, Henry grew intoxicated as the evening progressed.

Tallulah had told many witnesses that she'd gone to Hollywood mainly to fuck Gary Cooper. "I made a movie with him called *Devil and the Deep* (1932) for Paramount, but I found I had competition from my two co-stars, Charles Laughton and Cary Grant. Both of those homos wanted Gary too, but I got him, at least for the first week. Clara Bow had already told me he was hung like a horse and could go all night."

"By the second week, I met Andy here," she claimed. "He was Coop's steady piece, and they were living together at his house."

"I don't know how steady Coop is," Andy said. "It's true he lives with me when not going over to pound that Mexican spitfire, Lupe Velez. That bitch never said no to any man. In other words, we share Coop."

Later, Henry recalled to producer Arthur Beckhart, "Tallulah and Anderson are equally matched, a son and daughter of Alabama, each with an obscene tongue and a mocking laugh."

As the drunken evening reached midnight, Tallulah finally admitted she was exhausted, and she staggered to her feet and walked toward her bedroom. She turned back to address Henry. "Fonda, you are a *dah-ling*, and I think Andy agrees. Be my guest. You can share Andy's double bed."

When she was gone, Lawler asked Henry where he was staying "Nowhere," Henry said. "I left my lone suitcase with the baggage department downstairs. I'm low on cash, so I thought I'd try the YMCA tonight."

"Forget that," Lawler said. "I'm sure Tallu would be delighted if you shared my bed for the run of the play."

When Henry seemed leery, Lawler assured him, "Nothing to worry about. I'll stay on my side of the bed unless I get an invite to cuddle."

"It's a date," Henry said.

In the middle of the night in their shared bed, Henry was asleep when he was awakened by Lawler, answering a call from Tallulah's bedroom. He was gone for ten minutes. When he returned to their bedroom, he was blunt: "Tallu can't sleep until she gets fucked. I'm not the guy to do it, but you're on. Here's your chance to plug the clit that has satisfied everyone from John Barrymore to Sir Winston Churchill, not to mention many of the leading stage actresses of our day."

As Henry recalled later to James Stewart and others, "I was most hesitant to go into that dark chamber, I managed to do the dirty deed, and it was an ordeal. I wouldn't call it my command performance. She controlled the action, even issuing directions."

"After we'd finished, I fell into a deep sleep by her side. We didn't wake up until Andy arrived with black coffee at ten the following morning. I sure needed a cup. I think

Tallulah was disappointed with me. She would never invite me back to her bed again for a repeat performance."

"I stayed on, sharing Andy's bedroom, until the sudden arrival from Hollywood of Gary Cooper."

***

When they first met, Henry was both awed by Gary Cooper and secretly jealous of him. "He was this Montana cowpoke, who combined the best qualities of the American West with that of an English gentleman," Henry later said.

"He had me spellbound. This was the kind of man I wanted to be, but felt I was far short of my goal."

"Cooper possessed striking blue eyes with a kind of quiet intensity, seeing everything, but not commenting on what he saw," Henry said.

In Hollywood, Cooper had already developed a reputation for combining rakishness with innocence. He was lanky and very tall, looming several feet above most of his leading ladies. The press hailed him as "a true male beauty" long before he developed that rugged look of a true Western hero.

When Henry met him, he was morphing from a Montana ranch kid into a sophisticated man-about-town in Hollywood.

Cooper was embarrassed when both men and women marveled about his male beauty. "That doesn't sound masculine to me," he said.

In spite of the raves, he didn't seem narcissistic. He already enjoyed a reputation as "catnip for the ladies" and as a symbol of studly sexiness to homosexual actors and film crew members. His voice was deep, with a pleasant drawl, well-modulated.

Cooper arrived at Tallulah's suite at the Gotham after checking into his own suite at the Waldorf Astoria. To some degree, he was visiting to renew his acquaintance with Tallulah, which had begun when they'd co-starred in *Devil and the Deep*. More compellingly, he'd come over to retrieve Lawler, and to take him back to his hotel. Henry soon learned the nicknames they'd "assigned" each other: Cooper was called "Jamey," with Lawler nicknamed "Nin."

The evening marked the beginning of Henry's decades-long relationship with Cooper, although the two men would never be as close as Henry was with James Stewart.

Many film critics noted that Stewart, Henry, and Cooper specialized in the same kind of roles: "All three of these guys were bunched together as a prototype of the American hero," Joshua Logan said. "Take *High Noon* for example. Any of the three actors would have been suitable as the male lead, although Coop was the best choice."

Despite their rivalries, the friendship between Henry and Cooper endured, although they rarely saw each other. Later, after Henry signed a contract to star in a summer stock stage production of *The Virginian*, Cooper heard about it and sent Henry the spurs he'd worn in his film rendition of *The Virginian* (1929).

[In that film, he had co-starred with Walter Huston and Richard Arlen.]

Although Tallulah and Henry were left alone in her suite after Cooper departed with Lawler, she made no further sexual overtures toward him. He feared he'd have to move out soon, but Lawler phoned to say that he would return in a few days because Cooper had to fly back to Hollywood to film another movie.

An invitation to visit Cooper's suite at the Waldorf followed, and Henry escorted Tallulah there.

As he remembered it, it was a long evening of eating and drinking, with plenty of indiscreet revelations.

At one point, the subject of

Tallulah Bankhead was both adored and dreaded for the humor, naughtiness, and viciousness of her gossip.

Objects of her ire—especially as it applied to sexual overtures aimed at the object of her affection (Gary Cooper)—included, left to right, **Charles Laughton** (shown here with his understanding and indulgent "Bride of Frankenstein" wife, **Elsa Lanchester**); the promiscuity of the "Mexican spitfire" **Lupe Velez**, shown in center photo as a "coochie-coo" dancer in 1925; and **Cary Grant**, on the right with **Katharine Hepburn** in *Bringing Up Baby* (1938).

Lupe Velez was introduced. It was obvious from the expression on Lawler's face that he was jealous of Coop's sexy Mexican mistress.

The torrid affair between Velez and Cooper had begun during their filming of *Wolf Song* in 1929. "Our director, Victor Fleming, had me strip buck naked for a nude scene, but it didn't make the final cut," Cooper said.

"Had it been shown, you would have doubled your legion of admirers," Lawler responded.

"I agree, *dahling,*" a drunken Tallulah said. "Especially with size queens."

Cooper and Lawler, as both Tallulah and Henry learned, had met in 1929 when Lawler had visited the set of *Betrayal,* co-starring the German actor, Emil Jannings, and Esther Ralston.

Lawler had been impressed with sketches Cooper had made of his co-stars.

"I'm really thinking about becoming a newspaper cartoonist instead of an actor," Cooper told Lawler. "Would you like to come to my house tonight and see more of my work?"

"Would I!" Lawler said, as his eyes brightened.

That night, Lawler saw more than Cooper's etchings and moved in the next day. Word soon spread along the Hollywood grapevine.

Actor Jack Oakie went skinny-dipping with them. He later dismissed rumors of an affair. "Coop a queer? You gotta be kidding. But then again, it might be true. When we were lying nude sunning ourselves on a blanket, Andy's eyes never traveled north of Coop's waist. Indeed, it was a sight to see."

When director George Cukor heard the rumors, he believed them. He later reflected on that time in Hollywood, calling it "the Pre-Code era."

"When Mr. Cooper and Miss Bankhead hit town, everybody in Hollywood in those days seemed to be fucking everybody, usually without gender preference. Take Marlene Dietrich or Joan Crawford for example, and especially Errol Flynn who came along later. We called it 'free love.'"

In years to come, Henry would narrate a TV special about the Golden Age of Hollywood which prominently featured Cooper. By then, Henry knew a lot about the actor who by now had been nicknamed "The Montana Mule."

Long after both Lawler and Velez had been absent from his bed, Cooper engaged in a list of seductions, despite the validity of his marriage to Veronica (Rocky) Balfe at the time. The list included Marlene Dietrich, Ingrid Bergman, Claudette Colbert, Cary Grant, Howard Hughes, Randolph Scott, Carole Lombard, Barbara Stanwyck, and especially the American-born socialite, Dorothy, Countess of Frasso. Yet Cooper maintained that the love of his life was actress Patricia Neal, his co-star in *The Fountainhead* (1948).

"Certain men were more lovesick over Coop than women," claimed Loretta Young, his co-star in *Along Came Jones* (1945).

During his affair with Cooper, Lawler had at least one advantage over Velez: Like Cooper, he was a man of the outdoors, and he and Cooper went mountain climbing, boating, and swimming. Lawler even taught Cooper how to be an archer.

During all those outdoor activities, Velez did not remain alone. Born to a streetwalker in Mexico City in 1908, Velez, as a teenager, was sold by her mother to the highest bidder. At the age of fifteen, she was a "raunchy burlesque queen."

In Hollywood, she became known as a *de facto* nymphomaniac. Columnist Adela Rogers St. Johns said, "Lupe never met a man she didn't want to seduce."

When Cooper moved on, Velez found other playmates: Tarzan (Johnny Weissmuller), Clark Gable, Errol Flynn, boxer Jack Dempsey, and Douglas Fairbanks Jr., when he wasn't at home with his wife, Joan Crawford, and when she wasn't in bed with Clark Gable.

Beautiful people establishing (and maintaining) reputations for libertine hedonism in Pre-Code Hollywood.

Upper photo: **Gary Cooper** with **Marlene Dietrich** in *Morocco* (1930).

Lower photo: **Gary Cooper** on the set of *Morocco* (1930).

Henry Fonda, fresh from the cornfields of the Middle West, found navigations of the murky moralities of Hollywood tricky, indeed.

When Cooper flew back to Hollywood, Tallulah, Lawler, and Henry focused on the fine-tuning of *Forsaking All Others*. He learned that she had put up $40,000 of her own money to launch it on Broadway.

A week before its opening, she fired its producer, Arthur Beckhart, and replaced him with actor Thomas Mitchell. [*In years to come, Mitchell would immortalize himself playing Scarlett O'Hara's father, Gerald, in* Gone With the Wind *(1939).*]

Forsaking All Others could not have chosen a worse night to open on Broadway. Banks across America shut down for a "holiday" on March 1, 1933 when Franklin D. Roosevelt was in the White House.

Among those attending opening night was the doomed aviator, Amelia Earhart, who came backstage to greet the cast. "If you ever need a co-pilot," Henry said to her, "give me a call." Of course, he wasn't serious.

For the next fourteen weeks, attendance was sparse, and Tallulah was forced to shut down the play. She told Henry, "I should not have listened to that bastard, Leland Hayward. He told me that *Forsaking* would be a big hit. He is the most elastic reed I've ever leaned on."

She did recoup some of her money when she sold its film right to Hollywood for a movie starring Joan Crawford, Robert Montgomery, and Clark Gable.

Out of work and with no prospects, Henry found an ad in the classified section of *The New York Times*. "Florist's Assistant, Goldfarb's Florist, southwest corner, 72nd & Third."

Jobs were hard to come by during the Depression. When Henry arrived at the shop, some thirty guys were also there, but he won out by claiming that his lifelong ambition had been to be a florist. The job was much harder than he had thought. "What was needed was a weightlifter who could carry heavy pots of tulips, lilies, and other flowers from the basement to the street," where customers often awarded him with a nickel tip.

He would later jokingly refer to this temporary job as "My life among the pansies."

***

Although her *Foresaking All Others* had been a commercial failure, Tallulah would not abandon her theatrical ambitions. "In the theater, *dah-ling*," as she told Henry, "we often go from flop to flop, waiting to strike gold, which comes along occasionally, at least enough to make the struggle worthwhile."

She continued to receive scripts for plays, mostly from unknown writers. Going through the stacks she'd already reviewed, she found one by Owen Davis Sr entitled *Jezebel*. Davis was one of the most prolific playwrights in America, author of some two hundred plays, most of which got produced.

The role of the self-centered Southern beauty, Julie Marson, seemed ideal for Tallulah. The setting was New Orleans in 1852. She certainly would not need to learn how to speak with a Southern accent.

In her suite that night, she asked Henry to read the play with her, casting him into the role of Julie's suitor, a young banker named Press Dillard.

After the read, she told him, "You'd make the perfect Press. How about becoming my leading man?"

"It would be the greatest break of my life."

"We weren't great lovers in private," she more or less scolded him. "But on stage, we can pretend, can't we? Of course. I've got to get the approval of our director, Guthrie McClintic. I'll set up a meeting between you two. I think he'll really go for a handsome young man like you."

To Henry, it sounded like she was setting him up for a romantic date instead of a casting call.

The next day, McClintic indicated that he wanted to meet Henry at

FORSAKING ALL OTHERS
TIMES SQUARE THEATRE

Both photos, above: **Tallulah** in her (self-financed) Broadway production of the tear-jerking melodrama, *Forsaking All Others.*

MGM purchased the screen rights as a vehicle for Joan Crawford and Clark Gable.

What bombed on Broadway with Tallulah was raved about in 1934 as a Pre-Code Classic.

Photo shows **Clark Gable** emoting with **Joan Crawford** in *Forsaking All Others* (1934).

Young Henry Fonda, who by then had been steeped in the convoluted backstories associated with it, watched with fascination.

his residence instead of at his office. Henry had already attended McClintic's first major success on Broadway, *The Barretts of Wimple Street,* starring his wife, the venerable actress, Katharine Cornell.

As was widely rumored, their union was a lavender marriage, an arrangement designed to conceal their respective homosexualities.

As Henry admitted later, "I was very uncomfortable reading lines from *Jezebel* in front of McClintic. I felt he wasn't really listening to my reading but was appraising my sexual potential instead. He seemed to like what he saw. As I had been told, I would not be the first young actor he put on the casting couch."

After Henry had read, aloud, several pages of the script, McClintic told him, "No need to read more lines. You've won me over. You're my Press, and I think it's a case of dream casting since you're perfect for the role. Not only that, but as you read, I began to realize that you'd make the perfect Romeo opposite my wife as Juliet. I'm planning to bring the Bard's most famous work to Broadway in a few months. Of course, you may think that Hamlet is Shakespeare's finest, but we won't quibble about that now. You'll do *Hamlet* after you've had a few more years of living."

"I think you might become a major star on Broadway," McClintic continued, "with me directing you. I'm going to the Hamptons for the week, and I want you to come with me. I'd like to hear you read from certain key scenes. I'll select from plays with roles that might be ideal if they're cast with you. You certainly have the looks, the presence, and the voice."

Henry had been around the theater long enough to know that was a call for seduction, but it might also be his doorway opening onto Broadway stardom. He'd have to be cagey, deciding that if he wanted to succeed enough in the theater, he'd probably have to submit to the director and his casting couch. It was certainly something to ponder, and he had only days to make up his mind.

Fate intervened: *Jezebel* would eventually reach Broadway, but not with Tallulah as Julie or Henry as Press.

Spectacularly fashionable, and spectacularly sought-after, stage diva **Katharine Cornell** with her director/producer husband, **Guthrie McClintic** appear here in the library of their well-appointed home on Sutton Place in Manhattan in the 1930s.

Bound together by business in a highly strategic "lavender marriage," they were one of the two or three most visible "power brokering teams" on Broadway.

Young Henry Fonda was not the first actor to fall prey to their (separate) entrapments: A few years later, Kirk Douglas, among others, would find it hard to extricate himself from McClintic's trap, too.

Before rehearsals could get underway, Tallulah began to experience severe pains in her abdominal and pelvic regions. Her doctor was Mortimer Rodgers, the brother of the famous showman Richard Rodgers.

After an examination, he phoned an ambulance for her transfer to Doctors Hospital in Manhattan, where she remained for nine weeks. The press was alerted, and it was announced that she was suffering from kidney stones.

Later, she was struck with an emergency bowel stoppage and, again, by ambulance, she was sent to Lenox Hill Hospital.

On November 3, 1933, a hysterectomy was performed on the thirty-one-year-old actress.

Henry was among the few who learned the real story of her condition. Months before, she'd had an affair (or fling) with George Raft. *[Raft, along with Humphrey Bogart and Edward G. Robinson, had defined the movie gangster of the 1930s.]* It was discovered that Raft had given her a bad case of gonorrhea. The diagnosis from her doctors was that it had spread from her uterine cavity to her ovaries, her ovarian tubes, and eventually infected the membrane lining of her abdominal cavity. Her illness caused her weight to drop to seventy pounds, as her whole body, according to her doctor, was ravaged by pus.

During her recovery, Henry made periodic visits to her hospital room. "*Dah-ling,*" she said to him, "when you get to Hollywood, don't, under any circumstance let George Raft fuck you. He calls his thing 'Black Snake,' and it's as poisonous as a rattler."

Tallulah's "through the grapevine" broadcasting of **George Raft's** propensity for spreading gonorrhea didn't seem to affect his movie career.

By 1946, however, when *Whistle Stop,* a film noir, was released, Raft's career was winding down. Its producer blamed Raft for its low box offrice: "Raft had been a big name around the world but now he was on the skids and we could afford him...He looked like hell and who wanted to see this old man with Ava Gardner? We should have cast a young guy like Burt Lancaster."

"I'll fight the bastard off if he tries to plug me," Henry promised.

The producers of *Jezebel* could not wait for Tallulah's recovery, and the play opened on Broadway starring Miriam Hopkins, a daughter of Georgia, who seemed ideally cast.

Eventually, Hollywood wanted to film *Jezebel,* and both Hopkins and Tallulah ordered their agents to snare the role for them. Each was rejected, the role eventually going to Bette Davis for a classic released in 1938.

Coincidentally, Davis' leading man in the film was none other than Henry Fonda.

***

Although by now, he was divorced from her, Henry kept up with news about Margaret Sullavan. After their marriage ended, she had migrated to Hollywood for the filming of a Pre-Code movie, *Only Yesterday,* set for a 1933 release. It was the story of a vulnerable *["yeah, right!" Henry had commented sarcastically]* young woman who becomes pregnant by her boyfriend before he sails off to fight in World War I.

A Texan, John Boles, appeared in it as her leading man. *[A forgotten star today, Boles had had a big success in 1927 when he co-starred opposite Gloria Swanson in* The Loves of Sunya. *Later, he was noted for portraying Victor Mortiz in the hit movie,* Frankenstein *(1931). Future leading ladies as diverse as Barbara Stanwyck and Shirley Temple lay in his future.]*

Only Yesterday, released in 1933, became Universal's only hit that year. Yet despite its favorable ratings, Sullavan had been horrified by her appearance in the early rushes. Reacting almost violently, she had offered Universal all the money she had, $2,500, to buy out her contract. The studio refused.

Henry invited James Stewart to attend the movie's opening in Manhattan near Times Square. When it was over, Henry delivered his review: "It was a sentimental orgy."

Stewart had a different reaction. He did not share it with Henry, but with Joshua Logan: "I think I might be a movie star and have enough star power one day that I might order a studio to cast Maggie as my leading lady as frequently as possible."

Ironically, that romantic, starry-eyed fantasy came true—and in just a few years.

***

That summer, Henry could find no gigs as an actor, so he went to work at the Westchester Playhouse in Mount Kisco, New York, as a scenic designer. Within a stucco-sided barn that had been converted into a theater, as the organization's set decorator, he sketched the backgrounds of a dozen productions. He also managed to wangle walk-on parts in two of the season's plays.

The Westchester Playhouse was, after that, designated by *Life* magazine as "a grooming ground for movie stars." In any given season, such talents as Uta Hagen, Vincent Price, Anna Mae Wong, Montgomery Clift, and Herbert Bergdorf (one of the founders of Manhattan's Actors Studio and the husband of Uta Hagen) might appear. Even Hollywood royalty such as Joan Crawford and director Elia Kazan got professionally involved with it in some way.

To Henry's shock and surprise, Margaret Sullavan took time off from her commitments in Hollywood to star in a play at Mount Kisco that summer. Mostly they ignored each other, sometimes bypassing each other backstage without even a hello.

"As a recently divorced woman, Maggie was making the rounds," Henry asserted. "This was a man-grazing period for her, and she was seducing any good-looking guy she met. It was obvious to me that I had married and divorced a slut."

"I was not sitting alone in my room," he said. "I had met this

She was so horrified by the early rushes of her 1933 film, *Only Yesterday* that **Margaret Sullavan,** after many screaming denunciations tried, unsuccessfully, to prevent the studio from releasing it. She failed.

Henry Fonda, her estranged and embittered ex-husband, could do nothing but reflect on her ongoing abuse and, perhaps, gloat.

Its melodramatic plot? A romantic one-night fling during World War I results in a girl getting pregnant. Years later, she meets him again. Now a successful businessman who doesn't remember her, he tries to seduce her again.

sixteen-year-old usher at the theater. That fall would be her senior year in high school She looked much older. Frankly, I don't remember her name—maybe it was Phyllis—but she gave me a few tumbles. And unlike Tallulah and Maggie, she did not put me down as a lover. In fact, she told me I was the world's greatest lover, but I didn't let that appraisal go to my head. After all, I was the only male she'd ever known in bed."

He was assigned a small role in *Journey's End*. "The billing did little to boost my ego. Maggie was at the top of the hill, with me appearing near the bottom."

Journey's End, written by the English playwright R.C. Sherriff, was set during World War I, with much of the action taking place in a dugout of a British Army Infantry company in 1918. The play had first been performed at London's Apollo Theatre in 1928, with the lead role played by a young Laurence Olivier.

At summer's end, Sullavan didn't even bid Henry goodbye when she departed for Hollywood. She'd signed for her second movie, *Little Man, What Now?*. Douglass Montgomery had been designated as her leading man.

Henry returned to Manhattan, where James Stewart had gotten them a room at the Madison Square Garden Hotel. "It was so small, we were practically sleeping on top of each other," Henry recalled.

Finally, minor roles for both actors came through: They were cast in *All Good Americans*, which opened at the Henry Miller Theatre in early December, shutting down in early January of 1934.

The play was by S.N. Behrman, a son of parents from Lithuania who had emigrated to the U.S. Even though his parents had never learned much English, Behrman rose quickly and in time, became one of the leading Broadway writers of high comedy. Many of his plays were produced by the Theatre Guild and cast with such top stars as the husband-and-wife team of Lynn Fontanne and Alfred Lunt.

Soon, calls for Behrman came in from Hollywood. He was assigned to write scripts for Greta Garbo. They included *Queen Christina* and *Conquest*. He also wrote the script for *Two-Faced Woman*, the movie that ended Garbo's film career.

All Good Americans focused on a group of expatriate Americans living in Paris. They play "snob games" with newly arrived Yankees. As one critic put it, "Expect a tangle of romantic mix-ups and false identities and what-not."

Hollywood later bought the rights to the play and retitled it *Interlude*. None of the original stage actors was invited to replicate their performances on film.

In his memoirs, Henry remembered the New Year's party he and James Stewart had attended as *All Good Americans* was ending its short stage run.

"We got stinking drunk," he said. "Snowdrifts were piled up on New York streets. I came up with the bright idea of seeing who could piss the longest continual line in the snowdrift. I changed that to printing our names. We pulled out our dicks and started the contest. Jimmy won, spelling out, in urine, his full name, whereas I managed the initials H.F."

In need of a job, Henry welcomed the call of producer Arthur Beckhard, who had worked with him before. He, too, had turned to S.N. Behrman for his latest drama, *Love Story*, that would open in Philadelphia as a trial run before its Broadway premiere. Henry, once again, was given a small role, playing a character called Tavvy Schoenberg.

During rehearsals, Henry began a brief fling with actress Jane Wyatt, who was fast rising as a star. As he boasted to Stewart and others, "So many girls dream of stardom but never make it, of course, but Jane would go on to greater things. She made it all right, and I made her."

[In Hollywood, Wyatt would be cast as the love interest of Ronald Colman in the Frank Capra movie, Lost Horizon *(1937).*

She would later star with Cary Grant in None But the Lonely Heart *(1944); with Gregory Peck in* Gentleman's Agreement *(1947); and with Gary Cooper in* Task Force *(1949).*

In spite of these distinguished films, Wyatt would achieve her greatest fame as the devoted wife of Robert Young on the TV sitcom, Father Knows Best *(1954-1960).]*

Regrettably, their play, *Love Story*, didn't have such a long run, closing after only four performances. It faced bad reviews and never made it to Broadway.

At the end, Wyatt and Henry promised to meet again in Hollywood. But by 1935, she'd married investment broker Edgar Bethune Ward, a union that would last for the rest of the century. *[He died in 2000.]*

Henry would always remember what Wyatt said to him the first night he seduced her, and would often relay it as a joke on himself: After he had climaxed, she looked up at him and asked, "Is that all there is to sex? I don't know why people make such a

Jane Wyatt was as practical and no-nonsense during her (brief) affair with Henry Fonda as the character she eventually played, to almost universal acclaim, on TV.

Here she is with her "TV husband," **Robert Young**. Together, they starred for six seasons and 203 episodes of *Father Knows Best*, a TV series that helped define the nature of "the American family" during the go-go years of Sputnik, the Hula-Hoop, and the three-martini lunch.

fuss about it."

"I would not call that a very flattering review," Henry said.

***

At last, the major break Henry had long been waiting for came through when a struggling producer, Leonard Sillman, cast him, along with comedian Imogene Coca, in *New Faces*. The revue opened at the Fulton Theatre in Manhattan on the night of March 15, 1954 and ran until July.

The review demanded that Henry sing and dance with another new face, Coca.

This was the first of other "New Faces" that Sillman would introduce over the course of many years. Other actors who got involved included Eartha Kitt, Inga Swenson, Van Johnson, Carol Lawrence, Paul Lynde, John Lund, Madeline Kahn, and Maggie Smith.

"Leonard sure knew how to search out future stars, including yours truly," Henry said.

It was Glenn Anders, a casual friend of Henry's, who had introduced him to Sillman. He had set up an appointment for Henry to visit Sillman's one-room apartment at the Algonquin Hotel. At first, he eyed Henry skeptically: "So, young man, do you dance?"

"No," Henry said.

"Do you sing?" Sillman continued.

"No."

"Then what in hell do you do?"

"I impersonate babies from the age of one week to one year."

"Then go for it!"

Within minutes Henry had Sillman in stitches with his impersonation of infants.

"I'm hiring you for *New Faces*," Sillman said. "We'll teach you how to sing and dance during rehearsals. It pays $35 a week."

Sillman had assembled an array of talent for *New Faces of 1934*. It included Charles Walters, later a top musical director at MGM. Nancy Hamilton was brought in as a sketch writer, becoming one of the best in that field.

Henry, on his first day, was introduced to Imogene Coca. "She was not a pretty gal, but, what the hell, I developed hot pants for her."

He found out she'd launched her career as a child acrobat, later studying music and dance. Her greatest fame lay in her future (1950-54) when she co-starred with Sid Caesar on TV in *Your Show of Shows*.

Because of her rubbery face, one capable of almost any expression, *Life* magazine favorably compared her to both Charlie Chaplin and Beatrice Lillie.

In *Life's* words, "Coca can beat a tiger to death with a feather." One of the highlights of *New Faces* was a comic striptease wherein she made sultry faces and gestures while demurely removing only one glove.

"No man in the audience really wanted to see Imogene in the nude except for me," Henry recalled. "On the third day after meeting her, our affair began. I became her loving man for the duration of the show. She might have been a comic on stage, but in bed, she was a goddess like Garbo."

To get the show launched, Sillman had a big problem: No money. Henry revealed that he and Coca, among others, went through a staggering number of 196 auditions played out to potential backers, but none of them offered financing.

Suddenly, an "angel" emerged from Hollywood: Mary Pickford flew in from Los Angeles to attend opening night, sitting in the front row with Katharine Hepburn on one side and with Tallulah Bankhead on the other. Tallulah smoked one cigarette after another throughout the show, but no usher dared intervene to point out the "no smoking" signs.

The reviews that followed that night had nothing but praise for Henry and Imogene Coca. The Associated Press defined *New Faces* as "fairly witty...a pseudo-sophisticated revue." *The New York Times* claimed, "It lacks pace and polish, but contains enough wit to make it good entertainment."

Although Henry was relatively stoic in most of his future films, *New Faces* brought out his wacky side. He was referred to as "a jackal, loose, limber, and laughing hysteri-

Imogene Coca became a household name when she co-starred with Sid Caesar in the hit TV series, *Your Show of Shows*, seen by millions of viewers. Her rubbery face and comic style influenced an array of future stars—Carol Burnett, Lily Tomlin, Whoopi Goldberg, and Tracy Ullman.

She was rarely viewed as a sex symbol except by Henry Fonda.

43

cally." Another critic noted that when he emoted with the "pop-eyed *gamine,* Imogene Coca, he "flapped his arms and popped his own eyes."

Henry clipped out the good reviews and mailed them back to his parents in Omaha.

Amazingly, even though he didn't have a lot of talent for singing and dancing, his delivery of "She's Resting in the Gutter" and "She Loves It," became the hits of the show.

After the first night, producer Dwight Deere Wiman approached Henry with a year-long job offer that paid one hundred dollars a week.

Wiman felt that with lots of practice, Henry could be developed into a song-and-dance man.

The producer's vision did not fit Henry's own perceptions. He did not want to become, in the words of one author, "a gangly clown and piercing crooner, Ray Bolger crossed with Alfalfa."

[Carl "Alfalfa" Switzer was a child actor best known for Our Gang, the quirky comedy series of the mid-1930s. After leaving the series in 1940, he struggled to find future work, eventually becoming a dog breeder and hunting guide.

On January 21, 1959, Alfalfa was fatally shot by an acquaintance in a dispute over money. He was only thirty-one years old.]

In an ongoing search for new talent, Leland Hayward, one of the top talent agents in America, was in the audience that night. Once, Margaret Sullavan and Henry had arrived at his office, hoping to become clients, but he had rejected them. But after *New Faces,* he re-evaluated them, especially Henry, and would soon approach him for representation.

What happened to the romance of Henry and Imogene Coca?

"I had been enchanted with Imogene, but it was time for me to move on. She was a little clown and a talented one at that. In bed, it was no laughing matter between us."

When later asked about her affair with Henry, Coca said, "A ship that passed in the night."

***

In July of 1934, Henry returned to the Westchester Playhouse at Mount Kisco, north of New York City. To his delight, he learned that he'd been designated as the male lead in the romantic comedy, *Coquette.*

Then, to his horror and dismay, he was informed that Margaret Sullavan, his bitterly estranged ex-wife had been assigned a role as his leading lady, the object of his character's lust, desire, and adoration. Having taken a break from her involvement in Hollywood films, she had returned to the East Coast.

"Maggie treated me like she would have any other actor sent up from New York," Henry claimed. "There was no mention of our marriage, certainly not of our divorce. She acted as if our love affair never happened. I found out later that she was rooming with one of the stagehands. I met the guy, who looked much younger than Maggie. His pectorals bulged beneath his T-shirt, and he had a red mustache and lots of red hair. His tight jeans made his assets obvious. He was tall, tanned, tattooed, and terrific looking. How is a regular guy like me supposed to compete? He was George Clemont. In winter, he was a ski instructor at Lake Placid."

The only personal news Sullavan relayed to Henry was that she would be departing in a few weeks for a return to Hollywood. She was scheduled to shoot a film, *The Good Fairy,* set for a 1939 release. Its director would be William Wyler, helming a screenplay by Preston Sturges, with one-legged Herbert Marshall cast as her leading man.

A play by George Abbott, *Coquette* relayed the tale of a flirtatious Southern belle who choses to stand behind her father after he kills the man she loves. It had originated as a Broadway play featuring Helen Hayes.

In 1929, featuring Mary Pickford in her first talking role, Hollywood adapted it for

How Bad Advice Almost Derailed Henry Fonda

It happened after a Hollywood talent scout saw Henry flailing and spinning and (awkwardly) singing and dancing in a "flash in the pan" musical review, *New Faces* , a three-month theater gig he executed, like a trouper, early in 1934.

The scout offered Henry the then-substantial salary of $100 a week for a year-long gig as a "song and dance man" in the style of **Ray Bolger** (photo above). Bolger's stage gyrations, assembled into a collage, were publicized for his appearance as a "soft shoe' pro on the *Bell Telephone Hour* in 1963.

Henry, of course, who never considered himself either a singer or a dancer, disagreed heartily with the agent's assessment, and rejected the offer.

Although his detractors sometimes mocked his country-cousin similarities to **Alfalfa (aka Carl Switzer),** the cornpone kid from the hicks who frequently appeared in movies at the time, Henry never denied his cornhusker's roots as a Nebraskan.

44

the screen, bringing a Best Actress Oscar to Pickford.

Henry was cast as Michael Jeffrey, who is in love with Coquette. That role in the Pickford screen version had been played by the actor, Johnny Mack Brown.

After reading the script, Henry jokingly said to the director, "Imagine me playing the love of Maggie Sullavan. A case of miscasting if I ever heard of one."

At the first assemblage of cast and crew, Sullavan, now revered as a visiting star from Hollywood, addressed them all: "I never plan to give up the stage," she publicly vowed. "At Mount Kisco, I don't have to worry about all those damn close-ups and long shots."

At a provincial theater on the outskirts of New York, Henry was assigned the task of reprising, onstage, the screen performance of **Johnny Mack Brown**, an actor made famous by his romantic associations with "America's Sweetheart," superstar **Mary Pickford.**

Many in the audience had already seen Brown and Pickford in the 1929 screen version of the play, noteworthy, as it had been Pickford's first "Talkie."

The cast was collectively lodged at a large inn, the Kittle House. It was there, at the communal dinner table, that tensions between Henry and his former wife reached their boiling point.

Sullavan listened as Henry bragged about his reception on Broadway in *New Faces.* He claimed that he even had favorable write-ups in the columns of Walter Winchell and Leonard Lyons. "My picture ran in several newspapers, and for the first time ever, I was stopped on the street by some autograph seekers."

Suddenly Sullavan looked as if she could take no more of this talk: "It was just a forgettable, silly revue!" she said in a loud voice. "Hardly a big deal. You even tried to sing, which I guess was good for a laugh. You're carrying on like you just won an award for *Hamlet.*"

"And what in the fuck have *YOU* been doing, Princess?" he asked, sarcastically, in front of his fellow diners. "Placing your silly face on the screen? You must have given your makeup artist a fit. The boy faced the challenge of his career trying to get that chinless wonder of yours, that little face, to appear big enough for the screen."

She picked up a pitcher of ice water and dumped it over his head before storming out of the dining room.

Very quietly, he picked up a napkin and wiped the water from his face, then resumed eating his plate of fried chicken and mashed potatoes, asking for a second helping of green peas.

He spent his first evening with Aleta Freel and Ross Alexander. He had been surprised when the gay actor had married the actress on February 28, 1934 in East Orange, New Jersey.

That night, after Freel had retired to their bedroom, Alexander invited Henry to go for a walk in the moonlit woods. He confessed, "Aleta can't satisfy my desire, but you sure can."

Henry declined the invitation.

Three nights later, Sullavan and Henry had to execute a love scene on stage in the wake of her ice water assault. Each of them managed quite well and, in Alexander's summation, "were both most convincing. But off-stage they never spoke to each other."

***

At the end of her commitments at the Westchester Playhouse, without saying goodbye to Henry, Sullavan was driven to one of the New York City airports, where she caught a flight back to Los Angeles to resume her film career.

Henry stayed behind at the Westchester Playhouse to play the lead in Ferenc Molnár's *The Swan.* In it, he was cast as a tutor to a princess, alongside his co-star, Geoffrey Kerry, who played a prince. *The Swan* was billed as "a tale of surreal love and a triangle of needs." A dark comedy of the supernatural, it made frequent references to characters from Greek mythology.

As critic Stephen Holden explained it, "*The Swan* is more than a failure of communication, or even a biologically determined hormonal clash. As Dora, a part-time nurse who lives alone on the edge of a Nebraska highway, imagines it, men are born on the Planet Pluto, molecularly disassembled, and sent directly to Earth by radar. Their troubles arise from having to adapt to an alien ecosystem. An inability to adapt was the reason, she believes, why one of her three former husbands shot himself to death the day after they were married."

Henry was cast as a man who falls to Earth and into Dora's life. In the words of a local critic, "Mr. Fonda delivers a wrenching evocation of primal man as a lonely, wounded creature in need of nurturing."

Why was the play entitled *The Swan*?

Asleep in her bungalow beside the highway, Dora is startled by a violent crash against her front window. Rushing outside in terror, she finds a swan that is injured from having hurled itself against the glass. Gently, she places the wounded bird into a wicker basket and carries it indoors. Within a few moments, a naked, blood-streaked man, flapping his arms and emitting piteous cries, pulls himself away from the tangled bird feathers.

"It was the weirdest god damn play I ever appeared in," Henry recalled. "I needed someone to explain it to me. The director tried to tell me what it was about but ended up making me more confused. However, and you won't believe this, I got raves for my performance. Indeed, *The Swan* launched me indirectly into the big time."

Henry's British co-star, Geoffrey Kerr, was married at the time to the American actress June Walker. One Broadway critic put her in the same league as Helen Hayes or Tallulah Bankhead.

A New Yorker, Walker appeared on Broadway in such plays as *Green Grow the Lilacs* and *Twelfth Night.* She was the first actress to play Lorelei Lee in the 1949 Broadway production of *Gentlemen Prefer Blondes. [The character of Lorelei was later rendered far more famous in Marilyn Monroe's 1953 film.]*

Walker, who had married Kerr in 1926, divorced him in 1943 after producing a son who became the actor, John Kerr. He rose to greater fame than either of his parents starring in such films as *Tea and Sympathy* (1953) and *South Pacific* (1958).

On the evening of the third performance of *The Swan,* Walker arrived from Manhattan to see the play and her husband's performance in it. Afterward, she visited the dressing room that Henry shared with him.

She entered as Henry was in his underwear and as Kerr was removing his makeup. Speaking of Henry as if he weren't present, she said to her husband, "This Fonda guy is terrific. Marvelous, really. Of course, no one tops any performance of my husband, but he comes close. In fact, I'm calling Marc tonight to urge him to come to see this play. He's been searching for a leading man for my next play on Broadway. As far as I'm concerned, Henry is that actor."

"Well, thank you, ma'am!" Henry said from the adjoining dressing table.

[Walker had been referring to Marc Connelly, a son of Massachusetts who had begun writing plays when he was five years old. Later, he worked as a newspaper reporter for the Pittsburgh Sun-Telegraph.

Moving to New York, he often teamed to write plays with George S. Kaufman, the drama critic for The New York Times.

By 1930, Connelly won the Pulitzer Prize for his 1930 drama The Green Pastures. *It was a landmark production on Broadway, in that it featured an all-black cast.]*

The following night, Connelly arrived at Mount Kisco with producer Max Gordon.

It had taken a lot of persuading to get a producer of the stature of Max Gordon to commute to Mount Kisco to appraise an unknown actor like Henry Fonda.

[A New Yorker, the son of Polish immigrants, Gordon became one of the most successful producers of the Roaring Twenties, riding out the Depression, even scoring hits as late as the Eisenhower era.

He became known for such plays as My Sister Eileen, *a hit on both stage and screen. One of his early successes had been the original production of* The Jazz Singer, *which had electrified Hollywood in September of 1927.*

Other hits included The Bandwagon, *starring Adele and Fred Astaire, as well as* Born Yesterday *by the husband-and-wife writing team of Ruth Gordon and Garson Kanin. The movie version brought Judy Holliday an Oscar, beating out such formidable competition as Gloria Swanson in* Sunset Blvd., *and Bette Davis in* All About Eve.*]*

After sitting through Henry's performance in *The Swan,* both Gordon and Connelly agreed that Henry would be ideally cast in their next play, *The Farmer Takes a Wife.* Its producer and director met with Henry backstage and an agreement was reached whereby Henry would visit Connelly's apartment in Manhattan at the Gotham Hotel the following morning at ten o'clock. That was the same hotel where Henry had temporarily lived with Tallulah Bankhead and Anderson Lawler.

The next morning, Connelly, a late riser, greeted Henry at his door clad in white pajamas with red polka dots. After giving him a cup of coffee, he had him sit on the sofa as he acted out every part, both male and female, from his new play, *The Farmer Takes a Wife.*

When he finished, he handed the script to Henry and asked him to read the lines of the character named Dan Harrow.

Pleased with his "raw reading," Connelly offered him the role on the spot, telling

Max Gordon, depicted above, was the Broadway producer who with a lot of prodding, "discovered" a neophyte Henry Fonda.

To do it, he had to *schlepp* from Manhattan up to Mount Kisco, where young Henry was performing in regional theater in a play he hated, *The Swan* by the "mad Hungarian" playwright, Ferenc Molnar.

Although almost completely forgotten today, Cole Porter immortalized Gordon with these lyrics in the hit song "Anything Goes."

When Rockefeller still can hoard
Enough money to let Max Gordon
Produce his shows...
Anything goes.

him to go over to Max Gordon's office to sign four copies of a contract for a deal paying $200 a week.

After signing the contracts, he rushed back to Mount Kisco, arriving there only five minutes before the curtain went up on *The Swan*.

***

Leland Hayward, one of the top talent agents in America, had seen Fonda in *New Faces* and decided he wanted him as a client. He was tactfully reminded that he had previously rejected both Margaret Sullavan and Henry when they'd visited him for representation. "That was then, but this is now," he told Henry.

During their meeting, Henry also politely informed Hayward that Dwight Deere Wiman, who had hopes of turning him into a song-and-dance man on Broadway, had begun negotiating with him too: "He's willing to give me $100 a week for a year's contract," Henry told the agent.

"To hell with that. I can get you $750 a week," Hayward promised.

Henry was astonished at the figure but didn't dismiss it as a possibility. After all, Hayward was known in theatrical circles as "a hustler who could sell chewing gum to a man with lockjaw."

Although Hayward had assured him that his voice would record perfectly ("I could see you starring with some of my clients, perhaps Claudette Colbert"), the problem was that Henry didn't want to go to Hollywood to work in the talkies.

Despite that, two weeks later, during his involvement at Mount Kisco in *The Swan*, a three-page telegram arrived from Hayward, urging him to come to Los Angeles to sign a movie deal. "I'm talking you up big with producers, especially Walter Wanger, who is most intrigued."

Henry wired back a terse one-word response: "No!" Somehow, he just could not see himself as a movie actor, since he had worked so hard, and suffered so much, crafting his technique on the stage.

Hayward, however, was never a man to take "No" for an answer. Around Hollywood, he was known for his persistence, claiming "If a starlet rejects sex from me five times, I get lucky on the sixth request, even if I have to use a bit of force on the reluctant bitch!"

Hayward wired him again, this time including a round-trip ticket to California. "Are you out of your fucking mind? I'm offering you a fabulous deal, one that actors fantasize about. Get your god damn ass on the plane and cut the shit."

"Leland sure is blunt," Henry told his co-star, Geoffrey Kerr.

Finally, Henry decided to take that flight to California. Hayward had made it clear that he would meet him at the airport in Burbank.

Hayward kept his promise, arriving at the airport with a limousine that hauled them through the streets of Los Angeles to a suite at the then-new Beverly Wilshire Hotel.

As Henry looked out the window, he saw a city in transition, one in search of an identity. Oil rigs stood next to fields of oranges and grapefruit. Beverly Hills was sparsely populated, and Sunset Boulevard had not been paved yet.

The limo passed a restaurant, the Brown Derby, designed in the shape of a giant hat. This celebrity-haunted restaurant stood across from the Ambassador Hotel.

From his position in the back of the limousine, Henry asked, "Just who in hell is Walter Wanger? I've never heard of him."

Hayward provided a thumbnail sketch:

A son of San Francisco born in 1894, twelve years before the famous earthquake of 1906, young Wanger had migrated to Los Angeles, where he sought work in silent films.

His plans were interrupted by his entry into the Army during World War I. After his discharge in 1919, he returned to Los Angeles where he married the silent screen actress, Justine Johnstone.

A chance meeting with film producer Jesse Lasky changed his life. He was sent to New York to head an office that acquired books and plays for adaptations into films. He was the first to see the possibilities of a British novel, *The Sheik*, as the foundation of *The Sheik* (1921) Rudolph Valentino's spectacularly successful and

After affairs with such actors as Bing Crosby, Errol Flynn, and Spencer Tracy, the über-glam star, **Joan Bennett** (right) took producer **Walter Wanger** (left) as her third husband.

The marriage didn't go well. On December 12, 1951, Wanger, in a jealous rage, shot her agent and lover, Jennings Lang. Wanger was sentenced to four months in prison.

Lang survived, but lost a testicle.

most celebrated film.

Wanger was on his way to becoming a top film producer himself.

With the advent of Talkies in 1929, Wanger set out to sign actors who could talk. His clients included Jeanette MacDonald, Miriam Hopkins, Fredric March, Claudette Colbert, and even the Marx Brothers and Maurice Chevalier, despite his French accent. Directors he hired included George Cukor and Rouben Mamoulian.

In his hotel suite, Hayward told Henry to shower and change his clothes. Wanger was due at any minute.

"At my first meeting with Wanger, I stepped out of the shower," Henry said. "I was as naked as a jaybird. He handed me a towel and introduced himself. At least he got to see what he was buying."

"You're a bit on the lean side, and I've seen actors with bigger dicks, but Leland claims that you're very talented," Wanger said to him.

Fully dressed, Henry joined Wanger and Hayward for drinks and dinner, where both men wanted to sign him to

Right photo: Young romantic hero **Henry Fonda**, onstage with **June Walker** in *The Farmer Takes a Wife*. It made him a star.

a film contract. At this point in his life, he had little interest in becoming a movie star. Impulsively, he decided to ask an outrageous amount of money in an era when America was filled with breadlines and soup kitchens. "I can't work for less than a grand a week."

To his astonishment, both men agreed to that price.

The following day, a contract was signed, in which he agreed to make two pictures a year with time off for stage work. He recalled that he had once worked for five dollars a week.

"When I flew back to New York on their dime, I felt I'd been given two cakes to eat," he said.

Before he'd have to apply himself to any movie, he'd have time to "make his Broadway debut in *The Farmer Takes a Wife*."

***

Rehearsals for *The Farmer Takes a Wife* began in Manhattan. It was being produced by Max Gordon, directed by Marc Connelly, and cast with June Walker as Molly Larkins. Henry played the male lead of Dan Harrow.

The drama had been adapted from Walter D. Edmond's novel, *Rome Haul*. The setting was New York State in 1850, when the Erie Canal was a major transportation route. But the railroads were making fast inroads, threatening boat owners along the length of the canal.

Only ten days into rehearsals, Henry received devastating news from Omaha. His mother, Herberta Fonda, had fallen and broken her leg. A blood clot had developed and traveled through her bloodstream to her heart, killing her. The family went into mourning. Henry wanted to travel to Omaha to join them, but with the play about to open, he could not get away.

"In spite of our star's personal pain, he came through for us," Connelly said. "And although Gary Cooper was moving rapidly along as a film star, I saw Henry giving him competition when he, too, made it to Hollywood. Both of these actors had that *gee-gosh*, foot-dragging, *aw-shucks* quality. They also came from roughly the same part of America, Coop from the plains of Montana and Henry from the wastelands of Nebraska."

Henry and actress June Walker were backed up by a strong cast, notably Margaret Hamilton in the role of Lucy Gurget. The former schoolteacher was years away from menacing Dorothy as the Wicked Witch in *The Wizard of Oz*.

Working with Henry, she called him "a beautiful man."

She had launched her own film career in 1933 in *Another Language*. She would later be cast in the film version of *The Farmer Takes a Wife*. She would rejoin Henry one day in *You Only Live Once* (1937).

The Farmer Takes a Wife opened on Broadway at the 46th Street Theatre on October

Although she spent the latter decades of her life unable to shake the public's perception of her as Dorothy's Wicked Witch in *The Wizard of Oz* (1939), **Margaret Hamilton** was a fine actress in romantic comedies and a loyal lifelong friend of Henry Fonda.

30, 1934, running for 103 performances. Henry's performance was well-received, notably by the era's best-known critic, Brooks Atkinson of *The New York Times*. He wrote that "Henry Fonda gives a manly, modest performance in a style of captivating simplicity."

Arthur Pollock of the *Brooklyn Eagle* declared, "Henry Fonda is perfect in the role, giving an extraordinarily simple yet lustrous characterization." Another reviewer, Robert Garland, found Henry "a believable Dan Harrow, strong, sweet, and silent as Dan Harrow should be."

Yet another review found that "The Mask of Dan Harrow is a perfect fit for the young actor, Henry Fonda. He appears on stage as dependable as Mount McKinley."

***

Henry and "my best friend for life," James Stewart, were both working on Broadway and sharing a room at the decaying Madison Square Hotel. Although busy most of the time, they spent any spare moments constructing miniature model airplanes.

"We would not let a maid in to clean our bedroom," Henry said. "It was filled with wood shavings and balsa wood, the entire place stinking of glue."

Both actors were working on "our masterpiece," Stewart claimed. "A replica of a United States Army Air Corps Martin Bomber."

Like Henry, Stewart was using Broadway as a stepping stone to Hollywood. At least that's what it became. Actually, he had serious doubts he'd ever become a movie star. "I'm too awkward, lanky, and hesitant of speech," he confided to Henry.

A world famous director was soon to enter Stewart's life. He was Guthrie McClintic, the husband of Katharine Cornell, the theater's First Lady, or at least one of them. He cast Stewart in Sidney Howard's play, *Yellow Jack*, where he played Sergeant O'Hara. This was a saga about U.S. soldiers who were used as guinea pigs during the outbreak of yellow fever in Cuba. The original director was Jed Harris, fresh from his affair with Margaret Sullavan. When Harris dropped out, McClintic came in.

James Stewart, at the age of 25, made Broadway news in 1934 when he starred in the military drama, *Yellow Jack*. It marked the beginning of his deep, life-long friendship with an actor whose roles, it was argued, could easily have been interchanged: His roommate at the time, a young and equally lanky Henry Fonda.

In the photo above, players in the tense scene include, Left to right, : **Sam Levene, James Stewart** (who is standing), **Edward Acuff, Katherine Wilson** and **Myron McCormick** in the original 1934 Broadway production of *Yellow Jack*.

The play opened on March 6, 1934 at the Martin Beck Theater, winning critical praise. Stewart was hailed for giving a performance that was "simple, sensitive, and true."

Stewart became one of the most talked-about actors on Broadway. "It was McClintic who made Jimmy a star," said his friend, actor Myron McCormick. "During rehearsals, the two were inseparable. It was obvious to cast and crew that the director was falling in love with Jimmy."

Privately, Cornell told Tallulah Bankhead, "My husband usually falls for his leading man, and, in most cases, puts him on the casting couch. But his feelings for Jimmy are the strongest and the most powerful I've ever known. Jimmy is spending more time at our home than I am."

Henry noticed that instead of coming back to their room to work on model airplanes, Stewart would often get in at two or three o'clock in the morning. "I didn't need to ask where he'd been."

"I got a surprise one morning when I opened our closet and found five well-tailored suits hanging there. We usually paid no more that $20, but these looked like Savile Row $500 specials. There were also five pairs of shoes, one of them alligator from Florida."

In an interview with a reporter from the *New York Sun*, Stewart said, "I get wobbly in the knees thinking that such a great director of the theater has taken such an interest in my career. I owe him a lot. He has opened a whole new world for me, and I'll be forever grateful."

Henry summed it up: "McClintic is Jimmy's Svengali, or should I say that he is the director's Trilby?"

Impossibly famous, and impossibly prestigious, **Katharine Cornell** was one of the three or four stage actresses mostly likely to be fingered as "Queen of the American Theater." A lesbian, she maneuvered a double life in collaborative collusion with her sometimes predatory gay husband, Guthrie McClintic.

Estelle Winwood, McClintic's first wife, claimed, "My former husband had always been a promiscuous homosexual. As my husband, he never went to bed with me, but seduced many willing, handsome actors. Men were an obsession with him. Both Cornell and I agreed that his obsession with Stewart is the most serious yet."

Biographer Lawrence Quirk wrote: "Stewart had spent some six years or so struggling with his own bisexual impulses, and the great loves of his life emotionally, if not physically, had been Josh Logan, Margaret Sullavan, and Henry Fonda. Fonda was struggling with his own sexual identity problems."

What is known is that Stewart spent many nights at the Beekman Place residence of Cornell and McClintic. She lived on a separate floor.

Although both McClintic and Stewart had high hopes for *Yellow Jack,* the play proved too depressing for most audiences, and it soon closed.

Then McClintic found another showcase for his favorite actor. He cast Stewart in *Divided by Three,* which opened on Broadway on October 2, 1934. Stewart played the son of the formidable lesbian actress, Judith Anderson, who protested against his inclusion in the cast, but was overruled by McClintic.

Stewart, only ten years younger than Anderson, was cast in the role of her son, who is shocked by his mother's adultery.

Hedda Hopper was also in the cast, and she was a great supporter of Stewart when she went to Hollywood and became one of the two leading gossip columnists of Tinseltown, competing with her bitter rival, Louella Parsons.

On opening night, Henry was in a front row seat, sandwiched between such luminaries as Moss Hart and Irving Berlin.

When he went backstage to congratulate Stewart, he found McClintic kissing him on the mouth and hugging him. There were tears in McClintic's eyes, even though he had a reputation as a cold and cynical director.

Cornell came backstage to lure her husband away to meet some celebrities. But, as Henry stood watching, McClintic was soon replaced by Bill Grady, a talent scout for MGM. He strongly urged Stewart to take a screen test, scheduling it for the following Wednesday afternoon.

At the urging of Henry, a reluctant Stewart did take that screen test. It was sent to MGM, and the studio responded by offering him a seven-year contract at $350 a week.

The offer came at the right time because *Divided by Three* ran for only thirty performances.

Before Stewart was free to leave for the West Coast, Henry's play, *The Farmer Takes a Wife,* had closed too.

Henry arrived first in Hollywood and rented a home before Stewart got to town. He was at the railway station to meet him when the actor arrived there in April of 1935.

Henry told Stewart that when his own train had left Chicago, heading west, he'd vowed to fall in love, "wondering who the lucky girl would be."

"You mean 'girls,'" Stewart interjected.

Estelle Winwood, former (and very outspoken) wife of the gay director/producer Guthrie McClintic, was never as dotty or forgetful as she appeared.

In Alfred Hitchcock's *Rebecca* (1940) in a scene loaded with lesbian implications, **Dame Judith Anderson** (right) confronts the naive and timid "second Mrs. de Winter" (**Joan Fontaine**) with a sensual display of her predecessor's underclothes and transparent nightwear.

It all happened a few years after a neophyte actor, James Stewart appeared with Anderson onstage in the breakthrough role that sent him to Hollywood.

Although she later evolved into "the most poisonous bitch in Hollywood," thanks to her role as a syndicated gossip columnist, **Hedda Hopper,** depicted here as a seductive Jazz-Age flapper, performed in the same breakthrough play (*Divided by Three*) as James Stewart.

CHAPTER FOUR

REACTING TO HOLLYWOOD

HELLO, NEIGHBOR!

NOW ROOMMATES, HENRY FONDA & BEST BUDDY JAMES STEWART MEET AND SEDUCE
GRETA GARBO

HENRY'S OFFSCREEN ROMANCES AND/OR OFFSCREEN INTRIGUES WITH MARLENE DIETRICH, JEANETTE MacDONALD, LILY PONS, SYLVIA SIDNEY, AND A GAGGLE OF (REJECTED) MALE BISEXUALS

HENRY BECOMES A WORKING MOVIE STAR IN

THE FARMER TAKES A WIFE, WAY DOWN EAST, I DREAM TOO MUCH, & TRAIL OF THE LONESOME PINE

In Hollywood, Gary Cooper was sent a script for the movie adaptation of *The Farmer Takes a Wife,* the same vehicle in which Henry Fonda had starred on Broadway.

Coop wired back his regrets: "No way!"

The script was next sent to Joel McCrea, and he wired back: "It's the kind of role I could play, especially opposite Janet Gaynor, but I've already signed for two other pictures."

Victor Fleming had been selected to direct the film for Fox. At the end of World War I, he'd been the chief photographer for President Woodrow Wilson when the victorious Allies met at Versailles, a suburb of Paris.

After Fleming's return from that war, he directed his first Hollywood film in 1919. In part because of his love of sports, he became known as "a man's director," specializing in Westerns and action movies, some starring Douglas Fairbanks Sr.

Of course, Fleming was years away from 1939, when he directed two of the greatest films ever made, *Gone With the Wind* and *The Wizard of Oz*.

Faced with rejections from both Cooper and McCrea, Fleming met with the film's producer, Winfield Sheehan, Fox's chief of production from 1926 to 1935, when he was replaced by Darryl F. Zanuck.

Fleming had seen Fonda on Broadway in *The Farmer Takes a Wife* and was impressed with his performance. He asked Sheehan permission to let Henry repeat the role of Dan Harrow on the screen. It didn't take Sheehan long to agree. "Let's face it: The picture will be a star vehicle for that lezzie, Janet Gaynor. Her name alone will sell it to the public."

Gaynor, who had easily migrated from silents to the talkies, had become one of Hollywood's biggest box office draws, having signed with Fox in 1926. She became noteworthy in 1929 when she was the first winner of a Best Actress Academy Award for her performance in three films: *7ᵗʰ Heaven* (1927); *Sunrise: A Song of Two Humans* (1927); and *Street Angel* (1928). This was the only time an actress ever won an Oscar for three roles.

Giving his regards and goodbyes to Old Broadway, Henry headed to the West Coast for a new career and a new life.

As his Twentieth Century railway car roared west, he was filled with insecurity. What would his face look like when magnified on the screen? Would he "look like a horse's ass," the camera exaggerating all his flaws? At this point, he felt he had many.

As the train clicked along the rails, he recalled the lines he'd delivered in the play, *Merton of the Movies*: "Oh, God, make me a good movie star, make me one of the best. For Jesus' sake, Amen!"

Henry's first meeting was with producer Walter Wanger, to whom he was under contract. The producer said he had no immediate film role for him, and that was why he'd lent him to Fox for the filming of *The Farmer Takes a Wife*. Fox would pay Wanger $5,000 for hiring Henry, and he'd allow the actor to keep $3,000 of that.

"No more boiled rice," Henry said. "Steak whenever I want it." With his first paycheck, for $900, he purchased a Ford roadster with a rumble seat.

Wanger wanted his new star to meet the elite of Hollywood, so he decided that he should be introduced at Carole Lombard's lavish party at the Fun House Amusement Park, positioned on a steel pier jutting out into the Pacific. To that effect, Wanger phoned Eulalia Chapin, a houseguest of David O. Selznick, and asked her if she would accompany Henry to the Lombard *soirée*.

[Coincidentally, Chapin was the best friend of Frances Seymour Brokaw, who would become Henry's second wife in 1936.]

At the party, Chapin seemed to know everybody, and Henry was introduced to a galaxy of stars, beginning first with Clark Gable. *[In time, Gable would marry Lombard.]*

"When I met Carole, I got a wet kiss on the mouth," Henry recalled. "When I shook hands with Myrna Loy, she gave me a light peck on the cheek. I ended up talking with Norma Shearer, Jimmy Stewart's dream girl, and also to William Powell. I even met the Paramount blonde, Mae West. She invited me to come up and see her sometime 'if you've got something to offer in the bread basket.'"

Dolores del Rio came up to Henry, congratulating him for getting cast with Janet Gaynor in his first picture. "I think I'll demand that you be cast as my next leading man, too."

Del Rio had just seduced Greta Garbo and had had an affair with Joel McCrea during their co-starring in *Bird of Paradise* (1932). She was said to eat orchid omelettes for breakfast and to use butterfly wings as a back scratcher.

Before the party on the pier ended, Henry had met Kay Francis, Ina Claire, Ruth Chatterton, Constance Bennett, even the sultry Marlene Dietrich, who his best friend, James Stewart, would make pregnant when they co-starred together in *Destry Rides Again* (1939).

***

James Stewart would not arrive in Hollywood until April of 1935, a few months after Henry. Henry had promised in the meantime to search for lodgings for them to share. For the short term, Ross Alexander, his actor friend from New York, invited him to stay at his home, where he lived with his new wife, actress Aleta Freel, who had also become a friend of Henry's from New York. Henry volunteered to pay them for use of their guest room.

High in the Hollywood Hills, and accessible via the winding Woodrow Wilson Drive, their little villa evoked life in the country, with goats, chickens, and dogs roaming the grounds.

The first time Alexander maneuvered Henry alone into his guest room, he confessed "I'm still in love with you."

"Let's just be good friends," Henry cautioned.

Daytimes, when Alexander was away at work for Warner Brothers, Freel drove Henry around in his search for a cheap apartment.

One weekend, Freel was invited to join three other actresses in Palm Springs for a

Although the film version of *The Farmer Takes a Wife* was conceived as a vehicle for then-superstar **Janet Gaynor**, young **Henry** "also-ran" in this wholesome film about the virtues and bounty of fruitful hard work and home on the range.

Gable and Lombard (aka Clark and Carole): Press agents in Hollywood didn't know whether to depict them embracing in silk-upholstered drawing rooms or at home performing chores as icons of domestic bliss.

Here they are from around the time young Henry Fonda got invited to a party they hosted for *le tout Hollywood*.

Years later, Henry still remembered the guest list.

fashion layout for which she would be paid. She was struggling to launch a film career, and both she and Alexander needed cash.

That Saturday night, Alexander invited Henry to attend a party at the home of director George Cukor. It turned out to be very different from the previous Hollywood party he'd attended, the one hosted by Carole Lombard.

Before setting out, Alexander suggested to Henry that "You should suck up to George. He might cast you as a leading man in one of his films."

Born on the Lower East Side of Manhattan, the only child of Hungarian Jewish immigrants, Cukor as a child appeared in amateur plays and took dance lessons. At the age of seven, he performed in a recital with David O. Selznick, who in time became his close friend and mentor.

Photo shows the gay, barely closeted **George Cukor** during the peak of his fascination with the lesbian, barely closeted **Katharine Hepburn,** around the time he was directing her in her first film, *A Bill of Divorcement* (1932) and that great "trans-sexual riddle" film, *Sylvia Scarlett* (1935).

As a neophyte in the sexually ambiguous quicksands of Hollywood, Henry learned, fast, how to play things in ways that were "artfully noncommittal."

With the advent of Talkies, New York theatrical personalities were being hired. Cukor went west and made his solo directorial debut in *Tarnished Lady* (1931), starring Tallulah Bankhead.

After a stint at Paramount, Cukor was remembered by Selznick. At RKO, he gave him top assignments, including *What Price Hollywood?* (1932), and *A Bill of Divorcement* (also 1932), starring Katharine Hepburn. An avid movie goer, Henry had seen Cukor's recent films, *Little Women* and *Dinner at Eight,* both released in 1933.

The first person he met at the party was a drunken Edmund Goulding, the British screenwriter and director. Married to Marjorie Moss at the time, Goulding had helmed Greta Garbo in *Love* (1927) and again in *Grand Hotel* (1932) with Joan Crawford and John Barrymore. Even greater pictures lay in his future.

Edmund Goulding, the British director, liked to seduce his leading men, especially Tyrone Power during the time they filmed *The Razor's Edge* (1946).

Three of the films he directed were Best Picture nominated, not just *The Razor's Edge, but* Grand Hotel with Greta Garbo and *Dark Victory* with Bette Davis.

After only a few minutes with Goulding, Henry realized that he was not faithful to his wife. "Edmund made it obvious to me that the quickest way for an actor like me to get ahead was to lie on a casting couch, preferably his. Even though some of the actors were married, it was obvious that I was at a party of homosexuals."

"Cukor paid attention to me on and off throughout the evening, but I spent little time with him," Henry said. "I did get to talk to William Haines, who'd been a popular box office draw in the early 1930s. When he refused to give up his lover, Jimmie Shields, Louis B. Mayer gave him his walking papers. Haines told me that he bet his best friend, Joan Crawford, would love for me to be her leading man. To me, that was just so much drunken talk."

Gay, outed, disgraced, and dismissed from the film industry: Once an A-list movie star, handsome **William Haines** appears above in *Tell It To the Marines* (1926).

He survived in the years to come as an interior decorator to some of his many friends, including Joan Crawford and Ronald and Nancy Reagan..

[Coincidentally, Henry would become Crawford's leading man in Daisy Kenyon, *a Fox picture released in 1947.]*

One by one, Henry made the rounds, meeting many actors who were just getting launched in the movies. John Darrow had begun his film career in a 1927 silent, *High School Hero.* He would appear in a number of films before retiring from acting in 1935, when he formed a lifelong love affair with director Charles Walters.

Actor Tom Douglas seemed to have taken advantage of his good looks. The Kentucky-born teenager had enchanted both Cukor and Goulding, who spoke of his

"ethereal beauty." *Young Wooley* had been written just for Douglas by the gay playwright, John Van Druten. The Welsh actor, Emlyn Williams, in his memoir, had written "with Tom's short nose and wide, soft mouth that seemed not to know its potency, he casts a spell over his own sex."

Both Douglas and Williams had starred in stage versions of *Merton of the Movies,* the same play in which Henry had appeared at the Community Playhouse in Omaha in 1926.

Gavin Gordon was the typical

What's a man to do? Then-famous actors Henry Fonda met, partially or fully nude, around George Cukor's swimming pool in the early 1930s, at one of his "off-the-mainstream-record" Sunday afternoon parties. Left to right, above: **Tom Douglas, Gavin Gordon, David Manners, Alexander Kirkland,** and **Douglass Montgomery.**

handsome leading man type. He had worked to get rid of his Mississippi accent and went from being an unknown male secretary to co-starring as Greta Garbo's leading man in *Romance* (1930). He always told reporters, "My private life is off limits."

Hailing from Nova Scotia, David Manners, a clean-cut, good-looking young man, got his start lying on the casting couch of gay director James Whale. In time, he would appear opposite Katharine Hepburn, Barbara Stanwyck, Myrna Loy, and Loretta Young. He would be forever remembered for playing Jonathan Barker opposite Bela Lugosi in the horror classic, *Dracula* (1931). He confessed to Henry, "I've never seen that damned picture."

Talking to Alexander Kirkland, Henry soon realized that they had something in common: Tallulah Bankhead. Whereas Henry had lived with her in Manhattan, Alexander had starred with her in *Tarnished Lady* (1931).

Kirkland spoke of his experience in the early 1930s when he'd worked with the Group Theatre under the direction of Lee Strasberg and Cheryl Crawford.

Before coming to Hollywood, he had starred on Broadway in such plays as *Man in White* (1933).

During the course of his life, Kirkland married three times, so Henry assumed he must be at least bisexual. The surprise marriage that shocked Hollywood came in 1942 when he wed America's most famous striptease artist, Gypsy Rose Lee. The marriage lasted only a few weeks. Lee gave birth to a son, Eric, but its father turned out to be director Otto Preminger, Henry's future director.

A native of Los Angeles, Douglass Montgomery was a handsome, fair-haired young actor who came across as a bit effeminate in some scenes. At Los Angeles High School, he'd fallen in love with the captain of the football team.

On the screen, Henry had seen him emote in *Little Women* (1933), starring Katharine Hepburn.

He was later surprised when Montgomery wed the British actress Kay Young after her divorce from Michael Wilding. When their divorce came through, Wilding married Elizabeth Taylor.

The best-established star Henry met that night was the Swedish actor, Nils Asther, who began making silent pictures early in the movie-making game and was known as "The Male Greta Garbo." He is still remembered today for two films—*The Single Standard* and *Wild Orchids,* each with Garbo and each released in 1929.

With a touch of bitterness, he jokingly told Henry, "Greta objected when she had to play love scenes with me. She always said, 'I never know where your mouth was the night before.'"

When Henry was introduced to another son of California, Richard Cromwell, he had no clue that he would co-star with him one day. The actor would be cast in Henry's picture, *Jezebel* (1938) starring Bette Davis, and in *Young Mr. Lincoln* (1939). Cromwell would receive far better notices for his performance in *The Lives of a Bengal Lancer* (1935) starring Gary Cooper.

[Cromwell served in the U.S. Coast Guard during World War II, where he had secret affairs with actors Cesar Romero and Gig Young.

He surprised Hollywood insiders in 1945 when he married the English actress, Angela Lansbury. She was nineteen and her new husband was 35. It was later said that Cromwell

Pictured above are Swedish actors **Greta Garbo** and **Nils Asther** in 1929.

Their onscreen beauty contributed then and in decades to follow to the perception that Scandinavians are physically beautiful and "erotically combustible."

As their screen pairing progressed, Garbo became increasingly hostile to Asther, complaining that kissing him was "unsanitary" and effectively contributing to the demise of his American film career.

spent more time in the bed of Howard Hughes than he did of his wife. Lansbury later confessed that the marriage had been "a mistake."]

For Henry, the most memorable introduction at the party occurred when Alexander brought him over to meet Charles Laughton, who was sitting in an armchair. The English actor had been intrigued to learn that Henry had lived briefly in New York with Tallulah Bankhead. This otherwise talented actor's speech was slurred that night because of his huge consumption of Scotch.

"When I made *Devil and the Deep* in 1932 with Tallulah, Cary Grant, and Gary Cooper, Tallulah told me, 'Gary is divine. As for you, Charlotte, you are nothing but a repulsive mess of gob!' Let's face it: I have a face like the ass of an elephant."

"There are compensations," Henry told him. "Unlike many of the pretty boys in this room tonight, you can act."

"That is so true, my darling man, but I'd have preferred to be born pretty," Laughton said. "Since I'm ugly, I have to pay rent boys—you know, masseurs, hustlers, barmen, taxi drivers. In London, I patronize the hustlers who hang out at Piccadilly Circus."

Before Henry left Cukor' party that night, he was introduced to two late arrivals, Cary Grant and his lover, Randolph Scott.

At the end of the evening, Cukor approached Henry and gave him a kiss on both cheeks. "I want to invite you tomorrow afternoon to my Sunday swim party—no bathing trunks necessary."

As Henry recalled that night to James Stewart and others, he said, "In a way, the party marked a time of decision for me. I decided I was not cut out to be one of those casting couch boys. I would get movie roles based on my acting talent—and for no other reason."

He told his director, Victor Fleming, "When Jimmy Stewart arrives from New York, we'll develop our own set of friends. Instead of Cukor's pretty boys, we'll surround ourselves with beautiful starlets."_

Richard Cromwell (left) and **Angela Lansbury,** from a few years before their short and ultimately, embarrassing marriage in 1945.

Charles Laughton was the fill-in host for Ed Sullivan on September 9, 1958 when Elvis Presley made his first of three appearances on CBS's *The Ed Sullivan Show*, which generated 61 million viewers.

Laughton insisted on being Presley's "dresser," beginning with his jockey shorts.,

***

The Farmer Takes a Wife (movie; 1935)

Henry always remembered the day he arrived on the set of *The Farmer Takes a Wife*. As he did on the stage, he would play Dan Harrow. Used to June Walker as his leading lady, he had difficulty adjusting to Janet Gaynor, who "was day and night different from the acting styles of June."

By the afternoon of his first day, Fleming called him aside for a private chat. "You're playing Harrow like you did on Broadway. Your voice seems to be projecting to the top row of the balcony in a theater. You are, in fact, hamming it up far too much. Film, especially that all-seeing camera, calls for a different type of acting. Tone it down, kid."

For the next forty-six years on the screen, Henry would follow that advice.

As supporting actors for Henry and Gaynor, Fleming had hired a cast more talented and far better-known than Broadway's original roster.

The second male lead was cast with Charles Bickford, an actor called "tough as sandpaper with a voice to match." His greatest fame had come in 1930 when he starred opposite Greta Garbo in *Anna Christie*, her first talkie.

Margaret Hamilton had appeared on stage with Henry, and she repeated her role on the screen.

Slim Summerville, once listed as "the least sexy actor in Hollywood," starred as "Fortune Friendly." Born in the Territory of New Mexico in 1892, he got his start in those Mack Sennett "Keystone Kops" flickers, earning $3.50 a day.

From the territory of Arizona in 1905 came Andy Devine. He became known for his

Although the 1935 film version of *The Farmer Takes a Wife* had been conceived as a vehicle for the then A-list star Janet Gaynor, it was the Hollywood neophyte **Henry Fonda** who emerged as the victor in the aftermath of its release.

raspy, crackly voice and for playing the sidekick to Roy Rogers, "King of the Cowboys."

Andy Devine (who was anything but divine) would later work with Henry in *How the West Was Won* (1962).

Child actress Jane Withers had the small role of "Della." But by 1937 and 1938, she would be among the industry's top ten box office stars. Before that, she had starred with Shirley Temple in *Bright Eyes* (1934). She told Henry, "I detest Miss Lollipop. On screen, she's sickeningly sweet. Off screen, she's a fucking bitch."

The movie did so well at the box office that Henry was told that Janet Gaynor had been cast once again as his leading lady in his next picture.

In *The New York Times*, critic Andre Sennwald reviewed the movie as, "a rich and leisurely comedy of American manners," and he singled out Henry and Bickford for special praise. However, he felt that "Miss Gaynor is really too nice a person to be playing bad girls like Molly Larkins."

Eileen Creelman in *The New York Sun* wrote, "One of Mr. Fonda's most outstanding assets is his appearance of sincerity."

She had nailed it. Sincerity on screen would become one of Henry Fonda's most notable characteristics in his future films.

To a reporter, Henry gave his own review of *The Farmer Takes a Wife*: "That character up there on the screen wasn't me. He didn't even look like me, and he certainly didn't sound like me, or at least not like what I think I sound like. I'm pretty certain I'm going to be on the next plane heading back to New York."

***

Henry was in his dressing room when the latest copy of *Variety* arrived. In it came the report that Margaret Sullavan had "walked down the aisle for the second time." On November 25, 1934, she'd married film director William Wyler.

A reporter asked Henry about his reaction to his former wife's marriage. He sarcastically snapped at him, "I understand they're heading for Reno for their honeymoon," giving the union a slim chance of success.

It seemed that Wyler had fallen for Sullavan during his direction of her third film, *The Good Fairy* (1935). Her co-star had been the very charming Herbert Marshall, who had managed to become a leading man despite the fact that he'd had his right leg amputated during World War I.

Born in 1902 in Alsace-Lorraine, then part of the German Empire, Wyler would eventually make it to Hollywood where, as the press said, "He had a career of two decades of unbroken greatness."

Among his future films would be *Mrs. Miniver* (1942) with Greer Garson or *The Best Years of Our Lives* (1946) with Fredric March and Myrna Loy. By 1959, he was remaking *Ben-Hur*, this time a big-budget Technicolor blockbuster starring Charlton Heston.

In time, he would direct such stars as Olivia de Havilland, Audrey Hepburn, and Laurence Olivier. Henry got to know him when he helmed Bette Davis and himself in *Jezebel* (1938).

On the set, Wyler chastised Henry. "Why in hell didn't you warn me that Sullavan was an impossible bitch to live with?"

[Wyler had divorced her in March of 1936 after two unhappy years. During the filming of Jezebel, *Henry learned more details about their ill-fated union.*

On their honeymoon night, producer Jed Harris had gotten through to Sullavan on the phone in their bedroom. He threatened suicide if Sullavan didn't come back to him.

Her response? "Jed, darling, if you do kill yourself, why not donate your junk to the Museum of Natural History? A cock and balls like yours should be mummified." Then she slammed down the phone.

Henry claimed that Sullavan's marriage to Wyler was "an irresistible force meeting an immovable object."

The couple's battles actually began on their honeymoon. Henry could have predicted that.

Wyler later told him that "The bitch called me, among tamer names, a Kraut, Hogface, and Fart Blossom. But I shot back with even more colorful language: Cunt, Pussy Shit, Harridan, Slut."

Sullavan discussed both Henry and Wyler with a reporter, although some of her remarks would not be printed until years later.

"Wyler had something in common with my former husband, Henry Fonda.

The brief and fast-aborted marriage in 1934 of **William Wyler** (*left*) to the "terrifyingly self-willed" (and ultimately suicidal) **Margaret Sullavan** was even more unhappy and henpecked than Henry Fonda's very brief marriage to her in 1931.

Henry, with only a touch of revenge, told some of his friends that he could easily have predicted it.

Both of them are premature ejaculators, leaving me unfulfilled. Each one resembled the other in that they were fast starters, but lousy finishers."

Wyler attacked back: "Hell, Maggie knew about highway pickups before they became fashionable—or rather infamous. Sometimes, she would follow handsome young men down the street and propose to them. 'Won't you come back home with me?'"]

***

Lanky and still maintaining a Brooklyn accent, **Ross Alexander** fell in love with Henry Fonda during the time Fonda lived with the actor and his wife. But he got nowhere with Henry.

At the age of 29, he fatally shot himself.

Henry was finding it increasingly uncomfortable living with Ross Alexander and his new wife. "Every time I went to take a piss, Ross found some reason to follow me into the bathroom," he claimed.

Finally, he found a modest rental costing $65 a month, an amount he could easily afford.

"I'd been chaste for too long, unlike my former wife, Margaret Sullavan," he said. "My luck changed. At a party, I met a good-looking girl, actress Shirley Ross. As it turned out, she had been born in Omaha, Nebraska. At least we had something in common."

He'd never heard of her before. Neither had most of Hollywood, where she had grown up, attending Hollywood High and later, UCLA.

As she told him, "I never set out to be an actress. I was a singer. Even at the age of fourteen, I was giving recitals. Finally, I got a gig as the girl singer with the Gus Arnheim Band."

While singing one night, she was overheard by the songwriting team of Rodgers and Hart, who hired her to help sell their latest compositions to MGM. One of the early songs underwent several revisions, before being released across the country with the title of 'Blue Moon.'"

She was eventually assigned a small role in *Manhattan Melodrama* (1934), starring Clark Gable and William Powell. Long before she went to bed with Henry, she'd have a brief fling with each of these two leading men, although both of them would ultimately prefer Carole Lombard.

A photogenic beauty from Henry's home town of Omaha, **Shirley Ross.**

Famously, in 1938, she sang to the radio public what she ultimately said to Henry Fonda: "Thanks for the Memory."

Henry's affair with Ross lasted only two and a half months. "After my castration by Margaret Sullavan, Shirley made me feel like a man again."

Ross had already been cast in the screwball comedy, *Bombshell (1933)*, starring Jean Harlow, the platinum blonde of the 1930s. "But how could I be noticed with all the focus on Miss Hair Dye?" Ross asked Henry.

[Coincidentally, her director was Victor Fleming, who had helmed Henry in The Farmer Takes a Wife.*]*

The critic for *The Los Angeles Times* wrote, "At Paramount, Shirley Ross has one of the sweetest voices on the screen. She is hired mainly to smile and not step on the toes of her leading man."

To Henry's surprise, Ross became involved near the end of the decade with Bing Crosby and Bob Hope. Along the Hollywood grapevine, she made gossip fodder for her rumored affairs with both the singer and the ski-nosed comedian.

For a 1937 musical, *Waikiki Wedding,* she was cast as a local beauty queen with Crosby crooning "Blue Hawaii" in a palmetto setting of grass skirts, tropical sunsets, and a razorback pig named "Walford."

Ross moved from Crosby's bed to that of Hope when they co-starred in *Thanks for the Memory* (1938), which became his signature song for life. That was the name of the Oscar-winning song that had first been heard in *The Big Broadcast* of 1938.

Hope moved on to other starlets, and Ross married Ken Dolan in 1938.

Both Hope and Ross were reteamed in *Some Like It Hot* (1939). For that movie's screening on television in the 1960s, its title was changed to *Rhythm Romance* so as not to confuse it with Marilyn Monroe's classic comedy in which she appeared with Tony Curtis and Jack Lemmon, each portraying a drag queen.

***

57

Way Down East (1935)

Producer Winfield Sheehan hired Henry King to direct Henry Fonda's next picture, *Way Down East,* a 1935 remake of D.W. Griffith's famous silent screen version of 1920 that had starred Lillian Gish.

Henry had been assigned the role that in the original version had starred Richard Barthelmess. In one of the most iconic episodes in the history of the silents, he rescues Gish as she's floating downstream on a large slab of ice about to go over a waterfall to her certain death.

The plot focuses on a starving *gamine* who has lost everything after being tricked into a marriage by a wicked millionaire. He deserts her and she finds herself pregnant.

Her baby dies at birth, and she is taken in by a cold, puritanical family, later falling in love with the family's son.

Two views of **Rochelle Hudson.** *Left photo:* looking *über-glam* and *haute,* as in "couture," and (*right photo*) as a simple farm girl in publicity, with **Henry Fonda**, for the 1935 reprise of the classic silent film, *Way Down East.*

Henry was fortunate to be assigned King as his director. This native of Virginia, born in 1886, had started out as an actor in 1913, appearing in some sixty films before becoming one of the best filmmakers of his era. In time, he was nominated for two Oscars as Best Director, and seven of his films would compete for a Best Picture Academy Award.

Shortly before filming began, King phoned Henry to tell him that his projected leading lady, Janet Gaynor, had been involved in a car accident and would not be available. He had cast another actress, Rochelle Hudson, in her place.

A daughter of Oklahoma City, Hudson had been a WAMPAS Baby Star in 1931.   *[The WAMPAS Baby Stars was a promotional campaign that ran, with interruptions, for twelve years beginning in 1922. Sponsored by the United States Western Association of Motion Picture Advertisers (WAMPAS), it honored, each year, about a dozen young actresses believed to be on the brink of stardom. Except for Clara Bow, Janet Gaynor, Fay Wray, Dolores del Rio, Mary Astor, and Joan Crawford, many of them failed to match their promotional hype.]*

In 1930, when Hudson was only fourteen, she'd signed a contract with RKO. She had already appeared in *Wild Boys of the Road* in 1933 and would soon be starring as Cosette in *Les Misérables* (1935). Today, she appears in re-runs of James Dean's *Rebel Without a Cause* (1955) in which she was cast as Natalie Wood's mother.

Hudson is also seen on television in revivals of Mae West's *She Done Him Wrong* (1933). Cast as a fallen *ingénue,* Sally Glynn, Hudson gets some wisdom from West: "When women go wrong, men go after them."

Once again, in this, his second film, Henry found himself on the screen with Slim Summerville, Andy Devine, and Margaret Hamilton. New to him was the lesbian actress, Spring Byington, whose film career would span the years from 1904 until 1968. She had a seven-year run on radio and television as the star of *December Bride.* Once, she confided to Henry that her secret desire had been to become an airplane pilot.

Perhaps Hamilton was in an early rehearsal for her later role as the Wicked Witch in *The Wizard of Oz* (1939). In *Way Down East,* she was a scene stealer as the vicious gossip, Martha Perkins, digging up dirt on the poor young girl, Anna Moore (Hudson).

In contrast, Fonda's character of David Bartlett opposes "self-righteous bigotry."

To Henry's disappointment, his second film was, commercially speaking, rather unsuccessful, probably because the story was so dated. Henry, as an actor, however, was praised for his performance.

In a latter-day revival of the film, the *Motion Picture Guide* claimed, "As hokey as *Way Down East* is, Fonda delivers the *persona* that made him one of the screen's greatest actors, and he is the movie's saving grace."

André Senwald in *The New York Times* wrote: "In large measure, *Way Down East* is the personal triumph of Henry Fonda, whose immensely winning performance as the squire's son helps to establish an engaging bucolic mood for the drama in its quieter moments."

While working on *Way Down East,* Henry learned that his father had attended, in Omaha, a screening of *The Farmer Takes a Wife.* William had liked the film and, in a phone call to him, transmitted high praise for his son's acting talent.

He did admit that he was suffering from kidney trouble and wanted to retire from his profession as a printer. "I want to buy a spread outside Omaha and raise chickens."

Henry promised that he'd buy the land for him, but jokingly, said he'd have to ship him fresh eggs every day.

At the end of the filming, word arrived that Henry's father had died on October 7, 1935, almost a year after the death of his beloved wife, Herberta.

A saddened Henry flew home to mourn with his two sisters. "We are now orphans," he said with a melancholy sadness in his voice.

***

Under contract to Walter Wanger, Henry was told that he'd ordered his publicists to get his photos in newspapers and movie magazines. "The best way to do that is to take glamourous stars out to premieres at the Cocoanut Grove, and weekends in Palm Springs."

Henry almost could not believe that the first date arranged for him was with "the most glamourous star in the world, Miss Marlene Dietrich," a refugee from German cinema. He was told that he would be her escort at a Hollywood premiere.

As an escort, Henry joined the ranks of other suitors such as Douglas Fairbanks Jr., and the novelist, Erich Maria Remarque. Henry had seen Dietrich in her German-made film, *The Blue Angel* (1930) and in *Morocco* (also 1930) with Gary Cooper, and was enthralled with her screen image.

Marlene Dietrich living it up with **Henry Fonda** in 1939. She told him, "No man falls in love with me that I don't want to have fall in love with me. I don't intend to let you fall in love with me."

He showed up at her address, driving his modest Ford. But when she emerged and saw the vehicle, she said she didn't dare arrive at that premiere in such a vehicle. Quickly, she ordered a chauffeur-driven limousine to escort them.

Bejeweled and dazzling, she attracted massive attention from the press as flashbulbs popped when she, with Henry at her side, walked down the red carpet.

"I had the feeling I was with a goddess," Henry recalled. "Never before, and never again, would I have such a glittering date."

Sources differ over which premiere Henry and Dietrich attended. Even Henry, later, wasn't certain, claiming, "When you're out with Marlene, who looks at the screen?"

It appears to have happened on the night of November 16, 1935 at Warner's Hollywood Theatre. The picture was *Dangerous,* and it brought Bette Davis a Best Actress Oscar.

In one scene, Davis delivers an infamous insult to her leading man, Franchot Tone.

"Oh, you cheap, petty bookkeeper, you! Every time I think that those soft, sticky hands of yours ever touched me, it makes me sick. SICK! Do you hear? You're everything that's repulsive to me."

That was just the on-screen Davis, shouting vile insults. In private, she fell in love with Tone. Later, after fellating him, she gave him the nickname, "Jawbreaker."

At the time, he was romantically involved with Crawford, whom he later married. Crawford learned about his affair with Davis, thus launching the most famous diva feud in the history of Hollywood.

[Both Crawford and Davis would be, in years to come, lovers and co-stars of Henry.]

After the premiere and after three hours at the Cocoanut Grove, it was time to take Dietrich home. There, she invited him in for a nightcap, which was a signal that she planned, at this late hour, to seduce him.

He fully expected that she'd invite him into her boudoir, and that both of them would strip down for intimacies. Instead, she approached the armchair where he was seated with his third glass of champagne. She unbuckled his pants, pulled down his underwear, and fellated him.

"I would always remember it as the supreme blow-job of my life." Henry later said to director Josh Logan. *[As their respective careers unfolded, Gary Cooper, Yul Brynner, Maurice Chevalier, Kirk Douglas, Douglas Fairbanks Jr., President Kennedy, Howard Hughes, George Raft, Otto Preminger, Erich Maria Remarque, Mike Todd, Edward G. Robinson, and John Wayne would echo Henry Fonda's assessment.]*

When it was over and he was recovering on the sofa, she emerged fresh from her bathroom. She told him, "Men always want to put their things in. That's all they want. But I prefer what I just did."

"I loved it," he told her. "What great fun, what a climax I had! I didn't have to do one bit of the work. Glorious! I hope a repeat performance is called for."

"I will take it under consideration."

On occasion in the future, Dietrich would phone him to escort her to various Hollywood galas. It would be his best friend, James Stewart, who seduced (and impregnated) Dietrich during the filming of a Western, *Destry Rides Again* (1939). She would later have an abortion.

Henry later lamented, "I always wanted to be the leading man to Marlene in a film. But that was never arranged. I got Barbara Stanwyck instead."

Ironically, Stanwyck was having an affair with Dietrich at the time.

"I was subtle," Henry quipped. "When I suggested to Stanwyck that I might be in the market for a three-way, she looked at me like I'd asked to take a knife to her left nipple."

Young **James Stewart** with young **Henry Fonda,** around the time they shared a house together next door to Greta Garbo.

Many said their styles, *personae*, and acting styles were equivalent, if not "interchangeable."

***

Henry drove his Ford to the railway station to pick up Stewart, who had ridden across the country. He arrived late, having missed an earlier train.

When he got there, he rushed into Fonda's arms to give him a bearhug. As part of his luggage, he'd brought a crated "Martian Bomber," that model airplane on which they'd worked so hard in New York.

Henry drove him to the pseudo-Mexican styled farmhouse in Brentwood. As he pulled up in front, he pointed out the house next door. "Greta Garbo lives there."

"You're making that up," Stewart exclaimed, skeptical that their neighbor was the screen goddess.

Stewart was a bit horrified when Henry escorted him for a view of their backyard. It was filled with feral cats, perhaps thirty-five in all. "Don't try to pet them. They're wild and will claw you to pieces. They run wild, but I put out food for them every day. I've also got to warn you: They're covered with fleas."

"I'm already starting to itch," Stewart complained.

He had been instructed to report to MGM sometime the following week. For the upcoming weekend, Fonda had arranged a special treat for his best friend

As described by biographer Mark Eliot, one was "a long-legged, dyed redhead, gum-chewing starlet with a flair for comedy who could also dance. The other was a bleached blonde, tall-stepping dancer who'd been cast in a Fred Astaire movie." *[There has been speculation that the writer was describing starlets Ginger Rogers and Lucille Ball.]*

The shapely dancers would be their guests on Saturday and Sunday. Over breakfast that Sunday, Henry suggested that he and Stewart switch partners than night. As word had it, each member of the quartet involved agreed that that would, indeed, be enticing.

Details associated with Fonda and Stewart's encounters with Garbo, their neighbor, depends on which biography one reads. Some books claim that neither of them ever met the phobically elusive Garbo. Even Henry and Stewart disagreed on what happened. In reference to his friend, Henry later wrote, "When Jimmy doesn't remember something, he makes it up."

Norma Shearer, who was married at the time to Irving Thalberg, the "boy wonder" of MGM, remained Stewart's dream girl, followed by Garbo.

"Jimmy seemed obsessed with Garbo and sometimes went around quoting lines from her movies."

Of all the different stories, we'll focus on the account of Mercedes de Acosta, Garbo's socialite lover, the subject of a recent biography from Blood Moon Productions. In the mid-1930s, she often spent two or three nights a week in Garbo's bed.

Mercedes revealed that Garbo was eager to meet her next-door neighbors, and that Garbo had informed her, "I didn't have their number, so I went and knocked on their door one afternoon and invited them over for dinner. Both of them seemed eager to accept the invitation."

Garbo seemed more taken with Stewart than with Henry.

The most famously promiscuous lesbian in Golden-Age Hollywood, **Mercedes de Acosta** conducted affairs with female stage and screen divas who systematically rejected overtures from many dozens of men.

She's depicted above looking frumpier than she had during the glorious, well-connected days of her greatest youth and beauty.

In 2020, Blood Moon Productions published Darwin Porter's prize-winning biography of her extraordinary life as an acolyte and enabler to many of the most celebrated women of the 20th Century.

She was delighted to learn that she and the lanky actor would each be working at MGM, her home studio. It seemed that Garbo had a purpose for that dinner prepared by Mercedes.

When the men got there, she escorted them to her backyard and showed them a small boxing ring. "I like to box, and I need a sparring partner," she announced, turning first to Henry.

"There's no way in hell that I'll box with you," Henry protested. "Hitting Greta Garbo? That sounds insane."

"I'll do it!" Stewart volunteered.

That Sunday afternoon, Stewart, wearing boxing gloves and trunks, joined Garbo in the ring. Whereas he held back the force of his punches, she did not.

Mercedes had left Garbo's house early that Sunday morning. With the understanding that no one else was in residence, Stewart remained there, not returning to Henry's house next door until the following morning.

Henry was at the door to meet him. "You gotta tell me what happened!"

"Well, Greta and I got all hot and sweaty, and then we went in to take a shower. I guess I must have passed out. I don't remember what happened."

"Like hell you don't," Henry protested.

"You're not going to get any spice from me," Stewart said. "Now, if you'll stand out of my way, I've got to shower and get dressed. I have to report to the studio."

Over the course of the next three weeks, Stewart spent part of every Sunday with Garbo. Henry was excluded.

That event marked the beginning of what evolved, for Stewart, into an amazing string of seductions. A Hollywood columnist later reported that in the late 1930s, Stewart dated "263 glamour girls," many of them starlets. Over the course of his romantic career, he would seduce women from the "A-list," including his dream girl, Norma Shearer, after the death of her husband, Irving Thalberg. Other conquests would include Lana Turner, Olivia de Havilland, a young Rita Hayworth, Loretta Young, Rosalind Russell, and Katharine Hepburn.

To reporters, Stewart usually remained discreet, except he did admit to Louella Parsons, "My bachelor years, let me tell you, were wonderful…just wonderful. Boy did I have some good times."

Parson's verdict? "James Stewart is the most nearly normal of all Hollywood stars."

***

Josh Logan remains the only source that revealed Henry's sexual involvement with Greta Garbo, the odd and reclusive mega-star and screen goddess. Over drinks one night, a lot of alcohol, Henry revealed some details.

"She came over to our home one weekend when Jimmy was away, shooting a film," Henry said. "It seems she wanted a boxing partner in the ring, a role Jimmy had agreed to perform, but one I had refused. Boxing Greta Garbo—what a ridiculous idea! However, that Swede could be god damn persuasive. When Garbo wanted something, she usually got it."

"A seduction followed that afternoon, after I was invited into her house," Henry said. "I was jaybird naked in her bedroom, trying on Jimmy's boxing trunks, when she entered. She, too, was showing everything. For her, that was no big deal. Her nudism was widely known. I heard that in Sweden, nudity is commonplace, but only in summer. It was a hot and lazy afternoon. She changed her mind about sparring with me. Instead, she preferred love in the afternoon."

"We made love, but it was most unusual for me," Henry confessed to Logan. "I wasn't thinking about a sexual release on my part, I was an actor playing a role, and that role called for me to please Garbo. I was trying my damnedest but getting no response from her. She gave no indication that she was enjoying our intercourse. I was glad when we reached the final goal."

For the rest of the afternoon, she demanded he remain nude with her. A long talk with plenty of wine was followed by a light supper of herring.

She wanted to talk about "the first time." He revealed how he'd lost his virginity in an Omaha whorehouse to a much older woman. "The experience was so horrid I feared that it would turn me off women for life."

Contemporaries who met her described **Greta Garbo** as "self-centered," "narcissistic," "intellectually pedestrian," "emotionally evasive," and "dull."

Yet any fan of Pre-Code films describes her—on the screen, at least—as "incandescent."

Here's Garbo as she appeared with **Robert Taylor** in *Camille* (1936).

In reference to losing her own virginity, Garbo had quite a different experience, citing hers as occurring one midsummer evening in Sweden. She'd camped out in a tent by a Swedish lake in July.

"I lost my virginity with my sister. As a late teenager, I masturbated a lot, looking at photographs of my favorite film stars."

Like most of the American public, Henry thought that John Gilbert had been the love of Garbo's life, but she dispelled that idea. "Gilbert is a homosexual, and the sad truth is he can't admit it to himself."

"I'm supposed to be this great temptress on the screen," Garbo told him, "but MGM gives me leading men, one after another, who are disasters in the bedroom. Some of them wouldn't know what to do with a nude woman if confronted with one. Not just Gilbert, but so many others: Lars Hanson, Antonio Moreno, Conrad Nagel, Nils Asther, Edmund Lowe, Gavin Gordon, Ramon Novarro, Robert Taylor."

As Henry summed it up to Logan, "The sex with Garbo was memorable only in that I was having intercourse with Garbo, not necessarily for the pleasure of it. And in ways that evoke my sexual interlude with Tallulah Bankhead, I was not invited back for a repeat performance. Incidentally, did you know that Robert Taylor has a very small dick?"

***

Although beautiful starlets came and went from their Brentwood home, Stewart and Henry also entertained male visitors, too. In fact, between lodgings, Josh Logan once stayed with them for a while until he could get resettled. David Selznick had hired Logan as a voice coach for stars who were having trouble adjusting to the talkies.

After Logan left, John Swope, an actor-turned-photographer, moved in. Both Stewart and Henry had worked with him in New York. "He camped out at our house, with the feral cats and their fleas, until he found a modest apartment." In 1943, he married actress Dorothy McGuire, with whom Henry had worked onstage in Omaha. When she was only fourteen, she had starred with him in *A Kiss for Cinderella*.

Henry and Stewart often stayed home on weekends after inviting two starlets to come over for a visit. Once, one of the two actresses lined up for double date with Stewart and Fonda phoned and said that her sister was in town, and could she bring her over, too?

As a possible partner for the "third wheel," Henry called a young New Yorker he had recently met, Humphrey Bogart, a new-in-town actor with lisping speech and an ugly mug. Like Stewart and Henry, "Bogie" was torn between the Broadway stage and the pursuit of filmmaking success in Hollywood. When he got through on the phone, Henry invited him over as part of the Saturday night setup, promising him "a hot number," even though he had not yet met the sister.

Consequently, that weekend, three couples ate and drank the night away as the record player spun. Later that night, Bogie and the starlet were offered the guest bedroom. Henry and Stewart and their respective dates were forced to "make do" in a double bed in the main chamber.

The Petrified Forest

[As it happened, the trio of girls could spend only one night at the Stewart-Fonda home, as a yacht owner had invited them, along with eight of his male friends, for a boating trip to Catalina.]

Bogie emerged late on Sunday morning from the bedroom looking bedraggled. "Looks like you had a hot night," Henry said.

Bogie stared back at Henry: "Any guy who would stick his cock in that bitch would throw a rock through a Rembrandt."

[In 1955, Henry would co-star with Bogie and his actress wife, Lauren Bacall, in the television remake of The Petrified Forest.]

Their next guest was Orson Welles. Still years away from any involvement in *Citizen Kane,* he had taken a train to Hollywood for a screen test. Both Stewart and Henry had met him briefly in New York and had found him most in-

Here's the raconteur, producer, filmmaker, gourmand, and "shock jock' **Orson Wells**, often described as "the bad boy wonder" of Hollywood, as he appeared as a radio host in 1941.

In 1955, less than two years before **Humphrey Bogart's** death, TV producers decided to remake the 1936 film classic, *The Petrified Forest*, into a truncated version for the then-new-fangled medium of television.

It was **Lauren Bacall's** first time on TV, and it was obvious that **Henry Fonda** wasn't comfortable in the role of an embittered writer.

Reviewers savaged both the telecast and Bogart in particular as "stilted and tired, so tired."

triguing.

Later, Welles recalled, "I'd heard a lot of rumors about my hosts, claims that they were having a torrid affair to equal that of Randolph Scott and Cary Grant. I just assumed they were inviting me for a three-way. I came from the world of the theatre, where liaisons like that were common. I was intrigued, so I arrived on their doorstep. After an evening with them, I concluded that those two guys were either having the hottest affair in Tinseltown—or else they were the two straightest guys I'd ever met in my lusty days on Planet Earth."

Welles became intoxicated and passed out on their sofa. He joined them for breakfast the next morning at ten o'clock. Henry and Stewart were thin as scarecrows, and both of them were frequently being told to put on weight.

"My weight problem was the exact opposite of those two lean actors," Welles related to reporters on the set of the future *Citizen Kane.* As he told Joseph Cotten and others, "For Sunday breakfast, Fonda and Stewart drink eggnog, adding a lot of brandy. It was more nog than egg, looking like a dark rum drink. By noon, all of us were pissed."

***

I Dream Too Much (1935)

It came as a complete surprise to Henry when RKO producer Pandro S. Berman and director John Cromwell specifically requested him as the leading man for an upcoming production of *I Dream Too Much* (1935), his third feature film.

The opera diva, Lily Pons, the diminutive French coloratura soprano, had already been designated as the film's female lead.

As her career advanced, Pons had become skilled at promoting herself as a marketable cultural icon. Her opinions of cuisine and fashion were frequently reported in women's magazines, and she was featured in nationwide advertisements for Lockheed, Knox Gelatin, and various food and beauty products.

In the mid-1930s, after the success of singer Grace Moore in a singing role in *One Night of Love* (1934), Hollywood flirted with visions of transforming other opera divas into movie stars. But the trend quickly faded, as studios realized that opera was too high brow for most middle-class movie patrons.

Born in France in 1898, Pons had grown up near Cannes on the French Riviera. As a teenager, she'd sung for troops during World War I. By 1928, she'd made her operatic debut. Her greatest fame came at the Metropolitan Opera in New York City between 1931 and 1960, where she would appear almost three-hundred times (a record) as its principal soprano.

Henry was cast as Jonathan Street, the adoring husband of Annette (Pons). Although she has no musical ambition, he pushes her to become an opera diva. Its plot was ridiculous, and Henry knew it. He also realized how difficult it was to make the public believe that he and Pons could ever be a loving husband and wife.

According to the script, despite her lack of drive, Madame Street becomes a star anyway, leaving Henry—a would-be composer—with his career in tatters. The plot in some ways evokes *A Star Is Born,* but everything works out happily before the end of the final reel.

Henry's first "Franco-American alliance" was with the Provence-born opera and film star **Lily Pons.**

Fingered by Hollywood as the centerpiece of "musical movies" which were eventually appraised as "too highbrow," Pons became an aggressive marketer of luxury goods (especially cosmetics) and the assumption that all things French are "Ooooh-la-la": chic, charming, and desirable.

Henry Fonda appears here as her supportive husband and booking agent in the aria-studded melodrama, *I Dream Too Much* (1935).

John Cromwell was hired as the director who had to pull together this percolating stewpot of talent. His career had started in the early days of the Talkies and would last until the 1950s, when he was "blacklisted" and vilified as a Communist during the McCarthy "witch hunt."

Henry had been fascinated by Cromwell's direction of Bette Davis in the screen adaptation of W. Somerset Maugham's *Of Human Bondage* in 1934. *[Davis would soon become Henry's co-star.]*

Hoping for a big-hit musical like RKO's Astaire-Rogers movies, Berman employed top talent for *I Dream Too Much.* He hired Max Steiner as music director, and appointed Hermes Pan as its choreographer. Jerome Kern, backed up by lyricist Dorothy Fields, was assigned to write four new songs.

Berman even hired Pons' famous husband, André Kostelanetz, to conduct the film's musical sequences.

The movie would receive an Oscar nod for its sound recording. In spite of that, critic Graham Green reviewed the musical score as "ponderous."

Supporting roles went to Eric Blore, an English actor who was usually known for playing snobby butlers, valets, or "a gentleman's gentleman."

Osgood Perkins joined the cast as Paul Darcy. He later became far more famous for being the real-life father of Anthony Perkins, the star of Alfred Hitchcock's *Psycho* (1960).

Other roles were essayed by Mischa Auer as Darcy's pianist. Child actor Scotty Beckett was cast as "Boy on the Merry-Go-Round."

As a gum-chewing American tourist, Lucille Ball had only one line: "Culture makes my feet hurt." With her hair dyed blonde, she is a visitor to Paris, and Fonda is her tour guide. It's obvious that she'd rather sample the city's night life with him than view its monuments.

[Lucille had already appeared in small roles in three of the Rogers/Astaire musicals, Roberta *(1935);* Top Hat *(also 1935); and* Follow the Fleet *(1936).*

It was Rogers who told Lucille about her torrid affair with a young Cuban bandleader, Desi Arnaz.]

André Sennwald of *The New York Times* found Henry "the most likable of the new crop of juveniles descending on Hollywood from the New York stage."

After some chitchat on the set of their film with Lily Pons, young **Henry Fonda** and a then-brunette **Lucille Ball** met for a date. Here, they appear together when each of them were "relatively unattached."

Years later, reflecting on Lucille's spectacular success as an early purveyor of America's television industry, Henry ruefully remarked, "If I had played my cards differently, the studio that made all those *I Love Lucy* reruns might have been called "Henrylu" instead of "Desilu."

"As the husband of Lily Pons, Henry Fonda wants to be a composer, but can't make it. He is overshadowed by her success—and leaves her," wrote one critic. "He's quite creditable."

Variety disagreed, finding Henry not convincing in the role. "Perhaps that is the fault of the writing. Fonda just isn't made to wear top hat and tails."

***

Near the end of the shoot, Lucille Ball and Henry Fonda started dating. She remembered him as "unassuming, very kind, and quite handsome, but a little bit on the skinny side." She told her friend, Ginger Rogers, "I usually like men with more meat on their bones."

Rogers quipped, "Or meat somewhere else. Sometimes, those skinny guys make up for their deficiencies by being meaty down below."

After the wrap of *I Dream Too Much,* Rogers and Lucille went on a double-date "with those roomies," Stewart and Henry.

The evening began at the men's "farmhouse" in Brentwood. On that night, Rogers paired with Stewart, and Lucille emoted with Henry.

Henry cooked dinner while Rogers, in the living room, taught Stewart and Lucille how to dance the carioca. As Lucille remembered it, "I ended up doing the dishes."

After dinner, the quartet headed for the Cocoanut Grove, "where our table was in the boondocks" (Lucille's words).

Within the confines of the Ambassador Hotel, the quartet danced to Freddy Martin's band, later going for a late-night bowl of chili at Barney's Beanery. They ate under a sign that read NO FAGOTS *[Barney didn't know how to spell "faggots"]* ALLOWED.

Their collective double date lasted until dawn. By then, Lucille's nighttime makeup wasn't ready to face the sunrise. Henry took one look at her and said "Yuk."

He later lamented: "Shit! If I hadn't said that she might have named her production company 'Henrylu' instead of 'Desilu.'"

He called her the next day and apologized, stating that he'd had too much to drink. "I think you're beautiful," he assured her. "Hell, you're a natural beauty. You don't need all that studio guck on your face."

Somehow, he convinced her to go out with him again, and thus began an on-again, off-again affair that would endure for decades, acted out as romantic partners "in real life," and also in upcoming films together.

In the beginning, the press paid almost no attention to the romantic link between Henry and Lucille Ball. However, since Rogers was a big star because of all those Astaire/Rogers hit musicals, her dating of Stewart became a big event in the press.

Tabloid headlines blared:

HAS JIMMY HELPED GINGER FORGET LEW AYRES?;
CAN SHY SWEET JIMMY BE THE ANSWER TO GINGER'S PRAYERS?;
CAN GINGER CHOOSE BETWEEN FONDA AND STEWART?

That latter headline ran above a story that alleged that Stewart was involved in affairs with both Lucille and with Ginger.

The most memorable moment to that point in the careers of both Rogers and Stewart occurred on the night of February 27, 1941. He was photographed kissing her as they held their respective Oscars, she for Best Actress in *Kitty Foyle;* and Stewart for Best Actor in *The Philadelphia Story.*

***

Although his roles were most often minor, James Stewart was getting more film parts than Henry. In 1936 alone, he was cast in eight movies, whereas Henry, in larger roles, made three.

Ironically, each of the two actors, in future films, would work with Margaret Sullavan as his leading lady.

At this point, despite some beginner's mistakes, Stewart began to rise quickly toward stardom. By the end of his career, the American Film Institute would name him "The Third Greatest Male Star of All Time," with Henry in the Number Six position.

For a brief period, at least, studios interpreted the screen pairing of two Oscar winners, **Ginger Rogers** with **James Stewart,** as commercial and emotional dynamite.

Here, they appear together on the cover of the May 1938 edition of *Screen Romances*, percolating readers' involvement in the romantic complications of *Vivacious Lady.*

At first, MGM didn't know how to cast Stewart. Could he be a romantic leading man, or should he be used instead for comic relief?

He would prove to his early skeptics that he could excel in many genres: suspense thrillers, Westerns, family fare, biographic stories, and screwball comedies. Even in minor roles, he tended to get good notices, telling Henry, "I was all feet and hands, not knowing what to do with them."

Stewart's first film was *The Murder Man* (1935), with star roles going to Virginia Bruce and Spencer Tracy, who played a wise-cracking newsman who specialized in solving murder cases. In his final case, he admits that he is the killer.

Stewart plays a reporter, a tall, lean character nicknamed "Shorty." Although Stewart as an actor later became known for his hesitant speech patterns, in *The Murder Man,* he delivered his lines in a kind of *rat-tat-tat-tat* staccato.

During its filming, Stewart dated its leading lady, Virginia Bruce, who was both an actress and singer. She had arrived in Hollywood from the cold winds of North Dakota. In 1932, while filming *Kango* with Walter Huston, she met and fell in love with that silent screen heartthrob, John Gilbert. He was still suffering from a broken heart after Greta Garbo dumped him and took up with a woman.

Soon, Bruce and Gilbert were married in a quickie wedding in his dressing room on the studio lot. MGM's Irving Thalberg functioned as Best Man.

The marriage soon went sour. A divorce followed in 1934.

Stewart dated Bruce "between marriages." Sometimes, Henry noted, his roommate stayed at her residence over the course of several long weekends.

Stewart's fling with Bruce during the filming of *The Murder Man* marked a turning point in his life. Through the latter five years of the 1930s, the years before his marriage, he would often have affairs with his leading ladies.

"Maybe one or two of them said 'no' to Jimmie, but I don't know who they were," Henry said. "He seemed to score time and time again, making me envy his record of seductions. He was so god damn beguiling that women could not resist his manly charm. Even my wife, Margaret Sullavan—or should I more accurately say 'former wife'—fell for him."

Blonde and reasonably attractive, **Virginia Bruce** never achieved stardom in Hollywood's golden era.

She's known for two accomplishments: Her disastrous marriage (1932-1934) to screen idol John Gilbert, and her introduction of the Cole Porter hit song, "I've Got You Under My Skin" in the 1936 film, *Born to Dance.*

***

Greta Garbo had moved out, chased away, no doubt, by fleas from Henry's feral cats. As it happened, the owner of her rented home also owned the residence which Henry and Stewart shared. Each actor held a key to the house Garbo had just vacated, having agreed with the landlord to show it to prospective rentals.

It was Stewart who answered the door to discover singing star Jeanette MacDonald on his doorstep. Both of them stood looking at each other for a moment of discovery before she informed him she'd like to see the house where Garbo had lived. "I also need a place to rent," she told him.

He found her enchanting, as he showed her the rooms, finally inviting her into the backyard with its small boxing ring.

"I could see the fleas crawling up her stockings," he said. "No wonder she turned down the property. However, she rented a home four blocks away, so we became neighbors, anyway."

After MacDonald moved in, she once again knocked on Stewart's door. Something had gone wrong at her rental, and "I need a man to help me."

Stewart volunteered that Friday afternoon. He later phoned Henry to tell him he was staying over for the weekend to help her solve some problems around the house.

It was with a satisfied smile on his lips that Stewart greeted Henry back at his own home the following Monday morning. He needed a quick shower and a change of clothes. "I've been cast in *Rose Marie*. It's a musical starring Jeanette MacDonald and Nelson Eddy."

"But you don't sing and dance," Henry said to Stewart on his way to the bathroom.

Directed by W. S. Van Dyke, the screenplay had been adapted from a Broadway musical written in part by Oscar Hammerstein II.

In the revised plot, MacDonald was cast as a Canadian soprano, Marie de Flor. She learns that her brother Jack (Stewart) has escaped from prison and is hiding out in the northern woods, fleeing justice for having killed a Royal Mountie. Regrettably, the Mountie she loves, Sergeant Bruce (Nelson Eddy), is the one sent to find and arrest her brother.

Although he was miscast, Stewart managed to convincingly pull off his minor role, one critic stating that he performed it in fine form. It was clear, however, that *Rose Marie's* success belonged to the box office pairing of MacDonald and Eddy.

On location, its director, W.S. Van Dyke, took a liking to the nervous young actor and asked Stewart to be his bedmate during the on-location shooting of the film. As Stewart told Henry, "I played my accordian to put Woody (the director's nickname) to sleep at night."

"I hope that's all you and Van Dyke did," Henry said.

Back home, Stewart startled Henry by telling him that in his next picture, his leading lady would be Margaret Sullavan.

***

Eager to make new friends among the Hollywood colony, the roommates set out to befriend their new neighbor, Jeanette MacDonald, in her newly remodeled home down the street. Stewart had already spent a weekend alone with her.

Invited for dinner, with Henry, at MacDonald's new home, Stewart arrived on its doorstep to discover that Nelson Eddy—her co-star in *Rose Marie,* a film in which Stewart had also appeared—was already there. Stewart had heart rumors among the cast that Eddy was a homosexual.

Louella Parsons, the most widely read columnist in Hollywood, had "outed" Eddy in a recent column.

"The big laugh in Tinseltown these days is that Nelson Eddy is being pursued by female admirers. Come on, Eddy, even the hinterlands are wise to you."

Parsons had been made aware of Eddy's sexual orientation when one

Upper photo: **Jeanette MacDonald** in sensual satins. *Lower photo*: with **Nelson Eddy,** her singing partner.

They evolved into far more than co-stars. As one screenwriter phrased it, "They were crazy in love with each other...a little too crazy—wrenching fights, miscarriages, heavy drama."

She later married Gene Raymond, five years her junior, but continued her affair with Eddy.

of her gay assistants admitted to having had a fling with him the previous weekend.

Henry and Stewart bonded with Eddy, having collected recordings of his strong baritone voice. When MacDonald had to fly to San Francisco and leave Eddy behind, Henry invited him to dinner. He asked if he could bring a friend.

Eddy showed up with a blonde-haired actor named Gene Raymond. At the time, his hosts were vaguely aware of his past career, having only heard that he'd gotten his start on Broadway before becoming a film actor. Stewart and Henry had last seen him in the 1932 MGM film, *Red Dust,* starring Clark Gable and Jean Harlow. In that movie, Raymond had played the husband of Mary Astor.

By 1937, MacDonald had married Gene Raymond while continuing her affair with Eddy, a relationship that would last until her death in 1965. *[Eddy would die two years later.]* During the course of their long, clandestine affair, these singing sensations would unwind within any of several rented homes, including a converted cowboy bunkhouse in Beverly Hills.

Sometimes, they were invited to use the homes of friends temporarily out of town. On several occasions, Irene Dunne made her home available to the lovers, too.

Once, during the early months of her marriage to Raymond, MacDonald came home early and found her husband in bed with the musician, Buddy Rogers, husband of Mary Pickford. Nonetheless, her marriage to Raymond continued, and she later helped to conceal three of his arrests for soliciting young men in public toilets.

For some reason, it seemed that Raymond was incapable of fathering a child. It was also revealed that during her decades-long affair with Eddy, she underwent eight abortions.

On the set of *Sweethearts* (1938), the latest vehicle starring MacDonald and Eddy, she was obviously pregnant. After six months, she lost the infant. His father named the unborn child Daniel Kendrick Eddy and buried its fetal remains in Ojai, California.

It was at this time that MacDonald revealed to Eddy that Raymond was physically abusing her. That night, Eddy arrived at their 21-room mock Tudor mansion and severely beat Raymond, leaving him for dead. Fortunately, he survived, but spent a week in a hospital, recovering. A studio publicist reported that Raymond had fallen down the steps of his home.

The MacDonald/Raymond/Eddy love triangle, as Henry and Stewart observed, would soon be played out among others of their friends in months to come as various love affairs came and went in a tangled Tinseltown web.

Gene Raymond (above) was married to singing sensation Jeanette MacDonald from 1937 until her early death in 1965. Raymond was known for his "indiscretions."

On her honeymoon, MacDonald caught her husband in bed with Buddy Rogers, newly married to Mary Pickford.

The bisexual and spectacularly promiscuous *roué* **Errol Flynn** wields a frequently oiled saber in *Captain Blood* (1935).

When Henry met Flynn, the swashbuckler told him: "I'm just a goddamn phallic symbol to the world. Everyone's in love with me, from Howard Hughes to Hedy Lamarr."

***

Eventually, Stewart and Henry abandoned their rented home with its flea-infested feral cats. They moved into a much larger house, also in Brentwood, with two guest bedrooms.

Tragedy would strike one of their actor friends whom they each had known before they'd migrated to Hollywood. Ross Alexander had married actress Aleta Freel, with Henry serving as Best Man at their wedding. Even so, he told Stewart that he didn't think their marriage would last longer than a few months.

His prediction came true. On Broadway, Alexander had co-starred in *Let Us Be Gay,* with Rod La Rocque, a silent screen star of vintage renown. During the run of the play, La Rocque and Alexander had become lovers.

In Hollywood, Alexander had been cast in *Captain Blood* (1935), starring the screen's newest swashbuckler, Errol Flynn, replacing Douglas Fairbanks Sr. It took no more than a day for Alexander to transfer his romantic feelings to this handsome, dashing Australian.

The bisexual Flynn was only too willing to have intercourse with Alexander, who seemed ready and willing to indulge any time of the day or night.

Alexander began returning home later and later, often telling Freel that he had had a late shooting at Warners. When she inevitably learned of her husband's affair with Flynn, her response was deadly.

On December 7, 1935, she committed suicide by shooting herself in the head with a .22 rifle.

Years later, Henry said, "The death of Aleta Freel was my first suicide. As the years went by, my life seemed peppered with suicides."

In its aftermath, perceiving that Alexander needed to escape from the press, Henry drove him to his new home in Brentwood and gave him unrestricted, long-term use of its back bedroom. Throughout most of his stay, Alexander drank heavily.

"We had trouble getting him to eat," Henry said. "Finally, he pulled himself together and left us."

Henry was shocked to learn that on September 17, 1936, Alexander wed another actress, Anna Nagel. When, eventually, he talked to Henry about it, he admitted, "I hate having sex with a woman. But Warners has warned me that I have to get married to conceal my homosexuality. I don't love her. Actually, in addition to my long-running love for you, I'm also in love with two other men, both of them actors, too."

Alexander had met Nagel when each of them had co-starred in *China Clipper* and in *Here Comes Carter*, each released in 1936.

Henry was reading a newspaper and listening to the radio when a bulletin came on the air. On January 2, 1937, Alexander had committed suicide with a .22 pistol, not the .22 rifle that Freel had used.

As reported, his personal life had been in disarray. He was losing his movie contract; he'd become disenchanted with his recent marriage; and he was heavily in debt.

Both Henry and Stewart attended his funeral and his subsequent burial at Forest Lawn.

***

Other than a lingering sadness in the wake of Ross Alexander's suicide, there were many happy nights in Brentwood at the home of Stewart and Henry.

When Joshua Logan arrived to stay with them, he had suggested that they throw a house party. Henry was under contract to the producer, Walter Wanger, who agreed to provide the booze and the food. At the time, Wanger was deep in pre-production for a film that would feature eight "chorus girl hotties" emoting in the background. He volunteered to bring all of them to the Fonda/Stewart house party, with the understanding there would therefore be a date for each of the men there. Wanger, it was agreed, would also bring his assistant director. They were two men short, so Stewart invited actors Dick Foran and Alan Marshall.

Neither Henry nor Stewart provided any details about what happened that night, but Henry later said, "I attended my first orgy."

Girls were not always an essential element of the guest list. Sometimes Henry and Stewart hosted all-male (or mostly male) musical evenings, as was the case with two new friends, Hoagy Carmichael and Johnny Mercer.

Composer Alec Wilder described Carmichael as "the most talented, inventive, sophisticated, and jazz-oriented of all the great craftsmen of pop songs during the first half of the 20th Century."

And so he was, a Tin Pan Alley songwriter of the 1930s. The hosts heard Carmichael perform at their piano with his rendition of "Stardust" and "Georgia On My Mind."

The most famous son of Savannah, Georgia, Johnny Mercer was a singer and lyricist who became known over the course of his career for such hits as "Moon River," "Autumn Leaves," "Hooray for Hollywood," and "Days of Wine and Roses." He would win four Oscars for Best Original Song.

The musical events that Henry and Stewart staged became some of the most coveted invitations in Hollywood.

***

The Trail of the Lonesome Pine (1936)

Still under contract to Walter Wanger, Henry was assigned the third lead in his latest picture, *The Trail of the Lonesome Pine* (1936). Based on John Fox Jr.'s novel of

Silvia Sidney with **Henry Fonda** in *The Trail of the Lonesome Pine*.

Henry did some "heavy petting" with Sidney between her marriages. She'd just divorced Bennett Cerf, Publisher at Random House, after six months of marriage. In 1936, she wed character actor Luther Adler.

68

1908, it had been made twice as a silent film, in 1916 and again in 1923.

The adventure-romance was to be directed by Henry Hathaway, who became best known for Westerns starring John Wayne and for the seven films he directed starring Gary Cooper. Marilyn Monroe fans will be more likely to remember him for casting her in her breakthrough performance in *Niagara* (1953).

Billed above Henry were co-stars Sylvia Sidney and Fred MacMurry.

Sidney had begun working as an actress at the age of fifteen, hired as an extra in D.W. Griffith's *The Sorrows of Satan* (1926). She rose to prominence in the 1930s. Henry was just one of her leading men. He joined a list of actors who included Cary Grant, Gary Cooper, George Raft, Joel McCrea, Fredric March, and Spencer Tracy.

Henry always viewed Fred MacMurray as one of his major competitors, as the two actors often seemed suitable for the same roles.

Early in his career, MacMurray had worked as both a singer and a musician before becoming a leading man to Claudette Colbert, Katharine Hepburn, Joan Crawford, Barbara Stanwyck, Carole Lombard, and Marlene Dietrich.

As director, Hathaway had assembled a crew of strong supporting players who included Fred Stone, a veteran of minstrel shows and vaudeville. He had previously been cast in *Alice Adams* (1935) starring MacMurray with Katharine Hepburn.

The Trail of the Lonesome Pine was the second full-length feature film to be shot in three-strip Technicolor. It was also the first color film to have parts of it shot outdoors—in this case at Big Bear Lake in Southern California.

In a script that had been vastly revised from the Fox novel, the movie was set in the backwoods of Kentucky. It was centered on two feuding families, the Tollivers and the Falins. Henry played Dave Tolliver side-by-side with Sidney, who portrayed his sister, June. MacMurray was cast in the role of Jack Hale, a railroad engineer who becomes enamored of June.

At one point, Jack (MacMurray) saves Dave's (Henry's) life, but he is later shot by one of the Falin brothers. The families finally agree to end their feud and get along in the film's final scene. Of course, Jack and June will happily marry, but poor Dave—that is, Henry—is six feet under the ground.

A former circus and vaudeville performer, Fred Stone was cast as Judd Tolliver. When Henry met him, he was also appearing that year in *Alice Adams*, starring MacMurray and Katharine Hepburn.

Often cast as eccentric mothers, character actress Beulah Bondi would, during the course of her career, portray the mother of James Stewart four times, including in *Mr. Smith Goes to Washington* (1939).

An Englishman, Nigel Bruce enjoyed enduring fame thank to his long-running signature role of Dr. Watson in the Sherlock Holmes detective series (1939-1946). Alfred Hitchcock also cast him in *Rebecca* (1940) and *Suspicion* (1941).

At the *New York American*, Regina Crew wrote: "Henry Fonda combines another fine cinematic portrait to the galaxy he has given in the role of the somber mountaineer whose heart, filled with murderous tradition, is sometimes warmed by sunnier emotions."

Peter Colleir wrote: "*The Trail of the Lonesome Pine* established the Fonda *persona*—resolute, idealistic, and innocent. With the tensile strength beneath his implacable surface, he was the perfect westerner—speaking in a natural drawl that was hesitant and authentic, slightly stooped in posture, with a loping, Continental gait."

There were many critical comparisons of Henry to Gary Cooper, who had gotten his start in silent movies, especially in 1929 in *Wings*.

As amazing as it sounds, Henry inspired the cartoon character of Li'L Abner, which became one of the most popular comics of the 20th Century.

Al Capp had first created the character in 1934, but he later said he did not get Li'L Abner right until he'd seen Henry in *The Trail of the Lonesome Pine*.

The setting was the backwater of Dogpatch, Kentucky. Li'L Abner is a simple-minded son of the Yokum family, loutish but good-natured, an eternally innocent hayseed who lives with his parents, Mammy Yokum, scrawny but superhuman, and Pappy Yokum, shiftless and childlike. Sexy and well-endowed, Daisy Mae has her eye trained on Li'L Abner. Capp said that for her apparel, he invented the miniskirt.

After the release of *The Trail of the Lonesome Pine*, Walter Wanger told Henry, "You're on your way, kid. Super stardom is just around the corner. You and your boyfriend, Jimmy Stewart, are going right to the top."

That prediction overjoyed Henry, but also filled him with fear. He almost began to shake when he learned that his former wife, Margaret Sullavan, would be his next leading lady.

During the early heyday of Henry Fonda, even the most self-involved members of Hollywood's film community sensed that there were strident forces blossoming in other film communities within other political systems. Vibrant films were being crafted at the time (always with an eye toward what was happening in California) in France, England, and in increasingly pro-Nazi Germany at the time.

Monumental and utterly without humor, and often crafted as propaganda, they were a far cry from the romantic fluff in Hollywood that sometimes deeply depressed the American actors who made it.

Here (clockwise from upper left) are views of **Adolf Hitler** "prepping" members of the *Hitler Jugend*; an "ode to glory' from *Triumph of the Will* (1935); a portrait of **Leni Riefenstahl** (the notorious director of some of the most effective and technically innovative propaganda films ever made); and a view of her then-radical filming techniques, used at Heidelberg rallies and also at the Berlin Olympics of 1936.

It all made some of the simpering romances being fleshed out by Henry Fonda in faraway California look rather shallow and stupid—a perception that might have influenced some of his motivation for eventually joining the U.S. Navy for the protection of the American ideal.

CHAPTER FIVE

LOVE, POLITICS, & SHOW BIZ

(IT'S 1936)

BETWEEN PLAY DATES
WITH THE NATIVES IN LA-LA LAND,
HENRY MEETS, SEDUCES AND MARRIES
FRANCES SEYMOUR BROKAW
HIS WIFE #2

GOOD BUDDIES AND PARALLEL CAREERS
HENRY FONDA & JAMES STEWART

EACH EVOKES THE DECENCY OF "AMERICAN MANHOOD"
AND, IN AMICABLE COMPETITION, EACH POURS OUT A GAGGLE OF
ROUGHLY EQUIVALENT CLASSIC FILMS

"Sometimes a guy feels like a heel when he's screwing his best friend's wife."
—James Stewart, in reference to Margaret Sullavan

Margaret Sullavan's movies for Universal had brought the studio some badly needed cash. When she demanded James Stewart as her next leading man, her wish was granted, despite the fact that her director, Edward H. Griffith, had never seen a movie with either Stewart or Fonda.

Griffith, who had begun directing films in 1917 beginning with *The Law of the North,* managed to become the favorite director of the English screen goddess, Madeleine Carroll. He would helm her in seven movies, four with Fred MacMurray, including *Honeymoon in Bali* (1939).

Next Time We Love (1936)

Next Time We Love (1936)—a film built around Sullavan and her perceived allure—had been based on a novel by Ursula Parrott. With a plot akin to a soap opera, it also starred Ray Milland, the Welsh-born actor whose screen career would run from 1929 to 1985. *[Milland would be best remembered for his Oscar-winning portrayal of an alcoholic writer in Billy Wilder's* Lost Weekend *(1945). The director briefly considered Fonda for that role.]*

The story line has aspiring actress Cicely Tyler (Sullavan) marrying an aspiring

71

newsman, Christopher Tyler (James Stewart). Their marriage is frequently interrupted by his business trips abroad to Rome. A wealthy secret admirer, Tommy Abbott (Milland) enters the lonely wife's life when she becomes pregnant. Expect separations, reunions, and reconciliations to follow.

Ultimately, Stewart's character dies of a rare disease in China that allows the long-mooning Milland to marry his widow.

The title comes from Sullavan's last remark to Stewart, her dying husband: "The next time we love, maybe we'll have time for each other."

During the first three days of the shoot, Griffith wanted Stewart fired, based on his perception that he had imported many obnoxious stage mannerisms with him from his training on Broadway.

Sullavan, however, who had insisted that he be hired for the role, spent night after night helping him adjust to screen acting in front of a camera. He would later credit her with "making me a star. She had endless patience with me until I got it right."

When Sullavan's estranged husband, William Wyler, saw the rushes, he said, "Maggie took this lanky stage ham (Stewart) and made a movie actor out of him, something I didn't think possible. I bet she got something for her effort, too, notably some sticky white stuff."

A reporter later surmised that "nothing happened between Margaret Sullavan and James Stewart off screen during the filming of *Next Time We Love*. He is not her type."

When she read that, she said, "How in hell does this guy know what my type is? I don't even know what type I like. If he's wearing pants, I might go for him."

Milland said, "It had been obvious to me that Stewart and Sullavan were having an affair, one that lasted for several years…or so I heard. On the set, they were like two lovebirds."

Actor Myron McCormick, who had worked with Henry, Sullavan, and Stewart on Cape Cod, visited the set one day: "I was stunned to see Maggie so protective of Jimmy. She was downright motherly with him. If my pal Henry was still in love with her, he was the loser. Jimmy's love for her, which he had developed back on Cape Cod, finally won her over. He worshipped her."

Years later, when Sullavan heard of her purported "mothering" of Stewart, she retorted, "If that were so, then I'd call it incest."

Stewart was still living with Henry during his filming with Sullavan of *Next Time We Love*. He never took Sullavan to the house he shared with Henry, preferring to spend time with her at her residence instead. "The idea of me screwing Maggie with Henry in the next room listening to us was more than I could bear."

When *Next Time We Love* was released in 1936, it was not a success, although some critics cited Stewart's performance as "natural, spontaneous, and altogether excellent," at least within the pages of *Time* magazine. As for the movie itself, *Variety* reviewed it as "draggy. This complex romantic tale will have to be sold based on Sullavan's previous success."

Billy Grady, MGM's casting director, claimed, "As an actor, Jimmy returned to us a changed man. He knew how to act on camera, and he credited that to Sullavan. She taught him to march to his own drummer, to be himself on the screen. In the future, movie audiences would pay good money to see Stewart just be himself. In that respect, he and his roomie, Henry Fonda, were much alike."

Months later, the still-besotted Stewart said, "I will never marry unless I find a gal to match Margaret Sullavan."

At the end of the shoot, probably to her horror, Sullavan was informed that Walter Wanger had cast Henry Fonda as the leading man in her next picture.

Despite its apparent sincerity, the on- and offscreen romance of **James Stewart** and **Margaret Sullavan** during the filming of *Next Time We Love* was met with cynical disapproval—especially from each of Sullavan's bruised and embittered ex-husbands, William Wyler and Henry Fonda.

***

The Moon's Our Home (1936)

The Hollywood press viewed the re-teaming of Margaret Sullavan and Henry Fonda as an unusual event, speculating whether the once-feuding couple could get along this time—"or will there be fireworks?"

Henry found himself uncomfortably under contract to Walter Wanger for the purposes of filming *The Moon's Our Home,* an 80-minute Paramount feature released in 1936.

This screwball comedy was one of dozens formulaically released during the Depression years of the 1930s. Many Americans wanted to escape their woes through zany comedies, sometimes with Cary Grant or Carole Lombard.

The plot has Cherry Hester (Sullavan) emoting as a movie star in public, but as the understated Sarah Brown in private. Likewise, Henry Fonda plays a character who in public presents himself as Anthony Amberton, a high-profile author of adventure books. In private he emotes less flamboyantly as just plain "John Smith."

The couple meet as "Brown" and "Smith" in a private encounter. They fall in love and get married without any awareness of their respective public *personae.*

To have been paired as the lover of his deeply estranged ex-wife in a romantic comedy would have been paralyzingly embarrassing in the hands of a less professional actor.

Henry, however, perhaps with the impassive "cornhusker" neutrality he was becoming known for, pulled it off with grace. To make matters worse, however, **Margaret Sullavan** got top billing.

Expect trouble on the horizon: Mad, passionate love is followed by violent arguments. It sometimes seemed as if the pages of the script had been torn from Fonda and Sullavan's previous marriage.

William A. Seiter, its director, had been a bit player at Mack Sennett's Keystone Studios in 1918. In time, he became a director at Universal, sometimes casting his wife, Laura La Plante, in one of his movies. In time, he would direct some of the top box office stars of Hollywood: Shirley Temple, Barbara Stanwyck, Lucille Ball, Ginger Rogers, Fred Astaire, and Rita Hayworth.

To beef up a weak script, a married couple, Dorothy Parker and her gay husband, Alan Campbell, were hired. She was known for her wisecracks, sarcastic wit, and for her exposure of 20th Century urban pretentions. Some of the dialogue they'd written was said to have originated from their epic private battles.

An old geezer-like character actor, Walter Brennan, was cast as a forgetful and hard-of-hearing Justice of the Peace. At a key romantic moment in the script, he forgets how to conduct a marriage ceremony.

Once again, Henry had been cast in a picture with Margaret Hamilton, whom he was now calling "my good luck charm."

According to Seiter, "When Maggie came onto the set to greet Henry, she was a real Southern flirt, evoking Scarlett O'Hara."

Privately, Seiter told some members of the cast, "You could see the sparks fly between Maggie and Henry. As shooting on our picture progressed, they were turned into flames. Their love scenes became so hot I feared those damn censors, the ones enforcing that Code, would be after my ass. In one scene, Henry became so overheated, he gave birth to a hard-on. Maggie had to take him to her dressing room to take care of business before they returned to the set, minus the erection."

As Sullavan later confided to Seiter, "On our first night together in the wake of our divorce, when Henry mounted me, his technique had improved considerably, and he was a more satisfactory lover. Somebody must have given him pointers to improve his act."

"No doubt it was Jimmy Stewart," Seiter said, half-jokingly.

After the release of their film, *Variety* wrote: "Henry Fonda lends a fetching foil to Margaret Sullavan's madcapperies, as well as a personality that captures heaps of attention."

Graham Green of *The Spectator* found Fonda "fresh and absurd and civilized."

One critic referred to the actor's stature as "totem pole elegant," citing his

On the set, other cast and crew members marveled at how easily **Margaret Sullavan** and young **Henry Fonda** reinstated the intimacies of their former nuptials.

Author Howard Teichmann wrote, "Margaret Sullavan's Southern charm flowed as easily as maple syrup over hot pancakes, and the words melted Henry like butter."

"dangling Byronic forelock."

Another critic claimed it was "bedroom robbery the way Sullavan stole the picture from Fonda. Their on-screen feuds may have mirrored their former married life."

Back in Hollywood, Henry hinted to a reporter that he and Sullavan "might tie the knot once again."

However, after spending just one night back in the arms of James Stewart, Sullavan dashed all hopes of a remarriage to Henry. "Let's cut out this lovesick mush," she said to Henry. "We were just trying to get into character to make our acting more authentic. From now on, let's be friends, not lovers."

It appeared that this second heartbreak for Henry didn't put much strain on him.

Sullavan's divorce from William Wyler was legally finalized on March 13, 1936. In future movies in which they co-starred, she would continue her affair with Stewart.

But she shocked both Henry and Stewart when "all of a sudden," *Variety* announced that she had wed their agent, Leland Hayward, as her husband No. 3.

***

In the book, *Acting Male: Masculinity in the Films of James Stewart, Jack Nicholson, and Clint Eastwood,* appears this statement:

"When James Stewart began his film career as a studio contact player in the 1930s, his failure to fit the masculinity of a 'straight' leading man, his lithe physique and emotional demeaner confronted the studio publicity department with the problem of selling him as a 'real man,' since he was a personality that was evidently bisexual."

In 1936, Stewart was cast in more films than he'd ever made before in a single year, hoping that an identity would emerge so that MGM could more easily classify their offbeat new star.

Whereas Henry had one more film scheduled for release in 1936, his "roomie," James Stewart, had already released (or would soon release) a stunning array of six.

Spendthrift (1936)

Produced by Walter Wanger and directed by Raoul Walsh, *Spendthrift* cast Henry as Townsend Middleton, a profligate playboy who has run through his $23 million fortune but spends wildly until his debtors learn that he's broke.

Henry found Walsh sharp and brutal in his attacks on actors who didn't deliver the performances he wanted.

By now, Walsh was a Hollywood veteran, having starred as assassin John Wilkes Booth in D.W. Griffith's *Birth of a Nation* (1915). That same year, he had been the leading man to Theda Bara, the original screen vamp. Regrettably, the film in which they emoted together, *Carmen,* is lost, its love scenes turned to dust.

The Thief of Bagdad (1924), with Douglas Fairbanks Sr., cemented Walsh as a Hollywood director.

In 1926, he scored his biggest silent hit, *What Price Glory?* That was followed by *Sadie Thompson* (1928) opposite Gloria Swanson. Walsh wrote the script, directed, and starred in it.

The following year, a freak auto accident blinded him in one eye. That ended his acting career, and for the rest of his life, he wore a black patch.

During the first three days of the shoot, Walsh told Henry, "The script of *Spendthrift* is not worthy of me."

Even if that were true, *Spendthrift* marked a turning point in

As a self-indulgent wastrel, **Henry Fonda**, playing a spendthrift, seeks solace in liquor until love helps him mend his ways.

Frank S., Nugent in *The New York Times* wrote: "A slight and superficially diverting fable of a polo-playing Cinderella, Fonda is probably as morose a playboy as you would care to meet."

Henry's film career, as it became the first movie in which he got top billing. That was because his leading ladies, Pat Paterson and Mary Brian, were less well known than he was.

Produced during the depths of the Depression, the movie poked fun at the "filthy rich"

Its script prompts an attractive Southern gold digger (Brian) to marry Townsend (Henry) for his money, only to learn that he'd already spent most of it. Although she quickly dumps him, he finds true love in the arms of the Paterson character, the daughter of a stableman.

Townsend (Henry) goes to work for a living, getting hired as a sports announcer for $1,000 a week, big money in the 1930s.

"The Belle of Dallas," Mary Brian was born one year after Henry. She broke into silent films in the title role of *Peter Pan* in 1924. Later promoted as "The Sweetest Girl in Pictures," she would go on to star opposite Gary Cooper in *The Virginian* (1929) and with Ronald Colman in *Beau Geste* (1926).

Henry's other co-star, Pat Paterson, had fewer credits than Brian. If Paterson is remembered at all today, it's for her 44-year marriage to the French actor Charles Boyer.

In 1934, another French actor, Maurice Chevalier, invited Boyer to a screening of *Charlie Chan Goes to Egypt,* in which Paterson played the female lead. Later, at a cast party, when Boyer was introduced to Paterson, it was love at first sight, as the *cliché* goes.

Henry bonded with Boyer when he was brought onto the set of *Spendthrift* to have lunch with him and Boyer's wife. Soon, Henry would be sailing to England with Boyer.

[TRIVIA: In the same year that Henry was filming Spendthrift *with Boyer's wife, Boyer starred with Marlene Dietrich in* The Garden of Allah.

In 1943, the Boyers gave birth to their only child, Michael Charles Boyer. In 1965, at the age of 21, after breaking up with his girlfriend, he would commit suicide with a loaded pistol during a game of Russian Roulette.

In 1978, a few days after his wife died of cancer, Boyer himself would commit suicide.]

Spendthrift was promoted on posters with the following tagline: *HE RAN A FORTUNE INTO A SHOESTRING IN HIS HUNT FOR ROMANCE!*

Years later, when Henry was asked about the filming of *Spendthrift,* he said, "The title sounds familiar, but I have no memory of it."

Variety reviewed it with: "Fonda is handsome enough, and it is possible that he might be accepted as a spoiled young millionaire, if the things he does and says were acceptable. They're not!"

In *The New York Times,* Frank S. Nugent wrote, "If Walter Wanger is the prophet of a new social attitude, Henry Fonda provides an admirable mirror for the redeemed upper strata."

Spendthrift is remembered as the first film in which Henry Fonda got top billing. Why? Perhaps because he was more famous than either of the talented and (in Paterson's case) tragic actresses who appeared with him.

Mary Brian (left) adroitly made the transition from silent films to talkies and was repeatedly reinforced by the press in the years to come as "the sweetest girl in pictures."

England-born **Pat Patterson** married French superstar Charles Boyer and remained with him through multiple tragedies, including the suicide of their son, for more than forty years.

***

You Only Live Once (1937)

Next, producer Walter Wanger decided that the time had come to cast Henry in his most important film to date, *You Only Live Once.* He'd read a copy of Edward Anderson's 1937 novel, *Thieves Like Us,* and had acquired the film rights.

It was the tragic story of an ex-convict, Eddie Taylor, who tries to go straight after his release from prison. But the odds are against him: He gets wrongly convicted for involvement in a bank job in which six men are killed. He is tried and sentenced to death.

His long-suffering girlfriend is Jo Graham, cast with Sylvia Sidney, who got top billing over Henry. They had co-starred together before in *The Trail of the Lonesome Pine.*

When Eddie escapes from prison, he kills a chaplain. His ever-faithful girl-friend (now his wife) agrees to flee with him, hoping to cross the Canadian border into freedom. Eventually, they are ambushed by the police and killed.

As its director, Wanger hired the Austrian filmmaker, Fritz Lang, marking his second American film. The British Film Institute had dubbed him "Master of Darkness." In Europe, Lang had made the futuristic (and very *avant-garde)* film *Metropolis* (1927) and the influential *M* (1931). Starring Peter Lorre, the latter was the story of a psychotic child molester brought to justice by the Berlin underworld.

Like another director, Raoul Walsh, Lang wore a black patch over one eye. During the filming of *You Only Live Once*, Henry and Lang, men with very different temperaments, constantly clashed. Although Lang got the best performance of Henry to date, the actor later asserted that "working with this bastard was like living your worst nightmare."

In contrast, Henry and Sylvia Sidney worked together smoothly as they had in their first picture together. Personally, although he never found her sexually attractive, their on-screen love scenes were convincing.

Although the career of the Bronx-born actress would span seventy years, *You Only Live Once* remains one of her most memorable movies.

At the time Henry met her, she was married to publisher Bennett Cerf, but the marriage lasted only six months. She later wed actor Luther Adler, another ill-fated union.

She faded from Henry's life, although by chance he ran into her after the war. She was still struggling along as a film actress, despite the fact that exhibitors in the 1940s had labeled her as "box office poison."

Henry Fonda with **Sylvia Sidney** in a profoundly sad examination of the pathos of love. Fritz Lang (the Austria-born "Master of Darkness"), the film's demanding and very avant-garde director, drove both of them crazy.

Lang selected a strong list of supporting players, notably Barton MacLane, cast as Stephen Whitney, the public defender who comes to the aid of Eddie. MacLane would work in several movies with Humphrey Bogart, and with Glenda Farrell cast as reporter Torchy Blane. He made seven films with her.

Once again, Henry was cast with Margaret Hamilton, giving her a big hug when he saw her, after a long absence, on the set. "I may have to report you to the police as a stalker. It seems I can't make a film without you popping up in it."

He had a nearly violent encounter with the homophobic and emotionally unstable Guinn ("Big Boy") Williams. Confronting Henry, he said, "I hear you and that Jimmy Stewart guy are a couple of fags."

Instead of belting him, Henry walked on. He later heard that Lupe Velez dealt with him in her own special way. *[The "Mexican Spitfire" had briefly been engaged to Big Boy.]* At a party at the home of Errol Flynn, she took a framed, glass-covered publicity photo of Guinn and crashed it over his head, then pulled up her dress and urinated on it.

Velez would marry only one time, and that would be to movie Tarzan Johnny Weissmuller. Some of her most notable love affairs were with Charlie Chaplin, boxer Jack Dempsey, cowboy Tom Mix, and Gary Cooper.

When *You Only Live Once* was released Henry was drawing an annual salary of $56,000. It had been a commercial disappointment, not making back its production cost, which meant no raise for him.

In time, however, it became a film classic. In 1987, the *Motion Picture Guide* claimed, "Fonda gives a terrific performance as the social pariah fighting for his mere existence."

Variety wrote, "Fonda follows through brilliantly in showing the moral degeneration of a three-time con condemned to death for a crime he didn't commit."

Frank Nugent of *The New York Times* wrote "Fonda's characterization of Eddie Taylor is uni-dimensional, making us guess at—rather than realize—the inner honesty and goodness he is supposed to possess."

***

Wife Vs. Secretary (1936)

For James Stewart, as he raced from one picture to another, 1936 would mark his busiest year. During its course, director Clarence Brown met with him and offered him the second male lead in *Wife vs. Secretary*, a screwball comedy which had already been cast with Clark Gable, Jean Harlow, and Myrna Loy.

It marked the fifth of six collaborations between Gable and Harlow and the fourth of seven films with Loy. May Robson was cast as Gable's meddling mother.

Brown had worked in films since 1913. His glory days had been spent at MGM, where he directed Greta Garbo seven times and Joan Crawford in six of her movies. His films earned him a total of thirty-eight Academy Award nominations as director, winning awards nine different times.

In the plot, Gable is a publisher, Harlow is his sexy secretary, and Loy is his jealous wife. The story by Faith Baldwin had first appeared in *Cosmopolitan*. Baldwin, a romantic novelist, according to *The New York Times,* was popular because she enables "lonely working people, young and old, to identify with glamourous and wealthy characters."

After reading the script, Stewart told Henry, "I wish my part was bigger. Louis B. Mayer can't make up his mind. Am I leading man material or not? In your case, Hank, that decision has already been made. You're a star!"

As Brown, the film's director, had explained to Stewart, "Your role is that of a dangling boyfriend, suspended in the wings, waiting for her."

As Stewart later relayed to Henry, his one big line was: "Don't go looking for trouble when there isn't any, because if you don't find it, you'll make it."

MATING GAMES: **Jean Harlow** with **Clark Gable,** then "The King of Hollywood," in *Wife Vs. Secretary*

MORE MATING GAMES: **Jean Harlow** with **James Stewart** in *Wife Vs. Secretary.*

Typecast for her portrayal of "bad girl" characters, and famous as Hollywood's first platinum blonde, **Jean Harlow** was the most visible sex symbol of the early 1930s and one of the defining figures of pre-Code Hollywood.

Her early death, after only about nine years in the public eye, contributed to the, "live fast, die young, and leave a beautiful corpse" slogan that also applied to Marilyn Monroe, James Dean, and gaggle of other tragedy-soaked celebrities.

Like several other Hollywood players, both Henry Fonda and James Stewart, during the most intense period of their "bromance," each—for a short term, at least—became intimate with her

After *Wife vs. Secretary* was released in England, *The London Observer* gave Stewart his most favorable review: "James Stewart acts Harlow and Gable off the screen."

The highlight of the movie, for Stewart, had been his kissing scene with Harlow. According to Stewart, "I deliberately flubbed my lines so Brown would be forced to do six retakes. I got Jean all hot, and then invited her home with me that night. Hank was there cooking supper."

"Jean seemed attracted to him, too," Stewart said. "She suggested to me privately that we have a three-way, but selfish fart that I am, I wanted the platinum blonde goddess all for myself."

He later recalled, "For Harlow aficionados, I've got some news: Not only is she minus a bra, but no panties. All my life I've never found a kisser as good as Jean."

Harlow later told her director, Brown, "It was obvious that Gable and Stewart wanted to make it with me. But did you know that it was Myrna Loy who really came on to me?"

"After a night with Jean," Stewart said, "I had to report early to the studio. Jean had no scene to shoot that day, so she took the day off. I left her in my bedroom as Hank was asleep in the adjoining room. When I got home that night, Hank was in the kitchen cooking our dinner. Jean was in a bubble

Publicity photo for *Wife and Secretary* showcasing three of the most famous actors (**Harlow, Gable, and Myrna Loy**) of Classic, pre-Code Hollywood.

Each a legend in his or her time, they appear overheated in the California sunshine wearing the era's then-most-stylish finery.

James Stewart, who was considered an "also ran" and newcomer at the time, was NOT the movie's major draw.

bath. I just knew from the look on his face that he had seduced her. At first, he didn't give himself away, but later, he told me, 'Did you know Jean told me I have 2 ½ inches more than Gable?'"

***

Small Town Girl (1936)

On the final occasion when Henry and Stewart talked to Jean Harlow, she told them she'd been cast in *Small Town Girl* (1936) with Robert Taylor, the reigning pretty boy and matinee idol at MGM. Every day, he was getting hundreds of letters from lovesick fans, both male and female.

Two weeks later, the director, William A. Wellman phoned Stewart to tell him that he'd been cast in a minor role in *Small Town Girl.* That night, after its script was delivered, both Henry and Stewart threw it down on the floor, rejecting it violently.

"My character of Elmer Clampett is nothing but a country bumpkin, a hapless hayseed who goes around telling people to keep their chin up," Stewart claimed.

When Stewart reported to work Monday morning, he learned that Harlow had become ill, dropped out of the picture, and been replaced by Janet Gaynor, Henry's co-star in *The Farmer Takes a Wife.* At this point in her career, her box office clout was dropping, soon to be restored with her performance in *A Star Is Born* (1937).

Stewart expected no fireworks between Gaynor and himself. He had frequently been told of her sexual preference for young women.

In the plot, Kay Brannan (Gaynor) is bored with small-town life, finding it "too repetitious to tolerate." The dullness is broken with the arrival in town of Robert Dakin (Taylor), who has come to watch the Harvard vs. Yale football game.

When it's over, he invites her for a date at a roadhouse outside town. He drinks and drinks until he's staggeringly intoxicated. When he proposes marriage to her, she accepts, waking up a Justice of the Peace for a hasty wedding during the early hours of the morning.

When he wakes up, Taylor is shocked to find that he's an "entrapped" married man.

The quickie marriage meets with nearly rabid disapproval from his father, played by Lewis Stone, a New Englander born in 1879. Stone already had a claim to fame, as he'd starred in seven films with Greta Garbo. He would become even more famous playing Judge Hardy in MGM's popular *Andy Hardy* series starring Mickey Rooney.

When she learns about it, Taylor's girlfriend, Priscilla, a socialite played by Binnie Barnes, is furious. Barnes, a London-born actress, had been working in films since 1923. To date, her most famous role had been as Katherine Howard, the fifth wife in the 1933 British film, *The Private Life of Henry VIII,* starring Charles Laughton. She told Stewart, "One movie is just like another to me, just so long as I don't have to play a sweet little thing."

During the filming of *Small Town Girl,* Wellman told Stewart, "I'm forced to direct you in this hogwash."

When Billy Grady, casting director at MGM, came onto the set, he reassured Stewart. "Bigger roles at MGM are on the way. We'll soon turn you into a leading man, like your roommate, Henry Fonda."

On the set, Stewart met and bonded with Robert Taylor, although at first, he feared he would be jealous of him. Taylor was on the dawn of major success,

The fine print in the newspaper ad for *Small Town Girl* pumped Robert Taylor—then the hottest newcomer in Hollywood—and his romantic allure like this"

"IT'S HARD, GIRLS...To be platonically married to Hollywood's most fascinating new star (Garbo's most handsome man), and to know he is too chivalrous to kiss you for at least six months!"

Insiders guffawed, aware as they were of the private preferences of both **Robert Taylor** and his onscreen love interest, **Janet Gaynor.**

The posh, very British, and very glam **Binnie Barnes** provided an interesting cultural clash with the American homespun character portrayed by Janet Gaynor.

MALE BONDING on the set of *Small Town Girl* with **James Stewart** (right) and **Robert Taylor.**

The MGM matinee idol would become a close friend of "Hank & Jim."

78

and MGM, in time, would line up a bevy of leading ladies for him: Joan Crawford, Loretta Young, Jean Harlow, Vivien Leigh, Lana Turner, Hedy Lamarr, and ultimately, Greta Garbo. [*In 1936, when he co-starred with Garbo in* Camille, *she said about him: "So beautiful…and so dumb."*]

Intimacies between Garbo and Robert Taylor devolved into a one-night fling. During the shooting of *Camille,* in which he was cast as the beautiful Armand, whenever he wasn't needed on camera, he spent long hours in his dressing room with set designer Jack Moore.

[*John Gilbert, after being dumped by Greta Garbo, had fallen in love with Taylor, but later married Virginia Bruce. Ironically, Taylor would also seduce Bruce when they co-starred in* Times Square Lady *(1935).*]

[*In the 1930s, Taylor had maintained high profile homosexual affairs with aviator Howard Hughes, Errol Flynn, and Tyrone Power. Power and Henry would become close friends. In 1939, they appeared together in a Western playing the outlawed brothers, Jesse and Frank James.*]

"Bob (Taylor) seemed to want to hang out with Henry and me," Stewart recalled. "We thought he was trying to lure us into a three-way. After all, that was standard fare in Tinseltown. When he heard that Hank and I were planning to go away for a weekend in Palm Springs, he asked if he could have the use of our home for a seduction he'd planned. Request granted."

During the filming of *Small Town Girl,* Taylor had been attracted to an extra named Thelma Ryan. She was a virgin and, as she later publicly admitted, "I had developed a big crush on Robert Taylor."

Before finding work as a very minor bit part player in Hollywood, Thelma, born in a small mining town in Nebraska, had been a truck driver, drugstore manager, and telephone operator as she studiously worked her way through college. A professor told her, "You're like a good piece of literature on a shelf of cheap paperbacks," perhaps a reference to the shallow sorority girls he usually taught.

It was Robert Taylor who took Thelma Ryan's virginity in Henry's bedroom in Brentwood. At the time, she was also dating a young lawyer who had not yet seduced her. His name was Richard Milhous Nixon.

Few people were more surprised than Henry when Thelma Ryan changed her name to Patricia and married him, eventually becoming Second Lady of the United States (1953 to 1961) and First Lady (1969 to 1974, when Nixon resigned and left the White House in disgrace.)

In reference to his bedroom furniture, Henry later said, "Since a world-famous woman like Mrs. Nixon had lost her virginity to Bob Taylor in my bed, I should have held on to it. It might have been worth something as a curiosity object."

Both Henry and Stewart saw a lot more of Robert Taylor after he started dating Barbara Stanwyck. "Actually, I think Barbara spent very little time in bed with Bob," Henry claimed. "She much preferred Joan Crawford as a bedmate. In the meantime, Bob was spending most of his nights with Phillip Terry, Crawford's handsome stud of a husband."

***

Speed (1936)

James Stewart's next picture was *Speed* (1936), in which for the first time he got star billing. Admittedly, it had been shot on a very low budget. Much of its footage came from canned film from the Indianapolis 500 race. MGM publicists trumpeted news that Stewart had driven a special Falcon at 140 mph. [*Actually, it was driven by a lookalike—a professional race car driver.*]

In it, Stewart was cast as an auto mechanic, Terry Martin, the chief "car tester" for Emery Motors in Detroit. He spends much of his screen time trying to perfect a revolutionary design for a new carburetor.

Like Henry Fonda, **Thelma Patricia Ryan Nixon** was born in Nebraska.

In 1953, years after her traumatic and unsuccessful trial period as an actress in Hollywood, she appeared here with her famous and very controversial husband at the debut of his first year as Vice-President. .

Even at this "advanced early" state of their respective careers, directors and producers were still weighing the relative merits of Henry Fonda vs. James Stewart.

Here's **James Stewart** sharing a pre-race smooch with **Wendy Barrie** in the racecar adventure *Speed* (1936)

The irritable, undiplomatic racecar engineer he portrayed strikes some modern-day viewers as terminally crabby and hard to get along with. Still, he captures the girl in the end.

Both he and Frank Lawson (played by Weldon Heyburn) are rivals for the affections of Jane Mitchell (Wendy Barrie), who had been cast in the role of a publicist for an automobile manufacturer.

The highlight of the film is a car crash on the speedway that nearly kills Stewart as his cockpit is filled with choking fumes and he is severely injured.

[Don't worry: He recovers from his injuries and goes on to win the heart of the publicist (Barrie).]

"During the filming of *Speed*, Jimmy got the girl in more ways than one," said director Edwin L. Marin, "At the end of his first day on the set, he took Barrie back to that Brentwood home he shared with Henry Fonda."

Marin had been a director at Universal before signing with MGM in 1934. He'd hired Barrie after seeing her opposite Spencer Tracy in the 1935 romantic comedy, *It's a Small World*.

Educated in England and Switzerland, Barrie had been born in British Hong Kong to English parents. Her most notable role was that of Jane Seymour *The Private Life of Henry VIII*. By 1935, she'd moved to Hollywood, where, in 1942, she became a naturalized U.S. citizen. She had "borrowed" her stage name (Barrie) from J.M. Barrie, her godfather and the author of *Peter Pan*.

She soon became notorious for seducing her leading men, a roster that included Richard Greene, Basil Rathbone, and George Sanders.

Her director (Marin) would later claim that Barrie seduced some of the leading men he'd cast in films, "notably Randolph Scott when he wasn't being serviced by Cary Grant." Other conquests included John Wayne ("not enough there to mess up your mouth with"); movie gangster, George ("Black Snake") Raft; and Bela Lugosi.

Eventually, Barrie became the "gun moll" of the notorious gangster, Bugsy Siegel. With him, she produced a daughter named Carolyn.

Stewart later revealed, "Wendy got a reputation in the 1930s as The Fellatio Queen of Hollywood. The night I took her home to meet Hank, she drained both of us dry. The woman was insatiable. I'd never seen anything like it."

By the end of the 1940s, Barrie lost her queenly reputation to the MGM starlet Nancy Davis, widely identified, underground and before her marriage to Ronald Reagan, as "The Fellatio Queen of Hollywood."

Speed is sometimes defined as Hollywood's first racecar movie, mixing high-octane trials by racecar pros banging up classic cars worth fortunes today.

Depicted above is one of the "only for the movies" vehicles that evoke a sci-fi episode of Flash Gordon. As a hint of technologies to come, it went fast, but appeared only in the film's final minutes.

The rest of the "heavy on the Americana" film is part documentary, part "boy-meets girl' romance, part ode to American craftsmanship, and part "round and round the track we go."

***

The Gorgeous Hussy (1936)

When *Variety* heard that MGM had cast Joan Crawford and Robert Taylor together in the 1936 film, *The Gorgeous Hussy*, the paper asked, "But which one is the Gorgeous Hussy?"

Based on a 1934 novel by Samuel Hopkins Adams, its director was Clarence Brown, whose claim to fame would be that he directed seven of Greta Garbo's films and six of Crawford's. In time, he was nominated for thirty-eight Academy Awards. Nine of those nominations evolved into Oscars.

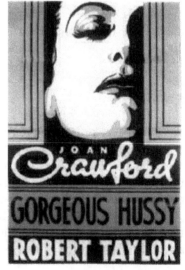

Crawford was cast as Peggy O'Neal, once the mistress of Andrew Jackson and now an innkeeper's daughter in 1830s Washington. She falls for a handsome young navy lieutenant, Bow Timberlake (Taylor). He is later killed in action, and in time, she turns her romantic attention to John Eaton (Franchot Tone), her husband in real life.

Lionel Barrymore had a key role as Andrew Jackson. Beulah Bondi was his pipe-smoking wife, Rachel, a backwoods woman with crude manners.

For her vivid portrayal, Bondi would be nominated for a Best Supporting Actress Oscar.

Stewart, cast as "Rowdy Dow," was Peggy's childhood friend and now her suitor. "My part isn't much," he told Henry after his first day on the set, "but at least I'm smartly frocked."

In his role, Stewart wants to fight a Southern senator, John C. Calhoun (Frank

Conroy), because he made insulting remarks about Peggy. However, she interrupts and—in a successful effort to calm things down—invites Rowdy to dance with her instead.

Melvyn Douglas also had a key role, that of John Randolph of Roanoke. Other supporting players featured Alison Skipworth, Melville Cooper, Gene Lockhart, and Sidney Toler as Daniel Webster.

Early during its filming of *The Gorgeous Hussy*, Crawford barged into the office of Louis B. Mayer, head honcho at MGM, demanding more lines for her husband. "Franchot's role is too small," she protested. "Take some lines from those two newcomers, James Stewart and Robert Taylor."

"Come on, Joan, just get through the picture," Mayer urged. "For your next film, I've lined up a real man, Clark Gable. It's called *Love on the Run*."

At the end *Gorgeous Hussy's* shoot, the aviator billionaire from Texas, Howard Hughes, appeared on the set to reclaim Taylor, with whom he was having an affair. That afternoon, he was to fly him for a vacation in Miami and a yachting trip in The Bahamas. *[Crawford had complained to Mayer that Taylor was "too effeminate," and referred to him as "Howard Hughes' kept boy.]*

The Gorgeous Hussy became one of MGM's highest grossing films of 1936. Frank Nugent in *The New York Times* claimed that "there was not enough hussy in Crawford's performance. Her Peggy O'Neal is a maligned Ann of Green Gables, a persecuted Pollyanna, a dismayed Dolly Dimple."

Howard Barnes in the *New York Herald Tribune* wrote, "In the title role, Joan Crawford is handsome, although century-old costumes do not go well with the pronounced modernity of her personality. She makes Peggy Eaton a straightforward and zealous figure."

One reviewer in Los Angeles singled out the performances of both Barrymore and Stewart: "They seem at ease and natural in a setting from 1836—and that's more than we can say about Joan Crawford. In the future, she should leave those costume dramas to Greta Garbo and Norma Shearer."

Henry was a dedicated Crawford fan, and he urged Stewart to invite her and her husband, Franchot Tone, to dinner at their home in Brentwood. They showed up that Saturday night. Over drinks and dinner, much of the talk—in fact, nearly all of it—was devoted to Crawford herself. She became very blunt, urging both Henry and Stewart to lie on the casting couch if they wanted better roles. "After all, the couch, at least, beats the hard, cold floor."

She was especially blunt about the dimensions of her husband's penis: "He has a thick, ten-inch cock and is nicknamed 'Jawbreaker.' Before he met me, he compelled women like Bette Davis to pay homage to his shaft. Before Franchot gets down to business, he spends about an hour sucking on my ninny pies."

BUT WHO IS THE GORGEOUS HUSSY?

Robert Taylor with **Joan Crawford** in the 1936 classic.

Same film (*The Gorgeous Hussy*), different coupling:

Joan Crawford with **James Stewart,** in the supporting role of a chivalrous defender of her honor.

Despite the other contenders for the affections of Joan's character, the real winner was **Franchot Tone**, Joan's then-real-life husband.

Behind the scenes, she frequently lobbied, mercilessly, for a bigger part and more lines for the man she, for the moment at least, loved.

During pre-production, everyone loved the concept and the *femme fatale* associations of its heroine, **Joan Crawford.**

But no one could reconcile her legendary sexual allure and reputation for *haute* fashion with the frumpy costumes associated with the 1830s, in which the film was set.

Crawford's reaction, after seeing one of the wardrobe department's dresses?

"Historical romance simply was not for me."

Making matters worse, banner headlines for the film, in reference to Joan, screamed, "No man who kisses her once will ever be content."

Both Stewart and Henry concluded later that that was a reference to her ample breasts. They also agreed that with enough alcohol in her, Crawford talked like a drunken sailor.

At the end of the evening, Crawford claimed that she'd welcome either of them as her leading man in future films. *[Actually, that would come true. Both Stewart and Henry eventually became not only her co-stars but her off-screen lovers, too. Stewart and Crawford would co-star in* Ice Follies of 1939, *and Fonda would be her leading man in* Daisy Kenyon *(1947).]*

***

Born to Dance **(1936)**

Henry could hardly believe it when Stewart came home one night to tell him that he'd been cast as the male lead in *Born to Dance* (1936), co-starring with tap-dancing Eleanor Powell, seven years before her famous marriage to Glenn Ford. "I'll have to sing and dance," Stewart said.

"But you can't do either one," Henry responded.

Defiantly, Stewart shot back, "So what?"

The third lead went to Virginia Bruce, with whom Stewart had had a brief fling when she was cast, the previous year, in his first motion picture, *The Murder Man.*

Stewart, cast as a sailor on leave, Ted Barker, who's out on the town, meets Nora Page (Powell) at the aptly named Lonely Hearts Club. It is owned by Jenny Saks (Una Merkel), the wife of another sailor Gunny Saks. Saks was portrayed by Sid Silvers, one of the writers of the screenplay.

Stewart arranges a date with Powell, but his naval commander, Captain Dinghy (Raymond Walburn), sabotages it. Lucy James (a Broadway star portrayed by Bruce) comes aboard the submarine as part of a publicity tour. When her beloved pet, a docile Pekingese, falls overboard, Stewart jumps in and saves it. Lucy is powerfully attracted to the gallant sailor, and he is ordered by his captain to escort her on a glamourous night of drinks and dancing. Thus, she intrudes on his developing romance with the hoofer aspirant, Eleanor Powell.

Correctly evaluating himself, early in his career, as a "non-singer" and "non-dancer," **James Stewart** (lower photo, where he appears in front of **Eleanor Powell**) was hired as a romantic foil in the "hoofer's extravaganza," *Born to Dance*, one of at least six movies he appeared in in 1936, the year of its release.

Also in the cast were singer Frances Langford and the tall, lanky, Buddy Ebsen, whose dancing with Powell is the highlight of the movie.

Roy del Ruth, the director, claimed that it was the homophobic Ebsen, who started the rumor that Stewart was collaborating on the casting couch of Cole Porter, who composed the music for the film. Although it was anything but ideal, Stewart's pipsqueak tenor was "enrolled" to sing "Easy to Love," and "Hey, Babe" with Powell.

One of James Stewart's potential pitfalls appeared that year in the form of songwriter **Cole Porter**, who fell madly in love with him.

Stewart more or less successfully managed to extricate himself from anything really dangerous or embarrassing associated with the sometimes suicidal songwriter.

Cole ("*Begin the Beguine'*") Porter appears here, having "drinky-poohs'" at a bar in the theater district with the gossipy hostess and professional matchmaker, **Elsa Maxwell,** in 1934.

After only a day on the set, Porter invited Stewart to his residence to rehearse. The next day, he told Del Ruth, "Jimmy has a squeaky voice both in his singing and in his speech patterns. And, oh, those long, lanky legs—they give Ebsen competition. I'm refusing to have his voice dubbed by a professional singer."

Soon, the director learned why: "Cole Porter was head over high heels in love with Stewart, who was resisting his advances. Word of this leaked out and was repeated, carefully phrased and with subtle innuendos in some of the columns of gossip maven Louella Parsons.

Del Ruth claimed, "Porter was smitten, and Jimmy didn't want to alienate him. But he also had to keep the composer leashed. Word of Porter's crush on

Stewart leaked to Louis B. Mayer, who had heard that Porter had invited Stewart home for an audition.

In response, Mayer ordered Eddie Mannix, the MGM-sponsored expert on covering up scandals, to "Tell Stewart never to be alone with Porter. A big scandal could wreck his career."

Mayer also ordered Mannix to begin featuring stories about a Powell-Stewart romance. Somehow, although Stewart was spending his nights with Virginia Bruce, she got left out of the rumors

Stewart admired Porter as one of the most talented composers and songwriters in the country, widely renowned for his witty, urbane lyrics. "But I didn't want him singing, 'You're the Top' to me."

After failing at inroads toward Stewart, Porter turned instead to a medley of sailors, truck drivers, longshoremen, rough trade, and male prostitutes. One Hollywood pimp claimed that on occasion, he supplied Porter with twenty young men a night, many of them ambitious chorus boys.

In New York, Porter patronized Clint Moore's notorious whorehouse in Harlem, staffed as it was with studly Mandingos.

Born to Dance would be the last time Stewart ever tried to imitate the rhythmic acrobatics of Fred Astaire. In future movies, he would only have to dance cheek to cheek, demurely, with his leading lady.

Henry accompanied Stewart to a screening of *Born to Dance* a week after its opening. He told his friend, "Jimmy, forget about dramas. From what I saw on the screen tonight, you're going to be the new singing and dancing sensation of Hollywood."

"And you're full of shit, good buddy," Stewart answered.

In 1945, after service in World War II, Stewart returned to Hollywood and—perhaps in an effort to re-familiarize himself with the Hollywood scene—asked for a screening of *Born to Dance*. His final verdict: "I wanted to vomit."

***

Wings of the Morning (1937)

Henry's next picture, *Wings of the Morning* (1937), involved location shooting in the English and Irish countryside. The experience would change his life, prompting him to move out of the Brentwood home he shared with Stewart. "No more would we be roomies," Henry said, "but friends for life with an occasional break-up."

As all of this was unfolding around Henry, Stewart had been miscast as a crazed, gun-toting murderer in *After the Thin Man* (1936), another MGM whodunnit starring William Powell and Myrna Loy as Nick and Nora Charles, amateur detectives.

A critic later said, "I didn't believe James Stewart was a killer. He wouldn't harm a fly."

Aboard the *Île de France*, Henry sailed to Southampton with his new friend, the French actor Charles Boyer. *[Although Boyer had recently married Henry's co-star, the English actress Pat Paterson, she was not available for the trans-Atlantic crossing.]* At their dinner table, Henry sat with Boyer and a young woman whom Boyer identified as "a family friend." She spoke absolutely no English.

The trio finished off three bottles of (the desirable, very posh, and very expensive) Pommery et Greno, 1926. The French woman "with Elizabeth Taylor's violet eyes" flirted with Henry, and he flirted back after realizing that she was not Boyer's on-board mistress.

During their second evening at sea, at around midnight, there was a knock on Henry's cabin door. When he opened it, he found the young woman there with a bottle of wine. He invited her inside and here she would remain, in his bed, every night for the remainder of the crossing.

As Henry told Boyer, "She did not speak English, and I did not speak French, so we communicated in the language of love."

The shipboard romance ended when the *Île de France* sailed into the Port of Southampton. Each member of the trio went their separate ways. Henry

Charles (*"Come with me to the Casbah"*) **Boyer**, who shared a table every night with Henry Fonda during a transatlantic crossing, appears here in his famous film of French colonial intrigue and deception, *Algiers* (1938).

With him are **Sigrid Gurnie** (left) and then-newcomer **Hedy Lamarr**. An unhappy runaway from a marriage to a Nazi munitions manufacturer, she was aggressively promoted by her Hollywood studio as "the most beautiful woman in the world."

boarded the train to London, studying the script for *Wings of the Morning.*

Interior scenes for that picture were to be filmed at Denham Studios outside London. The sprawling complex, part of it designed by Walter Gropius, had been built by producer Alexander Korda.

On the set, on the first day of filming, Henry met with the director, Harold Schuster, to discuss the script. Previously, he had edited two of Henry's films.

Wings of the Morning would be the first Technicolor film to be shot in the British Isles. The movie also marked the English-speaking debut of Annabella, an actress born in Paris who had become one of the most popular stars in French cinema.

The third lead would go to Leslie Banks.

[Born in 1890, Banks—known for his portrayal of gruff, menacing characters in the 1930s and 40s—had been working in films since 1911. He was also the chorus in Laurence Olivier's inspirational wartime production of Shakespeare's Henry V.]

The story opens in 1889, when Maria (Irene Vanbrugh), a Spanish gypsy, marries an Irish nobleman, Lord Clontarf (Banks), much to the horror of his aristocratic family. He is later killed in an accident.

Three generations later, the gypsy's granddaughter (portrayed by Annabella) returns to Britain. Although she's now the *Überglam* Duchess of Leyva, she disguises herself as a male jockey so that she can compete in a horse race on Derby Day at Epsom Downs.

At first, Henry, cast as Kerry Gilfallen, a Canadian horse trainer, views her as an effeminate pretty boy. He soon falls in love with her when he discovers that she's a young woman.

She will win the race.

During the shoot, Henry found Annabella enchanting. He would later remember long walks with her in the country, moonlit nights, and candlelit suppers.

Soon, word of their shared empathy leaked out. One day, the French actor Jean Murat, whom Annabella had married in 1934, showed up on the set and headed directly for Henry's dressing room, knocking loudly on its door. When Henry opened it, he found Murat in tears: "*M'sieur*, I have come to reclaim my wife. Please end your affair with her. I love her dearly. She is my life. She has written me, telling me you are a better lover than I am."

Henry invited the distraught man inside, and they had a talk that lasted about an hour. Henry denied ever having any sexual relations with his wife. At the end of their conversation, he promised he would have nothing else to do with Annabella. "She is your property, and I respect that."

That was a vow that Henry kept, in part because a new love interest had suddenly entered his life. He later learned that Annabella divorced Murat in 1938.

The French actress was not gone from Henry's life forever. In 1939, she would marry the bisexual matinée idol Tyrone Power, who by then had become one of Henry's friends. Also in 1939, Fonda and Power would co-star together in a Western as Frank and Jesse James.

During a break in the filming of *Wings of the Morning*, its producer, Robert T. Kane, invited Henry for a weekend trip with him through the English countryside, with stops at Windsor Castle and neighboring Eton.

With them were two attractive American women, Frances Seymour Brokaw, a Canadian-American socialite, and her brother's fiancée, Fay Devereaux Keith.

As author Peter Collier wrote in reference to Brokaw: "Henry was struck by her looks. She was a petite blonde with a smooth forehead and high cheekbones that narrowed her eyes into a look of sensual irony. He had seen more beautiful women in Hollywood. It was her frank and open manner that captivated him, the touch of class she conveyed, and also, the aggressive way she engaged him."

She was the aggressor, inviting him for dinner the night after their sightseeing trip ended. He was to pick her up at her suite at the Ritz Hotel in London.

When *Wings of the Morning* was released, he invited Frances to go see it with him. Afterward, she told him, "You

French *gamine* **Annabella** (later famously married to Tyrone Power) appears in a "dolled up and formal" romantic scene with **Henry Fonda** in the horsey melodrama, *Wings of the Morning*.

It was a spectacularly famous, and spectacularly unhappy (some said "undefined and inconclusive") marriage that didn't stop either from screwing around on the side.

Here's **Annabella** with then-megastar **Tyrone Power** in a press and PR photo for a movie they appeared in, *Suez* (1938).

looked glorious in Technicolor. The brilliant blue of your eyes was captured."

Critics had a hard time defining Fonda the actor, calling him "simple," "sincere," "honest," and "personable."

The Motion Picture Guide interpreted him as "affable in an engaging role which doesn't require much work on his part."

Annabella was cited by critics as "a woman of the world," "a *gamine*," even a "*hobbledehoy*," an old-fashioned synonym for "an awkward and gawky youth."

Another author noted, "Fonda seems more virtuous than Clark Gable, smarter than Gary Cooper, more melancholy than Joel McCrea, and more elusive than Spencer Tracy. His slow, hesitant speech stands in contrast to the bullet-like *rat-tat-tat-tat* spewing from the mouth of James Cagney in those gangster movies over at Warners."

***

The next day on the set, Henry confided to his producer, Robert Kane, "I can't say that Frances was thrilled to be going out with a movie star. She hasn't seen any of my movies, and she was not pleased that I was an actor, a lowly profession."

His mind seemed in a whirlpool. He was on the verge of "dumping" Annabella. However, by the time his next letter reached James Stewart in Hollywood, he sounded a different tune.

"Annabella is a delight, truly wonderful! Her beauty is of the ages. If Hollywood wants to make a movie of Helen of Troy, let the picture be cast with this French goddess. She's dear, dear, dear. Yes, we are very close, and, yes, I guess she will become the second Mrs. Henry Fonda. I want you to be my best man.

Love,
Hank"

Around the same time, he wrote to Margaret Sullavan, who had married their joint agent, Leland Hayward. He listed his return address as Brook Cottage, Station Parade, Buckinghamshire, England.

"I am living in a cozy cottage with my director, Harold Schuster. At a cast party there, Leslie Banks noticed that there was only one bedroom—and a double bed at that—he started the rumor that we are lovers. But that is hardly the case. We're just good friends.

I want you to know that even though you're married to Leland, I care more about you—your health and happiness—than I care about myself. You know how I feel about you. Regardless of what happens, you will be—and will forever be—my one true love. I've been a fool to let you go.

Love,
Hank"

Years later, Henry's daughter, Jane, said, "Maggie Sullavan was always in love with my father. She resented that she could not control him."

Back in Hollywood, Stewart had lunch one day with William Powell, with whom he had made *After the Thin Man.*

Powell said, "For Hank, Maggie—or Peggy as he insists on calling her—will always be the woman who got away. Now, she's married to Leland, as you know. He is not only my agent, but Maggie's, too, as well as Henry's. I'm in love with Maggie, too. Hollywood is a bit incestuous.:"

[*Coming from different backgrounds, and with different temperaments, William Powell and James Stewart had little in common. However, in the 1930s, they did have one romantic link. At various times, each of them had been entranced with both Jean Harlow and Carole Lombard.*]

***

Although Frances had invited Henry for dinner at the Ritz in London, their elegant meal was served not in the hotel's swanky dining room, but as part of a catered affair within her luxurious suite. As Henry looked around, he came to realize for the first time that his date must be very rich.

85

Their dinner lasted until ten o'clock the next morning. The newly minted lovers agreed to go out on the town the following evening after Henry finished his work at the studio.

Frances had entered his life so suddenly that he'd had no time "to wean myself" from Annabella.

He hugged and kissed Annabella goodbye, telling her that their affair was over.

"Our love for each other was just a flower that had not burst into bloom," she said. "There will be no tears. Perhaps we'll meet again, although that is most unlikely."

[She was wrong. They would meet again in Hollywood when their love lives were very different.]

During the preparations for her very grand transatlantic crossing aboard the *Île de France*, Frances had arranged the transport, within the bowels of that ship, her elegant Buick. It was part of her plan to motor her way through first the countryside of England, and then through The Continent, with the intention of dropping in on the 1936 Olympic Games in Berlin. She invited Henry to accompany her and, since he didn't have anything urgent on his immediate schedule, he accepted.

Rich, at loose ends, and eager to format a new life after the trauma of her previous husband's death: **Frances Seymour Brokaw.**

In London, before their departure, she took him out every night for dinners at the most expensive restaurants, often arranging the evening's transportation through limousines and drivers provided by the Ritz.

He felt like a kept boy yet enjoyed the luxury. Soon, he'd learn more about her "blue blood" background. "In Omaha, we didn't have blue bloods… just red bloods—especially Indians," he (quaintly) said.

Their favorite London pub became the Salisbury, where they met the West End's theatrical elite. One night, they drank beer with John Gielgud and Laurence Olivier.

Frances Seymour had been the second (and less illustrious) of her vastly wealthy first husband's two marriages.

Depicted above is **Claire Boothe** in 1923, during her marriage to George Tuttle Brokaw. Citing him as abusive at the time of their divorce, she later became a powerhouse writer, editor, and politician.

A devout Catholic, conservative, and Republican, she served as the U.S. Ambassador to Italy under Eisenhower, nurturing it back into the orbit of U.S. Allies after World War II, and becoming generally acknowledged as one of the most influential women in the world.

Frances, Henry Fonda's second wife, had a hard time competing with her predecessor's spectacular achievements.

The very rich, very unhappy, deeply alcoholic **George Tuttle Brokaw,** who died suspiciously in 1935, leaving his then-wife, Frances (Henry's future wife) breathtakingly rich.

One Sunday afternoon, Frances responded to Henry's constant questioning about her background. He'd gotten the impression that even though she derived from Canada, Brokaw's forebears had played an important role in U.S. history.

One of her ancestors, Horatio Seymour, born in 1810, had served two terms (1853-1854 and 1863-1864) as governor of New York. In the 1886 presidential election, he was the Democratic candidate running against Republican General Ulysses S. Grant, who won.

Frances Ford Seymour had been born in Ontario, Canada, in April of 1908. Her mother, Sophie Mildred Seymour, was descended from John Adams, the second President of the United States. Her father, Eugene Ford Seymour, was descended from the family of Edward Seymour, Duke of Somerset, a familiar and very influential player at the court of Henry VIII and its changing array of royal wives.

Henry later found that Frances had been the victim of sexual abuse when she was only eight.

The piano had needed tuning and a piano tuner, presumably Tarik Harren, came to work on it. For five hours, Frances was left alone in the house, staying in her upstairs bedroom.

As she would later relate to Henry, Harren came upstairs and discovered he was alone with her in the house.

"He came into my bedroom and raped me," she confided. "I screamed throughout the ordeal, and he left me bloody. He never tuned the piano, but he fled the house. When my mother got home, she found me in my bed bleeding and whimpering in pain. I was rushed to the hospital. My father wanted the police to go after this creep, a middle-aged man, but he had skipped town."

Frances had been married before. In 1931, she had tied the knot with George Tuttle Brokaw, the heir to a clothing dynasty.

[It was Brokaw's second marriage. He had previously been married (1923-29) to Ann Claire Boothe (aka Clare Boothe Luce). At the time of their divorce, his estranged wife cited him, after suffering four miscarriages, as an alcoholic and wife beater. Boothe, an astonishingly important voice in American politics and letters during and after World War II, would enter one of America's most famous marriages in November of 1935 when she wed Henry Luce, the publisher of Time, Life, *and* Fortune. *It was an "open marriage," within the context of which she conducted affairs with Ambassador Joseph Kennedy, Randolph Churchill, the famous author Roald Dahl, and U.S. Generals Lucian Truscott and Charles Willoughby.]*

Frances' marriage (1931–1935) to George Tuttle Brokaw was a disaster. He had gradually descended into madness and placed in an asylum, the Hartford (Connecticut) Retreat. There, on the night of May 28, 1935, he was found dead in its swimming pool. Was it suicide or accidental? *[An autopsy revealed that he was heavily intoxicated on the night of his death.]*

THE FINEST ACTOR MONEY COULD BUY

The very posh wedding of **Henry Fonda** to the socialite and recent heiress, **Frances Seymor Brokaw** was the most interesting interconnection of show-biz with high society that almost anyone could remember.

"How would it end?" was the question everyone was asking.

How much money he left her is the subject of debate. Some reporters suggested that he had been worth five million dollars in real estate and trust funds, an bequest that would allow her to live luxuriously for decades.

***

As part of their motor tour of Europe, Henry and Frances were booked into Berlin's legendary and very posh Hotel Adlon. Two or three times a day, they passed through the lobby, whose walls were festooned with Nazi flags and whose sofas and armchairs were occupied by "brown shirts" and black-uniformed members of the dreaded SS.

In the Adlon's dining room, they spotted Heinrich Himmler, dining with a party of eight Nazi officials. Himmler had recently been designated as head of the Gestapo, organizers of the concentration camps which systematically slaughtered Jews, homosexuals, gypsies, political prisoners, and *"Untermenschen" (inferior people and undesirables)*. In time, he would become second in Nazi command to the *Führer* himself.

Henry wanted to impress Frances. Remembering what Charles Boyer had ordered aboard the *Île de France*, when the wine steward approached, he asked for a bottle of *Pommery et Greno, 1926.*

In August of 1936, at Berlin's Summer Olympics, for $7 million, filmmaker Leni Riefenstahl was commissioned to film the games.

To the fury of Hitler, who would have preferred that athletes from "The Master Race" win all the events, Jesse Owens, an African-American, won four gold medals in the sprint and long jump events.

[In that year's official tally, Germany emerged first with 89 medals, vs. the Americans, who culled 56.]

Frances and Henry were so uncomfortable that they soon fled from Berlin, hurriedly navigating their way

It was an ill-chosen time for a honeymoon in Central Europe, as Henry and Frances soon discovered. Street fighting was frequent, arrests of "undesirables" by Nazi sympathizers were everywhere, and disdain for anything "NOT GERMAN' was common in both Berlin and Munich.

Depicted above from the German National Archives is a gathering of the **Freikorps,** a "Vanguard of Terror," and "shock troops" for the Third Reich that followed.

Henry and Frances, as newlyweds touring an increasingly unstable Europe, quickly ascertained that it was time to return to familiar venues in America and quietly headed out of town.

across (Nazi) Germany *en route* to the Austrian Alps. In any town they stopped, they saw Nazi soldiers strutting and rehearsing for war.

In Munich, where they hurriedly spent only one night, they stopped at the city's most famous beer hall, the *Hofbräuhaus*. It, too, was overrun with boisterous and usually hostile Nazi soldiers.

They left Munich the next morning, driving to Salzburg and later to Vienna, where they visited museums and attended an opera.

From there, they continued to Budapest, the highlight, they said, of their trip.

In Paris, Frances had booked them into a suite at the Ritz. As Henry later relayed to Stewart, "Traveling in Europe with a rich girlfriend sure beats being a starving actor pounding the streets of Broadway looking for work. I think I'll marry Frances unless Barbara Hutton wants me to help her share those Woolworth millions. If I wed Doris Duke instead, I'll never have to buy a package of cigarettes again as long as I live."

In Paris, after visiting Nôtre Dame, he invited Frances for a moonlit walk along the Seine. There, he proposed marriage, and she accepted. He put a modest ring on her finger.

The time had come to sail back to the Port of New York, where she had booked the most lavish suite at the Waldorf-Astoria.

The following day, two tailors arrived to fit Henry in a black coat with swallowtails and an ascot.

***

On September 16, 1936, it was with splendor and pomp that members of New York society arrived at Christ Church on Park Avenue in Manhattan. An elegantly attired Henry stood beside his Best Man, Joshua Logan, as the bride made her way down the aisle. Escorted by her brother, Fred de Villiers Seymour, Frances looked stunning in a pale blue gown and carrying a bouquet of pink roses. Her only bridesmaid was her sister, Mary. Elaborate masses of flowers filled the church.

Leland Hayward—the tough and very famous agent of Henry, James Stewart, and Henry's ex-wife, Margaret Sullavan—had been designated as one of the ushers,

The pews of the church were filled with some of the social elite of New York City. For the reception, fifty elegantly dressed guests gathered at the Roof Garden of the Hotel Pierre.

During the wedding ceremony, a crowd of onlookers, photographers, and members of the press had gathered. The size of the crowd surprised reporters, because at the time, Henry was only a minor movie star, and Frances' crowd was only a select élite.

It had been only two months since Frances had met an actor she had never before heard of. She would later tell her daughter, Jane Fonda, "I've gotten every man I've ever wanted. I recommend that you do the same. When I met your father and saw him for the first time, I made up my mind that he was going to be my next husband. At least I can afford him."

With their wedding and Manhattan behind them, Henry, with his bride, were *en route* to Chicago, where they would spend two nights as an extension of their honeymoon. As he later told some pals, "She wanted more, but I informed her that one blast-off a day was my limit."

After Chicago, as their train headed west for its long run across the midlands of America, Frances knew she was entering the strange new world of Hollywood. She'd heard disquieting stories of what was accepted there as "normal."

So far, Henry had more or less lived in a world that she had dominated. She knew that aspect of their life had ended. In Hollywood, as a rapidly rising movie star, her husband would be the focus of attention.

In letters to friends back in New York, Frances wrote, "I predict I'll henceforth be known merely as Henry's wife. For some reason, I fear trying to establish myself in a new life on the West Coast. I'll be meeting actresses who have slept with my husband, and I won't know which ones they are. They'll probably resent me, especially that Margaret Sullavan bitch."

Al Jolson, playing the ukelele, had made this song a nationwide hit in 1924, more than a decade before Henry Fonda and his bride, Frances, really understood the truth of its lyrics.

Their honeymoon—part of a posh and very expensive tour through *mitteleuropa* during the rise to power of the Nazis, was filled with dread at the political catastrophes (i.e., unimaginable bloodshed and genocides) to come.

CHAPTER SIX

How, Once Upon a Time in Hollywood, Henry Fonda Did It His Way with

FRANCES SEYMOUR BROKAW
His Disgruntled and Understandably Suspicious Wife #2,

BETTE DAVIS,
An Egomaniacal Jezebel in Real Life, Too

An Unhappily Remarried
MARGARET SULLAVAN
As an Ongoing Nemesis

JOAN BENNETT
Famous as the Erotic Flame whose Jealous Lover Shot Walter Wanger in the Testicles

And With Other Players Who Included

LORETTA YOUNG (impregnated by Clark Gable during *Call of the Wild)*; PHILLIS BROOKS ("The Face" and "The Ipana Girl"); ANITA COLBY (eventual wife of JFK's roommate at Harvard); KAY ALDRIDGE (one of the most visible fashion models in America); ILONA MASSEY ("a Hungarian bombshell like Zsa Zsa"); SIMONE SIMON ("a nymphomaniac from Marseilles famous for passing around her house keys"); JANE WYMAN (somber, business-like, and unfunny after her breakup with the future U.S. President); and celebrated Hollywood hostess ANITA LOUISE; with sidebars from bisexual matinee idols ROBERT TAYLOR AND PHILLIP TERRY; and insights from some of the most celebrated and sometimes most bitchy directors of Vintage Hollywood.

"I'm not going to let marriage stop me from having fun on the side."
—Henry Fonda

Henry's regrets about his New York marriage to Frances

Brokaw began shortly after his return to Hollywood for a reunion with James Stewart, his longtime friend and former roommate.

His two-month marriage to Margaret Sullavan had left him with a dim view of marital bliss. He did not think that his union with Frances would last forever. As he confided to Stewart and others. "I don't expect to grow old with her, and that we'll totter off into the sunset together."

He was envious of the track record Stewart was scoring in the romance department, one starlet after another and, on occasion, a really big-name movie star. His dream girl remained Norma Shearer, whom he had not yet seduced.

Henry spoke openly to the gay director, Edmund Goulding, who would soon put him in a film. "Jimmy is enjoying what surely will be the most promiscuous period of his life, seducing movie stars. It could be happening to me, too, and I'm not going to let all my chances pass me by because I was foolish enough to get married. I know this time will never come again in my life, and I think I'd be a real fool not to take advantage of it, married or not."

"When I'm an old man looking back, I might kick myself for trying to be faithful to just one woman. Frances wants to have children. What am I supposed to do in the meantime? Jerk off?"

"You could always come to me for relief," the director, Goulding, said, half-jokingly.

"I know. You first made that offer to me at George Cukor's party," Henry said. "My answer is still the same."

"But I simply can't make love to a woman if she's pregnant, even if it were only the first week of pregnancy. The thought of screwing her with my child, a boy or girl growing inside her, is just plain disgusting, bordering on incest."

A lot of what was going on in Henry's love life was not revealed until months after his marriage.

He had met Loretta Young at a Hollywood party, and both of them had become infatuated with each other.

Born in Salt Lake City, she had arrived in Hollywood at the age of three after her "Luxembourgeois" [*i.e., derived from the Western European nation of Luxemburg*] parents divorced. She and her two sisters became child actresses. In her early career, she was billed with her original name of Gretchen. By 1928, she was featured as Loretta Young, starring in *The Whip Woman* and later opposite Lon Chaney and Nils Asther in *Laugh, Clown, Laugh.*

In 1930, at the age of seventeen, she married actor Grant Withers, but within a month, the marriage was annulled. She would not marry again until 1940, when she wed producer Ted Lewis.

As an unmarried woman, she began a series of affairs in the 1930s. One of the most serious was in 1933, when she co-starred with Spencer Tracy in *A Man's Castle.* She fell in love with him but was unsuccessful in attempts to persuade him to divorce his wife to marry her.

By 1935, she'd begun her most infamous affair, and that was with Clark Gable during their on-location filming, in the Mount Baker National Forest (in Washington State) of Jack London's *Call of the Wild.* During the shooting of the film, she became pregnant with his child.

She did not appear in Hollywood for several months. Reports leaked out that she was recovering from an illness. After the birth of her child, Judy, she put the little girl in an orphanage, where she remained for about eighteen months.

Loretta then thought it was safe to bring the child to Hollywood, claiming that she had adopted her. Her name later became Judy Lewis, the girl taking the name of Loretta's next husband, Ted Lewis.

Hollywood insiders knew that Gable was the father, but Loretta always denied it. When news of Judy's real father eventually leaked out, Loretta claimed that Clark Gable had raped her during their only date.

Henry's fling with Loretta Young was brief. No more than a long weekend in Palm Springs.

Weeks later, he was surprised when, back in Hollywood, he learned that James Stewart also was having an affair with Young. He jokingly chided his friend, "So, you're reduced to taking my sloppy seconds."

"You've played that role to me many times, coming in for the second course, so shut your trap."

After a convent education and a personal history that included breaking into show-biz as a bit player when she was three, **Loretta Young** resurfaced at age 14 for a small role in *Naughty But Nice* (1927). In the photo above, she appears a year later in the also-silent film, *Laugh Clown, Laugh.*

Her performance led to a contract with First National (the precursor of Warner Brothers).

Within a few years, Young, by then deeply entrenched within Twentieth-Century Fox's orbit, had blossomed into a full-fledged star noted for her complicated emotional and romantic needs.

At that time, Young was gossiped about as a sexually voracious "super-manizer," in the words of one author.

Young later told Henry, "I desperately tried to get Jimmy Stewart to marry me, but he refused. Come to think of it, why didn't *you* ask me to marry you?"

"The thought didn't enter my mind, I guess," was his weak response.

Despite her inner torments, Young put up a good front, presenting herself as a very moral lady of high principals with a strong belief in the teachings of the Catholic Church.

However, actress Virginia Fields, who appeared with her in *Eternally Yours* (1939), called her "a complete phoney. She's two-faced, spewing morality out of her mouth while, in private, going against her own utterances. She had every man from George Brent to Darryl F. Zanuck, as well as writers, producers, and guys you've never heard of. Her longest-running affair was with Tyrone Power, when he wasn't out being a woman himself to his male lovers."

[*Many of his frenemies would have agreed with that uncharitably harsh assessment.*]

In 1937 alone, Young and Power starred in three pictures: *Love Is News, Café Metropolis,* and *Second Honeymoon.*

The last time Jimmy Stewart was photographed with Young was in 1992 when he attended her 79th birthday party.

The very elegant British-born **Virginia Field** in the 1940s, around the time she referred to Loretta Young as "a complete phoney."

***

After their status as congenial, full-time roommates had ended, Henry made a deal with James Stewart whereby each would hold onto copies of the door keys to their farmhouse-styled former shared home, and define it in the future as merely a "crash pad" where each of them would bring young actresses for off-the-record sexual trysts.

Henry, despite his new status as a "married man," also persuaded Stewart to serve as his "beard" whenever he wanted to escort a young woman for an adulterous date out on the town. The "*belle du jour*" would be introduced to whomever was interested as Stewart's date. Later, Henry and his date would retire to the farmhouse-inspired home, now controlled by Stewart, which Henry and Stewart had previously shared. Stewart would then, for the remainder of the evening, go on his own date, his seductions usually occurring at the residence of his conquest.

The excuse that Henry delivered on such occasions to his new wife, Frances, involved orchestrating a "catch-up" with his best friend, James Stewart. Frances might have been surprised that she was never asked to join in.

Stewart got a new roommate when actor Burgess Meredith came to live with him in the quarters since vacated by Henry.

Today's audiences might remember Meredith for playing "The Penguin" in the original *Batman* TV series (1966-68), or else for his role as he feisty manager of the boxer, Sylvester Stallone, in *Rocky* (1976). After her so-called marriage to Charlie Chaplin, Paulette Goddard wed Meredith.

Meredith later became a good source in revealing what was going on behind the scenes in the lives of Henry and Stewart.

"Before I met Henry, he and I had both shared the dubious charms of Miss Tallulah Bankhead," Meredith said. "But it was Jimmy, not Henry, with whom I shared the most conquests, notably Marlene Dietrich, although Henry, so I heard, had a one-night stand with the Kraut, too."

"Jimmy later knocked Dietrich up when they starred in that classic Western, *Destry Rides Again* (1939). She had to have an abortion. Also, Jimmy and I took our turns with Ginger Rogers and Norma Shearer. How's that for name-dropping?"

"There were a lot of lesser stars, mainly actresses in B pictures, some of whom were more successful as models. Let's see if I can recall," Meredith said. "Oh, yes, Phyllis Brooks, Anita Colby, Kay Aldridge, and Ilona Massey, a bigger star than those I just named."

"God knows I was not a dashing swain," said **Burgess Meredith.**

"In a kind of mongrel way, I chased the foxes, even ended up in a *ménage à trois* with a rich Nazi woman and her lesbian lover."

***

Hailed as "The Beautiful Blonde from Boise," Phyllis Brooks had entered the lives of Henry and Stewart after she'd earned a reputation as a "party girl."

"Jimmy and I expected Phyllis to have the whitest teeth in Hollywood," Henry said. "After all, she was the 'Ipana Toothpaste Girl.'"

At the age of twenty, Brooks had arrived in Hollywood, dreaming of superstardom, but settling for becoming a B-movie leading lady. Henry and Stewart met her through their friend Tyrone Power. He had started an affair with her when she had a minor role in his movie, *In Old Chicago* (1937), starring Alice Faye.

When Power was (soon) ready to drop her in favor of sexual trysts with Errol Flynn, he turned her over to Henry and Stewart.

Both Stewart and Henry were only too willing to remove Brooks from Power's list of possible dates. When the two actors tossed a coin to determine "who would get her first," Stewart won.

For a brief period, she came and went from their then-shared home on several different occasions.

In the years to come, Henry, on occasion, encountered Brooks. Once, in 1942, he met up with her when she had been named President of Parties Unlimited, Inc., an organization vaguely associated with morale-building during World War II. He saw her again when she was the first civilian woman to travel to the Pacific Theater of war for the USO. She traveled with and had an affair with Gary Cooper. She eventually appeared in almost three dozen feature films, portraying mothers, sisters, nieces, cousins, gold-diggers, debutantes, chorines, best friends, secretaries, nurses, debutantes, retail clerks, businesswomen, and showgirls.

Brooks was gay-friendly, and sometimes dated Cesar Romero, accompanying him to the Trocadero or Cocoanut Grove. At the time, both Romero and Brooks were enjoying the sexual favors of Tyrone Power. Henry also learned that Cary Grant had once proposed a "sexless marriage" to Brooks as a means of concealing his homosexual affairs.

The last that Henry heard of Brooks, she had settled down and married Torbert Macdonald, who had been John F. Kennedy's roommate at Harvard. Later, her husband became an eleven-term Congressman from Massachusetts.

Charming, non-judgmental, and fun, **Phyllis Brooks** appears above, in the 1930s as the collaborative and cooperative "lady friend, arm candy, and "beard" of two noted bisexuals, **Cesar Romero** (upper photo) and **Cary Grant.**

***

Once one of the highest-paid models in America, **Anita Colby**, appears as a pistol-toting "bad girl" in this *film noir* publicity photo from Jules Dassin's *Brute Force* in 1947.

Film reviewer Eddie Muller wrote that "the climax of *Brute Force* displayed the most harrowing violence ever seen in movie theaters."

Known as "The Face," Anita Colby was for a time the highest-paid model in America, gracing billboards and the covers of magazines.

She didn't marry until 1970, so for decades, she was viewed as "a hot date."

Henry was introduced to her by actress Dorothy McGuire, with whom he had first appeared on stage in Omaha when she was only fourteen.

From the very beginning, Henry viewed Colby as the most elegant woman he had ever known. Even David O. Selznick had hired her to teach some of his contract players beauty, poise, and publicity. With that intention, Colby worked with Joan Fontaine, Jennifer Jones (who later married Selznick), Ingrid Bergman, Shirley Temple, and even McGuire.

Colby's screen career eventually fizzled and died.

Henry had first seen her in *Mary of Scotland* (1936) starring Katharine Hepburn. According to Hepburn, "Anita brought Henry some class, which he desperately needed. Our boy still had that lingering trace of being a farmer on the fields of Nebraska. But when he started dating Anita, his wardrobe, style, and manners improved. She properly taught him which fork to use. I was told that she had him model various selections of underwear before making the final choice. Anita said that when it came to underwear, a man should be perfectly packaged."

For its edition of January 8, 1945, as World War II was entering its final months, *Time* magazine featured Colby on its front cover.

Her beauty was still intact when she performed in *Brute Force* (1947). When the cameras shut down for the night, she retreated into the arms of its star, Burt Lancaster.

***

A beauty from Tallahassee, Florida, Kay Aldridge was one of the most frequently photographed models in America. She had gone to Hollywood to later appear in *Vogues of 1938 [aka Walter Wanger's Vogues of 1938]* for United Artists. She stayed on to test for the Scarlett O'Hara role in *Gone With the Wind*.

Henry had been introduced to her by Nelson Eddy. Aldridge had been cast in his 1937 film, *Rosalie*, as an uncredited "Lady in Waiting."

Henry was immediately struck by her beauty and allure, in some way evoking an innocent, younger version of Barbara Stanwyck, assuming that that actress was ever innocent. On newsstands throughout America, Aldridge began appearing on covers of *Look* and *Redbook*, among other periodicals.

Although Henry began dating her, he opted to keep their relationship "down low" and secret because of his newly minted marriage to Frances.

Aldridge finally told Henry she didn't feel right going out with him as long as he was married. When she learned he had no plans to divorce Frances, she dropped him. She immediately found a number of unmarried young substitutes willing to take her out.

In 1940, she was cast in a small role in *Down Argentine Way*, starring Betty Grable and Carmen Miranda. She was soon dating the main star of the picture, Don Ameche.

That same year, she was cast in a low-budget movie called *Free, White, and 21*, whose title was later discretely changed to *Free, Blonde, and 21*.

***

On reflection, Henry viewed one of his most tantalizing conquests as the blonde goddess, Ilona Massey. The Budapest-born stage and film star was being billed at the time as "The New Dietrich."

Both Stewart and Henry were invited to a party at the home of Nelson Eddy, where they were introduced to Massey. At the time, Eddy and the Hungarian newcomer were making *Rosalie*, released in 1937.

Massey had already divorced her first husband, Nick Szavazd (married 1935-36), but had not committed herself to Alan Curtis (wed 1941-42). She defined her status at the time as "I'm free as a songbird."

After only six months of less than wedded bliss to Curtis, Massey was seen going out with other beaux. To her roster were soon added the names of James Stewart and Henry Fonda.

After seeing her at the Eddy party, the trio agreed to adjourn to the Cocoanut Grove for the rest of the evening.

Massey was next seen leaving the Stewart/Fonda home late the following Monday morning. One can only speculate what happened that weekend.

Eddy's on-again, off-again affair with Massey, however, continued for years, as did his affair with his other co-star Jeanette MacDonald. Massey and Eddy were

re-teamed in *Balalaika* (1939), in which she played a cabaret singer pursued by Eddy, cast as an ardent Cossack. The picture flopped, and MGM dropped her.

Massey's last picture with Eddy was *Northern Outpost* (1947), a musical composed by Rudolf Friml.

That was followed two years later by *Love Happy,* a comedy starring the Marx Brothers. In that film, Massey had to compete with a rising young starlet, Marilyn Monroe.

Massey tried to revive her career in 1954 by starring on television in *The Ilona Massey Show,* a variety show that teamed her with other celebrity guests. It went off the air after only ten episodes.

Henry last saw her in a 1959 newsreel filmed at the United Nations in Manhattan. Massey joined other protesters against Nikita Khrushchev because of the harsh treatment of her fellow Hungarians after the Soviets took over her native land.

Henry's final comment on Massey was this: "If there are any more like her in Budapest, I'm buying the next ticket."

***

James Stewart was completely turned off by his next co-star, Simone Simon, a French film actress who emerged from the depths of Marseille. Her father was a Jewish engineer and later, an airplane pilot in World War II. He would die in a concentration camp.

Before Darryl F. Zanuck brought her to Hollywood in 1935, she'd lived in Paris, Budapest, Turin, Berlin, and Madagascar.

Both Henry and Stewart had first seen her in *Ladies in Love,* which had cast, on-screen, Simon with Janet Gaynor, Loretta Young, and Constance Bennett. James Stewart had accompanied Young to one of its screenings, and Henry had as his date that night, Constance Bennett. She had married Henry de la Falaise (aka *Le Marquis de La Coudraye*) a French nobleman once known as "Mr. Gloria Swanson" during his marriage to the former silent screen vamp.

[Ironically, Henry Fonda would soon be co-starring with Constance's actress sister, Joan Bennett, in I Met My Love Again *(1938).]*

Around the same time, at Fox, Darryl F. Zanuck had decided to remake, for release in 1937, the Janet Gaynor-starring film, *Seventh Heaven,* a 1927 silent classic.

In a nutshell, it was the story of Chico, a Parisian sewer worker who falls in love with a beautiful prostitute.

As Stewart would find out, much to his regret, Zanuck wanted Tyrone Power as the male lead, but the reigning Fox matinée idol rejected the role. "I don't want to play someone working in shit all day."

On loan-out from MGM, Stewart, cast opposite Simone Simon, began filming it right before Christmas of 1936, with Henry King directing.

Right from the beginning, there was no on-screen chemistry between Stewart and the French *femme fatale.* Zanuck had hoped to build her up as Fox's answer to Greta Garbo and Marlene Dietrich. But it soon became evident to King that *Seventh Heaven* was not being made in heaven.

Throughout her life, Simon never married, so during her filming with Stewart, she was dating any number of men. She'd become infamous for handing out a gold-colored key to her apartment. Many men were said to have inserted that key into the door of her boudoir. Among her famous lovers was George Gershwin.

Simon made several sexual overtures to Stewart, and he rejected her. Finally speaking to her only when a camera was rolling.

Simon's luck changed after Henry showed up on the set to discuss Christmas plans with Stewart. King introduced Simon to Henry. Stewart then rejected an invitation to lunch with Simon and Henry. Before the end of that meal, Henry was presented with a gold-colored key for the door to Simon's apartment.

Two nights later, he turned the key within its lock. It led to "bliss itself" (his words).

Stewart was not impressed with Henry's conquest. "That thunderbolt from Paris

Simone Simon and a poster of the ill-fated movie she made with **James Stewart.**

After watching the first rushes of *Seventh Heaven,* Stewart said, "We should not have tried to remake this silent screen classic. Janet Gaynor took home an Oscar. Simone Simon (what a stupid name) got not only bad notices, but failed to lure me. In a love scene, she secretly grabbed my crotch. I don't like a woman that bold."

94

will screw anything from a studio grip to the man who delivers lunch to the set."

Opening to mixed reviews, the remake of *Seventh Heaven* died a miserable death at the box office. Stewart had been horribly miscast, and his pseudo-French accent was mocked.

"Simone Simon might be capable of doing many things," one critic wrote. "But acting is not one of her accomplishments."

[Editor's Note: As Henry would learn later, the most notorious lover of Simone Simon was Dusko Popov.Nicknamed "Tricycle" by the British M16 when he was head of a trio of spies passing on disinformation in a "Double Cross System" to the Nazis. He also worked as an agent of the Yugoslav Government-in-Exile in London.

By a long extension, his character lives on even in the cinema of the 21st Century. Popov (Tricycle) was the inspiration behind Ian Fleming's creation of the character of James Bond.

In August of 1941, the F.B.I. under J. Edgar Hoover made the mistake of his career by not listening to Tricycle's information. He warned Hoover and his agency that within three or four months, the Empire of Japan would attack Pearl Harbor on a Sunday morning raid when the island was for the most part asleep.

Hoover did not trust Popov since he was a double agent. Instead of alerting the President and the military, Hoover foolishly chose to invoke the Mann Act against Popov. In violation of that law, he had transported a seventeen-year-old girl from New York to Florida for purposes of sex. The spy was a notorious womanizer and heavy drinker. On hearing of his imminent arrest, Popov fled from the U.S., and it was good for the Allies that he did.

He later delivered one of the great services of World War II.

He was able to convince the Nazis that the Allied invasion of France would come at the Port of Calais and not on the beaches of Normandy, on June 6, 1944.

Nazi officers moved thousands of troops to Calais, allowing Operation Overlord, the name of the Allied invasion, to overtake the German fortifications and begin the march to liberate Paris.

When Henry Fonda finally learned of the exploits of Tricycle, he thought "it would make one hell of a movie." But he didn't promote the idea of a thriller strongly enough— or perhaps he lost interest.

He said, "At least Tricycle and I shared something in common: The world's best sex, as delivered in the sultry package of Simone Simon."]

***

Back on the West Coast, Henry and his new bride, Frances, rented a furnished house on Monaco Drive in the Pacific Palisades. They were only a block away from the home of Henry's ex-wife Margaret Sullavan and her new husband, Leland Hayward. Frances agreed that, after they'd had time to settle in, they'd invite Henry's agent and his former wife over for dinner.

Actually, Henry and Frances had gotten married before they really knew each other. Almost from the beginning, their interests, work schedules, and personalities were incompatible.

Within minutes of their arrival in Hollywood, they were showered with invitations, and Frances was eager to accept them.

Columnist Hedda Hopper met her and dubbed her "Lady Fonda. She was the most elegantly dressed at any party, showing up in a black velvet gown with a string of pearls, whereas other women were overly dressed, trying to show off as many diamonds as they could."

The talk of her fellow female guests bored Frances since it usually centered exclusively on movies and the drama and politics surrounding them. It soon became obvious that Frances preferred the company and conversation of men.

The notoriety of her romantic advenures made the French actress Simone Simon more famous for anything she ever did on screen.

One of the most astonishing was her ongoing affair with **Duško Popov (aka "Tricycle")**, the Serbian-born triple agent who managed to persuade the Nazis that the Allied invasion of Europe in 1944 would NOT happen at Normandy.

He was later morphed into the inspiration for Ian Fleming's spymaster, James Bond.

As newlyweds, **Henry Fonda** and his wife, **Frances.**

He did not like to be photographed in a bathing suit. "Let's face it: I'm no Johnny Weissmuller. No directorr is going to cast me as Tarzan."

Clark Gable met her one night and determined that her favorite subjects were "sex and money."

Frances would later label Hollywood parties as "incestuous."

She had taken over Henry's business affairs, telling him, "I like to buy cheap and sell high." His annual salary of $56,000 a year had tripled and she wanted to invest it wisely.

Frances' major vice involved consuming too much alcohol. By the time he drove her home after virtually anyone's party, she was nearly always intoxicated.

Henry was trying to adjust to his newly imposed role as a stepfather to Pan, Frances' daughter by her deceased first husband, George Tuttle Brokaw a four-year-old. Pan seemed to like him from the beginning. He asked her what she wanted to be when she grew up.

"A ballet dancer," she told him.

Their good relations continued. When she enrolled in the first grade, she gave her name as "Pan Fonda."

Politically, Frances was conservative. She and James Stewart seemed to have more agreement on politics than Henry, who was an ardent liberal. Henry grew upset whenever his wife and Stewart would attack "that horrible man in the White House," a reference to then-president Franklin Roosevelt.

As early as 1938, Henry joined a committee urging Roosevelt to cut trade ties to Nazi Germany. Frequently horrified during his motor trip through Germany with Frances, he had become convinced that Hitler was prepared to launch another World War.

Henry was a workaholic and Walter Wanger kept him going from one movie to the next, often without a break. At night, when Frances wanted to play and to party, he preferred to retire to his study after dinner to read scripts and memorize his lines for the following day. Many of his movies were rushed to completion as part of a shooting schedule of only fourteen weeks.

Constance Bennett at pierside in 1933 with the most stylish and newsworthy of her five husbands, **Henry, Le Marquis de la Falaise**, whom the American press quickly commandeered as "Hank."

He had a penchant for marrying demanding, "tarantula' divas: Prior to Bennett, he'd been (unhappily) married to Gloria Swanson.

He would often depart from the house before dawn, leaving her asleep in bed until 10AM. By the time he returned home at around 6 or 7PM, he was exhausted from a hard day at the studio. He not only had to consume a quick dinner and retire to learn his lines for tomorrow's shoot, but he was very low on energy. The idea of going out was more than his physicality could endure. Eventually, he began trying to arrange escorts to accompany her to night clubs and parties.

He wasn't a complete monk, however. At parties and at the studio, many women, secretaries and scriptwriters, flirted with him and made themselves available. On a few occasions, it would be his co-star herself who would invite him into her dressing room. [In those days, dressing rooms doubled as hideaways where adulterous affairs could transpire whenever its tenant wasn't needed on the set.]

Although Henry wasn't sure if Frances were having affairs with her escorts behind his back, he suspected that she might be, even though many of the young men who agreed to escort her—considering the circumstances—were gay.

At a party, Frances met Constance Bennett, who had recently dated Henry. They talked rather candidly about him.

"The first month of our marriage, I realized I'd married the wrong man," Frances said. "We live different lives with opposing interests. I like to booze, he doesn't. I desire more sex than he does. He wants to talk about scripts. I want to chat about stocks and bonds."

"Are you going to get an early divorce?" Constance asked. "Everybody's doing it. Let's face it: Tinseltown has some of the shortest marriages in America."

"I can't divorce him now," Frances said. "I already have one daughter from a previous marriage, and two days ago, I found out that I was pregnant again. I hope it's a boy."

***

Slim (1937)

Jane Fonda, years later, was quoted as telling a reporter that the movie *Slim* was her father's least-known picture.

Released in 1937, it was a drama about a telephone lineman, one of the "working men" movies that Warner Brothers was churning out at the time, many relaying tales of truck drivers and steel workers.

In this short-term loan-out from MGM to Warner Brothers, Henry would co-star with Pat O'Brien in a screen adaptation of a 1934 novel by William Wister Haines.

Produced by Hal B. Wallis and directed by Ray Enright, *Slim* was the story of an awkward farm boy who wants to desert his horse and plow to take on the dangerous job of a lineman dealing with high-voltage electricity.

In the story, an experienced electrician, Red Blayd (O'Brien), takes young Henry under his wing and teaches him how to scale a phone pole to restore electricity even during blizzards. Red's girlfriend is "Cally," cast with Margaret Lindsay, who takes a romantic interest in Slim.

Later, after Red dies while atop a pole whose wires have been tangled in a storm, Cally (Lindsay) is free to love him.

In *Slim*, **Henry Fonda**'s role called for an awkward, bashful, and underweight farm boy who suffers from unrequited love. By type casting, he was perfect.

Hard-drinking **Pat O'Brien** was his Irish counterpart, the other "reckless line man in love with the same girl," as pre-defined in the banner at the top of the movie poster displayed above.

"Love in the air" was poignant, but despite the high voltage publicity associated with this film, it wasn't electrifying.

Off screen, although both O'Brien and Henry found Lindsay an attractive actress, they surmised that as a lesbian, she was probably off-limits. *[Lindsay and Henry would soon be cast together once again in Jezebel (1938) starring Bette Davis.]*

O'Brien, who would amass a hundred screen credits, was called "Hollywood's Irishman in Residence." He often played cops, military figures, news reporters, pilots, and priests. His frequent co-star was James Cagney.

Two of O'Brien's best pictures were *Knute Rockne, All American* (1940) starring Ronald Reagan and, much later, *Some Like It Hot* (1959), which starred Marilyn Monroe in her best comic role.

[Later in life, when he was in his early 80s, O'Brien starred in a road show stage production of On Golden Pond *opposite his real-life wife, Eloise, appearing at dinner theaters in cities that included San Antonio and New Orleans. A few years before, Henry himself starred in the Oscar-winning film version of* On Golden Pond *(1981), alongside Katharine Hepburn and his daughter, Jane.]*

Even **Henry Fonda** realized that he was too thin (some said "skinny and emaciated") for the sexual preferences of some of his fans.

"But on the other hand," a film reviewer said, "As an American 'everyman' who was noted for his earnestness and sincerity, he wasn't so muscular that he threatened heterosexual men in his movie audiences, as might have been the case with Steve Reeves or Mickey Hargitay, each a spectacularly photogenic "Mr. Universe" title holder.

A heavy drinker, O'Brien, along with Spencer Tracy and Cagney, were part of a wild party crowd of men dubbed "The Irish Mafia." They met regularly, some of their drinking bouts lasting until the sun rose over Hollywood. On two different occasions, O'Brien invited Henry, even though he had no Irish blood.

Ray Enright had been designated as *Slim's* director. Over the course of his career (1927-1953), he helmed seventy-three movies starring such actors as Randolph Scott, Joan Blondell, and Joe E. Brown.

Enright cast Stuart Erwin into a minor role—that of "Stumpy"—in *Slim*.

At the time that he worked with Henry, Erwin had been nominated for a Best Supporting Actor Oscar for his role in *Pigskin Parade* (1936). That same year, he also co-starred with Cagney and O'Brien in *Calling Zero*. In time, Erwin would be reduced to replicating the voice of a tree squirrel in Walt Disney's *Bambi* (1942).

The small role of Stumpy's girlfriend went to Jane Wyman, then a contract starlet for Warners. "I may have gotten my dates wrong, but I heard Henry's wife was pregnant, and he was shopping around for a new sex partner," O'Brien said. "His roving eye fell on Jane, and on several occasions, I saw her visiting his dressing room, presumably for a quickie."

Wyman had divorced her first husband, Ernest Wyman, although she would retain his name for life. She had married Myron Futterman, a dress manufacturer, but the union lasted only three months. Her divorce from him would become final in 1938.

"I don't know this, but in my view, Henry was just using Wyman to get his rocks off," Enright said. "It was hardly a serious romance. Since he was married, he could not take her out in public."

In 1938, Wyman would co-star with Ronald Reagan in *Brother Rat,* and later with him again in *Brother Rat and Baby* (1940). Although they had many political disagreements, she would marry Reagan in 1940. At the time, she was a conservative Republican, and he was a liberal Democrat.

Wyman won a Best Actress Oscar for playing a deaf-mute rape victim in *Johnny Belinda* (1945).

When Ronald Reagan, her former husband, was elected 40th President (1981-89) of the United States, she became the first former wife of a President who was still alive when he assumed office.

In *Slim,* as a WPA daredevil pole climber, Henry gets to appear in hair-raising shots. One reviewer headlined his critique as *HENRY FONDA GOES ELECTRIC.*

Upon its release, the film created excitement at the box office. *Variety* suggested that it might generate a demand for Fonda and O'Brien as a screen team. It did not.

Years later, *The Motion Picture Guide* took a new look at *Slim,* finding that Henry "was perfect for the role because it embodied all the engaging sincerity needed to make the part of a naïve farm boy work.

***

Although Henry didn't really want to pursue it, Frances forged ahead and invited Margaret Sullavan and her husband, Leland Hayward, to dinner one Saturday night. All Henry's former wife and his agent had to do was walk half a block along a street in Brentwood to reach the Fonda home.

At the time, Hollywood insiders were buzzing with the cynical (but not unfounded) rumor that Sullavan had married the high-powered agent not for love, but to advance her career.

Months earlier, Sullavan had told Henry, "Although Katharine Hepburn is mostly *lez,* she still resents the fact that I stole Leland from her. She detests me. You ought to hear me do a mock imitation of her."

As Frances remembered, the "socially complicated" dinner for four went fairly smoothly. "There was no feeling that I had stolen Henry from Sullavan. She obviously didn't want him."

The talk was mostly about movies. At one point, each guest was asked to name his or her favorite actress. Sullavan cited Helen Hayes, Ina Claire, and Ruth Gordon. Not a movie buff, Frances said that she didn't have any one favorite. Hayward claimed he could not name his favorite out of fear of antagonizing one of his female clients. Then he took Sullavan's hand and gallantly said, "Actually, Maggie is my all-time favorite."

Finally, it was Henry's turn: He cited Bette Davis, Joan Crawford, and Barbara Stanwyck.

After her fourth drink, Sullavan referred to the rumor going around that Henry and James Stewart had been lovers during the time they roomed together.

"I know it's not true, but you guys certainly caused a lot of gossip," she said provocatively.

At that point, Hayward uttered a homophobic reaction and was quickly chastised by his wife: "If you were a homo, would you deny yourself love?" she asked. "I doubt it. So if the subject comes up again, keep your trap shut, if that's your only reaction."

She and Hayward quickly made up and were soon cuddling together on the sofa. "Leland is the only man I've ever loved, not Jed Harris," she said.

Frances could not help but glance at Henry's face. She found only that blank look he exhibited so often in his movie roles.

During the course of that dinner party, as the hour grew late, Johnny Swope, Henry's photographer friend, arrived from New York. Sullavan had known him, too, when he was part of the University Players on Cape Cod. She hugged and kissed him.

A former roommate of Henry and Stewart, Swope had planned, with Henry's cooperation, to stay for a few weeks in the Fonda's guest bedroom. He had dated

Since his death in 1979, historians have revised, for the better, their early interpretations of **Johnny Swope**, a photographer for *Life* magazine and a commercial pilot who trained Army Air Force pilots during World War II.

Here's the cover of a book celebrating Swope's work from 1936 to 1938, the peak years of his friendship within the inner circles of Henry Fonda and James Stewart.

One reviewer defined his phogtographs like this: "Swope photographs movie sets inside and out not from any useful angle, but with a theatrical sense of their usefulness."

Sullavan on the Cape, escorting her to a screening of *Mata Hari* (1931) with Greta Garbo, during one of their outings.

After the Haywards left and Frances had gone to bed, Swope and Henry had a catch-up session. For the first time, Swope admitted that he was in love with Sullavan and that he planned to get together in secret with her during his stay in Hollywood.

"When we come together, it's fireworks," he claimed. "I've got to keep Leland from finding out. Surely you're not jealous at this late date?"

"Maybe a bit, but not really," Henry said. "Actually, it gives me some delight to know that Leland, that smug bastard, is being compromised."

Sullavan phoned the next day to thank Frances for the dinner, promising that the two couples would get together more frequently.

Hayward was out of town on the occasion of Sullavan's next visit to the Fonda home, so Swope joined Henry and Frances in an attempt to entertain her. When their communal get-together ended, Swope departed alone with Sullavan and didn't return for three days and nights, forcing Henry to conclude that he had maneuvered his way into bed with Sullavan.

The next time she came over to the Fondas for yet another dinner, Swope was absent as he had had to fly to San Francisco. It was understood, at this point, that Hayward had still not returned from his business trip. Sullavan, in advance of her arrival at the Fondas, and with the understanding that Swope would not be there, asked Frances if she could bring "a friend" to dinner instead.

As it turned out, the mystery guest was Sullavan's *beau du jour*. Both Frances and Henry were surprised to see who her current lover was: Robert Taylor.

***

Three Comrades (1938)

The bisexual actor, Robert Taylor, had become a friend of "Hank and Jim" when they'd lived together as roommates in the house in Brentwood which Stewart still occupied. Henry, of course, had moved, favoring instead his new home in Pacific Palisades that he shared with his new wife, Frances.

Perhaps motivated by nostalgia, Stewart invited "Henry with his wife Frances" and "Sullavan with her acting colleague, Robert Taylor" back to the farmhouse-style dwelling in Brentwood for dinner. Sullavan's husband, Leland Hayward, it was revealed, was still in New York.

At the time, Taylor and Sullavan were shooting the final scenes of *Three Comrades* (1938), based on the novel by Erich Maria Remarque and a screenplay by F. Scott Fitzgerald. Their co-stars included Franchot Tone and Robert Young. The setting for the dark and gritty tale was Germany during the grim aftermath of World War I.

Taylor had been trying to live down rumors that he was a homosexual and his "Pretty Boy" reputation at MGM. He had tried to do so by dating some of his female co-stars such as Virginia Bruce in *Times Square Lady* (1935) and by sustaining a brief fling with Greta Garbo during their filming of *Camille* (1936).

This time, he was with Sullavan, Henry's former wife. What made the evening more complicated was that Stewart was also having a discreet affair with Sullavan. *[Their intimacies would continue into the future when*

Margaret Sullavan with **Robert Taylor** in a sociable scene from *Three Comrades*.

Their co-star, Robert Young, told reporters: "Taylor was perfectly capable as an actor, but he was so damn handsome that he, like Tyrone Power, looked almost feminine. He was what you might call a beautiful man. Not a handsome man, but a beautiful man."

The film version of **Three Comrades** began as a poignant testimonial to the allure of friendship and the power of love. Penned by Erich Maria Remarque, author of *All Quiet on the Western Front*, it morphed into a film released in 1938.

The senior co-author of this biography, **Darwin Porter**, shared after-theater drinks with Remarque one animated evening in 1961 in a sodden *soirée* that lasted till dawn.

Also present were Remarque's wife at the time, Paulette Goddard, their host, Tallulah Bankhead, and Tallulah's sometime mentor and muse, Stanley Mills Haggart.

99

they co-starred together in The Shopworn Angel *(1938), and later in* The Shop Around the Corner *(1940).]*

Because all three of the actors present had, at this point, seduced Sullavan, discussions about her—if they weren't avoided altogether—became awkward. Instead, talk centered mostly around their respective careers. Taylor discussed how the hairline of his "widow's peak" had become more pronounced.

"When I signed with MGM, I had a hairline that squared perfectly with my forehead. But Louis B. Mayer insisted that the makeup department "create" a widow's peak. Hair by hair was painstakingly pulled out from my forelock to create it, and it hurt like hell."

No mention was made that night of Sullavan's absent husband.

The evening ended with hugs and kisses, with promises to get together soon. That came later, when Taylor extended a party invitation to Henry and Stewart. Henry thought it might be wise to once again include Frances, but Taylor discouraged the idea, assuring him that that might happen "Some other time. This is a stag party."

MARRIAGE IN CLASSIC HOLLYWOOD
(AKA "HIGH HOPES")

Left photo: **Robert Taylor** during the course of his unhappy marriage to **Barbara Stanwick**

Right Photo: **Phillip Terry** during the course of his affair with Robert Taylor and his traumatic marriage to **Joan Crawford.**

***

When Henry and Stewart arrived at Taylor's home for the party he'd invited them to, they found him living with a very handsome aspiring actor, Phillip Terry. One author later described him as "an Anglicized, muscle-bound, six-foot-three-inch, 180-pound slab of beefcake."

Formerly, Terry had been both a football player and a worker in the oilfields of Texas.

Some students of Hollywood wondered how Taylor had met him. If a moviegoer lingered at the popcorn stand as the movie began, he would have missed Terry, who appears briefly in the opening scene of *Three Comrades*.

In 1943, he was assigned a more substantial role in *Bataan*, a wartime movie that also starred Taylor.

After her divorce from Franchot Tone, Joan Crawford married Terry, morphing him into her servant boy and publicly referring to him as "my caddy."

The affair between Terry and Robert Taylor spilled over into the dynamic of Taylor's marriage to Barbara Stanwyck. One day, when his wife picked up the phone and realized that Terry was on the other end, she called out, "Bob, your husband wants to speak to you."

***

Whereas Henry's two-month marriage to Margaret Sullavan never produced any children (as she later complained, "Henry didn't even know how to kiss"), her marriage to Leland Hayward stood in fertile contrast. As Henry sarcastically asserted, years later, perhaps with a tinge of bitterness, "Hayward was a virtual sperm factory."

Hayward and Sullavan's oldest daughter, Brooke, was born in 1937, the same year Frances and Henry celebrated the arrival of their daughter, Jane Fonda. Sullavan would have two more children with Hayward—Bridget, born in 1939, and Billy, born in 1941.

In 1977, when she was forty, Brooke Hayward would write a controversial autobiography, *Haywire*, documenting her traumatic childhood and adolescence with her suicide-prone mother and siblings.

In it, she referred to Leland Hayward, her father, as "the Toscanini of the

FROM AGONY EMERGES ART

This was certainly true in the case of Brooke Hayward's autobiography.

Its front cover artwork shows the "dream team" of **Leland Hayward** and **Margaret Sullavan** emoting together during a rare moment of marital happiness.

Telephone," making deals day and night for clients who included Greta Garbo, Ernest Hemingway, Judy Garland, Billy Wilder, Gregory Peck, Boris Karloff, and Fred Astaire.

In print, she referred to her mother as "a true star of Broadway and Hollywood, a superb actress, a spell-casting charmer, beautiful, and spirited."

When both of them were five, Brooke and Jane Fonda often played together at the Hayward home. Henry would on occasion drop in to "pick up Jane in the sandbox and take her home."

***

The Virginian (1937), Henry's Brief Return to Summer Stock Theater

Although his film career was on the rise, Henry still harbored powerful ambitions as a stage actor. When a break came in filming, he headed East for stage work, in spite of objections from his agent, Leland Hayward.

Back at the Westchester Playhouse in Mount Kisco, Henry accepted a major role (the male lead)   in a summer stock production of *The Virginian*. Based on a novel by Bowan Wister (1860-1938), the story had first been presented on Broadway in 1904. Two silent film adaptations had also been made, the first by Cecil B. De Mille in 1914 and later, in 1923, a version starring Kenneth Harlan and Florence Vidor.

Filmed again in 1929, this Pre-Code Western, directed by Victor Fleming, became Gary Cooper's breakthrough role. Coop's co-star was Walter Huston.

The Virginian was produced yet again in 1946 in a film starring Joel McCrea and Brian Donlevy.

Its plot focuses on a cowboy on a cattle ranch in northern Wyoming. Between sessions of tending the herd, he identifies and hangs a rustler; kills a notorious bad guy, and finally marries a school teacher who has come to Wyoming from the East.

"I should have followed Leland's advice," Henry recalled. In Mount Kisco, the actors were housed at the Kettle Inn, which was attached to a stable. Before he went on stage that night, the production's press agent instructed that everyone in the cast put on their cowboy costumes for a communal photograph.

"I was no Roy Rogers, much less Tom Mix," Henry said. "Horses and I were never buddy-buddy. After the press photographs were taken, we went for a ride."

On the way back to the stable, Henry was leading the pack along a country road in Westchester County, heading for the stable. Two cars suddenly approached them, fast. Henry's horse panicked and jumped over a station wagon, slamming into the sedan behind it. Henry was thrown ten feet, landing on his hand and breaking his wrist. That night, he went on stage in agonizing pain and with his wrist in bandages.

He was later sued by the owner of the sedan, settling the claim for $3,000.

On stage, his leading lady was Margaret Tallichet, with supporting players Henry Morgan and Dan Duryea.

[Coincidentally, Tallichet would later marry William Wyler months after he directed Jezebel with Henry and Bette Davis.

As Wyler later told Henry, "La Davis took too long to make up her mind about marrying me, so I ran off and fell into the arms of my 'Talli.'" (Talli was his nickname for Tallichet, his actress wife. Together, they produced five children and a 43-year marriage that lasted until his death.)]

Morgan would go on to make 100 movies but would be best known for his TV role of Col. Potter in M*A*S*H* (1975-1983).

Henry bonded and became friends with Dan Duryea, and they would sometimes go out drinking together. "I looked at myself in the mirror and knew I would never be a romantic leading man," Duryea said. "Not with my ugly puss and 155-pound weakling frame."

He would later decide to become "the meanest S.O.B. in the movies, learning to slap women around. In their future, both Henry and Duryea would co-star with Bette Davis. Duryea would star opposite Gary Cooper in a trio of movies and also make three with James Stewart.

The New York Times dubbed Duryea "a heel with sex appeal."

***

Blow Ye Winds (1937), A Broadway Play

September of 1937 found Henry back on Broadway starring in *Blow Ye Winds* at the 46th Street Theatre. His leading lady was Doris Dalton, an actress whose career was going nowhere. The comedy written by Valentine Davies closed after only 35 performances.

In the plot, Henry, as Hayden Chase, falls for Christine Lawrence (Dalton), a brilliant scientist. Together, they have to find their way in New York. Brooks Atkinson of *The New York Times* suggested that Henry "is not the chap to pick a placid script out of the doldrums."

When *Blow Ye Winds* opened, it had to compete with an array of other hit shows, notably *The Women* by Clare Boothe Luce, and *You Can't Take It With You*, the classic comedy by Moss Hart and George S. Kaufman. James Stewart, on film, would turn it into one of his most famous roles.

At the end of the play, a call from Hollywood came in for Henry. It was Leland Hayward on the phone, ordering him to come back right away. "Bette Davis wants you to be the leading man in her next film, *That Certain Woman*. You're due to report to the set on Monday."

***

That Certain Woman (1937)

Hal B. Wallis wanted audiences to see Bette Davis in a very different role than "the alleycat bitch" she'd played in *Of Human Bondage* (1934).

His director, Edmund Goulding, suggested they do a remake of *The Trespasser*, which had starred Gloria Swanson in her first talkie (1929). It had been produced by Joseph Kennedy, who was having a torrid affair with its leading lady at the time.

Having purchased the screen rights to *The Trespasser* (1929) from Swanson for $20,000, Goulding set about transforming the soap opera-ish story, eight years after its original release, into a new screenplay entitled *That Certain Woman.*

In one of their first conversations, Davis told Goulding that the one actor perfect for its male lead was Henry Fonda. She relayed to him the story of how, at the age of seventeen, he had given her her first real kiss in the rear of a Packard convertible. The year had been 1925. The next day, she had announced their engagement.

That Certain Woman was one of the lesser efforts of **Bette Davis** and **Henry Fonda**, who had first met and kissed in the mid-1920s. She decided that a "nice, juicy, hell-raising flirtation" with Fonda was in order. But that would mainly occur when she was cast with him in *Jezebel*, a year later.

"I'm not sure why," Henry said. "There was talk of my being a budding Casanova. Actually, all I did was give her a peck on the cheek."

When he had first arrived in Hollywood, then-neophyte Henry had first met Goulding at a party at the home of director George Cukor. Before the night was over, Goulding had propositioned the new man in town. Later, seeing him again, Goulding said, "Maybe during this shoot, I'll get lucky."

"And maybe you won't," Henry responded.

Goulding, a British screenwriter and director, would play a key role in the career of Bette Davis, forging between them a love-hate relationship. He would later direct her in two of her greatest box office successes: *Dark Victory* and *The Old Maid,* each released in 1939.

Like George Cukor, Goulding had a reputation as "a director of women's pictures," beginning with the release of *Grand Hotel* (1932), starring, among others, Greta Garbo, Joan Crawford, and John Barrymore.

Its costume designer was Orry-Kelly. During Cary Grant's early days in New York, he had been the "kept boy" of that then-famous fashion designer. "When he fits my trousers, he spends a hell of a lot of time fondling my crotch, taking the most intimate measurements there," Henry complained to Goulding.

STEEL MAGNOLIAS

Anita Louise with **Bette Davis** in *That Certain Woman* (1937)

Davis complained to her co-star, "This damn picture is a grab-bag of the most reprehensible romantic *clichés* I've encountered in any film so far."

"Orry is entitled to a little fun," the director had answered. "Otherwise, life would be so dull."

As Mary Donnell, Davis played the wife of a former bootlegger killed during the St. Valentine's Day massacre. She then takes a job as the personal secretary to Lloyd Rogers (Ian Hunter). A married man, he secretly falls in love with her. As the plot unfolds, it becomes apparent that she's actually in love with Jack Merrick Jr., the playboy son of the firm's richest client. The role of the senior Merrick was cast with Donald Crisp, who disapproves of his son's marriage and has it annulled.

Weeks later, Mary discovers that she is pregnant, but decides not to tell Jack. He goes on to marry socialite "Flip" Carson (Anita Louise). It is revealed that Carson was disabled, the result of a crippling car accident, during the course of their honeymoon.

Lloyd dies several years later in Mary's apartment, leaving her the bulk of his estate.

Her true love, Jack, eventually shows up and offers to adopt Mary's son, without knowing it is his own boy. He soon discovers he is the boy's father, which leads to his own father trying to take the child away from Mary, labeling her as an unfit mother.

Mary finally turns over her child to Jack and the crippled Flip. Mary then leaves America and wanders through Europe.

She hears of Flip's premature death, after which Jack tracks Mary down for a reunion and happy ending.

At this point in his directorial career, Goulding had developed his own special way of directing an actor, often acting out the scene for him or her. In a kissing scene between Henry and Bette Davis, he didn't like the way the actress was responding. He asked her to get up, and he sat down as her "replacement," reaching for Henry and hugging him tightly. The director's kiss on Henry's lips went on and on, leaving Henry red-faced, sweaty, and uncomfortable. He later told Davis, "I have never, in all my life, been kissed this passionately."

"Love scenes were difficult for me to perform on camera," Henry claimed. "I was never a great lover in my films. Nor was I in private life either. I'll leave that reputation for Errol Flynn. I made two good friends. Tyrone Power and Robert Taylor, who were called pretty boys in the 1930s. What millions of their women fans didn't know was that each of them were bisexuals. Chances are they were having sex with each other, but they also seduced a lot of beautiful women, as did my close friend, James Stewart. I could not match the records of those horndogs."

Davis later admitted that *That Certain Woman* was hardly her favorite script, but she had great admiration for its director "For the first time, I got star treatment."

Davis still had her keen eye focused on Henry as a possible conquest, and she flirted somewhat outrageously with him. One afternoon, when neither of them was needed on the set, he somewhat reluctantly agreed to visit her dressing room for a private rendezvous.

It didn't go well.

"Fonda was a premature ejaculator, like my first husband, Ham," Davis confided one day to Joan Blondell. *[The husband she was referring to was Harmon Oscar Nelson.]* "I was able to train him, but I'm too busy to take on another pupil like Fonda. Nonetheless, I'll remember his seduction of me as the easiest thirty seconds I've ever spent with any man."

Henry was far more attracted to Anita Louise, who played Flip, the beautiful woman his character marries and then cripples in an automobile accident. From the beginning he was smitten with her, especially her delicate features and blonde hair. Louise was noted for what one critic called her "ageless grace."

She had yet to marry producer Buddy Rich, so she was available on the dating market, and he took advantage of it. His wife, Frances, was pregnant at the time, and as he had clearly stated to multiple sources, he disliked sex with pregnant women.

When Henry met her, Louise had already been cast in the upcoming *The Sisters* (1938), co-starring Bette Davis with Errol Flynn, whom she loathed.

Louise was known for hosting lavish parties, and an invitation went out to Henry for a gathering of the Hollywood elite scheduled at her home for the upcoming Saturday night. Before the party broke up, she asked Henry to stay over for the weekend, and he gladly accepted.

"She and I had a wonderful time together," he recalled to Goulding. "She may sound and look like a lady, but once you get her panties off, she's a regular wildcat."

Their affair lasted until the end of *That Certain Woman's* filming.

In the role of "the other man," Ian Hunter had been born in Cape Town, South Africa, when it was a British colony. At the age of 17, he had fought with British forces during World War I. By 1924, he was starring in British films. Later, director Alfred Hitchcock gave a big boost to Hunter's film career.

The year of 1929, as the films learned to talk, found Hunter in Hollywood, starring for RKO in *Syncopation* for his first sound film. By 1935, he was making *The Girl from 10th Avenue* with Bette Davis. He became known to audiences when he co-starred with "clothes hound" Kay Francis in seven films from 1935 to 1938.

Cast as Merrick Sr., Donald Crisp would go on to win a Best Supporting Actor Oscar for *How Green Was My Valley* (1941). Actually, he'd been working in films since the days of the silents, cast by D.W. Griffith as General Ulysses S. Grant in the controversial *Birth of a Nation* (1915). He'd go on to star with Henry and Davis in *Jezebel*, and would appear with the actress yet again in *The Old Maid* with Miriam Hopkins. He rated that as his favorite Davis picture, ranking *That Certain Woman* as the worst.

Publicists set about marketing the Davis/Fonda collaboration, falsely and outrageously defining it as *AMERICA'S GREATEST ACTRESS IN THE GREATEST ROLE OF HER CAREER*. Subheads blared, "I Wouldn't Remarry

My Baby's Father," and "I Kissed You Goodbye on Our Wedding Night."

"*That Certain Woman* sinks into a morass of suds, syrup, and sacrifice," wrote Matthew Kennedy.

The New York Times was the most optimistic, claiming that "tragic heroines like Kay Francis are invited to move over to make room in their potential niche for Miss Bette Davis."

England's *Film Weekly* found that the movie was a "waste of Bette Davis' talent and will do nothing to further her career."

Frank Nugent of *The New York Times* claimed: "The lanky Mr. Fonda is his usual self."

In *The Films of Henry Fonda*, Tony Thomas wrote: "Henry Fonda often claimed he could barely remember some of his early films. In the case of *That Certain Woman*, he could be forgiven for claiming he never appeared in it."

In spite of critical assaults, producer Hal B. Wallis liked Henry and Davis so much in *That Certain Woman* that he ordered both of them to be cast in one of his major films, that upcoming ode to Southern love, obsession, heroism, and drama, *Jezebel*.

***

I Met My Love Again (1938)

To launch his 1938 movie career, Henry's producer, Walter Wanger, phoned him to tell him that he had cast him in a romantic drama, *I Met My Love Again*. He had talked about its plot for only three minutes before Henry realized it was "yet another woman's picture."

His co-star would be Joan Bennett. As Wanger explained it, Henry was about the only actor he could trust to appear opposite Bennett. Wanger was very jealous of her since he was falling in love. "I believe you won't slip into Joan's dressing room. Not like those poontang hounds Jimmy Stewart and Gary Cooper."

Henry had once dated Joan's older sister, Constance Bennett. The first time he met Joan, he realized that her striking beauty, sultry eyes, and husky voice would steal the picture from him.

The screenplay was based on *Summer Lightning*, a novel by Allene Corliss.

The role of Ives Towner, a rather dull academic, went to Henry. While a professor at a small-town college in Vermont in 1927, he falls quickly in love with Julia Weir Shaw (Bennett).

But one snowy night, Julia gets lost in a storm and is stranded until she finds a refuge in a small cottage owned by Michael Shaw (Alan Marshal), a pulp fiction writer.

He seduces and soon marries her, taking her to live with him in Paris, where they produce a daughter.

He becomes an alcoholic and a decade later is killed in a brawl.

Julie returns to that Vermont town where the still-unmarried Ives is being pursued by a local beauty, Brenda Lane (Louise Platt).

The battle is on as regards which woman will win Ives.

Three different directors would be called in to helm the picture—Arthur Ripley, Joshua Logan, and the uncredited George Cukor. Ripley emerged as the major director.

Joining Mack Sennett in 1923, Ripley had originally written comedies with Frank Capra. He later directed short films starring such actors as W.C. Fields and Edgar Kennedy. He later joined Academia, helping to establish the Film Center at U.C.L.A. Robert Mitchum asked Ripley to direct his movie, *Thunder Road* (1958).

Logan and Henry bonded, pouring out their frustrations over the way their Hollywood careers seemed to be going downhill. Logan was humiliated when Cukor was brought in to refilm some of the scenes with Henry and Joan Bennett that he had helmed.

Logan eventually returned to Broadway, where he became a huge success, later directing and co-writing *South Pacific* (1949) and winning the Pulitzer Prize. In time, he would go back to Hollywood to turn out such hits as *Picnic* (1955) with William Holden or *Bus Stop* (1956) with Marilyn Monroe.

Cukor invited two of the actors he was directing, Henry and Joan Bennett, to lunch. He had known Henry since he'd invited him to a gay party at his home when the then-unknown newcomer had first arrived in Hollywood.

[*Later, when Cukor—during its early stages—was directing Gone With the Wind, he*

Henry Fonda with an uncharacteristically blonde **Joan Bennett** in *I Met My Love Again*. *(1938)*.

He agreed with David Niven's assessment of his leading lady: "Joan seems to be the quintessence of a movie star. Everything about her shone—her burnished head. Her jewels. Her famous smile. Her lovely long legs. And the highly publicized fact that she pulled in $30,000 a week."

104

would select Bennett as one of the four finalists in the race for the role of Scarlett O'Hara. Her competitors would include Paulette Goddard, Jean Arthur, and ultimately, Vivien Leigh.]

In the 1940s, Joan Bennett was on the dawn of her greatest fame. She had gone from a winsome blonde *ingénue* in the 1930s to a sultry brunette *film noir* goddess in the 1940s.

Bennett had begun an affair with Wanger around the time that her divorce from the producer, screenwriter, and highly decorated Naval officer Gene Markey was coming through.

[Markey was and had been a puzzle to Hollywood. Famous for marrying beautiful and famous actresses, he would not only "bag" Joan Bennett, but would go on to marry (1939-1941) Hedy Lamarr, hailed as the most beautiful woman in the world. After the war, he married (1946-1950) Myrna Loy, and after that (1954 until his death in 1980), Louise Wright, the philanthropist and horsebreeding/racehorse guru behind Calumet Farms, four-time winner, during her stewardship, of the Kentucky Derby.]

"What has the guy got?" Henry asked. "He looks so ordinary, like an average Joe."

When not servicing these beautiful actresses, Markey spent a lot of time with his good buddy, John Wayne.

Louise Platt grew up in Annapolis, Maryland, the daughter of a dental surgeon in the Navy. She broke into summer stock "from Maine to Virginia to Minnesota."

Today, she is best remembered for playing an officer's pregnant wife in John Ford's *Stagecoach* in 1939, starring John Wayne.

That was the year she married producer Jed Harris, who had broken up Henry's marriage to Margaret Sullavan. After suffering through months of physical abuse, she would divorce him in 1941. After her latest picture with Henry, she would also star with him in his upcoming picture, *Spawn of the North*.

Born in Australia, the rather handsome Alan Marshal, who was Henry's on-screen competition for the love of Julia, appeared on Broadway in *The Swan* (1924) at the age of 15. In time, David O. Selznick would spot him and bring him to Hollywood.

Right before working with Henry, he had made *The Garden of Allah* (1936) with Marlene Dietrich and Charles Boyer.

He'd also appeared in *After the Thin Man* (1936) that had starred William Powell and Myrna Loy. Henry's friend, James Stewart, had the role of the killer in that movie.

Marshall had just finished starring in *Conquest* with Greta Garbo and Charles Boyer. The actor was destined to have a short life. He was found dead in his hotel room at the age of 52. He'd been in Chicago starring with Mae West in her play, *Sextette*.

A daughter of Liverpool, Dame May Whitty played "Aunt William," a name, of course, usually reserved for males. She was the first of two women to be awarded the title of "Dame" in England.

After a successful career there, she gravitated to Hollywood at the age of 72.

One of her best-known films was *Night Must Fall* (1937) with Robert Montgomery. For that role, she had received a Best Supporting Actress Academy Award nomination. Another classic in which she starred was the Alfred Hitchcock thriller, *The Lady Vanishes* (1938).

Variety claimed, "This yarn of love finding its way after a decade's delay will have to find its favor with the *femmes*. It lacks just about all they requisites for the trouser-wearing slice of film fandom. Fonda's character at all times isn't sympathetic."

Frank Nugent of *The New York Times* was never impressed with Henry's "Indian-like façade." In his review, he wrote, "I didn't know whether to hope for his return to Miss Bennett or to encourage him to accept the frank offers of Louise Platt."

I Met My Love Again did not make a profit and lost $65,000.

***

[Henry was among the most shocked in Hollywood when news came over the radio. On December 13, 1951, Walter Wanger had shot the agent, Jennings Lang, when he caught him in a car with his wife, Joan Bennett. One bullet hit his thigh, the other "the family jewels." He was rushed to the hospital for emergency treatment of his groin.

Wanger would have to serve a four-month prison term for attempted murder. Bennett would divorce him in 1965.

The incident, broadcast across the nation, ended up putting Joan Bennett's once-flourishing career on hold. In essence, she was blacklisted, later saying, "It was as if I pulled the trigger myself."]

***

Jezebel (1938)

Based on a play by Owen Davis Sr., *Jezebel* was a Warner Brothers release in 1938. Produced by Hal B. Wallis, its direction was, after many detours, awarded to William Wyler and starred Bette Davis and Henry Fonda in the lead roles.

Davis had gone to see *Jezebel* on Broadway. It had starred Miriam Hopkins. Davis later called Hopkins "a total bitch, impossible to get along with."

Back in Hollywood, Davis urged Jack Warner to acquire the film rights. At first, he balked, claiming "There is no one to root for in this play."

On Broadway, the play had flopped, but because of the massive sale of the book, *Gone With the Wind,* Jack Warner decided that he, too, wanted his studio to make a movie about a flirtatious Southern belle "up to no good."

As it turned out, Hopkins owned part of the film rights. Warners paid her $12,000 for her share, with the promise that it would cast her in the lead. Since that provision had not been written into the bill of sale, Warner phoned her later to tell her that he'd cast her arch enemy, Bette Davis, instead. "Tough luck, kid," he told the enraged actress.

Edmund Goulding, who had helmed Henry and Davis in *That Certain Woman,* was *Jezebel's* original director. In a letter to Warners, he wrote, "Julie is a Southern bitch, and Pres [*a.k.a. "Preston," the male lead eventually portrayed by Henry*] is prissy. A rewrite is needed for these leads. The picture is nothing but the triumph of bitchery."

The day he received Goulding's letter, Jack Warner fired him and hired Michael Curtiz to replace him. Curtiz himself then abandoned the project a few days later. He said, "I'd rather direct Errol Flynn in *The Adventures of Robin Hood."*

As noted above, Wyler was ultimately selected as its director.

As the male lead, Wyler and Warner had originally wanted Franchot Tone, who had married Joan Crawford in 1935. Crawford, however, was aware of Tone's previous affair with Davis back when they'd co-starred together in *Dangerous* (1935) and refused to allow her new husband to accept the role.

Within a week, Wyler, with the approval of Jack Warner (who had from the beginning wanted Bette Davis as Julie Morrison) cast the other leads: Henry Fonda as Pres Dillard; George Brent as Buck Cantrell; and Margaret Lindsay as Amy Bradford.

Wyler had known Davis for a long time. In 1931, when she had auditioned for him for a role, he had rudely dismissed her as a "hopeless little wren," and since then, he'd seen at least three of her previous films. By now, he was fully aware that somehow he'd have to restrain her, suppressing some of her exaggerated mannerisms and overacting. "Even in some mild scenes with her requiring control, she often became hysterical, although her leading man had done no more than pass the salt," he said.

Early in the shoot, Wyler told Davis, "In this picture, I want you to change from a Southern Belle bitch to a self-sacrificing Angel of Mercy." Later, in a moment of exasperation, he warned her, "If you don't stop moving your head so wildly, I'll put a chain on it."

During the first week of filming, Davis argued with Wyler over his direction. But by the second week, they had become lovers. The first evidence of their affair was revealed to Henry when they arrived, as a couple, an hour late to screen the first rushes of *Jezebel.*

"When Wyler entered the room, Bette was with him," Henry said. "There were traces of lipstick over his mouth, which he had not bothered to wife off."

When the film's producer, Hal B. Wallis, heard of the affair, he said, "I hope all this screwing doesn't lead to overtime and run-up costs."

William Wyler had been born in Alsace-Lorraine, then part of the German Empire. In time, he would become one of the most successful directors in Hollywood. As one critic phrased it, "After he directed *Dodsworth* in 1936, starring Walter Huston, he entered a sparkling two-decade career of almost unbroken greatness."

After *Jezebel,* he scored one hit after another, pictures such as *Wuthering Heights* (1939) starring Laurence Olivier.

After World War II, he turned out such classics as *The Best Years*

Jezebel was the film that entrenched **Bette Davis'** affinity for roles portraying ruthless, reckless, and emotionally cruel vixens with streaks of barely suppressed hysteria.

The movie-going public loved it.

Off-screen, perhaps taking her cue from Margaret Sullavan, **Bette Davis** began treating the real-lfe **Henry Fonda** the way her character in *Jezebel* had treated Henry's character, Pres: Cavalierly, provocatively, and indifferently.

of Our Lives (1946) and later, a "wide screen" remake of Ben-Hur (1959) starring Charlton Heston. Wyler went on to create star vehicles for Gary Cooper, Audrey Hepburn, Gregory Peck, and Barbra Streisand.

Wyler (who had married Margaret Sullavan after her divorce from Henry) sometimes appeared jealous of Henry and critical of his acting, demanding one retake after another before, often rejecting his later takes and often using the first one.

Almost everything about both Henry and Davis had changed since 1925 when they'd each been part of a double date on Cape Cod. He had been twenty and she was seventeen.

He had fled from the scene, but he encountered her once again, much later, when she was an usher at the Cape Playhouse in Dennis, Massachusetts. She still harbored a crush on him, but he managed to elude her bed again.

Davis' seduction of Henry finally occurred while they were filming *That Certain Woman*, but she had found him an unsatisfactory lover. Coming together with Henry again, this time in *Jezebel*, Davis set out to seduce him, even though she was not particularly attracted to him. She had an-

Naughty **Bette Davis** (aka Julie Marston), cheekily wearing scarlet, shocking her neighbors, and toying with the grace and chivalry of the man **(Henry Fonda)** she loves, in this keynote *("I Could Have Danced All Night but They Wouldn't Let Me")* scene from *Jezebel* (1939).

other motive: She wanted to make Wyler jealous. On occasion, she summoned Henry to her dressing room for seduction, and made certain that Wyler became aware of that.

These revelations came from her former suitor, George Brent, one of her most consistent on-screen, off-screen lovers in such movies as *Special Agent* (1935) and *The Golden Arrow* (1936).

Henry began an affair with Davis on nights when Wyler was not otherwise occupied with his star. "I don't think Bette was all that hot for Henry, the way she had been with me on a few of the pictures we did together," Brent said. "She was just using Henry to get back at Wyler, whenever she felt he had neglected her for too long."

Brent, a handsome, Ireland-born actor, is known today for having made eleven pictures with Davis, most notably *Dark Victory* (1939) in which her character is going blind. She developed a crush on him in the wake of his divorce from Ruth Chatterton.

"In several films, Bette declared her love for me," Brent recalled years later during his retirement. "I had sex with that wildcat, but it was not filled with any great passion on my part."

In 1937, shortly before they re-teamed for *Jezebel*, Brent married Constance Worth, divorcing her a few months later.

Brent quickly realized that as regards Davis on the set of *Jezebel*, Wyler and Henry had replaced him. Actually, his desirability as a romantic leading man had weakened, and he found himself in the third lead. He had wanted the role Henry had been assigned.

Against her wishes, Davis was reunited on the set of *Jezebel* with Margaret Lindsay, an actress she despised. Her most recent work with Lindsay had been in *Dangerous*, where Lindsay had played the third lead.

She was aware by this time that Lindsay was sexually attracted to women.

Davis told Henry, "I'll eat up the scenery in any scene I have with this lez. Her part in *Jezebel* is namby-pamby so that won't be hard to do. She's not right for the role, but she's under contract. Since she's getting paid every week, Jack Warner has to keep her busy."

Richard Cromwell, cast as Pres's younger brother, Ted Dillard, was one of the first actors Henry had met when he first arrived in Hollywood and was invited to one of George Cukor's gay parties.

By the time he joined the cast of *Jezebel*, Cromwell had already made his best-known picture, *The Lives of a Bengal Lancer* (1935), starring Gary Cooper and Franchot Tone. Gos-

BELLES IN CRINOLINE WITH GRIT

Margaret Lindsay (left) plays a demure but straightforward Northern beauty.

Bette Davis as the arrogant, tempestuous Jezebel is a Southern belle who doesn't stumble into deadly trouble— she causes it.

Davis herself was a person of assorted perversities and rebellious quirks. Off screen, she pitted her lovers, director William Wyler and her co-star, Henry Fonda, against each other

Jezebel—pre-dating the poignant and epic sweep of *Gone With the Wind* (1939) by more than a year—left audiences of 1938 wondering how David O. Selznik would match (or surpass) it.

107

sip spread at the time that Cromwell had offered to "service" each of the two leading men. Henry and Cromwell would reteam to make another movie, *Young Mr. Lincoln* for release in 1939.

Jezebel's most sympathetic role was essayed by Fay Bainter portraying Aunt Belle Massey. She delivered the line that justified the film's title: "I'm thinking about a woman called Jezebel, who did wrong in the sight of God."

Davis was horrified to learn that Bainter was drawing the same salary that she was: $2,000 a week.

Also in supporting roles is a strong list of talented and at the time well-known actors who included Spring Byington. As Mrs. Kendrick, she added her usual charm, and Donald Crisp, who portrayed Dr. Livingstone. Also in the cast was John Litel as Jean LeCour.

Davis told Henry that *Jezebel* was her consolation prize for not getting the role of Scarlett O'Hara in *Gone With the Wind*. She could have had the part, but foolishly lost it when she refused to co-star with Errol Flynn as Rhett Butler. "I would not budge from my decision," Davis claimed. "I'd agreed to take the role only if Rhett was cast with Gary Cooper or Clark Gable."

Fay Bainter (center) used her 1938 Oscar win with *Jezebel* to compete for other high-visibility, supporting roles in her near future.

Above, once again portraying a kind-hearted but ferociously protective matriarch, she appears wtih **Mickey Rooney** and **Judy Garland** in *Babes On Broadway* (1941).

The producer withdrew his offer from Davis.

Many critics later noted the similarities of the characters of Scarlett O'Hara and Julie Morrison.

Jezebel is set in the (supposedly) halcyon days of 1852 in New Orleans, an idealized re-creation of the antebellum South of plantation houses with huge pillars, near Spanish moss hanging from nearby trees.

The script called for what the writer called "pickaninnies" rushing after just-arrived carriages carrying elegantly dressed men and women in those days of slavery. Young children yell, *"Carriage comin'!, carriage comin'."*

Julie Marston (Davis) is a self-centered Southern beauty intent on having her own way, especially when it came to men. A haughty, arrogant daughter of plantation aristocracy, this willful, egocentric, woman is engaged to banker Preston ("Pres") Dillard, the role acted by Henry. As the second male lead, George Brent as Buck Cantrell also has his eye trained on Julie. His character is described as a "horse-and-hounds aristocrat."

The pivotal scene in *Jezebel* occurs when Julie defiantly wears a scarlet gown to the Olympus Ball, the highlight of New Orleans' social season. All of the other young women—unmarried, that is—are attired in virginal white. The scene just screams for Technicolor, but the film was formatted in black and white. To photograph properly, Davis' gown was crafted from rust-colored fabric.

Pres is outraged, and Julie, too, becomes embarrassed at her own behavior. To punish her for her outrageous flaunting of precedent, he insists that she waltz with him, alone on the dance floor, in full view of the deeply offended guests, who have gathered on the sidelines in disapproving silence to watch this arrogant, headstrong display.

Julie's entrance in that shocking gown was described as "part peacock, part vulture." In contrast, throughout every measure of the waltz they dance together, Henry, as Pres, rigorously maintains his poker-faced ferocity.

Pres then abandons both Julie and the dance floor, migrating north to Philadelphia, where he remains for the next three years.

The film's beguiling musical score was by Max Steiner before the fame that would come to him after he scored the music to *Gone With the Wind*.

The ball episode of *Jezebel* gobbled up fifteen minutes of screen time. By anyone's estimate, it's the highlight of the film.

As part of further social embarrassment that mortifies everyone there (including many members of the audience), Julie asserts to everyone there that Pres has dishonored her, and she turns her attention to Buck.

This outrages Pres's young brother, Ted Dillard (Richard Cromwell). He challenges Buck to a duel in the early dawn outside New Orleans. Ted shoots and kills foolish, arrogant Julie's other suitor.

Julie's competition for Pres is Amy Bradford (Lindsay), a demure Northern woman Pres brings back with him to the South. This arouses the jealous fury of Julie, who confronts him. "Marriage is it? To that washed-up little Yankee thing?"

In 1853, New Orleans was in the deadly grip of a yellow fever epidemic. It killed 8,000 residents. To prevent the spread of the disease, victims were hauled away, usually in overburdened horse-drawn carts, to Lazarette Island, the last refuge of the dying.

Pres comes down with the yellow fever and must be carted off to quarantine with other victims. Perhaps to amend for her miserable previous behavior, Julie announces that she will go with him to care for him. After a lot of persuasion—with Davis reaching new heights of repressed hysteria—Julie persuades Amy to stand back and let her (Julie) accompany him (Pres) to the "death camp." Will she survive? Will Pres?

At the end of the film, in a grim horse-drawn procession resembling a funeral *cortège*, Julie heads off in Pyrrhic triumph, perhaps never to return.

The Davis/Wyler affair had continued throughout the course of *Jezebel*'s filming, with the real-life Henry providing merely a minor diversion for her. The rendezvous point for Davis and her director was a rented hideaway that Wyler maintained not far from the studio.

They often dined there at night before going to bed. One of Wyler's assistants came by most evenings to prepare their dinner.

"We made mad, passionate love throughout the night," Davis later confessed. "But on the set the next morning, he would attack me, demanding retakes. He came down even harder on Henry."

Henry sometimes fought back, accusing Wyler of making a film "with the pace of a snail."

In the end, Davis concluded that Wyler was "a homely, handsome dynamo. With him, I met my match. He was the only man who ever tamed me."

Somehow, word of Davis' affair with Henry reached Frances Fonda in New York. She obtained the number of Davis's private home and called her after midnight one Sunday night.

On the other end of the wire, Davis heard the screaming voice of Henry's enraged wife, who violently denounced her as "a brazen hussy," "slut," "bitch," and "cunt."

"I know exactly what you're doing with my husband!," Frances shouted into the phone. "If you don't stop, I'll go to the press. You'll be disgraced. Such a scandal will certainly hurt Henry, but it will also destroy your career. If you don't let him alone, I'll get on the next plane to Los Angeles, where I'll scratch out your bug eyes."

Regardless of whether or not he had finished shooting all his scenes, Henry, according to the terms of his contract, had arranged to fly to New York on December 17 to await the imminent birth of his child.

Having left the set of *Jezebel* before the end of shooting, Henry, at the airport, told a reporter, "I will never again make a picture with Bette Davis."

In New York, his wife would soon give birth to a baby girl. Later, as Jane Fonda, she'd be hailed as "The Next Bette Davis."

After the final scenes of *Jezebel* were filmed, Wyler also ended his affair with Davis. She had hesitated when he'd asked her to marry him.

Instead, in October of 1938, he married Margaret ("Talli") Tallichet, a union that would last until he was hauled off to Forest Lawn in the summer of 1981.

In the wake of her divorce from Ham, Davis launched an affair with the aviator/producer Howard Hughes, luring him away from Katharine Hepburn. Davis later claimed that she helped Hughes recover from his impotence.

During the course of her marriage (1932-1938) to Ham (Harmon Nelson), her husband burst in on his wife in bed with Hughes. The billionaire paid him $70,000 to forget the indiscretion.

In January of 1938, at the end of the filming of *Jezebel*, Davis went to her doctor to discover "my first nightmare. I was pregnant. Who was the father? Willie or Hank? I was married to neither of them. I had an absentee husband, but a husband nonetheless. The only alternative for me would be to have an abortion, which was eventually arranged though the studio doctor."

Years later, Davis revealed, "Willie was the love of my life. No question about it! I always wished that I had married him and that I'd had his child instead of aborting it. Perhaps the films we made together are our children. First, *Jezebel,* then *The Letter* (1940), and finally *The Little Foxes* (1941).

On reflection, Davis recalled, *Jezebel* made me a far better actress than I had ever been and paved the way for all those great movies I made beginning in the late 1930s."

After attending the premiere of *Jezebel*, columnist Hedda Hopper confronted Davis: "Don't kid me. I can tell you've fallen in love with Henry Fonda. An actress can fake just so much on the screen. That look in your eyes as you gazed into his face is the look of love. You're smitten, kid."

"The gossipy bitch didn't know how I did those close-ups alone, since Fonda had flown to Manhattan to await the birth of his baby. He told me he was naming the kid Henry Fonda Jr. They say the camera doesn't lie. Well, in this case it did. That look of

love in my eyes might really have been aimed at my director, not Henry.

***

To promote the film, Warner publicists went to great lengths:

HALF ANGEL, HALF SIREN, ALL WOMAN!

THE MOST EXCITING HEROINE WHO EVER LIVED IN DIXIE!

HEARTLESS SIREN FOR WHOM MEN DIED!

HER LIPS WERE A CHALLENGE TO EVERY MAN!

THE STORY OF A WOMAN WHO WAS LOVED
WHEN SHE SHOULD HAVE BEEN WHIPPED!

THE SCREEN'S GREATEST ACTRESS WHO COMES TO YOU
IN THE HIT PICTURE OF HER CAREER!

On the day it opened at Radio City Music Hall in Manhattan, *Jezebel* took in a million and a half dollars, and put Davis on the cover of *Time* magazine.

Archer Winston of the *New York Post* wrote, "Henry Fonda performs up to the high Fonda standard, adding a bit of stiffening to the more willowy character he has made."

Howard Barnes of the *New York Herald Tribune* claimed, "Henry Fonda makes an adequately disgusted hero. No amount of sincere acting would turn *Jezebel* into a sincere tragedy, though the story is still bad, even if it is persuasively enacted and resourcefully staged."

Another critic noted, "As the obstinate, determined *beau* of Julie (alias Jezebel), Henry Fonda managed to hold his own and did so stoically."

When *Gone With the Wind* was finally released, comparisons with *Jezebel* were inevitable. *Time* magazine compared the two movies "as chicory is to coffee."

Jezebel would bring Davis her second Best Actress Oscar, having previously won in 1935 for *Dangerous*.

In the 1938 sweepstakes, she competed against Margaret Sullavan, Henry's former wife, for her starring role in *Three Comrades* opposite Robert Taylor.

Ironically, both Sullavan and Davis competed against Fay Bainter, who had only a supporting role in *Jezebel*. She was nominated for a Best Actress Oscar for her lead role in *White Banners*. This was a rare moment in Oscar history when one actress was up for Best Actress and Best Supporting Actress in the same year.

When Bainter walked off with the Best Supporting Actress Academy Award, she competed with Spring Byington, part of the cast of *Jezebel*. Byington this time was nominated for her key role in *You Can't Take It With You.*

For Best Picture of 1938, *Jezebel* competed with such movies as *Boys Town* with Spencer Tracy. *Jezebel* lost to *You Can't Take It With You,* starring James Stewart and Jean Arthur.

Because of their similar themes, Warners rushed *Jezebel* into release one year before *Gone With the Wind,* hoping to dim some of the impact of Margaret Mitchell's "classic tale."

In that, Warners did not succeed. Released in 1939, *Gone With the Wind* won as Best Picture of that year, and became one of the highest-grossing movies of all time.

With all its flaws, the release of *Jezebel* signaled the beginning of the reign of Bette Davis as the unofficial Queen of Hollywood.

In contrast, Henry had a way to go before he moved into super stardom.

Henry Fonda

FONDA: Some women preferred him as a matinée idol over Tyrone Power and Robert Taylor.

CHAPTER SEVEN

STARTING A DYSFUNCTIONAL FAMILY &
BECOMING A MOVIE STAR

VOWING NEVER TO WORK WITH *JEZEBEL* (BETTE DAVIS) AGAIN,
HENRY RUSHES TO NEW YORK TO AWAIT THE BIRTH OF HIS FIRST CHILD, "LADY JANE." YEARS
LATER, TO HENRY'S CHAGRIN,
SHE'S DESCRIBED IN THE PRESS AS **"THE NEXT BETTE DAVIS."**

FRANCES SEYMOUR BROKAW FONDA BUILDS HER DREAM HOUSE IN THEN-RURAL BEVERLY HILLS.
ALWAYS A LONER, HENRY BECOMES EVEN MORE OF ONE
DURING HIS RARE MOMENTS AT HOME

"Sometimes, I'd do naughty things just to get his attention."
—Jane Fonda

BLOCKADE
WILLIAM DIETERLE DIRECTS HENRY IN A FILM ABOUT
THE SPANISH CIVIL WAR

SPAWN of the NORTH
HENRY CO-STARS IN A COLD-WEATHER FEATURE WITH
"THE SARONG QUEEN," DOROTHY LAMOUR

THE MAD MISS MANTON
PLAYING PRANKS AND SOLVING MURDERS WITH BARBARA STANWYCK

JESSE JAMES
BUSHWHACKING THROUGH RURAL MISSOURI WITH TYRONE POWER
AS A GUERILLA EX-CONFEDERATE

INVENTING ALEXANDER GRAHAM BELL & THE TELEPHONE
SOMEWHAT RESENTFULLY, HENRY PLAYS SECOND FIDDLE TO DON AMECHE

*"Those jerks should have given me, not Don Ameche,
the role of Alexander Graham Bell."*
—Henry Fonda

YOUNG ABRAHAM LINCOLN
HENRY, AS DIRECTED BY JOHN FORD, MORPHS "AW, SHUCKS!" NEBRASKAN FOLKSINESS
INTO AN ICONIC FILM CLASSIC ABOUT HONEST ABE

Leaving the set of *Jezebel*, as pre-arranged with the producers, before the picture was wrapped, Henry flew to New York, fearing he would not arrive in time for the birth of his son. A fortune teller at Laguna Beach had predicted that the infant would be a boy, and he'd already told Bette Davis and others that he was naming him Henry Fonda Jr. "I want someone to carry on my name, although I don't know why."

When he arrived at Doctors Hospital in Manhattan, and rushed to his wife, Frances' room, he learned that the signs of an imminent premature birth had been wrong. Nonetheless, the doctor advised, "The baby could come any day, however...so stick around."

Although suffering from occasional pain, his wife seemed in good spirits. "We already have my dear daughter Pan, and the birth of our son will make us the perfect family. And there's no need for a third child, so I want you to exercise caution."

No longer standing, Doctors Hospital, founded in 1929, stood at 170 East End Avenue, in Manhattan, between 87th and 88th Streets, overlooking the East River. It was erected opposite Gracie Mansion, the official home of New York's mayor.

In time, the 14-story, fully equipped hospital would be where celebrities would check in, none more famous than future patients like Marilyn Monroe and Michael Jackson. Playwright Eugene O'Neill was once a patient. Other illustrious guests had included Clare Booth Luce, novelist Jacqueline Susann, and humorist James Thurber.

On the lower floor was a busy restaurant with a gourmet chef. Even though they might not have been associated with any patient inside, many of the neighborhood's social elite stopped in for lunch. During the course of several consecutive days, Henry was spotted dining alone there, with interruptions from fans seeking his autograph.

On December 21, 1937, "the blessed event" arrived, the birth, by Caesarean, of an infant girl: A disappointment to both of her parents, each of whom had wanted a boy.

Frances was the one who named her, calling her Jane Seymour Fonda. During her early years, the girl would be known as "Lady Jane."

[Her name derived from Jane Seymour (1509-1537), one of Frances' distant ancestors. The third wife of the Tudor King, Henry VIII, she became officially betrothed a day after the execution of Henry's second wife, Anne Boleyn. Jane died of postnatal complications a few days after the birth of her only child, the (sickly and short-lived) future King Edward VI. She was the only wife of Henry to receive a queen's funeral or to be buried beside him in St. Georges Chapel at Windsor Castle.]

Proud parents with Baby Jane. The lower photo dates from 1943, the darkest year of World War II.

Josh Logan, the best man at the wedding of Henry and Frances, remembered her: "A patrician kind of beauty, which she passed on to Jane. The bride could talk only of four things: Money, babies, sex, and clothes. She had no interest in Henry's movie career."

At first, Henry (Fonda) bragged about "his golden-haired beautiful daughter, Jane," although in time, her hair grew darker. As described by author Fred Lawrence Guiles, "Within a few months, the contours of her face would take the shape that they would have throughout her life. She had a high and slightly bulging forehead, a good American nose on the snub side, an ample upper lip and generous smile, strong with a prominent jawline."

When Jane arrived back at the Fonda home in California, Frances' first daughter, Pan (Henry's stepdaughter), was jealous because of all the attention heaped on the newly born, but in time, the girls became friends.

With Henry's increase in salary, he could employ a full-time nurse for his daughter. He also hired a chef, who turned out his favorite foods, many of which were radically different from the menus Frances preferred for herself.

Henry VIII married **Jane Seymour** in May of 1536, but she was dead by October of 1537 at the age of 28.

In 1933, the actress Wendy Barrie played Seymour opposite portly Charles Laughton in Alexander Korda's highly acclaimed film, *The Private Life of Henry VIII.*

"That matronly nurse used the Bitch of Buchenwald as a role model," Henry protested. "She wouldn't even let me kiss my daughter, fearing germs. Every time I came into the nursery, I was forced to wear a mask."

Later in her life, Lady Jane did not remember her then-young father ever kissing her at all. He had never shown a lot of emotion, although initially, he told her he loved her. Jane's mother, Frances, according to Jane, was even more aloof, bonding more with her daughter Pan from her first marriage. From that first four-year marriage to George Tuttle Brokaw, the widowed Frances had emerged as independently wealthy, and never had to ask Henry for anything.

Although Henry was not much for smooching, he was an avid photographer, frequently photographing "Lady Jane" with his Leica. "She became," he boasted, "the most photographed baby girl in Hollywood."

Ironically, as time passed, the grown-up Jane would spend a good part of her life in front of a camera.

The first visitors to Henry and Frances' new home were James Stewart and the *Life* photographer, Johnny Swope. Each became more or less a godfather to Jane.

Jane's memory of her life as a child was fairly pleasant. In recollection, she called herself "my father's son. I was a real tomboy. Sometimes, he took me fishing, and I was horrified but put up a good front when I had to bait the fishhooks with bloody worms."

Even at home, Henry was somewhat of a loner, often retreating to his study to read scripts. "I was desperate for his attention," Jane said. "Sometimes I'd do things that were naughty just to get that attention."

With Henry at the studio working almost every day, Frances started to explore various neighborhoods of Los Angeles in her Buick convertible, looking for building sites for the construction of a larger home for her family. After many difficulties, she finally located the ideal site in Brentwood, where Henry had lived with James Stewart.

The property she "uncovered," occupied nine scenic acres on a hillside along Tigertail Road, south of Sunset Boulevard. The final address of the two-story house they built was a 255 Chadbourne Street, in a landscape of pine trees and acacias.

In a surprise move, Leland Hayward and Margaret Sullavan would relocate to a new home a block away. Their daughter, Brooke Hayward, later described the area at the time her family moved there:

"The wilds of Beverly Hills in the early 1940s was still unspoiled land but treacherous. The sky belonged to the patrols of turkey buzzards circling leisurely. The hills swarmed with jackrabbits and deer, and packs of coyotes gathered to howl at the moon. The tall grasses were alive with king snakes and rattlers."

Sunflooded, idyllic, and underpopulated: **Coldwater Canyon**, circa 1910.

"We moved here at 600 Tigertail Road in 1941," Henry said. "Our home looked like a rambling, 100-year-old Pennsylvania Dutch farmhouse surrounded by vines and flowers. Inside, it was a combination of antiquity and efficiency."

Since Henry was making one movie after another, it had been left to Frances to deal with the many architects, builders, electricians, and plumbers. She ordered that a swimming pool be dug into the arid landscape out back. When the house, with its long front porch, was completed, she embarked on an antique-buying visit to New England for furniture to ship back to California. The rustic objects she bought included a cobbler's bench and three lamps crafted from 19th-centruy butter churns.

***

Blockade (1938)

Henry's first movie after his return from Broadway to the West Coast was *Blockade* (1938), set during the Spanish Civil War.

[At the time, its theme and setting were all the rage, generating animated controversy throughout the U.S. and Europe. In 1936, war had broken out between Republican anti-fascist socialist-leaning Loyalists (on the left) and Falangist fascist forces of Francisco Franco (on the right). A lot of Catholic support was generated for the dictator, Franco, in the United States. In contrast, the Loyalist Cause drew support from artists and celebrities like Ernest Hemingway and Hollywood producer Walter Wanger, who still had Henry under contract.]

Henry played Marco, a farmer who takes up arms to fight for the Republicans. He's in love with Norma, the daughter of an international arms agent profiting from the Civil War's bloody hatreds. Norma is a traitor, but Marco (Henry) exposes her to the suffering of civilians, and she changes her mind. She then directs him to the hangout of spies.

Cast as Norma, Madeleine Carroll, a native of Staffordshire, England, was a blonde goddess, one of the most beautiful co-stars Henry had ever had. At the time he worked with her, Carroll was at the peak of her career—in fact, she was the world's highest-paid actress. Her greatest fame had come in 1935 when Alfred Hitchcock cast her in *The 39 Steps,* where she played a cool, glib, smart blonde.

When Henry met her, Carroll was in the final months of her marriage to Colonel Philip Reginald Astley. Her divorce would come through in 1939. Two

The agonies of love, war, and blockade on the eve of World War II.

In it, **Henry Fonda** and **Madeleine Carroll** re-enacted a then-very-popular theme, made prominent in published form by Ernest Hemingway and the "Lost Generation," of everyday anguish during the Spanish Civil War.

years later, when she was cast in *Virginia* (1941) opposite Sterling Hayden in his first major screen role, she fell in love with him and they were married the following year.

A native of Bavaria, Germany, the director, William Dieterle, had only recently become a citizen of the United States. He'd acted in German films since 1921, often playing country yokels or simpletons. In 1923, he financed and directed his first film, the silent *Der Mensch am Wege (aka The Man by the Wayside),* based on a Leo Tolstoy short story. In it, he cast a young, then virtually unknown, Marlene Dietrich.

Before working with Henry, Dieterle had helmed Bette Davis in *Fog Over Frisco* (1934) and *Satan Met a Lady* (1936). What turned him into a top Hollywood director was the 1934 *A Midsummer Night's Dream,* starring James Cagney and Olivia de Havilland.

Dieterle also became known for his bio pictures such as *The Story of Louis Pasteur* (1936) and *The Life of Emile Zola* (1937), which won an Oscar for Best Picture. In 1939, he went on to score a major success with *The Hunchback of Notre Dame* starring Charles Laughton.

The producer of *Blockade,* Walter Wanger, hired writers such as Clifford Odets and James M. Cain to create the script.

Henry played a simple, perhaps miscast, farmer who evolves into a guerilla fighter. As reviewed by one writer, "He made a peculiarly stringy revolutionary hero, lacking virility in his movement."

As *Blockade's* third lead, Leo Carrillo, who was able to trace his Spanish ancestry back to 1260, became deeply intrigued with the historical implications of the script. The censors at the Hays Office were worried that the film, by siding with the anti-Fascist Loyalists, would violate America's commitment—rigorously enforced in those years before Pearl Harbor—to neutrality in Europe.

Blockade was released into a spectacularly polarized environments in both the U.S. and Spain, with some of the best commercial artists in Spain expressing the evils of Fascism as represented by the military *junta* of General Franco and his anti-Royalist, anti-communist forces.

Motivated by short-sighted "non-interventionist" policies at the time, even Hollywood censors resisted what they called *Blockade's* anti-fascist "propaganda"—at least until the Japanese attack on Pearl Harbor in 1941 rendered their objections obsolete.

To that effect, changes were made in the script to please these enforcers of the Motion Picture Production Code. Later, during and after the film's release, studio publicists falsely asserted, "*Blockade* doesn't attempt to favor any cause in the present conflict."

*Block*ade was openly anti-Fascist and critical of nations that stood by and let dictators commit atrocities. Its 1938 premiere at Grauman's Chinese Theater was inexplicably canceled, and it was controversial upon its nationwide release. The film was banned in several cities and denounced by conservative elements of the Catholic Church.

The New Republic wrote, "Henry Fonda does very well at coming through silly rubbish to establish himself as a good man, an honest, troubled, but steady spirit in his country's service."

Henry didn't like the film. "I was synthetic in the role. My dialogue was not that of a farmer, but a political activist."

In a concluding speech, his character is virtually crying out propaganda: "We're part of something, something greater than ourselves. The people out there…we've given them hope again."

In his character's final oration, he shouts [*at least as loudly as Henry could shout*] "We're the conscience of the world."

***

Spawn of the North (1938)

Variety carried the news that a new Paramount picture, *Spawn of the North*, scheduled for release in 1938, would be cast with Cary Grant, Randolph Scott, and Carole Lombard. Hollywood gossips were aware that Scott and Grant were off-screen lovers. One wag joked, "Who will get Cary at the end of the picture? Scott or Lombard?"

When that casting combination fell through, the movie had to be recast.

Thus, its director, Henry Hathaway, phoned Henry Fonda and asked him to co-star in the reconfigured project alongside George Raft. Henry had long admired the work of Hathaway, who, two years previously had guided him through *Trail of the Lonesome Pine* (1936) with Sylvia Sidney.

Then the director added a tantalizing piece of additional information: "Dorothy Lamour will be your leading lady, and John Barrymore has signed for a supporting role."

Before anything could be finalized with his agent, Henry met for lunch with Hathaway to discuss the picture. It was revealed that it would not be shot on location, as the script had called for, in the wilds of Alaska. Instead, the northern frontier's fishing port would be replicated on Paramount's back lot.

In addition to Henry, George Raft, and Barrymore, *Spawn* would also star Louise Platt as the second female lead. Henry had recently starred with her in *I Met My Love Again* (1938) alongside Joan Bennett.

The script by Jules Furthman had been based on a novel by Barrett Willoughby, with music by Dimitri Tiomkin. Hathaway gave Henry a copy of the novel to read over the weekend.

Henry would play Jim Kimmerlee, the owner of an Alaskan salmon cannery who has been plagued by Russian pirates stealing fish from his traps. He has an ongoing feud with Red Skain (Akim Tamiroff), a Russian suspected of the thefts.

An old friend from years ago, Tyler Dawon (Raft) arrives in town and hangs out with Jim. In time, Jim learns that Tyler is collaborating with the thieves.

The drab fishing port comes alive when Nicky Duval (Lamour), the world-weary owner of the local hotel, appears. When the movie opens, she's Tyler's sweetheart. The plot's other love interest is provided by "Di" Turlon (Platt).

Barrymore as Windy Turlon is the editor of the local newspaper (*The Gazette*), although he spends much of the time in the saloon. At this time in his career, the aging actor was "truly in his cups," as one writer defined it. Yet he summoned up a bit of yesterday's *razzmatazz* to pull off the role. When they weren't otherwise occupied on the set, he and Henry had many talks about stage acting.

The Great Profile loved to shock people. One day, a group of female schoolteachers appeared on the set and were awed by him until he began telling them stories of how he always demanded that "My leading ladies suck me off."

No one knew quite what to do with the title of Henry Fonda's then most recent movie.

Were the conflicting romances between its male and female leads as earthy and "biologically essential" as the title implied?

And would **Dorothy Lamour** wear, perhaps, a fur-lined version of her trademark sarong?

115

They fled in horror.

Frank Nugent of *The New York Times* wrote of Henry's puzzled brow during confrontations with crumbling icebergs and the Alaskan salmon run. "Scorning such effeminacies as marlin spikes, the movie's huskies go at it with harpoon guns, sealing knives, lengths of chain and gaff. The bloodshed is beautiful."

At the end, Jim shoots his old friend Tyler (Raft), who stays alive long enough to crash his Russian adversary's boat into a glacier, killing not only the salmon bandits but himself in the final valiant act of atonement.

Although Henry had seen only two of Raft's films—*Scarface* (1932) and *Night After Night* (also 1932), the latter with Mae West—he'd heard many stories about his background. He had been a gigolo in Manhattan when he'd roomed with Rudolph Valentino in 1914. Later, he was a "wheel man," piloting getaway cars for gangster Bugsy Siegel.

When Raft had danced onstage in London in 1926, his most ardent fan was the Prince of Wales (aka the future King Edward VIII and later, the Duke of Windsor). Raft told Humphrey Bogart and others that "His Highness went down on me."

Raft called his penis "Black Snake," and inserted it into such stars as Carole Lombard, nightclub owner Texas Guinan (*"Welcome, suckers!"*), Mae West, and Lana Turner. His longtime friend, Mack Grey, claimed, "George averages two women a day, nearly always a hooker." After her unhappy fling with Raft, Betty Grable claimed that he was a latent homosexual. "Instead of screwing me, he used to get off beating me up."

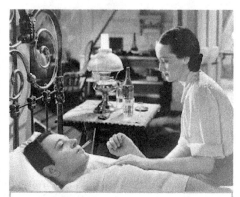

Spawning in Northern Climes: In the sickbay photo above, **Dorothy Lamour** manages to look more demure than Florence Nightingale in this "giving aid to the sick" scene with **George Raft.**

In other roles, Raft usually managed to look ready for a tumble or a rumble with anyone outfitted in a sarong.

"The Belle of New Orleans," Dorothy Lamour had shot to fame in *The Jungle Princess* (1936), earning her an undying reputation as "The Sarong Queen."

Her greatest fame would come during World War II, when she made all those Road Pictures with Bing Crosby and Bob Hope, both of whom she seduced.

[As a side note, Lamour may have been one of the very few women who ever became sexually intimate with J. Edgar Hoover, the dreaded and very vindictive homosexual chief of the FBI. According to biographer Richard Hack, their one-time fling occurred one drunken night in a hotel in Washington D.C. Years later, when asked to verify that, Lamour said, "I cannot deny it."

Henry's reaction? "Any gal who would go to bed with J. Edgar Hoover would also bed a buffalo."]

During the shoot, Henry and Lamour bonded, and Hathaway thought she was definitely in pursuit of Henry. "I wasn't there to catch on camera what happened between them, but he always emerged from her dressing room with a smile on his face." At that time, Henry and Jimmy Stewart were known for seducing their leading ladies.

When Lamour first met Henry, she was in the throes of divorcing her first husband, orchestra leader Herbie Day. When Hathaway introduced the pair, Lamour turned to Henry. "Too bad you've gotten married. I'm shopping around for a new husband and I'm conducting auditions."

Spawn of the North was a moderate success, although hardly a milestone in Henry's career.

In her 1980 memoir, Lamour added a footnote. "I must have been in love with Hank because I married a man that could be his twin. There was one difference: Hank had blue eyes and Bill had brown."

[She was referring to her second husband, William Ross Howard III, a captain in the U.S. Army. Incidentally, one of Lamour's sarongs is on display at the Smithsonian Institution, presumably as an item of "enduring cultural or historical significance".]

Informally, at least, two historical figures, **Madame Récamier** and **Dorothy Lamour,** taught the world how to lounge.

The *upper photo* shows the neoclassically inspired portrait of the Parisian socialite, **Mme Récamier,** painted in 1800 by J.J. David, as it hangs in the Louvre,

In the lower photo, **Dorothy Lamour** shows why Hollywood press agents began referring to her as *The Jungle Princess* (1936).

***

The Mad Miss Manton (1938)

When Henry read the script of his new movie offer, *The Mad Miss Manton,* scheduled for a 1938 release, he didn't like it.

It was penned, in part, by Philip G. Epstein. He and his twin and writing partner, Julius I. Epstein, would have more enduring success with their script for *Casablanca* (1942), starring Humphrey Bogart and Ingrid Bergman.

Although at first, Henry protested its shortcomings to Walter Wanger, who was still in control of his contract. Henry eventually agreed to get involved in it after learning that Barbara Stanwyck, as a fun-loving socialite, would be his leading lady.

It had initially been proposed as a vehicle for Irene Dunne, but she had another commitment. It was then offered to Katharine Hepburn, who rejected it.

Finally, Stanwyck accepted. "It's about time I gave that bitch, Carole Lombard, some competition in screwball comedies. Besides, I'm tired of waiting by the phone for David O. Selznick to say that he's cast me as Scarlett O'Hara in *Gone With the Wind*."

Barbara Stanwyck *(The Mad Miss Manton)* and **Henry Fonda**, the skeptical editor of the local newspaper...until he falls madly in love with her

Stanwyck would be paid $60,000 for her star billing. In contrast, Fonda earned $25,000, from which Wanger and his agent, Leland Hayward, would take their cuts.

A New Yorker, Leigh Jason, helmed the movie, as he had done since 1928 when he directed *Prince of Fear*. Before *The Mad Miss Manton*, he had released *New Faces of 1937* and *Wise Girl* (also 1937) with Miriam Hopkins and Ray Milland.

As a side note, Hattie McDaniel was cast as Stanwyck's grumpy, wise-cracking maid. Unlike Stanwyck, she would get that call from Selznick when he cast her as Mammy in *Gone With the Wind,* bringing her an Oscar.

In the script, Melsa Manton (Stanwyck) takes her little dogs for an evening walk. When she sees a man fleeing from a house, she goes inside to investigate. There, she finds the body of George Lane, a rich banker, dead on the floor.

But after she phones the police, the body mysteriously disappears. Sam Levene, as a bumbling police detective, accuses her of pulling a prank.

In the second lead, Henry was cast as Peter Ames, editor of *The Morning Clarion*. He, too, is dubious. He accuses Melsa of playing a trick on the police, noting that as a rich society dame without a lot to do, she takes up valuable time from the city's police.

Defiantly, she rounds up a similar group of "dizzy debs," all rich and with time on their hands, to investigate the murder. Peter defines them in his paper as "Park Avenue, mink-clad dames, useless members of a rapidly vanishing class."

But when he meets Melsa, he starts to fall in love, even though on occasion, she plays rough and ties him up.

Eventually, these rich girls find the murderer and Melsa is redeemed. By that time, Peter is so smitten he wants to marry her, suggesting, "We'll honeymoon in Europe—on your money."

The Mad Miss Manton had moderate success. With tongue-in-cheek, Frank S. Nugent of *The New York Times* wrote: "One of the story's loudest hoax-criers is Peter Ames, who looks too much like Henry Fonda to make a convincing metropolitan newspaper editor."

Harold Barnes of the *New York Herald Tribune* sat through all this wacky harum-scarum, which he found drew upon both *The Thin Man* with William Powell and Myrna Loy and *My Man Godfrey* with William Powell and Carole Lombard. "The fact is that the nonsense in the motion picture almost never mixes with its hair-raising interludes," he continued.

The question was later asked, "Did Henry Fonda have an affair with his leading lady, Barbara Stanwyck?" He responded, "Everyone close to me knows I've been in love with Barbara since I met her. A delicious woman like her can act the hell out of any part. She's also a lotta fun. She almost became the mother of my daughter, Jane."

What did that enigmatic statement mean? Did he have an affair with her or not? It was suggested that he wanted "to get back at her *beau,* Robert Taylor, who had appeared around town with his ex-wife, Margaret Sullavan, making it obvious that they were having an illicit affair.

117

***

Jesse James (1939)

When enlarged and displayed in the lobbies of movie palaces in 1939, this poster had a LOT of information to convey to movie fans about who and what they'd see.

Lights! Camera! Movie Stars! Pop Americana! Sex Appeal! Action!

Henry had long detested Darryl F. Zanuck at Fox, but when Fox sent him the script for *Jesse James,* he agreed to play the brother of the outlaw Jesse James, that role portrayed by his friend, Tyrone Power.

Henry knew that Power would steal the film. He was Fox's heartthrob, hailed at the time as the best-looking actor in Hollywood. Every day, he took a nude steambath with Zanuck. Rumors spread that Power *[widely known as a bisexual]* performed fellatio on Zanuck.

Film historians cite 1939 as the greatest year in movie history, as studios turned out more classics than ever before...or after.

Although Henry found the *Jesse James* script intriguing, he knew it would never rank among the best pictures being turned out that year.

Future classics being filmed at the time, each scheduled for release in 1939, included *Dark Victory* with Bette Davis; *Goodbye, Mr. Chips* with Robert Donat; *Love Affair* with Charles Boyer and Irene Dunne; *Ninotchka* with Greta Garbo; *Of Mice and Men,* based on the John Steinbeck novel; *Stagecoach* with John Wayne; *The Wizard of Oz* with Judy Garland; and *Wuthering Heights* with Laurence Olivier and Merle Oberon—stiff competition indeed.

The legend of the American outlaw and folk hero, Jesse James, had long fascinated movie-goers, especially Zanuck. He named Nunnally Johnson as his newest film's co-producer and scriptwriter and set about launching it.

Zanuck's keen sense of showmanship proved correct, as the eventual movie would be the third highest-grossing film of 1939, ranking behind *Gone With the Wind* and *Mr. Smith Goes to Washington,* starring Henry's best friend, James Stewart.

Snapped on location on the set of *Jesse James*, this publicity photo delivers up-close-and-personal views of two of the most famous male movie stars of their era, each with his own distinctive allure: **Tyrone Power** (*left*) and **Henry Fonda.**

Zanuck hired Henry King, a son of Virginia born in 1886, as its director, ordering him to line up "the best supporting team we've ever had."

By 1925, King had appeared as an actor in some 60 films before becoming one of the most successful directors in Hollywood. He'd be nominated for a Best Director Oscar twice, and his pictures would be up for a Best Picture Academy Award seven times. His preferred stars were Tyrone Power and, new to the business, that handsome hunk known as Gregory Peck.

Zanuck immediately tangled with King over his choice of Henry Fonda as Jesse's brother, Frank. According to Zanuck, "That guy Fonda has no business playing Frank James. He's a lousy actor and has been knocking around for years without finding major stardom. When he appears with Bette Davis, he's like a dress dummy."

King overcame Zanuck's objection, and the producer actually came to like and respect Henry. In fact, it was the release of *Jesse James* in Technicolor that made Fonda, at long last, a major motion picture star.

The first day he saw Henry on the set, Zanuck told him, "You'll fit in perfect with the people of the Ozarks, where the movie will be shot. I hear you're from Nebraska. That state is where I lost my virginity at the age of thirteen. I screwed this virgin, the daughter of a local Baptist pastor, in a field outside Oakdale."

The script by Johnson had little to do with the real Jesse James (1847-1882), the outlaw, bank and train robber, and guerilla fighter. His family derived from a section of western Missouri known as "Little Dixie," and the two became sympathizers of the Confederates and atrocity-committing "bushwhackers" for their cause. *[In some parts of North America during and after the Civil War, the term "Bushwhacker" specifically referred to guerilla-fighting Missourians who resisted the Union Army's occupation of border counties.]*

After the war ended in 1865, the James gang continued their rampage of robbery and pillage, gaining national

WANTED
DEAD OR ALIVE

JESSE JAMES

NOTORIOUS ROBBER OF
TRAINS AND BANKS $5,000.00

REWARD

They were a lot more "homespun" than many of their "fans of the Old West' might have realized.

Here's a Daguerrotype portrait of **Frank** (*right*) and **Jesse James.**

fame and notoriety for their brutality.

On April 3, 1882, James was shot and killed by Robert Ford, a new recruit to the gang. He hoped to collect a reward and be granted amnesty for his previous crimes.

Jesse James became immortalized as a colorful figure of the long-faded Old West of yesterday. The Johnson script actually made the James brothers sympathetic, imbuing them with a degree of romantic gallantry.

Much of the movie was shot on location near Pineville, Missouri. In the late 1930s, the town and its environs looked a bit like they did during the heyday of the James outlaws. Even today, Pineville—reinforced by the memory of the film that was shot there—celebrates "Jesse James Day" every year.

When word spread of the shoot, hundreds of people from the surrounding area and neighboring states flocked to the site.

Power, and to a lesser degree, Henry, was swamped with fans seeking autographs—"and a piece of our flesh," as an annoyed Henry said. Most of the cast and crew were housed in the Shadow Lake resort at Noel, on the shores of Oklahoma's Elk River.

On location, King met and had many long conversations with the son of Frank James, who still lived in the area.

Henry had sustained an affair with Annabella, Power's wife-to-be, when they'd co-starred in *Wings of the Morning* (1937) shot in England. Power may have known about that, but there seemed to be no jealousy between the two actors. Power told him that he would wed Annabella upon her return from Paris, after her divorce came through from actor Jean Murat.

In Paris, Annabella was asked by a reporter if she planned to marry Power after her divorce became final. She looked up, puzzled: "Tyrone Power? He is still a boy. That is all."

The remote location of the *Jesse James* shoot drew reporters and photographers from newspapers and photographers from across the nation. *Life* sent the fabled Alfred Eisenstad to shoot a photo essay. In one picture, he shot Henry and Power sitting on top of a railroad car, handing out autographs to fans below.

At the beginning of filming, King, as the film's director, instructed Henry, "I want you to be a slow starter and a buzz saw finisher."

Cast as "Zee Cobb," Nancy Kelly was cast as Jesse's love interest. As a child actress, she had played in numerous Silents in the 1920s. She returned to the screen and by the late 1930s had established herself as a leading lady, making two dozen movies before 1945. The same year, after working with Henry and Power, she would star opposite Spencer Tracy in *Stanley and Livingstone.*

In the film's fourth lead as Marshal Will Wright was Randolph Scott, a veteran actor of Westerns who had usually been paired with actresses who included Mae West and Shirley Temple. A co-starring role with Marlene Dietrich loomed in his future. Scott lunched with Henry, telling him he was in the throes of divorcing heiress Marion DuPont, whom he and married in 1936. "I'm moving back in with Cary," (a reference to Cary Grant, his longtime lover), he told his friends.

Early in the picture, agents of the St. Louis Midland Railroad arrive at the James property to try to force the family to sell their land for a pittance. When the James boys stand up against Barshee (Brian Donlevy), a fight ensues. Barshee later orders his men to return and set the homestead on fire, killing Mrs. James. To seek revenge, Jesse goes after Barshee, eventually gunning him down. Both he and Frank become wanted men on the run, embarking on a life of banditry.

Here's a detail from a "movie star glam" press photo, autographed by **Tyrone Power**, in tennis clothes, and his enigmatic French wife, **Annabella**—often viewed as a stranger in the strange LaLa land of Southern California—wearing a sundress.

Both of them were bisexuals.

Character actress Jane Darwell played the mother of Frank and Jesse. A star of stage, screen, television, she would later immortalize herself in a roughly equivalent role as Henry's mother in their classic, *The Grapes of Wrath* (1940). She felt at home on the location shot in Missouri, as that was her home state. Short, stout, and plain-faced, she appeared in five films with Shirley Temple. Immediately after working with Henry, she was assigned a minor role in *Gone With the Wind*.

The cantankerous father of Zee (Kelly) was played by Henry Hull, cast as Major Cobb. A character actor from Kentucky, Hull had recently become known for his star role in *Werewolf of London* (1935). Before that, on stage, he had created the character of Jester Lester in the long-running *Tobacco Road* (1933), based on the novel by Erskine Caldwell.

On location, Hull was assigned lodgings on the ground floor of a building in Noel, Missouri. Every day, fans assembled outside, looking into his windows. He finally decided to go around naked to scare them off.

Donald Meek was cast as McCoy, the railroad rep, who promises Jesse a light sentence if he'll turn himself in. After acquiescing, the outlaw is betrayed, and his hanging is hastily scheduled for within a few days.

Frank and his cronies react by riding into town to rescue Jesse. Thus begins their campaign of ravaging banks, trains, and often killing gunfight opponents during their narrow escapes.

At a point near the end of the picture, character actor John Carradine plays the infamous Bob Ford, a recent addition to the James' gang. After appearing at the home of Jesse and Zee and realizing that they're on the verge of escaping to California, he assassinates Jesse with the intention of collecting a reward and pardons for his crimes.

No one played rural matriarchs better than **Jane Darwell.**

She was so convincing as the "home on the range" mother of Frank and Jesse James that she was later reprised as Henry Fonda's mother, Ma Joad, in *The Grapes of Wrath* (1940).

Henry was later to learn of a embarrassing sexual indiscretion by his new friend, Tyrone Power. He had picked up a sixteen-year-old girl from an Ozarkian mountain family and had housed her in his temporary residence for two weeks. During her sojourn with him, he took her virginity and impregnated her.

After filming ended, and after Power "abandoned" Missouri, his son was born in June of 1939. Years later, Power learned of the child's birth and tried to locate him. Adoption records, however, had been sealed and he never found him.

When Henry learned this from Power years later, he said, "Some very good-looking young man is walking around Missouri today. He's attracting a horde of young gals with his good looks. I bet he gets one question over and over. 'Did anyone ever tell you you look like Tyrone Power?'"

Back in Hollywood, when Henry was otherwise occupied and could not join him, and while Annabella was still in France, Power visited his studio's headquarters to see early rushes of *Jesse James*. After leaving the screening room, he ran into a handsome and charming young man, J. Watson Webb Jr., a scion of the Vanderbilt family. At the time, Webb was working as a messenger boy to learn the film business "from the ground up."

Power was immediately attracted to the tall, patrician-looking young man with the perfect manners and invited him for dinner with his mother in their rented home in Bel Air.

That following morning, Webb moved into Power's home.

When Anabella, a worldly sophisticate, returned from France, she accepted Webb as a member of her new family. In many ways, his presence allowed her to continue some outside lesbian affairs of her own.

Henry dined or sometimes went out "clubbing" with Power and Webb, referring to it as "a night out with the boys." He later said, "I think Ty, a promiscuous kind of guy, found his anchor, the love of his life. He always could come home to Webb."

When Power joined the Marines in World War II, he wrote to Webb faithfully two or three times a week. The young man sent Power a letter every day.

One of those letters (dated June 2, 1942) eventually surfaced:

"Believe me, Watson, the things you say about friendship, especially ours, I agree 1,000 percent. You are the only one close to me. After all our nights together, you should know that I don't have to tell you all the things you already know."

J. Watson Webb, the ultimate long-term survivor of the fickle, sometimes heterosexual love affairs of superstar Tyrone Power.

As it turned out, their Power/Webb relationship evolved into one of those "bonded-at-the-hip" lifetime links. As Power once told Henry, "Watson fulfills needs in me no woman can. Somehow with him, part of myself comes alive. A day away from him, even if I get a phone call, is like a day in hell."

Tyrone Power died on November 15, 1958. Henry joined mourners who included Loretta Young, James Stewart, Gregory Peck, and Yul Brynner.

His body ended up buried near the remains of Rudolph Valentino and Marion Davies, the former mistress of press baron William Randolph Hearst.

Webb had remained his steadfast friend for life—"and for eternity."

He had a memorial inscribed in Power's memory: GOOD NIGHT, SWEET PRINCE.

Love under pressure: **Henry Fonda** and **Maureen O'Sullivan**—"The Pride of Ireland"—in a *film noir* misunderstanding of mistaken identity.

***

Let Us Live (1939)

When Henry signed to co-star in *Let Us Live,* scheduled for release in 1939, he found himself in a familiar role of a victim wrongly convicted. It was evocative of the 1937 movie, *You Only Live Once,* in which he had co-starred with Sylvia Sidney. Under different circumstances, he would repeat a similar role in a far better picture, *The Wrong Man,* in his future.

Let Us Live was directed by the German *émigré,* John Brahm, born in Hamburg in 1893. He later became the director of the Deutsches Theatre *[aka the Friedrich-Wilhelm-Städtisches Theater]* in Berlin. When Hitler rose to power, Brahm fled to England and later migrated to Hollywood. One of his previous films had been *Broken Blossoms* (1936), a remake of the D.W. Griffith 1919 movie with the same name.

Film historian Andrew Sarris claimed that Brahm had really hit his stride in a series of mood-drenched melodramas that ended the 1930s with *Let Us Live.*

The plot was based on a real-live event: Cab drivers Brick Tennant (Henry) and Joe Linden (Alan Baxter) are falsely accused of a murder at a movie house. Seven of eight eyewitnesses identify them as the killers. Accused and convicted of murder, they are sentenced to die in the electric chair.

Brick's *fiancée,* Mary Roberts (Maureen O'Sullivan), knows he is innocent because he was in church with her at the time of the murder. She works desperately to free him. In her frantic search for the real culprits, she is aided by Lieutenant Everett (Ralph Bellamy). As part of a tense but happy ending, Brick and his partner, Joe, are freed only an hour or so before facing execution.

When she first met Henry, O'Sullivan revealed that autograph seekers often confused her with his first wife, Margaret Sullavan.

"Other than a similarity of name, you two actresses are as different as a robin to a vulture," he said.

O'Sullivan as Jane to **Johnny Weissmuller's** Tarzan.

When Tallulah Bankhead met him, she said, "*Dah*-ling, you're the kind of man a woman like me must shanghai and keep under lock and key until both of us are entirely spent. Prepare a leave of ten days!"

O'Sullivan was known for making all those Tarzan movies, starring as Jane, in the 1930s, with Johnny Weissmuller. She also had roles in such classics as *The Thin Man* (1934) with William Powell and Myrna Loy; *Anna Karenina* (1935) with Greta Garbo and Fredric March; and *A Yank at Oxford* (1938) with Robert Taylor.

Director John Farrow had married O'Sullivan in 1936, and from that union emerged a famous actress daughter, Mia Farrow. When she came of age, she wed Frank Sinatra. Her mother said, "Ol' Blue Eyes should be marrying me, not my daughter fresh out of her diapers."

In 2020, O'Sullivan was listed as number eight on the *Irish Times'* list of Ireland's greatest film stars.

A son of Chicago, Ralph Bellamy would have a career spanning 62 years on Broadway and in television and the movies.

He was nominated for a Best Supporting Actor Oscar for his 1937 film, *The Awful Truth,* starring Cary Grant and Irene Dunne.

Henry's durable and always reliable co-star, character actor **Ralph Bellamy.**

His signature role came when cast as President Franklin D. Roosevelt.

In that role, he virtually created the screen character of "The Other Man." He would play that role again and again. In the words of one critic, *"The Other Man* represented a character who has solid values and is honest and dependable, in contrast to his competition, a male who is likely to be a bit wild. Bellamy always loses the girl in the final reel."

The fourth lead, playing a taxi driver wrongly accused, was cast with Alan Baxter, an Ohio-born actor who once went to school with director Elia Kazan. In New York, he joined the Group Theater and appeared in such stage plays as John Van Druten's *The Voice of the Turtle.* Although he worked steadily from 1935 to 1971, he never rose above his B-picture status.

Whereas Columbia had, during the planning stages of *Let Us Live,* set out to make it an A-list feature, they began receiving legal pressure and eventually, threats of upcoming lawsuits from the State of Massachusetts. The Old Bay State objected to their state's law enforcement and judicial systems being portrayed as incompetent venues whose citizens might be wrongly accused and convicted of crimes they did not commit.

Bowing to pressure, Columbia removed many of *Let Us Live's* most controversial scenes and reduced its length to about an hour, thereby formatting it into the shortest Henry Fonda movie in his repertoire.

Nonetheless, Henry delivered—although greater roles were at his doorstep— one of his best performances of the decade. In it, he's effective from beginning to end, starting out as an idealistic youth whose faith in American justice is shattered. Even though his character is later freed from prison, it appears that his faith in the U.S. justice system will never be restored.

***

The Story of Alexander Graham Bell (1938)

Henry had so little regard for his next movie, *The Story of Alexander Graham Bell* (1938), that he didn't even mention it in his memoirs. It was a somewhat fictionalized biopic of this Scottish-born eccentric, an inventor who patented the first practical telephone.

"Don Ameche was cast as Bell," Henry said, "and I was given the thankless role of Tom Watson, his assistant. Watson's claim to fame was that he heard the first words ever spoken over a telephone. The movie became the most famous Ameche ever made."

A recent survey of high school students found that only eight out of 100 knew who Alexander Graham Bell (1847-1922) was. Ironically, this son of Edinburgh had both a mother and a wife who was deaf. Although he patented the telephone on March 7, 1876, he found the instrument so intrusive that he would not allow one in his study.

Graham had, during his heyday, been so famous that at his funeral, phones across America went silent to honor their inventor.

Early in its planning stages, Darryl F. Zanuck, the CEO at Fox, summoned the film's newly appointed director, Irving Cummings, Sr. to his office to cast the leads. It was Zanuck who suggested Ameche and Loretta Young for the lead roles of Mr. Bell and his deaf wife. As Tom Watson, Cummings recommended Fonda.

Henry met Cummings over lunch at the Fox commissary. He had learned of the director's background, which began as a stage actor. Once, he'd appeared on-stage with the fabled showgirl, Lillian Russell, the subject of an upcoming biopic

It was an era of "instructional" and "inspirational" films coming out of Hollywood, ones which would probably not be considered economically viable today.

Lower photo, the real-life inventor, Scotland-born **Alexander Graham Bell,** in 1885 with his wife, **Mabel Gardiner Hubbard**, and daughters **Elsie May Bell** *(far left)* and **Marian Hubbard Bell.**

in which Henry would eventually co-star.

Beginning in 1909, Cummings began evolving into a leading man in silent pictures. When he starred in Fred Niblo's movie, *Sex* (1920), it marked the first time that "The Flapper" had ever appeared on a screen. *[Flappers, known for short dresses, flat bosoms, and loose morals, became famous during the Roaring Twenties for dancing the Charleston.]*

In time, Cummings turned to directing, being nominated for a Best Director Academy Award in 1929 for *In Old Arizona.*

Eventually, he became known for directing such stars as Shirley Temple in *Little Miss Broadway* in 1938, along with musical stars such as Alice Faye, Betty Grable, and Carmen Miranda.

Handsome, debonaire Don Ameche, a native of Wisconsin, had been a leading man at Fox since 1935. The year he worked with Henry he also released *Hollywood Cavalcade* (1939) and had starred as Stephen Foster in the bio picture *Swanee River (also 1939).*

Beautiful actors (**Don Ameche** and **Loretta Young**) emulating real-life historical figures, Alexander Graham Bell and his hardworking (deaf from scarlet fever since the age of five) wife, Mabel Gardiner Hubbard.

Off screen, Ameche was seen so often in the company of Tyrone Power that Louella Parsons spread the rumor that they were lovers. Alice Faye, who would co-star with both actors, was convinced that they were each gay (or at least bisexual but preoccupied with each other) "because neither of them ever made a pass at me, although I sent out signals. One day, in my frustration, I asked Power, 'Why not try a gal for a change?'"

[Actually Ameche had married Honore Prendergast in 1932, a union that lasted until her death in 1986.]

When Cummings told Henry he'd be working with Ameche and Young, he quipped, "I bet those two will fight over boudoir rights to Ty."

Coincidentally, Power had starred in 1938 in *Suez*, in which his co-stars had included Loretta Young, with whom he was having an affair, and Annabella, whom he would marry in 1939. Henry had made love to the French actress when they had co-starred in *Wings of the Morning* (1937).

Henry Fonda (left) regretted the limited range of his role, a portrayal of Bell's assistant, Tom Watson. Here, he's listlessly waiting for a phone to ring.

On the right, as "Father Bell" himself, **Don Ameche** steals the scene.

Henry had long admired the talents and other charms of Loretta Young. Born in Salt Lake City in 1913, she had moved to Hollywood, where she became a child actress in 1917.

Her first marriage to Grant Withers in 1930 had lasted only a few months, leaving her free to play the field for the remainder of the 1930s. Coming and going from her bed, were Douglas Fairbanks Jr., Clark Gable (with whom she'd already produced a daughter "out of wedlock"), and Spencer Tracy. Henry's best friend, James Stewart, also found time to seduce her.

Young told Henry that playing the deaf wife of Alexander Graham Bell was one of the most challenging roles of her career. "Being deaf means you have to be more sensitive," she said. "In a love scene, you have to feel his lips to hear that he loves you."

In a surprise casting, all three of her sisters were also in the movie. Loretta had been involved in a love affair with Norman Foster a few years earlier. He had married Claudette Colbert, but they occupied different houses. Their divorce would become final in 1935.

By this time, Sally Blane, Loretta's sister, was already dating Foster and wed him that same year. Young was responsible for getting Sally cast within the Alexander Graham Bell movie in the role of Gertrude Hubbard, one of the sisters in the Hubbard family. Its "reigning patriarch" was the wealthy Gardner Hubbard, as portrayed by Charles Coburn. Her other sisters were Polly Ann Young (Grace Hubbard) and Georgiana Young (Berta Hubbard). Georgiana would go on to marry that Latin lover of the screen, Ricardo Montalban.

Spring Byington, whose character was married to Gardner Hubbard (Charles Coburn), played the mother of these daughters. A lesbian, Byington told Henry, "I can't tell you how hard it is to be convincing as the wife of this old goat. He's from redneck Georgia and still believes that slaves should not have to be freed. He's a member of the White Citizen's Council, a white supremacist group."

Gene Lockhart, a Canadian American, played the minor role of Thomas Sanders. He became a U.S. citizen that year and would go on to nab parts in three-hundred other movies.

He had a very sympathetic role as one of the early financial backers of Bell's experiments with the telephone.

At the movie's opening, Bell is a struggling inventor, having to make a living teaching deaf people. He meets Mabel (Young) who is the daughter of the wealthy man Coburn played. She persuades her father to help finance Bell's scientific research. Ameche, as Bell, hires Tom Watson (Fonda), an electrician, as his assistant.

Near the end of the movie, Bell gets ensnared in a high-profile legal challenge from Bell Telephone, its lawyers falsely claiming that the communications giant had been the first to file a patent for the telephone. Thanks to the intervention of Mrs. Bell (Loretta Young), her husband wins the case and is cut in on one-fifth ownership of the Bell Telephone Empire.

Before that, a pivotal scene takes place in London, where Queen Victoria (Beryl Mercer) is introduced to this new-fangled invention. She orders that telephones be installed in Buckingham Palace, predicting that they'll soon be installed throughout the British Isles. After praising the inventive spirits of the Americans, she is informed that Bell is from Scotland.

Variety claimed that Henry slugs through his role as the "faithful and tireless assistant." Critic Michael Kerbel found that Henry provides "comic relief with his laconic sarcasm."

Another writer said that Henry "poured a little acid on the refined sugar of co-stars Ameche and Young."

A critic for the *New York Herald Tribune* wrote, "If one were inclined to find fault, one might reason that the comedy contrast of Thomas Watson, who is a loyal but unimaginative soul, is a bit too finely drawn. However, one would have to admit that these strains of levity, furnished by the increasingly capable Henry Fonda, are welcome safety valves when the situations are most tense."

The Bell film sent Don Ameche, who walked away with the picture, over the top. As for Loretta Young, it was widely acknowledged that no one portrayed a deaf mute better than her until Jane Wyman came along with her Oscar-winning portrait in *Johnny Belinda* (1948).

"For me," Henry said, "It did nothing to help my career, but whimper not, Fonda. John Ford was about to enter my life with the motion picture for which I would be forever associated."

***

Young Mr. Lincoln (1939)

As executive producer of *Young Mr. Lincoln*, Darryl F. Zanuck, the autocratic CEO of 20th Century Fox, hired Kenneth Macgowan as its producer. Early in that film's creative life, when casting issues were raised, Zanuck had already made up his mind.

He adamantly endorsed John Ford to direct the film, and Henry Fonda as the best choice for the portrayal of a 23-year-old Abraham Lincoln. Both men were stunned when the proposed director and the proposed star each rejected any involvement in the film, for which a budget of $1,500,000 had already been allocated.

Ford explained his reasons for not wanting the job: "We've already worked Young Lincoln to death." He cited two recent Broadway plays that had dealt with Lincoln's young days as a lawyer in Illinois. One of them had been *Prologue to Glory*, followed by Robert Sherwood's *Abe Lincoln in Illinois*, which won the Pulitzer Prize.

Ford was told that he'd be paid $75,000 to direct the picture. With that in mind, screenwriter Lamar Trotti arrived at his home to review the script with him. They spent the afternoon reading and talking about the story line.

By six o'clock that evening, Ford had changed his mind, claiming that he found the script original, fresh, sensitive, and graceful—unusual praise for a script that depicted a tall, bumbling, gawky young lawyer from the backwoods.

The next day, he was informed that Fonda had refused the role and that it would be wise to instruct his crew to begin evaluating and testing other actors. In response to that, Ford phoned Fonda at his home. "What in the fuck is all this shit that you don't want to play Lincoln?"

"I fear that it's beyond my range," Fonda answered. "It would be like playing Christ."

"To hell it is—fuck that idea,"

The historical melodrama that propelled **Henry Fonda**'s career into the big time.

Its director, John Ford, recognized that the Midwestern origins, gangly limbs, thoughtful cadences, and relentless earnestness of the young actor would be valuable assets in his portrayal of Honest Abe.

Many of Fonda's latter-day fans believe that he was born to play it.

[Henry soon realized that Ford could not utter a sentence, any sentence, without using profanity.]

"You don't have to play the Great Emancipator, presiding over the Civil War. In our script, you're a jacklegged, lanky young lawyer arriving in Springfield on a mule because you can't afford a horse."

"That's a role I could play," Henry said.

He later told Ford that he was a "Lincoln buff," and that he had read every book on Lincoln in the Omaha library. As related earlier, he had also toured the Midwest with George Billings, the country's leading Abraham Lincoln impersonator. On stage alongside him, Henry had played John Hay, Lincoln's secretary, a tall, skinny young man.

In makeup the next day, Henry recalled the grueling experience, a ritual of "pancake and prosthetics." In his early days, Lincoln had not grown a beard, so the makeup artists went to work transforming his face without the benefit of any additional "camouflage."

He was given a *faux* nose, and even an imitation big wart was glued to his face. Hairdressers went to work on his existing coiffure: he would not have to wear a wig—only submit to a restyling.

In wardrobe, two gay costumers ordered him to strip to his underwear and then proceeded to redress him. He was fitted with unpressed black trousers, a heavily starched white shirt, a string necktie, and a knee-length frock coat topped off by a stovepipe hat.

As he surveyed his image in a full-length mirror, Henry decided that he did resemble the young Lincoln, and that he was ready to shoulder this challenging role, shooting for which was scheduled during February of 1939.

John Ford had emerged in his life, and their long and famous association had begun.

***

Henry rapidly came into Ford's orbit. He would later tell the director's grandson, Dan Ford, that, "John was full of bullshit, but a delightful kind of bullshit. He had a great instinct as a director—fantastic, sensitive, and keen, a man who did everything instinctively."

As Henry remembered him, "He wore baggy clothes that looked like something he'd picked up at the Salvation Army. Under his floppy hat, he always wore a pair of dark glasses. Most often, he went around smoking a briarwood pipe. In all, he was a hard-drinking Irishman, stout of flesh."

As his grandson, Dan, wrote, "Pappy was born Sean O'Feeney in 1895, and rose from obscure beginnings as the son of an Irish-born bootlegger-saloon keeper to become one of Hollywood's greatest directors. Starting his career at the height of the silent era, he went on to make some eighty feature films, many of them classics, and many starring Henry Fonda."

During the shoot, Henry called Ford "Pappy," and the director referred to him as "Toots." Privately, one drunken night, the (semi-closeted gay) director alarmed Henry when he confessed "I always fall in love with my leading man. A lot of people can't believe that because I come off as so rugged and masculine."

[Ford's homosexuality has already been "outed" in many latter-day articles and biographies. He was alleged to have put a young John Wayne on the casting couch. Later, he warned Maureen O'Hara, "There's not enough there to mess up your mouth with." Although Ford and the Duke became close friends, Ford later admitted, in reference to Wayne, that "He's really a big idiot."

O'Hara revealed in her 2004 biography, 'Tis Herself, that she had walked in on Ford one day, finding him lip-locked with Tyrone Power.]

Whereas Ford sometimes expressed admiration for Henry, he could

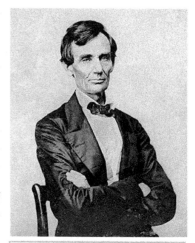

Abraham Lincoln (aka Honest Abe, the Rail-Splitter, or the Great Emancipator; 1809-1865)

Henry Fonda emulating "The Great Emancipator," using every aspect of his "actor's instrument," including his height, for a realistic replication.

Murky, complicated, self-tormenting, brilliant, and a dutiful and very Catholic, hard-drinking son of Ireland: **Director John Ford**

125

also turn on him if he didn't like his performance in any particular scene. During a rehearsal for one of the film's episodes, they got into an intense argument, and Ford bashed his face, bloodying his nose. They quickly made up when the bleeding stopped.

Ford was very clear in issuing orders that one scene should be cut from the script. It was of a young John Wilkes Booth who meets the man he will assassinate years later—in 1864—at a theater in Washington, D.C.

Most of the characters in *Young Mr. Lincoln* were fictional, but Mary Todd, Ann Rutledge, and Stephen A. Douglas were personalities inspired by living historical figures.

Abe's first love, Kentuckian Ann Rutledge, was born in 1813, the third of ten children. Most aspects of her life have been lost to history. In his own later life, Lincoln sometimes spoke of her, lamenting her early death in 1835.

["It is true—true indeed. I did love the woman dearly and soundly. She was a handsome girl—would have made a good, loving wife. I did honestly and truly love the girl and think of her often."]

Young **Mary Todd Lincoln** in 1846 at the age of 28, four years after her marriage to Abraham Lincoln, and shortly before his election to the U.S. House of Representatives from Illinois

Mary Todd, of course, became the wife of Lincoln nineteen years before he became 16th President of the United States. Her reign as First Lady lasted from 1861 until her husband was assassinated in 1865. She and Lincoln had four sons, three of whom died young.

She was depressed throughout most of her life and was put in an institution for "psychiatric disease" in 1875. She died of a stroke at the age of 65 in 1882.

She was once courted by Stephen A. Douglas, the longtime political opponent of Lincoln. Born in 1813, Douglas had previously defeated Lincoln after the famous Lincoln-Douglas debates of 1858. Douglas was elected Senator from Illinois. Lincoln came back and defeated the Democratic party nominee in the 1860 presidential election.

During the first year of the U.S. Civil War, Douglas contracted typhoid fever and died on June 4, 1861. On that day, the first skirmish of the Civil War, the Battle of Philippi, was fought.

In the plot of *Young Mr. Lincoln*, the setting is 1832 in New Salem, Illinois, where Abe Lincoln is part owner of a general store. The Clay family is passing through in their covered wagon. Abigail Clay is the mother of three children (Eddie, Matt, and Sarah) traveling with her.

They have no money, but they're willing to barter away some of their possessions, including their collection of books, including *Blackstone's Commentaries*. After reading that book, Lincoln is inspired to become a lawyer.

He receives encouragement from his first sweetheart, Ann Rutledge. She soon dies and, one wintry night at her grave, he vows to study law and get a license to practice it in Illinois.

In the plot, in 1837, Lincoln arrives in Springfield, Illinois' capital, to establish his law practice. He soon meets Mary Todd, who invites him to a *soirée*.

Here, he meets the very polished Stephen Douglas, who will, later in life, become his political opponent.

When Springfield celebrates Independence Day, it turns raucous. A tragedy ensues. The Clay brothers encounter two roughnecks, Jack Cass and Scrub White. White is killed when he draws a gun during a fight. Abigail, the mother of the Clay brothers, witnesses the shooting.

Later, her sons are fingered as the murderers. Since the actual killer is not known, both of the brothers end up in jail awaiting trial. Lincoln becomes their lawyer.

Before the trial, an angry mob assembles, and its members demand to be let into the jail, capture the (innocent) brothers, and hang them. One man expresses the mood of the mob, claiming that they're "hungry for a lynching."

Lincoln shows his skill as an orator by convincing the angry men to go home and await the results of the trial.

Marjorie Weaver and **Henry Fonda** portraying the First Lady and President Lincoln in *Young Mr. Lincoln* (1939).

A beauty contest winner from Tennessee, Weaver has a dubious footnote in Hollywood history: During her four-year marriage to Naval officer Kenneth Schacht, she saw him for only 16 days.

Lincoln has to face off against veteran trial lawyer, Stephen Douglas, who is also wooing Mary Todd.

Since the mother of the two accused boys witnessed the killing, she is asked to name which of her sons actually killed the victim. Faced with that horrid request, she refuses.

Eventually, Cass is exposed as the real killer, and the Clay brothers are free to continue their westbound transit aboard their wagon train to a new life.

At the end of the trial, Douglas tells Lincoln that he will never underestimate him again.

After screening the film's final cut, Ford called Henry's courtroom style "folksy shim-sham, which I was going for. You brought Lincoln down from a monument and made him a man."

The soundtrack swells to the sounds of "The Battle Hymn of the Republic." Lincoln had already suggested that he is thinking about entering politics.

Ford carefully selected a supporting cast with no household names, yet each was a talented thespian ideal for the part he wanted them to play. Cast as Mary Todd, Marjorie Weaver had appeared in pictures in the 1930s and stuck around until the early 1950s as film roles dwindled. Before working with Henry, she had appeared opposite his friend, Tyrone Power, in *Second Honeymoon* (1937).

Alice Brady as Abigail Clay, the mother in the covered wagon, was the daughter of the famous producer William A. Brady. She was only four by the time she walked onto her first stage, and by 1931, she was on Broadway starring with John Barrymore. In one decade, she starred in fifty-three silent pictures.

Her most famous role was as Mrs. Molly O'Leary, a fictional version of Catherine O'Leary, whose temperamental cow kicked over an oil-burning lantern and burned down Chicago.

In the 1937 film, *In Old Chicago* starring Tyrone Power, Brady had won a plaque for Best Supporting Actress of the Year. *[The Academy at the time gave only plaques, not statuettes, for supporting roles. Unable to attend, Brady learned that an imposter had accepted her award, and it was never seen again.]*

Shortly after making *Young Mr. Lincoln,* in October of 1939, Brady died, suffering from cancer.

Richard Cromwell was cast as her son, Matt Clay. *[He had recently made* Jezebel *with Henry.]* He frequently made sexually suggestive passes at Henry, once or twice telling him, "Since that first night I met you at the home of George Cukor, I've had the hots for you. When are you going to relent?"

"The next picture we appear in," Henry jokingly promised.

As the Clay family's second son, Adam Clay was portrayed by Eddie Quillan. He came from a family of vaudeville performers, having made his stage debut at the age of seven. His career thrived in the silents and continued into the talkies before his television debut in the 1980s. Occasionally, he would have a minor role in a classic, as when he appeared with Clark Gable in *Mutiny on the Bounty* (1935). Quillan would soon be working with Henry on the set of *The Grapes of Wrath.*

The fourth member of the Clay family was actress Adeen Whelan, cast as Sarah. She'd made her debut in *Frankenstein* (1931) and had continued to appear in films as late as 1958, often in B-picture Westerns. Her biggest moment had come when she nabbed the female lead in Robert Louis Stevenson's *Kidnapped* (1938).

The role of Abe's first sweetheart, Ann Rutledge, went to Pauline Moore, who in time appeared in a number of Westerns and other movies in the 1930s and '40s. She'd made her film debut in *Frankenstein* (1931) and starred with Shirley Temple in *Heidi* (1937) before ending up in "oaters" with Roy Rogers or in one of those Charlie Chan detective stories.

The villain of the Lincoln film, John Palmer Cass, was cast with Ward Bond. Like Henry, he was a native of the rough winters and hot summers of Nebraska.

In Hollywood, Bond formed a trio of best buddies that included John Wayne and John Ford. Before the end of his career, he starred in two-hundred films, none more notable than *It's a Wonderful Life* (1946) with James Stewart. In Ford's *The Searchers* (1956) he appeared with The Duke (John Wayne) himself. The year he worked with Henry and Ford, he'd had a minor role in *Gone With the Wind.*

Two views of **Alice Brady,** a venerable hoofer from the days of vaudeville and the silent screen, was instrumental in the development of Humphrey Bogart as a cinematic giant.

Noted for her role in *Young Mr. Lincoln* as a Great Plains matriarch, she died shortly after the release of the film that made Henry Fonda a household name.

Lincoln's chief rival, Stephen Douglas, was cast with veteran actor Milburn Stone. The former vaudeville performer hit it big in the role of "Doc," starring in the CBS Western series, *Gunsmoke* (1955-1975).

Fred Kohler Jr. was cast as the ruffian Scrub White, the young man who was killed after he pulled a gun in a fight. His murder becomes the centerpiece of the trial that followed.

As the prosecuting attorney, John Felder, actor Donald Meeks had gone on the stage at the age of eight. Before working with Henry, he had made his two best-known films, *You Can't Take It With You* (1938) with James Stewart, and *Stagecoach* (1939) with John Wayne.

Cliff Clark, cast as Sheriff Gil Billings, had been in the film industry only two years before he worked with Ford on *Young Mr. Lincoln.* He'd go on to appear in minor roles in some 200 other movies, often as a sheriff, a detective, or a police inspector.

Spencer Charles, as Judge Herbert A. Bell, was "discovered" in 1890 working as a machinist for the Chesapeake nail factory in Harrisburg, Pennsylvania. By 1910, he was on the Broadway stage, eventually, in the 1930s, evolving into a busy character actor portraying befuddled judges, doctors, clerks, managers, and jailers.

On December 22, 1941, he committed suicide from a mix of sleeping pills and carbon monoxide poisoning.

Young Mr. Lincoln met with critical success, Otis Ferguson in *The New Republic* writing, "You will not forget, I hope, the lanky, eager, common sweetness of Henry Fonda, whose Lincoln was high and far above the studied caricatures of Raymond Massey."

Herbert Cohn of the *Brooklyn Eagle* claimed, "It will be no small task in the Lincoln films to come to match the work of Henry Fonda. His Lincoln might have stepped out of a picture gallery and come alive to stride through the streets of Springfield. We can't remember when Fonda has been better."

The critic for *The New York Times* wrote: "Mr. Fonda supplies the warmth and kindness, the pleasant modesty, the courage, resolution, tenderness, shrewdness of wit that kindles the film and makes it a moving unity, at once gentle and quizzically comic."

Matthew Lucas in a review pointed out "John Ford would go on to make grander, greater films. But none were quite as discreetly powerful as *Young Mr. Lincoln*. It's one of the most assured, accomplished works, an expertly crafted slice of Americana that portrays our nation, not necessarily as it is or was, but as it was always meant to be."

Variety commented, "Fonda has not compromised on the popular conception of the ungainly Lincoln. The makeup is authentic and highly affective on both the physical, exterior and Fonda's own serious interpretation."

During the course of his career, Ford became the recipient of six Academy Awards, four of which were for Best Director. In a career that spanned half a century, he helmed 140 movies. Orson Welles considered him the greatest director of all time.

Even though *Young Mr. Lincoln* was hailed as a triumph for both Henry Fonda and for John Ford, the movie lost $100,000 upon its initial release.

Screenwriter Lamar Trotti was nominated for an Oscar for Best Writing of an Original Story.

In 2003, *Young Mr. Lincoln* was selected for preservation in the U.S. National Film Registry for being "culturally, historically, and aesthetically significant."

***

Tactless, crude, predatory, and universally loathed, **Darryl Zanuck** did a lot to build America's entertainment industry into the profit-motivated monster that many critics claim that it is.

Here's the cover of the June 12,1950 edition of *Time* Magazine, whose illustration includes a flattering portrait wearing a depiction of a celluloid crown.

Film publicists have defined *Drums Along The Mohawk* (1939) as a classic John Ford western about the relationship between civilization, anarchy and barbarity.

Here's **Henry Fonda** with French-born **Claudette Colbert** portraying frontier settlers in upper New York State shortly after the U.S. War of Independence, taming the wilderness (and obliterating the natives) with grit, determination, flair, and enormous personal suffering.

In *Drums Along the Mohawk*, **Claudette Colbert's** character wasn't at all like the confident, "modern" society women she had portrayed so convincingly in the past.

Here, she protects the safety of frontier colleagues and their children with the ferocity expected at the time of any man.

Drums Along the Mohawk **(1939)**

Even though it had not generated the box office bonanza that he had hoped for, *Young Mr. Lincoln* pleased the boss at Fox, Darryl F. Zanuck. He assigned Henry and John Ford to work together on his next picture, *Drums Along the Mohawk*, set for a 1939 release in Technicolor.

Once again, the screenwriter was Lamar Trotti, based on the novel by Walter D. Edmonds.

On loan from Paramount, Claudette Colbert would get top billing in her role of Lana Magdelan, with Henry cast as her husband, Gilbert ("Gil") Martin. The third lead (Mrs. McKlennar) went to Edna May Oliver, who often played tart-tonged spinsters. John Carradine and Ward Bond were the leading supporting players. Each of them had worked with Henry before.

Henry felt a personal connection to *Drums* since his early Dutch ancestors had settled in upper New York State during the early Colonial period, the era and location for the movie.

Lana and Gil head for the Mohawk Valley to find a life for themselves during the American Revolutionary War. Before peace is restored to the Valley, the frontier couple will suffer attacks from both the British and from the Indians.

At the time of the drama, the homeland of the "Iroquois Six Nations" was under threat from the arrival of increasing numbers of white settlers. The Indians broke into different factions, some siding with the British, others with the Americans.

Warned of an imminent Indian attack, Gil and Lana take refuge in the nearby Fort Schuyler. A pregnant Lana suffers a miscarriage. Then they learn that a raiding party of Seneca Indians has burned their home to the ground. With winter on the way, the Martins take refuge in the home of a rich widow, Mrs. McKlennar.

Later, Gil is almost slain fighting British-backed Indians, having joined forces with the local militia.

When the Indians and the British invade the Valley, Gil outruns the attackers to get help. In that, he succeeds, as Continental forces sweep in as the fort is about to be overrun.

Zanuck wanted Gil's twenty-mile run to be featured as the highlight of the movie. "This scene can be whipped into one of the most unusual and exciting climaxes ever seen on the screen, and we can afford to let it run a thousand feet, taking up eleven minutes of screen time."

Drums Along the Mohawk was released at a delicate time in world politics. World War II had recently broken out, and the British had emerged as the main bulwark against Hitler's invading armies.

At such a delicate moment in world history, Zanuck did not want to portray the British in a bad light. "I don't want to portray the Brits as harsh villains." Therefore, British soldiers were seldom referenced in the film, and celluloid hostilities remained mostly between the Indians and the Tories.

"Claudette was a true professional, but I think Loretta Young could have made her character more convincing," Henry later commented.

Claudette Colbert, who had been born in France, was appearing regularly on Broadway in the 1920s. Later gravitating to Hollywood, she worked first for Paramount. At Columbia Pictures, she won a Best Actress Oscar for *It Happened One Night* (1934) alongside Clark Gable. That same year, she had a big success playing *Cleopatra*.

She was so short that many members of the crew called her "The Dwarf" be-

Although you'd never know it from **Claudette Colbert's** frontier-swoman garb in *Drums Along the Mohawk*, she was an international fashion icon and symbol of Gallic grandeur, especially during her film heyday in the 1930s.

Everyone in Hollywood said everything conceivable about **Marlene Dietrich**, including frequent "accusations" of predatory "non-gender preferenced" debauchery.

Here she is as she appeared in male drag in *Morocco* (1930)

hind her back. She was luminous on the screen, with her charming aristocratic manner enhanced by her big eyes and round face.

Her brilliance in both light comedy and emotional drama made her one of the best-paid stars of the 1930s and 40s. An actress in sixty movies, she appeared most frequently with Fred MacMurray (seven films) and Fredric March (four movies).

On the set of *Drums Along the Mohawk,* Colbert was relentlessly demanding of the way she was photographed, restaging some shots of herself with Henry. She felt that the right side of her face was flawed, so she demanded to be photographed only on the left. The crew dubbed the right side of her face "the dark side of the moon" because no camera operator ever "officially" saw it.

Although that requirement was widely reported at the time, a close study of the film's final cut revealed that her right side, on that rare occasion when it was shown at all, appeared only in long shots, angled and shadowed.

While Henry's closest friend, James Stewart, was wildly seducing his leading ladies of the 1930s, Henry didn't even try to move in on Colbert. He had been advised that she was off-limits, even though he wasn't sexually attracted to her anyway.,

She had a reputation of being a lesbian, especially when Marlene Dietrich was in town. However, on rare occasions, she'd seduce her leading men. Such was the case when she'd worked with Fred MacMurray on *Gilded Lily* (1935). Before that, Gary Cooper had seduced her when they co-starred in *His Woman* (1931).

During her first marriage, to Norman Foster, the couple lived in different homes and pursued radically different lives. Her final marriage to Dr. Joel Pressman, a union that lasted thirty-five years, was equally unconventional.

"When I did see him, he never wanted to talk shop, that is, my making films. It's my belief that he never went to see any of my pictures."

In 1958, Colbert met and began a longtime affair with Verna Hull, a photographer and painter and one of the Sears & Roebuck heiresses.

Colbert ultimately settled into the Caribbean island nation of Barbados, where she became its alltime most famous resident.

Frances Fonda recalled that a few years after its release, she took her stepdaughter, Jane, for a screening of *Drums Along the Mohawk.* "It may have been the first time she saw her father on the screen. She became hysterical when she saw her dad being chased by Indians."

Most critics found that although *Drums* made very few demands on Henry's acting talent, he nonetheless created a believable portrait of an American pioneer facing great odds. *Variety* found him "lacking as a romantic male lead, but giving a good, steady performance nonetheless."

The film became a major success for Fox, grossing a million dollars in the first year. Edna May Oliver was nominated for a Best Supporting Actress Oscar.

In *The New York Times,* Frank S. Nugent summarized key points about the movie like this: "It is romantic enough for any adventure story lover. It has humor and its full compliment of blood and thunder make it a first-rate historical film. Fonda and Colbert have done rather nicely as Gil and Lana. Miss Oliver could not have been better as the warlike widow."

***

By the time *Drums Along the Mohawk* was released, John Ford had evolved into a key player in the life of Henry Fonda.

For his next film, Darryl Zanuck opted to overlook his many differences with Henry and commissioned John Ford to once again direct him in what became his most memorable film, *The Grapes of Wrath,* based on the seminal novel by John Steinbeck.

Diehard fans of John Ford Westerns interpret **Henry Fonda**'s portrayal of a settler along the Mohawk as a precursor of future "cowboy movies of the Wild West' to come.

CHAPTER EIGHT

MAIN STREET AMERICA IS DIVIDED BY

WAR IN EUROPE

EVEN THOUGH THE U.S. ISN'T YET INVOLVED,

AS A DEPRESSION-ERA REFUGEE FROM THE DUST BOWL
HENRY FONDA SHOOTS TO MAJOR STARDOM WITH

THE GRAPES OF WRATH

"Watching The Grapes of Wrath *is a reminder that Americans have been fucked for a very long time
—and remain fucked for many today.*
—Henry Fonda

HENRY JEALOUSLY STANDS ON THE SIDELINES AS HIS BEST FRIEND
JAMES STEWART
STARS IN ONE CLASSIC AFTER ANOTHER
(& SEDUCES GREATER NUMBERS OF GOLDEN AGE DIVAS, TOO.)

THE BIRTH OF HENRY'S SECOND CHILD, PETER
*AN INCREASINGLY UNSTABLE FRANCES FONDA
DEMANDS POSTPARTUM TIME ALONE, WITHOUT HER CHILD OR ITS FATHER,
IN MANHATTAN WITH HER SOCIETY FRIENDS*

MORE ABOUT MARGARET
(SULLAVAN)
STEWART IS STILL IN LOVE WITH HENRY'S EX-WIFE

GONE WITH THE WIND
OLIVIA DE HAVILLAND WANTS HENRY AS ASHLEY WILKES, BUT SELZNICK HAS OTHER PLANS

HENRY SIGNS A SEVEN-YEAR
"SLAVE CONTRACT"
WITH DARRYL "FUCK IT ALL" (HENRY'S WORDS) ZANUCK

IN THE 1940 BEST ACTOR OSCAR RACE,
HENRY IS OSCAR-NOMINATED FOR
THE GRAPES OF WRATH
BUT LOSES TO JAMES STEWART FOR *THE PHILADELPHIA STORY*

FONDA VS. STEWART

FONDA'S CAREER TEMPORARILY DE-ACCELERATES

AS JAMES STEWART GRABS HEADLINE-GENERATING ROLES IN AN ASTONISHING ROSTER OF HEROIC LEADS
(*MR. SMITH GOES TO WASHINGTON, DESTRY RIDES AGAIN, THE PHILADELPHIA STORY*,) AND LOVERS (GINGER
ROGERS, LORETTA YOUNG, CAROLE LOMBARD, NORMA SHEARER, JOAN CRAWFORD, OLIVIA DE HAVILLAND,
CLAUDETTE COLBERT, ROSALIND RUSSELL, MARLENE DIETRICH, & KATHARINE HEPBURN).

As the value of John Steinbeck's socialist novel, *The Grapes of Wrath,* became widely obvious after its publication in April of 1939, Americans began listening intently to breaking news from Europe. In September of 1939, Hitler's Nazi forces launched its massive invasion of Western Poland, overcoming its meager defenses. Since France and England had an ironclad defense agreement with Poland, World War II, the most destructive in the history of the world, was immediately unleashed.

Most of the sympathy of the American people, of course, was with the British, French, Polish, and other Allies, The United States—at least until Japan's bombardment, on December 7, 1941 of Pearl Harbor—continued to assert its neutrality.

Both Henry and *The Grapes of Wrath's* director, John Ford, each speculated that within months America would join the war against the Nazis. Although a land invasion of the U.S. by Germany seemed remote at that point, many predicted that an attack on some remote American outpost might be launched by the forces of Imperial Japan, which at the time maintained a defense treaty with Nazi Germany.

The U.S. Declaration of War on December 7, 1941, changed Hollywood, the world, and Henry Fonda's career overnight.

The Grapes of Wrath **(1940)**

As an actor lusting after his next juicy role, Henry had read *The Grapes of Wrath*, soon after it was published. In reference to its advocacy of issues pertinent to working class Americans ravaged by the Great Depression, Steinbeck had claimed, "I've done my damnedest to rip the readers' nerves to rags."

Many conservatives interpreted the novel's vivid description of the Dust Bowl tragedy as an attack on America itself, labeling the book as either "subversive" or as "radical communist propaganda." Particularly hostile to its message was Louis B. Mayer at MGM, who refused to purchase its (potentially profitable) movie rights.

[In contrast to its denunciation by conservatives, the novel, for the most part, met with academic and popular praise. In the first year of its release, it sold 430,000 copies, and during the course of its lifetime, it would sell more than fourteen million copies. It won the Pulitzer Prize the year of its publication, and by 1962, its author won the Nobel Prize for Literature. Eventually, Darryl F. Zanuck, the much-loathed head honcho at Twentieth Century Fox, paid $100,000 for the rights, partly in defiance after Mayer famously rejected them.]

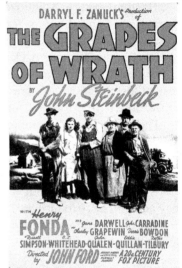

John Garfield immediately lobbied for the role of Tom Joad, but Zanuck interpreted his New York accent as too pronounced. Tyrone Power was considered but rejected as "too beautiful" for the role. And there was a fear that the suave and very urban Don Ameche might be a joke as an Oakie.

From the beginning, Fox's director, John Ford, had wanted Henry as the film adaptation's male lead, but warned him, "Do less, suggest more."

Steinbeck himself had worried, "I trust Henry Fonda as Tom, but I have no idea what that cigar-smoking womanizer, Zanuck, is going to do to my story."

Henry himself made no secret about desperately wanting the lead role of Tom Joad. Although he'd urged his agent, Leland Hayward, to arrange it with Fox, he'd qualified his enthusiasm for the role by telling him, "I loathe that bastard Zanuck. All he's interested in is box office gross and getting his cock sucked every day by some starlet."

Leland's arrangements did not go well. Zanuck would give Henry the lead role only if he signed a seven-year contract with Fox. Henry desperately wanted to remain a freelancer, without permanent and binding links to any studio. Yet he longed for the role of Tom Joad so desperately that, against his better judgment, he signed what he defined as "a slave contract."

"I have to insist on signing you," Zanuck demanded. "Otherwise, as a freelancer, you'd go off and make a movie with Joan Crawford."

Nunnally Johnson was hired to adapt Steinbeck's novel into a screenplay. Zanuck met with him, outlining what he wanted and warning him to tone down some of the "socialist" content. "In some scenes, we can't be as daring as Steinbeck."

One scene in particular would never get past the censors. That is when "The Rose of Sharon Joad Rivers," the oldest Joad daughter, produces a stillborn baby.

Almost the same day, Ma Joad encounters a young boy and his father. The older man is obviously dying of starvation. Ma realizes there's only one way to save him. She signals to Sharon, who, left alone with the man, lets him drain her of her breast milk.

Basically, Zanuck wanted his writer to "let politics take a back seat to the personal travails of the Joad family and their caravan heading west."

Ford hired Gregg Toland, one of the best cinematographers

EVEN ON THE GREAT PLAINS OF NORTH AMERICA, THE APOCALYSE SEEMED NEAR

On April 14, 1935, after a prolonged drought across the Central Plains, the infamous "Black Sunday Storm" whipped up millions of tons of dirt and dust so dense that some local witnesses believed that the Apocalypse was near.

Blowing away the topsoil and destroying crops, and later blamed on erosion and a lack of soil conservation techniques, it reduced millions of acres of farmland into a "Dust Bowl" which demoralized thousands of impoverished "Okies."

Thousands of them, like the Joads, began a long migration, as described poignantly in *The Grapes of Wrath*, to more favorable regions like California.

in Hollywood, to shoot the film. As one author put it, "Gregg set out to film murky silhouettes against light skies, plus grim figures bent against the wind." *[In 1941, Toland would craft the cinematography for Orson Welles' masterpiece,* Citizen Kane.*]*

Both Henry and Zanuck "devoured" Johnson's final script. It was later defined as "the definitive example of a novel-to-film adaptation."

The clouds of war were raining down on Europe as filming began that September of 1939. Some scenes were shot on location in the San Fernando Valley; others in the Oakie refugee camps on the outskirts of Los Angeles. Alfred Newman's theme song, "Red River Valley," enhanced the nostalgic aspects of the film.

The film opens as Tom Joad is released from prison after serving four years of a seven-year term for manslaughter. "It was self-defense," he says.

Hitchhiking his way back to his family of sharecroppers, he meets a half-crazed hobo, Jim Casey. Years before, he had baptized Tom, but now he has "lost the spirit." He travels along with Tom back to the little farm-house, only to find the Joad family gone.

They meet Muley Graves, a neighbor, who has decided to stick it out. At the end of one of his early scenes, the mortgage holders of the deeply-in-debt farmers begin tearing down their shanties with bulldozers.

BUT WILL IT MAKE IT TO SAN DIEGO?

Being homeless and broke during the Great Depression meant very little money for gas—and almost no money for spare parts.

Here's the broken-down jalopy (a 1926 Hudson "Super Six") the Joad family used for their exodus to other promised lands.

Tom eventually hooks up with other members of the Joad family and becomes a passenger in their overloaded jalopy, a 1926 Hudson "Super Six." Early in their saga, they view California as the Promised Land. That's before they actually have to face the harsh and unforgiving reality they'll confront there.

The elderly Grandpa Joad did not want to leave his native land and dies during the early stages of their trip. Before their saga is over, his wife, Grandma Joad, will also die during her transit across the Mohave Desert. She had lost her will to live.

The arrival of the Joads in California is very different from the dream they'd envisioned. At first, they anchor in a campground for workers, where they encounter other starving, desperate migrants, all of them seemingly with hungry children. In the understated, folksy way for which Henry Fonda had become known, his character (Tom) says, "Sure don't look too prosperous."

In another camp, they encounter striking workers who have been paid only five cents an hour for picking fruit.

Later, Casey is killed by one of the guards. When Tom tries to defend his friend, he accidentally kills a guard, thereby becoming a wanted man. He suffers a serious wound on his cheek, which can be used to identify him. Although Ma Joad hides him temporarily, he knows he must flee. During his tearful goodbye with Ma, he tells her:

"I'll be all around in the dark. I'll be everywhere. Wherever you can look, wherever there's a fight so hungry people can eat, I'll be there. Wherever there's a cop beatin' up a guy, I'll be there. I'll be in the way guys yell when they're mad. I'll be in the way kids laugh when they're hungry, and they know supper's ready, and when the people are eatin' the stuff they raise and living in the houses they build, I'll be there too."

As the family moves on again, they discuss the fear and difficulties they've had. Ma Joad concludes the film, saying:

A REBEL AND HIS MOTHER

Jane Darwell with **Henry Fonda** as Tom Joad in *The Grapes of Wrath.*

The open, honest acting of this pair helped define it as a movie classic, and still shines from celluloid today in countless revivals.

"I ain't gonna be scared no more. I was, though. For a while, it looked as though we was beat. Good and beat. Looked like we didn't have nobody in the whole wide world but enemies. Like nobody was friendly no more. Made me feel kinda bad and scared, too, like we was lost and nobody cared. Rich fellas come up and they die, and their kids ain't no good and they die out, but we keep a comin'. We're the people that live. They can't wipe us out. They can't lick us. We'll go on forever, Pa, cos' we're the people."

As Ma Joad, Jane Darwell was given "the role of a lifetime," virtually immortalizing herself in Hollywood's film history. She had previously appeared with Henry and Tyrone Power in *Jesse James* (1939), and she'd soon be working with Henry again in the Fox production of *Chad Hanna* (1940).

As Casey, the "defrocked" and half-crazed pastor, John Carradine had a more sympathetic role than he'd had in Henry's previous film. *[Cast as Bob Ford, Carradine's character had assassinated Jesse James.]*

Russell Simpson as "Pa Joad" is a hard-working man whose spirit is broken at the loss of his livelihood. Ma, his wife, has to take over as the leader of her brood.

Born in 1880, Simpson was a character actor who had appeared in 1914 in a film by Cecil B. De Mille called *The Virginian*. Gaunt, lanky, and rustic, he was known for playing grizzled old men. In the future, he would work under the direction of John Ford again in several other movies.

In the role of Grandpa Joad, Charley Grapewin, born in 1869, began his career as a circus and vaudeville performer. From silents to sound, he had roles in a hundred films, most notably as "Uncle Henry" in *The Wizard of Oz* (1939). In *Grapes of Wrath,* he didn't want to leave his native land, so Ma gave him a "soothin' syrup," which drugs him into a stupor so that he can be placed in the jalopy. But he dies soon after the Joads set out on their trip. His family buries him near the western border of Oklahoma.

Eddie Quillan, cast in the role of Connie Rivers, plays the husband of "The Rose of Sharon," the eldest daughter of the Joad family. Only nineteen years old, and overwhelmed by his marriage and his pregnant wife, he abandons her and the Joad family shortly after their arrival in California.

Quillan had recently appeared as one of the Clay brothers with Henry in *Young Mr. Lincoln*.

Cast into the role of "Rose of Sharon Joad Rivers," Dorris Bodon played the oldest daughter of the Joad clan. When she gets married, she is only eighteen, a "dreamy" teenager who is quickly thrust into the problems of a mature woman. Her baby is stillborn.

One critic wrote that she "acted her role like a figure in the mainstream of history rather than as a shallow bit of make-believe."

Perhaps she was the only one in the list of character roles who thought Henry was miscast. She told a reporter, "I heard that Fonda was Zanuck's third choice. He originally wanted Tyrone Power or Don Ameche. Each of them, I'm sure, would have been better than Fonda."

Winfield, the youngest member of the Joad family, was portrayed by Darryl Hickman. Born in 1931, he was often confused with his older brother, Dwayne Hickman, also an actor. Discovered by a Paramount casting agent, he played Ronald Colman's son in *The Prisoner of Zenda* (1937). In the 1930s and '40s, he appeared in a number of pictures, including *Men of Boys Town* (1941). A critic wrote, "He almost ran away with the picture right under Mickey Rooney's nose."

Ward Bond, who played the killer in *Young Mr. Lincoln,* was reduced to a very minor role as a policeman in *The Grapes of Wrath.* After complaining bitterly to his friend and director, John Ford, for giving him a mere walk-on, Ford responded, "Don't worry. I'll triple your paycheck and have you shipped a six-month supply of whisky, buster."

John Qualen played Muley Graves, a neighbor of the Joads. He doesn't want to join the westbound march of the Oakies, preferring to remain in Oklahoma. The Joads leave him two of their dogs, taking the third animal, who is killed in a car accident.

Queland would soon have a minor role in another classic movie, Humphrey Bogart's *Casablanca* (1942).

Cast as Muley's wife was Mae Marsh, a fabled veteran and star of silent pictures. She had even appeared in D.W. Griffith's controversial *Birth of a Nation* (1915). She'd also worked with Mack Sennett in her early days.

By the arrival of the talkies, her career began to fade. Ford, however, liked her and put her in such future films as *How Green Was My Valley* (1941); *3 Godfathers* (1948), and *The Searchers* (1956).

It's been said that most of Marsh's footage of *The Grapes of Wrath* ended up on the cutting room floor. That's not quite the case. Actually, Ford himself destroyed most of her unused footage, fearing that Zanuck might rescue it and insert some of her scenes back into the film.

After an eventful career that had spanned half a century, Marsh died in 1968.

O.Z. Whitehead took the role of Al Joad, the third-youngest member of the clan. He plays "a smart-aleck 16-year-old who cares mainly for cars and girls. At first, he looks up to big brother Tom, but begins to discover his own way of life.

As a member of the informal John Ford Stock Company, Whitehead would play a bizarre range of characters throughout his career. Twenty-two years after *Grapes* found him in his fifth film for Ford—*The Man Who Shot Liberty Valance* (1962). He told Henry, "My real name is Oothout Zabriskie. No one could pronounce it, so I shortened it to O.Z."

Opening in January of 1940 at the Rivoli Theatre in Manhattan, *The Grapes of Wrath* drew some 13,000 people in just one day. The next day and for several days thereafter, that movie house was packed, creating a traffic jam in the heart of the city.

Frank S. Nugent of *The New York Times* wrote *"The Grapes of Wrath* is just about as good as any picture has a right to be. If it were any better, we just wouldn't believe our eyes. Henry Fonda's Tom Joad is precisely the hot-tempered, resolute, saturnine chap Steinbeck had in mind."

Variety wrote, "It took a pile of money and John Ford to film the story of the Dust Bowl and the tribulation of the unhappy survivors, who sought refuge in inhospitable California. Picture is *The Grapes of Wrath* adapted from Steinbeck's bestseller. It is an absorbing, tense melodrama, starkly realistic and loaded with social and political fireworks. It is off to a smash box office career, hot on the heels of *Gone With the Wind,* which precedes it by a few weeks."

The critical response was the best of Henry's career. Critic Tony Thomas wrote: "Fonda's portrayal of Tom Joad can be considered the triumph of his film career."

Legal battles among **John Steinbeck's** heirs over his literary estate are still, more than 50 years after his death in 1968, at high heat.

The once-radical, "socialist" novels of the Nobel Prize winner are still required reading in high schools and universities throughout America.

Some recent trade papers have hinted that *East of Eden* (1955) a film that figured prominently into the superstardom of James Dean, and *The Grapes of Wrath* (1940), which did so much for the public recognition of Henry Fonda, might get reinterpreted and remade.

Robert Nash said that the role "established Fonda as one of the world's top actors."

In *The Village Voice,* Andrew Sarris said, "What stands up to every test of time is Henry Fonda's gritty incarnation of Tom Joad, a volatile mixture of the prairie sincerity of *Young Mr. Lincoln,* and the snarling paranoia of Fritz Lang's *You Only Live Once.*"

Some critics noted that most novelists dream of writing "The Great American Novel," and that Steinbeck had done just that. In many regions of the United States, *The Grapes of Wrath* was banned and even burned in ways that evoked Josef Goebbels and his burning of books in Nazi Germany.

During the peak of its *brouhaha,* Steinbeck received dozens of death threats and took to carrying a gun. "I want to kill my would-be assassin before he mows me down," he famously stated.

Not all reviews of the movie were positive. William Bayer wrote, "The picture is inferior to the novel. "It suffers from being so tiresomely predictable that it is best forgotten."

Dan Ford, grandson of John Ford, later wrote, "*Grapes of Wrath* is both a political and social document, but the film is remembered for its austere and tender beauty. Its first focus is human, and it's the people who ultimately count. The characters are bathing in idealistic light and presented with love, compassion, and human dignity."

Onstage at the Academy Awards of 1940, *The Grapes of Wrath* lost to *Rebecca* for Best Picture. *Rebecca,* which starred Laurence Olivier and Joan Fontaine, was the first movie David O. Selznick had released since *Gone With the Wind. Grapes* had stiff competition from other major films in the running that year: *All This and Heaven Too, Foreign Correspondent, The Great Dictator, Kitty Foyle, The Letter, The Long Voyage Home, Our Town,* and *The Philadelphia Story.*

Henry was nominated for Best Actor, competing against Charles Chaplin for *The Great Dictator;* Raymond Massey for *Abe Lincoln in Illinois;* and *Laurence Olivier in* Rebecca. The winner was Henry's best friend, James Stewart, for *The Philadelphia Story.*

Jane Darwell won as Best Supporting Actress for her role of Ma Joad, and Ford was named Best Director.

Stewart later told the press, "Hank deserved to win."

Actually, Henry later admitted that he was too embarrassed to attend the Oscar ceremony and opted instead to go fishing along the Gulf of California.

In the history of American cinema, *The Grapes of Wrath* emerges near the top. In 1989, it became the first of some two dozen movies selected for preservation by the Library of Congress.

Years later, when the movie was screened once again for Steinbeck, he said, in relation to Henry, "a lean, stringy dark-faced piece of electricity walked out on the screen—and he had me. I believed in my story once again."

Orson Welles weighed in with his view, too: "I looked into the face of Henry Fonda and saw America."

***

According to his wife, Frances, after his huge success as Tom Joad in *The Grapes of Wrath*, Henry sank into deep despair.

"What's bothering you?" she asked him.

"I feel I've completed my masterpiece. Never again will I have such a triumph. I'll make future pictures, maybe a few good ones, but I feel my one chance to ever win an Oscar has come and gone. Even Jimmy (James Stewart) admitted that that Oscar was mine."

Although Henry's despair was momentary, Frances, a short while later, suffered from a much more severe case of what she called "the nerves." She always seemed in a nervous state. Her medicine cabinet overflowed with cod liver oil (her drink of choice) and pills for her nerves.

At one time, she was seeing five doctors at the same time, never letting the other know the wide circles from which she was receiving medical advice and, presumably, medications. Most of them offered the same verdict, suggesting that her condition was mental and/or emotional rather than physical. When one of her doctors suggested that her problem was hypochondria, she stormed, in a rage, out of his office.

The depressed but newly married, increasingly unstable **Mrs. Henry Fonda** tried to forget her domestic problems with an upscale tour through South America.

Oblivious to the simmering conflicts in Europe and Asia, she sent back, to friends in New York, postcards like this one from Ecuador, circa 1941.

Instead, she took the advice of another physician, who recommended that she spend a few weeks at the Scripps Clinic near La Jolla, where she hoped to find some relief from the anxiety she suffered day and night.

After she returned to Henry and their home, she delegated most of the responsibilities associated with her growing children to her nurse. Day after day, she shut herself alone into her study, where she was fascinated by the rise and fall of her investments in the stock market. Whereas she seemed to have made good choices in her own stocks, she lost money whenever she lured Henry into the purchase of others. As her own portfolio increased in value, that of her husband declined.

Finally, in an attempt to help matters, Henry requested and received a month-long vacation from Zanuck and 20th Century Fox. He suggested that he and Frances go on a whirlwind tour of South America as a sort of second honeymoon.

During her holiday, she wrote to friends in New York, who remembered getting postcards from such remote places as Ecuador. One card from Peru depicted "squat, grim-faced Indian women." On it, she wrote to a recipient in Los Angeles, "Of course, we haven't faced the legendary beauties of Argentina and Brazil. There, I may have some real competition."

Less than a month later, when she and Henry returned home, she was pregnant. He immediately set about tending to his farm. *["My first movie role was as a farmer, and I intend to become one myself," he said.]* Every morning, he collected eggs from his cackling henhouse. He watered the vegetables in his garden, paying special attention to Swiss chard and eggplant. He even grew a prize-winning apple tree, which usually did not do as well in Southern California as it did in other, more temperate regions.

He built a small stable for Pan and presented her with a five-gaited gelding she named "My Boy."

Whimsically, or perhaps superstitiously, Frances wanted her next baby to be born in Manhattan, so Henry flew her to New York and checked her into the LeRoy Sanitarium, where she gave birth by Caesarian, exactly at noon on February 23, 1940. The infant was later christened Peter Henry Fonda.

At last, a boy, which both his mother and father had wanted. Instead of announcing that the child was a boy, Henry proclaimed to all who listened, "Frances has given birth to a fullback." *[At the time, that newborn fullback weighed ten pounds.]*

When Frances was released from the hospital, she checked into a lavish suite at Manhattan's elegant Pierre Hotel. Here, she entertained her socialite friends and frenemies from years past. For some reason, the newborn Peter remained in the hospital for another three weeks until Henry arrived to rescue him and fly with him back to California. Frances wanted to remain behind for another three weeks.

For a while, at least, Henry was a "hands-on father." He showed Pan and Jane pictures of Frances in bed at the hospital, and later, photographs of the newborn. For some reason, Jane ran from his study in tears.

After Frances returned, Henry arranged Sunday afternoon picnics for his whole family, evocative of the ones his mother used to organize in Nebraska. "Sometimes, a bobcat or rattlesnake would want to join in our fun," he said.

With the family reunited again—father, mother, two daughters, and an infant son—life began at their Pennsylvania-style farmhouse for which he had paid $27,000. It was situated on nine acres of land, which had cost $3,000 per acre.

In the beginning, Jane Fonda recalled how at first she had thought her father was a farmer instead of a movie star. One of her first memories of him was watering the vegetables in his "Victory Garden."

In contrast, one of Peter's earliest memories involved waking up in his nursery and looking at walls painted with pictures of the characters from *The Wizard of Oz*, including "the Cowardly Lion."

Later on, his most painful memory was of hugging and kissing his father goodbye as he left to join American forces battling the Japanese.

But that memory dated from several months before what actually happened to Henry in the early 1940s.

***

Despite an unrelenting schedule of film production, where one role immediately followed another, Henry still maintained his long-enduring friendship with James Stewart. Of course, their get-togethers were much more limited than when they'd been roommates. Stewart was now rooming with actor Burgess Meredith.

Both Henry and Stewart entered the busiest film schedules of their careers, each of them turning out an occasional masterpiece, before getting sucked up into World War II.

Henry looked forward to hearing about Stewart's sexual adventures. At the time, he was seducing some of the most famous female stars of Golden Age Hollywood.

"That lanky, long-legged friend of mine, a kind of 'aw shucks' fellow, was not only making classic movies, but screwing really top names," Henry said. "To name a few, Ginger Rogers, Norma Shearer, Olivia de Havilland, Loretta Young, Joan Crawford, Carole Lombard…and beat goes on."

"He never stopped screwing my former wife, Margaret Sullavan, especially when they started making all those movies together, which was an excuse for them to be together, since she was still married to Leland Hayward."

"In spite of his getting all that nooky, Jimmy made a confession to me," Henry recalled.

"Of the dozens of gals I'm dating," Stewart said, "my most trustworthy mistress remains my fist. I call it polluting myself. I'm still a chronic masturbator. Of course, having lived with me, you already know that."

"Jimmy was years away from getting married and settling down," Henry said. "Of all those marquee dazzlers he was poking, he was never serious about marriage except in the case of Olivia de Havilland or perhaps Loretta Young. MGM also hooked him up on publicity dates from its stable of female stars. He was seen a few times with tap-dancing Eleanor Powell before she settled down and started getting it from her new husband, Glenn Ford. Most of these arranged dates were off-putting to Jimmy."

One day, when Stewart was working, Henry drove over to have lunch with him at MGM's commissary. During their meal, an MGM publicist interrupted to inform Stewart that for the first time, his weekly fan mail topped that of all their leading matinee idols, including Clark Gable and Robert Taylor.

After the publicist left, Stewart said, "I don't get it. These poor love-starved gals…Clark Gable is more studly, Robert Taylor prettier, Robert Montgomery more suave. But these hot little pussies want to lie in bed buck naked with me."

To better understand the Fonda/Stewart friendship, one must take a trip down memory lane.

***

Vivacious Lady (1939)

Stewart and Ginger Rogers had a brief fling when they double-dated with Henry and Lucille Ball. At the same time, Rogers was having an affair with a young Cuban bandleader named Desi Arnaz.

Henry claimed that Jimmy and Rogers were not really pursuing a serious romance but a sexual fling "just for the fun of it," Stewart said. "I'm crazy about hitting the dance floor, but would you believe this, she's a better hoofer than I am."

The Stewart/Rogers affair drifted off until they came together again to co-star in a movie together.

Ginger Rogers with **James Stewart** in *Vivacious Lady.*

Lanky, long-legged Jimmy was added to a list of Rogers intimates who also included Desi Arnaz, Cary Grant, Howard Hughes, George Gershwin, David Niven, Dick Powell, and Rudy Vallee.

Director George Stevens cast them in a romantic RKO comedy, *Vivacious Lady* (1938). The movie's plot is that of love at first sight when a botany professor meets a nightclub singer.

Someone on the set quickly learned of their affair, and during the first week of the shoot, the romantic duo made a newspaper headline—GINGER MUST CHOOSE BETWEEN FONDA AND STEWART.

"I was seen a couple of times with them," Henry said, "but I wasn't shacked up with Ginger. Nor were we involved in a three-way as was rumored."

"One thing I don't like about Ginger," Stewart confessed to Henry, "is that when I go to bang her, she orders me to get on top of her. Her command is, 'Prove it to me, buster!'"

In spite of the casual nature of their affair, Rogers was the last star Stewart requested "for a marathon of love-making" before he got caught up in World War II.

***

The Shopworn Angel (1938)

Stewart phoned Henry to tell him that he'd been cast as Margaret Sullavan's leading man in *The Shopworn Angel* (1938). It marked their second screen pairing. Henry told his wife, Frances, that "Jimmy is still in love with Maggie, and she—my difficult ex-wife—is in love with love."

MGM cast rising star Walter Pidgeon as *Shopworn Angel's* second male lead.

Sullavan had been assigned the role of Daisy Heath after its original star (Jean Harlow) had died. Her death was so sudden and unexpected that she didn't even complete her final film, *Saratoga* (1937) with Clark Gable. *[Harlow had collapsed on set during the making of that film, and her unfinished scenes were completed by a stand-in actress, Mary Ella Dees. Joan Crawford was then given the role but dropped out to make another movie. The role then went to rising star Rosalind Russell, but for some reason, that didn't work out either. Finally, the director cast Sullavan in the role.]*

The current version of *Shopworn Angel* was a remake of a 1928 film that was part silent, part talkie. The Paramount original had starred a young Gary Cooper with Nancy Carroll, then the mistress of Joseph P. Kennedy Sr. when he wasn't with his other mistress, Gloria Swanson.

Sullavan had been cast in it as a sophisticated Broadway star, Stewart as a naïve young soldier from Texas.

When Louis B. Mayer sat throught the rushes, he told his associates, "Those two are hot on the screen with some real chemistry. Find the right vehicle and team them again."

Stewart and Sullavan in *The Shopworn Angel*. Walter Winchell claimed, "Maggie Sullavan is shopworn all right—but hardly an angel. She's right at home playing a 'man manipulator'; on screen."

When Stewart conveyed Mayer's remark to Henry, Stewart boasted, "Maggie is even hotter off the screen."

"Not with me," Henry complained. "Maggie was usually the top, riding me. She looked like she was just enduring it."

***

You Can't Take It With You (1938)

Stewart's biggest career break came when Frank Capra cast him and Jean Arthur in *You Can't Take it With You*, a Columbia romantic comedy, released in 1938. It was based on a play by George S. Kaufman and Moss Hart, which won the Pulitzer Prize. The film became Stewart's most important critical and commercial success, receiving seven Oscar nominations, winning Best Picture and (for Capra) Best Director Award.

Its plot concerned the son of a rich family who falls in love with a company stenographer. She comes from a good-natured but decidedly eccentric family. Supporting players included Edward Arnold, Lionel Barrymore, Ann Miller, and Spring Byington.

Since Stewart and Henry felt they weren't seeing enough of each other because of their back-to-back film roles, either of the two actors visited the sets of each other when one of them had a break in filming.

One day, Henry showed up on the set of *You Can't Take It With You*, where he was introduced to Jean Arthur, a former model from New York. She had struggled through small roles before gaining recognition for her fetching style in comedies. Before meeting her, Stewart had mused, "This is one leading lady I won't be seducing. She's a lesbian."

As they chatted, Arthur told him that she'd been the second choice for the role. "Capra really wanted Olivia de Havilland, but Jack Warner refused to lend her out."

During lunch with Stewart and Arthur, Henry told the actress that she seemed perfect for the role, based on what he'd seen this late morning.

"Thanks, and I certainly hope so," she said. Perhaps you'll be my leading man in an upcoming picture." Then she glanced at Stewart and smiled. "I guess Jimmy has told you, I don't put men on my casting couch."

"I understand. What a great loss that will be when we eventually work together."

After he'd seen Stewart and Arthur emoting together in *You Can't Take It With You*, Henry told a reporter that the picture realistically depicted Stewart as he was in real life.

James Stewart and **Jean Arthur** in the comedy classic, *You Can't Take It With You.*

"Doing a love scene with Arthur was trouble," Stewart confessed to Henry.

"She had to stop every few minutes to check her face in the mirror, fearing she had aged. If not that, on several occasions, she cut off her love scene to go to her dressing room to vomit."

***

Even though Stewart had a line of beauties, including a major star now and then, his ultimate dream girl remained Norma Shearer, the First Lady of MGM. When he was properly introduced to her at a costume party, his first words were, "You are the most beautiful woman in Hollywood."

She shot back, "I hear that every day of my life."

Right after midnight, Shearer and Stewart were seen leaving the party together. He left his car where he'd parked it and disappeared into the night in her yellow limousine.

The first person he phoned after a weekend spent at Norma's home was Henry himself. "Norma really goes for me. After our first night together, she almost proposed to me."

As each year moves on into the 21st Century, the public's memory of Norma Shearer grows dimmer. However, in the Hollywood of the 1930s, she reigned as First Lady of MGM and rated among the top ten most famous women in America.

Born in Montréal, she later moved to Hollywood, where, starting in 1919, she became active in silent films. Her career lasted until 1942, when she disappeared from the screen.

She was often cast as spunky, sexually liberated *ingénues* during the Pre-Code years of Hollywood. Unique in film history, she was said to have been the first actress who made it both acceptable and even chic to appear single and "unvirginal" in films.

Shearer became the first five-time Academy Award nominee, winning the Best Actress Oscar for the 1930 *The Divorcee.* Her co-star was Robert Montgomery, with whom she had an affair.

This marked the beginning of many of her high-profile affairs, including one with the aviator/producer Howard Hughes and with director Victor Fleming. She also seduced such matinee idols as John Gilbert and Clark Gable.

Her sexual flings progressed despite her marriage to Irving Thalberg Jr., the "Boy Wonder" of MGM, as early as 1927. Alongside Louis B. Mayer, he was running MGM, issuing such classics as *Grand Hotel, Mutiny on the Bounty,* and *The Good Earth.*

He not only made Shearer the leading star of the studio, giving her all the choice scripts (much to the regret and rage of Joan Crawford). Thalberg was also instrumental in making stars out of Greta Garbo, Clark Gable, John Gilbert, Lionel Barrymore, Spencer Tracy, and Jean Harlow. He guided Luise

Norma Shearer of "The Cheating Heart' poses with MGM's *Wunderkind,* **Irving Thalberg** in 1928.

Although married to him, he was in poor health, and she turned elsewhere for sex. Pint-sized Mickey Rooney claimed, "She was hotter than a half-fucked fox in a forest fire."

Rainer into two films, allowing her to win back-to-back Best Actress Oscars.

It is not known if Thalberg knew about his wife's many affairs. Rumors were rampant that his sexual powers were waning because of his affliction with congenital heart disease. Eventually, that led to his early death in September of 1936 at the age of 37.

Before dating Stewart, Henry's friend, Tyrone Power, had told him that he had rejected Shearer's sexual advances. This was in spite of the fact that she was responsible for getting him cast as her co-star in the historical drama, *Marie Antoinette* (1938), in which he played the dashing Swedish nobleman, Count Axel Fersen, at the French court of Louis XVI.

"Norma lost her head in that movie, and again fell head over heels for Tyrone Power, constantly praising his male beauty," Henry said.

"I detest women who come on too strong with me," Power told Henry. "I feel differently, however, if a handsome stud comes on to me."

Henry later noted, "Jimmy came along at the right time to make Norma feel desirable again in the wake of that harsh rejection from Tyrone."

The Shearer/Stewart affair became tabloid fodder, as she arrived at parties and premieres with him, together in the back seat of her yellow limousine.

Whenever she emerged from that impressive vehicle, arm in arm with him, photographers wildly snapped away. Stewart soon became known in gossipy Hollywood circles as "Norma's Toy Boy," a title he bitterly resented.

During Stewart's weeks-long affair with Shearer, Henry was often seen going with them to the Cocoanut Grove or the Trocadero. Sometimes, they were entertained at her private home. Somehow, Frances never seemed to accompany him. As Henry remembered it, "Most of our talk was devoted to her playing Scarlett O'Hara in *Gone With the Wind* (1939). She felt that David O. Selznick, its producer, had more or less made up his mind to cast her, perhaps opposite Ronald Colman or Errol Flynn as Rhett Butler."

"Norma thought I'd be ideal cast as Ashley Wilkes, the husband of Melanie, and the Southern gentleman with whom Scarlett is in love," Henry claimed.

"I felt she had the power to get me cast, although Selznick, not Louis B. Mayer, would make the final decision."

At home, I began reading through this horribly long novel. I soon skipped pages until I came to a scene where Ashley appears. From what I read of the character, I thought Margaret Mitchell must have had me in mind."

Shearer ultimately lost both Scarlett O'Hara and Stewart, as their romance faded with the summer winds of 1938.

Stewart was soon replaced with Shearer's brief fling with the much younger and pint-sized Mickey Rooney. But she soon fell in love with movie gangster George Raft, who was married at the time.

Raft had wed Grayce Mulrooney back in 1927, and, as the years drifted on, this former social worker from New York's Welfare Island [*it's name was later changed to Roosevelt Island*] always refused to divorce him, in spite of his many affairs. She was still married to him at the time of her death in 1970.

***

After his highly publicized affair with Norma Shearer, Stewart got at least half as much press coverage when he began "hot dating" Olivia de Havilland, the sister of Joan Fontaine.

De Havilland was a celebrated beauty and had been a skilled actress since her debut, as a teenager, in Max Reinhardt's spectacular 1934 stage production of *A Midsummer Night's Dream* at the Hollywood Bowl. [*She also appeared in its film adaptation a year later.*]

Born in Tokyo to British parents, she was brought to Hollywood and reared by her mother after her parents separated.

At Warner Brothers, she would achieve early fame as the co-star of swashbuckler Errol Flynn. Warners liked their pairing so much that they'd eventually make eight films together, including *Captain Blood* (1935) and *The Adventures of Robin Hood* (1938). Flynn would be called "the love of her life," but the extent to which they went in off-screen lovemaking is still being debated today among film historians.

Flynn himself added a tantalizing revelation about Olivia's sex life when they co-starred with Ronald Reagan in *Santa Fe Trail* (1940): "Olivia may be resisting my overtures, but she succumbed to the charm of this young actor named Ronald Reagan."

Stewart immediately brought Henry up to date on the state of his affair with Olivia when the hot-and-in-demand rising male star confessed, "I'm going out with these big-name movie stars. But for sex, I often prefer fly-by-night pickups, the flashy and trashy kind. These broads will do anything you ask, but to clean up my act, I've also begun an affair with Oliva de Havilland."

On several occasions, it was suggested in print at the time that Olivia "would make the perfect wife" for Stewart.

"So far," he told Henry, "Olivia is the only woman in Hollywood that I would take for a wife. She is a real lady. Her sister, Joan Fontaine, even more so."

Like Henry, Burgess Meredith was also a close observer of the burgeoning romance between Stewart and Olivia. "I was the second person Jimmy told that he had proposed marriage to Olivia. She didn't say yes, but neither did she say no."

Apparently, as the days drifted by, there seemed to be no more talk of marriage.

"I think he was still in love with Margaret Sullavan, especially whenever the two of them made films together," Henry said. "She was still married to Leland Hayward, and I suspected she would be for many years to come. It took time and a few more co-starring roles with Maggie before he came around to the point of view that the bitch was a real ball-buster."

Stewart told Henry that he and Olivia were compatible in many ways. "I love to dance. She loves to dance. We have fun attending parties and premieres."

Stewart, in fact, would accompany her, as his "date," to the world premiere of *Gone With the Wind* in New York.

Olivia de Havilland, the estranged sister of fellow actress Joan Fontaine, wanted Henry Fonda to play the role of Ashley Wilkes, her character's husband in *Gone With the Wind* (1939).

Instead, the role went to British actor, Leslie Howard.

She also sustained a long and competitive relationship with Errol Flynn, her spectacularly promiscuous co-star in, among others, *Captain Blood* (1935).

Before James Stewart started having an affair with her, Errol Flynn contemptuously warned him, "I don't think she has a hole between her legs."

"We're spending many loving nights together," Stewart confessed. "Maybe she likes older men. I'm about thirty and she's twenty-one."

Years later, when asked what lingering disappointment she might have had about not marrying Stewart, Olivia said, "I don't think I was ready to settle down. Romantically, I was confused. Howard Hughes wanted to marry me, but John Huston loomed large in my life, too. So did my continuing fascination with Errol Flynn."

She went on to say that she regretted never having made a film with Stewart.

Whenever Henry spent time with Olivia and Stewart, the talk was mainly about how ideal he'd be as Ashley Wilkes in *Gone With the Wind.* She promised to lobby David Selznick to cast Henry in that part. She had already signed to star as Melanie.

She later reported back to Henry, "David said he thought you were the ideal type, but his wife, Irene, wants Ray Milland. If he's not available, she said she'd prefer Humphrey Bogart. How wrong can a casting suggestion be? Maybe Vincent Price would be even worse as Ashley."

There was other speculation in the press, with suggestions that Melvyn Douglas might be perfect for the role.

Columnist Hedda Hopper had her own recommendations, asserting that Joan Crawford should play Scarlett, with Franchot Tone cast as Ashley. "They are divorcing," she observed, perhaps with a touch of sadism. "How novel it would be to see an estranged couple like Tone and Crawford making love on the screen."

Many readers wrote letters to Hopper and to MGM, suggesting that the English actor, Leslie Howard, would make the best choice for Ashley Wilkes.

According to Henry, "After I waded through that long, long book, I decided that Norma and Olivia were right. There was no actor in Hollywood, certainly not Bogie, Vincent Price, Milland, or even Leslie Howard, who could bring to the role the quality of Ashley that I could. The part was written for me. Guess what? I didn't get it. That so-called ladies' man, Leslie Howard, got that plum role. Since he was to die in a plane crash in 1943, maybe it was just as well that he immortalized himself as Ashley."

In the 1930s, Leslie Howard had earned his self-proclaimed label of "ladies' man," in part by seducing screen legend Mary Pickford. Others of his seductions included Ingrid Bergman, Kay Francis, Marion Davies, Myrna Loy, Merle Oberon, Maureen O'Sullivan, Ann Harding, and Claudette Colbert. (Not a lot of men had succeeded in making it with Colbert.)

Although he lost out on portraying Olivia's husband in *Gone With the Wind,* Henry co-starred with her in the 1942 film, *The Male Animal.* He would later appear on Broadway with her.

It was not Henry, but Stewart's roommate, Burgess Meredith, who began an affair with Olivia after she and Stewart broke up. News of that was revealed when Meredith took her to parties hosted by the Thursday Night Beer Club, an early version of Frank Sinatra's Rat Pack.

Stewart and Henry were charter members. Signing up were director Josh Logan and actor Myron McCormack. Newly divorced from Joan Crawford, the charming, well-educated, debonair Franchot Tone was invited to join, too. One night at a party, Olivia met him. Within a week, she told Burgess Meredith goodbye, and began a short romance with Tone.

***

Made for Each Other (1939)

Although the genre known as "the screwball comedy" was beginning to wane during the late 1930s, columnists who included Louella Parsons speculated that Stewart and Carole Lombard would be ideal for the next one.

Finally, it was announced that Lombard and Stewart would co-star in *Made For Each Other,* set for a 1939 release. This time, David O. Selznick cast them in dramatic roles as a Depression-era young couple who get married after knowing each other for only a day. The plot unfolds as she becomes discouraged by his unpaid bills.

Henry was fully aware of the brief fling of Lombard with Stewart, not taking it seriously. He knew she was growing more and more involved with Clark Gable, trying to wean him from what he called his "chick-a-birdies."

As an escape from the dying genre of screwball comedy, **Carole Lombard** turned to soap opera dramas such as *Made For Each Other* with **James Stewart**.

At one point, within the plotline, her maid, Louise Beavers, advises her, "Don't let the seeds spoil you from enjoying the watermelon."

[Gable told Walter Pidgeon and others at MGM that he'd seduced Joan Crawford, Mary Astor, Marion Davies, Jean Harlow, Norma Shearer, Lupe Velez, and Loretta Young. In his future lay more conquests: Lana Turner, Hedy Lamarr, Nancy Davis (later Reagan), Yvonne De Carlo, Paulette Goddard, Grace Kelly, Shelley Winters, and Marilyn Monroe. He later claimed, "They're all beautiful, and I've had every one of them."]

Before Gable, Lombard had been married to William Powell, her co-star in *Man of the World* (1931). She'd also had a serious romance with musician Russ Columbo before his early accidental death.

Before Gable, she'd hopped in and out of the beds of various actors, a string of whom included Gary Cooper, John Barrymore (her co-star in *Twentieth Century,* released in 1934), John Gilbert, director Ernest Lubitsch, David Niven, David O. Selznick, Preston Sturges, and George Raft.

On at least three occasions, Lombard and Stewart were seen at both the Trocadero and the Cocoanut Grove. They were also part of a double date with Henry and Lucille Ball. Henry and Ball would later co-star in another drama, *The Big Street* (1942), wherein Henry played a docile character with the unlikely name of "Little Pinks."

It was suggested that the only reason Lombard dated Stewart was to make Clark Gable, her true love, jealous. Even though claiming a commitment to her, she heard rumors he was having outside affairs.

Food for Scandals had been the only movie Lombard made in 1938, so she had a lot of free time on her hands.

Four years after teaming with Gable in *No Man of Her Own,* they were reunited at a Hollywood party and began a torrid romance in 1936.

At the time, Gable was separated from his wife, Ria Langham, who was refusing to give him a divorce. She later agreed to dump him only after he paid her $500,000, a king's ransom during the Depression years. Lombard and Gable would elope in March of 1939, the year he starred as Rhett Butler in *Gone With the Wind* (1939).

At a party, Henry talked with William Haines, who had been a big box office attraction until Louis B. Mayer learned about his gay life. After his "demotion," he became an interior designer. A close friend and confidant of Lombard, he told Jimmy that, "Carole photographs like a virginal princess, but she sure isn't. She lives like a tiger and flutters her wings like a colorful butterfly."

Henry found Lombard outrageous and delightful, with a real potty mouth. "Honey," she said. "I've got everything but breasts. On the set, whenever I make a picture, I call out to wardrobe 'Bring me some tits, you damn queens!'"

Haines was right in his assessment of Lombard. She soon dumped Stewart.

"Jimmy took the rejection very well," Henry said. "He only called her a brittle dame, an unpredictable bitch, and no one he'd want to spend more than a night with for a quick fuck."

Lombard had a much more flattering appraisal of Stewart. "He is a bottomless pit of passion."

"Frankly," Stewart told Henry, "I don't go for a dame who takes out a ruler to measure a man. She told me that if Gable's dick was only an inch smaller, he'd be the Queen of Hollywood—and not its king."

***

More about *The Story of Alexander Graham Bell* (1939)

When Henry starred in *The Story of Alexander Graham Bell,* he found the film's leading lady, Loretta Young, very seductive. She was most flirtatious with him and seemed to be openly soliciting a pass from him. He was gearing up to seduce her because, in his words, "her reputation has preceded her."

As biographer Marc Eliot wrote, "Loretta Young was known in Hollywood circles as a charter member of leading ladies who sexually devoured their male co-stars. She was in the front rank of 'manizers.' The top crown, however, went to Marlene Dietrich, who fucked every man or woman that moved."

Of course, Henry knew if he seduced Young, he would be but one on her long list of other lovers.

Young had married actor Grant Withers in 1930, but their union was annulled a few months later. After that, she spent most of the 1930s flitting from one affair to another.

Loretta Young and **James Stewart** sustained a torrid affair, and she added him to her long string of seductions.

"Every time Loretta 'sins,' she builds a church," claimed Marlene Dietrich, who loathed her. "That's why there are so many Catholic churches in Hollywood."

Her most serious romance was with the married Spencer Tracy in *A Man's Castle* (1935). But he would not leave his wife and children.

Her most notorious affair had been with Clark Gable during location shooting, in the forests of Washington State, of Jack London's *Call of the Wild* (1935). During the course of that affair, Gable impregnated her. Quietly, she left Hollywood for a few months and later returned but not with her daughter. When the girl mysteriously reappeared a few months later, Young claimed that she had been adopted.

At the top of her list of romantic and sexual associations was Fox's studio chief Darryl F. Zanuck. She often sustained affairs with actors, sometimes with her leading men. When she filmed *They Call it Sin* (1932) she had flings with both of her leading men, George Brent and Louis Calhern.

That same year, she made *Playgirl* and was attracted to Norman Foster., taking him home with her. Other actors who came and went, so to speak, were Ricardo Cortez, Wayne Morris, Gilbert Roland, and her most serious love affair, Tyrone Power, beginning on the set of *Love Is News* (1937).

Directors, too, ended up on Young's casting couch: Joseph Mankiewicz, Gregory Ratoff, Edward Sutherland. A studio executive, Irving Asher, also bedded her.

For a while, she became emotionally involved with tennis star Fred Perry, but soon was going out with Jock Whitney, the business executive and socialite once engaged to Tallulah Bankhead.

An occasional lawyer such as William Buckner was one of her conquests as was newspaperman John McLain. Sometimes she dated men who had once been married to famous stars, notably restaurateur Herbert Somborn (the former Mr. Gloria Swanson), and screenwriter Robert Riskin (the former Mr. Fay Wray).

After appearing with and having an affair with Richard Green in *Kentucky* (1938) Young signed to play the role of the wife in *The Story of Alexander Graham Bell* (1939), appearing in it with Henry Fonda and Don Ameche.

During filming, James Stewart showed up to take Henry for lunch, where they were joined by Young. "They spoke to the waiter, but had little words for me," Henry said. "All their talk was centered on each other. It was obvious to me that Jim was going to do what I had been postponing. He was getting ready to run off with Loretta. Those two clicked, and they soon departed, leaving me with the bill."

"They'd had a brief fling before, and now, or so I gathered, they started up again like gangbusters. I was the best friend left out in the cold. After a weekend in Palm Springs, their affair turned more serious."

The columnist Adela Rogers St. Johns was the first to hear of their affair. "Loretta carried this big torch for Jimmy Stewart. She was shameless in her pursuit of him and begged him to marry her."

As Stewart confessed later, "Her intensity was so powerful it scared me away."

Two months after filming the Alexander Bell film, Henry attended a party with Frances where he met Young again.

This time, she was with an executive she introduced as Ted Lewis, the head of the radio department of Young & Rubicam (aka Y&R New York), an advertising agency in Manhattan.

He and Henry talked for a while. Lewis told him that he had launched himself in his first radio show by casting Judy Garland, Joan Crawford, and Jack Benny.

As she told Henry goodbye, Young said, perhaps with a touch of irony, "I'm no longer the bride of Alexander

Graham Bell or the would-be girlfriend of Mr. Stewart."

She later said, "I've been in and out of love so many times… but I wonder if I were ever in love at all."

In 1940, Young married Lewis, and later, he formally adopted the daughter she'd had with Gable, re-naming her Judy Lewis.

The couple also produced two sons of their own: Peter Lewis (later associated with the San Francisco rock band, Moby Grape) and the film director, Christopher Lewis.

Lewis and Young endured a bitter divorce in 1969. She then immediately launched an affair with actor Glenn Ford.

In 1993, Young, who by that time was not so young, married fashion designer Jean Louis.

Her last words in 2000 were, "I've lived to see the birth of the 21st Century." She was dead that summer at the age of 87.

When Stewart finally married his first and only wife, Gloria, McLean, in 1949, Young told a reporter, "I think his marrying Gloria was the right choice for Jimmy. I'm convinced that if I had wed him, it would not have worked. After all, we're both actors, hogging the spotlight. Henry Fonda's marriage to Margaret Sullavan lasted only two months."

A reporter from *Parade* asked her if she'd ever had an affair with Stewart's best friend, Henry Fonda.

"Maybe I did and maybe I didn't," she said, enigmatically. "My memory grows dim about such things."

***

The Ice Follies of 1939 (1939)

The next picture Stewart made found him cast opposite Joan Crawford in *The Ice Follies of 1939*. Lew Ayres, once married to Ginger Rogers, had the third lead along with Lewis Stone. Set against a show biz backdrop that featured the International Ice Follies, it was directed by Reinhold Schünzel.

The plot spun around Mary McKay (Crawford), an inept skater who marries Larry Hall (Stewart), and then drags down his career because of his links with her. In time, however, Larry's Ice Follies becomes a smash hit, and Mary's ice-skating skills improve.

The early press releases were misleading. It was announced that Crawford had morphed into a singing sensation, and that she'd be performing six songs with her own voice. A press agent (absurdly) claimed that "Miss Crawford is such a sensation that she's been asked to co-star at the Met in Manhattan."

When the final cut was released, however, Crawford's songs had been reduced to two numbers, each of which was dubbed.

[Stewart had had a small role in the Crawford movie The Gorgeous Hussy *(1936) in which Robert Taylor was her leading man. He flirted with her at the time, but she shunned him because she was heavily involved romantically elsewhere.]*

On the set of *Ice Follies*, he met a very different Crawford. She was most charming to him, inviting him to her dressing room. She had recently filed for divorce from Franchot Tone.

Soon, Stewart was invited to spend the night at home in her boudoir.

[Years later, after the war, when Henry co-starred with Crawford in Daisy Kenyon *(1947), she talked about Stewart: "He was not my type, but he came along when I desperately needed to get involved with another man after that Franchot Tone disaster. Jimmy and I were just reaching an orgasm with each other. What's love got to do with it? I've had better in bed than your friend, but, believe me, I've had worse, much worse, including getting raped by my brother and his gang of thugs."]*

When Henry talked to Stewart about Crawford, he was told, "I found Joan more aggressive in her pursuit of me than Norma Shearer was. She's a wildcat in bed. One night, she even showed me two blue films she'd starred in back in the 1920s. One was *Velvet Lips*, the other was *The Casting Couch*."

"She liked a lot of foreplay. On the first night, she asked me to make love to her 'ninny pies.' I asked her, 'What in hell are those?' It turned out to be her breasts. She liked me to chew down on her nipples. Not my usual scene."

At the end of their first session in bed, Crawford told Stewart, "Your

James Stewart, Joan Crawford, and **Lew Ayres** in roles all three of them hated: *The Ice Follies of 1939*.

Stewart seduced Crawford almost a decade before Henry Fonda took her to bed.

145

prick is ample, just fine, but nothing like the ten inches on Tone. I call him 'The Jawbreaker.' But you're satisfying. I'll want you for one repeat after another, at least until we get through with this stinking piece of shit called *The Ice Follies of 1939.*"

Months later, Henry recalled, "Jimmy and Crawford invited me to a sneak preview of that *Ice Follies* crap. The movie was trash. During the screening, Jimmy sank lower and lower in his seat. Joan and Jimmy should not have disgraced themselves by appearing in that disaster. At the end of the screening and over dinner, I tried to put a good face on it. But they knew how awful it was."

Joan Crawford's seduction of Henry would come much later when they co-starred in *Daisy Kenyon.*

***

It's a Wonderful World (1939)

One afternoon in late in 1938 or early in 1939, after James Stewart arrived at Henry's home, they retreated together to his study. With him, Stewart had carried the script of *It's a Wonderful World* by Ben Hecht and Herbert J. Mankiewicz, and eventually released in 1939. These two writers wanted to create one of those screwball comedies of the type made famous by Carole Lombard and others.

Both actors agreed that this new filmscript had been inspired by Claudette Colbert's Oscar-winning performance in *It Happened One Night* (1934), in which she had appeared with Clark Gable. The script was also inspired by *The Thin Man,* which had starred William Powell and Myrna Loy.

The new movie would star Colbert as the female lead. Since Henry had recently worked with the French actress in *Drums Along the Mohawk* (1939), Stewart wanted to know what the experience of acting with her was like.

She received a good report from Henry. "She's very professional, graceful, and courteous, even when you fuck up a scene."

The silly plot, later denounced by critics as "more leaden than laughable," depicts Stewart on his way to prison. He escapes from a train and steals the car of a female poet, portrayed by Colbert. Somehow, he wins her confidence, and she aids in his search for the true murderer, a crime he did not commit. Along the way, they fall in love.

In later years, the title puzzled viewers who confused it with that "other" Stewart classic film, *It's a Wonderful Life* (1946).

"Our director, whom I call 'Speedy,' was 'Woody' Van Dyke," Stewart said. "As a director, he's like a premature ejaculator. He likes to wrap a scene with just one take. He completed the damn picture in just two weeks. Speedy, or 'Van Dyke,' as he's called, wasn't the only dyke on the picture. It was obvious to me that Miss Colbert prefers the charms of the fairer sex, too."

Colbert shared her own opinion of her co-star with "Woody" Van Dyke. "Stewart denies it, but I'm convinced that he and Fonda are lovers. I think those two ladies protest too much that they are straight shooters."

Colbert later told Louis B. Mayer that she preferred Fonda as her leading man over Stewart. "Actually, my favorite leading man is Gary Cooper."

Mayer opened *It's a Wonderful World* in certain key theaters in big cities, but it was such a failure that he soon withdrew it from general release.

***

Mr. Smith Goes to Washington (1939)

The bruising that Stewart's battered ego suffered from the release of *Ice Follies* was repaired when he was cast in his next film, *Mr. Smith Goes to Washington,* also released— in rapid-fire succession with many others—in 1939. Directed by Frank Capra, the MGM drama starred Jean Arthur in the lead, with supporting players Claude Rains, Edward Arnold, Guy Kibbee, Thomas Mitchell,

Not to be confused with James'Stewart's "Every Year at Christmas" special, *It's a Wonderful Life, It's a Wonderful World* was a bit more forced and a lot less popular—and not particularly associated with Christmas.

Eugene Pallette, Beulah Bondi, H.B. Warner, Harry Carey, Ruth Donnelly, Grant Mitchell, and William Demarest.

Columbia had originally purchased an unpublished story, *The Gentleman from Montana* by Lewis R. Foster, intending it as a vehicle for Ralph Bellamy. When Frank Capra came aboard, he wanted to cast Gary Cooper in the lead, but he was not available. Stewart was his second choice. He had to "steal him" (his words) from MGM. The director said, "I knew he would make a hell of a Mr. Smith. He looked like a country kid, an idealist. It was very close to his own heart. If Stewart had been tied up with another movie, the role would have been perfect for Henry Fonda."

Joseph Breen, the much-disliked director of those dreaded censors at the Hays Office, warned MGM, "It looks to me like this story is loaded with dynamite, both for the motion picture industry and for the nation at large. It paints an unflattering picture of American democracy. With the world on the verge of war, this is a crucial time to paint such a crude portrait of American democracy, at the very time we should be depicted as a beacon of light to a world growing increasingly dark."

Once again, Jean Arthur was cast as Stewart's leading lady.

He was on hand to embrace her after her arrival on the set. "I hope we can be a big smash like before." He was referring to their co-starring roles in *You Can't Take It With You* (1938).

Cast as Clarissa Saunders, Arthur played the secretary to Smith's predecessor as senator. That predecessor had died in office, which led to the appointment of Stewart, cast as Jefferson Smith, the idealistic and newest Senator in town, a sort of bumpkin with a loving heart and an innate sense of honor.

At first, Arthur comes off as hard-boiled, a cynic who has been around Washington for years, and who knows how it works. Over time, she develops faith in Smith's honor and decency. As the plot progresses, she falls in love with him.

Stewart, cast as Jefferson Smith, was selected because corrupt political bosses handpicked him as a "stooge" (aka "useful idiot") to send to Congress as their senator, filling in for a recently dead crony. Happy Hooper (Kibbee), portraying the governor of an unnamed western state, has been pressured by a political boss, Jim Taylor (Edward Arnold), to choose Smith, with the assumption that he can be manipulated.

James Stewart and Jean Arthur were such a by-then famous couple, that the name of the film (*Mr. Smith Goes to Washington*) wasn't judged as essential for the poster that promoted it.

It took a lot of persuasion, but **James Stewart** finally convinced Frank Capra to assign him the lead in *Mr. Smith Goes to Washington*. Capra had wanted Gary Cooper to play the role.

According to Stewart, "The filibuster scene took three weeks to shoot and nearly destroyed my throat."

Columbia borrowed **Claude Rains** to play the senator who starts off as James Stewart's role model.

In the words of one critic, "Rains ends up embodying every ethically bankrupt politician."

Mr. Smith Goes to Washington brought Rains his first Oscar nomination.

In the third lead, Claude Rains plays Senator Joseph (aka "Joe") Harrison Paine, an esteemed powermonger who's a secret crook. Mendaciously taking Smith under his wing, he lures Smith into proposing a bill that later leads to scandal and disgrace for him.

To defend himself from the charges levied against him, Smith launches a filibuster that will postpone the bill and prove his innocence on the Senate floor, just before a vote is taken to expel him. This is his best chance to prove his innocence, and he speaks nonstop for more than 24 hours. Eventually, after many setbacks, he will triumph as an honest man.

Stewart told Henry, "The hardest part for me was maintaining a 'sore throat' kind of voice after that marathon talk. That filibuster scene required a shooting schedule of three weeks. It was the most difficult performance of my career, totally exhausting. I feared I may have destroyed my vocal cords."

"I bet you'll be terrific," Henry said. "Sounds like you're gonna be a cinch at Oscar time."

In October of 1939, the film's premier in Washington, D.C., was a disaster attended by 4,000 guests who included 45 U.S. Senators. After about twenty minutes, many senators rose to their feet and shook their fists at the screen. Within two-thirds of its way through, one senator after another stormed out in disgusted expressions of protest.

Senator Alban Barkley, a future vice president under Harry S Truman, denounced it as "grotesque." Joseph P. Kennedy, the U.S. Ambassador to Great Britain, called it "Nazi propaganda," claiming that "Joseph Goebbels will love it." He even offered to purchase and destroy the negative as a means of preventing its release across the nation.

In spite of all these attacks, *Mr. Smith Goes to Washington* morphed into a huge success at the box office, earning $3.5 million in the United States alone and evolving into the second-highest-grossing film of 1939, a year loaded with hits. In terms of revenue generated in the 1930s, it emerged behind only *Gone With the Wind* and *Snow White and the Seven Dwarfs*.

"I told Jimmy it was his role of a lifetime, while at the time, trying to hide my professional jealousy," Henry said.

In what emerged as one of the most competitive races in Hollywood history, that year's competition for the Best Actor Oscar, Stewart had to compete against Clark Gable for his role of Rhett Butler in *Gone With the Wind;* with Laurence Olivier in *Wuthering Heights;* and with Mickey Rooney in *Babes in Arms.* Robert Donat walked off with the gold for *Goodbye, Mr. Chips.*

All that Henry had to (publicly) say about the race was, "Jimmy got my vote."

As Best Supporting Actor, Claude Rains was nominated for his performance as the crooked senator. That award that year went to Thomas Mitchell for his performance in *Stagecoach*, starring John Wayne and Claire Trevor. Mitchell also garnered rave reviews for his role as the father of Scarlett O'Hara in *Gone With the Wind.*

***

Destry Rides Again (1939)

Still in 1939, in a year already studded with masterpieces, James Stewart was the lynchpin in yet another classic, *Destry Rides Again,* a Western that emerged as one of the all-time bests in that genre.

His previous leading lady, Jean Arthur, had been a lesbian. This time around, his leading lady was the sultry, seductive, sometimes predatory Marlene Dietrich. *Destry* represented a sort of comeback picture for her, since she had been recently labeled "box office poison."

When she was unexpectedly summoned to Hollywood to make a Western, Dietrich was deep into a prolonged vacation on the French Riviera and involved in affairs with Joseph P. Kennedy and his son, John F. Kennedy.

Back in Hollywood, after meeting Stewart in the wardrobe department, he was soon added to her list of suitors who included Gary Cooper, Edith Piaf, General James Gavin, General George Patton Jr., Frank Sinatra, and Barbara Stanwyck.

It was somewhat of a casting secret at the time, but producer Joe Pasternak had originally wanted to cast Paulette Goddard and Henry Fonda in the lead roles.

After the two leading roles were cast, director George Marshall personally selected a strong supporting cast to back up his stars: Mischa Auer, Charles Winniger, Brian Donlevy, Irene Harvey, Una Merkel, Billy Gilbert, Bill Cody Jr., and Lillian Yarbo.

Even though the opening credits "suggested" that *Destry Rides Again* had been inspired by a novel by Max Brand published in 1930, the movie's screenplay bore little resemblance to it. [*In 1932, the cowboy hero of the silent screen, Tom Mix, had filmed a "Talkie" adaptation of the novel that adhered more stringently to its original plot.*]

Destry provided Dietrich with one of her most classic songs, a ditty she'd sing in stage performances in Europe and the U.S. for the rest of her life: "See What the Boys in the Back Room Will Have."

On his first visit to the set for lunch with Stewart, Henry greeted Marlene Dietrich. As he remembered it years later, "She was dressed in cowboy drag." She'd been cast as Frenchy, a saloon singer, with Stewart configured as Tom Destry, the town's new deputy sheriff. The picture marked his first western, a natural genre for him, although he would not return to this type of film until 1950.

One of the most iconic scenes in film history involved a catfight in a saloon be-

No one in the audience really believed that **Marlene Dietrich** was a washed-uip saloon singer in *Destry Rides Again*—least of all **James Stewart.**

tween Dietrich and Una Merkel, cast as Lilybelle Callahan.

It is the catfight of all catfights, with hair-pulling and kicking, until Stewart pours water over the ladies to cool them down. Frenchie grabs a gun and starts firing, sending the sheriff fleeing from the saloon.

Henry found Dietrich a bit dismissive of her leading man. "Stewart comes off as a mumbling, baby-faced beanpole," she said. "I think you, my darling, would have been a better choice as the sheriff."

But by the third week of her involvement with the movie's filming, she had a more favorable opinion of her co-star. "I think I'm falling in love with Mr. Stewart…if only he could figure out what to do with those gangling legs of his."

"Speaking of legs, Miss Dietrich, I want to congratulate you for recently being hailed for having the best gams of any dame in Tinseltown," Henry said.

Later, and privately, Stewart shared one of Dietrich's sexual secrets: "She prefers giving fellatio more than receiving penetration from a man in any of nature's 'old fashioned' ways."

Months later, Henry told Frances and others that, "Jimmy must have done more than that. He made Dietrich pregnant, and without telling him, she aborted his child."

Erich Maria Remarque, the author of the novel, *All Quiet on the Western Front*, had been one of Dietrich's longtime lovers. He wrote, "Marlene became pregnant after the first time she slept with James Stewart. In her apartment, she assembled, with photos, flowers, and candles, a makeshift shrine to him. For a brief period, she was obsessed with him until she became uncomfortable and soon grew bored, returning to me, her ever-faithful admirer."

In spite of that sad ending to their affair, Stewart and Dietrich would return to the screen in 1951 when they starred together in the Fox thriller, *No Highway in the Sky*.

As regards *Destry Rides Again*, *Time* magazine cited Stewart for turning in an even better performance than he'd generated for *Mr. Smith Goes to Washington*.

The New York Times made the same claim. Its critic, Bosley Crowther, wrote, "Stewart's rendering of Sheriff Destry is a masterpiece of underplaying in a deliberately sardonic vein—the freshest, most offbeat characterization the popular actor ever played."

The film generated good box office. Frank S. Nugent of *The New York Times* wrote, "It is difficult to reconcile Miss Dietrich's Frenchy, the cabaret girl at the Bloody Gulch saloon in the fictional Western town of Bottleneck with the posed and posturing Dietrich we saw in Ernst Lubitsch's *Angel*, a Paramount release in 1937."

Destry put Dietrich back on the "most wanted" list of Hollywood casting circles. She immediately followed Destry with a string of other movies, beginning with the 1940 Universal picture, *Seven Sinners* , in which she starred opposite John Wayne who told his cronies, "Best sex I ever had."

***

The Shop Around the Corner (1940)

Stewart launched 1940, a milestone year in his career, with two back-to-back films starring his long-enduring lover, Margaret Sullavan. At the time, Henry was often seen in the company of Sullavan, his ex-wife, with Stewart, still his best friend. In inner Tinseltown circles, there were rumors of a *ménage à trois*.

The very savvy Leland Hayward, one of the most informed men about behind-the-scenes Hollywood, obviously knew about his wife's continuing affair with Stewart. He did nothing about it, probably because he, too, was having adulterous relationships.

In addition to Stewart, Sullavan that same year launched an affair with Glenn Ford when they co-starred in *So Ends Our Night*. Directed by John Cromwell, the film was based on a novel by Erich Maria Remarque and starred Fredric March and Erich Von Stroheim.

Sullavan had long believed that Stewart was heading for major stardom. She was less optimistic about Henry, her former husband, telling Stewart and others, "He is just too stone-faced."

She had helped Stewart's career by insisting that he be her leading man in *Next Time We Love* (1936). She liked their on-screen chemistry. In contrast, when cast with Henry in *The Moon's Our Home* (1938), she reviewed him as "pallid."

James Stewart and **Margaret Sullavan** as they appeared in *The Shop Around the Corner*.

Some reviewers wrote that Stewart was "too American to be convincing as a Magyar."

Once again, she found Stewart effective as the sweet, naïve Texas soldier in their co-starring film, *The Shopworn Angel* (1938). She reviewed that venture as "a mite superficial but good, clean fun."

Fresh from his triumph in Greta Garbo's *Ninotchka* (1939), Ernst Lubitsch was eager to help Stewart and Sullavan. In the third lead was Frank Morgan, a key player in *The Wizard of Oz* (1939).

The screenplay of *The Shop Around the Corner* had been adapted from a 1937 Hungarian play, *Parfumerie*. The American version positions the male and female protagonists as employees at a leather goods shop in Budapest. Stewart played Alfred Kralik, with Sullavan, also an employee, cast as Klara Novak. During the day, they can barely stand each other. But nevertheless, they're falling in love, thanks to their habit of writing anonymous letters to each other off-hours.

Henry privately predicted that Lubitsch and Stewart "would come to blows after the first week," but he was wrong. The "mating" of these artists worked well together. Frank Morgan later said, "Jimmy and Maggie were supposed to be falling in love on the screen. From what I observed, they were already in love as shooting began. Lots of his visits to her dressing room."

Upon its release, and despite generally good reviews, *The Shop Around the Corner* bombed at the box office. Filmed at a cost of $500,000, it took in $380,000. Film historian David Thomson credited it with "being among the greatest of all films. The movie is a treasury of hopes and anxieties based on the desperate faces of Stewart and Sullavan."

In June of 1941, Lux Radio Theatre promoted and broadcast it as a sound-only remake with Claudette Colbert and Don Ameche. A movie adaptation entitled *In the Good Old Summertime* (1949) co-starred Judy Garland with Van Johnson.

***

The Mortal Storm (1940)

Early in 1940, in the tenuous months before the U.S. got involved in the growing conflicts in Europe, James Stewart invited Henry to his home to work with him one weekend on a new script, a very serious anti-Nazi drama, in which he had been cast, reuniting him with his love and former co-star Margaret Sullavan.

Its plot had been adapted from the 1937 novel, *The Mortal Storm,* by Phyllis Bottoms. In essence, it recorded what she saw about the spread of fascism in Germany, the rise of the Nazi Party, and the transformation of Germany into (one of) the worst evil empires the world has ever known.

In their rehearsals, Henry read the role of Sullavan, Freya Roth, and Stewart personified Martin Breitner, the character he'd soon play.

The opening of *The Mortal Storm* takes place in 1933, the year in which Hitler became Chancellor of Germany, and the head of the Nazi Party, which takes over the country, ending democracy and ruling with unlimited and murderous power.

Freya is a young German girl, who is engaged to Fritz Marberg (Robert Young). Soon, his true nature as a Nazi racist becomes unbearable to him. She turns to a friend, Martin Breitner (Stewart), with whom she falls in love. Her father is Professor Roth (Frank Morgan), who will face death by the Nazis. His stepsons are Erich (William T. Orr) and Otto (Robert Stack), each a member of the Nazi Party.

In the movie's final reel, Martin and Freya take to their skis to flee the Nazis, but she is shot while crossing the border. Martin takes her in his arms, crossing the border with her as she dies.

During his first day on the set of *The Mortal Storm*, director Frank Borzage had called for a reading of the script by most of the supporting players. He had helmed Sullavan recently in *The Shining Hour* (1938), in which she had starred with Joan Crawford.

That day, she and Stewart rehearsed with the other members of the cast and enjoyed a catered lunch. In supporting roles were Robert Young, Robert Stack, Frank Morgan, Dan Dailey, Ward Bond, and the incomparable Maria Ouspenskaya.

Some sources assert that *The Mortal Storm* was the first anti-Nazi film made in America. However, Charles Chaplin had also appeared in *The Great Dictator* and *Confessions of a Nazi Spy* had also been released.

America was still officially neutral when this movie was shot, although it really wasn't. One strong-willed movie house operator in Omaha, Nebraska, advertised free admission to *The Mortal Storm* to anyone willing to confess they were a fifth columnist.

150

After press and promotional announcements of this upcoming movie were released, there emerged conflicts at certain film distribution centers in Western Europe, and it was denounced and banned in territories under German control. But by the time *The Mortal Storm* reached general circulation, America was at war, and the delicacy and political caution of its pre-war plot negated its appeal at the box office.

This marked the last time Sullavan and Stewart would co-star.

"By the time Jimmy starred with Maggie (in *Mortal Storm*), the wild passion of their early affair had begun to flicker," Henry claimed. "Passion was replaced with a deep and abiding love for each other. I believed that except for his wife, Gloria, Maggie was the only woman Jimmy really loved."

Henry was asked for his reaction to his friend's latest movie: "I wish I had played that part, but my best buddy got it."

Henry could see himself cast in nearly every role Stewart played, but that did not damage their friendship. However, in the months ahead, Henry and Stewart would find themselves competing for the Best Actor Oscar.

***

No Time for Comedy (1940)

One weekend, Henry was invited to spent two nights with Stewart and his new co-star, Rosalind Russell. Henry had raved about her performance in *The Women* (1939) in which she had co-starred with Norma Shearer and Joan Crawford, two of Stewart's former conquests.

To be directed by William Keighley, *No Time for Comedy* (1940) was based on a play of the same name (1939) by S.N. Behrman. Its screenplay was by Julius J. Epstein and Philip G. Epstein, who would soon go on to greater glory with their screenplay for *Casablanca* (1942) starring Humphrey Bogart and Ingrid Bergman.

During the reading of the script, Stewart read the lines of Gaylord Eastbrook, a reporter from a minor newspaper in Minnesota. He writes a play about high society in Manhattan, a city he'd never visited. Russell read from her lines as Linda Paige, a leading lady on Broadway. At first, her character mistakes his character for a theater usher.

Henry was assigned to read all the lines associated with members of the supporting cast, including Genevieve Tobin, Charlie Ruggles, Allyn Joslyn, and Louise Beavers, who competed with Hattie McDaniel for black maid roles.

What Henry didn't tell either of the two other stars was that he had originally been envisioned as the production's male lead. On Broadway, he'd seen Laurence Olivier perform the role opposite Katharine Cornell. *[Olivier was starring on Broadway at the time, while his brilliant but unstable lover, Vivien Leigh, was in Los Angeles portraying Scarlett O'Hara in* Gone With the Wind.*]*

Stewart had gone out on two dates with Russell, causing speculation about a big romance, which she denied. "We admire each other's acting talents, but that is that. Don't make any big romance out of it."

"Technically, Rosalind was right," Henry said. "There was no big romance, but there had been some rolls in the hay. Personally, although I admired the talents of Miss Russell, she was no sex symbol for me," Henry said.

Years later, Henry recalled, "This dame could play any role assigned to her. The same year she worked with Jimmy, she made *His Girl Friday* with Cary Grant. She was also good at portraying professional women—judges, psychiatrists, and newspaper gals—the kind of role she played in *His Girl Friday* (1940). She was never better than when she was cast as *Auntie Mame* in 1958 and Rose in *Gypsy* (1962).

The title of the **Rosalind Russell/James Stewart** film, *No Time for Comedy*, turned out to be a liability, as critics "fully agreed with the title's assessment."

In a re-release, the studio came up with an even worse title, calling it *Guy With a Grin*.

In the course of her career, Russell was nominated for a Best Actress Oscar four times.

During the weekend, when Russell went into the study to take a phone call, Henry whispered to Stewart, "You and Roz? I can't believe it. What about all this talk that she's a lez?"

"Maybe she is, but that doesn't mean that on occasion she might want to sample what I've got dangling. Do you know why I can easily get an erection for her? Like me, and unlike you, she's a Republican. We both hate Roosevelt."

In reference to the part she'd played in *His Girl Friday*, Russell revealed to Henry, "Your former wife, Margaret Sullavan, rejected it." Russell continued: "So did Katharine Hepburn, Irene Dunne, Claudette Colbert, Jean Arthur, and Ginger Rogers."

Henry later learned that Stewart and Russell had been invited to attend a party at the home of Cary Grant. There, she met a man she called "This Danish guy." His name was Frederick Brisson, a producer who, at the time, was Grant's lover. By 1941, Russell married him. Grant served as Best Man at their wedding. Their union, known in Hollywood circles as an open marriage, continued for 35 years until her death in 1976.

***

The Philadelphia Story (1940)

Stewart's next picture, a role that Henry also coveted, was *The Philadelphia Story*, eventually released in 1940. A stylish romantic comedy, it had been cast with Cary Grant and Katharine Hepburn in the two leads, with George Cukor directing.

Based on the Broadway play by Philip Barry, the film was about a socialite (Hepburn) whose wedding plans are complicated by the simultaneous arrival of her ex-husband (Grant) and the visit of two tabloid journalists played by Stewart and Ruth Hussey. It is considered one of the best examples of a film about remarriage.

On the movie set of *The Philadelphia Story*, as Katharine Hepburn eagerly awaited her introduction to James Stewart, she was fitted for costumes by Adrian. He'd designed for Garbo, and Hepburn felt that he'd dressed her appropriately for the role of Tracy Lord. She was also delighted at the perfect sets created by Cedric Gibbons, pronouncing them "an abode for the rich but with nothing ostentatious. Old money."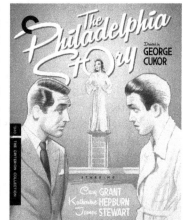

The real man of her character's dreams, Stewart, soon walked onto the set. As he approached her, his body reminded her of Howard Hughes in that it was tall, underweight, and gangly. He was cheerful and most engaging, with a slightly adolescent air about him.

'Kate," he said immediately, calling her not only by her first name but a nickname at that. "It's wonderful to meet you at last. I'm Jimmy Stewart."

If there was one thing she was determined to do, it was to make Stewart forget the charms of Ginger Rogers and Olivia de Havilland.

In spite of his emaciated body, Hepburn thought that he was one of the most handsome men she'd ever met. There was a soft-spoken quality to him that endeared him to her. She felt an innate kindness in him. She told Cukor that it was an "appealing diffidence, a certain boyish earnestness that I find most fascinating."

"Oh, darling, where have you been?" Cukor responded. "He's one of the most sought-after studs in Hollywood, now that his long fling with Henry Fonda is over and he's back to women again."

"*Fonda*?" she said in astonishment. Surely Hollywood could hold no more surprises, yet she managed to find something surprising every day.

During the filming of *The Philadelphia Story*, Kate was entertained frequently by Cary Grant and Randolph Scott. Grant informed her that his contract called for a salary of $175,000 for *The Philadelphia Story*, all of which he planned to donate to the British War Relief.

At a picnic lunch, Kate said, "Oh what the hell! I'm tired of waiting." She leaned over and gave Stewart a passionate kiss on his lips.

Three big stars *(left to right)*, **James Stewart, Cary Grant,** and **Katharine Hepburn** look startled in this scene from *The Philadelphia Story*.

On Broadway, Hepburn had both financially sponsored and starred in the play that inspired the movie, but rejected her onstage co-stars, Joseph Cotten and Van Heflin, for the movie adaptation.

"I know you don't like women like Loretta Young and Joan Crawford chasing after you, but I simply could not resist."

At first surprised, he must have decided he liked the kiss. He reached for her and took her into his arms, kissing her far more passionately than she had him. After he'd done that, he invited her out for a date that night.

As Hepburn was later to say, "Jimmy stood six-foot-three and weighed—oh, I don't know—one-hundred and twenty five pounds, give or take. Although he mumbled and stammered, he was actually quite smart. All that 'Aw, shucks, ma'am,' act was, I think, just an act. Looking at him, he was everything that Lotus Land disdained in its male stars. Ironically, he went on to become the best loved star in Hollywood."

As Hepburn was to relate to her friend, Anderson Lawler, and as he was to tell virtually everybody else, Stewart finally got around to explaining his beliefs about "pollution" to Kate. It was discussed during a "pillow talk" moment, when Margaret Sullavan's name was mentioned once again.

Sullavan had seriously damaged the sexual reputations of both Fonda and Stewart, denouncing both of them as "faggots" to the Hollywood community whenever she wasn't attacking Hepburn for her lesbianism.

Hepburn quickly learned that "pollute" meant to masturbate. The actor, Burgess Meredith, Stewart's roommate for a number of months beginning in 1940, revealed later that the actor would come home "hot and bothered" from a date and announce that he had to go and "pollute myself."

Apparently, not all of Stewart's many romances with Hollywood stars led to seductions. He confessed to Hepburn he'd been polluting himself since he was six years old—sometimes as often as five times a day.

He said that when he turned fourteen, his mother had urged him to "save your clean and godly body until the right woman comes along. Bring to your marriage bed an undefiled, uncorrupted, and unpolluted temple of manhood."

"For years I took my mom's advice," he claimed, "but she didn't say anything about using my fingers. I'm a bit excessive with them."

Hepburn found all this intriguing, especially when he told her that he could go "the stretch" with a woman but always had to pull out at the last minute and let his fingers do the rest of the work. He said that Sullavan had accused both her former husband, Henry Fonda, and himself of being "adolescent boys." She said that whereas Henry was "quick on the draw," I take forever. At least I don't suffer from premature ejaculation like Hank does. In fact, it's Hank's marriage bed horror stories that have kept me from committing to one woman."

"Let me understand this," she said. "You penetrate but pull out and call your right hand into duty to finish off the night. Absolutely fascinating!"

"I wanted you to understand that before giving me a try," he said. "That way you won't be disappointed. I once went the full run with Marlene Dietrich, but she ended up getting pregnant."

"Let's give it a go," she said. "If it's really bad, I can take you home to father. He's a doctor and knows about such things."

What happened to make their romance a quickie, lasting no more than two weeks? Stewart was never certain, and Hepburn never explained.

In New York, film adaptation of *The Philadelphia Story* opened on Christmas Day, 1940, at Radio City Music Hall. When the sum of box office receipts became available on January 21, 1941, figures revealed that the film had broken the all-time attendance record, which till then had been set by Walt Disney's *Snow White* in 1937.

The Philadelphia Story marked the end of an era, the twilight of the so-called screwball comedies that had dominated the screens of the Thirties. Although Kate and Cary Grant would remain friends, the film would be her last screen appearance with him.

***

Contingent with the receipt of his role as Tom Joad in *The Grapes of Wrath,* Henry had been pressured into signing a seven-year contract with Darryl F. Zanuck.

"I was no longer Walter Wanger's boy under contract to that fucker. I hoped Zanuck would stop drooling over Tyrone Power in the steambath and give me some strong, meaty roles. It wasn't long before that I realized that I'd been sold into slavery to this cigar chomper and starlet deflowerer. I just hoped he wouldn't make me suck his dick like he'd demanded of that moppet, Shirley Temple."

Henry had submitted to Zanuck's control at the time the mogul was at the peak of his career as chief of Fox. Hollywood biographer George F. Custen wrote: "Darryl F. Zanuck transformed himself into a purveyor of colorful but basically escapist entertainment into the film industry's pre-eminent serious producer."

[Zanuck, for example, had been the producer of How Green Was My Valley, *voted Best Picture of 1941 and starring*

Walter Pidgeon and Maureen O'Hara.]

As Fox's newest contract player, Henry joined a galaxy of established stars who churned out, on cue, movies for the entertainment of a wartime public. Alice Faye, the reigning queen of Fox musicals, was gradually replaced by Betty Grable, the pinup girl of World War II. Other leading stars were Don Ameche and Loretta Young, each of whom Henry had co-starred with in *The Story of Alexander Graham Bell*. Sonja Henie was also under contract. She could not act, but she could skate better than anyone else on ice.

A cold dose of reality soon hit Henry. He detested many of the movies he'd made before he went off to war in 1942, and in his memoirs, he sometimes failed to even mention them, despite admitting that a few of them were pretty good. *[Actually, The Ox-Bow Incident (1943) became a classic.]*

What Henry didn't say is that his female co-stars were some of the biggest and most famous women in Golden Age Hollywood: Gene Tierney, Dorothy Lamour, Linda Darnell, Barbara Stanwyck, Joan Bennett, Olivia de Havilland, Rita Hayworth, Lucille Ball, and Maureen O'Hara.

To demonstrate his disdain for his new boss, Henry, behind his back, began to refer to him as "Darryl Fuck-It-All Zanuck. He cast me in movies he wanted me to make, not in film scripts I wanted to shoot."

[The authors of this book do not share Henry's disdain for his movies of the early 1940s. We will preview them in the following chapter, with special emphasis on how he related to his famous leading ladies. We'll include what Henry said about his male co-stars, too.]

Blunt and intense, with a touch of melancholy and a direct, "in-your-face" honesty, **Henry Fonda** had a face and mannerisms that evoked his era's quintessential American male.

CHAPTER NINE

DARRYL ("THE DEMOLITION KING") ZANUCK

"My boss at Fox forced me to film trash, but gave me great leading ladies."
—Henry Fonda

ON FILM, HENRY COURTS
THE EDWARDIAN AGE'S QUEEN OF BROADWAY
COMPETING WITH DIAMOND JIM BRADY FOR THE HAND OF
LILLIAN RUSSELL

*"Henry taught me you don't have to be married to a man to make love to him.
JFK convinced me of that, too."*
—Gene Tierney

LOVING LUCY
JANE FONDA CLAIMS THAT LUCILLE BALL
WAS THE LOVE OF HER FATHER'S LIFE

"THE WORLD'S MOST BEAUTIFUL WOMAN"
Henry Seduces "That Dizzy Blonde,"
MARION MARTIN

HOLLYWOOD'S SPIN ON COLORFUL CHARACTERS
YOU'RE LIKELY TO MEET IN NYC,
TALES OF MANHATTAN

HENRY DALLIES (AND SOMETIMES DANCES) WITH DIVAS
GENE TIERNEY, LINDA DARNELL, DOROTHY LAMOUR, MARY BETH HUGHES, OLIVIA DE HAVILLAND, ETC.

THE OX-BOW INCIDENT

DARK, DEPRESSING, AND VIOLENT, IT'S A RADICAL FILM ABOUT SELF-RIGHTEOUS "CITIZENS" WHO LYNCH.
SHORT ON BOX OFFICE CASH, IT MORPHS INTO SOMETHING HUGE IN THE PAGES OF FILM HISTORY

STANWYCK

(A.K.A. "BLOODY BABS," A.K.A. "THE LADY EVE")
"DO YOU REALLY BELONG TO ME?"

"Barbara Stanwyck gave me the best fuck of my life."
—Henry Fonda

PLUS A GAGGLE OF
MINOR, FORGETTABLE FILMS
RARELY OR NEVER MENTIONED IN HENRY'S MEMOIRS: *WILD GEESE CALLING, THE MALE ANIMAL.*

WITH HIS MARRIAGE ON "LIFE SUPPORT,"
AND PERHAPS SUFFOCATING FROM TOO MUCH DOMESTICITY,
HENRY JOINS THE NAVY
TO FIGHT "THE JAPS" IN THE SOUTH PACIFIC

ALTHOUGH TEMPORARILY THWARTED BY DARRYL ZANUCK,
HENRY PERSEVERES

As an infant, Lady Jane (the nickname for Jane Fonda) didn't receive the love and support she needed either from Henry or Frances. Her parents were mostly absorbed in their own activities, hiring a series of nannies to deal with the day-to-day demands of their daughter. Frances' daughter, Pan, was to some degree, at least, able to pursue her own interests, and Peter was still in diapers.

Jane wanted a closer bond with her father, but he was often distant and aloof, absorbed as he was in his private world of plowing his acreage, hanging out with close friends who included James Stewart, and churning out, one after another, a stream of pre-war films. When he wasn't farming, he and Stewart sometimes "flight-tested" model airplanes in the windswept hills of Brentwood.

When she was very young, Jane at first thought her father was a farmer—not a movie star. On most nights after dinner, he retreated to his study to memorize his lines so he'd be ready to face the cameras in the morning. Frances, too, was involved in her own affairs, spending hours handling not only her own financial affairs, but those of her husband, too. When she did visit the nursery, it was to lavish attention on the infant Peter, whom she seemed to adore, as she had long wanted a son. Fortunately, she could well afford nannies, maids, and any maintenance that needed to be done to their home.

Frances seemed discontented with her life, which she found relatively barren after the hectic social activities she'd cultivated in the East. She often expressed her hopes that Henry would take her to more of the gala Hollywood parties to which he was invited as a rising film star at 20th Century Fox.

***

As Henry recalled, his daughter Jane was "all questions. She wanted to know not only about earth but the moon. She asked me if people lived there and, if not, and had they ever inhabited that planet she could see shining at night from her bedroom window?'"

Often, he didn't even attempt to answer her questions, instead looking vacantly into space, absorbed with his many problems.

She didn't like the frilly little frocks Frances purchased for her. At the age of five, she preferred blue jeans and lumberjack shirts, sometimes following her dad around as he plowed his fields. At an early age, although she seemed far too young to learn how to swim, he took her in his arms and went into the pool with her.

She developed a love of horses and enjoyed the visits of her father's newly minted "coyboy" friends: John Ford, Ward Bond, and John Wayne, whom they called Duke. She believed that he might rule over a castle somewhere. These men often showed up dressed as cowboys, and she hoped that one day she could go riding with them.

One night she remembered the arrival at her parents' house of Tyrone Power with his new wife, the French actress Annabella. Later in life, Jane learned that her father had had an affair with her when they'd co-starred together in *Wings of the Morning* (1937), shot in England.

One of Jane's early playmates was Brooke Hayward, the daughter of Leland Hayward and Margaret Sullavan. Brooke lived on the same street and had been born in the same year (1937). Later, Jane was somewhat shocked to learn that her father had, in 1931, been briefly married to Sullavan. Leland Hayward, the father of her friend Brooke and the (present) husband of Sullavan, was Henry's film agent.

Brooke, who later became a stage, film, and TV actress, was the eldest of three children born to this powerhouse couple. Doomed to a tragic life, Bridget was born in 1939, William (nicknamed Bill) in 1941.

In the early years, Jane viewed Brooke as living in an ideal world, one of three beautiful, wealthy, and privileged children with parents who were one of the most glittering couples of Hollywood.

Jane would live to see their magical world end destructively. But in those glory days of growing up, Jane saw a parade of famous men and women cross the threshold of the Hayward/Sullavan home.

They included Greta Garbo, on the verge of abandoning the film world forever. Everyone from Ernest Hemingway to Judy Garland arrived to see Hayward. Jane found Gregory Peck very handsome, and both Brooke and Jane agreed that was the kind of man they would marry in the future.

Both of them thought Boris Karloff was scary.

"My mother Frances was well trained in the social graces, but Maggie had her beat," Jane later recalled. "An actress, she was both high spirited and charming. My father was rather subdued, but Brooke's dad, Leland, was flamboyant, even magnetic. He sure wooed the greats of Hollywood. But their world came tumbling down."

One summer day, Jane witnessed firsthand how temperamental Sullavan could be. The Haywards invited the Fondas for a picnic in their backyard. Henry arrived and started soliciting contributions for a big Fourth of July fireworks display. Leland had retreated into the house to retrieve something.

When Henry asked Sullavan for a contribution, she not only refused but picked up a pitcher of cold water and doused

The statuesque grandeur **Alice Faye** pumped into her portrayal of the real **Lillian Russell** (shown in the two lower photos as she appeared in 1904 and 1890, respectively) was applauded by many who had actually been fans of "the real, diamond-studded deal" during her heyday in gaslight operetta.

A darling of what became known as "the papparazzi," Russell did dramatic things in her personal life that often upstaged her music, including being "racy" in ways then unbecoming for a lady.

She came to New York from Iowa in 1878 to become an opera star, arranging for private lessons with Leopold Damrosch, whose son Walter, coincidentally, was closely involved in the creation of Carnegie Hall.

In short order, she scandalously breezed through four stormy marriages with an actor, a politician, a composer and a newspaperman, but she would be most famous for the one man she didn't marry — Diamond Jim Brady, an ongoing emissary for conspicuous consumption (including gluttony) during the Gilded Age.

his head. Then she sat down and ordered more potato salad as if nothing had happened.

From that day forth, Jane did not regard her in a good light. "She was mean to my father. I will never forgive her for that."

Jane was later quoted as saying, "This was the first time I watched one person humiliate another. It would not be the last. I would go on to know triumph and tragedy in my own life. In fact, every year, as a New Year's celebration, I asked myself, 'What new humiliations will I have to face this year?'"

***

Lillian Russell (1940)

After *The Grapes of Wrath,* Henry was bitterly disappointed when Darryl F. Zanuck, his new boss at Fox, cast him in the third lead in the bio film, *Lillian Russell.* The stars were Alice Faye and Don Ameche, with direction by Irving Cummings Sr., who had helmed Ameche and Henry in the recent *The Story of Alexander Graham Bell* (1939). Only a few months earlier, Ameche had been Faye's leading man in *Hollywood Cavalcade* (1939).

Cummings was a good choice as a director, having actually appeared on stage with the real Lillian Russell back in the 1908 play, *Wildfire.*

"Billed after Ameche and Faye, I was just one of the suitors pursuing Russell in that film," Henry said. "I played a newspaper reporter, Alexander Moore, who marries her at the end."

Edward Arnold was cast as Diamond Jim Brady, and Warren William was yet another suitor, Jesse Lewisohn.

Although hardly known by today's generation, Lillian Russell and Diamond Jim Brady were legendary figures at the turn of the 20th Century. Born in 1860 at the start of the Civil War, Russell was the foremost singer of operettas and musical theater of her era on the Broadway stage. She was known for her hour-glass figure, her beauty and style, and for her voice and stage presence. Composer Edward Solomon (Don Ameche) created roles for her in several of his comic operas in London.

Leo Carrillo, who had co-starred with Henry in his film *Blockade* (1938), played a vaudeville impresario who hires Russell to sing at his theater. Diamond Jim Brady financed her lavish lifestyle for four decades. When Alexander Graham Bell introduced long-distance phone service on May 8, 1890, Russell's voice was the first one carried on the line.

Arnold had already starred in the 1935 biopic named. *Diamond Jim* before being offered the role again in this newest version with Fonda, although the scripts were very different.

Born on the Lower East Side of Manhattan in 1890, Arnold had appeared on Broadway at the age of twelve and went on to star in several other stage roles in the 1920s and 1930s. In Hollywood of 1937, he took star billing over Cary Grant in *The Toast of New York.* He would also co-star with James Stewart in *You Can't Take It With You* and in *Mr. Smith Goes to Washington.* "I played character roles. The bigger my waistline got, the more parts I got."

The real-life Diamond Jim Brady lavished diamonds and other precious stones on Russell for four decades. Born in New York in 1856, this son of a saloon owner started out as a messenger boy in Grand Central Station. In time, he would make millions selling railroad equipment to a transportation industry pushing itself Westward at epic speeds.

He also became famous for owning the first automobile (1895) in New York. He also collected jewelry, amassing a fortune in gems, which would be worth

Alice Faye (aka "Lillian Russell"), then the Queen of Fox and one of the highest-paid actresses in Hollywood, with **Don Ameche,** then at his (well-paid) career peak, too, recently famous for playing bandleaders who knew how to persuade audiences to "get down and rhumba."

Everyone agreed that **Henry Fonda's** role in *Lillian Russell* was shallow, peripheral to the plot, and unfocused.

But here, at least, perhaps tapping into his Midwestern sense of chivalry, he defends the honor of a damsel then in distress, Alice (Lillian) Faye (Russell) from an "unsuitable suitor."

Alice Faye as Lillian Russell, sharing secrets with **Edward Arnold,** portraying her mentor, Diamond Jim Brady.

Arnold later commented on how "unbeneficial" it would be for him to lose weight: He spent the rest of his career portraying "likable fat guys" with "large" personalities.

about $65 million in 2022 dollars.

As a glutton, his appetite became the stuff of legend. A typical dinner would consist of three dozen oysters, six crabs, two bowls of green turtle soup, seven lobsters, two canvasback ducks, a double portion of terrapin, a thick sirloin steak, vegetables, and a platter of French pastries. He finished it off with two pounds of chocolate. When he died of diabetes in 1917, an autopsy revealed that his stomach was six times larger than that of an "average" man.

In reference to his casting decisions, Cummings, as director of the biopic, made many wise choices. He cast Helen Westley as Russell's feisty grandmother. She had previously appeared as Aunt Sophie in *Alexander's Ragtime Band* (1939), which had starred Alice Faye with Don Ameche and Tyrone Power.

In the late 1930s, Faye was one of the top box office stars in America, and she was cast in *Rose of Washington Square* alongside Power once again. Fanny Brice later sued Fox "for ripping off my life story."

When Henry worked with Faye, she was the "Queen of Fox," one of the highest-paid stars in Hollywood. But the crown would soon be ripped off her head by Betty Grable.

"*Lillian Russell* was my most challenging role," Faye said. "On several occasions, I passed out because of those tight corsets I was forced to wear."

"My marriage to singer Tony Martin was heading for the divorce courts," Faye claimed. "I never got Ty Power to seduce me, and I also struck out with Henry Fonda. Thank god Phil Harris, a real man, lay in my immediate future."

When Ameche was cast in *Lillian Russell,* he was at his career peak, ranking no. 21 as a box office draw. That same year, he starred in *Down Argentine Way,* which made stars out of both Betty Grable and Carmen Miranda. His take-home pay was $250,000 a year, an astonishing salary in the pre-war 1940s.

Warren William's career was in decline when he worked with Henry and Ameche. Hailed in the 1930s as "The King of Pre-Code Hollywood," he was a leading man to such stars as Mae West and Bette Davis. He was also the first film actor to portray the fictional defense attorney Perry Mason on the big screen.

Nigel Bruce, as William S. Gilbert, had previously starred with Henry in *The Trail of the Lonesome Pine* (1936). Eddie Foy Jr., son of the famous vaudeville star, was one of the "Seven Little Foys." Throughout the 1930s and 1940s, he starred in dozens of B movies. In *Lillian Russell,* he was cast in a romanticized portrayal of his own father, the vaudevillian comedian, Eddie Foy Sr.

Bosley Crowther in *The New York Times,* wrote, "Fonda paces monotonously through the weakly conceived role of Alexander Moore." In *The Films of Henry Fonda,* Tony Thomas wrote, "It is doubtful if Henry Fonda ever saw [the final cut of] *Lillian Russell.* Mention of it in his presence brought an expression of disgust. It is easy to see how such a shallow role displeased him after having proved his calibre in *The Grapes of Wrath.*"

After being shown in theaters, *Lillian Russell,* a voice-only adaptation of it was aired on the *Lux Radio Theater* in October of 1940. Henry's role was cast with voice of Victor Mature.

***

The Return of Frank James (1940)

Darryl F. Zanuck was pleased with the box office grosses of *Jesse James,* that 1939 Western that had starred Tyrone Power as Jesse and Henry Fonda as his brother Frank. He ordered Sam Wellman, a screenwriter, to develop a sequel. His attempt to replicate those profits resulted in *The Return of Frank James* (1940) a Western where Frank goes on a rampage to seek revenge on the Ford Brothers who had killed his brother, Jesse. Wellman concocted a fairly original drama, with scant attention to historical accuracy.

The movie was a success and earned a note in film history in that it was the first motion picture that involved Gene Tierney, who became a major star at Fox later in the 40s. She played a reporter for the newspaper *The Denver Star.*

On a mission to avenge the death of his father, Jackie Cooper was cast as Clem James, Jesse's grown-up kid.

Henry became furious when he was told that Fritz Lang, "a real son of a bitch," would direct him again. During the making of *You Only Live Once,* the director and its star had clashed, at times almost violently.

It seemed too much like a "forced" (some said "unnecessary") sequel, and its ending was weak. But the 20th Century Fox studio boss, **Darryl Zanuck**—was famous for his "in your face" involvement with scripts, film editing, and production values.

It was Zanuck himself who ordained that it should be so, and indeed, so it was.....

Before shooting began, the Viennese director assured Henry that this time, he'd be much more considerate. But after the second week, he forgot about that and relaunched his feud with Henry.

Henry came to the aid of Tierney when Lang attacked her acting and physicality. She had a tendency to keep her lower jaw open even when she wasn't speaking. Marilyn Monroe in the 1950s would get away with that, but not Tierney in 1940. "Would you keep your god damn mouth shut when you're not speaking, you buck-tooth bitch! What an overbite!" Lang shouted at her.

Tierney burst into tears, and Henry stepped in, threatening to bash in Lang's face. After a few hours, tempers had cooled, and shooting resumed.

Tierney later confessed, "That afternoon forth, Henry became my gallant knight." In a memoir, she admitted to having developed a crush on him. Jackie Cooper interpreted it as far more than a crush. Since Henry was married, he had to slip around and visit Tierney in private. The relationship became sexual, partly because, as he admitted one afternoon to Burgess Meredith, "I've grown tired of Frances."

At the time, Cooper was transitioning from child star to adult roles. This son of California became the youngest performer ever nominated for a Best Actor Oscar, an honor bestowed on him for his role in the film *Skippy* (1941).

As part of a "roundup" of the actors from the original film, *Jesse James,* Henry Hull was tapped once again to play the crusading newspaper editor. The malevolent Ford brothers were cast again with John Carradine and Charles Tannen.

For her debut performance, the *Harvard Lampoon* cited Tierney as "The Worst Female Discovery of 1940." In spite of that put-down, she would again co-star with Henry in the 1941 *Rings on Her Fingers.* Two years later, she would star in the classic film noir, *Laura,* and in 1945, she received a Best Actress Academy Award nomination for *Leave Her to Heaven.*

Otis Ferguson, in *The New Republic,* wrote of Fonda, "Durn if I don't like that boy. I remember the first picture he played in, with about as much expression as a brown paper bag."

Theodore Strauss, writing in *The New York Times,* said, "Henry Fonda plays the role with his accustomed honesty and understatement, though we thought him a little phlegmatic for one of the West's most noted killers."

Tierney told Power and others, "When I arrived in Hollywood, I believed that a woman should only have sex with the man she married. Hollywood, Henry Fonda, and Howard Hughes changed my impression."

Jackie Cooper himself had been a virgin until Joan Crawford took the then-seventeen-year-old to bed. Crawford,

AMERICAN GOTHIC

Like it or not, **Henry Fonda** couldn't seem to escape his midwestern origins when it came to scripts that called for poker-faced stone during his interactions with other characters, including beautiful women.

Here he is, evoking stalwart, no-nonsense reliability, in a publicity still for *The Return of Jesse James* with the actress who later, briefly, became JFK's party girl, **Gene Tierney**

The Return of Jesse James, to Henry Fonda's regret, was directed by Fritz Lang, a temperamental Viennese with a penchant for associations with ghoulish horror.

Perhaps that's why this publicity photo of the film's moody protagonist (**Henry**) was shrouded, sepulchre-style, with cobwebs.

In a tense scene from *Chad Hanna,* its three stars, *left to right,* include **Linda Darnell** as Caroline; **Dorothy Lamour** as Albany; and **Henry Fonda** in the title role of Chad.

He marries Caroline, but is tempted to have an affair with Albany. That is, until he realizes how much he loves Caroline.

Originally, Chad had been so smitten with Albany, a beautiful bareback rider, that he joined the circus as a roustabout with the single-minded intention of pursuing her.

Former child star **Jackie Cooper**, is wholesomely depicted here in the 1930s, with girl singer **Deanna Durbin**, a "operatic sensation" who competed for roles (usually unsuccessfully) with the post-adolescent Judy Garland.

By his own admission, teenaged Jackie was hot, hip, and sexually curious, as noted months later by the patient and generous older and more experienced Joan Crawford.

along with five older female friends of his mother, taught him additional boudoir lessons. He later revealed that he'd lost his virginity at the age of thirteen. At the time that he worked with Henry, he told him he was seducing Judy Garland.

Henry and Tierney would remain in contact for years, and he followed chapters of her troubled life. Shortly after her affair with Henry, she married fashion designer Oleg Cassini. The couple had two daughters, one of whom contracted German measles. During an advanced stage of her pregnancy, Tierney was greeted, close up and personal, by a crazed fan who had risen from her sickbed, having contracted German measles *[identified as a cause of birth defects in unborn children]*, to get her autograph. A few months later, Tierney's daughter was born deaf, partially blind, and mentally disabled.

This incident became the plot of the Agatha Christie mystery novella, *The Mirror Crack'd*, starring Elizabeth Taylor, Rock Hudson, and Tony Curtis.

When Oleg Cassini and Tierney separated in 1946, she began an affair with a young naval officer, John F. Kennedy, who refused to marry her. After a fling with Kirk Douglas, she began dating Prince Aly Khan. Tierney herself would suffer from mental illness, eventually requiring hospitalization.

***

Chad Hanna (1940)

Director Henry King and producer/screenwriter Nunnally Johnson cast Henry Fonda as *Chad Hanna* opposite two of the most glamourous female stars of the 1940s, Dorothy Lamour and Linda Darnell. Henry had worked with Lamour previously in *Spawn of the North* (1938).

Henry had come close to appearing alongside Darnell in the movie he'd made with Claudette Colbert, *Drums Along the Mohawk* (1939), but Darnell's role went to Dorris Bowdon instead.

However, in *Chad Hanna*, casting was the inverted. When filming began, Dorothy Lamour and Bowdon were each engaged as the female leads. But during the first week of filming, Zanuck changed his mind, preferring Darnell in Bowden's role, believing that she was a big star in the making. He fired Bowdon, replacing her with Darnell, who took over her part. However, as a cost-saving measure, he retained some of the production's early footage, including long-distance shots filmed while Bowdon was still on the payroll.

Chad Hanna had been adapted from a best-selling novel, *Red Wheels Rolling*, by Walter Dumaux Edmonds. It marked the third time Henry had starred in a screen version of an Edmonds novel, the first being *The Farmer Takes a Wife* and later, *Drums Along the Mohawk*.

Chad Hanna was the third picture in which Henry had been directed by Henry King, Zanuck's favorite director. Earlier pictures included *Way Down East* and *Jesse James*. In spite of all this exposure to a famous director like King, Henry made no mention of him in his memoirs.

The setting for *Chad Hanna* is along the banks of the Erie canal in Canastota, New York. Henry plays a naïve stable boy who is captivated by the visiting circus. He falls in love with the star of the ring, bareback rider Albany Yates (Lamour). He joins the circus and although he initially pursues Albany, he eventually falls for and marries Caroline (Darnell), who is fleeing from an abusive father.

Although she and Chad face problems and interruptions in their marriage, everything ends well. He even saves the circus from financial ruin.

Among the supporting cast, Jane Darwell had previously played Henry's mother in *The Grapes of Wrath*. John Carradine was fresh from starring with him in *The Return of Frank James*. Guy Kibbee was a well-known character actor. Henry had met him on the set of *Mr. Smith Goes to Washington*, the 1939 movie that had become a landmark in the career

Henry Fonda as Chad appears here with a coquettish **Linda Darnell** as Caroline. "Henry and i are married in the film, so I thought it appropriate that we have a fling off screen to be more convincing in our roles."

"I've got more balls than most men do. If there's anybything I detest, it's a weak man. Henry Fonda was strong. That's why I went for him. Of all my lovers, Zanuck had the biggest weapon, and Kirk Douglas was what I delicately call 'parlor size.'"

of his friend, James Stewart. Henry had first seen Kibbee onscreen when he'd played the innkeeper in Joan Crawford's version of *Rain* (1932).

Meeting Lamour again, Henry was told that her role had originally been cast with a lesser-known actress, Mary Beth Hughes. According to Lamour, "Zanuck decided she had no marquee value. He tapped me for the female lead instead."

In a memoir, Lamour wrote: "Hank's only memory of *Chad Hanna* is the scene in which he is asleep in a barn. He is awakened by a playful pachyderm determined to save my show. The elephant slobbers all over Henry. I enjoyed making *Chad Hanna,* not knowing it was a mere rehearsal for a bigger circus picture twelve years later."

[She was referring to Cecil B. De Mille's The Greatest Show on Earth *(1962).]*

Darnell later admitted that "Henry and I had a brief fling, but, frankly, I preferred Tyrone Power."

She eventually sustained affairs with Darryl F. Zanuck; the aviator/producer Howard Hughes; Kirk Douglas; and Milton Berle, among others, before burning to death in a fire in 1965.

In *The New York Herald Tribune,* Robert Dana wrote: "Henry Fonda's portrait of Chad Hanna is something else, the something that proves an actor can be somebody else if he is good enough. He makes Chad terribly ingenuous, almost stolid. It is one clear-cut aspect of the movie, perfect in every respect."

Theodore Strauss in *The New York Times* claimed, "Henry Fonda was the most natural selection for the gauche, simple-minded and resourceful fellow that Chad was, and he carries the role perfectly."

One critic described Henry's role as that of a "clod-kicking juvenile" even though he was thirty-five at the time. "He mouths phony 'hillbillyishs' and totes slop to feed the hogs."

Fox released this dud as "Santa's gift to America."

On Henry's return from World War II, John Ford cast him in *My Darling Clementine* (1946) in which Henry renewed his affair with Darnell.

***

Henry didn't accept every role Darryl F. Zanuck sent to him. He read the script for the 1941 Western, *Belle Starr,* a very loose retelling of the life of the notorious outlaw.

Gene Tierney was to play Belle, and she wanted to work with Henry again. But he felt there was too much focus on the female role, and that his part of Sam Starr was weak. Randolph Scott accepted the role, with Dana Andrews in the third lead.

Henry made a wise choice in bowing out, as a short while later, he was lent to Paramount to co-star in a much better role with Barbara Stanwyck in *The Lady Eve.*

***

The Lady Eve (1940)

Based on *Two Bad Hats* by Monckton Hoffe, *The Lady Eve's* script had been written and directed by Preston Sturges.

As the female lead, Stanwyck would play a con artist, Jean Harrington, (aka Lady Eve Sidwick). Henry, nicknamed "Hopsie," was second-billed in the role of a rich heir, Charles Poncefort Pike. Aboard an ocean liner, he is a woman-shy snake expert returning from a year-long expedition in the Amazon. As a handsome "babe magnet" and millionaire, he is viewed by her as a potentially valuable catch.

Charles Coburn was cast in the third lead as "Colonel" Harrington, Jean's conniving and larcenous father. Both are out to fleece the somewhat naïve Charles. In the film's most memorable scene, Henry, wearing a dinner jacket, enters the hotel dining room, facing avaricious looks from the "greedy" dames at the various tables. After all, he's the most desirable "male catch" on this voyage. It's obvious that many of the female passengers want both his body and his gold.

To Stanwyck, he appears as "the perfect pansy." As he strolls by her table, she extends her shapely leg and trips him, causing him to fall at her feet. A love game (or a war game) has just been declared.

William Demarest was cast as "Mugsy," Charles' (Fonda's) sidekick. He warns him

162

that Jean (Stanwyck) is a trickster after his gold. Meanwhile, Jean is falling fast in love with Charles, and attempts to protect him from the other hustlers on board. By now suspicious of her motives, Charles dumps her.

Jean does not give up easily and stages a comeback, this time disguised as a titled English aristocrat, The Lady Eve. Amazingly, he accepts her reincarnation, falling into the same trap again. He marries her, but the drama morphs into a madcap second act, a battle of the sexes. As one reviewer phrased it, "Charles has about as much chance as a man with an umbrella under Niagara."

Originally, *The Lady Eve's* female lead was to have gone to Paulette Goddard, but she was having personal difficulties with her presumed husband, Charlie Chaplin, and had to drop out. Stanwyck almost immediately agreed to replace her and the next day, appeared at Paramount for the fittings of costumes designed by Edith Head. The famed designer became the star's favorite and would create her wardrobes for another twenty-two films.

Early in the shoot, Henry learned that Preston Sturges, the film's writer and director, had originally offered his role to Joel McCrea, one of Sturges's favorite actors.

In the most "madcap" scene from *The Lady Eve*, **Henry** "falls" for **Barbara Stanwyck** when she puts out her foot and trips him in the dining room.

"If there's anything I hate," Stanwyck said, "it's a god damn phoney. Hollywood is filled with 'em, pretending to be what they're not. Some of them never were. Henry was real—no fancy airs, no pretensions, a real man, unlike my closeted husband, Robert Taylor."

Stanwyck appreciated Sturges as a director more than Henry did. Her favorite line of dialogue from her role in the film was, "I need him like a turkey needs an axe."

One reviewer wrote, "It is not uncommon for a Sturges character to deliver an exquisitely turned phrase and take an elaborate pratfall within the same scene. Such versatility and dexterity can be seen in *The Lady Eve* where a tender love scene takes place between Fonda and Stanwyck, which is enlivened by a horse as it repeatedly pokes its nose into Fonda's head."

The Lady Eve featured a strong supporting cast, especially Charles Coburn, who had co-starred with Henry in *The Story of Alexander Graham Bell* (1939). "I admired his talent, but this old son of Georgia was the biggest racist I've ever met," Henry said. "He believed that slavery should never have been abolished in America."

A veteran of the silent era, Kansas-born Eugene Pallette had met Henry before, when he had a role in James Stewart's *Mr. Smith Goes to Washington* (1939). This time, he was cast as Horace Pike, Henry's father, the influential owner of Pike Ale ("The Ale that Won for Yale").

Eric Blore, as Sir Alfred McGlennan Keith, was an English actor known for playing in some sixty films, mainly cast as a fluttery, gay-ish butler. Melville Cooper, as Gerald, was another English import, whose stocky frame and basset-hound eyes popped up in many a film.

Fonda may have shown his contempt for Sturges by not even mentioning him in his memoirs.

Born in Chicago in 1898, Sturges was an influential Hollywood director, playwright, and screenwriter. The same year that he helmed Stanwyck and Henry, Sturges won an Oscar for Best Original Screenplay, an honor for the screwball comedy, *The Great McGinty* (1940). He had famously agreed to work for one dollar in exchange for Paramount allowing him to direct.

Around the time that he worked with Henry, Sturges was at the peak of his career, turning out *Sullivan's Travels, The Miracle of Morgan's Creek,* and *Hail the Conquering Hero,* each of which is viewed today as a classic.

In his memoirs, Henry writes, "Everyone close to me knows I've been in love with Barbara Stanwyck since I met her. She is a delicious woman. We've never had an affair. She's never encouraged me, dammit. Stanwyck can play the hell out of any part and can turn a chore into a challenge. She's fun, and I'm glad I had the chance to make three movies with her, beginning with *The Mad Miss Manton* (1938), a little murder mystery comedy."

Henry told a different story to James Stewart, Burgess Meredith, and other friends. "Barbara Stanwyck gave me the best fuck of my life."

"Hank was friends with her husband, Robert Taylor," Meredith said. "But he didn't feel that he was betraying his buddy all that much, since Bob was turning tricks with a lot of males, including Phillip Terry, the husband of Joan Crawford. Babs wasn't getting much from Bob."

As was known among Hollywood insiders, Stanwyck, a bisexual, had a string of adulterous affairs during her long marriage to Taylor. The list features Joan Crawford, Marlene Dietrich, Gary Cooper, director Frank Capra, William Holden (aka "Her Golden Boy"), and—later in life—a long affair with her *Titanic* co-star, Robert Wagner, that is, when she could lure him away from the salivating Clifton Webb.

In his review of *The Lady Eve,* critic Andrew Sarris referred to Henry as "the funniest deadpan comedian since Buster Keaton."

At its premier at the Rialto in Manhattan, Bosley Crowther in *The New York Times* called *The Lady Eve* "a sparkling romantic comedy."

In 2008, *Esquire* named *The Lady Eve* among the fifty greatest films of all time. *The New York Times* ranked it among the 1,000 best. *Time* magazine brought it in among the top 100.

In 1956, the plot was badly recycled for *The Birds and the Bees,* starring Mitzi Gaynor, David Niven, and George Gobel.

***

Wild Geese Calling (1941)

At Fox, Henry's home studio, he was reteamed in *Wild Geese Calling* (1941) with director John Brahm who had helmed him in *Let Us Live* (1939). Likewise, Brahm had previously directed both Henry and this newest film's co-star, Joan Bennett, in *I Met My Love Again* (1938).

Its screenplay was by Horace McCoy, based on a novel by Stewart Edward White. The music score was by Alfred Newman, a composer, arranger, and conductor of film music, later winning nine Academy Awards.

When Henry came together with Bennett, she was at the peak of her *film noir* career. She referred to that period of her screen life as "before I became the mother of Elizabeth Taylor." *[She was, of course referring to* Father of the Bride *(1950) and its sequel* Father's Little Dividend *(1951). In both of those films, Spencer Tracy played her husband.]*

Bennett and her real-life husband, Walter Wanger, had formed a production company with Fritz Lang, a director Henry detested. Lang would helm her in four *film noir* movies, including *The Woman in the Window* (1944) with Edward G. Robinson.

Her future leading men would include Walter Pidgeon, Gregory Peck, Robert Ryan, Charles Bickford, and James Mason.

In the plot of *Wild Geese Calling,* Henry starred as John Murdock, a lumberjack who journeys to the lusty Seattle of 1895. He heads north to Alaska in search of gold. There, he meets a saloon dancer, Sally (Bennett). He falls in love with her and marries her.

At the time, he doesn't know she is the ex-girlfriend of his closest buddy, Blackie Bedford. That role went to Warren William, who, in *Lillian Russell,* had competed as a rival suitor to Henry for the

Warren William *(left)*, **Joan Bennett**, and **Henry Fonda** in *Wild Geese Calling.*

After reading its script, Henry labeled it "a second-rate melodrama where I play a lumberjack with a wanderlust in lusty Seattle of 1895. Warren William plays a man who's short on scruples.

Henry falls in love with Sally (Joan Bennett), a pretty dancer in a waterfront saloon, who is no innocent when it comes to men and their desires.

stage actress.

When John finds out that Blackie and Sally are lovers, and he catches them alone together, he thinks about leaving her, until he learns that she is pregnant.

Blackie is fleeing from Pirate Kelly (Barton MacLane), who has learned that he won a hotel in Alaska from him in a game with loaded dice. MacLane and Henry had previously worked together in *You Only Live Once*.

Ona Munson was cast as Clarabella, a prostitute with a heart of gold. Privately, she told Henry that after playing the whorehouse madam (Belle Watling) in *Gone With the Wind*, she feared that she'd forever after be cast as a prostitute.

Henry knew that Munson was a lesbian, concealing her affairs with "lavender marriages." Her lovers had included socialite Mercedes de Acosta and Alla Nazimova, the Queen of MGM in the early 1920s.

[Editor's note: In 2021, the authors of this book published a biography of Mercedes de Acosta, perhaps the most notorious lesbian in pre-Code Hollywood. Entitled The Seductive Sapphic Exploits of Mercedes de Acosta, Hollywood's Greatest Lover, *it contains a detailed overview of the tragic life and eventual suicide of Ona Munson, one of Mercedes' genuinely devoted lovers.]*

"There was something tragic about Ona," Henry said. "A sense of doom."

He was right. On February 11, 1955, she was found dead in her Manhattan apartment, having committed suicide by a barbiturate overdose.

Near the end of *Wild Geese Calling*, Blackie shows up and fatally wounds Pirate Kelly. He and Clarabella take a sailboat through stormy seas to John's cabin, where Sally is giving birth.

John settles down and becomes a family man, no longer hearing the sound of *Wild Geese Calling*.

Robert W. Dana, in the *New York Herald Tribune*, wrote, "The action is studied and believably commercial for the most part, but some good acting by the principals is submerged by the excess weight, mood, and thought. Fonda, splendid as always, plays with as much reality as possible, the strong-armed dreamer. Bennett isn't able to do much with the role of the wife."

Variety found that "Fonda is perfect casting for the wandering lumberjack, giving the role every bit of the simplicity and strength it requires."

***

You Belong to Me (1941)

Based on the success of *The Lady Eve*, Columbia wanted to borrow Henry from Fox to co-star with Barbara Stanwyck again in a romantic tale of a playboy heir who falls in love with a female doctor.

You Belong to Me was based on an original story by Dalton Trumbo and directed by Wesley Ruggles. Regrettably, in spite of its notable co-stars, it did not do well at the box office.

When released in the United Kingdom, its title was changed to *Good Morning, Doctor*. In 1950, it was remade as the lackluster but provocatively entitled *Emergency Wedding*.

In this latest picture, Henry was once again cast as a millionaire heir, but in this case he was the pursuer—not the pursued.

According to the plot, Henry, as playboy Peter Kirk, spots Helen Hunt (Stanwyck) at a ski resort and crashes into her, landing in a snowdrift. As she treats his minor injuries, he falls in love with her. This leads to marriage. But he soon becomes jealous of her profession as a doctor, spending time away him and (presumably) examining all those nude male bodies.

Helen wants her (idle and rich) husband to find something useful to do instead of leading a wasted life. Submitting to her pressure, he takes a job as a lowly clerk in a department store. Eventually, he will undergo a change of character and, with his inheritance, purchase a bankrupt hospital, making her chief of staff and appointing himself as its director.

The supporting cast consisted of some famous character actors whose faces were familiar at the time to movie audiences.

As the groundskeeper, Edgar Buchanan, as Billings, tries to interest his boss in gardening. Over the course of his career, Buchanan would ap-

IN SICKNESS AND IN HEALTH

Henry, playing the spoiled, n'er-do-well scion of a Gilded-Age fortune, managed to convince audiences that during scenes like this, he really was MADLY in love with **Barbara Stanwyck.**

pear in some 100 films, working with co-stars Irene Dunne, William Holden, Glenn Ford, Cary Grant, Ronald Colman, Jean Arthur, Joel McCrea, John Wayne, Doris Day, and Clint Eastwood. The peak of his fame came in the 1960s on television in such sitcoms as *Petticoat Junction, Green Acres,* and *The Beverly Hillbillies.*

Cast as Emma, Ruth Donnelly had met Henry when he visited James Stewart on the set of *Mr. Smith Goes to Washington.* This stage and film actress began her stage career at the age of 17. In 1914, she appeared in a silent picture and in 1931, she became a supporting actress in numerous movies until her semi-retirement in 1957.

Equally famous as Donnelly, Mary Treen, cast as Doris, worked steadily in some forty movies from the 1940s to the 1960s, including an appearance with Ginger Rogers in her Oscar-winning drama, *Kitty Foyle* (1940).

Character actor Melville Cooper had worked with Stanwyck and Henry in *The Lady Eve.* This time around, he played a character nicknamed "Moody."

Joseph Walker, the cinematographer, was one of the best in the business, not only for Henry but for James Stewart, on such pictures as *Mr. Smith Goes to Washington* (1939) and, after World War II, *It's a Wonderful Life* (1946).

In one of its first reviews, Bosley Crowther of *The New York Times* wrote: "The Stanwyck/Fonda coupling is the right combination. He, with his loose-jointed bumblings and charming diffidence, and she with her forthright manner and ability to make a man forget, are the right team for this sort of dalliance. *You Belong to Me* is a bit of well-tuned fun."

Howard Barnes of the *New York Herald Tribune* defined the film as "lightweight and second rate, even with the popular stars."

Tony Thomas wrote: "The movie was not a good vehicle for Fonda because his role was too silly, with little sympathy for his so-called plight as the idle husband of a busy wife."

On the set, Henry resumed his affair with Stanwyck, seducing her during discretely private visits to her home when Robert Taylor was away with his buddies on his hunting trips. He enjoyed camping and sleeping with some very desirable men, often actors trying to break into show business.

Biographer Patricia Bosworth wrote, "Fonda remained outwardly faithful to Frances, but he continued to see Stanwyck for months after the wrap of *The Lady Eve.* She provided a diversion from his shifting career, dying marriage, and needy children. He had other affairs, too, as women found him irresistible. One of his lovers said, 'He didn't talk much, but could do everything well. He was a magician with his hands.'"

Frances first learned of her husband's adulterous affairs when one of his conquests filed a paternity suit against her husband. She privately settled the suit out of court, using her own money.

***

The Male Animal (1942)

Henry's next film, *The Male Animal,* was a 1942 comedy drama released by Warners. Although it starred Olivia de Havilland and Henry as a married couple, it has not aged well.

Henry, as Tommy Turner, is a college professor with horn-rimmed glasses. Olivia is his wife, Ellen. His first kissing scene with Olivia marked her 100th screen kiss. Errol Flynn, her frequent co-star, had been the recipient of much of her smooching.

Gene Tierney, Henry's former co-star in *The Return of Frank James* (1940), was originally set to be his co-star, but instead, she was assigned to film *Tobacco Road* (1941), based on the bestselling novel by Erskine Caldwell.

Henry had known Olivia since she was engaged in a torrid affair with his best friend, James Stewart. To Henry, she clearly expressed her disappointment that David O. Selznick had not cast him as Ashley Wilkes in *Gone With the Wind.*

On the set, Olivia had a reunion with Hattie McDaniel, who had played Mammy in that "impossibly famous" 1939 Civil War drama.

During the shoot of *The Male Animal,* McDaniel ruined several of her early takes by referring to Olivia as "Melanie," the role she'd played in *Gone With the Wind.*

The Male Animal first opened as a stage play on Broadway in 1940, the work of

The Male Animal: A heavy-handed story of idealistic, dysfunctional love with an overlay of socialist politics and free speech.

In the photos above, **Henry Fonda**, as a shy quasi-academic, grapples his way through mating games with **Olivia** (aka Melanie, in *Gone With the Wind*) **de Havilland.**

166

Elliott Nugent and humorist James Thurber. On the stage, Nugent had portrayed the character that Henry was essaying in the movie. Ironically, two years later, Warners assigned Nugent to direct the movie version. Nugent, now the production's director, and fully aware that he had virtually no marquee value himself, agreed to the casting of Henry.

The film's script was the work of Julius J. Epstein and Philip G Epstein, who were, at the time, also writing *Casablanca* that year, the movie classic which eventually, in 1942, starred Humphrey Bogart and Ingrid Bergman.

Henry is an English teacher at a football-crazed "rah-rah" college in the Middle West. He becomes involved in a controversy about free speech when one of his students, with the endorsement of the editor (Michael Barnes portrayed by Herbert Anderson) of the school newspaper, wants to publicly present a controversial document.

[The document—defined as an example of eloquent composition, was the statement delivered by Bartolomeo Vanzetti before his execution in Boston in 1927. Vanzetti, an Italian immigrant and anarchist of the 1920s, was probably the most famous victim of possibly wrongful prosecution in the history of Massachusetts. He generated worldwide interest before his execution on the questionable charge of murder. Despite nationwide protests and numerous appeals at the time, his death sentence was upheld.

In 1977, on the 50th anniversary of his execution, Massachusetts Governor Michael Dukakis issued a proclamation that Vanzetti, along with his co-defendant, Nicola Sacco, had been unfairly tried and wrongly convicted and that "any disgrace should be forever removed from their names"]

Every scene of *The Male Animal* had to be carefully scheduled, since Olivia was running back and forth between two sets. *[She was simultaneously shooting* They Died With Their Boots On, *starring swashbuckling Errol Flynn, who was chasing after her to become "in like Flynn.']*

The rotund Eugene Pallette, fresh from the set of *The Lady Eve,* played Ed Keller, the reactionary college trustee who threatens to expel Tommy if he publicly reads aloud Vanzetti's emotional and eloquent but very controversial statement.

As the plot advances, a love triangle emerges, threatening Henry's marriage. Joe Ferguson (played by Jack Carson), Ellen's ex-boyfriend, still with designs on her, arrives on the scene.

Carson was often typecast as a beefy lug who added comic relief to any scene he was in. A few years later, he played the rejected suitor of Joan Crawford in her Oscar-winning movie, *Mildred Pierce* (1945).

In a secondary love triangle, Herbert Anderson, portraying the editor of the college newspaper, is in love with Joan Leslie, who plays Patricia Stanley, Ellen's sister. She, however, seems smitten with Don DeFore, cast as Wally Myers, the lusty halfback on the football team.

DeFore had appeared in the Broadway stage version in *The Male Animal* and was repeating his role on the screen. *[Ironically, he would also star in its 1952 remake,* She's Working Her Way Through College, *starring Virginia Mayo and Ronald Reagan.]*

In *The New York Times,* Bosley Crowther wrote, "Henry Fonda plays the young professor with a floppy doggedness which is completely pat, still conveying a sense of integrity which gives his character more than comic point.   H i s reading of the Vanzetti letter is a profoundly moving performance. It gives genuine significance to this film."

This photo of a protest rally in Union Square, NYC, in 1927 shows the passions aroused by the **Sacco and Vanzetti** case.

After seven years of court proceedings based on sometimes circumstantial evidence, a questionable death sentence was imposed upon two recent Italian immigrants with poor English-language skills and histories of union activism.

Some movie fans said that the moral "message" in Henry Fonda's call to arms is the only thing that salvaged this otherwise lackluster movie.

***

Rings on Her Fingers (1942)

Henry had been disappointed that Gene Tierney had not co-starred with him in *The Male Animal.* "I got Olivia de Havilland instead," he recalled, "and she was still in mourning over the loss of Jimmy (James Stewart)."

A top director, Rouben Mamoulian, rectified that to some degree when he cast

Henry with Tierney in *Rings on Her Finger* (1942), a film released by Fox. The director was fulfilling the last of a three-picture deal he'd made with Fox. *[He'd already released* The Mark of Zorro *and* Blood and Sand, *the latter a bullfight film starring Tyrone Power. Before that, Mamoulian had filmed such classics as* Dr. Jekyll and Mr. Hyde *(1931) and* Queen Christina *(1932) with Greta Garbo cast as the lesbian Swedish monarch.]*

On greeting Henry again for the first time in many years, Mamoulian recalled how he'd cast him in his Broadway debut in a play called *The Game of Love and Death.* Henry had had only a bit part as "Soldier-Citizen," in this production of the Theater Guild. Opening on Broadway in January of 1930, it had starred Alice Brady, Otto Kruger, and Claude Rains.

On the set, the director was almost apologetic in casting Henry "in this silly little flicker, *Rings on Her Finger,*" in which he'd play a poor man mistaken for a millionaire who is swindled out of his life savings.

Zanuck, Henry was told, had ordered his writers to "come up with something similar to *The Lady Eve.*"

Two of its supporting players included Laird Cregar and Spring Byington, cast as con artists "Warren" and "Mrs. Maybelle Worthington," respectively.

Henry and Tierney had had a brief fling when they'd co-starred together in *The Return of Frank James* (1940). On the third day of the shoot, Tierney signaled that he'd be most welcome if he'd opt to visit her dressing room whenever the director didn't need them on camera.

The two tricksters enlist Susan Millar (Tierney) in their scheme to bilk this "millionaire." She is a beauty sure to attract a rich beau. Actually, they find her working as sales assistant specializing in girdles in a large department store. She dreams of living rich and "on the other side."

Warren explains to Susan why he and the Byington character are swindlers: "We are merely bees that take a little nectar from the flowers that have so much. You, too, can have some."

Thinking that Henry is a millionaire, the crooks sell him a sailboat for $15,000, which represents his entire life savings. Actually, he is a $65-a-week accountant. Before the final reel, Susan falls in love with the intended victim.

At one point during filming, Henry shared his disappointment with the script with Tierney. "The huge amount they pay us at times doesn't seem worth it if we have to star in crap like this."

Gene Tierney plays an otherwise "nice girl" who's "enlisted" to swindle an unwitting **Henry Fonda** out of millions, which the plot eventualluy reveals, he doesn't own.

As part of the complicated melodrama, love predictably blossoms.

Step One: Meeting "the millionaire."

In this beach scene from *Rings on Her Fingers,* **Gene Tierney**'s character sets up the initial stages of Henry Fonda's seduction. and, it's assumed, swindle.

But a problem arises: She begins to fall in love, too.

"In spite of his disappointment, Henry gave it his all," Tierney said. "Of all the actors I worked with, Henry and Gary Cooper had the best sense of timing in and out of bed."

The yacht used in the film actually belonged to character actor John Carradine, with whom Henry had recently co-starred in two movies related to Jesse and Frank James.

In *Rings on Her Fingers,* character actors **Laird Cregar** (*left*) and **Spring Byington** (*right,* sometimes reviewed as "the sweetest matriarch in movies"), play con artists who maneuver the other characters (especially Henry Fonda) into embarrassing straits.

At one point, Mamoulian visited Henry in his dressing room, requesting him "to get buck naked."

"Are you a homo?" Henry asked.

"No, we're shooting a beach scene tomorrow, and I need to know what you look like stripped down."

When Henry pulled off his shirt, revealing a hairy chest, the director ordered him to go to makeup and have it shaved.

Cregar, too, was to have a scene in a bathing suit. The corpulent actor came onto the set, all 285 pounds of him. He made a swan dive. But, as an observer noted, "It looked like Dumbo's old Ma had learned to fly." The director ordered that the scene be shunted onto the cutting room floor.

Henry had recently worked with Spring Byington before, including in *The Story of Alexander Graham Bell* (1939). "She was a gracious, charming old lez," he told Tierney.

This was his first picture with Cregar. This son of Philadelphia had first appeared on stage at the age of eight. He'd been educated in England and had starred on the stage there.

In the early 1940s, he appeared in some film classics, including *Blood and Sand* with Power. One of his best *film noirs* was *I Wake Up Screaming,* a 1941 release with Victor Mature and Betty Grable.

In 1943, David Bacon, who had just been voted "the handsomest actor in Hollywood," was found murdered on a California beach. He was involved at the time in a "lavender marriage" to the fabled Viennese chanteuse, Greta Keller.

[Editor's Note: The Austrian stage diva, Greta Keller, whose roots as a cabaret entertainer went back to the early days of the Weimar Republic before she was evicted from Germany by the Nazis, lived in Magnolia House, the Staten Island home of the co-author of this book, Darwin Porter, for two years, reciting her memoirs and kibbutzing with friends who included Jolie Gabor and Leni Riefenstahl, before her death in 1977.]

At the time, Bacon was involved in romantic trysts with both Howard Hughes and Cregar. When Hughes told Bacon he was breaking up with him, having fallen for actor Jack Beutel, Bacon threatened to write an exposé of their affair. A few days later, he was murdered.

Cregar himself was also to die young, at the age of thirty-one. He was on amphetamines and a rigid diet, trying to lose weight.

Two views of **Greta Keller**, a well-known entertainer and *demi-mondaine* of the Weimar Republic. Near the end of her life, she became a friend and housemate of this biograaphy's co-author, **Darwin Porter.**

In exile from Berlin during the 1930s and 40s in Los Angeles, she was associated—at least peripherally—with Laird Cregar through his affair with her notorious husband, David Bacon, whom she believed had been murdered after threatening to expose the bisexuality of his lover, Howard Hughes

When *Rings on Her Fingers* was released, Theodore Strauss of *The New York Times* wrote, "To this overworked escapade, Henry Fonda brings his stupefied sort of charm, injecting some humor into his character of the fleeced accountant."

Jay Robert Nash, writing in *The Motion Picture Guide,* claimed, "A trivial picture that looks better than it actually is, because of Fonda's comic timing and Tierney's radiant presence."

The best review was in *The Philadelphia Enquirer:* "It's the funniest story since Eve double-crossed Adam out of a rib."

Henry's silly little froth could not have been released at a worse time. The United States had gone to war, and few people were interested in sitting through a picture watching Henry deal with these con artists.

When the bombing of Pearl Harbor occurred on December 7, 1941, the cast and crew of *Rings on her Finger* were location shooting on Catalina Island off the coast of southern California. Because of its exposed position, Catalina was deemed vulnerable to either a submarine or aerial attack.

As Tierney fled from the island on a boat with the crew, she recalled Henry holding onto her hand. "As we sailed east," she said, "it was twilight time. The sky had turned a brilliant blood red. That seemed to me like a sign of all our brave soldiers who were to die—or had already died."

The Magnificent Dope (1942)

According to Henry, "Director Walter Lang should be ashamed of himself, not only letting Zanuck con him into helming *The Magnificent Dope,* but for casting me in the lead of this New Englander hayseed. The movie was also called *The Magnificent Jerk, Lazy Galahad,* and *Strictly Dynamite.* I was the dope or the jerk, hardly Joe Dynamite. I played Thadeus Winship Page, a yokel from the small town of Upper White Eddy in Vermont. I run a small little business of renting boats to tourists, but I spend my winter sitting by the fire waiting for the spring in May."

A son of Memphis, Lang originally wanted to be a painter, joining a coterie of artists in the Montparnasse district of Paris. That did not work out, and by 1925, he was in Hollywood, directing his first movie, *The Red Kimino,* a silent.

He worked steadily throughout the 1930s and 1940s, reaching the pinnacle of his career in 1956, when he directed Yul Brynner (it brought him a Best Actor Oscar) in *The King and I.* Lang himself was nominated for an Oscar for his direction of this adaptation

Henry Fonda disliked his image in this poster, alleging that the only item that would captivate viewers was its view of the backside of his co-star, **Lynn Bari.**

Even its creative team disagreed frequently, arguing about whether a dope could be magnificent, and frequently changing its title.

of the Rodgers and Hammerstein musical.

"My only joy working with Lang was to be playing the lead with Don Ameche in the third slot," Henry said. "His career seemed to be fading as mine was on the rise because of all the hit movies I was making."

Henry was a bit premature in delegating Ameche to the Forest Lawn graveyard of actors. It was true that Ameche—once the golden boy of Fox—faced a diminishing career after the war, but in 1943, he earned $247,000, making him the second-highest grosser at that studio other than its bossman, Spyros Skouras.

As one Hollywood career rises **(Henry Fonda's)** another contender's **(Don Ameche,** *right)* declines.

In the center of this cast photo of *The Magnificent Dope* appears its center of gravity, the charming and very durable **Lynn Bari.**

The film's plot might have been taken from a Frank Capra movie, although that director would have done it better. Dwight Dawson (Ameche) runs a hype-driven self-improvement course, a rip-off of the more popular Dale Carnegie course. His partner is the "King of Gay Camp," Edward Everett Horton, in the fluttery role of Horace Hunter.

Elevated to leading lady status, Lynn Bari, a daughter of Virginia, was cast as Claire Harris, Dawson's secretary and *fiancée.*

To help his sagging business, she conceives a publicity stunt, seeking the biggest loser in the country. The winner in a radio contest is given $500 and free lessons at Dawson's School, where career advancement is taught.

Henry, as bumpkin Thadeus, wins the top prize and heads for Manhattan. On his first night on the town, he falls for Claire.

After all sorts of comedic complications, Henry wins the girl and converts the tense, fast-talking city slickers to his easy-going lifestyle.

On the first day on the set, Henry was introduced to his leading lady, Lynn Bari. She claims she had an uncredited role in his second film, *Way Down East* (1935), but he didn't recall ever seeing her. As an actress, Bari specialized in "man killer" roles, often losing her love interest to the leading lady. She worked at Fox in the 1930s and 40s until her career faded.

Bari appears in many biographies of Judy Garland, since she was married to Sidney Luft (1943-1950, before his marriage (1952-1965) to Judy Garland.

Henry later described what happened between Bari and himself to reporter George Salle: During the second week of the shoot, she came to his dressing room, ostensibly because she wanted to talk to him. "When we were alone, she shocked me by grabbing my crotch, a first for me. I didn't want to look like a homo, so I seduced her, and I visited her place two or three times before shooting ended. She sure knows how to please a dude. In her case, vast experience counts." *[Other actors, including John Payne and George Montgomery, also cited Bari as a crotch-grabber.]*

During World War II, Bari became the second-most-popular pinup girl for American GIs, topped only by Betty Grable, the era's most visible and best-known cheesecake queen.

Unlike Henry's assessment of his own picture, many movie-goers liked the film, wanting to escape the unrelentingly bad news from the battlefields of Europe and the Pacific.

Theodore Strauss in *The New York Times* wrote, "Fonda gives a joyous portrait of rural inertia." *Variety* claimed that "both Fonda and Ameche groove solidly in their respective roles."

***

Tales of Manhattan **(1942)**

Sam Spiegel, sometimes identified as "S.P. Eagle," had been born in the Polish-speaking region of the Austro-Hungarian Empire in 1901. At an early age, he turned to film production, working in Berlin. But because he was a Polish Jew, he had to flee in 1933 when the Nazis took over. As an independent producer, he turned out several films in Europe before arriving in Hollywood.

There, he would achieve his greatest success. Billy Wilder nicknamed him "The Velvet Octopus," because of his propensity for entwining women in the back seat of taxis and for managing Hollywood pictures with a deft, delicate, and sometimes manipulative touch.

Spiegel's great success came in the 1950s with *The African Queen* (1951), starring

Humphrey Bogart in his Oscar-winning portrayal opposite Katharine Hepburn. Best Picture Oscars also went to him for *The Bridge on the River Kwai* (1957) and *Lawrence of Arabia* (1962).

Tales of Manhattan was Spiegel's somewhat complicated "anthology film." Five sequences with different casts would be filmed, the plot following the "decline and fall" of an elegant tailcoat as a metaphor for the ironies of urban life. Cursed by its cutter, who was fired after crafting it, its story was concocted by a team of some of the film industry's best screenwriters: Ben Hecht, Ferenc Molnar, and Donald Ogden Stewart. It also included some of the era's major stars, including Henry Fonda.

Its famous French director, Julian Duvivier, had fled to Hollywood when his native country was overrun by the Nazis. Jean Renoir had defined him as "a great technician, a rigorist, and a poet." After *Tales of Manhattan,* he would helm *Flesh and Fantasy* (1943) with Edward G. Robinson, Charles Boyer, and Barbara Stanwyck.

With so many marquee names in its cast, the order of billing was touchy and contentious. Their names were arranged in this order: Charles Boyer, Rita Hayworth, Ginger Rogers, Henry Fonda, Charles Laughton, and Edward G. Robinson. In supporting roles was an array of almost-as-famous players who included Elsa Lanchester, Thomas Mitchell, Gail Patrick, George Sanders, and James Gleason. The film's final sequence, the one that focused on the "ruin and degradation" of the once-elegant tailcoat, starred African Americans Paul Robeson, Ethel Waters, and Eddie ("Rochester") Anderson.

The film opens when the obviously expensive tailcoat is new and meticulously tailored. The opening sequence starred Boyer, Hayworth, and Mitchell. Paul Orman (Boyer) is a renowned stage actor who seeks to rekindle his romance with his former flame, Ethel Holloway (Hayworth), now married to John Halloway (Mitchell). John offers to show Paul his weapons collection, which leads to Boyer's getting shot by the jealous husband. The story, however, has just begun.

In the film's second sequence, the players are Ginger Rogers as Diane, Henry Fonda as George, and Cesar Romero as Harry Wilson. Supporting roles were handled by Gail Patrick, Roland Young, and Marion Martin as "Squirrel."

The now used and second-hand coat has a bullet hole in it from the shooting in Sequence One. The fickle Romero is dating Diane, who fishes through the pockets of his dinner coat, finding a torrid love letter from another woman. Romero calls his "best man," (Fonda) and asks him to assert that the coat (and the letter inside) are his.

Things don't go as planned, as the Ginger Rogers character is attracted to the mild-mannered George (i.e., Henry) and eventually falls for him. Then Romero returns to his mistress ("Squirrel") played by Marion Martin.

Two other sequences add further adventures to the history of the increasingly threadbare tailcoat.

In the film's final sequence, the coat is stolen from a second-hand shop by a con artist who wears in during his robbery of the patrons of an illegal gambling parlor, stuffing $43,000 loot into its pockets. During his escape in an airplane, the jacket catches on fire and the panicked thief throws it out the plane's window with the money still in its pockets. After it lands, it's discovered by an impoverished black couple, Luke and Esther (Paul Robeson and Ethel Waters), who take it to the minister ("Rochester") of their church before donating the money to its congregation. The now torn and ragged tailcoat ends up adorning a scarecrow in a lonely field.

The sequence with the interaction between Fonda and Rogers generated the best reviews. *The New York Times* defined them as "very amusing in their romance-switching episode."

Tales of Manhattan was defined as "an anthology film" with five specific "chapters," each illustrating the decline and fall of a once-elegant waistcoat—a metaphor for "the human condition."

In this, the opening chapter, an "on top of the world" stage actor, **Charles Boyer** *(upper photo)* makes love to another (very jealous) man's wife **(Rita Hayworth)** before he's shot and killed in an act of reprisal.

Henry Fonda *(above, lower photo)* gets involved in the second of the five chapters, morphing his character into the love interest of **Ginger Rogers.**

Even hardcore fans of vintage *I Love Lucy* won't necessarily love **Lucille Ball** portraying the meanest piece of sidewalk trash since Bette Davis tackled the sadistic, self-involved bitch role of Mildred in *Of Human Bondage* (1934)..

The Big Street (1942)

In 1940, Damon Runyon published a short story entitled "Little Pinks" in *Collier's Weekly* magazine. RKO purchased its screen rights, engaged Leonard Spigelgass to craft a film script, and designated Runyon as its producer.

The studio knew that naming its film adaptation "Little Pinks" would not incite fans to line up at the box office, and two or three other titles were considered before *The Big Street* was chosen. *[Manhattan's Broadway used to be nicknamed "The Big Street."]*

At first, Runyon, the newspaperman and short story writer, had recommended Charles Laughton and Carole Lombard as the leads, but that ended, of course, with the tragic death of the actress in an airplane crash in Nevada.

Born in the small town of Manhattan, Kansas, Runyon wrote about America's entertainment industry (especially its theater industry) during Prohibition. New Yorkers depicted in his work spoke in *rat-a-tat-tat* slang and were a rough and tough gang of gamblers, crooks, hustlers, actors, and gangsters, men nicknamed "Harry the Horse" or "Dave the Dude." He peopled his stories with what one critic defined as "loud-mouth, arrogant twits." Runyon's greatest fame came with the adaptation of two of his short stories ("The Idyll of Miss Sarah Brown" and "Blood Pressure") into the Broadway musical *Guys and Dolls* (1950), which Marlon Brando and Frank Sinatra made into a film in 1955.

With Lombard dead, RKO wanted the lead role of a tough-talking gun moll in *Little Pinks* to be cast with either Barbara Stanwyck or Jean Arthur. But before those offers went out, columnist Walter Winchell introduced Runyon to Lucille Ball in the RKO commissary one day at lunch. On the spot, Runyon decided that she'd be just what he'd had in mind for the character of Gloria Lyons, nicknamed "Your Highness" in the film adaptation of his short story.

Henry Fonda had already signed on as the male lead, a character cursed with the absurd name of "Little Pinks." *[Lucille Ball's husband, Desi Arnaz, told her that he thought the name was "faggy."]* Fonda's character was a simple, naïve busboy who falls in love with Gloria, the gun moll of gangster Case Ables, portrayed by Barton MacLane. Case and Gloria have a fight, and he pushes her down the stairs, which cripples her for life.

She is befriended by Pinks, who has very little money. He maneuvers her wheelchair during their long transit to Florida, getting picked up as hitchhikers by passing motorists.

Gloria hopes to recuperate in the home of "Little Pinks'" friends, Violette Shumberg (Agnes Moorehead) and her stocky husband, "Nicely Nicely" Johnson, who is overweight and speaks with the voice of a croaking frog. Moorehead, having recently appeared in Orson Welles' *Citizen Kane* (1941), was on the fast track to becoming one of the most formidable character actresses in Hollywood.

Lucille had reservations about portraying a manipulative, conniving bitch on the screen. She met with one of her admirers, Charles Laughton, who still was mulling the possibility of co-starring with her one day if they found the right vehicle. "Here's what you do," he advised. "Play the bitch like the bitchiest bitch there is, and you can't go wrong. You might even win an Oscar."

As the vixen, Gloria (Ball) believes that "love means you'll live in a one-room apartment, develop two chins, and hang your clothes on a tenement washline." Unsure if she'll ever walk again, Gloria is a gold-digger who is just using Little Pinks.

She's got her radar trained on a millionaire boyfriend, Decatur Reed (William T. Orr).

Despite his matinee idol good looks and a physique that was exhibited and often photographed on a Florida

Newsman and novelist **Damon Runyon**, is shown here with his second wife, **Patrice Amate del Grande** (married 1932-46).

His name inspired the adjective ("Runyonesque') that describes any urban character noted for street humor and *bee-bop*, fast-talking, Depression-era hip

Weird Alliances on The Big Street

Although its script followed the premises of Damon Runyon's short story, none of **Henry Fonda's** fans believed that he was the infatuated and subservient boyfriend to a harridan as horrible as the one brought to the screen by a wheel-chair confined **Lucille Ball.**

To Runyon fans, he was just *"some guy doin' it, and going crazy for, some doll."*

beach in a bathing suit, Orr never became "another Robert Taylor." But in the long run, he did fine professionally, eventually put in charge of television for Warner Brothers.

Rounding out the cast of *The Big Street* was a string of other well-known character actors, including Ray Collins as "The Professor." Like Moorehead, he, too, had appeared in *Citizen Kane.*

The African American actress Louise Beavers was cast in the film as Ruby. Throughout the 1940s, she consistently vied with Hattie McDaniel for black maid roles.

Ozzie Nelson and His Orchestra provided the music. His great fame would come later when his family appeared in the 1950s in a hit TV series.

Directing this cast of varied personalities was the relatively untested Irving Reis, who was known mostly for his work in radio, for which he wrote plays. *[He later became a scriptwriter for Paramount Pictures.]* He would receive more renown in 1948 when he helmed Arthur Miller's play, *All My Sons.]*

Since he was not working at the time, Desi showed up every day at the set of *The Big Street* as a kind of self-anointed guardian of his wife. "I'm protecting my investment," he told the director. "Lucy used to go out on double dates with Fonda, Jimmy Stewart, and Ginger Rogers. I think a lot of stuff went on when she and Fonda co-starred together in *I Dream Too Much* (1935). I'm here to see that Fonda doesn't bang my Lucy just for old time's sake. He can't be trusted around co-stars. I know for a fact that when he made *Jezebel* (1938) with Bette Davis, he plugged her."

For her performance in *The Big Street*, Lucille got some of the best reviews of her career, and felt she did her finest work. *Life* magazine called her performance "superb—that girl can really act." Also, most reviewers agreed that in some scenes she had never looked more glamourous.

The *New York Herald Tribune* asserted: "Lucille Ball gives one of the best portrayals of her career as the ever-grasping, selfish Gloria, who takes delight in kicking the hapless Little Pinks around."

Time magazine wrote: "Pretty Lucille Ball, who was born for the parts Ginger Rogers sweats over, tackles the emotional role as if it were sirloin, and she doesn't care who is looking. Good shot: Miss Ball, crippled and propped up in bed, trying to do the conga from the hips up."

A.W. Walker, in *The New York Times,* wrote, "Fonda as 'Little Pinks' makes an acutely sympathetic hero opposite Ball's portrayal of the singer."

The noted critic, James Agee, claimed, "Carefully solemn Henry Fonda has the dignity of a wax grape among satiated little foxes."

Variety found that "Fonda as the mooning but intensely loyal Little Pinks is at his best."

Another critic, Michael Kerbel, disagreed: "Although Fonda is appealing, if excessively dour, in his early scenes, his character's self-abasement and utter blindness to Gloria's mean nature becomes too unbelievable for anyone to have portrayed convincingly."

In 2021, as a celebration of "The American Century" and an acknowledgment of the woman who changed the face of television, Blood Moon Productions crafted and published a double-volumed biography of **Lucille Ball.**

Each went on to win a "best in its category' award from the New York and the New England Book Festivals, respectively.

***

MARION WHO?

HENRY FONDA
& THE WORLD'S MOST BEAUTIFUL SHOWGIRL

"Marion Martin *[EDITOR'S NOTE: Not to be confused with Mary Martin, the Broadway star of* Peter Pan *and* South Pacific*]* was not only blonde and beautiful, at least in the late 1930s and early 1940s, but she epitomized the flashy, gold-digging blonde," Henry said. "She was sultry, sensuous, and sexy. What was a man, even a married one, to do when she presented me with her wares?"

Martin deserves a footnote in Henry's love and sex life.

Born in 1909 in Philadelphia, the daughter of an executive from Bethlehem Steel, Inc., she was four years younger than Henry. It was said that on Broadway, she got launched by being auditioned on the casting couch of showman Flo Ziegfeld, who gave her career as a showgirl a big boost.

Hollywood beckoned. She made her film debut in *Sinner in Paradise* (1938) starring Madge Evans and directed by James Whale. Later, she was cast as a dizzy blonde or showgirl in many leading B pictures. She also accepted an occasional role so small that she was uncredited.

She soon developed a reputation as "an easy lay." Clark Gable found that out when she appeared in a minor role in his film *Boomtown* (1940), in which he co-starred as a "get rich quick" oilman with Spencer Tracy, Claudette Colbert, and Hedy Lamarr.

That was followed with Martin's role in *His Girl Friday* (also 1940). "In that movie, I had a better chance seducing its lez star, Rosalind Russell, than I ever did Cary Grant," she said.

Marion was rumored to have had a lesbian fling with Barbara Stanwyck during their appearance together in *Lady of Burlesque* (1943).

[HOLLYWOOD TRIVA: What was Martin's most famous line in that film?

Stagehand to Martin, after knocking on her dressing room door:
"Are ya decent?"
Martin to other showgirls inside:
"Oh, I wish he wouldn't say that! It sounds so cheap!"]

Elliott Roosevelt, the son of FDR and Eleanor Roosevelt, had a brief affair with her during World War II, and she also seduced two sons of press baron William Randolph Hearst.

She was cast in three films with Lupe Velez, the "Mexican spitfire" in the 1930s. When Marion made *The Big Store* in 1941 with the Marx Brothers, it was rumored that she seduced all three of them, eventually awarding the best score to Harpo.

She didn't hook up with Henry until both of them were cast in the same sequence in his film *Tales of Manhattan* (1942). In that movie, she played "Squirrel," the mistress of Cesar Romero.

"Marion didn't get any action from Cesar, who was still mooning over Desi Arnaz, but Squirrel came knocking on my dressing room door, perhaps looking for some nuts," Henry claimed.

To his surprise, she was cast again in his film, *The Big Street,* in which Henry co-starred with Lucille Ball. In that pictur4e, as "Mimi Venus," she was married to a gangster while having an affair with a younger man, played by William Orr.

"Orr wasn't married at the time, so he was fair game," Henry said. "But I was married when she came once again knocking on my dressing room door. What was I to do? Turn her down? No way!"

Marion finally ended her career of off-screen seductions in 1950 when she married Jerry Krzykowski, a repairman for Singer sewing machines.

***

The Ox-Bow Incident (1943)

Henry had been disappointed with every movie he'd made since his landmark *The Grapes of Wrath* (1940). But that was about to change when he received a call from director William A. Wellman.

He had long admired the screen output of this director. He had come to Henry's at-

WOMEN WE LOVE: MARION MARTIN

The perennial "good time chorus girl," **Marion Martin**, one reviewer said, "always carried the aura of the kickline about her, no matter the distance traveled."

No one, it was said, played dance hall girls, gun molls, or floozie night club singers better than Marion, who fully realized her comic allure, successfully playing a blonde (again and again and again) who wasn't altogether dumb.

Henry Fonda, on the set of *The Big Street*, found her intoxicating. So did her fans—especially when she was given screen credit for whatever part she was in at the time.

She saw a lot and met a lot of people during the course of her eventful life (1909-1985), including many of the leading comedians and actors of her era.

Sometimes, as a blonde goddess with a fine body and good-looking legs, she evoked Lana Turner Other times, depending on her wardrobe, she reminded viewers of Dorothy Lamour, especially when she wore a sarong. Henry remembered **Marion Martin**, shown in the "girlie postcard" displayed above, as a realistic survivor of the Hollywood wars, self-deprecating and amusing till the very end.

tention when he'd gone to see that classic 1927 silent film, *Wings,* which had starred Clara Bow with Gary Cooper in a supporting role. The male leads were Richard Arlen and Charles ("Buddy") Rogers. *Wings* had become the first movie to win the Best Picture Academy Award.

Wellman was coming to visit, arriving with the promise of having a great script, ideal for Henry. What he didn't tell him was that he had first gone to Gary Cooper, who had rejected it.

Henry didn't know what to expect from Wellman. Some industry insiders referred to him as "Wild Bill." The story was that he'd had a reckless youth, getting kicked out of high school for dropping a stink bomb onto the principal's head. He'd also been arrested for car theft, even though his mother was a probation officer.

During World War I, he'd joined the French Foreign Legion, and his plane was later shot down by the Germans. He survived the crash but walked with a limp for the rest of his life.

After practically every other producer in Hollywood had rejected it, Wellman paid $500 for the screen rights to *The Ox-Box Incident.* It had originated as a novel by Walter Van Tilburg Clark, and had been converted into a screenplay by Lamar Trotti.

The afternoon that Wellman arrived on Henry's doorstep, the two men spent several hours going over the script. By midnight, it had won Henry's approval. "This is the kind of breakthrough role I've been looking for after *The Grapes of Wrath,* and Zanuck has had me mired in horseshit."

One problem remained—and it was a big one. How to get Zanuck to greenlight the script? After all, this Western was not a Roy Rogers/Gene Autry gig, where the hero is a good guy shooting it out with the outlaws. Zanuck had immediate objections to the movie's subject matter: A lynching in Nevada in 1885, two decades after the end of the Civil War. "American fighting men, as well as War II audiences—that is, the guys—want to see the tits and legs of Betty Grable and Rita Hayworth. If they want to see fighting, they prefer Errol Flynn or Duke Wayne blowing up jack-booted Nazis or bombing those yellow Japs with their buck teeth."

It took several days, but the actor and his director finally badgered Zanuck into financing the film. Zanuck demanded concessions from them before acquiescing: They'd have to appear in or direct future film projects that they'd otherwise have preferred to avoid.

In addition to maneuvering beautiful actresses into bed, Zanuck was obsessed with the war, and 1942 was one of its darkest years. The Japanese had overrun the Philippines, and "The Desert Fox" (Rommel) and his *Afrika Corps* had chased British forces westward from Egypt into Libya. The Soviet southern flank was on the verge of collapse from Nazi forces, and the horrific battles of the Coral Sea and Midway were on the horizon.

For *The Ox-Bow Incident,* Wellman assembled talented co-stars and an array of supporting players, each carefully chosen. Henry's co-stars would include Dana Andrews, Harry (sometimes billed as "Henry") Morgan, Frank Conroy, Anthony Quinn, and, in the female lead, Mary Beth Hughes.

Cast into the minor role of "Ma Gries," Jane Darwell was greeted by Henry with a bear hug. To him, she would always be his "Ma Joad" from *The Grapes of Wrath.*

The Ox-Bow Incident, in a nutshell, was about mob rule in the Old West and the lynching of three innocent men based on inadequate evidence in a spirit of hysterical over-reaction to a perceived crime. As the movie opens, Gil Carter (Henry) is riding into a small Nevada settlement with his scruffy sidekick, Art Croft (Morgan). They head for Darby's Saloon.

Henry's character was best described by Manny Farber in *The New Republic* as a reckless, raunchy, roughneck. Farber wrote: "Fonda is magnifi-

The Ox-Bow Incident cemented **Henry Fonda's** reputation as a tight-lipped man of the West—not unlike Gary Cooper—with a firmly entrenched set of morals.

Here, he ponders the implications of "Fake News," the kind that unleashed events that ultimately sent three innocent men to the gallows.

Standing behind him is **Paul Hurst.**

The publicity department at Fox recognized that the dismal, dark, and depressing *Ox-Bow Incident* was a hard sell to the movie-going public.

Therefore, they tried to make posters for it as provocative and violent as they could.

He wasn't witty, and he certainly wasn't funny, supportive or comforting.

Actors and actresses alike, in fact, asserted that **Darryl F. Zanuck,** kingpin at 20th-Century Fox, "had everyone in his studio by the balls," according to Henry Fonda "and seemed to enjoy squeezing them as hard as he could."

cent in his projection of the unremarkable, bored, sexually frustrated cowboy who has been on the range for too long. In the saloon, he studies a nude painting over the bar as he gets drunk fast. A violent streak in him comes out as he beats one of the cowpokes half to death out of meanness. Along with his sidekick (Morgan), he creates an insensitive, moronic cowboy, a masterpiece of restrained playing."

At first, the cowboys in the saloon suspect that Gil and Art might be cattle rustlers. Into the bar comes a cowboy reporting that a rancher, Kinkaid, has been murdered and his cattle stolen.

An angry mob begins to form, many of them drunk, and most of them in a "hang 'em high" mood.

An old storekeeper, Davies (Henry Hathaway), tries to cool down the crowd, but to no avail.

Opposing him is Major Tetley (Frank Conroy), who quickly positions himself as a leader of the lynch mob, replete with references to (and the uniform of) his alleged long-ago "glory days" as an officer in the Confederate Army.

William Eythe portrayed his sensitive and rather delicate son, who urges him to call off any lynching, and who, by all indications, secretly loathes him.

At first, Gil and Art are reluctant to join the lynch mob, but since they don't want to be mistaken for cattle rustlers, they go along.

En route through the desert, the hastily assembled posse comes across a stage-coach moving by night at high speeds along rutted roads. At first, the security guards traveling with the coach assumes that the men are bandits, and he starts shooting, wounding Art.

A passenger inside the coach is Rose Mapen (Mary Beth Hughes), the former girlfriend of Gil. She is now married to a Mr. Swanson (George Meeker). His honor is at stake, and complications arise.

As the night progresses, the lynch mob comes across three men sleeping beside their campfire in Ox-Bow Canyon.

The posse grills them, especially their spokesman, Donald Martin (Dana Andrews) and "an Old Man," played by Francis Ford.

The third member of the trio is a sophisticated, probably well-educated Mexican, Juan Martinez (Anthony Quinn). He is recognized as a notorious high-stakes gambler, Francisco Morez. With him, he happens to have Kincaid's gun.

Nearby is a herd of cattle, but no bill of sale. Martin insists that he paid cash for them and that no bill of sale was ever generated.

Gil and Art, among others, want to haul the men back into town for a trial, but the other members of the posse are in the mood for a lynching. The trio is condemned to die at dawn. Martin (Dana Andrews) is granted permission to write a letter to his wife and children before being hanged.

At sunrise, after they're lynched, the mob heads back to town. On the way there, they encounter the sheriff (Willard Robertson), who tells them that the cattle were not rustled and that Kinkaid is still alive.

The lynch mob must come to terms with their murder of three innocent men. In the bar, Gil, with great emotion, reads the letter that Martin wrote to his wife.

In the film's final scene, Gil and Art ride off to give Martin's wife the letter and $500 they have raised in cash.

Amazingly, *The Ox-Bow Incident* was shot in only one month, using a desert location near Chatsworth, California, and sets constructed on the Fox lot. Because wartime rationing of building supplies was being rigorously enforced at the time of filming, the crew had to tear down an older set and recycle its materials. What emerged as a backdrop for *The Ox-Bow Incident* was the largest ever constructed on the Fox lot. It would be used again, later, for the filming of Gregory Peck's *The Gunfighter* (1950).

Henry was impressed with the acting talent of his co-stars, especially Dana Andrews. A son of Mississippi, he became a celebrated actor in the

In this "early in the screenplay" incident from *The Ox-Bow Incident*, **Henry Fonda**, with his sidekick, **Harry (aka "Henry") Morgan** makes it clear that he is NOT a cowboy driven by moral or self-righteous concerns.

In fact, it's made clear that after a few months rustling cattle on the range, he's a two-fisted drunk who enjoys a rocking brawl at any saloon lowbrow enough to have him.

Falsely accused, and eventually hanged, **Dana Andrews**, *center*, plays an unwitting ("wrong time, wrong place") victim whose dignity emerges, in understated ways, before the end of the film.

The prairie cowboy played by **Henry Fonda** *(left)* ingests the random vengeance of the mob with a haunted and horrified kind of stoicism.

1940s, starring in such classic *noirs* as *Laura* (1944) with Gene Tierney. His greatest role was as a returning war veteran in *The Best Years of Our Lives* (1945), with Fredric March, Myrna Loy, and Teresa Wright.

Andrews was the brother of Steve Forrest, an actor who changed his birth name so as not to be confused with his brother.

Other directors praised Andrews' performance, including Lewis Milestone, Otto Preminger, John Ford, and Fritz Lang.

Andrews later claimed, "I seduced most of my leading ladies, notably Joan Crawford, Gene Tierney, Susan Hayward, and Merle Oberon. Greer Garson and Maureen O'Hara told me, 'No way!'"

Harry Morgan claimed that his moviemaking gig with Fonda influenced, for the better, one of his greatest performances. He appeared, during the course of his career, in a hundred films spanning six decades of moviemaking, co-starring with Joan Crawford, John Garfield, Walter Matthau, Peter Lorre, and other major stars. He also became a TV star in sitcoms, including eleven seasons (1972-83) of M*A*S*H.

Fifth-billed in the film was the Mexican actor, Anthony Quinn, the most flamboyant of the trio of lynched victims. He would go on to greater glory, becoming a super star in such pictures as *Lawrence of Arabia* (1962) with Peter O'-Toole; *The Shoes of the Fisherman* (1968); and his Oscar-nominated titular role in *Zorba the Greek* (1964). He won a Best Supporting Actor Oscar for his performance in *Viva Zapata* (1952) starring Marlon Brando. In 1956, he would win another Best Supporting Actor Oscar for his performance in *Lust For Life,* playing Paul Gauguin, the friend of Vincent Van Gogh, as portrayed by Kirk Douglas.

Quinn became well known for his portrayal of earthy, passionate characters marked by, in the words of one critic, "brutal and elemental vitality."

He also became notorious as one of Hollywood's most "hot-blooded" seducers, sustaining affairs with everyone from George Cukor to Rita Hayworth, from Claire Bloom to Evelyn Keyes, who "reviewed" him as: "There was simply too much of Tony Quinn—yes, down there, too." Others he was intimate with included Maureen O'Hara, Carole Lombard, Inger Stevens ("he is the perfect embodiment of the virile man all women sub-consciously seek"), Mae West, and Shelley Winters.

At the age of 78, Quinn fathered his last child with a woman reported to be his "secretary."

His first wife was Katherine De Mille, daughter of director Cecil B. De Mille.

"Wherever I went, there was always a lovely local lady to lie beside me in bed," he told Henry.

Mary Beth Hughes later confessed, "Wellman cast me as the female lead of *The Ox-Bow Incident* only because the Western needed a beautiful girl."

Almost completely forgotten today, except for her appearance in *The Ox-Bow Incident,* Hughes became known for her roles in B pictures. In 1940, she appeared in *The Great Profile,* a swan song for a drunken John Barrymore who was near his death.

She became scandalous around Hollywood for having affairs with Mickey Rooney, Franchot Tone, Lew Ayres, and Robert Stack. When she met Henry, she was involved in a fling with James Stewart. He begged Henry "to take this gal off my back. I've moved on."

Henry didn't necessarily want an affair with her, only a night or two with her on location. It was later revealed that she was also having flings with George Montgomery and Milton Berle.

But by the time *The Ox-Bow Incident* was being shown, Hughes had settled down and married Ted North, the first of her three husbands.

After the movie was in the can, Zanuck held it up for several months, not knowing how to popularize it. When it was at last released, he claimed, "As I told Fonda and Wellman, the movie would be a flop in spite of its significance and dramatic value. Our records showed that it failed to pay its way. In fact, its pulling power was less than half of a Laurel and Hardy comedy we made at the same time."

The Ox-Bow Incident has stood the test of time and remains not only a classic, but one of Henry's favorite films. It was nominated for a Best Picture Oscar but lost to Humphrey Bogart's *Casablanca.* Henry had hoped that he might be nominated for a Best Actor Academy Award, but he was not. Paul Lukas carried off the Best Actor Oscar that year for *Watch on the Rhine,* a movie co-starring Bette Davis.

The Ox-Bow Incident has been called "one of the most important Westerns in the history of American cinema."

In a cast filled with actors portraying taciturn men of the Great Plains, Mexico-born **Anthony Quinn** portrayed a flamboyant exotic, revealing under questioning his sophistication and well-educated, perhaps Castilian, flair.

None of it mattered: The vigilantes hanged him anyway, unfairly, randomly, vengefully, and without a trial.

Reviews were mostly positive, although *Harrison's Reports* found it "depressing, unpleasant, at times, horrible melodrama. Whoever was responsible for selecting such sordid material should be awarded the Booby Prize."

Variety weighed in too: "It is a powerful preachment against mob lynching. Director Wellman has skillfully guided the characters and driven home the point that hanging is unwarranted. Fonda measures up to the challenge."

The Motion Picture Guide found that "Fonda is prosaic and compassionate as the observer in this powerful anti-lynch film."

Phil Hardy, writing in *The Western* claimed, "The members of the posse are delineated with a sharpness that still impresses, including Fonda and Morgan as ineffectual doubters cast in the role of observers."

Bosley Crowther of *The New York Times* wrote, "In a little over an hour, the film exhibits most of the baser short-coming of men—cruelty, blood-lust, ruffianism, pusillanimity, and sordid pride. It puts Henry Fonda in a very dubious light. He is cryptic and bitter as one of the stauncher hold-outs for justice. *The Ox-Box Incident* is not a picture which will brighten or cheer your day. But it is one which, for sheer, stark drama, is hard to beat."

In spite of *The Western's* prestige, Zanuck forever after called it a flop. "Our records show that it lost us dough. Maybe if Gary Cooper had taken the role, it would have made some money, But no, that long-legged bastard insisted on doing that film written by his buddy, Ernest Hemingway, a closeted fag acting macho in my opinion. At least, Coop got to screw Ingrid Bergman during the shooting of *For Whom the Bell Tolls.*"

***

QUIRKY HOLLYWOOD LORE
"Who In Hell Is Paul Hurst?"
Asks Henry Fonda

On the set of *The Ox-Box Incident,* director William A. Wellman told Henry that Paul Hurst was arriving later that day. "I've cast him in the role of Monty Smith, the drunken and sadistic vigilante"

"I've never heard of him," Henry said.

"Didn't you see *Gone With the Wind?*" Wellman asked.

"Three times. I'm still pissed that I didn't get to play Ashley Wilkes."

"Hurst played the villain in one of the most famous scenes in the history of movies," Wellman said. "He was that Yankee deserter who invades Tara and gets his head blown off by Scarlett O'Hara."

"So that's the guy," Henry said.

Every movie fan around the world remembered that scene, but very few fans could identify Paul Hurst, even though he appeared in more than 250 movies during the 1920s, '30s, and '40s.

Half-Cherokee, half-Seneca, he was reared on a ranch in Traver, California, where he was born in 1888.

By 1911, Hurst was working as an actor, writer, and even a director. He mostly appeared in low budget Westerns, most of them produced on "Poverty Row."

[Poverty Row was the slang term for a number of mostly short-lived filmmaking studios centered around today's Gower Street in Hollywood. Most of the films that emerged from them were Westerns, some of them shot inexpensively in less than a week.

Despite their low budgets, some of the films crafted on Poverty Row were noteworthy and in some cases, profitable. One had been Billy the Kid, *starring Buster Crabbe. The comic series* The Bowery Boys *was shot at Monogram. Mickey McGuire (later known as Mickey Rooney) had worked there in the late 1920s, and within a decade—after moving to MGM— he had become the top box office star in the world.*

Among the under-funded studios of Poverty Row, some of the biggest box office was generated by Republic Pictures under the baton of Herbert J. Yates. Many of the most profitable starred Roy Rogers, Gene Autry, and a young John Wayne. At a nearby competitor, Grand National, James Cagney got his start in gangster movies.

From yet another Poverty Row studio, the Producer's Releasing Corporation, Edgar G. Ulmer turned out the film noir *classic,* Detour, *in 1945. Six years earlier, in 1939, that same studio had released the "hiss and boo" anti-Nazi low-budget thriller,* Hitler, Beast of Berlin.*]*

Hurst, stocky and squinty, with a raspy voice, found steady work, usually from studios on Poverty Row. Even if moviegoers didn't recognize his name, his face became familiar, usually because of his success at portraying villains, cops, and sidekicks.

In the 1940s, Hurst often appeared as the cowboy sidekick to Monte Hall in a number of Westerns usually shown as part of a lineup of Saturday matinees.

Hurst's last film appearance was in *Giant* (1956), for which he taught James Dean to use a lariat.

In addition to *Gone With the Wind*, and *The Ox-Bow Incident*, Hurst also cropped up in such classics as *Mr. Deeds Goes to Town* (1935) with Gary Cooper; *In Old Chicago* (1938) with Alice Faye and Tyrone Power; and *Alexander's Ragtime Band* (also 1938), again with Alice Faye and Tyrone Power).

Before all those classics, Hurst had starred as Captain Donahue in the 1932 *Island of Lost Souls*. It was the first sound film adaptation of H.G. Wells' 1896 novel *The Island of Dr. Moreau*. Kathleen Burke, as "The Panther Woman" lures men with the intention of destroying their bodies and souls. A horror movie, it starred Charles Laughton, Richard Arlen, and Bela Lugosi. *[Burt Lancaster and Marlon Brando would each star in future adaptations.]*

John Wayne remembered Hurst from their days together on Poverty Row, and cast him in *Angel and the Badman*, a 1947 Western starring Gail Russell, with whom the Duke had an affair. Hurst was cast as a crotchety old rancher who refuses water to a thirsty Quaker family until Wayne's character convinces him to share.

Vivien Leigh as Scarlett O'Hara made history many times during the exhausting filming of *Gone With the Wind* (1939).

Among many others, she showed how a self-respecting Southern woman can blow the head off any maurading Yankee before he plunders Tara and perhaps rapes her.

The upper photo shows **Vivien** on the staircase at Tara, concealing a weapon before shooting the lecherous Yankee renegade, played by **Paul Hurst** *(right photo)* directly in the face.

In 1952, Wayne once again hired Hurst to appear with him in *Big Jim McLain*, a political thriller about investigators from HUAC (House Un-American Activities Committee) hunting down "commies" in postwar Hawaii. When he hired him, the Duke knew that Hurst was dying from terminal cancer.

An old friend, John Ford, cast Hurst in his final picture, *The Sun Shines Bright*, in 1953. It was based on those puckish, often romanticized tales about small town life in Kentucky, the "Judge Priest" stories, published in *The Saturday Evening Post*.

It depicts "The Judge" defusing a mob from lynching a young black man. Right after the movie was wrapped, Hurst, suffering from acute pain, committed suicide at the age of 64.

***

HENRY PREPARES FOR WAR

In the wake of the Japanese attack on Pearl Harbor on December 7, 1941, residents all along the U.S.'s West Coast—Washington, Oregon, and California—feared bombing raids from Japan or else an enemy submarine surfacing and firing into a port city. For a while, at least, almost the entire West Coast, including the lights of Hollywood, went dark every night.

Studios began frantically converting to wartime propaganda films. Scripts about the raging worldwide battle and the heroism under fire of U.S. troops were in heavy demand.

Clark Gable was joining the military, as were Henry's friends—James Stewart, Tyrone Power, and Robert Taylor.

Because of Henry's age (37 at the time, married, and with dependents), he was not subject to the draft.

One weekend, he had a prolonged talk with Frances—not with Jane or Peter—during which he insisted that he wanted to join the U.S. Navy. The prospect brought her to tears. Her main fear, of course, was that he'd be killed in action.

Eventually, they spoke of his hopes of returning, when and if the war ever ended, to Hollywood and what that might be like. His pre-war popularity in films might have faded.

"There's a strong possibility that many pre-war players will return when the fighting is over and find that the sun has set on their careers," she warned. "For example, I don't know if Gable, the so-called 'King of Hollywood,' will ever regain his popularity of the 1930s."

"That's a risk I'll have to take," he responded. "I don't want to become one of those celebs touring the country selling War Bonds. Or like the Duke, winning the war on film but not in the military. I don't want to be asked, 'Why don't you sign up?'"

By Monday morning, Henry's mind was set. As soon as the last scene on *The Ox-Box Incident* was finished, he was going to join the U.S. Navy—"That is, if they'll have me. Let's face it. I'm no spring chicken."

He was a man of his word. The day after the film was wrapped, he drove to the center of Los Angeles, a section he rarely visited, and walked into U.S. Naval Headquarters.

En route to the office where he was to be interviewed, he was stopped several times by young men signing up for duty or else by personnel, each asking for his autograph.

That afternoon, along with twenty-four other men, each younger than himself, he pledged allegiance to the U.S. Constitution.

After signing up, he was given twenty-four hours to go home and say goodbye to his wife and kids and to settle any last-minute business affairs. He did the former but not the latter. Still under contract to Darryl F. Zanuck, he did not inform his boss that he had joined the Navy.

That night, he packed only essentials, leaving all but a handful of civilian clothes behind in favor of the sailor's uniform he would be given.

He was driven to the induction center at the vital port of San Diego, a zone that would play a large part of the war effort because of its strategic location.

Less than two hours after checking in, two officers of the Shore Patrol come to him and more or less placed him under arrest without explaining why.

He was driven back home in a military car, where three men representing Fox waited to explain to him what was happening.

In his powerful position, Zanuck had intervened with Naval authorities in Washington, claiming he needed Henry to star in a war propaganda film, which he predicted would greatly increase enlistment across the country. The Fox boss prevailed, and Henry's entry into the Navy would be delayed until one final movie was shot.

Frances and the children, especially Jane, were thrilled that he was home again. One newspaper reported a comment from his daughter, although there is doubt that she actually said it: "Only one day in the Navy, and my dad caused the Japs to surrender."

That night, Henry read a new, hot-off-the-press script entitled *The Immortal Sergeant*, later telling Frances, "It's a lot of hokum. Guess what? According to the plot, I win the war single handedly. How improbable is that?"

The following morning, he again kissed Frances, Pan, Jane, and Peter goodbye and headed for California's Imperial Valley to shoot desert scenes.

When James Stewart was told that Henry had joined the Navy, he told friends, "Hank is willing to face death, perhaps in the South Pacific, rather than a slow death by domesticity."

Years later, a reporter claimed a quote from Jane: "My father was a patriot opposed to the Fascists. I could be wrong, but I think he also wanted to escape life as a family man, at least for a period."

***

The Immortal Sergeant (1943)

During the filming of Fox's *The Immortal Sergeant*, its cast and crew suffered the summer heat of California's Imperial Valley at 110°F in the shade. Actually, the desert setting was supposed to be the Libyan Desert during the early years of World War II.

In the film, Henry received lead billing for his performance as a poker-faced corporal, Colin Spence, an unassertive Canadian volunteer.

Burly Sergeant Kelly (Thomas Mitchell) was his superior officer. Henry had worked with Mitchell before, always referring to him as "Scarlett O'Hara's father."

The war transforms the previously timid corporal (Fonda) into a man of courage and daring. In one heroic maneuver, he and his handful of men attack a German base during a sandstorm, emerging victorious, although Colin (Fonda) is wounded.

Recovering in an Egyptian hospital, he writes a letter to his girlfriend Valentine (Maureen O'Hara) in England. Scenes from their love affair, including a beach scene, are relayed in flashback. Within three months, they marry.

In smaller but vital roles are Allyn Joslyn, Reginald Gardiner, and Melville Cooper, veteran character actors of countless pre-war movies.

180

In *The Immortal Sergeant*, Henry worked with director John M. Stahl for the first and last time. Born in Baku, Azerbaijan, in 1886, to Russian Jewish parents, the young boy later settled in New York. By 1931, he was in Hollywood directing his first film.

As a producer and director, he is more than a footnote in Hollywood. He signed with Louis B. Mayer in 1919 and was later one of the men who founded Metro-Goldwyn-Mayer.

He also became one of the founding members of the Academy of Motion Picture Arts and Sciences. Two of the most celebrated movies he directed include *Imitation of Life* (1934) with Claudette Colbert, and, in the following year, *Magnificent Obsession* with Irene Dunne and Robert Taylor. After finishing his assignment with Henry, Stahl cast Gene Tierney in *Leave Her to Heaven* (1945), which earned her a Best Actress Oscar nomination.

Lamar Trotti wrote the film's screenplay based on the novel by John Brophy. *[Trotti had also written the script for* The Ox-Bow Incident.*]*

The best aspect of the film was the work of cinematographer Arthur Miller. *[He bore no relation to the famous playwright who married Marilyn Monroe.]* During the course of Miller's career, he would be nominated for an Oscar in his field six times, carrying home the gold three times for *How Green Was My Valley* (1943); *The Song of Bernadette* (1944); and *The King of Siam* (1947). "Among my most dubious achievements, I also did the cinematography for all those Shirley Temple movies."

A daughter of Dublin, the Irish beauty, Maureen O'Hara, was Henry's love interest in the movie. She was brought to world attention when she co-starred with Charles Laughton in *The Hunchback of Notre Dame* (1939). In time, she became "The Queen of Technicolor," partly because of her famous mane of auburn hair, her high cheekbones, and bright eyes.

She often worked with John Ford, co-starring with her friend, John Wayne. Her most memorable movie with Duke was *The Quiet Man* (1952). Shown every year at Christmas is the classic *Miracle on 34th Street* (1947) in which she starred with John Payne and Edmund Gwenn playing Santa Claus. Natalie Wood, then a child ingénue, was in it too.

Upon its release, *The Immortal Sergeant,* despite its mixed reviews, drew $2.2 million at the box office. Jay Robert Nash in *The Motion Picture Guide*, wrote, "This was not one of Henry Fonda's favorite films, but he is nevertheless effective as a timid citizen-soldier."

David Lardner of *The New Yorker* found the desert scenes the most solid aspect of the picture. "However," he wrote, "I found I was distracted by the strange difficulty of O'Hara pronouncing polysyllabic words."

In *Harrison's Reports* appeared this comment, "Although it does not reach great dramatic heights, and it's somewhat drawn out, the performances are so good that one's interest is held consistently."

In *The New York Times*, Theodore Strauss wrote: "I found the film disappointing, but Fonda gives a creditable performance of a timid man learning to make decisions under stress. It was occasionally a warm and human study of man's triumphs over his own fears, but the romance was vapid. O'Hara's role of Valentine was very dull."

In the history of wartime movies, *The Immortal Sergeant* is hardly memorable, but it does merit a footnote: It was the first Hollywood picture to depict the British Army's military campaigns in North Africa during World War II.

***

Only a day after completing *The Immortal Sergeant,* Henry said goodbye to Frances and his children and left Hollywood to join the U.S. Navy in its

In retrospect, it's easy to interpret **Henry Fonda's** final pre-War film as a macabre rehearsal for the rigors to come.

To Henry and the other volunteers who joined him after *The Immortal Sergeant* was wrapped, it was hard —at least at first—to grasp the ironies.

WARTIME HEARTBREAK & BATTLEFIELD YEARNING

Even though it was conceived and filmed before America's involvment in armed conflict, **The Immortal Sergeant** weirdly conveyed the anguish of romance with a soldier who might not come back.

Here's **Henry Fonda** and **Maureen O'Hara** emoting ferociously in ways inspired by thousands of equivalent wartime couples to come.

battles against the forces of the Empire of Japan.

In the months leading up to Henry joining it, he was known for having a number of flings with beautiful women. "What I'm not getting at home, I find outside the home!" he confided to James Stewart and others. By now, his faltering marriage to Frances was on life support.

On July 4, 1943, a scandal arose. As reported in the *San Pedro News Pilot,* Barbara Thompson, 25, called a "blue-eyed brunette," filed a paternity suit against Henry. She was demanding that he pay her $2,000 a month in child support, plus $17,000 for expenses, including her lawyer's fees.

It was at first printed that the child's name was Henrietta, and that her name had been inspired by Henry's. But, as it turned out, her name was Sharon. She was one of Thompson's four biological children.

In her court brief, Thompson charged that during the location shoot of *The Immortal Sergeant,* she met Henry in a bar. After a few drinks, she was said to have gone back with him to his hotel room, where he seduced her "without protection." She also stated that she remained his bed partner until he returned, at the end of filming, to Los Angeles.

Since Henry was serving in the Navy and could not be reached by reporters, the newsmen sought information from the public relations division of the Navy. Their answer was blunt: "No comment."

Frances, however, opted to respond to reporters, denying the charge. "He never knew this girl. Her suit is ridiculous."

At Fox, the PR director said, "Miss Thompson approached us months before filing suit. She demanded $50,000, but was turned down."

During one of his shore leaves and back in Los Angeles, Henry did encounter some reporters.

His answer was brief: "Let me be clear: The charges are false."

Thompson's private life was investigated. At an earlier trial for vagrancy and disorderly conduct, she had failed to appear in court. She had married a second man, although she was legally wed to another at the time. She faced charges of bigamy.

She tried to get an October, 1943 court date, but Henry was protected under a wartime "sailor's relief act" that stipulated that "no case could be brought against a military man until two months after the end of his tour of duty."

On December 3, 1946, an item appeared that Thompson's case against Henry had been dropped.

He said, "I rue the day I decided to become an actor. I would have been better if I'd been a farmer. Case closed."

Thompson's charge was buried but hints of it rose again in 2005 when Jane published her autobiography. In it, she claimed that her father, years into his marriage, began to have affairs. "Frances was ignorant of them until the paternity case arose."

Confronted with a lawsuit, Frances, it was reported by Jane, paid off the woman, and the suit went dormant.

The Immortal Sergeant

A MATURE & DOMESTICATED FATHER OF THREE JOINS THE NAVY

HENRY FONDA AT WAR WITH "THE JAPS"

"I don't want to be a fake in a studio simulating war. I also don't want to be a civilian on the home-front. I want to see action in the Pacific. Clean up those islands from the Japs. I'm tired of being a spectator. I'm enlisting because I want to be a sailor—not a movie star."
—Henry Fonda to a reporter after enlisting in the Navy

BUT WHO'S REALLY FIGHTING THE WAR?

WHEREAS HOLLYWOOD'S DUKE & ITS SWASHBUCKLING ROBIN HOOD REMAIN IN CALIFORNIA TO FIGHT WORLD WAR II ON CELLULOID, "FOLKSY" TOM JOAD (AKA HENRY FONDA), OAKIE OF THE PRAIRIES, TACKLES IT UP CLOSE AND PERSONALLY

HOW HENRY FONDA, A LOW-RANKING ENLISTED "QUARTERMASTER, THIRD GRADE," GOT DRENCHED IN THE BLOOD BATHS OF THE SOUTH PACIFIC

TOKYO ROSE

JAPAN'S "MISTRESS OF PROPAGANDA" PREDICTS, IN BROADCASTS AIMED AT U.S. SERVICEMEN, THAT HENRY FONDA WILL DIE IN A WATERY GRAVE

THE ENOLA GAY & ITS NUCLEAR PAYLOAD

AFTER A TEETH-GRINDING TOP SECRET TRANSIT TO THE SOUTH PACIFIC ISLAND OF TINIAN, HENRY PERSONALLY DELIVERS UPDATES TO THE CREW JUST BEFORE THEY DROP "LITTLE BOY" ON HIROSHIMA

HENRY'S UNDERWHELMING HOMECOMING

"CALIFORNIA, HERE I COME! I'M HENRY FONDA! HE'S BACK! WILL ANYONE CARE?"

AS A SEASONED & CYNICAL WAR VETERAN, FONDA STRUGGLES TO FIND HIS PLACE IN THE SUN

THE FILMMAKING CULTURE OF POSTWAR HOLLYWOOD HAS RADICALLY CHANGED. SO HAS AMERICA. SO HAS HENRY

JOHN FORD TO THE RESCUE!

HOLLYWOOD'S MOST INFLUENTIAL DIRECTOR, A FELLOW NAVY VETERAN, DEFINES HENRY AS "THE QUINTESSENTIAL AMERICAN MALE" AND POSITIONS HIM, AGAIN AND AGAIN AND AGAIN, AGAINST BIG SKIES AND BARREN LANDSCAPES

AFTER SOME SEXUAL EXPERIMENTS AND SOME
"ENTERTAINMENT OF TROOPS" AT THE HOLLYWOOD CANTEEN,
FRANCES SEYMOUR BROKAW FONDA
ENTERS THE TWILIGHT ZONE

MY DARLING CLEMENTINE
RED, WHITE, BLUE, AND BASHFUL,
HENRY SHINES AS WYATT EARP
IN A WESTERN THAT PRESIDENT HARRY TRUMAN
DEFINES AS HIS PERSONAL FAVORITE

DOLORES DEL RIO
THE PORCELAIN-SKINNED MEXICAN BEAUTY TELLS HENRY:
"I ALWAYS SEDUCE MY LEADING MEN."

THE FUGITIVE
HENRY PLAYS A ROGUE PRIEST IN A VENUE WHERE RELIGION IS OUTLAWED.
JUDGED AS "EXCESSIVELY ARTSY," IT BOMBS AT THE BOX OFFICE.

"**At boot camp in San Diego,** I was treated like a regular gob," Henry recalled. "I stood in a line of nude sailors-to-be and got my balls juggled by a young medic. I was examined like the next guy in line, no special treatment, no big movie star from Hollywood."

Getting up at four in the morning was no big deal for him. Movie stars are accustomed to rising early to be at their studios for wardrobe and makeup before any actual shooting begins.

"Unlike my usual light breakfast, I began to eat like a farmer," Henry said. "I was pushing forty and facing a three-mile run. That was rigorous, consuming all my energy, leaving me totally exhausted as I hit my bunk at night when lights out was called."

"For dinner, I joined a line of hungry boys and served slop from steaming gigantic hot pots," he said. "For my taste, none of the cooks would ever make it as a chef, not even as a short-order cook."

After the bombardment of Pearl Harbor, America went through a time of fear, uncertainty, and neurosis. Henry confronted it head on, by joining the Navy and heading out to sea.

184

Over his bunk at night was a large poster that read "LOOSE LIPS SINK SHIPS. "Sleeping next to me was this likable cute kid named Barry Riley of Bakersfield. The Navy didn't treat me like a movie star, but this kid did. A film addict, he'd seen all my movies, some more than once. His favorite was *Jezebel*, that film I made with Bette Davis. I didn't want to take advantage of Barry, but he made life in the barracks easy for me. He even shined my shoes. He saw that I always had clean shorts, and he used his meager pay to buy me thoughtful little gifts, like he brought me a better brand of toothpaste. What to call his affection for me? Puppy love? His first serious crush?"

After two months of training, Henry could don his white Navy cap as in "Ordinary Seaman Third Class," the lowest of the low rankings. At boot camp, it seemed that petty officers tried to make my life miserable just to show me that my being a movie star didn't mean a damn thing in this man's Navy." For the most part, higher-rated officers treated me with respect."

"Although one's request could be shot down by a superior officer, a sailor at least could be asked exactly what position he was seeking. I told my superior officer I wanted to be a gunner's mate. That way, I could get to kill Japs."

After his request was submitted, he was summoned to the Chief Petty Officer for an interview. "Years from the date of that interview—in 1954, to be exact—I would see Ernest Borgnine on the screen in *From Here to Eternity* (1953). The burly actor looked like my petty officer and talked just as rough."

"In this war, you're not shooting some god damn movie," the officer said.   "As a gunner's mate, you'd probably be killed on your second day on duty. I've heard that a lot of movie stars have a turkey brain, but your test scores show you have enough sense maybe to become an officer. I've checked with my superior, and they told me you might have the intelligence to make it as an officer."

"I know I don't have a hell of a lot to say about what happens to me, but what I want to do is see some action, kill some Japs as a revenge for what they did to our boys at Pearl Harbor."

"Okay," the officer responded. "If you want to be a fucking wise-ass, I'll get you assigned to four months in the Quartermasters' School."

"The coming weeks were hell for me," Henry said. "The hardest training of my life. What did I know about trigonometry? I excelled in English and in history. In arithmetic, I managed to learn that two plus two equals four. I've never studied so hard in my life. I learned to do a 'wigwag'—that's Morse Code using flags to send signals. My final rank was not impressive. I emerged as a quartermaster, third grade. That would be like getting 20th billing in a roster of characters on a movie set."

Actually, he graduated among the top ten in his class of 200 men, each much younger than himself.

He was briefly assigned to the destroyer USS *Saterlee*, "Where he had to double up as both a navigator and a signalman, I sorta pulled off the navigator position, but sucked as a signalman. One of my jobs was to look out into the night sea to see if I spotted any Jap submarines that might blow us all to hell."

The *Saterlee* was part of a convoy escorting a British aircraft carrier, HMS *Victorious*, to the Panama Canal.

On the second day of the Saterlee's association with the much larger *Victorious*, stormy seas arose and the smaller ship was tossed about. Henry's partner that night was a handsome, blonde-haired young man who knew nothing about the ocean, having grown up in the wheatfields of Western Kansas.

"He vomited and vomited until there was nothing left in his gut to throw up. I felt sorry for him. Sailing through the Panama Canal was smooth, but once we emerged into the Atlantic Ocean, it was stormy seas again. For my mate, it was puke time again."

"I was not a happy sailor when the *Satterlee* glided into the ship-filled port of Norfolk, Virginia," Henry said. "Fear ruled the night. Norfolk blacked out at sundown, fearing an air strike from the Luftwaffe, or a submarine shelling of the port."

In Norfolk, sailors from the *Satterlee* were given shore leave. "I went out with this same kid. He had recovered but he got so drunk with me that he vomited right in the bar. That boy sure knew how to throw up."

"I didn't throw up, but I had the drunk of my life. When I headed back with him to the *Satterlee*, my head was spinning like a merry-go-round."

"I zigzagged into the naval training station in Norfolk, where a petty officer took mercy on me and filled me with black coffee. He finally put me on the most overcrowded train in history, heading for New York."

In Manhattan, Henry checked into the local YMCA in Chelsea, a few blocks north of Greenwich Village. "The damn place was a bordello after dark. It

CAMERADERIE AND (GO NAVY!) ESPRIT DE CORPS

Photo above shows crew members from the **USS Saterlee** a few years after Henry Fonda joined its ranks and was eventually transferred to other vessels.

Rarely, before or since, was the American population as carefully focused on a shared agenda: Winning the War!

seemed that half the young men were getting blow-jobs."

Sobered up, he reported to duty the following morning at 90 Church Street in Lower Manhattan.

There, he was discharged as an enlisted man, and then sworn in again, along with seven other men, this time as a Lieutenant Junior Grade in the U.S. Navy. A report from his commanding officers claimed that "Henry Fonda has demonstrated officer-like qualities of leadership, military bearing, loyalty, judgment, and intelligence."

[Ironically, that description fitted the quasi-fictional character of Mister Roberts, *a title role that he would play beginning in 1948 on Broadway. In 1955, that "Six-year stage smash" was adapted into a movie, again featuring Henry. And in the years to come, he would also star in such World War II-themed movies as* Battle of the Bulge *(1965),* Midway *(1976), and* The Longest Day *(1962).]*

He was immediately given new uniforms in Navy blues and whites. In December of 1943, he joined a lot of other military men *en route* by train to Washington, D.C., to get briefed on their new assignments.

Meeting with a superior officer—an empathetic and solicitous fan of his movies— it was suggested that he might want to be assigned to the development of training and "propaganda" movies for the Navy. But he was opposed to that offer, claiming he'd prefer active duty in the Pacific theater instead.

It was finally decided that Henry might be best suited for an assignment in combat intelligence.

That meant, once again, another stint in boot camp, this time at the Officer Candidate School in Quonset, Rhode Island.

In this newest boot camp, he was no longer surrounded with young boys from the wheat fields of Kansas and the cotton fields of Mississippi.

Henry Jaynes Fonda, in uniform, as displayed on the U.S. Navy's Memorial website, with the following awards and citations:

BRONZE STAR MEDAL
NAVY PRESIDENTIAL UNIT CITATION
AMERICAN CAMPAIGN MEDAL
ASIATIC-PACIFIC CAMPAIGN MEDAL
WORLD WAR II VICTORY MEDAL
NATIONAL DEFENSE SERVICE MEDAL

This time, his fellow classmates were intelligent and mature; many had been lawyers, even mayors, of small towns, and in some cases, judges. Each of them seemed to have enough drive, experience, and "applied intelligence" to make it as a commander.

With his own brightness, ambition, and motivation, Henry moved to the head of his class, sincere in his desire to help save American democracy. He detested Nazis and the Imperial Officers of Japan.

After weeks of intense training, Henry was assigned to Air Combat Intelligence, known as ACI. He was given a one-week leave before being shipped out.

Shortly before boarding an overcrowded cross-country train to Los Angeles, he shopped at the Post Exchange, buying hard-to-find nylons for Frances and Hershey bars and other gifts for his children. He also bought cartons of cigarettes and fourteen bottles of the most expensive bourbon. His petty officer had told him he might use it to bribe some of his superior officers into granting him a favor or two.

That was a mistake: After his luggage was recklessly thrown around, all the bottles were broken. His quarters began to smell like a distillery, and since liquor was not allowed aboard naval vessels, he was chastised severely.

After his return to Brentwood, his family treated him like a wartime hero. Frances wanted sex twice a day, and the children devoured the chocolate bars and liked the other gifts.

Afternoons were spent around the swimming pool, and the best food he'd had in months was served.

He caught up on all the children's activities, and also learned that Frances had volunteered to work at the Hollywood Canteen, which in part had been founded by Bette Davis and John Garfield.

Once again, he told his kids goodbye, leaving them in care of a nanny. Frances had volunteered to drive him to the Mark Hopkins Hotel in San Francisco for a "honeymoon night" before his morning departure. There were tearful goodbyes. When they were over, he found himself on yet another overcrowded train, this one heading north to Seattle, where he'd report for duty once again.

A rumor was spread around the Hollywood Canteen that Frances did not return to Los Angeles alone. *En route* south, she picked up three soldiers

Dark shadows, despite the streaming sunlight.

Frances Seymour Brokaw Fonda with her young husband, **Henry Fonda.**

186

from the U.S. Army, each of them on leave. A night was spent in a motel with her military trio.

Meanwhile, from the Port of Seattle, Henry was shipped, along with many fellow sailors, to Hawaii, which had rapidly recovered from the Japanese attack of December 7, 1941 and which was now busier than before the Declaration of War.

In Hawaii, on the island of Oahu, Henry was assigned to what was known at the time as the Naval Air Station at Kaneohe Bay. There, he underwent an intensive two-week course in anti-submarine warfare.

When it was over, his superior officer told him he'd "passed the course with flying colors." He was then assigned to the staff of Vice Admiral John S. Hoover. Hoover—and thousands of other enlisted men and officers in the U.S. Navy—were now under the brilliant guidance of Fleet Admiral Chester W. Nimitz, whom President Roosevelt had designated as U.S. Commander in the Pacific.

[It was with many touches of irony that Henry would star in the 1976 film, Midway, *in which he would portray Admiral Nimitz.]*

Vice-Admiral Hoover, born in Ohio in 1887 and nicknamed "Johnny," had distinguished himself as a naval officer during World War I. In the new war, he'd been assigned awesome responsibilities. He had risen quickly, evolving into one of the best and most trusted of Nimitz's underlings.

In the early stages of the war, he had been charged with protecting Puerto Rico, the Virgin Islands, and other islands of the Caribbean and The Bahamas.

Some of the greatest roles in the history of the U.S. military lay in his future, most notably during his battles against the naval might of the Empire of Japan. Eventually, Hoover emerged as a brilliant strategist during the U.S. takeover of Tarawa, Kwajalein, and Eniewetok *[aka Enewetok Atoll; aka Brown Island]* in the Gilbert and Marshall Islands. He was also effective in leading future campaigns in Saipan, Guam, and in the Mariana and Palu Islands. He plotted land-based attacks deep within Japanese-controlled territories, bombing and strafing the enemy's formidable defenses—fortifications on which they had labored feverishly for months.

Admiral Chester W. Nimitz, in Guam on April 1, 1945 during an interview broadcast worldwide.

In it, he revealed the U.S. invasion of Okinawa, 325 miles from Tokyo.

The commander of U.S. forces in the Pacific Theater, Nimitz has been cited as one of the greatest naval commanders of all time.

According to Henry Fonda, "It was a great honor to me to potray this 'admirable admiral' in *Midway* for a release in 1976. What a challenge! I had to look like I knew how to defeat Japan."

His forces would also join the Battle of Iwo Jima during January and February of 1945. John Wayne brought dramatization of the conflict to American audiences in one of the best movies to emerge from World War II, *The Sands of Iwo Jima* (1949).

Henry would later "dine out" on telling his fellow servicemen about his first meeting with Hoover, who said to him, "Some of my men tell me you used to be a movie star. Is that true? Or is it just gossip?"

"Yes, sir. I've made movies," Henry said modestly.

"I'm not a movie fan myself, but I did see John Gilbert in *The Big Parade* (1925). I also saw Gary Cooper years later in *Sergeant York* (1941). Have you heard of that one?"

"Only vaguely, sir," Henry answered, trying to conceal his amusement.

[It's ironic that a naval officer with almost no interest in the entertainment industry would have family links to show business. But in time, Hoover evolved into the great-uncle of Jim Morrison of The Doors.]

Before the end of the war, Henry told anyone who was vaguely interested that statues should be erected in every state capital to his supreme commanding officer, Chester W. Nimitz. A Texan born in 1885, he became a historical legend as Fleet Admiral of the U.S. Navy, playing a major role in overseeing the incredible battles of the Pacific theater.

That awe-inspiring title had been assigned to him only ten days after Japan's attack on Pearl Harbor. He took over at the most critical moment of the war, when the U.S., almost overnight, had to fast-rebuild its Pacific fleet. Despite pressing shortages of industrial parts and raw materials, Nimitz set out to halt the Japanese advance. Fortunately for him, brilliant men under his command had already cracked the Japanese code. Nimitz faced overpowering forces in the Battle of the Coral Sea and the Battle of Midway.

"After Midway," Nimitz said, "Japan has nowhere to go but down in defeat."

The Battle of Midway as seen from the decks of the *U.S.S. Yorktown*, just before it was fatally hit by a Japanese missile and abandoned.

In time, Nimitz moved his headquarters from Pearl Harbor to the recaptured island of Guam. His "Operation Starvation" cut off badly needed war materials to Japan.

On September 2, 1945, Nimitz was aboard the USS *Missouri* in Tokyo Bay to participate in the Japanese surrender. October 5, 1945, was officially designated as "Nimitz Day" in Washington, D.C.

***

Henry's military file at the National Archives in St. Louis, Missouri laboriously but flatteringly states: "He preferred to be enrolled in the naval service as an enlisted man, depending on his performance of duty to establish his qualifications for appointment to a commissioned rank, rather than endeavoring to secure immediately his commission, which would have been very much to his advantage financially and from the point of view of rank and prestige."

His pre-enlistment salary at Fox was $150,000 annually *[i.e., $2.3 million in today's currency]*. After enlisting in the Navy, his salary fell to $1,600 a year *[i.e., about $25,000 in 2022 currency]* In February of 1944, Henry's official designation was written as "Lt. (j.g.)."

The time had come for him to sail to the Eastern Islands of the Pacific, where fierce battles were raging. As an officer-courier, he carried a dispatch with him, containing military secrets. His plane landed on the recently captured Kwajalein Atoll, one of the southernmost of the Marshall Islands.

"I was awed by what I saw in the lagoon," Henry said, "a whole armada—battleships, carriers, destroyers, cruisers, each seemingly prepared for a massive invasion of the homeland of Japan. This force would be part of our revenge on the Japanese for that sneak attack on Pearl Harbor."

Henry's first assignment involved taking a highly secret dispatch satchel from Admiral Hoover to Admiral Nimitz, whose headquarters were aboard the USS *Essex*. In a small boat, two Navy men transferred him to the Fleet Admiral's vessel. Once he delivered the satchel to the Admiral's executive secretary, Henry returned to the *Curtiss*.

When he got there, he was told he'd been assigned to new quarters: A five-by-eight-foot cabin he'd share with Lt. Commander John Dinkelspiel, a former lawyer from San Francisco.

"I wouldn't exactly compare it to anything glamourous like island-hopping in the Caribbean, but the *Curtiss* was on the move," Henry said. "Next stop was Eniwetok Atoll that the Americans had captured. "We steamed in and made anchor—the Navy calls it 'winging on the hook.' It was terrible to see how battered everything was, but the Seebees had gone to work. They leveled the ground and built an airstrip and Quonset huts before you could say, 'Where's the warm beer?'"

"Let's face it," Henry said. "The *Curtiss* was a rusty bucket that had not fully recovered from the wounds it suffered at Pearl Harbor. But it was still seaworthy, and was able to indulge in the Pacific sea battles of 1943, 1944, and 1945. Names unfamiliar to Americans—Saipan, Iwo Jima, Guam—became household words back in the States."

Henry then faced a terrifying enemy bombardment of the *Curtiss*. "I was scared shitless," he recalled. "I was down below, where I put on my helmet and rushed to battle stations. I also had on a life preserver in case the ship was blown up. It was hell for about an hour, but we managed to fight off these bastards. We wouldn't be so lucky in our future."

In early 1944, Kwajalein in the Marshall Islands became a base for the *Curtiss*. "Our men were right in the heart—dead center—of the Pacific theater. Our vessel was a seaplane tender. We were not a battleship, but a repair and supply vessel for destroyers engaged in the epic battles going on at the time, mostly in the Marianas and the Solomons."

"Frankly, I hated my job as an ACI officer. Life was hell on the stormy seas, the constant nausea, living like packed sardines with other men, the daily sound of bombardment, of men dying, of seeing guys burned alive. I often lay drenched in sweat in unbearable heat in my smelly bunk, wondering how long this will last. Could I endure until the bloody end?"

Launched in April of 1940, the USS *Curtiss* was the first purpose-built seaplane tender constructed by the U.S. Navy. It had been named in honor of Glenn Curtiss, a naval aviation pioneer. For the most part, it was stationed at Pearl Harbor, where it operated as a local guard vessel, making frequent trips to the mid-Pacific refueling station of Wake Island, 2,300 miles away, and carrying crews and cargo to reinforce the military garrison there. Nearly 2,000 men and officers could be carried aboard the *Curtiss* at a time.

In Honolulu on that Sunday morning of December 7, 1941, the *Curtiss* had returned fire from the attacking Japanese aircraft.

Her crew had begun firing when they sighted the periscope of a Japanese Midget submarine. Right after 9AM, the vessel was hit by weapons from a Japanese plane, which then crashed into her. That was followed by an attack from a dive bomber, which damaged the crane of the *Curtiss* and exploded below deck.

The end result was that nineteen men from the Curtiss died in the attack that Sunday, and many crew members were wounded. It was able to motor its way to San Diego for repairs, and she was back in Pearl Harbor, repaired and reconfigured, in January of 1942.

***

One by one, Pacific islands fell into American hands after fierce battles. Henry remembered visiting Saipan, although he later said, "I think I got the order of my island-hopping mixed up."

Today a Commonwealth of the United States, Saipan was and is the largest of the northern Marianas. It survived both Spanish and German colonial eras before it was captured during World War I, in 1914, by the Empire of Japan.

It was one of the most strategic islands of the Pacific, a last line of defense before a possible invasion from the Japanese homeland.

The Battle of Saipan (June 14 to July 4, 1944) was one of the most brutal campaigns of World War II, costing Americans 3,426 lives, with 10,364 wounded. Of the Japanese defenders, a total of 30,000, only 921 were taken alive.

[In the wake of its capture, Henry visited Saipan's "suicide cliff," (aka Laderan Banadero) where, in July of 1944, an estimated thousand Japanese civilians and soldiers committed suicide by jumping to their deaths to avoid capture by the United States. Nipponese propaganda had emphasized, for months, a bloodthirsty, mutilation and rape-based treatment of Japanese by "American Devils"].

While on Saipan, Henry heard his name mentioned in an English-language propaganda broadcast from the notorious Tokyo Rose, who noted that he was anchored in harbor on Saipan aboard a vessel that had been seriously damaged during Japan's December, 1941, attack on Pearl Harbor.

"Japanese forces will soon send Mr. Henry Fonda, former motion picture star, and his motley crew aboard the tired old *Curtiss* to the bottom of the ocean. All of them face a watery grave."

***

In a desperate move to save the homeland from an invasion, the military forces of Japan devised a new technique of warfare so horrible and ghoulish that it shocked the world. A special style of aerial bombardment, the Kamikaze or "divine wind," was conceived by diabolical minds.

Young idealistic, and fervently nationalistic Japanese pilots were recruited for suicide attacks on U.S. naval vessels, with the understanding that their mission would result in a "sacrifice with honor" of their own lives.

The final act of the Pacific campaign of World War II had entered its second, more vicious, stage, with future horrors to come.

Kamikaze pilots could destroy Allied shipping better than any "conventional" air attack. Before this terror ended, 3,800 young pilots from Japan gave their lives, Many U.S. ships were damaged, and some 7,000 naval personnel were killed as a result.

Kamikaze aircraft were essentially pilot-guided explosive missiles, purpose-built or converted from conventional aircraft.

Pilots would attempt to crash into enemy ships in aircraft loaded with bombs, torpedoes, or other explosives. About 19% of Kamikaze attacks on U.S. naval vessels directly hit (and severely damaged or sank) their targets,

Japanese illustration, circa 1942, of the damage a **Kamikaze** pilot could inflict on a U.S. ship.

This style of aerial assault began late in the course of the conflict, in October of 1944, in fact, as Japan sacrificed its best pilots in a hopeless war. Even so, they lost command of the air, as their aircraft also became outdated.

One of the most devastating attacks was on the USS *Bunker Hill* on May 11, 1944. It resulted in 389 sailors killed or missing, and 264 wounded.

The *Curtiss* survived two separate Kamikaze attacks. The first came early in 1944 as the Americans were fire-bombing Tokyo, and after Iwo Jima had fallen to American forces. The Japanese pilot of an already-damaged-by-gunfire plane wanted to crash it onto the deck of the *Curtiss*. He went down into the water about twenty-five yards from his goal.

Henry and a volunteer sailor put on dive suits and went out into the open water. In the open sea, at a depth of about thirty feet below the surface, they spotted the pilot and his bombardier, each dangling from their cockpits by their safety belts.

"It was a sight I will never forget," Henry said. "The bastards wanted to kill all of us, and they went to a watery grave instead. Years from now, a diver might discover two skeletons in a decaying cockpit."

The second Kamikaze attack came on July 21, 1944 as the *Curtiss* was cruising in the waters off the Ryukyu Islands in the vicinity of Okinawa. A Japanese pilot appeared only 800 yards from the *Curtiss*, and flying right into it. Gunfire from the *Curtiss* came too late, and a half-ton bomb was dropped. The explosion ripped through Henry's ship, destroying compartments everywhere, even Henry's sleeping cubicle.

Henry was not harmed. *[He and his bunkmate were on shore leave in Guam at the time.]* Thirty-five sailors and others were, however, wounded in the attack.

Badly damaged once again, the *Curtiss* was able to power itself back to the naval shipyards in San Diego. There, it was made seaworthy again, cruising on the high seas until 1952. In 1972, it was sold for what the Navy defined as "scrap."

***

It was on Guam that Henry heard of V-E Day, during which Nazi armies had surrendered to Soviet forces recently arrived in Berlin from the East and to Allied forces from the West. News leaked out that Hitler had committed suicide in his bunker with his mistress, Eva Braun, whom he had married in his final hour. Josef Goebbels and his wife, Magda, had also committed suicide after she poisoned all her children.

The devastating news about the collapse of the Third Reich was received in Tokyo. Many of the Allied forces on sea and on land in Europe had, almost immediately, been re-directed to the Pacific theater.

Months before that, Henry and his fellow sailors on Guam had become deeply involved in the Battle of Tinian (July 24-August 1, 1944). Tinian, part of the Marianas, was the site of a vital, 8,000-man garrison that Japan had previously installed as a "front line defense" of the Japanese motherland.

The battle that raged there quickly evolved into one of the bloodiest of World War II. After many casualties, U.S. forces overwhelmed the heavily fortified Japanese garrison.

Retaining firm control of Tinian was interpreted by the Japanese as vital to the Imperial Army's defense of its homeland. The U.S. arrived there with three battleships, sixteen destroyers, and five cruisers.

In early stages of the battle, the USS *Colorado* was struck twenty-two times. Forty-three men were killed and 198 were wounded.

Sir Winston Churchill in London waving to the crowds from Whitehall on May 8, 1945, celebrating the end of the war in Europe,

During the battle's final hours, 4,000 Japanese soldiers committed suicide when it appeared that they had lost.

[At the small Japanese garrison on Aguijan Island, near Tinian's southwestern tip, a military force stationed there held on until the end of the war. Its last Japanese soldier, Murata Susumu, lived there in a cave until he was captured in 1953.]

Once the American Army took over the Tinian, the mainland of Japan came under dire threat, since it was within striking distance of the B-29 Superfortress bombers of the United States. "For the first time, my buddies and I were seeing victory, but a lot of horrible crap was yet to descend on us. Even more horror was to descend on Japan, a kind of terror that no country had ever known before. Believe it or not, I played a minor role in that. I'll tell you about it."

After the U.S. takeover of Tinian, it became the base for more Allied operations in the Pacific, and a site where camps were established for 50,000 U.S. troops. Seabees turned the island into the busiest airfield of the war. B-29 Superfortress bombers were flown in for the final assault on the failing Empire of Japan. Planes took off from here for firebombings of Tokyo. "The war was over, but the bastards refused to surrender," Henry said.

Fonda served under the Commander of Air Operations in the area, and both Henry and that commander were still under the control of Admiral Hoover.

U.S. Marines wading ashore at Tinian in 1945.

Some of these brave Americans were given an awesome task. They not only had to create a mass grave for soldiers killed by fighting on both sides, but also for the 4,000 Japanese soldiers who committed suicide before the Allied landing.

190

On Guam, his superior officer called Henry into his office for a secret confab, the results of which suddenly brought the island of Tinian looming into his own life.

It was decided that as part of a secret mission, he was to fly with a crew—with strict orders not to divulge any aspect of the project to anyone—to Tinian. Even Henry himself was not told why they were flying there.

He later said, "I could not help speculating. At one time, I thought it (Tinian) might become the setting for the Jap surrender."

Time and time again, Henry was warned not to tell anyone of this flight from Guam to Tinian. He and his commander carried a dispatch to the captain and crew of an aircraft with the (rather odd) name, *Enola Gay*. Little did he know that it would one day be hailed as one of the most famous airplanes in world history. [*Its name derived from Enola Gay Tibbets, the mother of Colonel Paul Tibbets, the pilot of the craft.*] After handing over the dispatch, and before hastily departing, Henry shook the hand of the pilot—soon to become one of the most famous in the history of World War II. Months later, when secrecy no longer mattered, Henry divulged that his dispatches conveyed to Tibbets and his crew the weather conditions then prevailing over Southern Japan, site of Hiroshima.

Back on Guam, Henry, along with the rest of the world, learned that on August 5, 1945, the *Enola Gay* had dropped the world's first atomic bomb, destroying the city of Hiroshima.

"Little Boy" was the most destructive weapon in history. It took only 53 seconds to fall from the aircraft at an altitude of 31,600 feet. An estimated 70,000 to 80,000 residents died in the blast, with another 70,000 injured, some with health repercussions that lasted the rest of their lives. Of those killed, 20,000 were Korean slave laborers.

After dropping its lethal "payload," the *Enola Gay* returned safely to its base on Tinian, 1,500 miles south of Tokyo.

***

Henry and "my buddies" got drunk celebrating the end of the war. "I knew that perhaps, in a matter of days, I'd be heading back to Brentwood and my farm to see Frances and the kids. I wanted to see how much Lady Jane and boy Peter had grown in my absence. The Japs would be idiots to continue the war now. "

But to Henry's dismay, the war continued.

He was still on Guam when more news shocked the world. This time, a nuclear bomb nicknamed "Fat Man," from a B-29 Bockscar, was dropped on Nagasaki, a bustling port city on the southern island of Kyushu.

Less than a second after its detonation, the entire northern tier of that city was destroyed, with 35,000 people killed, many of them instantly.

"Now we knew that surrender was a matter of days," Henry said. "My buddies, who got drunk with me, called me a lucky son of a bitch when I told them I was heading home."

As he recalled, "I was drunk the next day."

As part of the almost interminable transit back to the US mainland, he found himself *en route* to Christmas Island, an Australian territory in the Indian Ocean, 220 miles southwest of Java and Sumatra. [*Following their attack on Pearl Harbor, Japan had invaded it for its phosphate deposits After the war, the United Kingdom transferred sovereignty to Australia.*]

The next stop for Henry during his homeward Odyssey was Johnston Atoll, 860 miles southwest of Hawaii. [*Since December 29, 1934, it had been under the control of the US Navy, which established an air station there. The island later came under the command of the US Air Force. The Japanese failed to take the atoll in the wake of the December bombing of Pearl Harbor.*] "I was trying to sober up, so at Johnston, I drank only water, hoping to clear my head."

At last, his plane flew into Honolulu. His first reaction was "My God, they've rebuilt the place! From there,

Gamechanger at Hiroshima, August 5, 1945.

"The Japs should have surrendered that night, but the stubborn bastards held on to get another city bombed," Henry said. "Harry S Truman was under great pressure to arrange for that next bomb to be dropped directly on Tokyo."

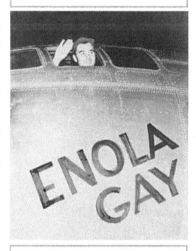

In the immediate aftermath of World War II, **Enola Gay,** a Boeing B-29 "Superfortress Bomber," became the most famous piece of military equipment in the world.

It was named after Enola Gay Tibbets, the mother of its pilot, **Colonel Paul Tibbets**, who waves from its cockpit before embarking, on August 6,1945 for the atomic bombardment of Hiroshima. The resulting explosion flattened into rubble an estimated three-quarters of the city.

As such, perhaps to the horror of the woman it was named for, Enola Gay, became the first aircraft to be used for the launch of an atomic bomb.

aboard a commercial Pan Am flight, he landed at San Francisco.

"California, here I am!" he shouted as he got off the plane.

***

En route aboard the flight from Honolulu to San Francisco, Henry had sat up front with an admiral, who immediately recognized him as the actor, Henry Fonda. "I used to be a movie star before the war," Henry told him. "Who knows if they'll want me now, an old man of 40."

"Sure, they will," the admiral assured him. "You'll be a bigger star after the war than ever."

The admiral learned that Henry had been summoned for a debriefing in Washington before he was discharged from the Navy. "I can pull some strings and delay your visit," he promised. "In San Francisco, I've got this little eight-seater and a pilot who plans to fly me to Los Angeles. You can go with me and pay a surprise visit to your family."

"I'm game for that," Henry said.

His homecoming at Brentwood didn't go as well as anticipated. Without any advance notice, he arrived unexpectedly on his doorstep. He tried the door. Finding it unlocked, he stood for a moment in the entrance vestibule, listening for any sound, and eventually hearing some noise coming from the kitchen. "Frances!" he called out in a loud voice. "Jane! Peter!" He left out his adopted daughter, Pan, because he'd learned in a letter that she was away at camp.

His wife emerged from the kitchen—as he noted—not with a look of joy, but one of surprise. Finally, adjusting to the reality before her, she ran to him and into his arms. As he held her and kissed her, he had the worrisome feeling that she was not all that thrilled at his homecoming.

Jane was upstairs studying. Hearing noises from the hallway, she ran downstairs and into his arms. When he had a chance to look at her, he noted many changes. She was growing up before his eyes, amply demonstrating that she'd evolved into a beautiful young woman. Whereas Frances did not have tears in her eyes, Jane did.

"Where's my boy?" Henry asked.

"At school," Frances answered. "He'll be getting out in about twenty minutes."

"Give me the keys to the station wagon," Henry said. "I'm going to be there waiting for him as he comes out."

Within ten minutes, when the Brentwood Town and Country School let out, Henry immediately spotted Peter in the distance as he stood before his car. The boy seemed to recognize the station wagon, but who was that man standing in front of it?

Suddenly, he realized who it was. "Chad!" he yelled. "It's Chad!"

"I picked up my boy and raised him above my head. "It's not Chad, son. I'm your father. Home from the war."

That night, Frances explained why Peter had called him Chad. During the war, she had taken him to see *Chad Hanna*, the first movie he ever saw of his father. Peter had become hysterical when he recognized his father, trapped in a lion's cage. He'd started screaming and had to be ushered out of the theater by an attendant, with Frances trailing.

On Henry's first night back home, he made love to his wife. As he later confided to James Stewart, Burgess Meredith, and other male friends, "I was just going through the motions. I managed to climax. But in my heart, I came to realize I no longer loved her."

After a brief stay, Henry told his family goodbye and flew to Washington for his final duties. He was surprised when the Office of Public Information assigned him to host four radio shows devoted to *The Navy Hour*. In this weekly broadcast, he was to perform in some skits and in some dramatizations of the battles of World War II.

With time off, he shopped for a new civilian wardrobe on the streets of Washington, where he was often stopped and asked for an autograph. He felt good that fans still remembered him. His first purchase was a gray charcoal suit, with an assortment of shirts, shoes, and underwear. He bought eight ties as well.

As soon as he could, he was going to hunt down an Air Force pilot named James Stewart, whom he had heard had returned temporarily to his hometown of Indiana in Pennsylvania.

Stewart's triumph as a pilot flying over Nazi Germany had been widely heralded in the press. "The messenger boy of the Pacific would soon be meeting a true American war hero," Henry said.

During his Navy-mandated sojourn in Washington, Henry was awarded the Bronze Star and a Presidential citation for service abroad. Years later, he was asked what happened to that Bronze Star.

"I'm not sure," Henry said. "One day Peter put it on and went off to play war games with his pals. He lost it."

On September 11, 1945, he performed his final duties for the U.S. Navy and left the Office of Public Information to fly home to Los Angeles.

He went on inactive duty until he resigned in 1953, citing "overage in rank."

Back in California, he had that long-delayed reunion with Stewart. "We literally fell into each other's arms," Henry said. "Neither one of us was much into man-kissing, but we kissed and hugged like two long-lost lovers. After all, he was my projected lifelong companion. We had a thrill feeling two live bodies come together, unlike the thousands upon thousands of corpses slain on battlefields. We were going to face our futures as two guys who weren't kids anymore."

Back home once again in Brentwood, Henry began a new chapter in his life, one of tragedy and film-related triumph.

***

Before the Japanese attack on Pearl Harbor, James Stewart had accumulated 400 hours of flying time. He had joined the Army in March of 1941, becoming the first American movie star to wear a uniform in World War II.

Enlisting as a private, he was promoted to second lieutenant in January of 1942.

In the European theater of war, he flew dangerous missions over Germany. In 1944, he was promoted to the rank of an Air Force Major. As the command pilot of the new B-24 airplanes, he led bombing raids over Nazi targets.

For his heroic efforts, he received the Distinguished Flying Cross and the *Croix de Guerre*. He was later named Chief of Staff of the 2nd Combat Bombardment Wing of the British Air Force. By war's end, he'd been promoted to a colonel in the U.S. Air Force, one of the very few Americans who went from private to colonel in just four years.

In the post-war years, Stewart continued to play a role in the Air Force Reserve. He was elevated to the rank of Brigadier General in the summer of 1959.

***

During his first weeks back at home in Brentwood, Henry returned to plowing his fields. He had developed a self-admitted "fetish" for growing strawberries.

He later confessed that although he'd been looking forward to being "a family man again," he wasn't living the life he'd dreamed about on Pacific Islands such as Guam. In fact, he was having a hard time adjusting to civilian life after the wartime hostilities of the Pacific.

Author David Downing described the Fonda household during the immediate post-war years:

"Frances' social position ensured that care of Jane and Peter would be entrusted to nurses and governesses. There was something almost austere about the Fonda household—Henry the distant, awe-inspiring patriarch and Frances the preoccupied hostess and domestic manageress. As with children of the upper Victorian and middle class, the lives of Jane and Peter were sheltered. Money, celebrity, and social status cocooned the growing children against the joys and pains of the workaday world and buffered their mother and father against the demands of parenthood."

Home from the War: **Henry Fonda** with his precocious daughter, **Jane,** in 1945.

He is explaining to her the dynamics of sailing by using this miniature vessel. A photographer snapped their picture beside the family pool on Tigertail Road in Brentwood.

Throughout her adolescence, instead of playing with dolls, Jane seemed more interested in becoming "a tomboy."

Even at the age of five, Jane showed the instincts of becoming a cowgirl, perhaps a precursor to how comfortable she'd be in her future hit movie, *Cat Ballou*, a Columbia release in 1965.

She'd developed advanced riding skills early in life, which went along with her love of horses. In time, Henry attended her horse shows, watching with a bit of trepidation as his daughter jumped hurdles, collecting Blue Ribbons.

Instead of the pretty frocks Frances bought for Jane, her closet was filled with riding crops, leather gloves, spurs, and cowboy boots.

As she grew older, Jane secretly came across pages of a manuscript Frances was writing and defining as "my autobiography."

One day, when her mother was at the beauty parlor, Jane sat down to read it, and was shocked at how her mother described "my miserable childhood."

When Frances was only eight years old, she had been sexually abused by a piano tuner inside her family home.

After her shame-soaked, forced introduction to sex, she confessed that by the time she was ten or so, her life became filled with (her words) "boys, boys, and more boys."

In high school, Frances wrote about having sex with the football captain and described other sexual trysts and peccadilloes with young men much older than herself. Meeting college boys had been easy for her, since she grew up in the leisurely world of high society, with winters in New York and summers in East-hampton—a self-contained cocoon of chic parties, tennis tournaments, elegant balls, regattas, and lavish banquets.

Lady Jane's upbringing was very different from that of her socialite mother.

She hated dressing in those silly frocks Frances bought for her, forcing her to attend Hollywood parties where she'd meet children of her own age, most of them the sons and daughters of other movie stars.

In Henry's view, "I think my daughter wants to be the next Dale Evans." *[He was referring to the wife of Roy Rogers, billed in Westerns as "The Queen of the Cow-girls."]*

Once, Jane was invited to the home of Joan Crawford to attend a party she was hosting for her adopted daughter, Christina Crawford.

According to Jane, "I think Christina, from the look of things, hated her mother, but I found Crawford charming and gracious to me. She would soon be co-starring with my father in a romantic drama."

Jane was impressed with Candice Bergen, the daughter of Edgar Bergen. "I admired her style and grace, but I felt I looked a little puffy back then."

At a party, Jane met the four sons of Bing Crosby, noting that each of them seemed to hate their father. She also met Cheryl Crane, the daughter of Lana Turner. *[Despite her status as a minor, Cheryl would later be accused, tried, and (perhaps falsely) convicted of fatally stabbing her mother's lover, the gangster, Johnny Stompanato.]*

Both Jane and Peter were enrolled at the Brentwood Town and Country School, several blocks from the Fonda home. Many sons and daughters of movie stars attended the school. Jane may have been seen walking down the hall with Maria, the daughter of Gary Cooper, or she might have been spotted with Susan, the daughter of Fred MacMurray. There were so many other friendships she could have pursued, but she much preferred to hang out with classmate Sue-Sally Jones.

Sue-Sally was unlike the other girls. Like Jane, she preferred lumberjack shirts and cowboy jeans. Some of her female classmates whispered "lez." Jane's new best friend was the best athlete at school, and her fashion accessories included buckskin jackets and leggings, cowboy outfits, and sometimes, garments with vague references to Native American drag.

Sean, the son of Errol Flynn, had an unusual (some said "illegal") way of collecting the lunch money of Brentwood girls. For a negotiated fee, he would escort one, two, or even three of the schoolgirls to a concealed area of the gym where he would unzip and expose his penis.

Most of the girls had never seen a (human) penis before. Some of them were awed and wanted to feel it; others were repulsed, finding it didn't look at all sexy.

Jane's older sister, Pan, began dating in her early teens. It appears that it was up to her to transmit to Jane information about the "facts of life," very little of which either of them was getting from their parents.

***

Even at an early age, Jane sensed her father's lack of interest in everything to do with Frances. Many of her friends and classmates also had fathers who had recently returned home from the war. The word was out: "War changes a man." Many pre-war and wartime marriages did not survive.

In a memoir, years later, Jane wrote, "Side with the man if you want to be a survivor. Go out there and listen to jazz with them and pour their whiskey and even bring them women, if that's what they want. Learn to find that ex-

Although **Henry Fonda** was often accused of being an absentee father, this picture depicts a loving Daddy.

He holds one-year-old **Peter Fonda** on his lap while looking lovingly at his three-year-old daughter, **Jane**

This photo was snapped in 1940, two years before he joined the Navy and headed off to war.

citing. Better be perfect if you want to be loved." She also added a postscript that might have been aimed at her post-war mother. "And don't walk around naked."

Not long after his return from the Pacific, Henry began to learn of his wife's affairs while he'd been away. Hollywood was still a small town—when its denizens weren't making movies, they gossiped.

Frances was said to have been sexually intimate with several of the servicemen she met at the Hollywood Canteen. According to the rules, hostesses were not supposed to make out with anyone from the Army, Marines, Navy, or Air Force. Bette Davis had been one of the founders of the Canteen, and even she had violated the rules. Perhaps Frances figured that if the Canteen's founder could breach the bylaws, she could, too.

On several occasions, Frances met Marlene Dietrich, who didn't follow the rules either. "I think it's only fair that we girls offer aid and comfort to young men about to be shipped off to the Pacific, perhaps never to return," Dietrich said.

Dietrich herself had volunteered several times to entertain Allied servicemen amid some of the most ferocious fighting of wartime Europe, sometimes showering, when other options weren't available, in close proximity to the horny, lonely, and sexually frustrated "boys abroad." She didn't spend all her time with enlisted men, as General James Gavin and General George Patton Jr., might testify if their lips weren't (discreetly) sealed.

Within only ten days of his return to home and hearth, Henry had an embarrassing close encounter with one of his wife's boyfriends, Johnny Shields, a 22-year-old sailor on leave from Honolulu. Unannounced, he arrived on the Fonda doorstep, intoxicated.

"Who in hell are you?" Henry asked.

"Move aside, Grandpa," Shields answered. "Johnny's here now to claim his piece. You look to me like you're due for retirement. What branch are you in?"

"If you don't get the hell off my property, you're going to end up a bloody mess," Henry threatened, slamming the door in the sailor's face.

Later that afternoon, he forced Frances to admit to the affair. She said it was over because one drunken night, he'd shot a hole into the wall of their bedroom. "I felt he was too dangerous to have in the house with Jane and Peter."

Henry said nothing, but got up and left the bedroom, never to return. He knew he had no right to condemn her, because, during his time abroad, he had engaged in numerous affairs with willing young women on such islands as Saipan and Guam. They had made themselves readily available to the invading Americans, and often could be had for the presentation of a Hershey bar.

It turned out that Shields had been an aspirant musician, skilled at playing the guitar. He figured into some advice Frances later gave Jane: "Whatever you do, don't fall in love with a musician."

On leave from the U.S. Navy in the war-torn year of 1943, **Henry** came home for a short visit with his growing family.

Standing with him is **Pan**, Frances' daughter from her previous marriage. **Jane** dominates the center between her stepmother, **Frances,** (seated) and young **Peter**.

***

Young Peter and **young Jane** often spent afternoons playing in a sandbox with the children of their neighbor, Fred MacMurray, a former co-star of Henry's.

Here, the future movie stars are seen as they looked in 1942, the worst year of World War II.

When James Stewart returned to Hollywood, he was told that the couple he had leased his home to had the legal right to continue living there for another three months, and that he couldn't move back in until then.

In the meantime, Henry invited him to live in what he called his "Playhouse" in the back yard.

The quarters were the size of a small studio apartment, with a living room and a sofa that converted into a bed. It also had a bathroom, a small kitchen, and a study overlooking the swimming pool.

After such a long absence from each other, the two movie stars renewed their friendship, often sitting around drinking and sharing their very different experiences during World War II. Stewart had more dramatic tales to tell.

Stewart related that Hitler had ordered his Nazi forces to capture Clark

Gable, himself, and Tyrone Power alive "and breathing, at least," with the intention of "stripping us naked and putting us in cages for exhibit in Berlin."

"I don't think the monster knew I was even in the war," Henry said.

Stewart and Henry attended A-list galas together, almost always without Frances. Rumors about a possible romantic link between then surfaced once again.

In terms of their social desirability, they surfaced near the top of the "glam factor" at the lavish parties Marion Davies hosted at her beach house in Santa Monica. *[Davies, of course, had been the long-time mistress of the legendary press baron, William Randolph Hearst.]*

Sunday afternoons were often spent with Fred MacMurray and his wife, Lillian Lamont. *[After she died of cancer in 1953, MacMurray married actress June Haver.]*

When Henry returned from whatever event he'd attended, he and Frances retreated to their separate bedrooms. Sometimes, if they'd had too much to drink, Henry bunked with Stewart in the Playhouse.

Still a bachelor, Stewart, even after the war, didn't seem at all interested in "tying the knot," as he called it. "Putting a noose around my neck is not my idea of a good time."

In his future lay such enticing targets as June Allyson, who fell in love with him; the dancing star Mitzi Gaynor, Diana Barrymore, and later Grace Kelly when he co-starred with her in Alfred Hitchcock's *Rear Window* (1954).

Most of his conquests were with unknown starlets, one of whom stood out. Her name was Peggy Rogers, who claimed, "I'm going to be the Lana Turner of the 1950s." After he accidentally made her pregnant, he drove her to Mexico for an abortion. He later paid her $5,000. She ended up returning to her hometown of Lawrence, Kansas, where presumably, she got married and settled down.

As he told Henry, "When you're screwing a chick, accidents happen."

It came as no surprise to Henry when Stewart began secretly dating—once again—Henry's ex-wife, Margaret Sullavan. *[At the time, she was still married to agent Leland Hayward, but by 1947, she would file for divorce after learning of his affair with the socialite, "Slim" Keith. Sullavan had once invited Stewart and Henry for a "three-way." It is not known if the two suitors accepted the invitation.]*

Sullavan had taken a break from filmmaking in 1943, preferring to return to the stage. After Henry made a series of post-war movies, she urged him to do the same, and he would follow her advice.

With a dramatic flourish, she had told the press, "As long as the flesh-and-blood theater will have me, it is to the flesh-and-blood theater I'll belong. I really am stage-struck. And if that is treason, Hollywood will have to make the most of it."

[Sullavan would return to Hollywood in 1950 to make one more film, aptly titled No Sad Songs for Me. *Her co-stars were Wendell Corey, Viveca Lindfors, and Natalie Wood. At the time, Sullavan was losing her hearing. Her decline continued throughout the rest of the decade.]*

Long known for making model airplanes, Henry and Stewart at Brentwood discovered a new hobby—the construction of massive kites. Sundays were often spent flying these kites in the windy hills nearby.

THE *BRAVE* PICTURE OF THE YEAR

No Sad Songs for Me (1950) features **Margaret Sullavan** (Henry Fonda's wife from his disastrous first marriage) in her last film role as a woman dying of cancer who stoically keeps the news from her husband, played by Wendell Corey.

(At the time, Corey is falling in love with another woman, a situation which the dying protagonist —Sullavan—manages to cope with gracefully.)

Shamelessly sentimental, and based on a premise ("Keep your terminal illness a secret from your family!") that has since fallen out of favor with most medical counselers, it's viewed today as a post-war Hollywood tearjerker.

A decade after its release, Sullavan herself committed suicide.

Later in her life, the tumultuous uncertainties of **Marion Davies** calmed down as she grew more secure with her status as the long-time companion to billionaire press baron, William Randolph Hearst.

Upper photo shows Marion from around the time she entertained Henry Fonda, James Stewart, and a coterie of other A-list movie stars at her sprawling beach house in Santa Monica.

Lower photo shows a postcard of the Georgian-style mansion shortly after its construction in the early 1920s, perhaps with a fantasy replica of the "Ziegfeld Showgirl Who Made Good," the popular and widely admired Marion Davies, herself, "the most successful courtesan since Madame de Pompadour.

Once, they constructed a kite so big that on a particularly windy day, Henry almost shot skyward, as Stewart screamed for him to let go. Finally, he did and fell back to the ground. Fortunately, he did not injure himself. "Buster," Stewart told him. "You almost flew back to your native Nebraska."

***

When Stewart moved out of Henry's guest cottage, renewed his career, and began having affairs, Henry became morose and sometimes sulked for a week, not wanting to talk to anybody, even his kids. This period could be likened to a reverse metamorphosis—that is, like a butterfly entering a cocoon and emerging as a caterpillar.

Brooke Hayward, Leland's daughter, wrote of Henry as "melancholy and saturnine."

He was returning to the film world, which he held in contempt.

Author Peter Collier wrote: "The situation in which he found himself made Henry focus on what he hated about Hollywood—the indifferent quality, the triviality of most projects, and most of all, the constant devaluation of the actor's craft. For a film star, acting was sitting around and waiting, doing small takes over and over without seeing the results, and never having a chance to do a complex and extended characterization—that escape from the mundane self which had made him want to be an actor in the first place."

Post War Hollywood was seething with changes, that sent actors like Henry Fonda reeling.

The revolution was a by-product of, among many others, new venues in entertainment (i.e., television), and the introduction of controversial subject matter that in earlier days would have been censored as obscene.

From upper left, clockwise, 1) An American family watching that new-fangled medium called TV; 2) one of the fascinating gurus who promoted it (That's **Lucille Ball** pumping *I Love Lucy* from the cover of TV guide; and 3) A marquee for a movie about sex, career-building, existential depair, and death in Hollywood, **Sunset Blvd.**

For a period, at least, Henry and many other players were baffled.

***

Back on his home turf after the trauma, pain, inconvenience, and exoticism of World War II, Henry faced a new era: Post-War Hollywood, a time of change and turmoil. He spent some time reading extensively about what had happened while he was away.

He learned that the U.S. government had used the medium of film for massive propaganda purposes. Most importantly, movies became a morale booster, always ending with a patriotic message about (our) brave men fighting to save American democracy.

Although they were not directly involved in any military conflicts, Errol Flynn and John Wayne frequently fought World War II on the screen.

Perhaps with touches of envy, Henry imagined that he might have been the star of some of these films had he never signed up to join the Navy.

Flynn had been become famous as a heroic swashbuckler in movies of the late 1930s. Now he was heroic in such movies as *Dive Bomber* (1941); *Desperate Journey* (1942) with Ronald Reagan; *Uncertain Glory* (1944); and *Objective, Burma* (1945), arguably his best war picture.

Wayne's decision to avoid joining any branch of the Armed Forces was controversial. At the time, he was not the top star he became. Author Randy Roberts wrote: "Clark Gable, Tyrone Power, Robert Taylor, Henry Fonda, and James Stewart—far more important stars than Wayne—were willing to share a foxhole or a cockpit or a ship deck with teenaged American soldiers and sailors."

As a warrior on the screen, however, Wayne appeared in such movies as *Flying Tigers* (1942), a saga of the Construction Battalion of the U.S. Navy.

With each war film, although he remained a civilian, Wayne came to embody the spirit of the American fighting man. He was particularly moving in *They Were Expendable* (1942) and *Back to Bataan* (1943).

After the war, he appeared in the classic *Sands of Iwo Jima* (1947), glorifying the

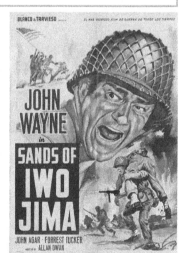

Officially and Ostentatiously Macho: John Wayne, noisily fighting World War II from home:

Henry defined himself as a Roosevelt Democrat and a "loyal fighting American" defending America.

Here's the party roster he probably voted for in 1940, the year this poster was issued. Notice the photo in the top tier, left, showing **Harry S Truman** on the ticket as a Democratic candidate to the U.S. Senate from Missouri.

U.S. Marines. Henry had each of these films screened for him, sarcastically concluding, "Without Duke, we could not have won World War II."

On the dawn of resuming his film career, Henry faced a different Hollywood from the one he'd left. The Golden Years of peak box office lasted from 1939 to 1946, but change was in the air.

Television was beginning to loom on the horizon. In a few years, nine out of ten homes would have a TV set, with box office receipts dropping one half from their 1946 peak.

The great movie moguls were fading, notably Harry Cohn at Columbia and Louis B. Mayer at MGM. But tenaciously (some said, "obsessively"), Darryl Zanuck at Fox still held onto Henry's pre-war contract.

Westerns and musical were still being churned out in Hollywood, but more realistic small-scale dramas were also being shot, many of them dealing with controversial and provocative themes. *Gentleman's Agreement* (1947) starring Gregory Peck dealt with anti-Semitism. *Smash-Up, The Story of a Woman* (1947)

Some players promoted their loyalties to Home, Hearth, and the US of A.

Here's **Ronald Reagan,** then President of the Screen Actors Guild, testifying against alleged communists at Congress's HUAC hearings in October, 1947.

featured Susan Hayward in a poignant (and timely, for its era) drama about alcoholism. Mental illness was the issue in Olivia de Havilland's *The Snake Pit* (1948).

When the Nazi menace ended ghoulishly in a Berlin bunker, the new threat, as perceived by many Americans, was Communism. An ally during World War II, the Soviet Union was now interpreted as a bomb-wielding menace to the civilized world. The House Un-American Activities Committee was formed to ferret out "The Commies in Hollywood," blacklisting them and ending their careers.

Henry watched on television as actors were called to deliver their versions of the menace: Ronald Reagan, Gary Cooper, and Robert Taylor each appeared as witnesses.

Henry, however, felt safe: "I was in the Navy, a loyal fighting American defending his country. I was a Roosevelt Democrat. In other words, I'm clean and won't have to go to jail like the Hollywood Ten," a reference to writers such as Dalton Trumbo who went to prison for refusing to testify.

Nonetheless, day after day, Henry waited for the phone to ring. Then one day, John Ford was on the other end of the line.

***

My Darling Clementine (1946)

After the rigors of war, Henry's comeback picture had been in the stew at 20th Century Fox weeks before he had any knowledge of it. John Ford still owed Fox one more picture, as did Henry himself.

Darryl F. Zanuck decided it was time to film a new and updated version of the fabled *Gunfight at the OK Corral.* Samuel G. Engel, who once owned a string of drugstores in Manhattan, was assigned the task of writing the script. The original title was *Frontier Marshall,* but Zanuck objected. "It sounds like your typical Western. Come up with something novel."

[The title Frontier Marshall *had been used by Fox in 1934 (with a different plotline) and again in 1939, that time with a similar story line to the present version.]*

Its name was therefore changed to *My Darling Clementine,* the words taken from the folk ballad *"Oh, My Darling Clementine,"* with the intention of having it sung,

When the agent for **Linda Darnell** notified her that she had been cast in *My Darling Clementine,* with Henry Fonda, she just assumed that she would play Clementine.

However, that role went to Cathy Downs. Darnell's role was that of the "spitfire Mexicana," Chihuahua, a dance hall girl of shifting alliances and loose morals.

with quavering nostalgia for the Old West, both in the opening credits and again at the end of the film.

[Before Ford signed on to direct My Darling Clementine, *he had wanted to film, instead,* The Quiet Man, *a romantic story set in (and to be shot in) Ireland. It had first appeared as a novella in the* Saturday Evening Post *in 1933, and he bought its movie rights in 1936. With the war looming and with Hollywood otherwise preoccupied with other, more crucial issues, the script gathered dust on a shelf. It was Ford's desire that* The Quiet Man *be Henry's first post-war film, one in which he'd be paired with the flame-haired Irish beauty, Maureen O'Hara. To Ford's frustration, Zanuck nixed the project.*

Henry Fonda, Linda Darnell, and **Victor Mature** pretend it's a threesome in this publicity photo for *My Darling Clementine.*

Ford eventually got financing for it from Republic Pictures, but by now, the male lead had changed. Henry had dropped out of films and returned to the stage.

Ford kept O'Hara in the cast but assigned John Wayne the male lead. The Quiet Man, eventually released in 1952, became a classic, the biggest-grossing picture Republic ever released.]

During the course of one long, contentious afternoon, Ford and the Fox CEO cast the leading characters in *My Darling Clementine*. Zanuck wanted Jeanne Crain for the role of Clementine but decided not to give it to her, saying, "The role is too small. She's currently the star bringing in the most bucks to Fox, so I've got to get her a more featured film."

It was decided, however, to cast Henry as Wyatt Earp, the sometimes unwilling marshal of Tombstone, Arizona. The role of Doc Holiday went to Victor Mature, despite Ford's objection. "I always found the big hunk sleazy," Ford, to no avail, protested.

Linda Darnell was assigned the other female lead, that of a "spitfire Mexicana," with Cathy Downs cast as the Boston-bred schoolteacher, Clementine.

Other key roles were assigned to Walter Brennan, Tim Holt, Ward Bond, Don Garner, Grant Withers, John Ireland, Jane Darwell, and the British actor, Alan Mowbray as the vaudevillian stage actor, Granville Thorndyke, drunkenly reciting lines from *Hamlet*.

One afternoon, as Henry was working the fields at Brentwood, that call he'd been waiting for came in. It was from "Pappy," Henry's nickname for Ford, who had famously helmed him in the pre-war *The Grapes of Wrath* (1940).

"Congrats on killing all those Japs," Ford said. "Legend now has it that you helped load the atomic bomb onto the *Enola Gay*."

"I had some help in becoming a mass murderer," Henry responded in jest.

"Zanuck wants you to play Wyatt Earp in a new version of that gunfight at the OK Corral which has already been written about in at least a dozen dime store Westerns.

"That old thing?" Henry said. "Who will play Doc Holiday?"

"Liverlips himself. The Greaseball."

"I'm not familiar with this actor," Henry said.

"Victor Mature! He was forced on me by Zanuck. And your leading lady will be Linda Darnell. If you can lure her away long enough from getting fucked by Howard Hughes, she might give you a renewed tumble."

"Perhaps," Henry said. "The Aviator is strong competition. Will she play Clementine?"

"No, she'll be a prostitute in love with Doc Holiday," Ford said. The title role goes to this former model Fox has signed, Cathy Downs.

"Never heard of her," Henry said.

"She's a little wren with no sex appeal," Ford said. "But she's supposed to be a schoolteacher, so I guess that'll be okay."

Bidding Frances and his children goodbye, Henry drove by himself to the sweltering heat of Monument Valley, straddling the border of Utah and Arizona. Ford had instructed him to grow a beard for the role.

One of the first actors he met on the set was Jane Darwell, who had played his mother in *The Grapes of Wrath* and now found herself cast in yet another movie with him. "In every picture I make with you," she told him facetiously, "I keep waiting to play a torrid love scene with you."

"That day will come," he said with gallant humor. "We'll be nude and we'll heat up the screen."

Henry, as before, worked smoothly with Ford. Walter Brennan, however, did not, vowing that he would never be directed by him again. The veteran old Hollywood cowpoke kept his word.

Victor Mature and Ford clashed repeatedly, and in almost every scene, Ford criticized Mature's performance. "The Hollywood Hunk," this time around, wasn't sexy at all. The story line called for the character he was playing

(Doc Holliday) to suffer from tuberculosis, and therefore, to cough a lot. "His character knows he's at death's door and is perhaps expecting to be sentenced to hell's fire," Ford claimed.

In the film's opening scene, Wyatt Earp (Henry) and his brothers are driving their herd through the arid terrain of Monument Valley westward to California. Cast as Earp's brothers are Tim Holt as Virgil; Ward Bond (Henry's longtime friend) as Morgan; and Don Garner as James (aka Jim). Along the route they encounter the aimiable but vaguely sinister Old Man Clanton (Walter Brennan), who offers to buy their herd. Wyatt turns him down.

Later, the brothers set out to explore the wicked frontier town of Tombstone, leaving their youngest brother, 18-year-old Jim behind as a watchman. When they return, they find him dead and the cattle stolen. Old Man Clanton and the sinister, surly members of his gang emerge as the chief suspects. Grant Withers plays Clanton with John Ireland cast as Billy Clanton.

Wyatt (Henry) becomes the town marshal of Tombstone, plotting to (legally) pursue and arrest the Clanton gang.

Arriving on the scene is Clementine (Cathy Downs), Doc's former love interest from Boston. He wants her to return there, but Wyatt, by now, has become smitten with her.

After the sweet temptations of "Darling Clementine," **Henry Fonda** posed, the quintessence of the strong, taciturn, "heroic-when-necessary" American male, once again against a background of Big Skies and barren landscapes.

In spite of his ill health, Doc is romantically (albeit brutally) involved with Chihuahua (Darnell), a dance hall girl.

As the story moves on, just before she confesses to who actually killed Wyatt Earp's brother, Bill Clanton (Ireland) shoots Chihuahua through a window (she eventually dies) and flees on horseback.

With more shooting on the way, Doc decides to join the Earp brothers for the ultimate fight at the OK Corral at sunup. The Clantons are killed, as is Doc.

The marshal (Henry) and Clementine (Downs) survive. She becomes the new schoolteacher of Tombstone. *[Fox would drop Downs in 1947, and she would never be employed by a major studio again.]*

As Zanuck sat through the early rushes, he sent Ford a devastating memo conveying his opinion of the Western: He'd found it disappointing. "We face a major recutting and the insertion of a few new scenes. I'm an old hand at film editing, and I personally will do the job. I performed the same job on *The Grapes of Wrath* and *How Green Was My Valley,* and both of them won Oscars."

After Ford—humiliated, frustrated, and furious—sat through the doctored film, he told his friends, "It's no longer my picture."

When it was released, *My Darling Clementine* recouped its high cost of production and went on to gross $4.5 million. *Variety* claimed, "Major boost to the film is given by the simple, sincere performance of Henry Fonda. As a boomtown marshal, he pulls the reins taut on his part, charging the role with more excitement than it really has."

Bosley Crowther in *The New York Times* wrote: "Henry Fonda plays Wyatt Earp such as we've never seen before—a leatherly, laconic young cowpoke who truly suggests a moral aim. Through his quiet yet persuasive self-confidence—his delicious intonation of short words—he shows us an elemental character who is as real as the dirt on which he walks. The eminent director, John Ford, is a man who has a way with a Western, like nobody else in the picture trade."

The Christian Science Monitor gave a perceptive review: "Wyatt Earp, portrayed by Henry Fonda, is a superb interpretation—shy, slow-moving, and easy-going, imperturbable, and likable. The marshal getting a haircut, dancing a two-step, and walking a lady to church is as funny as though he were in a comedy, yet Fonda's characterization of a down-to-earth Westerner, free as air, is so persuasive that his Wyatt Earp becomes one of the great Western heroes."

More than half a century later, *Clementine* was still getting good reviews. Roger Ebert wrote, "It is one of the sweetest and most good-hearted of all Westerns. It is unusual in that it makes the romance of Wyatt Earp and Clementine the heart of the film rather than the gunfighter."

As time went by, Henry was credited with being the finest Earp, topping such other actors as Randolph Scott, Errol Flynn, and James Garner.

Burt Lancaster and Kirk Douglas starred in yet another recycling of that bloody saga of the American West, *The*

Gunfight at the OK Corral in 1957. In it, John Ireland, as he had in *My Darling Clementine*, appeared in it too.

Henry's greatest review came from the Oval Office in Washington, D.C. President Harry S Truman wrote: "*My Darling Clementine* is my favorite movie."

***

The Long Night (1947)

The Long Night was conceived as a remake of a politically troubled and at the time, very controversial French-language film, named *Le jour se lève*, (aka *Daybreak*). Released in 1939 and later suppressed as "nihilistic and depressing." by France's Nazi-collaborating Vichy government, it was written by Jacques Prévert, directed by Marcel Carné and based on a short story by Jacques Viot. Modern-day critics still cite it as one of the best examples of the short-lived French film tradition of "poetic realism."

Perhaps fearing that widespread distribution of the (subtitled) French original would alienate American audiences in advance of the remake's release, after RKO bought the screen rights just before the fall of France to the German Nazis, they acquired as many copies of the French-language original that they could find and destroyed them.

[Fortunately, they didn't succeed. A copy of the French-language original surfaced in the 1950s. Now remastered and redigitalized, it's revered by fans of Jean Gabin and his co-star, Arletty, for their poignant performances and their replication of gritty, "between-the-wars" Paris.]

At this point in trying to re-establish his career, Henry was not interested in some "romantic piece of French fluff," with a "controversial, censorship-prone Nazi past." Instead, he preferred a taut melodrama in which he could reveal to America his new maturity.

Handsome and "*noir*": **Henry Fonda** in *The Long Night*.

"The 1939 original version starring Jean Gabin had been a big hit in 1939 France," Henry said. "But I fell on my ass in the Hollywood remake."

But the great director, Anatole Litvak, convinced Henry that the Americana-soaked remake would be the perfect vehicle for him. He would play Joe Adams, a soldier returning from the battlefields who finds it hard to readjust to life in a small Pennsylvania mill town. Getting a job as a sandblaster, he becomes romantically entangled, leading to his murder of a jealous rival.

Henry had long admired the films of Litvak, who had once been married to Miriam Hopkins. His first words to Henry were, "Miriam is still mad at you. She thinks you should have held out for her playing in *Jezebel*, not that dreaded horror, Bette Davis."

"Miriam is smart enough to know that I didn't cast the picture," Henry answered.

Until its takeover by the Nazis, Litvak had previously worked in the German film factory, UFA. Being a Jew, he had fled from Berlin to France and then to England as a refugee. He achieved international recognition with the release of *Mayerling* (1936), starring Charles Boyer and Danielle Darrieux. The success of that film brought him to Hollywood, where he had a long stint at Warners. Later, as war clouds gathered, Litvak directed one of Hollywood's first anti-Nazi "propaganda" films, *All This and Heaven Too* (1940), starring Bette Davis and Charles Boyer.

He joined the U.S. Army where he worked with Frank Capra on the *Why We Fight* series. He was later put in charge of combat photography during the D-Day Allied Invasion of Normandy in 1944.

In 1948, months after helming Henry, Litvak turned out two of the greatest films of the late 1940s, *Sorry, Wrong Number* with Barbara Stanwyck and *The Snake Pit* with Olivia de Havilland.

During the pre-production of *The Long Night*, Henry was told that his leading lady would be Barbara Bel Geddes. Based on her prominence on Broadway, RKO had signed her to a seven-year filmmaking contract. Right after starring with Henry, she was Oscar nominated for the George Stevens film, *I Remember Mama* (1948).

In supporting roles were Ann Dvorak, the "creepy" Elisha Cook Jr., and Vincent Price.

A stage and screen actor, the eventual star of some 100 films during the course of his lifetime (often horror movies), Price had already immortalized himself by his performance in the *film noir, Laura* (1944), starring Gene Tierney.

A Yale graduate, and a brilliant one at that, Price was also an art collector and gourmet cook. One day in RKO's

201

kitchen, he prepared a gourmet meal for Henry. "I think he wanted me for dessert, but NO WAY!" Henry told Litvak.

On the third day of the shoot, Henry met the second female lead, Ann Dvorak. The New Yorker told him her family name was pronounced *"vor-shack,"* the "D" being silent. "Everyone mispronounces my name. I've been called everything from Balzac to Bickelsrock."

Dvorak had made her film debut at the age of five in the silent film, *Ramona* (1916).

After an intimate relationship with Howard Hughes in the 1930s, she entered the peak of her career with an appearance in *Scarface* (1932) as Paul Muni's sister; and in *Three on a Match* (1932) with Bette Davis and Joan Blondell. Dvorak continued with appearances in numerous modern romances and melodramas throughout the 1930s.

During the war, Dvorak was an ambulance driver in England. But in the post-war years, when she worked with Henry, her film career—in her words—was "on the skids." By 1951, she had retired from the screen.

Before going off to war, Henry had seen Elisha Cook as the baby-faced killer in *The Maltese Falcon (1941)* starring Humphrey Bogart. From that point, he went on to play in numerous films, including *Rosemary's Baby* (1968), often as a deceptively mild-mannered villain.

Two worldly and sophisticated actors, each dolled up and ready to "lip-lock" in *The Long Night:* **Ann Dvorak** and scary **Vincent Price**

Although he stood 5 feet 6 inches tall and weighed only 120 pounds, the U.S. Army accepted him for service.

He told Henry that after that *Falcon* picture, he became typecast as weaklings, sadistic losers, and hoodlums. "My character is usually murdered, strangled, poisoned, or shot. If the role calls for a homicidal maniac, a shady, pugnacious little creep, I get a call. I'm also great in dim-witted parts."

Most of *The Long Night* was relayed in flashback, as a frightened and deeply depressed Joe (i.e., Henry) has locked himself into his shabby boarding house, having shot Max the Magician (Price), his jealous rival. The viewer learns that his motivation involved falling in love with Max's assistant, Jo Ann (Bel Geddes).

In his dingy room, he holds off the police for the duration of *The Long Night* as they plan to use tear gas to smoke him out. Jo Ann arrives on the scene, urging him to surrender, but he refuses. He remains holed up in the room until his inevitable death.

The Long Night lost $1 million and was poorly reviewed. Bosley Crowther in *The New York Times* wrote, "Henry Fonda, while moody and pathetic as the holed-up fugitive, is not the wrath-tortured killer that Jean Gabin was."

Nathan Cohen, in the *Toronto Star,* wrote, "Henry Fonda enacted with stunning perceptiveness a quite ordinary man who goes berserk when his sweetheart is lured away by a carnival magician."

The noted film critic James Agee claimed, *"The Long Night* depends too heavily on huge, lugubrious close-ups of Fonda looking adenoidal."

***

The Fugitive (1947)

Once again, "Pappy" (Henry's nickname for John Ford) was on the phone, wanting to cast him as a priest in his latest film, *The Fugitive.*

Dudley Nichols had written its screenplay based on Graham Greene's 1940 novel, *The Power and the Glory.*

The setting was a brutally anti-clerical police state in an unnamed Latin American country where religion was outlawed. It's the tale of a priest in love with a prostitute, or, in the words of one critic, "The saga of flesh battling the call of Jesus." In the book, flesh wins, but in the strife associated with getting the movie made, major surgery was required from Nichols, the frustrated screenwriter, who was ordered to "remove the sex."

This was another film that Ford had wanted to make as early as 1940. But with the coming of the war, he relegated it to his archives, the same way *The Quiet Man* had nestled there for years.

As Henry would learn, the plot had been rejected, because of censor-

Henry Fonda behind bars in *The Fugitive:*

Grim and configured as a moral mandate whose lust-inspired spiritual torments somehow got camouflaged by the censors.

ship fears, by every major studio in Hollywood.

Ford seemed aware that *The Fugitive* would have limited appeal to movie audiences, viewing it instead as "a possible vehicle for art houses."

His grandson, Dan Ford, wrote, "Working with an all-Mexican crew and free from the restrictions of Hollywood, Pappy went after dramatic angles, shadows, backlights, stylized compositions, and ravishing pictorial effects."

Budgeted at $1.5 million, the film was set for a November 3, 1947 release. Shooting would be at various locations in Mexico, including Cuernavaca and Taxco de Alarón, with interior scenes at Churubusco Studios in Mexico City.

Its plot is the saga of a charismatic but nameless and conflicted Catholic priest, a fugitive, as stated earlier, in an unnamed Latin American state where religion is outlawed. He performs mass in secret and develops a following among the local farmers and laborers.

In his biography, *John Ford: The Man and His Films,* Tag Gallagher wrote, "In Mexico, Ford jettisoned most of the script and, giving way to his fancy, made a highly abstract art film. *The Fugitive* lost a lot of money, caused a rift between writer Dudley Nichols and Ford, and has posed problems among Ford's most devoted followers."

Some of the scandals associated with Henry's leading lady, Dolores Del Rio, cast as the prostitute, Maria Dolores, had preceded her. Henry had read about her exploits for years.

Is She Good or Is She Bad?

Dolores Del Rio as a "fallen Madonna" in *The Fugitive*.

As she told Henry, "Men are playthings, toys to amuse for a while until you get bored with them."

Del Rio never told anyone her age, claiming, "I am an ageless beauty." *[Actually, she was born in Durango, Mexico, in 1904, which made her one year older than Henry.]*

When Henry met her, he asked the first question on everybody's mind: "Is it true that you rarely appear in daylight—only if you're forced to in your work—and that you thrive only on orchids?"

"Legends, my darling man, legends," Del Rio answered. "The most accurate legend about me is that I'm usually successful at seducing my leading men."

That wasn't quite true, as she missed a few along the way. Into her boudoir(s) marched Bruce Cabot, Joel MacCrea, George Sanders, and Orson Welles, who called her "the most beautiful woman I've ever seen, and I was once married to love goddess Rita Hayworth. Dolores looked like her face was dipped in porcelain."

Del Rio didn't confine her conquests to actors. She made love to the novelist Erich Maria Remarque, too. "My biggest thrill came from that stud from the Dominican Republic, Porfirio Rubirosa. My most amazing conquest was Walt Disney, although I suspected he was mostly homosexual. As for women, I name the one and only Greta Garbo."

She told Henry, "As long as a woman has twinkles in her eyes, no man notices whether she has wrinkles under them."

The question not answered by Fonda biographers is, "Did Dolores Del Rio ever seduce him?"

The only clue came from Ford himself. "On location one afternoon, when neither of them was needed on set, he visited her dressing room for three hours. Perhaps he didn't seduce her. Maybe they spent all that time reading Balzac out loud."

Del Rio enjoys a footnote in Hollywood history. In the 1933 film, *Flying Down to Rio,* she introduced the two-piece bathing suit to American women.

When Ford directed her, he put her beauty "in a class with Garbo. But when she spoke, out came Minnie Mouse."

Her cruelest rejection from a leading man came when she starred with Elvis Presley in *Flaming Star* (1960), cast as his mother. When she suggested that the singer visit her dressing room, he said, "I don't do it with grannies."

In the third lead, Pedro Armendáriz was cast as an unnamed police lieutenant. In the 1940s and '50s, he became one of the best known Latin American movie stars.

Dolores Del Rio, Katy Jurado *(High Noon)*, and Armendáriz formed one of the most legendary trios in the history of Mexican cinema. Ford became fond of the Mexican actor and cast him in three movies, two with Henry.

The star's final appearance on screen would be in the James Bond film, *From Russia With Love* (1963). At the time, he was terminally ill with cancer and could not complete his commitments. His final scenes were executed by his double, director Terrence Young.

Before the film was released, Armendariz committed suicide by shooting himself in the chest. He was 51 years old.

During part of the shoot, Henry roomed with his longtime friend, Ward Bond, cast as "El Gringo." To allow the priest to escape from police troops, El Gringo holds off the troops in a gun battle.

When the priest (Henry) hears that the bandit is dying, he risks his own life and returns to give him his last rites. The priest is captured and as payment for his kindness, he's sentenced to death.

J. Carroll Naish had the unattractive role of the police informer. Even if movie fans didn't know his name, Naish earned 200 credits during Hollywood's Golden Age.

"Naish could play almost any role," Henry said. "Mad scientist, gangster, an assistant to Boris Karloff in *House of Frankenstein* (1944). He could also play all sorts of ethnicities. Some people called him 'Hollywood's one-man United Nations.'"

Cast as the chief of police, Leo Carillo had first worked with Henry in *Blockade* (1933).

Michael Kerbel wrote, "Fonda, who has played fugitives before, here seems stilted, but his almost constant solemnity and bewilderment have a comparatively pathetic effect."

Movie critic Jay Robert Nash found that *The Fugitive* "is movie-making at its technical best, and it offers a performance from Henry Fonda that the sensitive actor seldom matched."

Bosley Crowther of *The New York Times* called it "a symphony of light and shade of deafening din and silence of sweeping movement and repose."

Co-producer Merian C. Cooper wired Henry with this: "I think your performance is one of the truly great ones in the history of motion pictures."

Bret Wood has written, "Ford is best remembered today for his boisterous adventure films, such as *The Quiet Man* (1952), *The Searchers* (1956), *She Wore a Yellow Ribbon* (1949); and for his crusty, unpretentious demeanor, often denying the existence of thematic subtext in his work and refusing to discuss his artistic intentions as a director. But *The Fugitive* belongs to an earlier, lesser-known faction of his work, self-consciously 'arty' films that demonstrated his interests in German expressionism, English literature, and religious ideology. Films such as *The Informer* (1935), *The Prisoner of Shark Island* (1936), or *The Long Voyage Home* (1940), remind us that beneath Ford's growling *machismo* were a sophisticated mind and a brilliant visual sense, even though Ford was later to deny both gifts. ('I make Westerns' is how he typically summarized his career). *The Fugitive* is perhaps Ford's last great 'art film', a high-minded show of faith, a lovingly crafted paean to his own Catholicism."

When Henry and Ford learned of just how big a financial failure *The Fugitive* was, they dined together to discuss their respective futures. "We've got to come up with a blockbuster, a sprawling, Western saga," Ford said. "I'll cast you in one of two male leads. What do you think about working with both John Wayne and Shirley Temple?"

"You've got to be kidding," Henry answered.

***

As Ford contemplated his next picture, young Peter ran outdoors and called to his dad. "There's a guy on the phone that sounds like a fucking Nazi. Want me to hang up?"

"No, son. I'd better take it. Could be a German director."

Picking up the phone, he heard the booming voice of Otto Preminger: "Fonda, can I drive over and talk? Joan Crawford demands that I cast you in her next picture coming up."

To the astonishment of many of his film industry associates, no longer young **Henry Fonda** opted to join the Navy, horrifed at the attack it had suffered at Pearl Harbor in December of 1941 by the Empire of Japan.

Here, surrounded by motivational "Join the Navy" posters, is a view of Henry on his way to boot camp (*upper photo*), and a view of him, uncomfortable and perhaps rueful, "at ease" on the deck of a U.S. Naval vessel somewhere in the South Pacific in 1944.

CHAPTER ELEVEN

ON STAGE WITH *MISTER ROBERTS*

(1948)

HENRY STARS IN A COMEDY/DRAMA ABOUT WORLD WAR II.
IT MORPHS INTO ONE OF THE MOST POPULAR PLAYS EVER PRODUCED ON BROADWAY

BATTLING COCHISE AND THE INDIANS WITH JOHN FORD

A CLOSETED GAY DIRECTOR TEAMS WITH HENRY FONDA AND JOHN ("THE DUKE")
WAYNE IN ANOTHER SAGA OF THE OLD, OLD WEST

THE SAD, TRAGIC, AND UTTERLY POINTLESS SUICIDE OF
FRANCES SEYMOUR FONDA

JOAN CRAWFORD

HER "NINNY PIES," AND *DAISY KENYON*

WITH THE UNDERSTANDING THAT SHE'S "A HELLUVA DAME,"
HENRY AND DANA ANDREWS TRY TO FIGURE HER OUT

SUSAN BLANCHARD

SHE'S YOUNG, SHE'S BEAUTIFUL,
SHE'S A SOCIALITE MEMBER OF THE HAMMERSTEIN CLAN,
AND HENRY HAS FALLEN MADLY IN LOVE WITH HER

PETER FONDA

"Your son has shot himself. He's dying."
— A SPOKESPERSON FOR THE U.S. COAST GUARD, TO HENRY,
DURING HIS HONEYMOON IN THE U.S. VIRGIN ISLANDS.

"WE CAN WORK IT OUT"

MORE ABOUT JAMES STEWART

STAGE AND FILM OFFERS THAT MADE IT, OTHERS THAT DIDN'T

I don't want anybody to get to know me. I fear I would disappoint them. You see, most of my life I've spent play-acting other people. James Stewart is the only friend who ever looked deeply into my soul. I ain't Henry Fonda, that man on the screen or stage. Nobody could have that much integrity."

—Henry Fonda

"

Daisy Kenyon (1947)

Henry owed Fox one more picture before he could release himself from that "slave contract" he'd signed with Darryl F. Zanuck before joining the U.S. Navy. He was disappointed when Otto Preminger, the director, told him that his final film for Fox would be the third lead in a Joan Crawford "soap opera" in which Dana Andrews' name would be billed above his own.

Its "love triangle" plot has Crawford, in the title role, living in New York's Greenwich Village and working as a commercial artist. She is in love with Dan O'Mara (Dana Andrews), a high-powered and successful attorney who is married to Lucille (Ruth Warrick) and has two daughters.

One night, when he breaks a date with her, Daisy goes out with Peter Laphan (Fonda), a widower and former boat designer who is returning from the battlefields of World War II. In time, he falls in love with her and marries her, taking her to live in his cottage on Cape Cod.

In the meantime, O'Mara divorces his bitchy wife and comes back into Daisy's world, urging her to divorce Peter and marry him.

For those who haven't seen the end, we won't reveal her choice of beau, but many fans who saw the movie knew in advance which man she will allow a close-up view of her "Ninny Pies," a cute name she had devised for her breasts.

After reading the script, Andrews phoned Preminger, telling him he didn't like the role and wanted out. Preminger tried to talk him into it. In the meantime, he pitched the part of the cheating attorney to Walter Pidgeon, Wendell Corey, and Joseph Cotten, to no avail.

Andrews later said, "I was cajoled into playing the part, although I would

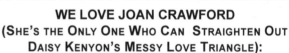

WE LOVE JOAN CRAWFORD
(SHE'S THE ONLY ONE WHO CAN STRAIGHTEN OUT
DAISY KENYON'S MESSY LOVE TRIANGLE):

America has won the war, and now, different kinds of conflicts are busting out all over. What's a Girl to Do?

Joan Crawford, as Daisy Kenyon, gets confused in her love for **Dana Andrews** (*left photo*), the mogul who trivialized and tormented her; and her affection for the introvert she married on the rebound, **Henry Fonda** (*photo above*).

have preferred the role of the soldier given to Fonda."

He was delighted, however, that his billing appeared over Fonda's. *[In the* Ox-Box *Incident (1943), Andrews had been billed as the second lead, behind Fonda. Perhaps he felt vindicated.]*

The screenplay by David Hertz was based on the bestselling 1945 novel by Elizabeth Janeway. Peggy Ann Garner was cast as one of Dana's two daughters. The child star had won a Juvenile Oscar for her role in the memorable *A Tree Grows in Brooklyn* (1945).

Martha Stewart (no, not the lifestyle guru and television personality of the 1990s) had a minor role of Mary Angelus. After a talent scout discovered her singing at Manhattan's Stork Club, she went to Hollywood. In time, her greatest role was as the murder victim, Mildred Atkinson, in the classic *In a Lonely Place* (1950), in which Humphrey Bogart delivered one of his best performances. From 1946 to 1948, Stewart was married to the famous comedian, Joe E. Lewis.

Warrick recalled the shooting weeks later. "Otto and Crawford were known tyrants who could explode at any minute. Never once did they show their ferocity, completely concealing it. Neither seemed to want to declare World War III, as both of them were desperate to make a good movie. The boys (Andrews and Fonda) disliked their roles but carried bravely on."

Newspaper reporters Walter Winchell, Damon Runyon, and Leonard Lyons appeared in cameos, as did actor John Garfield.

A makeup artist and shadowy cinematography were employed to disguise Crawford's forty-three years, since the character in the novel was much younger.

According to Warrick, "During interior scenes, Crawford was having hot flashes, and she insisted that the temperature be kept at 52° F. I wore a fur coat between takes. She presented Hank and Dana with long underwear."

When her best friend, William Haines, former movie star, now interior designer, came to visit the set, Crawford confided a secret to him: "I had two choices—seduce both Dana and Henry, or just one of them. I chose Henry. To signal my intentions to seduce him, I had wardrobe design a jockstrap for him, made with gold sequins, red beads, and rhinestones."

Crawford then invited Henry to come to her dressing room later that day and model it for her. That led to their off-screen affair, which lasted only until the end of the picture.

Preminger brought the film in on time and right under its $1,850,000 budget. Exterior shooting occurred during the hot summer days of June 16 to August 12, 1947.

On her final day, Preminger told Crawford, "I honestly believe this picture will bring you an Oscar. And you don't have to play a mother like you did in *Mildred Pierce*. Fox tried to get Gene Tierney or Jennifer Jones to play Daisy, but they bowed out. I'm so glad you accepted."

At the end of the shoot, Henry told the press, "My bondage to Fox is over. Today, I'm a freelancer, seeking roles better suited to my brand."

Zanuck responded in anger at his remark: "I don't know why Fonda sounds so pissed off. Under that contract, he made two masterpieces, *The Ox-Bow Incident* and *My Darling Clementine*. The other pictures were good entertainment and performed well at the box office. A lot of actors have more to complain about than Fonda."

Crawford, too, was interviewed after the completion of *Daisy Kenyon*: "Working with Dana Andrews and Henry Fonda is like putting chocolate icing on a chocolate cake.

Variety reviewed *Daisy Kenyon* as "A *True Confessions* yarn with a *Vogue* sheen." It also cited Fonda as "the right actor for the part. He goes from dreamer to man of iron."

The critic for *The New York Times* found Fonda "likable and somewhat more sympathetic than a husband in such circumstances has any right to be."

Jay Robert Nash in *The Motion Picture Guide* claimed, "Dana Andrews is strong, but not strong enough. Fonda is as bland as a mayonnaise sandwich on supermarket white."

Although it faced many negative reviews at the time of its release, *Daisy Kenyon* has stood the test of time. Today, it enjoys a small cult following. Many critics consider it "a misunderstood masterpiece of Otto Preminger."

Ruth Warrick in 1947. Warrick was an actress very skilled (remember *Citizen Kane*?) at playing rich, unhappy wives.

One night she told Darwin Porter, the co-author of this book, "If I sat down with you and told you all the secrets I know about Hollywood in the 1940s, and you published them, there would be rioting in the streets."

The brilliant and always-reliable **Otto Preminger** was known in some circles as Hollywood's harshest, most abrasive director. Born a Jew during the heyday of the Austro-Hungarian Empire, he consistently pushed taboos and made a name for himself, early, in *film noir* as an expatriate in Hollywood.

He didn't daunt Crawford, a diva who was used to maneuvering her way around moguls.

"Otto," she said, "was the sweetest person. Contrary to his legend, he was a doll to work with, although he appears like a Nazi officer from central casting."

Mike D'Angelo gave the film a grade of 99 out of 100, calling it "the most brutally realistic melodrama I've ever seen."

***

On Our Merry Way (1948)

At last, a director—in this case, King Vidor—devised the idea of casting those best buddies, James Stewart and Henry Fonda, in the same movie. *On Our Merry Way* was subdivided into four separate segments, evocative of Henry's *Tales of Manhattan*, which he had shot before joining the U.S. Navy.

Based on his past record, King Vidor gave Henry faith that he would pull this one off, in spite of it being rather disjointed.

A Texan, Vidor would spend 67 years of his life making movies, going from the silents (*The Big Parade;* 1925), to such hit Westerns as *Duel in the Sun* (1946). He would be nominated for a Best Director Oscar five times, and would helm such stars as Robert Donat, Wallace Beery, Barbara Stanwyck, and Lillian Gish.

Henry and Stewart would join an all-star cast headed by Paulette Goddard and Burgess Meredith months before they went to the divorce court. Henry's friend, Fred MacMurray, was also in the cast, as was Henry's former co-star, Dorothy Lamour.

Meredith had, for a while, been Stewart's roommate after Henry moved out. So the two former "roomies" spent time talking together about former adventures.

Henry was entranced by Goddard, but put no moves on her, fearing Meredith's watchful eye.

Very flirtatious, Goddard, during the course of her adulthood, became famous for at least three of her sensational marriages, one of which (believed to have been "common law") had been with Charles Chaplin. After dumping Meredith, she would go on to wed the fabled German-born novelist Erich Maria Remarque.

Her affairs with various well-known celebrities had been widely bruited in the tabloids: Attorney Greg Bautzer, Clark Gable, Gary Cooper, Bruce Cabot, George Gershwin, John Huston, Aldous Huxley, Sir Alexander Korda, Mervyn LeRoy, Anatole Litvak, David Niven, Aristotle Onassis, Artie Shaw, Spencer Tracy, H.G. Wells, and John Wayne.

As an editor, Martha Pease (Goddard) gives her husband an assignment. He is a newspaper want ad clerk who dreams of becoming a reporter. To advance his cause, she assigns him the job of a roving reporter to interview people asking the question, "What great influence has a little child had upon your life?"

He interviews two musicians, Slim (Stewart) and Lank (Henry), a pair of footloose, down-on-their-luck pals. Slim works the piano as Lank plays the cornet. Lank's big (musical) moment is when he impersonates a jazz musician in a rocking rowboat, blowing himself, in the words of one critic, "into a volcanic eruption of *mal-de-mer.*"

When it was released, most reviews were dismal, although the Stewart/Fonda sequence was hailed as the best. David Shipmen, in *The Story of Cinema,* wrote: "Its failure was three parts deserved, but the fourth segment was a very funny take about two unemployed musicians, incisively but casually played by Henry Fonda and James Stewart."

Bosley Crowther in *The New York Times* claimed, "Playing a couple of beat-up musicians, Fonda and Stewart whip a purely ridiculous script into an act of low comedy mugging that is a good bit of slapstick fun."

Ragtime with **Henry Fonda** *(right)* and **James Stewart** in *On Our Merry Way*.

The movie was first released as *A Miracle Can Happen*, but its title was soon changed. John O'Hara wrote the sequence featuring Stewart and Fonda. The two former roommates were told to play their roles "Like hip but hapless jazzmen."

Burgess Meredith met his third wife, **Paulette Goddard**, when they co-starred in *Second Chorus* (1940). She was legally separated from Charlie Chaplin, but not quite divorced. To win her over, Meredith had to compete with Fred Astaire, another co-star of that same picture. "One afternoon, when I stood with Fred at the urinal, I realized I had him beat by a country mile."

"Paulette was more attractive in person than on film," Meredith claimed. "She was bright, funny, and sensual—when she walked into a room, you felt the vibration. She understood the id of the male animal."

"I was surprised when she agreed to marry me, since I was not a dashing swain. She flew from man to man in a game of *roulette d'amour.*"

"She also liked diamonds. No ice, no dice.'"

208

Variety panned it: "The cast couldn't have been better. The story's execution falters because a scene here and there is inclined to strive too much for whimsical effect."

The *New York Daily News* described the dynamic of the film as "a million dollar cast in a ten-cent film."

***

Fort Apache (1948)

During the course of his prolific career, director John Ford made three classic Westerns about the U.S. Cavalry. The first was *Fort Apache* (1948) starring John Wayne and Henry Fonda. The "cavalry trilogy" was completed with *She Wore a Yellow Ribbon* in 1949 and *Rio Grande* in 1950. The latter two were made without Henry, but starred "The Duke."

As Tony Thomas wrote, "*Fort Apache* has a gritty quality. It provided Fonda with an opportunity to broaden his screen image. In it, he's a martinet, a ramrod of a soldier—no affability, no folksy charm."

As Lt. Col. Owen Thursday, he is a dedicated and inflexible officer who acts his role with chilly authority, dealing with such issues as a rebellious daughter and sloppy, undisciplined troops on the verge of mutiny at a remote outpost.

In time, *Fort Apache* has emerged as a Western masterpiece, one of the first major movies to present an authentic and often sympathetic view of Native Americans.

After the colossal success of *The Grapes of Wrath* (1940), Henry had complete faith in John Ford to guide him through this latest Western.

Over the years, Henry and countless others left descriptions of Ford's personality—intelligent, sensitive, and sometimes sentimental. He preferred to be known, in his words, as a "tough, two-fisted hard-drinking Irish son of a bitch."

Author Nancy Schoenberger states, "Ford, having grown up with brothers he idolized in a rough-and-tumble world of boxers, drinkers, and roustabouts, found his deepest theme in male camaraderie, especially in the military, one of the few places where men can express their love for other men."

Ford's sexual preference has been much debated over the years. In her 2004 autobiography, *'Tis Herself,* Maureen O'Hara wrote of walking into a room where she discovered Ford kissing "a famous actor." She didn't name him, but the year was 1954 and that actor was Tyrone Power. Ford and he were filming *The Long Gray Line* (1955) at the time.

An inveterate pipe-smoker, Ford became known for chewing on a linen handkerchief. Each morning, his wife, the former Mary McBride Smith, would give him a dozen fresh handkerchiefs. At the end of shooting every day, the corners of the handkerchiefs would be chewed to shreds.

Whereas Ford evolved into a major player in Henry's life, he had a far greater influence in the career of Marion Michael Morrison. Ford and the future John Wayne met when the young man was a student at the University of Southern California. One summer, before his junior year, Morrison got a job at Fox as a "swing-gang" laborer," striking sets and moving props from one stage to another.

He was tall and thin, and quite handsome, an Irish-looking schoolboy. Over the years, rumors have claimed that in those early years, Ford fell in love with the future John Wayne and over a period of at least three years, performed fellatio on him.

Fort Apache was based on a 1947 story, "Massacre," by James Warner Bellah, which had appeared in *The Saturday Evening Post.* In part because of his idealistic, empire-building patriotism, some scholars have referred to Bellah as "The American Rudyard Kipling." But he had a bias. It was said that "the only Indian he liked was a dead Indian."

However, when Frank S. Nugent worked on the script, he got rid of all that

This triad of the most important actors in *Fort Apache* (1948) includes three of the most famous actors of their era:

1. A haggard-looking **Henry Fonda**, *left*, made up to look older than his age of 43 at the time;

2. A fast-blossoming **Shirley Temple,** made up to make her look more "womanly" (i.e., older) than her "barely legal" age of 20 at the time; and

3. **John Wayne**, a long-standing *protégé* of the director (John Ford) made up to look younger than his age of 41 at the time.

Whereas Wayne was the hero of the film, Henry played its unpopular and unbending "authority figure."

"I've never had such an unattractive role before," he said.

anti-Indian bias, portraying Native Americans instead with sympathy and respect.

As the arrogant Col. Owen Thursday, a former Civil War hero, Henry's character arrives at a frontier outpost, Fort Apache, to assume command. "With him is his fast-growing, late teenaged daughter, "Philadelphia" (Shirley Temple).

Thursday soon clashes with the level-headed Captain Kirby York (Wayne). The colonel is determined to engage the Indians, leading them in battle for his own glory.

Despite the warnings of York, the soldiers at the fort ultimately declare war against the forces of Cochise (Miguel Inclan)—an act of folly that will have dire consequences.

Philadelphia will fall in love with the handsome Lt. Michael Shannon O'Rourke (John Agar). The actors (Temple and Agar) playing these characters had become deeply involved with each other romantically. (They were engaged, in fact,) They'd eventually enter what evolved into a disastrous marriage (1945-1950). Agar's father in the movie was Sgt. Major O'Rourke, cast with Ward Bond, a close friend of both Henry and Ford.

Ford had assembled an awe-inspiring cast, arguably the best he had ever assembled. Many of the actors had been fabled stars of yesteryear.

Pedro Amendáriz, as Sgt. Beaufort, had recently co-starred with Henry in *The Fugitive* (1947).

The role of the corrupt Indian agent, Silas Meacham, went to Grant Withers, who had co-starred with Henry in *My Darling Clementine* (1946)..

Three former A-list stars, now reduced to minor roles, included Victor McLaglen as Sgt. Festus Mulcahy; Mae Marsh as Mrs. Gates; and George O'Brien as Capt. Sam Collingwood.

[McLaglen would star in seven movies with Wayne and Ford, and he had won an Oscar for his 1935 role in The Informer.

Before that, he had starred in the World War I classic, What Price Glory? *(1926). Over the years, he had worked with such stars as Marlene Dietrich and Humphrey Bogart. He would later be nominated as a Best Supporting Actor Oscar for his work in* The Quiet Man *(1952), that John Wayne classic.]*

By the time of her involvement in *Fort Apache*, Mae Marsh had morphed into a legend of the silent screen, having worked with Mack Sennett and D.W. Griffith. In *The Birth of a Nation* (1915), she had famously leaped to her death in lieu of submitting to the lustful advances of the so-called "Renegade Negro" who is later lynched by the KKK.

On the set of *Fort Apache*, Marsh had a reunion with Shirley Temple, with whom she had famously starred in *Rebecca of Sunnybrook Farm* (1932). Marsh had also appeared, previously, with Henry in *The Grapes of Wrath*.

George O'Brien had been a star in silent pictures, having appeared in Ford's "semi-Western," The Iron Horse (1924). A former boxer, he was proud of his physique and liked to be body-worshipped. He attracted the attention of the homosexual director F. W. Murnau, who maneuvered him frequently onto a casting couch.

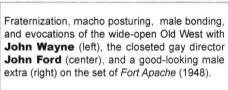

Two views of **George O'Brien** from the set of *Fort Apache*.

In the right photo, he's with **Henry Fonda,** in the broiling sunlight and between takes.

By the time O'Brien made Ford's *She Wore a Yellow Ribbon* (1949), his career was at twilight.

Location shooting was in Monument Valley, the setting of Henry's movie *The Immortal Sergeant* (1943), where it replicated the World War II landscapes of North Africa, and *My Darling Clementine,* in which it (accurately) evoked the arid landscapes of "the Great American West."

At the start of filming, Ford told Frank S. Nugent, "How can I go wrong with this film? Not with my two favorite men, Henry and The Duke, as the male leads!"

Since *Fort Apache* called for filming during young Peter Fonda's school vacation, it was decided that he would visit his father on location. It evolved into a memorable trip. He was driven there from Los Angeles by John Wayne in his ivory-colored convertible with flashy red upholsteries.

During the first day of shooting, Ford met with his actors, telling Henry, "I want you to appear as if there is a cold fire raging within you." To Wayne, he said, "I want you to play a brawler by instinct, yet one who has self-discipline."

Ford later said, "In the 1930s, for some four years, Shirley Temple was the top box office star in America. I felt *Fort Apache* might propel her into adult stardom. In fact, I paid her $100,000, the same as I did for Fonda and The Duke. But I was wrong about Miss Lollipop. She'd have a grand future, but not as a movie star. In her dressing room, that lollipop was replaced with John Agar's dick."

The handsome young Agar evolved into Ford's whipping boy throughout the production. "Everything I did was wrong. He shouted at me, humiliating me in front of cast and crew."

Temple had met Agar when she was 15, in 1943, and was immediately very attracted to him. Despite her young age, she married him two years later.

Agar detested Ford, but liked Wayne, and would appear with him in two more hits, *Sands of Iwo Jima* (1949) and *She Wore a Yellow Ribbon* (also 1949).

Agar would also try to salvage a final celluloid success with his wife, Shirley Temple, *Adventure in Baltimore* (1949) for RKO. *[It recorded a fiscal loss of $875,000.]* Major stardom would elude him, as did the success of his marriage to Temple. It ended in 1950.

Agar told Henry that he preferred to have two women in bed with him at the same time. "Otherwise, I'm not sexually satisfied, but Shirley refuses to grant my wish."

Back in Hollywood for interior shots, gossip columnist Hedda Hopper showed up one day on the set. She arrived after Henry had consumed three or four beers and was in a festive mood. He waltzed her around the floor. At one point, he removed his six-shooter from its holster and "mock-fired" three times into her back. He had been told that the gun was not loaded.

"Hedda nearly shit her pants," Ford said. "I warned Fonda never to do that again. He might have killed her."

Fort Apache earned $4.5 million at the box office. A leading film critic, James Agee, wrote, "Henry Fonda does well, if thinly, as the megalomaniacal martinet." Bosley Crowther of *The New York Times* found Henry, in his portrayal of the colonel, "fiercely stubborn and stiff with gallantry."

The movie was such a success that it saved Argosy from bankruptcy, taking in more receipts at the box office than *My Darling Clementine.*

Fort Apache would be Henry's last film before he (temporarily) transferred himself to Broadway as the star of *Mr. Roberts.*

***

The Broadway Play, *Mr. Roberts* (1948)

A freelancer at last, Henry, with a sense of what he called "quiet desperation," searched for his next film project. He thought he had found it the weekend he devoted to reading John O'Hara's novel, *Appointment in Samarra.*

[Henry's praise of O'Hara's 1934 novel was justified. Modern Library *now ranks it 22nd on its list of the 100 Best English-language novels of the 20th Century. Its plot concerns the self-destruction of a fictional character named Julian English, a rich Cadillac dealer, who, over the course of three days, destroys himself with a series of impulsive acts which culminate in suicide.*

Blue-nosed critics of the day attacked the book's depiction of sexuality. Sinclair Lewis, however, defined the novel's sensuality as "nothing but infantilism—the erotic visions of a hobbledehoy behind the barn."]

Leland Hayward was no longer Henry's agent, the job having been transferred to Lew Wasserman.

[Wasserman, a talent agent and studio executive, has been described as "the last of the

AMERICA'S GREATEST PLAY!
LELAND HAYWARD presents
HENRY FONDA
(IN PERSON)
Mister Roberts
THOMAS HEGGEN and JOSHUA LOGAN
ROBERT BURTON   CURTIS COOKSEY   DON FELLOWS

legendary movie moguls." He was the most powerful and influential Hollywood titan in the four decades that followed World War II. His career spanned nine decades, more or less flourishing until as late as 2000.

Wasserman's first job was as an usher in a movie theater. At his peak, he was president of MCA, spearheading that company's efforts to take over Universal.]

Wasserman quickly ascertained that a film adaptation of *Appointment in Sammara* had been green-lighted, and that Henry had nabbed the role and was already being outfitted for costumes. But after Henry's meeting with one of his long-time friends, the Broadway producer and director Josh Logan, Henry phoned his (new) agent (Wasserman), begging him to get him out of the picture.

"That I can do," Wasserman told him. "But you'll owe me one. And I always collect on my debts."

[During Henry's reunion with Logan, they had discussed the director's newest project, a Broadway-bound play called Mr. Roberts.

After rendezvousing with Logan after a long absence, Henry had cautioned him, "Let's don't go down memory lane and that summer back in Falmouth in 1928. We had our fights, we made up, and we argued again after that. But our best times happened when you came to live with Jimmy (Stewart) and me. All those fun nights. Now, let's bury all the secrets and never unearth them again."

Logan did, however, issue a latter-day appraisal of Henry: "No matter our differences, Henry Fonda is part of me, and I'm part of him. He is so intermingled in the intricacies of my web that I cannot ever be free of him. May he live forever."

When the director saw Henry's children, Jane and Peter, again, he was amazed at how they'd grown. "I think both of them are flashing some kind of frantic semaphore to the world as if to say, 'Look at me, I'm as big as he is.' It must be hard to grow up in the reflected light shed by an American symbol."

In 1945, after serving during World War II in the U.S. Army, Logan, a bisexual, returned to Broadway and married his second wife, Nedda Harrigan.

His success on Broadway was amazing. It began with the musical, Annie Get Your Gun *(1946-1949), which ran for 1,147 performances. He followed that with Anita Loo's* Happy Birthday *(1948; 563 performances), and Norman Krasna's* John Loves Mary *(1948-1949; 423 performances). Next would come his latest play,* Mr. Roberts, *the one he discussed during its early stages with Henry Fonda), which he both co-authored and would eventually direct. It would run for 1,157 performances and earn Tony Awards for Henry (as Best Actor), and Logan (as Best Director), and Leland Hayward (as Best Producer).*

After *Mr. Roberts,* Logan would co-author *South Pacific* (1949-1954), which won a Pulitzer Prize for Drama and another Tony for Logan.

To his fateful, long-delayed reunion with Henry, Logan brought with him a rough draft of *Mr. Roberts,* which he read to Henry over beers. It had been adapted in collaboration with the author—the doomed Thomas Heggen—of the novel on which it had been based.

Heggen, who had emerged from Fort Dodge, Iowa, had set his million-copy best-selling novel in World War II. Its hero was Lt. (j.g) Doug Roberts, the fictional alter ego of Heggen. During the war, Heggen had spent fourteen months aboard *The Virgo,* a broken-down rust bucket which he described as "sailing from Tedium to Apathy and back again, with an occasional side trip to Monotony."

Throughout the course of his novel, the protagonist butts heads with *The Virgo's* commander, a crude martinet, who repeatedly (some said sadistically") denies his request for transfer to a destroyer. In retaliation, Roberts throws the commander's palm trees—"pets" which have been lovingly cultivated—overboard.

During their long-overdue reunion, Henry sat across from Logan, listening intently as he read the play's script. When Logan was finished, Henry stood up, announcing, "I've got to take a beer piss, but I'll be back." When he returned, he had another announcement: "Fuck John O'Hara. I'm going to play Lt. Roberts. Call me Doug."

Logan then confessed, "Tom (Heggen) and I had you in mind as the star when we drafted the first page of our script."

From Tedium to Boredom And Back Is a Brisk Literary Sail

In 2016, the *Oklahoman*, a newspaper of record from his (and Henry's) home state, published an overview of **Thomas Heggen,** the author and naval veteran who had penned the at-sea saga of the play (*Mr. Roberts*) that made Henry Fonda a Broadway star.

Whereas he'd complained of being unable to cope with failure as a writer, Heggen had an equally hard time coping with success. Despite the spectacular box office success of his script for *Mr. Roberts*, he died of an alleged suicide after months of subsequent "writer's block" seemingly paralyzed him from writing anything else.

The next day, the first person Henry phoned about how he was temporarily abandoning Hollywood for the Broadway stage was his closest friend, James Stewart. "I want to go back on the stage to restore my soul. Forgive me for sounding so high-faulutin'. I've been stalking around the house always in a foul mood. I'm bored with Frances, bored with farming, and not getting off being a father. I might play a father in the future, but I'm not sure I actually want to be one. The kids know how frustrated I am, and I'm afraid I unfairly take it out on them."

"We'll miss you, brother," Stewart said. "Don't write me off. I'll be right there sitting in the front seat on opening night. You can bet your left butt cheek on that."

For a farewell party at his home, Henry was disappointed that Stewart could not make it, but John Wayne, Ward Bond, and movie stuntman Frank McGrath could attend. Duke (Wayne) and Bond dressed in what Henry called "cowboy drag."

At the end of the drunken evening, he embraced his friends, telling them, "Broadway here I come, right back where I started from."

Henry set out to fly East by himself, leaving Frances and the kids behind. His excuse for getting away by himself had to do with the fate of the play. "If it closes after two nights or a week, I'm coming back. But if it looks like it's in for a long run, I'll rent us a home outside the city. Greenwich, Connecticut, was recommended to me as an ideal place for a family with kids."

At this point in his life, Henry would not have been eligible as either "Husband of the Year" nor as "Father of the Year.".

An observer at that time wrote: "When Fonda came back from the horrors of the Pacific in World War II, he had crystallized into a hardened, distant man. He family got the worst of it. He had extreme difficulty expressing his emotions, and whenever he suspected that his wife or children were demanding feelings from him, he would have terrifying outbursts of anger that reverberated through the house."

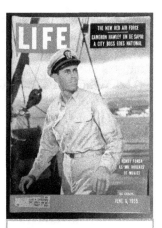

By the time he nabbed the leading male role in Broadway's ultimate "The Sacrifices of War" play, **Henry Fonda** had earned his stripes as one of the most admired actors in America's Entertainment industry.

Here, representing the play, the Navy, and probably America's new role as the world's pre-eminent superpower, he appears on the cover of *Life* magazine.

In another comment made about him, an insider said, "Fonda did a number on both his children in awful ways. Peter claimed that he never heard his father say, 'I love you' until he was elderly. Jane said that her father told her that 'unless you look perfect, you will never be loved.'"

Since his return from the war, Henry noticed that to an increasing degree, Frances had slipped into hypochondria, which in time would evolve into a serious case of mental illness. He no longer wanted to be her husband.

***

Back in Manhattan once again, Henry found a suite waiting for him at the Lombardy Hotel, where Josh Logan lived with his wife, Nedda.

After checking in, he wanted to walk the streets around Broadway, which he had first trod as an out-of-work actor. This time, there was one big difference: He was often stopped by an autograph seeker.

The next day, he reported to work at the Alvin Theater, where he had a reunion with Leland Hayward, who by now was no longer his agent, but his producer in this most recent stage endeavor, *Mr. Roberts*.

Hayward introduced Henry to key players in the cast right before the first read-through. His supporting players included David Wayne, Robert Keith, Jocelyn Brando, and William Harrigan. Harrigan, Logan's brother-in-law, had been cast as the ferocious captain. In minor roles were such actors as Harvey Lemeck, Ralph Meeker (who was headed for stage and screen stardom), Steven Hill, Lee Van Cleef, and Murray Hamilton.

The play was set in the Pacific theater during World War II. The U.S. cargo ship, the *Reluctant* (aka "Rust Bucket") and her crew sailed the backwaters of the war-torn ocean.

The full rank of the character Henry played was "Executive Officer and Cargo Chief Lt. (j.g.) Douglas A. Roberts. He tries to shield his disenchanted crew from the harsh commands of the crazed captain.

One by one, Henry got to know the other members of his cast. David Wayne would eventually cultivate a stage and screen career spanning half a century. In film history, he appeared in more Marilyn Monroe films than any other actor. They included *As Young as You Feel* (1951); *We're Not Married* (1952); *O'Henry's Full House* (1952); and *How to Marry a Millionaire* (1953).

The ship's doctor was played by Robert Keith, a character actor born in Indiana in 1898. His best-known roles were in future movies with Marlon Brando: the ineffectual police chief in *The Wild One* (1953) and a tough, no-nonsense cop in *Guys and Dolls* (1955).

Cast as the sailor Mannion, the brazenly macho Ralph Meeker would soon get his big break as a replacement for Marlon Brando in the stage role of Stanley Kowalski in *A Streetcar Named Desire* (1949). He also achieved Broadway success in William Inge's *Picnic* (1953), although he lost the role to William Holden when it was converted into a movie.

Many hopefuls tried, unsuccessfully, for the sailor roles, including Lee Marvin and Jack Lemmon. Ironically, Lemmon would be given the key roles of Ensign Pulver in the movie adaptation.

When Henry had a reunion with Jocelyn Brando, sister of Marlon, she said, "The last time we met, I was seven months old and I sat on your lap."

"Now you're older enough to do more," he said jokingly. *[Or did he mean it?]*

They talked of their days together in Omaha, and he expressed his life-long appreciation of her mother, whom he called "Doe," for having launched him into the theater.

In her role as a nurse, Brando was the only female in the cast. She told Henry that the part at first had gone to Eva Marie Saint until Logan concluded that she was "too beautiful."

"You're beautiful, too," Henry assured her.

Logan later said that during the early weeks of *Mr. Roberts,* Jocelyn and Henry had a fling that didn't last long.

In little more than a walk-on, Fess Parker was cast as one of the sailors. He later became a household name when he was cast in Walt Disney's *Davy Crockett: King of the Wild Frontier* (1955).

Near the end of the play, Lt. Roberts gets the transfer he desperately wants, to active duty aboard a destroyer. Shortly after his departure, his friends who remain onboard receive two letters: The first is from Roberts, who glowingly communicates his enthusiasm for his new assignment aboard a destroyer, the USS *Livingston,* during heavy bombardments near Okinawa. A follow-up letter, posted a few days later and laden with existential ironies, reveals that Roberts was killed in a Japanese kamikaze attack very shortly after being posted to the active wartime duties he so desperately yearned for.

"Fonda became Doug Roberts," Logan said. "He has deep within him a small but inextinguishable flame that burns in worship of the art of the theater. He is one of the high priests of that art. When he feels laxness, insincerity, dilettantism around him, Hank can fly into short-lived tantrums, and his votive flame can become a Holocaust. He was giving me the best of himself during the rehearsals of *Mister Roberts.*"

Ironically, a victim of the *Mister Roberts* saga—one who ended tragically in real life—was Thomas Heggen, the creator of the original *novella* on which the play was based. Bewildered by the fame that accompanied the play's success, enormous pressure was aimed at him to churn out another bestseller. He found himself with a crippling sense of writer's block. He evolved into an insomniac, trying to cure himself with alcohol and drugs.

On May 19, 1949, he was found drowned in his bathtub after overdosing on sleeping pills. He was only thirty years old.

After tryouts in Baltimore and New Haven, *Mr. Roberts* opened in Philadelphia on December 28, 1947 and got good reviews before it made its Broadway premiere on February 18, 1948.

From Philadelphia, columnist Walter Winchell was the first to signal that *Mr. Roberts* might be a hit. "The play appears to be a gilt-edged investment. It is being hounded by censors in the stix *(sic.)* and serenaded by reviewers, a surefire combination."

As was revealed later, the play's backers included Frances' mother, Mrs. Sophie Seymour. Columnist Hedda Hopper, and director Billy Wilder also put up cash. Leland Hayward confronted Wilder, reminding him that he had lent him $2,500 during the war, and "I'm going to deduct that amount from your first royalty check."

On opening night, the *glitterati* turned out to see it. James Stewart, as he'd promised, sat in the front row.

After the curtain went down to wild applause, a parade of distinguished visitors headed for its star's dressing room. Lee Wasserman joined Helen Hayes and her husband, Charles MacArthur, along with Irene Mayer Selznick, Henry Luce, Moss Hart, and Noël Coward.

Greta Garbo, who had known Stewart and Henry intimately when they were neighbors, came backstage. Without saying a word, she wet-lipped him and then hastily departed.

Other glittering guests included Marlene Dietrich, Dorothy Parker, and novelist John Steinbeck. Dorothy McGuire, who at the age of fourteen had starred onstage with Henry in Omaha, showed up with her husband, Johnny Swope, one of Henry's best friends.

Brooks Atkinson in *The New York Times* led off the critical appraisals of *Mister Roberts:* "Now that Mr. Fonda is back after eleven years, it would be nice to have him back for good. He has brought quite a lot of good will with him this time. As Roberts, he is lanky and unheroic, relaxed and genuine. He neatly skirts the maudlin and skillfully underplays the bombastic scenes."

Howard Barnes in the *New York Herald-Tribune* claimed, "Henry Fonda plumbs to the depths of the play's inner significance. He is every inch a star at the Alvin."

William Harking in the *New York World-Telegram* weighed in: "As Doug Roberts, Fonda is giving a great performance. He performs with innate simplicity, blending in undertones of charity and anguish that not only make the character a true person, but more importantly verify the passionate masculine devotion of the crew."

John Chapman in the *New York Daily Mirror* added a personal note: "Last night at the Alvin, the audience wouldn't go home until Mr. Fonda made a speech. Said he: 'This is all Tom and Josh wrote for us. If you want, we can start all over again.' I hung around for a while, hoping they would."

Louis Kronenberger in *PM Exclusive* shared his appraisal like this: "Henry Fonda gives an exemplary performance as Doug Roberts, neither ostentatiously underplaying his manly role in the British manner, nor somewhere hamming it after the manner in Hollywood."

Both *Newsweek* and *Life* put Henry on their respective covers, and Logan was given a spread in *Life.* At award season, Henry received a Tony for Best Male Performance, *Mister Roberts* was honored as best play of the season, winning the Antoinette Perry Award.

Two years after opening night, it was estimated that 1.3 million people had seen *Mr. Roberts* on Broadway.

Columnist Earl Wilson, writing in the *New York Post,* called the drama "one of the greatest plays of the decade."

John Lardner of *The New Yorker* wrote: "Logan and Heggan have written the best comedy, the best war play—to come right down to it, the best new play of any kind—that has been seen this season."

For a London opening, Tyrone Power was cast as Mister Roberts, signing a six-month contract for which he would be given ten percent of the gross. However, many among local theatre-goers denounced the play as "too American."

John Forsythe was also one of the actors who toured with the play in American cities, as did Henry himself.

***

Jigsaw (1949).

During the run of *Mister Roberts* on Broadway, Henry received a phone call from Franchot Tone, an actor he'd known during Tone's marriage to Joan Crawford in the late 1930s.

He asked Henry to join several stars who had agreed to appear in a cameo in his latest movie, a *film noir* crime thriller named *Jigsaw* (1949).

His co-star was the blonde-haired former fashion model, Jean Wallace. At the time, her marriage to Tone was breaking up. In 1946, she had attempted suicide by overdosing on sleeping pills. In 1949, she would attempt to fatally stab herself, but was rushed to the hospital in time to avert her death. After that, she married actor Cornel Wilde.

On the set of *Jigsaw,* Henry had a warm reunion with his longtime friend, Myron McCormick, a star of radio, film, and stage. He had worked with Henry in the late 1920s at the Cape Playhouse at Dennis (Cape Cod), Massachusetts.

Signing up for cameos were Marlene Dietrich, cast as a nightclub patron, Marsha Hunt, Burgess Meredith, Everett Sloane, and columnist Leonard Lyons.

Bosley Crowther reviewed this star cameo casting in *The New York Times:* "An irresistible temptation to get a few recognizable stars to play roles in the picture was accepted, unfortunately. John Garfield is seen as a loafer, and Henry Fonda as a waiter in a club, among other cameos. This tomfoolery doesn't help the picture. It gives the whole thing a prankish look."

Jigsaw bombed at the box office, doing little to advance the careers of its co-stars, **Franchot Tone** and his suicidal real-life wife, Jean Wallace. The cast was rounded out by Myron McCormick and Betty Harper.

Tone, the former "Mr. Joan Crawford," played a DA who investigates a murder. As the plot unfolds, he discovers an organized group of racial and religious bigots.

Henry appears in a cameo as a waiter in the Blue Angel night club, serving **Tone** and **Betty Harper,** the couple depicted above.

***

Since *Mr. Roberts* seemed to have acquired long-term squatter's rights at the Alvin Theater on Broadway, Henry decided the time had come to move his family to Greenwich, Connecticut. He also rented himself a one-room apartment in Manhattan, with the stated belief that he would visit his family briefly every week after the Saturday night show.

Neither Peter nor Jane wanted to leave California, but they had no choice.

Henry was in Manhattan when Frances arrived at their newly rented home, a historic home known throughout Greenwich as the Count Palenclar House.

It stood on twenty-three acres and took in two ponds, one suitable for swimming, and contained far more rooms than they needed. The building was painted white with black shutters and red doors. It had a four-car garage and an elevator inside, which Peter rode up and down endlessly during the first week.

In the basement, Henry discovered a mammoth walk-in vault filled with hundreds of canceled checks. At first, he thought he was rich until someone explained to him that a canceled check was worthless.

Ironically, after divorcing Leland Hayward, Margaret Sullavan had settled nearby. In those days, Greenwich was known as "very white, very Republican, and anti-Semitic." When its snobbish mayor heard that the Fondas had moved in, he said, "I think the family should have settled into the bohemian enclave of Greenwich Village. Our town is filled with respectable people, not Hollywood riffraff."

Brooke Hayward renewed her friendship with Jane, learning that she was no longer to be addressed as "Lady Jane." Whereas the Sullavan daughter saw Peter as "very fragile, Jane is made of tempered steel."

At least Jane could continue her passion for horseback riding in the fields of Connecticut. On occasion, she joined some of the locals in traditional fox hunts, equivalent to the kind they had in England.

As an example of the town's intolerance, yachtsman and producer David O. Selznick arrived aboard his yacht at one of the marinas in Greenwich with the hopes of picking up the Fondas. Port Authorities refused him docking space because he was a Jew.

The children didn't really want to change schools, but had to, with Peter being admitted to the Brunswick School. Jane became a uniformed student at Greenwich Academy, an all-girl's school. *[No fan of the prevailing snobbery at the time, she suggested that if a play were to be written about the town of Greenwich, it should be titled* Pretense and Prejudice.*]*

Henry's adopted daughter, Pan, was not part of the just-migrated new household in Greenwich, as she was enrolled at a boarding school in Baltimore.

There, she fell in love with Charles ("Bunny") Abry, the grandson of the chain store mogul R.H. Kress. When he impregnated her, the very young couple, each member of which was seventeen at the time, agreed to get married.

Henry and Frances each attended the wedding. Henry's last, and perhaps tactless, advice to Pan was, "You can always get a divorce."

In a surprise move, the newlyweds invited Frances to accompany them on their honeymoon in Europe. As a trio, they were photographed on France's *Côte d'Azur.*

Regrettably, after her return to the States, Pan had a miscarriage, although, according to some reports, a premature daughter was born and lived outside the womb for two hours.

Josh Logan noted that Henry seemed reluctant to take that trip from Manhattan to Greenwich even on his day off. He remained distant from his wife but took the kids fishing or engaged in some other activity. He told Logan, "I'm a restless soul."

"It was only later that I found out what was keeping him in town," Logan said. "He had taken a 20-year-old, socially connected, beautiful girl as his mistress."

As Henry told James Stewart back in Hollywood, "My self-esteem has been restored after some of those dumb movies I did for Zanuck. The audiences for *Mr. Roberts* have brought me back to life again. And a beautiful young, very young, gal joins me in bed at night."

***

Jane adjusted to life in the East more easily than her brother, Peter. Once he wrote on the walls of their home, "Fuck the East!"

He claimed that in California, they lived on fresh fruit and vegetables, but he remembered the meals served by the household staff in Greenwich as consisting of "Spam and tongue."

Eventually, for several reasons, Henry and Frances agreed to leave the Count Palenclar House and move into the Boomer House, also in Greenwich. Jane called it "an uncomfortable, Charles Addams-y, gloomy old house that was dark and chilly."

The grounds bordered a hardwood forest, and the house overlooked a tollgate on the Merritt Parkway.

Frances was often seen, in fair weather, chasing butterflies across nearby fields with a net.

Their mother would often disappear sometimes for weeks at a time. Upon her return, she never explained her absence. During those times, Sophie Seymour, the grandmother of Peter and Jane, would look after the children and run the household. Henry often stayed in Manhattan, even on his day off.

At one point, Sophie took Jane and Peter to visit their mother at Johns Hopkins Hospital, where she remained for two months, having suffered from a painful operation for a "floating" or "dropped" kidney. It left a huge and ugly red scar. Frances feared that her beauty had been seriously damaged.

She was moving into middle age, and she feared that Henry would never find her attractive again. He had long ago moved into a separate bedroom. She was the first to be aware of rumors that her husband was having an affair with a beautiful young girl in Manhattan.

At school, Jane was no longer allowed to wear the Western garb she had in Brentwood. Her new school demanded a uniform dress. She said that most of her schoolmates spoke "as if their jaws were wired together."

At the age of twelve, her height had begun to rapidly increase, and she intensely disliked "my puffy face. I look like a chipmunk with nuts stuffed in his jaw."

Widely analyzed in New York gossip columns, news about Henry's affair with a young woman even reached Jane's school. One particularly nasty classmate provocatively told her, "I hear your father has a teenaged mistress, who is a sex fiend. I'm told she wears him out so much that he can hardly get through his Broadway performance at night."

Jane turned and walked away, feeling hurt and depressed.

Finally, the time had come for Henry to tell Frances that he wanted a divorce. She was sitting up in bed when he came into her room and sat down beside her. He put his arm around her and said, "I want you to know I will always love you, as I will always love the two beautiful kids you gave me. But..." he hesitated. "I've fallen in love with someone else, and I want a divorce. You're still young and plenty charming enough to find a new love and a new life. In show biz, it will become known as your second act."

On the surface, Frances took the news calmly. "Well, all right, Hank, if that's your choice, I wish you all the happiness in the world."

He'd been amazed at how well she assimilated the information. But it was all a front. The very next day, Sophie walked in on her in the bathroom, where she was feeling her throat. "I'm trying to figure out where the jugular vein is."

Two hours later, Henry departed from their home after loading a lot of his wardrobe and personal possessions into the back of a rented station wagon. He was transferring his residence to Manhattan but promised Peter and Jane that he'd visit as often as possible.

Frances faced the new decade of the 1950s morbidly depressed—"My nerves are a wreck." That January, she checked into the Austen Riggs Psychiatric Hospital in Stockbridge, Massachusetts.

For a while, she seemed to recover a bit, but then her depressions returned. One afternoon, she pulled off her wedding ring and tossed it out the window. Later, she changed her mind and told the staff that she wanted it back.

It could not be found in the grass outside.

After checking out of the hospital, she went home. Jane and Peter found her very distant. During their talks with her, her mind seemed somewhere far away.

Day after day, dark depressions descended. Sophie phoned Henry in Manhattan to tell him about his wife's condition. Although he thanked her for looking after Jane and Peter, he made it known that he was too busy to return, even briefly, to Greenwich,

He cautioned Sophie that "I don't want Frances committed to some god damn loony bin. How would that look for me, a star on Broadway? The tabloids would have a field day."

One afternoon, after Frances went into a fit of screaming hysteria, Sophia

ACTOR, SOCIETY BEAUTY TO WED

Mrs. George T. Brokaw and daughter, with Henry Fonda, inset

From Paris comes news of a surprise engagement between Henry Fonda, rising young romantic screen star, and Mrs. George T. Brokaw, New York society leader. Mrs. Brokaw, the former Frances Seymour, is pictured above with her daughter, Frances De Villers Brokaw. Fonda is shown, inset. No date for the wedding has been set.

JUST MARRIED

made arrangements to have attendants arrive and strap her into a straitjacket. She was delivered to Craig House Sanitarium, a gloomy scattering of buildings, some of which housed the criminally insane, at Beacon, New York. The doctor assigned to her was Courtney Bennett.

When spring came, Frances expressed a desire to return home. "I want to see the dogwoods burst into bloom. It will give me hope."

That didn't happen. Henry agreed to release her so she could visit Peter and Jane on April 1, 1950. When the time arrived, her children watched from a second-floor window of their rented house as an ambulance carrying her pulled into the driveway.

Two white-jacketed attendants escorted her into the house. Although she was too emotional to have any meaningful dialogue with her children, she told each of them how much she loved them. She was especially affectionate with Peter, her favorite, hugging and kissing him.

She disappeared briefly into an upstairs bathroom and emerged with a small white box. She said she wanted to take it back to the hospital with her as a "keepsake." Unknown to attendants there, the box contained a razor that she used to shave her legs.

When she left, Jane and Peter stood out front waving her goodbye. They could not have known at the time that it was their final farewell.

The last words Jane heard were, "I didn't get to tell Jane something I want her to know." For the rest of her life, Jane wondered what that last communication might have been.

Back at the Craig House Sanitarium, a week went by. At 6:30AM on the morning of April 14, 1950, a nurse, Anne Grey, carried a breakfast tray to Frances' room. The patient was not in her bed. A note pasted to the outside of her (closed) bathroom door read "Don't enter the bathroom. Call Dr. Bennett."

The night before, Frances had phoned her mother, telling her, "I will not live to suffer through that divorce from Henry."

Within minutes, Bennett and an intern broke into the bathroom, where they found Frances lying in a pool of blood. With the razor, she had slashed her throat, but she was still alive—at least she'd be for twenty more minutes—as the doctor tried to stanch the flow of precious blood from her bleeding throat.

It was her birthday. She had committed suicide.

Dr. Bennett spotted yet another note on the toilet seat. It read: "I'm sorry, but I feel this is the best way out."

Henry was the first person Sophie called with the tragic news.

He remembered "driving like a bat out of hell," arriving at a mortuary in Hartsdale, New York. Her body had been moved there from the Craig House Sanatorium.

Sophie and Henry agreed that there would be no funeral, only a few words said over Frances' casket by a local pastor. A hearse then carried her body to be cremated, followed by a burial in the Seymour family plot at a cemetery in Hartsdale.

Both Sophie and Henry agreed that Peter and Jane would be told that Frances had died of a heart attack.

Dr. Bennett later told the press, "I detested Henry Fonda, a completely self-absorbed narcissist."

Henry had been cut out of Frances' will. Her cash assets were valued at $650,000, with sixty percent going to Sophie, the rest to Peter and Jane.

While still married to the suicidal Frances, Henry launched an affair in Manhattan with a beautiful young woman, **Susan Blanchard.**

When Jane met her, she said, "Susan is everything I aspire to be." Susan became like a big sister to Jane.

When Peter met Susan, he said, "She's young enough for me to marry—not a middle-aged guy like dear ol' Dad!"

***

As a teenage girl, Susan Blanchard had developed a crush on Henry, going to see all the movies he made in the late 1930s and early 1940s. Her favorite was *Jezebel*, in which he had co-starred with Bette Davis. Susan had seen that film three times.

While starring on Broadway in *Mr. Roberts*, Henry had been invited to a party by Billy Hammerstein, Susan's half-brother. Henry accepted the invitation, and soon found that at the age of 45, he was the oldest person there. Nevertheless, guests at the party were aware that he was a big movie star.

It was Billy who introduced Henry to Susan.

A young socialite, Susan Clurman, witnessed the event. "When Fonda met Susan Blanchard, his face lit up with a kind of moon glow. No wonder. She was a marvelous-looking girl—no makeup, a simple hairdo. She was my friend. When not dressed up for a party, she wore jeans and a T-shirt. She was the most honest and real human being I had ever met. I can understand why Fonda was drawn to her. The moment he met her, I truly believe he had started to fall in love, in spite of the fact that he was old enough to be her Dad. And married."

Henry also recalled his coming together with Susan: "Her long, blondish hair hung down her back, and she looked like Alice in Wonderland." He would later change that description to, "Susan looked like what the Madonna looked like before she gave birth to Jesus. She was almost 21, and unbelievably pretty, a real tomato after my own heart."

Weeks later, when Jane heard her father referring to Susan as a tomato, she said, "If Susan is a tomato, then she is the sweet, sun-ripened kind that grows in the fields of California."

At the time, although Henry was still legally married to Frances—against his better impulses—he made a play for Susan. She wanted to respond to him in like measure, but she held him off for at least three weeks. However, she was falling in love with him.

"He was so sad and lonely," she told Clurman. "He said to me that Frances had not been his real wife for the last three years. They had grown apart. Even if staying under the same roof, which was rare, they were completely alienated from each other. That's what Hank told me, and I believe him."

Susan became Henry's mistress, and, for the most part, spent her nights with him at his apartment on the top floor of a brownstone on East 77th Street.

As they grew more confident about their relationship, she introduced him to her family.

She was the daughter of Dorothy Blanchard, a native of Australia, and of Henry Jacobson, a New York businessman. After her mother got a divorce, Susan chose to use her mother's maiden name of Blanchard. Dorothy then wed Oscar Hammerstein II. The composer therefore became Susan's stepfather.

On October 28, 1950, Henry delivered his final performance of *Mister Roberts* on Broadway. He had to leave the cast because of a painful injury to his (torn) knee cartilage, which would require surgery. He was told that it would take two months of recuperation "before your knee is back in circulation."

Jane was introduced to Susan when she went to call on her father in a Manhattan hospital after his knee surgery. When Jane entered his private room, she spotted what she later described as "the most beautiful woman I've ever seen." Susan was nine years older than Jane.

"Her hair was pulled back tightly into a large *chignon* that accentuated her pale blue, slanted eyes, not unlike my mother's. The angels must have climbed over our prostrate hearts to bring Susan to us."

In the aftermath of Frances' suicide, Henry made a remark to Josh Logan that he considered insensitive.

"Now that Frances is dead, I can marry Susan right away and not have to go through the horror of an awful divorce."

Three days after celebrating Christmas of 1950, Henry and Susan were married by Dr. Everett Clinchy, the president of the National Conference of Christians and Jews.

The wedding was held at the Hammerstein townhouse on East 63rd Street in Manhattan. The Hammersteins were busy that day: Later, they attended the wedding of John Steinbeck to Elaine Scott, the former wife of actor Zachory Scott.

The first night of the Fonda/Blanchard honeymoon was spent in a suite at the Plaza Hotel in Manhattan. The next morning, they flew to St. Thomas in the U.S. Virgin Islands. There, they transferred, by boat, to the neighboring island of St. John. They registered at the Caneel Plantation House, where they planned to spend two idyllic weeks.

However, on the second night of their honeymoon, they were awakened by a loud pounding on their door. A member of the Coast Guard, via his short wave radio, had received horrible news.

Susan Blanchard with **Henry Fonda.**

The daughter of Dorothy Hammerstein from a previous marriage, often dressed only in a T-shirt and jeans, Susan was part of theatrical "high society" in New York City.

"She does not need to enhance her natural beauty," Henry said. "She is 21, I am 44. But we are of the same age."

Susan Blanchard wore white during her wedding to **Henry Fonda.**

Teenaged Peter Fonda was skeptical of the union, fearing that the bride would get more of a headmaster than a husband.

"He's astonishingly restrictive," he warned her. "Whatever you do, don't cry in front of him. He finds tears disgusting."

Staggering to the door, Henry opened it to hear "Your son has shot himself. He's dying."

***

On St. John, during the early morning hours, Henry and his bride, Susan, packed hurriedly and boarded a boat to St. Thomas, where a taxi rushed them to the airport. An early morning plane was leaving for Bermuda. They boarded it, knowing that from Bermuda, they could transfer via frequent air links, to New York. At stopovers *en route*, Henry put through calls to Manhattan, learning more details.

His son was still fighting for his life. Peter's grandmother, Sophie Seymour, explained as best she could.

It was later detailed what had happened: For Christmas, teenaged Peter had pleaded with Henry to give him a .22 rifle, and to teach him how to use it.

While his dad was away on his honeymoon, he had convinced Sophie to unlock the rifle and let him carry it, with two other boys, to the fields. He knew the gun was unloaded, but he just wanted to carry it and pretend to be a hunter on a bird shoot. She agreed, and off he went with two of his friends, Tony Abry,

Teenaged **Jane,** her father **Henry**, and young **Peter** around the time of his "hunting accident."

Perhaps because of the sweet, innocent look on the faces of his kids, Henry had not a clue that Peter would ride a motorcycle into film history, and that daughter Jane would become both an intergalactic sex kitten and a leftist radical nicknamed "Hanoi Jane."

Pan's brother-in-law, and Reed Armstrong, her husband's nephew. A chauffeur drove them to the Abry estate, which had a shooting range.

Armstrong showed Peter a historic antique pistol that had belonged to a distant relative during the Civil War.

As Peter later confessed, "The trigger laid up against the stern like a derringer. I put in the shell, and when I closed it, the whole fucking mechanism spun around and discharged right into me. The bullet hit my rib cage, blew off a piece of my liver, and tumbled into my stomach. It just missed my aorta, slammed right through the center of my kidney, and made just a lump on the skin of my back next to my spine."

The chauffeur hustled him into the back seat of his car and rushed him to the hospital at nearby Ossining, which was near the Sing-Sing prison.

On the operating table, Peter's heart stopped beating three times, but was revived. Fortunately, the chief prison doctor at Sing Sing, Charles Clark Sweet, was available. As the prison doctor, he was on expert on gunshot wounds.

"I was out and didn't know a thing," Peter recalled. "But this wonderful doctor saved my life with all his probing, digging, sewing, stitching, and patching me up to live again."

After the doctor emerged from the operating theater, he faced Henry, Susan, and Peter's sister, Jane, who had recently arrived on the scene.

"It's a fifty-fifty chance for Peter," Sweet said. "the wounds are very, very serious."

"Dear god!" Jane almost screamed. Henry looked grim-faced, and Susan, who didn't really know Peter, was on the verge of tears.

It took an entire week of tears, bitter remorse, and fear until the doctor told the Fondas that Peter's condition had stabilized.

That was followed by a month of recuperation before he could be released for home care with around-the-clock nurses.

In the meantime, the tabloid press heralded fake news that Peter had attempted to commit suicide in the wake of his mother's suicide.

Peter retained a lingering memory of sitting out on a porch overlooking the Sing-Sing prison: "On certain nights, the lights in the hospital dimmed. That meant it was 'fry day' at Sing-Sing. Some poor guy was being dragged to the electric chair. Probably fighting, kicking, and screaming all the way until he was bolted in and given the fatal juice."

During his recuperation, Peter got to know Susan, his new mother, who took loving care of him, nursing him back to health, even partially holding him up as he took awkward steps from the wheelchair, learning to walk again.

Peter later said, "Susan was like a good mother to me, and she was beautiful, full of fun and all the right things. I found her loving and kind and she came into my life when I really needed a mother."

He concluded that "when I grow up, I'm gonna marry a gal like the gal who married dear 'ol Dad."

When he was at last able to return to school, his classmates greeted him with a cake on which was written, in icing, "HAPPY BIRTHDAY TO LEAD BELLY PETER."

***

FONDA REACTS to
James Stewart and Donna Reed in
It's a Wonderful Life (1946):

Both Henry and James Stewart, still his best friend, joined a list of former movie stars returning home after the rigors of World War II. All of them wondered if they would find a niche in a post-war Tinseltown. By now, many box office star attractions of the 1930s were out of work, at least some of them scrounging for any part on "Poverty Row."

Henry and Stewart joined war veterans like Tyrone Power, Robert Taylor, and Clark Gable, hoping to re-establish their image on the screen.

New stars had emerged during the 1950s, and many others were on their way. Gregory Peck and Robert Mitchum each became major postwar stars in the Eisenhower era. Others included James Dean, Marlon Brando, Rock Hudson, Tab Hunter, Montgomery Clift, Steve McQueen, and Paul Newman.

Although Louis B. Mayer talked with Stewart about renewing his contract with MGM, he opted to be a free lancer instead.

After the war, Stewart and Henry spent a lot of time together, mulling over what to do with the rest of their lives and careers.

During one of their long weekends together, Stewart became more despondent than ever about his future movie career. He told Henry that his father wanted him to return home, marry a nice girl, have kids, and open, perhaps, a hardware store.

Henry urged him to "Hang in there. Your day will come."

That day would, indeed, come for Stewart. But not immediately, and not with his next movie. He had been careful with his money and considered becoming an investor in Southwest Airways, founded by his former agent, Leland Hayward. If his film career didn't ignite, he thought he might aim for an executive post in the aviation industry.

As a free lancer, MCA took over his career, morphing him into one of the first big name, independently contracted, actors with the freedom to choose his roles.

Frank Capra arrived one day with a script called *It's a Wonderful Life*. It would morph Stewart into an involvement in his third (and final) Capra movie. The producer had paid $10,000 to acquire the rights from RKO. The newly established Liberty Films offered its female lead, in this order, to Ginger Rogers, Olivia de Havilland, Ann Dvorak, and Martha Scott.

Each of those actresses turned him down. Jean Arthur, Stewart's co-star in *Mr. Smith Goest to Washington*, later revealed that Capra had first come to her with the script, too.

Henry Fonda and about six other actors had rejected the male and female leads in what has become a Christmas classic, *It's a Wonderful Life*, and even its "turned around" hero (James Stewart) had, for a while, referred to its script as "a piece of shit."

But later, after it burst into the public eye as a joyfully durable classic, he changed his mind.

In the press photo above, **Henry Travers**, playing a guardian angel, "rescues" **James Stewart** from a life of bitterness and regret.

After all these rejections, Donna Reed (real name, Donna Mullenger) gladly accepted the role. *[Her name had been changed from Mullenger to Reed based on the anti-German sentiment that followed the grisly ending of World War II.]*

Before her movie gig with Stewart, Reed had been a popular pin-up girl during the war and had made Andy Hardy movies with Mickey Rooney. She had also portrayed a nurse in John Ford's *They Were Expendable* (1945) with Duke Wayne.

The screenplay for *It's a Wonderful Life* had had a long and somewhat rugged history. In November of 1939, Philip Van Doren Stern wrote the original story, *The Greatest Gift*. It was rejected by fifteen publishers. Eventually, it ended up on the desk of RKO producer David Hampstead, who tried to interest Cary Grant in it.

Grant had instead preferred to make *The Bishop's Wife* instead. It, too, evolved into a Yuletide morale booster.

[RKO had acquired its rights for $10,000, and hired three different writers (one of whom was Dalton Trumbo) to develop a script.]

After four years of crafting World War II documentaries, Frank Capra returned to Hollywood and "Fell in love with the script of *It's a Wonderful Life.*"

[Before it reached the screen, its script included lines written by Clifford Odets, Marc Connelly, and even Dorothy Parker, who had been imported for "polishing." Some scenes had actually been written by Capra himself, aided by Albert Hackett and Frances Goodrich.]

Its lead role of George Bailey was first offered to Henry Fonda, who had already signed for another movie. Capra then presented it to Stewart, who he had last directed in *Mr. Smith Goes to Washington.* Stewart defined it as, "The biggest piece of shit I've ever read." Obviously, he later changed his mind.

Rounding out the cast were such strong supporting players as Thomas Mitchell, Beulah Bondi, Frank Faylen, Ward Bond, and Gloria Grahame.

In the plot, George Bailey is frustrated with his small town life financial woes. He has abandoned his personal hopes and dreams. On Christmas Eve, he contemplates suicide, but is saved by the intervention of his guardian angel (Henry Travers). The angel reveals to George how he has enriched the lives of his family and community, and what the town of Bedford Falls would have lost had he never been there.

After its release, *It's a Wonderful Life* received mixed reviews and a poor box office. Even so, it was nominated for Best Picture Academy Award, losing to Samuel Goldwyn's *The Best Years of Our Lives.* Stewart lost the Best Actor Oscar to the star of that Goldwyn hit, Fredric March.

Ultimately, Capra's Liberty Pictures filed for bankruptcy. The copyright on *It's a Wonderful Life* expired and was not renewed. Today, it's shown on television sets across the nation every year at Christmas.

Stewart's alltime favorite review came from Harry S Truman at the White House. "If Bess and I had a son, we would want him to be Jimmy Stewart."

***

Best Buddies In Magic Town (1947):
Jane Wyman Emotes with Jimmy Stewart, as "Reviewed" by Henry Fonda

Lew Wasserman, recently configured as the agent for both Henry Fonda and James Stewart, secured roles for both actors in the immediate post-war era.

Looking back, Stewart reflected to Henry, "Lew shopped me around like a Saturday night whore going from bed to bed at United Artists."

Before most of his Wasserman-era films were released, Stewart faced a reporter from *The New York Times.* He had flown to Hollywood to write an article to be headlined *The Rise and Fall of James Stewart.*

Stewart assumed that as an actor, he was in "safe hands" when director William A. Wellman helmed him in *Magic Town,* a 1947 comedy for RKO. In it, he'd co-starred with Jane Wyman, who was still married at the time to Ronald Reagan.

In 1943, after its release, Henry had invited Stewart to a screening of *The Ox-Bow Incident,* and Stewart had been impressed with the way Wellman had helmed his best friend.

After the war, *Magic Town,* written and produced by Robert Riskin, and directed by William Wellman, was one of the first films about the then-newfangled "science" of public opinion polling.

According to the plot, the little town of Grandview is said to fairly accurately reflect the opinions of small towns throughout America.

"Rip" Smith (Stewart) is a former basketball player and ex-military man who runs a company which conducts polls and consumer surveys. He lands in Grandview, where he meets Mary Peterman (Wyman), a newspaper reporter.

James Stewart, getting *goo-goo* and *gaa-gaa* with Ronald Reagan's "First First Lady"," **Jane Wyman**, in *Magic Town.*

Eventually they fall in love, but not before she writes an angry editorial attacking Rip in the local newspaper.

At least temporarily, Grandview blossoms as "the public opinion capital of the United States."

On their first day of work, Wellman greeted both Stewart and Wyman, predicting that "Both of you will walk home with the gold after this picture is released."

How wrong he was.

Stewart and Wyman had sustained a fling during her days as a starlet in the 1930s. They lunched together in the Commissary, where she confessed that her wartime marriage to Ronald Reagan was falling apart.

Over hamburgers, he said, "Do Fonda and I have to apologize for taking advantage of you when you were just a pretty but innocent gal struggling up the Hollywood ladder?"

"Innocent, my foot!" she answered. "I had screwed around with Errol Flynn, Clark Gable, and Robert Taylor and had already been married twice. I'd later fall in love with John Payne before marrying Reagan on the rebound."

A bespectacled **Jane Wyman** comforting her soon-to-be husband, **Ronald Reagan,** later President of the United States, in *Brother Rat and a Baby.*

Silly and superficially collegiate, it was released in 1940, the year of their marriage.

She later chided him: "I know that you and Hank played the field, seducing some really big stars, and that he is now married. But Hedda Hopper is still convinced that you guys are queer. She's suspicious because, unlike Fonda, you're forty years old and still unmarried."

"I enjoy the bachelor life too much to settle down, although I'm still waiting to meet the right gal."

"Well, please consider me if I go ahead and divorce Ronnie?" Wyman said. "I think I'd be great as the first Mrs. James Stewart. If *Magic Town* is a big hit, we might become a screen team like Hepburn and Tracy."

"That's a very interesting proposition," he answered.

To beef up a sagging box office, RKO ran a sexy picture of Stewart and Wyman under the headline

THEIR LOVE JEOPARDIZED THE HAPPINESS OF THOUSANDS.

One critic asked, "Just who is Wyman impersonating? Perhaps Irene Dunne. No, Claudette Colbert. No, definitely Jean Arthur."

Producer Wellman certainly changed his mind. "The picture stinks," he said. "If you think *Magic Town* has anything good about it, there's something wrong with you."

Henry went to see it and, officially, at least, had nothing but praise for his friend and his performance. He phoned Stewart. "Kid, you were just great. You showed us you still have that old Jimmy Stewart magic."

"You wouldn't be bullshitting me, would you, Hank?"

***

Call Northside 777 (1948)

On March 7, 1947, it was announced in the arts section of *The New York Times* that Henry Fonda's next picture would be called *Call Northside 777.*

Its script was based on the life story of a real victim, Joseph Majczek, who had been convicted in Chicago of a murder charge in 1932, about a year before the end of Prohibition, during one of the most violent years in the history of organized crime.

Warners had pioneered gangster films during the 1930s, nurturing the careers of

All the tenets of *film noir* appear in this press photo for *Call Northside 777:* Spooky lighting, high tensions, and neuroses pouring from its lead players, **James Stewart** (left, a last-minute replacement for Henry Fonda) and an early-in-his-career **Lee J. Cobb.**

"tough guys" who included Edward G. Robinson, George Raft, Humphrey Bogart, and James Cagney.

But after World War II, Hollywood *film noir* and *cinema verité*, "ripped from newspaper headlines," were enjoying a profit-generating vogue. A new wave of actors had walked into the spotlight: Dan Duryea, Dana Andrews, Richard Widmark, Richard Conte, Victor Mature, and Robert Mitchum, who evolved into a key player in these new dramas.

Two months later, *Variety* reported that Henry had bowed out of *Call Northside 777* to co-star with Joan Crawford in *Daisy Kenyon*. His replacement was James Stewart. Henry Hathaway, who had helmed Henry in *Spawn of the North* (1938), was assigned to direct.

Henry called Stewart to discuss the ironies and perhaps to chide him. "So now you're reduced to taking my sloppy seconds, not only in women—Margaret Sullavan comes to mind—but in movies, too."

"Cut the crap!" Stewart answered. "You know I'm a better actor than you are. You're known as Mr. Stone Face."

"We should be jealous rivals," Henry said. "Why aren't we?"

"Hell if I know," Stewart said. "Why don't you go fly a kite this weekend?" Then he paused. "With me, your best buddy, by your side to keep you from lifting off from the ground."

In *Call Northside 777*, the city editor of the *Chicago Times* (Lee J. Cobb) assigns his ace reporter, P.J. McNeal (Stewart) to investigate if Joseph Majczek had been wrongly convicted. *[For the film, his name was changed to Frank Wiecek.]* Richard Conte agreed to portray him. Actress Helen Walker played the female lead. She had divorced her first hus-

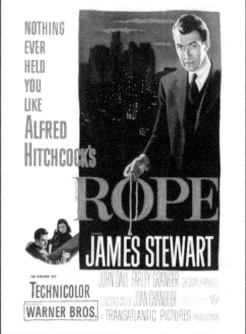

band, Robert F. Blumofe, and had not remarried. As Stewart told Henry, "Helen was ripe for the picking, and I plucked her right off the vine."

"Is 'pluck' the word you meant to say?" Henry asked, jokingly.

Brusque and pragmatic, and committed to cinematic "authenticity," Hathaway later took the cast and crew to Chicago for location shooting.

After seeing *Call Northside 777* with his wife, Susan, Henry told her, "This movie has put Jimmy back on the auction block, and he'll get a lot of job offers. But he was too lovable to be a tough-minded reporter. The role really called for a son-of-a-bitch like me."

***

Alfred Hitchcock and his "experimental' murder thriller, Rope *(1948)*

The great English director, Alfred Hitchcock, born during the last summer of the 19th Century, had long wanted to cast Henry Fonda in one of his movies. In time, he would get his wish, but not at first.

For his 1942 spy thriller, *Saboteur*, "Hitch" thought Henry might play the lead of Barry Kane, who is falsely accused of torching a wartime aircraft factory in Glendale, California.

Henry had not been his first choice. Hitchcock had envisioned it as a film that would star Gary Cooper and Barbara Stanwyck. Coop had practically tossed the script back at the director. Hitchcock later offered the role to Henry, with the hope of pairing him with one of Henry's favorite actresses, Barbara Stanwyck. After pitching his casting idea to both of them, they each rejected his offer.

As the key players in *Saboteur*, Hitchcock ended up with two lesser stars, Priscilla Lane and Robert Cummings, who—although he could be effective in drama—had been more frequently associated with comedic roles. Hitchcock would cast him again in *Dial M for Murder* (1954).

In 1944, Hitchcock made a wartime movie, *Lifeboat*, which evolved into the final film role Tallulah Bankhead ever accepted. That film is set entirely aboard a lifeboat launched from a cruise line's passenger ship torpedoed by a Nazi U-boat.

Once again, Hitchcock wanted either Gary Cooper or Henry as the male lead, knowing that each of them had had affairs with Bankhead

Lovers and thrill-seeking murderers (played by **Farley Granger**, *left*, and **John Dall**, *right)*, evade the questions of their suspicious professor, played by James Stewart (*center*).

It's the philosophical tenets of the professor, the viewer learns, which have inspired the "hate crime."

in the 1930s. "As it turned out, neither of them wanted to get in that lifeboat with the mink-clad Tallulah. I had to settle on John Hodiak, who ended up on her casting couch."

Once again, Hitchcock came across a property he felt would be ideal for Henry in the lead. The original story with its homosexual theme was based on the play, *Rope* by Patrick Hamilton. Its plot focused on a real-life murder committed by two Chicago students, Nathan Leopold and Richard Loeb, who in 1914, with the intention of committing "the perfect murder," killed 14-year-old Bobby Franks.

An English actor, Hume Cronyn worked on the screen adaptation alongside Arthur Laurents, who finished the final script. Laurents' greater successes lay in his future: The stage version of *West Side Story* (1957), *Gypsy* (1959); and *The Way We Were* (1973).

Homosexuality could not be openly depicted on the screen at the time, so Hitchcock knew he had to be subtle. Leopold and Loeb—each a brilliant but twisted young aesthete—ended up being played by John Dall as Brandon Shaw and Farley Granger as Philip Morgan.

At the time, Granger and the film's scriptwriter, Arthur Laurents, were lovers, and Dall was seducing any member of the crew who "measured up."

These young actors had second and third billing. The actual star role was the character of Rupert Cadell, a professor of philosophy for both of the young men. He taught them lessons from the writings of Nietzsche. He suspects they are guilty of murder, and he visits their apartment to investigate the crime because he fears that his teachings may have unintentionally inspired it.

The body of the dead boy is actually hidden in an antique chest in their living room. The closed lid of the coffin serves as a table from which a buffet is served.

Hitchcock asked both Henry and then Cary Grant to play the role of the professor, but each of them turned him down.

Hitchcock then asked James Stewart, who accepted the role even though he was miscast. Stewart's triumph with Hitchcock lay in his future in such pictures as *Rear Window* (1954) and *The Man Who Knew Too Much* (1956).

Midway through the shoot, Stewart talked to Henry, fearing that the homosexual context of the movie might revive old rumors that he and Henry had themselves engaged in a homosexual relationship in the 1930s.

"Don't worry about it," Henry said. "Those rumors will never go away."

When Stewart was finally able to screen the final cut of *Rope* for Henry, the star of the picture said, "As you can plainly see, this film just doesn't work. Only Hitch would have tried it."

Warners earned about $3 million at the box office, and *Rope* was banned in both Chicago and West Germany.

***

Henry Fonda with Susan Blanchard, on Tour with Mister Roberts:

From Charleston, South Carolina, to Cleveland, *Mister Roberts* was a stage hit on a nationwide tour. For most of it, Henry's wife, Susan, joined him. Peter and Jane were away at boarding schools.

Many times, Henry visited a city for the first time, delivering performances in Denver, Kansas City, or St. Paul.

There was the occasional mishap: The Fort Des Moines Hotel caught fire one night, but the cast escaped. The elevator operator, a teenaged girl named Joan Galuska, passed out during her escape, and firemen asked Henry to give her artificial respiration. The 17-year-old spent the rest of her life dining out about the night she went "mouth to mouth" with Henry Fonda.

Leaving Minneapolis late one night by train after a performance, the cast and crew faced a violent storm. It was so disruptive that they did not reach Henry's hometown of Omaha in time for that night's performance.

Even when the props still hadn't arrived by the following evening, Henry had to go out and explain to residents of his hometown where each of the props would otherwise have been placed on the stage, including the towering hull of *The Reluctant,* the (sociopathic) captain's palm tree, and the ship's turrets and hatches.

After additional performances in Seattle, the company moved on to San Francisco, where they confronted the play's director, Josh Logan, who wanted to see what had happened to "my play" during its interim on the road.

Logan sat through a performance of his "gently revised" production and was bitterly disappointed. He assembled the cast after the curtain went down and accused Henry of having drained all the comic relief from the play, which Logan interpreted as "too solemn, too grim."

In the explosive confrontation that followed, the long-time friends became almost violent.

Henry phoned Leland Hayward the next day, knowing he was involved in selling *Mister Roberts* to the movies. He told him, "I will not be your star if Logan is the director."

Hayward wasn't particularly disturbed at this news. Only the day before, he'd learned that Warners thought Henry was too old for the movie role he'd previously "perfected" on the Broadway stage.

In fact, Jack Warner had ordered Hayward during his discussion about Warner's possible involvement in a film adaptation of *Mr. Roberts,* "NOT FONDA! Give us Marlon Brando, or maybe William Holden."

At this point in his career, **Henry Fonda**, had emerged as a "*vedette* (star) *du cinema,*" even in Paris, a long long way from the dusty plains of Oklahoma and *The Grapes of Wrath.*

Here, he appears in a French postcard from 1954, smiling out at a world that was gratefully—albeit with confusion about what would come next—celebrating a world no longer at war.

In a 1962 edition of *The Village Voice,* Andrew Sarris claimed that Henry Fonda "is our most truthful actor. His body commands the screen without appearing hyper-virile. His bearing suggests something like morality, a sort of ethics of posture and gait: Upright and humane, empathetic if also stoic and withdrawn. On film, he repeatedly bears the values and burdens of civilization."

Barry Monush gave his summation: "Many have revered Fonda as the best actor there ever was. In his quiet, unmannered, straightforward way, he is a front-runner for that honor. A star for more than 45 years, he was the very embodiment of an idealistic level of integrity, shy yet forceful, manly yet sensitive, deliberate of speech with both thought and feeling behind each word, and stubbornly All-American."

Director Josh Logan wrote, "Henry Fonda's mind, his dedication to his art, and his brooding, sad face have always been one of the great influences of my life. No matter what our differences, Fonda is part of me, and I'm part of him. He is so intermingled in the interstices of my web that I cannot ever get free of him. May he live forever, for when Fonda smiles, the theater smiles."

WHILE FACING A MIDLIFE CRISIS ABOUT WHAT TO DO AND WHO TO BE,
AND REJECTING SEVERAL GOLDEN OPPORTUNITIES IN CLASSIC FILMS

HENRY RETURNS, AGAIN, TO BROADWAY

MORE ABOUT JOAN CRAWFORD

"She was still hot for me."
—Henry Fonda

THE LOVE GODDESS OF THE 40s

AFTER DEFINING HENRY AS "COLD AND DISTANT,"
RITA HAYWORTH FALLS FOR JAMES STEWART

THE COLD AND BLOODY SANDS OF IWO JIMA

AFTER HENRY REJECTS THE CHANCE TO PLAY ITS MALE LEAD,
IT GOES TO JOHN WAYNE AND BECOMES HIS MOST MEMORABLE WAR DRAMA

IT'S HIGH NOON

BUT HENRY TURNS DOWN THE MALE LEAD

"I made the mistake of my life in rejecting that role, and the easy access to Grace Kelly that came with it. To make matters worse, it became Gary Cooper's Greatest Western classic."
—Henry Fonda.

THE CAINE MUTINY COURT-MARTIAL

HENRY BATTLES WITH ITS DIRECTOR, DICK POWELL
("THE MAN WITHOUT A SPHINCTER")
AND WITH ONE OF THE UGLIEST (AND SOME SAID, "MOST TWISTED")
ACTORS IN HOLLYWOOD, CHARLES LAUGHTON
("YEAH, HIM! THE ONE WHO EROTICIZES FECES!")

HENRY REMAINS DISCREET ABOUT HOW HIS BEST FRIEND, JAMES STEWART.
IS DIDDLING AROUND WITH POWELL'S WIFE, JUNE ALLYSON

How and When **James Stewart,**
("after sexual interludes with 263 'Glamour Girls'")
Found "The Right Woman!"
(Pssst!! Was it really cursed? Her former mother-in-law once owned the Hope Diamond)

Broadway Musicals Want More of Henry
But How? As a "Song Speaker" Like Rex Harrison?

Tedium at Sea
A Cinematic Version of Mr. Roberts
This time, after too much meddling from, among many others, Josh Logan,
it's "Tedium on Celluloid."
The Producers make it clear that they'd have preferred Marlon Brando

> *"Henry Fonda's subtle, naturalistic acting style*
> *preceded by many years the popular style of Method Acting."*
> —Joshua Logan

Dino De Laurentiis' **War & Peace**
With Audrey Hepburn
A Tolstoyan Tragedy of Manners about Why Men Go to War

> *"I was miscast"*
> —Henry Fonda

Touring with the Stage Version of Mr. Roberts

After Henry left the Broadway stage production of *Mister Roberts* and entered a hospital for knee surgery, his recovery was routine. Soon, he was able to walk around again, enough so that he signed with his producer, Leland Hayward, for a nationwide tour of a road show production of that hit play.

During that national tour of *Mister Roberts*, he would deliver about 550 performances from February until the end of August 1951.

Sometimes, he was booked into cities that usually didn't get road tours.

It began in Pittsburgh, where he played to a full house. Often, he received standing ovations. "I kept the role fresh," he later claimed, "like every night, it was my first time out."

***

Partying with Joan Crawford

During the course of the tour, Henry, with Susan at his side, flew into Los Angeles for a brief visit. They had business to tend to and friends to see.

James Stewart was the first person Henry phoned. He learned that invitations had been extended to a Saturday night party at the home of Joan Crawford, who had seduced Henry on and off the screen during the filming of *Daisy Kenyon* (1947).

Stewart agreed to pick up Susan and Henry, but he chose not to tell him who his date would be that evening. He did admit, in a voice lower than usual, "She's a bit young."

Ann Blyth, seductively conspiring with her mother's boyfriend, **Zachary Scott** in *Mildred Pierce.*

For decades after, its release, Blyth's character was defined as the ultimate example of betrayal of a mother by an ungrateful daughter.

"I hope you won't be arrested for jailbait," Henry said, jokingly.

"I've got this powerful crush on her," Stewart confessed.

That Saturday night, Stewart arrived right on time. In the front passenger seat, Henry recognized Ann Blyth sitting beside him.

En route to Crawford's house, both Henry and Susan lavishly complimented Blyth on her portrayal of Veda Pierce, Joan Crawford's bitch-scheming, ungrateful daughter in *Mildred Pierce* (1945), the film which brought Crawford a Best Actress Oscar. Although she was only sixteen when she played the role, Blyth herself was nominated for a Best Supporting Actress Oscar.

Although many of the women who'd worked with Crawford in the past had condemned her, Blyth had nothing but praise for her co-star.

"Our director, Michael Curtiz, didn't want me," Blythe admitted. "He said I was too young, too sweet. But Joan took me home and coached me night after night. I'll always be grateful to her. She taught me how to be a bitch."

"Joan knows a lot about that," Henry said.

At the party, Crawford hugged and kissed Blyth, Stewart, and Henry, but virtually ignored Susan. Crawford had a young man, who looked to be in his twenties, beside her. Although it was obvious he was her date for the night, or maybe longer. she chose not to introduce him. She had divorced Phillip Terry in 1946 and would not remarry for a decade.

At the party, Henry "played catch-up" (his words) with a lot of friends and acquaintance, most of whom urged him to leave the stage and return to Tinseltown.

At around 1AM, Crawford hugged and kissed Stewart and Henry at the front door.

After she lip-locked with Henry, she broke away only to invite him to make another picture with her. "This time, without Dana Andrews," she added.

"It's a deal," Henry said. "You find the script."

Stewart dropped Henry and Susan off, and then drove off into the night with Blyth.

Henry told Susan, "Jimmy usually confided in me about his romances. But he's strangely quiet about Blyth. I don't know if they're making it or not."

A week later, Susan told him that she'd read in Hedda Hopper that Stewart appeared to have dropped Ann Blyth. "Hopper reports he's planning to marry Rita Hayworth."

A look of shock appeared on Henry's face.

***

Red-Hot Rita (Hayworth)

It seemed that Stewart had dated Rita Hayworth on at least three occasions in the early 1940s. But the locales were in out-of-the-way places, so their brief fling passed virtually unnoticed.

After the war, Stewart and Henry attended a showing of *Gilda* (1946), the classic film which helped to establish her image as the Love Goddess of the 1940s.

Rita later said, "Men went to bed with Gilda but woke up with me."

After running into her at a party after the war, Stewart resumed his affair with her.

As he described to Henry, "I caught her between her divorce from Orson Welles and her affair with Prince Aly Khan."

Shifra Haran, Orson Welles' secretary, said, "Rita's only security was knowing someone would want to be with her."

Welles himself admitted, "All of Rita's life was filled with pain ever since her father, Eduardo Cansino, took her virginity. I regret all the pain I've caused her, too."

As one reporter wrote, "Rita Hayworth had a fondness for bisexual men, including Howard Hughes, Victor Mature, David Niven, James Stewart (who had an affair with Henry Fonda), Robert Mitchum, Tyrone Power, and Peter Lawford."

That report assumed that Stewart and Henry had been lovers, a common assumption about them, a belief that still exists to this day in some quarters.

Peter Lawford was not very charitable, calling Rita "the worst lay of my life." In contrast, the Latin lover, Gilbert Roland, proclaimed, "A night with Rita is a trip to pussy heaven. It was the fuck of my life, and I've had a string of the hottest dames in Hollywood. Rita once confessed to me that the best head she'd ever received was from Marlene Dietrich."

As Stewart later confessed to Henry, "My fling with Rita was brief, too brief. She ran off with some prince, or so I was told."

"Yeah, right," Henry said. "Just pick up any newspaper. Aly Khan and Rita generate the biggest news since we dropped the bomb on Hiroshima."

Rita later discussed her affair with Stewart: "He was the sweetest, dearest man I ever met. A bit lean and lanky for my taste, but endearing nonetheless. I think he truly understands a woman's needs, unlike Howard Hughes, Harry Cohn, and a long string of other lovers. I felt that if I needed something, Jimmy would come running."

"I never understood his friendship with Fonda," she said. "He was a cold, distant man, totally unlike Jimmy. I mean, he even drove his wife to suicide. This is just a guess. If you were troubled and broke down and cried, chances are that Jimmy would offer you a handkerchief and put his arms around you to comfort you. When you recovered, he might even make love to you. With Fonda—and I'm only guessing—he would never show any emotion. He would probably tell you that tears disgust him. He might even say, 'Quit your whimpering, bitch, and get on with your life.'"

Henry was on the road when news broke of the upcoming marriage of Rita Hayworth and Prince Aly Khan. He phoned Stewart, telling him, "The marriage will never last. He's a whoremonger. Probably on his honeymoon, he'll have at least ten more girls. I predict that after a few months, she'll come running back to you. You are her real prince, not this satyr."

Previously, Otto Preminger had told Henry that Khan had only two interests—women and horses.

Zsa Zsa Gabor, one of Khan's lovers, had said, "A woman was not in the swim—really *déclassé, démodé*, nothing, and hardly counted—if she had not gone to bed with Aly."

Rita Hayworth, her portrait from *Gilda*. Her dazzling beauty set the standard for a generation. She was also the first Hollywood star to become real-life royalty.

She was the love goddess of the 1940s, acting with Glenn Ford, Gary Cooper, Fred Astaire, Cary Grant, James Cagney, Tyrone Power, Victor Mature, and Robert Mitchum, among others.

Rita Hayworth with the Prince Aly Khan at their wedding reception at the Chateau de L'Horizon on the French Riviera in 1949.

To celebrate their nuptials, the prince ordered that his swimming pool be filled with champagne. In the ferocious sunlight of Provence, It immediately went flat and attracted flies.

***

Helen Walker

The next time Henry talked to Stewart, he found that he had recovered quickly from the loss of Rita. As it turned out, he was having a fling with Helen Walker, his co-star in *Call Northside 777*.

Walker had made her film debut in the 1942 film, *Lucky Jordan*, a comedy about a gangster (Alan Ladd) who gets drafted into the Army. Walker's character later reports him AWOL.

That same year, she had married Robert Blumofe, an attorney for Paramount. She'd also played the romantic interest of Fred MacMurray in the comedy, *Murder, He Says* (1945).

Before meeting Stewart, she had starred in Tyrone Power's most controversial film, *Nightmare Alley* (1947), in which his character morphs from magician to circus geek.

Henry met Walker only once, when she had dined with Stewart and him. After dinner was served, as dessert was on the way, Stewart had excused himself to go to the men's room. As she watched him walk away, she turned to Henry and said, "There goes my next husband."

Her fantasy marriage to Stewart never happened. In 1950, Walker married Edward DuDomaine, a department store executive. She divorced him two years later.

In 1960, Henry and Stewart read that Walker's home had burned down. She was said to be broke and in dire need of money. Along with other stars, they organized a benefit for her, raising enough cash to get her life back in order.

Helen Walker at play. Her life was filled with controversy and scandal. She took Gail Russell under her wing, and taught her the tranquilizing benefits of vodka, pushing her along the rocky road towards alcoholism.

On the last day of 1946, driving while drunk, she picked up three hitchhikers . While speeding, she had a horrible accident, killing a young soldier and seriously injuring the other two, who filed lawsuits against her.

Following a nine-year illness, she died of cancer at the age of 47.

***

FONDA'S FOLLIES: ROLES THAT GOT AWAY

Battleground

In the four years that immediately followed the end of World War II, Hollywood producers were warned that the public had tired of its steady diet of war movies. However, before the dawn of the 50s, there was a return to the battleground.

At MGM, William Wellman was assigned to direct *Battleground* (1949). It would star Van Johnson, the male version of America's so-called "Sweetheart" of the 1940s, a title he shared with his female counterpart, June Allyson.

Wellman met with Dore Schary, who had recently ousted Louis B. Mayer as head of MGM.

"I think Johnson is too faggy for the role," Wellman said. "The role should go either to Robert Taylor or Henry Fonda."

At the time, *Battleground* was entitled *Prelude to Love*, which hardly described either the context or the plot. It dealt with U.S. soldiers coping with the siege in France during the Battle of the Bulge. The squad leader was named "Holley."

Taylor rejected the role, as did Henry. When Wellman reported this to Schary, the studio chief ordered him to cast Van Johnson. "You can butch him up."

Henry later saw the picture and liked it, claiming, "It portrayed American soldiers as human beings, very vulnerable."

Sands of Iwo Jima

Around the same time, another war picture, *Sands of Iwo Jima* (1949) was being cast at Republic Pictures, one of the film industry's minor studios. It contained a starring role for a "tough-as-nails" Marine sergeant named John Stryker. According to Henry, "At least during the war, my ship sailed into Iwo Jima after it was conquered from the Japs. Even so, I turned the movie down"

John Wayne was cast instead. It became one of his classic pictures.

"I was shocked when The Duke was nominated for a Best Actor Oscar," Henry said. "Stars at Republic almost never got such an honor."

Director Vincent Sherman wanted to cast Henry in yet another World War II drama, *The Hasty Heart* (1949). He was offered the role of "Yank," an American in a British mobile surgery unit in the Pacific Theater. The makeshift hospital is in the jungle.

It receives a Scot, "Lachie" MacLachlan, who will die in a few weeks. Henry felt that picture belonged to Lachie, not Yank.

Richard Todd, as Lachie, proved that Henry's forecast had been correct. The role of Yank went instead to Ronald Reagan, who had an affair offscreen with its female star, Patricia Neal, helping her get over her lost lover, Gary Cooper.

***

Broken Arrow

Henry wasn't ready to place himself under the thumb of Darryl F. Zanuck at Fox again, so he rejected an offer to appear in *Broken Arrow*. It was scheduled to begin shooting in the spring of 1949 on location in the Cocomino Mountains of Arizona. Director Delmer Daves pitched the role to Henry. He would play Tom Jeffords, who conducts a peace agreement, set in 1870, between the Apache tribes, led by Cochise, and the U.S. government.

Henry liked the script, since it presented Indians, as they were called back then, in a sympathetic light, one of the first Westerns to do so. The subplot has him falling in love with an Indian girl named Sonseeahrayn. That role had already been cast with Debra Paget, who was only fifteen at the time.

It came as a surprise when James Stewart phoned and told him that he had signed with Fox for the role of Jeffords, the one that Henry had recently rejected.

"Jimmy," Henry said. "You'll get arrested for child molestation. Paget, I heard, is jail-bait."

After *Broken Arrow* exploded into a success at the box office, Stewart phoned Henry. "I think I've found my post-war niche. I'm going to become the new Gary Cooper."

***

Detective Story

Director William Wyler thought Henry might be ideal cast as the lead in *Detective Story* (1951). It was the story of an angry New York City detective, who fights a grim daily battle with the scummy underbelly of the city.

He rejected it, the role eventually going to Kirk Douglas, who morphed it into one of his most iconic films. *Detective Story* was eventually nominated for four Academy Awards.

Although Henry often thought he was too old for some of the roles offered to him, when Columbia suggested that he play Willy Loman in *Death of a Salesman* (1951), he thought he was "too young."

Henry Fonda's decision to reject the script for *Detective Story* was celebrated by **Kirk Douglas**, who's shown here "roughing up" a participant in a grubby scam.

The film had originated in 1949 as a play by Arthur Miller. In it, Loman, a dogged salesman who suffered through six decades of failure soon begins to lose his grip on reality and slips between the past and present, frantically trying to discover where he went wrong.

The studio eventually cast the title role of Willy Loman with Fredric March. *Death of a Salesman*, a prescient and very appropriate film for its era, won five Golden Globe Awards and five Oscar nods.

***

Above and Beyond

Henry was tempted when another World War II drama came his way: *Above and Beyond,* set for a 1952 release. Its producers and directors, Melvin Frank and Norman Panama, thought he would "jump at the chance" to play Lt. Col. Paul W. Tibbets Jr., the pilot of the *Enola Gay,* the bomber from which an atomic bomb had been dropped on the Japanese city of Hiroshima.

232

As a naval officer, early in August of 1945, Henry had flown to the small island of Tinian to deliver weather reports before Tibbets made his crucial flight into the pages of history.

Henry told Wasserman, his agent, "I just don't have it in my heart to play a pilot responsible for the deaths of thousands of innocent Japanese."

The role went to Robert Taylor and is cited as one of his best performances. In 1952, the *National Board of Review* cited *Above and Beyond* as one of the best films of that year. It was nominated for two Academy Awards.

***

High Noon

The male lead in one of the greatest classic Westerns, *High Noon* (1952), was offered to Henry, but he "made the mistake of my life" by turning it down.

Both its producer (Stanley Kramer) and director (Fred Zinnemann) had wanted Montgomery Clift to play the role of the town marshal, newly married to a pretty young Quaker girl, as eventually portrayed by Grace Kelly.

Henry was not that enthralled with the script and was the second actor to reject it.

Gary Cooper accepted the role, admitting, "I might have been born a long time before Grace Kelly. She looked like a real cold dish until you got her panties off, and then, she'd explode."

***

Come Back, Little Sheba

Henry had another major regret when he rejected the male lead in the William Inge play, *Come Back, Little Sheba* (1952). The script told the story of a loveless marriage between a recovering alcoholic and his frumpy wife. His life is rocked when a pretty young collegiate rents a room at their home.

The movie would win a Best Actress Oscar for Shirley Booth, who had originated the role on Broadway. The male lead went to Burt Lancaster. Ever since, *Come Back, Little Sheba* has been considered one of his greatest roles.

After all these roles became triumphs for its male stars, Henry told his agent, Lew Wasserman, "Regrets...I've had a few."

***

Point of No Return

Although Henry turned down several movie roles after the Broadway and road show versions of *Mr. Roberts*, when producer Leland Hayward offered him the lead in another stage play, this one entitled *Point of No Return*. Henry said yes. He had already read the best-selling novel by John P. Marquand it was based on.

[One of Marquand's major themes was the confining nature of life in America's upper classes and those who aspired to join them. In 1938, he had won the Pulitzer Prize for his novel, The Late George Apley.*]*

HENRY FONDA
Point of No Return

Henry was not impressed when given Paul Osborn's stage adaptation of Marquand's novel, but he believed at the time that its problems with *Point of No Return* could be worked out in rehearsal.

He returned to the Alvin Theatre *[it was later renamed the Neil Simon Theatre]*, where he had performed for so long in *Mister Roberts*. There, he met his director, H.C. Potter.

In some respects, Henry found that the script mirrored his own problems, personal and professional, as he drifted into middle age.

He was cast as Charles Bray, an executive competing with another officer for the vice presidency of a bank. The tension that builds is shared with his wife, Nancy. *[Henry worked smoothly with the actress, Leora Dana, who had scored a hit on Broadway in* The Madwoman of Chaillot. *Her most recent success had been in the Broadway smash,* Happy Time.*]*

233

Henry's character is also a troubled father to his children. He later said that the film's title might have been *The Man in the Grey Flannel Suit,* a movie that Gregory Peck would make in 1956.

Point of No Return was the story of a Madison Avenue executive struggling to get ahead and to find meaning in life.

To finance the play, Henry invested $10,000 of his own money. Other "angels" included Hedda Hopper, Billy Wilder, Irving Berlin, and Mary Martin.

After ten days of rehearsal, the play still wasn't working for Henry, who labeled it as a "high-toned slog." He had conflicted with his director, H.C. Potter, who was known mainly for having helmed a number of pictures. *[One of them,* The Farmer's Daughter, *had won the Best Actress Oscar for Loretta Young in 1947.]*

"If there's a weakness in the play, Potter can't fix it," Henry told Leland Hayward. After sitting through a dress rehearsal, Hayward agreed and dismissed him.

Called in at the last minute, Elia Kazan became its "play doctor." After tweaking the script, the show was ready for its "out of town" opening. For its upcoming Broadway opening night, the play had already had advance ticket sales of $500,000, more than *Mister Roberts* had generated prior to its own opening, a few years earlier.

Late in its rehearsals, Henry was almost forced to drop out of the show. A doctor discovered that his vocal cords were riddled with what he called "bleeding volcanic craters."

Point of No Return had its world premiere in New Haven on October 29, 1951. From there, it moved to the Colonial Theatre in Boston for a three-week run, followed by a short run at the Forrest Theater in Philadelphia, beginning on November 29, 1951.

At the Alvin in Manhattan, *Point of No Return* opened on December 23, 1951, where it would run for 356 performances.

Brooks Atkinson in *The New York Times* wrote, "Henry Fonda bestows on the play one of those unbelievably easy and engaging performances that do not seem like acting at all. He is a most ingratiating male star."

Richard Watts Jr. said, "Fonda may not ever quite indicate any great inner turmoil of spirit, and he seems at the end of the play just about what he was at the beginning. But his portrayal has all the charm, directness, earnestness, and vast likeableness that he invariably gets into his performances."

xxx

In Manhattan, Henry and Susan Buy the Fleischman House.
Jane & Peter Attend Boarding School

After nurturing it through thirteen months of performances on Broadway, Henry took *Point of No Return* on a road tour for seven months (November 1952 to June of 1953). The tour began in Baltimore. In every city, it played to standing-room-only audiences.

Surprisingly, he told his new wife, Susan, "I feel I'm cheating the audience in every possible way."

In spite of that, he signed with Leland Hayward as the male lead in the play's adaptation into a film, a movie that was never made. "I'm trying to stop thinking about it, but I've had several dreams about suicide," he confided to Susan.

For now, at least, since he'd expressed a desire to appear in no more movies unless something really special came along, Henry and Susan had decided to make Manhattan their permanent home. To facilitate that dream, they bought a five-story brownstone on East 74th Street, right off Lexington Avenue, in Upper Manhattan.

Its previous owner had been Raoul H. Fleischmann, owner of a string of bakeries associated with Fleischmann's Yeast. He had grown weary of the tedium of mass market bread-making when a well-known editor, Harold Ross, suggested that they start "a new comic paper." The result was *The New Yorker,* which was first published in February of 1925. Fleischmann poured $700,000 into it before it turned a profit.

Thanks to their associations with what evolved into a respected and prestigious magazine, the literary and theatrical elite of New York and visiting "royalty" from Hollywood had already passed through the brownstone's portals.

As part of his purchase of the house, Henry had acquired some of its furnishings, and liked to point out, "Ethel Barrymore sat in that chair," and "See that corner over there? Ethel's brother, John, once pissed in it when he was too drunk to get to the toilet."

Since he and Susan were on the road together most of the time, they tended to see Peter and Jane only during holidays or summer vacations. When Jane came home, Susan would assume the duties of not only her stepmother, but those of a stylist and mentor, too. She introduced Jane to the Manhattan of her own girlhood—the theaters, the chic luncheon spots, the elegant clothing stores, the movie palaces, the best hairdressers, and the greatest museums.

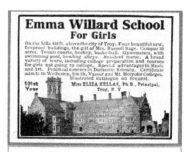

One day on Third Avenue, they spotted Greta Garbo.

As one of her girlhood ambitions, Jane had expressed a wish about becoming a ballerina. Susan did not encourage that goal. As she told Henry, "I just can't see Jane as the next Pavlova."

Both Henry and Susan were in agreement about where to send Peter and Jane to school. They chose two of the finest boarding schools in America, one just for girls, the other for boys only.

Jane was enrolled in the Emma Willard School on Mount Ida, a promontory near Troy, New York.

It had been established as the Troy Female Seminary in 1814 by Emma Willard—a women's rights advocate—as the first higher education institution for women in the United States. Jane was housed in a dormitory, a medieval-looking building with turrets and crouching gargoyles.

Today, Jane Fonda is listed among the school's most distinguished alumnae. Another notable graduate, born in Troy during the Gilded Age, had been Lilian Warren Price, later known as Lily Spencer-Churchill, Duchess of Marl-borough (1854-1909).

Because she was the daughter of Henry Fonda, Jane was encouraged to join the Campus Players, but she held off for many months, fearing that she would not be judged for any talent she might have, but would be seen only as the daughter of a famous stage and screen star.

But finally, she joined the Campus Players, in whose productions male roles were performed by cross-dressing young women. Jane made her stage debut in Christopher Fry's *The Boy With a Cart*.

At that period of her life, Jane had not yet blossomed into the sexy siren she became in the years ahead. She was often referred to as "cute" or "pugnacious."

She liked to eat, and sometimes she would splurge outrageously, perhaps downing a gallon of strawberry ice cream in one sitting. Then, she'd go to a bathroom as part of the "binge and purge" process, forcing herself to vomit. This rite became part of her life. At least, despite the many health problems such a practice catalyzed, it kept her fig-ure intact.

Jane recalled her first date. It transpired in Manhattan. Her beau was Daniel Selznick, the son of producer David O. Selznick, who had immortalized himself as the producer of *Gone With the Wind* (1939). Selznick and his wife, the actress Jennifer Jones, went with Daniel and Jane to a performance of the Broadway play, *Dial M for Murder*.

Previously, Daniel had dated one of Jane's best friends, Brooke Hayward. When he introduced Brooke to his father, the elder Selznick had raved about Brooke's potential as a future movie star. In vivid contrast, when Daniel introduced Jane to his father, Selznick said nothing.

At Emma Willard, Jane was only an average student. It was reported that she broke the rules by escaping from her dorm after curfew, climbing over the walls to date young men from the nearby colleges.

One of them, William Robertson, who had been born in Troy, boasted to his fraternity brothers that he was the lucky stud who took the virginity of Jane Fonda. That turned out to be an idle boast, since, as was later revealed, she did not lose her virginity until she attended Vassar. In the meantime, her dates were punctuated only with "heavy petting."

In her memoirs, Jane was most candid, even revealing that at the age of sixteen, she was menstruating. "I thought I was bleeding to death. In the bathroom, as she was showering, Susan came to her aid, offering her a Kotex. Later, she explained more about the facts of life to her stepdaughter, saying to her, "Welcome to womanhood, with all its joy and pain."

The following day, Susan sent Jane to her gynecologist, telling her, "You need to know about contraception."

Meanwhile, Peter was enrolled at an all-boys boarding school, the Fay School. Founded in 1866, it occupied a 66-acre site in Southborough, Massachusetts, about 25 miles from Boston.

In the aftermath of his shooting accident, Peter was a year behind in school. The restrictions at Fay did not readily appeal to him, especially the sewing of name tags into all of his clothing.

He was rescued from boredom when he met Judy Rankin, the beautiful daughter of Fay's assistant headmaster, with whom he indulged in extended "kissing sessions." Prior to Judy, Peter had enjoyed kissing Bridget Hayward, the daughter of Leland Hayward and Margaret Sullavan.

Whereas Jane had played male roles in school theatrics, Peter made his stage debut in drag as one of the "fair maidens" in a school production of *The Pirates of Penzance*. In the weeks that followed, other students began referring to him as "Fairy Fonda." Three of the more aggressive ones, thinking he was gay, tried to date him or entice him into a toilet stall with them. He angrily rejected them, later informing his school's drama coach that he would never again appear as a woman onstage.

At the Fay School, Peter would appear in two plays before he starred in one of his own creation. He portrayed Sir Andrew Aguecheek in Shakespeare's *Twelfth Night,* and the Lord High Executioner in Gilbert & Sullivan's *The Mikado*.

In Manhattan, he'd gone to see the Broadway rendition of *Stalag 17*, a saga about a group of American airmen imprisoned and scheming in a German internment camp.

He was so inspired by the drama that after his return to Fay, he wrote *Stalag 17½* , a 33-minute play about boys in a boarding school. It was actually produced by the Fay School, and well-received.

"I decided then and there that I was going to become the greatest living American playwright."

Stalag 17 was released, in 1953, as a movie directed by Billy Wilder. Peter had urged his father to try out for the male lead, even though technically, at least, he was too old. *[Wilder cast William Holden instead, who won a Best Actor Oscar for his performance.]*

Peter's involvements with Judy Rankin would continue for many months. As he put it, "I was in the seventh grade, and we would huddle together in the low light, hugging and kissing. It wasn't that I was in love with Judy or she with me, but we could trust one another. We explored the beginning of a boy-girl relationship to see how far we could go. Judy was right there at the right time with the right response."

Peter would later be named as one of the famous alumni of Fay School. Other notable graduates included Robert E. Sherwood, the four-time Pulitzer Prize-winning playwright, and Efren Zimbalist Jr, the Golden Globe-winning actor.

***

The Fonda household was about to have another addition. Susan could not get pregnant, and she urged Henry to adopt a child. Against his better judgment, he did.

At a foster home in the spring of 1953, she found an eight-week-old girl whom she wanted as her own. Henry agreed and signed the papers, naming the child Amy.

Susan was very protective of the infant, but Henry had little in common with "a baby who's not even a year old. Once or twice, I tried to pick her up. I found she had shit her diapers. I called Susan to the rescue while I was out the door. Fatherhood was never really my calling in life."

In his memoirs, he made himself out to be a much more loving and caring father to Amy, even describing how he rose at five o'clock in the morning to give her her bottle and to burp her.

Actually, he was on the road most of the time, and a nurse was on hand to tend to the baby's needs, including the diaper-changing that Henry deplored.

***

Henry Fonda poses with his two fast-growing kids, **Jane** and **Peter**, before boarding a Pan American Airways flight from New York in 1957.

Although both would eventually become movie stars, too, Jane was known at the time as "Henry Fonda's daughter"—at least until she morphed into her own legend.

Peter, on the other hand, never matched his sister's super-stardom.

Ad for American boys' clothing in the mid-1950s. Conformity reigned at schools that included the **Fay School,** young Peter's *Alma Mater.*

The Caine Mutiny Goes to Broadway

Henry had rejected many offers, both stage and screen roles, but when Paul Gregory and Charles Laughton presented him with the Broadway-bound script of *The Caine Mutiny Court-Martial*, he found this two-act courtroom drama irresistible. Author Herman Wouk had adapted the drama from his best-selling 1951 novel, *The Caine Mutiny*.

The Pulitzer Prize-winning novel had evolved from Wouk's own experiences aboard two destroyer-minesweepers in the Pacific theater of World War II.

In a nutshell, the drama spins around the court-martial trial of Navy Lt. Maryk, the executive officer aboard *Caine*. He incites a mutiny against his tyrannical and neurotic commanding officer, Lt. Commander Queeg. Maryk is defended by a young Jewish lawyer, Lt. Barney Greenwald.

As a team, Gregory and Laughton had toured America in late 1949 and early 1950, playing to full houses in a table-reading rendition of the works of Stephen Vincent Benét and George Bernard Shaw.

For their highly praised readings, they garnered $200,000. After producing the court martial play, Gregory would go on to launch seventeen more Broadway plays in the 1950s and 1960s.

Susan Blanchard, with the daughter, **Amy,** she adopted, with her then-husband, **Henry Fonda,** a few years after their wedding.

Henry was well-acquainted with the memorable film roles of the Yorkshire-born Laughton, including *The Private Lives of Henry VIII* (1933); *Mutiny on the Bounty* (1935) with Clark Gable; and *The Hunchback of Notre Dame* (1938).

"From Shakespeare to monsters and misfits, Laughton could take any role," Henry said of him.

He had heard that Laughton and Gregory were "two gay blades who put aspiring young actors on the casting couch."

Laughton was married to the English character actress Elsa Lanchester, who was very tolerant of the sexual proclivities of her spouse.

Gregory would not wed until 1964, when he entered into a "lavender marriage" with Janet Gaynor, the actress who starred in the first version of *A Star Is Born* (1937), long before Judy Garland and Barbra Streisand tackled the role.

Because of his major success with *Mister Roberts*, Laughton and Gregory presented Henry with a choice: He could play Captain Queeg or else Lt. Barney Greenwald, the lawyer who defends Stephen Marky, Queeg's second-in-command, who led the mutiny.

Henry chose the role of the defense attorney, Barney Greenwald. After signing for the role, he learned that the production would be directed by Dick Powell.

John Hodiak, married at the time to actress Anne Baxter, originated the role of Lt. Maryk. His career had zoomed upward after appearing in *Lifeboat* (1944). Directed by Alfred Hitchcock, it had also starred Tallulah Bankhead. One of Hodiak's best-known film roles was as the male lead in *The Harvey Girls* (1946) starring Judy Garland. His most recent film had been *Malaya* (1949) with Spencer Tracy and James Stewart.

Because the play gives spectators access only to the court martial, the audience knows only what various witnesses say about the events that took place aboard the *Caine*.

A meeting was set up among Wouk, the producer (Paul Gregory) and Laughton, who was in partnership with Gregory.

Henry was introduced to Wouk, who was rather reclusive. He congratulated the novelist on his Pulitzer Prize for *The Caine Mutiny's* original format.

[The key role of Captain Queeg in the movie that emerged in 1954 had gone to Humphrey Bogart as one of his final roles. His performance would later be widely acclaimed, bringing him his third and final Oscar nomination.]

In Henry's stage production, the character actor Lloyd Nolan played Captain Queeg. Although he could play many different parts, he was best known at the time for originating the role of private investigator Michael Shayne in a B pictures series

Charles Laughton in 1933 as Henry VIII with a wench.(upper photo), and with his "indulgent and understanding wife (lower photo), Elsa ('Bride of Frankenstein") Lanchester.

Here's a "squeaky clean" portrait from Pre-Code Hollywood, in 1931, of Dick Powell's second wife, the saucy and very kind **Joan Blondell,** a loyal personal friend and house guest of this biography's co-author, Darwin Porter.

It was she who provided some of the details that appear within this chapter.

Here's **Dick Powell** with **Ruby Keeler** as Broadway hoofers in *42nd Street* (1933), twenty years before he became a director responsible for directing and guiding a "just-returned from Hollywood pro, the formidable Henry Fonda."

in the 1940s. When he heard of Henry's casting, he said as part of a mordant and sarcastic joke, "How ideal. I've always thought of Fonda as a young Jewish lawyer"

Almost from the first, Henry had serious doubts about Powell as a director. He had seen only one of his musicals in the 1930s, and that was the hit *42nd Street* (1933). In the 1940s, he'd tackled more hard-boiled roles, playing private detective Philip Marlowe in *Murder, My Sweet* (1944).

Powell had been married to Joan Blondell (1936-44) until June Allyson stole him away and married him herself. Allyson— once hailed as "America's Sweetheart" — was appearing with James Stewart in *The Stratton Story.*

Before directing Henry and the cast, Powell had just helmed *Split Second* (1953), a *film noir* thriller about escaped convicts and their hostages in a ghost town. The film co-starred Stephen McNally and Alexis Smith. In reference to Powell's first time as a director, *The New York Times* wrote: "Mr. Powell's initial directorial debut effort is not likely to startle the cinema world, but it is a long step in the right direction."

Rehearsals for *The Caine Mutiny Court-Martial* became a clash of egos. Henry frequently disagreed with Powell's directions, fearing he was ruining the dramatic impact of the play. As one of the financial backers, Charles Laughton was at the rehearsals every day, and he, too, weighed in with suggestions which were far more valid than those of Powell.

Henry conspired with the two leading actors, Hodiak and Nolan, to get Powell fired. Gregory was reluctant to do so because Powell was a friend of his.

But only two weeks before the play's opening, he fired Powell and named Laughton the director instead.

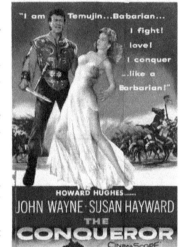

During his last day of rehearsals, (Powell by now had been fired as the production's director) Powell and Henry bid each other a chilly farewell. "I never thought you were right for the role," Powell said. "There's nothing Jewish about you. Also, the part called for a young lawyer. Another reason I detest you is that your so-called best buddy is fucking my wife, June Allyson."

Henry said nothing, only remarking later that "I found Powell distasteful. He had some serious toilet issues." After Powell was fired as director of *The Caine Mutiny Court-Martial,* Henry told Paul Gregory, "I think he wears a diaper."

Gregory assumed that Henry was referencing his lack of experience as a director, but it was not until later that he and the cast learned what Henry had meant.

For decades, a Hollywood rumor persisted that Powell had been born without an anal sphincter, which is clinically defined as the ring-shaped muscle that controls the exit of fecal matter from the large intestine. To manage his condition, it was also rumored not only that he wore some form of a diaper, but that he took medications—one to induce constipation, another a laxative to release fecal matter at (in theory at least) convenient moments.

[As it turned out, the Court-Martial play was just a minor disaster

The deadliest movie in film history: **The Conqueror**, where most of the cast and crew died from nuclear fallout after filming. In it, **John Wayne** (photo above) had to emulate Ghenghis Khan, the Mogul conqueror; **Susan Hayward** his barbarian consort. The critics hated it, too.

238

in Powell's career. He later faced the horror of his life after Howard Hughes hired him to direct The Conqueror *(1956), starring John Wayne as the Mongol warrior, Genghis Khan, with co-stars Susan Hayward, Agnes Moorehead, and Pedro Armendáriz.*

Exterior scenes were filmed near St. George, Utah, which is 137 miles downwind from the government's Nevada National Security Site. This area received the brunt of the nuclear fallout from the testing of atomic bombs in 1953. Later, Howard Hughes shipped sixty tons of dirt from this region back to Hollywood in an attempt to match the colors of the location in Utah that had been used in earlier shots, as a means of matching it for re-shoots.

Of the 220 members of the film's crew and cast—including Susan Hayward and John Wayne, 91 of them developed cancer before the end of their lives. Even the director himself, Dick Powell, died of cancer in January of 1963, only seven years after the movie's release.

A legacy of poisoning from nuclear fallout was not the only horrible after-effect of The Conqueror. *Critics "declared war" on it and its male lead, John Wayne, portraying Ghenghis Khan. Almost universally, reviewers agreed that it was "the worst movie ever made."]*

***

As part of a sexual fetish that many associates found disgusting, Charles Laughton was said to derive sexual satisfaction from eating the feces of young men he admired and often hired for various purposes. That included "rent boys" from Piccadilly Circus in London, masseurs, chauffeurs, barmen, and sexy movie extras.

Tensions continued to rise. With only ten days before *The Caine Mutiny Court-Martial's* California premier, Laughton and Henry clashed.

Henry became so furious at Laughton at one point that he denounced him: "You're fat, you're grotesque, and you're a miserable old fag."

The premier of *The Caine Mutiny Court-Martial* was staged at the Granada Theatre in Santa Barbara on October 12, 1953, receiving good reviews.

From there, it began a nation-wide tour before it reached Broadway. A large bus carried cast and crew from city to city, from El Paso to San Diego. It played only for one-night stands. Meandering eastward, with many stopovers, it finally opened on Broadway on January 20, 1954 at the Plymouth Theatre.

John McClaine in *The New York Journal-American* wrote, "Here is easily the most ambitious part Fonda has handled in his recent stage renaissance."

In the *New York Post,* Richard Watts Jr. claimed, "The deceptive simplicity of Fonda's acting style suits the role of Greenwald splendidly."

Robert Coleman of the *Daily Mirror* found Henry "deeply moving."

For John Chapman of the *Daily News,* Henry was "wonderfully artful."

Brooks Atkinson of *The New York Times* wrote, "Henry Fonda's talent for underplaying has never been so apposite, or cut so sharply into the veracity of a person. He makes a heroic character out of unheroics."

Columnists also weighed in, Earl Wilson rating it as "one of the great shows of our time."

The biggest rave came from another columnist, Mel Heimer: "I feel the play may be the finest thing I have ever seen in the theater."

The Caine Mutiny Court-Martial would run for 405 performances, but Henry dropped out on the last night of May in 1954. He had been lured back to Hollywood at last.

His replacement came in the handsome form of a studly actor named Jack Bumgarner, who was born in Oklahoma in 1928. He was advised to get rid of the "Bum" in his name, and he did so, becoming James Garner, future movie star, who would appear on TV and in films for seven decades.

He became a household name when he played Bret Maverick in the 1950s Western series, *Maverick.*

Hodiak later privately spoke about how Garner got the role: "Gregory and Laughton really drained that guy dry on their much-used casting couch," Hodiak claimed.

***

Because of their differing work schedules, Henry and James Stewart had not seen each other for several months. On Henry's next trip to Los Angeles, he spent the weekend with his friend, eager to learn whether the rumor that he was having an affair with June Allyson was true.

Powell didn't seem to be joking when he made that accusation about Stewart sleeping with his wife, whom he had married in 1945 after his divorce from Joan Blondell.

239

Before Powell, Allyson had fallen in love with John F. Kennedy, with whom she had had a brief fling. She had also had a brief fling with another future U.S. President, Ronald Reagan. Others of Allyson's suitors included Peter Lawford and David Rose, the conductor and composer.

Soon, Henry learned that the rumors about an affair of Stewart with Allyson were true. Both of them had been physically attracted to each other during their filming of *The Stratton Story* (1949), which was based on the life of Monty Stratton, a Major League baseball pitcher for the Chicago White Sox from 1934 to 1938.

The picture would a box office bonanza and would win an Academy Award for Best Writing in a Motion Picture.

It was a story of bravery and endurance followed by ultimate triumph in 1938. Stratton had accidentally shot himself in his right leg while hunting on his farm in Texas. The leg, which was eventually amputated, ended his career. But, with the support of his wife, and on his wooden leg, he worked hard year after year until he staged an inspirational minor-league comeback in 1946.

The Stratton Story became Stewart's first film for MGM since he appeared in *Ziegfeld Girl* in 1941.

As Stewart confessed to Henry, "I know June is married, and I didn't mean for it to happen, but it did. I mean, she came to my dressing room. I didn't pursue her. I'm only human."

"I certainly am not one to pass judgment, considering my record." Henry said. "Powell knows about it. You think a divorce is in the offing?"

"Not at all," Stewart answered. "Powell is a very forgiving husband."

What amazed Henry was the willingness of Powell to accept his wife's affairs. Once, from the podium of a banquet which Stewart attended, Powell said, "And now, let me introduce my wife's husband—JIMMY STEWART."

On another occasion, he said, "June must have made a good wife for Jimmy. He married her three times."

[Powell was referring to the fact that June Allyson had already portrayed the wife of a character Stewart was playing three separate times. The other two were in The Glenn Miller Story *(1954) and* Strategic Air Command *(1955).*

Henry privately believed that Powell's knowledge of his wife's adultery would lead to their divorce. But they remained married until his death, at which time, he left her so rich she would never have to work or worry about money for the rest of her life.

Henry came to believe that the marriage was going to survive when he read in *Variety* that Powell was going to direct his wife in a 1956 Technicolor and CinemaScope musical comedy, *You Can't Run Away from It.* Allyson's co-star would be Jack Lemmon.

The new movie was a remake of the classic *It Happened One Night* (1934) that brought Best Actor and Actress Oscars to its co-stars, Clark Gable and Claudette Colbert. The Gable/Colbert movie had also been remade into a musical comedy in 1945 as *Eve Knew Her Apples.*

In her future, Allyson was often asked if rumors of her affair were true. She always delivered the same answer: "Jimmy is so thin he's a fright. But women fall madly in love with him. He has a hidden talent: Once you fall for him, it's almost impossible not to fall out of love with this wonderful guy—so tender, so sweet, so lovable."

One night, Stewart phoned Henry and said, "June and I are still on and off, but I've finally—now in my forties—found the woman I'm gonna marry."

***

Henry was eager to meet the woman who had captured the heart of his best friend. "Jimmy had to audition 200 gals before he found the one he wanted to marry."

Born in Larchmont, New York in 1918, Stewart's *fiancée* was a former actress, the beautiful and elegant Gloria Hatrick McLean.

[In 1943, Gloria had married Edward Beale McLean Jr., whose father was heir to The

They were plugged and plugged again in silly ads everywhere as "America's sweethearts," despite **June Allyson's** alleged nymphomania and **Van Johnson's** widely acknowledged status as a gay man.

Here they are in a promotional photo for one of the films that got them typecast, *The Bride Goes Wild* (1948).

James Stewart with "the woman of my dreams," **Gloria Hatrick McLean**

Washington Post.

McLean, Jr.'s mother, the gold-mine heiress, Evalyn Walsh McLean, was one of the most gossiped-about eccentrics of the Gilded Age, famous as the (unlucky) last private owner of the 45-carat Hope Diamond.

Gloria's marriage to McLean lasted from 1943-1948. Within nine months of their divorce, her ex-husband went on to marry Manuela "Mollie" Hudson, the former wife of Alfred Gwynn Vanderbilt Jr.

Stewart would later adopt Gloria's two sons, Ronald, age five, and Michael, age three. Michael would die in 1969 in Vietnam during service as a first lieutenant in the U.S. Marine Corps.

James Stewart and Gloria, during the course of their marriage, would produce twin daughters, each born on May 7, 1951.

As Stewart told Henry, "After the war, my movie career had some rough spots. But I didn't have to worry where my next steak was coming from. Gloria ain't po'. When I passed the Big 4-0, I figured I'd better get married before I get so ancient I couldn't get it up anymore."]

When Henry met Gloria, he found the former model a lovely woman, highly polished, full of charm and grace. "She told me she fell in love with Jimmy on the golf course. Both of them are golf addicts, and she's a better player than he is."

Gloria confessed to Henry, "A lot of male stars throw away their money gambling in Las Vegas or buying Tiffany diamonds for prostitutes. But Jimmy is tight with the dollar. When we were dating, he made an agreement with me. He would pay for the first dinner, but I had to pick up the tab on our next date."

As it turned out, Stewart had been introduced to Gloria in the summer of 1948 when both of them dined with Gary Cooper and his wife, "Rocky," who fancied herself a matchmaker.

It was later rumored that Rocky had offered Gloria the choice of two *beaux*, Stewart or Ronald Reagan. Jane Wyman, by then, had divorced the future president.

"I hear Reagan talks politics all night. So I'll take Stewart," Gloria had said.

Their first-date dinner had unfolded at the celebrity-studded Chasen's Restaurant, followed by dancing at Ciro's, where Nat King Cole at the piano was one of the attractions.

The joint agent of both Henry Fonda and James Stewart was Lew Wasserman, who hosted Stewart's bachelor party at Chasen's. Fellow invites Spencer Tracy and Jack Benny sat on the sidewalk curb waiting for Stewart's arrival. Inside the restaurant, a fifty-foot sign announcing—JAMES STEWART'S LAST PERFORMANCE—had been erected.

Beneath the sign were life-sized cutouts of characters from the actor's most disastrous motion picture flops.

After drinks at the bar, the (all male) guests retired to a table, where the largest silver platter in town was hauled out, one almost big enough, it seemed, to hold a whole roasted pig. When its gigantic lid was removed, two of the town's smallest midgets squirted water pistols at Stewart. Nearby diners thought the liquid that squirted was yellow piss, but Stewart later ascertained that it was apple juice.

When dinner was served, an English butler came out and stood "at attention" behind Stewart's chair. Every time he ate a bite, the butler wiped his mouth.

Because he was starring on Broadway at the time, Henry could not attend the wedding of Stewart to Gloria on August 9, 1949. Bill Gray was best man. Early in Stewart's career, Gray, then a talent scout, had spotted Stewart and arranged an MGM contract for him.

After the wedding, Stewart and Gloria, his bride, flew to Hawaii for their honeymoon. The following day, they encountered Helen Hayes and her husband, playwright Charles MacArthur. They were in mourning for the death of Mary, their nineteen-year-old daughter, who had recently died from polio.

Stewart had known Hayes back in the 1930s in New York. Now, years later, in Hawaii, he and Gloria spent a lot of time with the actress and her husband, helping them cope with their loss.

Sometimes, when Henry was in California, he slept over at the Stewart home on North Roxbury Drive in Beverly Hills. Even though he called the small mansion "Mediterranean ugly," Stewart purchased the residence from director Charles Vidor. Stewart would live in the home until his death.

As Henry said, "Gloria provided the style, Jimmy the comfort."

The first night Henry stayed over, he and Jimmy were up until the early hours, long after Gloria had retreated upstairs for her beauty sleep.

Stewart told him, "Now that I'm married to the greatest gal in the world, my whoring days are over. I plan to remain faithful to my wife except for an occasional tryst with my mistress, June Allyson."

***

John Steinbeck's Cannery Row Morphs into Pipe Dream—a Theatrical Flop

While appearing on stage in *Point of No Return* at the Alvin Theatre (later the Neil Simon Theater) in Manhattan, Henry was approached by two leading producers and offered the lead in an upcoming Broadway musical.

"But I can't sing a note," he warned Ernest Martin and Cy Feuer, who had produced the original stage version of *Guys and Dolls* (1951). It was later adapted into a hit movie musical starring Marlon Brando and Frank Sinatra. The co-producers would reign supreme in the mid-20th century, going on to receive nine Tony nominations, winning the Pulitzer Prize for *How to Succeed in Business Without Really Trying* (1962), *Cabaret* (1972) with Liza Minnelli, and the long-running stage version of *A Chorus Line* (1985).

Henry was informed that the two men had acquired the rights to John Steinbeck's *Cannery Row*, a novel published in 1945. The setting was Monterey, California, on a rundown street lined with sardine canneries. Taking place during the Depression, the story is a saga of a motley group trying to survive, often under harsh conditions.

As it turned out, it was Steinbeck himself who recommended Henry for the role. The novelist once told his wife, Elaine, that "I see Henry's face and lanky torso in every book I write."

In an effort to persuade Henry to accept, Martin and Feuer pointed out that Rex Harrison was not a singer, yet he starred in one of the biggest hit musicals, *My Fair Lady*, in entertainment history.

Henry was also reminded that Walter Huston had starred in the Broadway musical, *Knickerbocker Holiday*, cast as peg-legged Peter Stuyvesant. He had introduced the classic Kurt Weill "September Song," which became a classic.

Intrigued, Henry agreed to show up for an audition in an otherwise empty theater with Martin and Feuer sitting, concealed, in two of the darkened seats.

Accompanied by a piano, Henry chose to sing, "If I Were a Bell, I'd Be Ringing" from *Guys and Dolls*.

At the end of the song, the producers were silent. Finally, Feuer stood up, calling out from the darkened audience area to Henry, who remained onstage: "You were awful, Yet you're perfect for the part."

Martin also rose to his feet. "We want you to work with our vocal coach, Herbie Green, for several weeks." Henry followed through, morphing from *falsetto* to *vibrato* to *basso* during the course of his "training."

After a few weeks, the composer, Frank Loesser, was brought in to hear Henry sing. He had won Tonys for both *Guys and Dolls* and for *How to Succeed in Business Without Really Trying*. In time, he would write songs for more than sixty Hollywood films and for the Broadway stage.) Eventually, he won an Oscar for his song, "Baby, It's Cold Outside," which was sung at an Academy Awards presentation during the unlikely pairing of Mae West with Rock Hudson.

At the end of Henry's audition, Loesser came up onto the stage, telling Henry, "You're hopeless, but the boys think you might pull it off."

Henry had to interrupt his singing lessons to go on the road with *Point of No Return*. Feuer promised him that when he returned to New York, the musical would be ready and waiting for him to begin rehearsals with a cast.

However, when he returned for further negotiations after his gig with *Point of No Return* ended, he learned that the co-producers had sold the performance rights to Rodgers and Hammerstein.

Henry also learned that his role of the marine biologist had been completely altered. It had been radically reconfigured into a female character who runs the local bordello.

The role, he learned, had been cast with Helen Traubel as the star. A concert and opera star, she was known for her success with high-minded but ferocious Wagnerian roles, especially Brünnhilde and Isolde.

When the musical opened, the title had been changed to *Pipe Dream*. Henry attended and went backstage to congratulate Traubel, telling her of his early involvement with the musical.

Margaret Truman, seated with her mother, **Bess**, and her father, then-president **Harry S Truman**, who's standing, tried to cash in on her fame as the First Daughter.

"Poor Margaret just didn't have what it takes," said Mary Martin after hearing her sing at a concert in Washington, D.C.

In a widely publicized rebuttal to one of his daughter's critics, "Give 'Em Hell Harry" wrote to the reviewer: "I've just read your lousy review of Margaret's concert... Some day I hope to meet you. When that happens you'll need a new nose."

She was not optimistic for the future of *Pipe Dream*, telling Henry that she dreaded reading the early morning reviews, especially from *The New York Times.*

She relayed to Henry that then-U.S. President Harry S Truman, in the late 1940s, as a favor, had asked her to take his daughter, Margaret, under her wing and help her with her dream of becoming a classical singer.

"Margaret envisioned herself as a potentially great musical star, but I found her hopeless. I fear I have seriously damaged my reputation trying to coach her."

"Well, congrats anyway," Henry said. "You're a fine replacement for me, the first time I've ever been replaced with a soprano." Then he turned and left the theater.

Pipe Dream, as Traubel had predicted, flopped at the box office.

Oh Men! Oh Women!

Pipe Dream wasn't the only stage role Henry was offered at this point in his career. Edward Chodorov, the playwright, wanted him for his latest work, *Oh Men! Oh, Women!*.

He told Henry, "Psychoanalysis is merely an attempt to give proper direction to people's sex urges. Men and women will never, but never, get along together because they want different things. Men want women and women want men."

"Not in every case," Henry said in disagreement. "Some men want men, and some women want women."

He rejected the role. He didn't even go to see the film version, released in 1957, starring Ginger Rogers, Dan Dailey, and David Niven. It marked the film debut of Tony Randall, who had played Dailey's role on Broadway.

André Gide and The Immortalist

Henry was also offered the lead in a tense, then-being-developed stage drama, *The Immortalist,* based on a novel by André Gide written in French in 1902,

In a nutshell, it was the story of a gay archeologist who weds in the hope that his marriage to a woman will cure his homosexual impulses. Nonetheless, even despite having "tied the knot," he's still not able to consummate their marriage on his wedding night.

The couple decide to go to Algeria for their honeymoon. There, he falls for their good-looking Arab houseboy. Somewhere along the way, he also manages to sleep with his wife, impregnating her.

Henry rejected the role, which, for its Broadway opening, went to Louis Jourdan, who, as a bisexual himself, was better suited for the part.

The Immortalist opened at the Royale Theatre on Broadway and ran from February to May of 1954., attracting hordes of homosexuals in the audience.

Geraldine Page starred in the role of the wife. A then-virtually-unknown James Dean was cast as the Arab houseboy.

Elia Kazan showed up on opening night and offered Dean the star role in his upcoming film, *East of Eden* (1955).

That very night, Dean dropped out of the play and headed for Hollywood.

It was the birth of a legend.

***

Henry Reprises Mr. Roberts as a Movie

The Hollywood Reporter announced that after a seven-year absence, Henry Fonda was making a film "comeback," repeating his role of Lt. Doug Roberts, this time as part of a movie, then in pre-production at Warners.

At the time, Josh Logan, who owned a financial interest in the picture, thought he would be the director. Henry, however, had said he would never work with Logan again after a blow-up they'd had over the way *Mister Roberts* was being performed onstage in San Francisco.

Since he'd first starred in the role on stage, Henry had aged a bit and was pushing fifty. The character he played, Lt. Roberts, was that of a 27-year-old naval officer.

Logan had met several times with Marlon Brando, who had already signed to make *The Egyptian* (1954), a big-budget script he loathed. He thought he could get out of his commitment and take the lead in *Mister Roberts.*

Jack Warner, however, had a different actor in mind for the film version of *Mister Roberts:* "William Holden would be perfect," he told his associates.

Three days later, Logan read in *The Hollywood Reporter* that John Ford had signed on as the director. Logan was bitterly disappointed and put through a call to Warner, finally getting him on the phone.

"We'll make a lot more money with Ford as director," Warner told Logan. "You'll benefit financially, since you own some of the rights. I also heard you and Fonda aren't even speaking to each other. My decision is final. It's Ford, with Fonda in the lead."

Ford had attended the stage production of *Mister Roberts* in Manhattan. He watched only the first ten minutes before retreating to a saloon across the street. After the curtain went down, Ford joined Henry in his dressing room, praising his performance, despite the fact that he had not seen it.

On the way out of the theater, a reporter from the *Daily News* spotted him. "Are you going to direct the film version?"

Ford shot back, "I'm not known for directing homosexual plays."

Before signing for the role, Henry had worried that he was too old to play the rebellious young lieutenant, thinking he might be better suited to the role of the older doctor. Jack Warner talked him out of that, and brought the aging William Powell out of retirement to play "Doc." It would be Powell's last motion picture.

Assigned the role of the tyrannical Captain Queeg, James Cagney returned to Warner's after 25 years. Back in the 1930s, he had made all those gangster movies at the studio.

The key role of Ensign Pulver went to Jack Lemmon, who had been rejected as one of the sailors in the Broadway production. He was eager to take over the role of the lackadaisical officer in charge of morale and the laundry.

Other key parts went to Betsy Palmer as the nurse. Ford always hired "my most reliable old friend," Ward Bond. Other players included Phil Carey, Nick Adams, and Martin Milner.

On the first day that Cagney showed up to impersonate Captain Queeg, Ford confronted him, suggesting that they "tangle asses" before the picture was completed.

By the second week, Cagney was enraged. "I want to kick out Ford's brains!" On the afternoon of the day that Cagney could take it no more, Ford was publicly shouting insults about his acting.

"I reminded Ford of that 'tangled asses' comment," Cagney later said. "I dared him to step outside where I planned to beat his ass to pulp. He turned down my challenge. For the rest of the shoot, he showed a little respect, as both of us concealed our loathing."

In their previous films, including *The Grapes of Wrath,* Ford and Henry had gotten along reasonably well. At this point in his illustrious career, Ford had a reputation for being tough on his actors, even calling John Wayne "the big idiot." It was said that the only man who could bring The Duke to tears was Ford himself.

For some faraway location shooting, the U.S. Navy flew cast and crew to Midway Island, scene of some of the bloodiest fighting in World War II. The director and his stars were housed in the Bachelor Officers Quarters.

Ford had always been a heavy drinker, but in most cases, he confined his boozing until nighttime, and remained sober throughout most of the day. On Midway Island, however, he began to drink heavily early in the day and was often intoxicated before noon.

It was said that the more macho the film, the more its director, **John Ford**, drank on the job.

On postwar Midway Island, long after the heroism of the war had morphed into sentimental retrospective, he was sometimes incoherent after lunch from too much alcohol. At moments like that, his feud with Henry Fonda got serious.

Henry, still dedicated to the precepts of the (very successful) Broadway play in which he had starred, complained to Cagney, Powell, and others about Ford's direction and the "silly scenes" that he had ordered inserted into the script. Word of his complaints reached Ford, who firmly believed that Frank Nugent, a former film critic for *The New York Times,* had distorted the original script.

One night from the officer's quarters, Ford sent a messenger to summon Henry to his room. Although he resented being summoned like this, Henry went anyway, finding Ford hostile, drunk, and seated imperiously in a large wicker chair.

"I hear you don't like the new script or my direction," Ford said.

"That's right. I think both of them are shit."

On unsteady feet, Ford rose from his chair, crossed over to Fonda, and bashed him in the face, bloodying his nose. Henry fell back against a table, knocking it over and breaking the glass vase which had stood on it.

Rising in rage, Henry was ready to strike back, but did not, realizing that Ford was not only half blind, but drunk and in obvious ill health.

Two hours later, Ford staggered to Henry's room, pounding on the door. When Henry opened it, the director said, "I've come to apologize."

The door was slammed in his face. For the rest of the location shooting in Midway, although the tension between Ford and Henry was intense, there was no more violence.

However, Ford showed his contempt for Fonda by turning to him after every scene was wrapped and asking, with elaborate good manners, "Mr. Fonda, did the way I directed that scene meet with your approval?"

Henry never answered such questions, always turning and walking away.

Producer Leland Hayward was of no help. From Midway, he was flown to Los Angeles, where he entered a hospital, suffering from internal hemorrhages.

After the shooting ended on Midway, cast and crew were flown to Hawaii for a month's location shooting on Kaneohe.

Ford collapsed on the set and was rushed to a hospital, where he was operated on for a gall bladder infection. When it became obvious that his recovery would be slow, Jack Warner sent Mervyn LeRoy to take over as director.

When Warner sat through the rushes, he was horrified at some of the scenes Ford had inserted. Neither was he pleased with LeRoy's work, either. He phoned Josh Logan to reshoot some scenes and to add some new ones.

Previously, Henry and Logan had feuded over the performances of Henry and his fellow actors in the San Francisco production of *Mister Roberts*. Although Henry had vowed never to work with Logan again, to save the movie, he and his longtime friend made up, merely as a means of getting through a final cut.

For the most part, the critical appraisals of the film adaptation of *Mister Roberts* were favorable. The critic for *The New York Times* found that "Fonda evolves as a beautifully lean and sensitive characterization, full of dignity and power."

Variety suggested that "Talent such as Fonda's should be used more frequently on the screen."

Of course, there were the usual detractors. Devin McKinney wrote, "A story that calls for a poet's sad touch is covered with Ford's fumbling thumbprints. The skeletal play becomes a wide-screen whale spouting gouts of buffoonery and sentimentality."

As another critic wrote, "The humor of the play has been junked and some silly scenes inserted instead. The subtitles of the Broadway play have been tossed aside, and some of the best lines rewritten into meaningless dribble."

Made on a budget of $2.5 million, *Mister Roberts* garnered $2.3 million at the box office.

The film was nominated for three Academy Awards, including Best Picture and Best Sound Recording. Lemmon won the Best Supporting Actor Oscar.

On looking back, Henry said, "John Ford and I have had a long and abiding love for each other. However, that love affair is over."

***

Henry Fonda's Early Experiments with TV

Only his most devoted fans recall Henry's first venture into television drama. Performing on the new medium—in vivid contrast to shooting a movie or appearing on stage—he was on and off rather quickly.

On July 13, 1953, Henry performed live in front of a "studio audience" on a Chrysler-sponsored, 30-minute drama. It was *The Decision of Arrowsmith,* based on Sinclair Lewis' Pulitzer Prize-winning novel, *Arrowsmith,* published in 1926. In it, Arrowsmith searches for a cure for the plague in the West Indies.

Tad Mosel, who had adapted the novel for the screen, claimed, "It was the worst experience for both Hank and me."

In the studio audience on the night of its telecast, checking out the venue, was Ronald Reagan, who was to star in the Chrysler Theater's next drama, *A Job for Jimmy Valentine,* adapted from a short story by O. Henry.

He met with and talked to Henry, telling him that his role would be that of a safecracker just released from prison. He has returned to his criminal behaviors until he falls in love with the daughter of a banker.

"Type casting!" Henry said, jokingly.

He and Reagan met again when Henry agreed to appear on the General Electric Theater on CBS, a series hosted by Reagan. *The Clown,* broadcast on Sunday, March 27, 1955, paired Henry with actress Dorothy Malone as the episode's co-stars

The Clown was based on the life of circus clown Emmett Kelly (1898-1979), who created the character of "Weary Willie." He became America's most famous clown, with his sad-sack, shuffling antics of the unkempt, downtrodden hobo.

As one reviewer wrote, "Through Fonda's character, we see the serious business of being funny and the personal price paid for success. The strains of life under the Big Top take their toll on one, and Fonda's role leaves us with feelings of a lifetime."

Producer Fred Coe scored a big success when he got Henry to co-star with Humphrey Bogart and his wife, Lauren Bacall, in an episode entitled *The Petrified Forest*, an hour-long live show that was televised as part of NBC's *Producer's Showcase* on May 30, 1955.

[The original version of The Petrified Forest *had been a 1935 play by Robert E. Sherwood. It had been adapted into a movie in 1936 with Leslie Howard, Bette Davis, and Humphrey Bogart.*

Bacall made her TV debut in its much- revised televised remake as Gabrielle Maple, who works in a dusty gas station café, but yearns for a better life. A hitch-hiking writer, the disillusioned Alan Squier (Henry Fonda), appears and revitalizes her dream. Duke Mantee (Bogie) and his gang of "thugs" show up and take hostages.]

One critic wrote, "It's a sad, sad disaster. Fonda is stilted in his role. Bogart is back as the gangster Mantee, but he is tired, so tired. He may have already known he was dying."

Two views of **Dorothy Malone:** Upper photo: With **Henry Fonda** in the General Electric Theater's TV drama, *The Clown*.

Everyone agreed that Malone, especially her legs, looked a lot better than Henry's—and more convincing as part of a high-wire act.

At the end of the telecast, Henry was invited to join Bogie and Bacall for a party at their home. There, Henry greeted Frank Sinatra at the bar. He was pushing an after-dinner drink *[one part crème de cacao, one part crème de menthe, one part fresh cream]* called 'the grasshopper."

Henry agreed to try one, although he had never heard of such a concoction. He liked it and ordered another….and another. As the night wore on, he drank even more until he passed out on Bogie's sofa in his living room.

After midnight, Sinatra asked Bogie to help half-carry, half-drag Henry to Sinatra's car.

The drunken actor was driven to the Beverly Hills Hotel, where he was taken to a suite, undressed, and put to bed.

When Henry awakened at 10AM the next morning, he found himself completely nude under a sheet. He had no memory of how he had gotten there. In the hotel lobby, at the front desk, he learned that Bogie and Sinatra had "transferred" him to his room.

Henry phoned James Stewart and did his best to describe what had happened: "Both guys completely undressed me until I was jaybird naked. I think they raped me."

"Is your rosebud sore?" Stewart asked.

"No."

"Then you weren't raped. Sinatra probably wanted pictures of your junk to sell as postcards along Hollywood Boulevard."

Henry stayed in bed at the hotel until noon, trying to recover "from the worst hangover of my life."

After he'd dressed, he stumbled through the lobby with a blinding headache, seeking some medication at the newsstand.

***

Dino De Laurentiis, *War and Peace*

En route to the newsstand in the lobby of the Beverly Hills Hotel, an unidentified young man with an Italian accent approached him. He was accompanied by the most smartly dressed man in Hollywood.

The younger of the two men said to Henry, "Sir, I would like to introduce you to Dino De Laurentiis." After Henry shook his hand,

and said a few words, the Italians moved on.

Back in his suite, the phone rang. It was that assistant again. "Mr. De Laurentiis is in Hollywood casting roles for his latest movie, Tolstoy's *War and Peace*. There is a role in it for you, should you accept."

"Go on," Henry urged. "I read the book. A fabulous story."

"I'll have the script delivered to your suite at once." He kept his word. Within ten minutes, there was a knock on his door. When he opened it, he was handed a thick script.

Ordering a pot of black coffee, he sat down to read it. He immediately became aware that he had not been told which character De Laurentiis had earmarked for him.

He later said, "The part I really wanted was that of Pierre, the central character and a voice from Tolstoy's own beliefs and struggles. If only I were thirty years younger."

[In the novel, Pierre is the socially awkward and illegitimate son of Count Kirill Vladimirovich. Educated abroad, Pierre has returned to Russia but remains something of a misfit. However, his unexpected inheritance of a huge fortune has made him socially desirable.]

After making some phone calls, Henry learned a lot more about the upcoming epic. Indeed, De Laurentiis wanted him for the role of Pierre, in spite of Henry's age. He later learned that King Vidor had been named as director. This was the same director who had helmed James Stewart and Henry in *On Our Merry Way* in 1948. Henry had reservations about working with Vidor again, because Vidor had objected to his being cast as Pierre. Instead, Vidor preferred Marlon Brando.

When Brando was dropped, Vidor then recommended Peter Ustinov or Paul Scofield. De Laurentiis rejected both of them, claiming that neither had enough box office appeal.

Vidor, however, kept recommending other actors, each of whom fitted—more closely than Henry—the character's age: Montgomery Clift, Stewart Granger, Gregory Peck, and Richard Burton. De Laurentiis, however, rejected all of them. "I WANT FONDA," he said. "AND THAT'S MY FINAL WORD."

[De Laurentiis was a name familiar to Henry. Along with Carlo Ponti (married to Sophia Loren) he was one of the Italian producers who had brought Italian cinema to the international arena in the aftermath of World War II. In time, he would produce or co-produce a remarkable total of five hundred films, thirty-eight of which would be nominated for Academy Awards.

He'd come a long way since, as a kid, he used to hawk spaghetti, fresh from his father's pasta factory, in and around Naples.

De Laurentiis came to world attention when he directed such films as Bitter Rice *(Riso Amaro) in 1949, marrying its star, Silvana Mangano. He also received worldwide acclaim when he produced Fellini's* La Strada *(1954).]*

Leo Tolstoy had published *War and Peace* in 1869.

Over the years, many producers considered filming a movie adaptation, most notably Alexander Korda in 1941, when he wanted Orson Welles to direct it. Mike Todd once wanted to produce it with Elizabeth Taylor cast in the principal role of Natasha.

The plot begins its spin in 1805 when Napoléon was trying to conquer much of Europe, including parts of Russia.

Epic battle scenes, many of them filmed in Yugoslavia, would add to the flair and allure of the De Laurentiis film.

Eventually released in 1956, De Laurentiis' *War and Peace* would begin in 1812 when Napoléon crosses the River Neman into Russia, despite a treaty. The novel relays in detail the story of the war's effect on five families—the Rostovs, the Kuragins, the Drubetskoys, the Bezukhovs, and the Bolkonskys.

Before he arrived in Rome to make the film, Henry learned the names of the other cast members and the roles they would play.

The key characters would be Natasha, Pierre, and Andrei. Receiving top billing would be Audrey Hepburn, at the time, one of the biggest stars in the world. *[Actually, she had been the second choice after Jean Simmons rejected the offer.]*

Natasha, according to the novel and the script, was a singer and dancer, "not too pretty, but full of life, romantic, impulsive, and highly strung."

Hepburn insisted that her husband, Mel Ferrer, be assigned the third lead of Andrei. *War and Peace* would be the only time Hepburn and Ferrer would co-star together in a movie.

A member of the Bolkonskys, Andrei was described as "strong but skeptical, thoughtful and philosophical as an *aide-de-camp* during the Napoleonic Wars."

The Italian actor, Vittorio Gassman, emerging from his divorce from Shelley Winters, was also assigned a key role. He would play Prince Anatole Vasilyevich Kuragin, a handsome and amoral pleasure-seeker who is secretly married but tries to

Audrey Hepburn with **Mel Ferrer** on the set of *War and Peace.*

Hepburn not only insisted that her real-life husband be cast in the movie with her, but that his fee be doubled.

elope with Natasha anyway.

The most glamourous member of the Kuragins, Princess Hélène, is a beautiful and sexually alluring woman who has many affairs, including, or so it is rumored, with her brother, Anatole.

Arlene Dahl had been set to portray her but had to drop out because of illness. In her place, the Swedish actress, Anita Ekberg, was cast as Hélène. The role would elevate her to an international celebrity, especially after she starred, four years later, in Fellini's *La Dolce Vita* (1960).

At the time of filming, Ekberg was married to the British actor, Anthony Steel, but would not be faithful. *[She conducted affairs, it was widely acknowledged, with Frank Sinatra, Yul Brynner, Tyrone Power, Bob Hope, Errol Flynn, Rod Taylor, and John Wayne.]*

Fredric March was originally slated to appear as Field Marshal Kutuzov, but before filming began, he was replaced with Oskar Homolka, a Viennese star who became one of the most employed actors in film history. *[He starred in four hundred plays before he was thirty, and before the end of his life, in some 100 movies. Prior to making* War and Peace, *he had appeared in Marilyn Monroe's* Seven Year Itch *(1955).]*

As one of the Rostovs, Natasha had a cousin, Sonya. That role went to the blonde beauty from Stockholm, May Britt, who had been discovered as a teenager by Carlo Ponti. She would become notorious in 1960, when she married Sammy Davis Jr. At that time, interracial marriage was banned in 31 U.S. States.

Cast as Napoléon, the Czech-born British actor, Herbert Lom, would have a career spanning six decades. He often portrayed criminals or suave villains but became best known for his skill as a comic actor in *The Pink Panther* franchise.

The English actor, John Mills, was cast as Platon Karatayev, the archetypal good Russian peasant, whom Pierre meets in a prisoner-of-war camp. His career would span seven decades and take in some 120 films. In 1971, he would win a Best Supporting Actor Oscar for his performance in *Ryan's Daughter*. In time, he would be knighted by Queen Elizabeth II.

The best-looking actor in the cast was a Viennese, Helmut Dantine, who almost made a decades-long career cast in various film productions as a Nazi. In *War and Peace*, he played Fyodor Ivanovich Dolokhov, a cold, almost psychotic officer. He ruins the life of Nikolai Rostov (Jeremy Brett), a Hussar and the beloved eldest son of the Rostov clan. Fyodor lures him into an outrageous gambling debt after unsuccessfully proposing to Sonya Rostov (May Britt). His character was widely rumored—it was suggested in both Tolstoy's novel and in the film—to have had an affair with (the widely promiscuous) Hélène (Anita Ekberg).

Dantine was seen by American audiences when he played the downed Nazi pilot in *Mrs. Miniver* (1942) opposite Greer Garson. That same year, he was seen as a desperate refugee in *Casablanca* opposite Humphrey Bogart.

Dantine was signed to a contract by Warners, and ended up at least three times on the "casting couch" of Errol Flynn. Their co-starring roles were in *Desperate Journey* (1942); *Edge of Darkness* (also 1942); and *Northern Pursuit* (1943).

During his reunion with King Vidor, Henry told him, "You already know what a son of a bitch I can be."

Many of the conflicts Henry had with De Laurentiis were about the physical appearance of Pierre. The producer wanted Henry to be dashing and romantic, but Henry preferred that he follow the description composed by Tolstoy: "a guy with two left feet, clumsy, a little too heavy, and not very good looking." Henry also wanted Pierre to wear glasses, but the producer did not.

[Whenever the producer was not on the set, Henry put on "my specs."]

Henry also clashed over changes being made to the original script. Henry called these last-minute rewrites "a farrago of fiddlings."

Their disagreements became so intense that Henry announced that he would not see the finished film. "Why should I?" he said. "I know how lousy it is already!"

Henry even told a reporter, "We are making the *Reader's Digest* version of the Tolstoy novel. Based on letters coming in, fans would rather see Rock Hudson in my role."

Bosley Crowther in *The New York Times* praised the movie as "massive, colorful, and exciting as anything of this sort I've ever seen. However, the characters are second

Agog, then, with all things Italian, including Dino De Laurentiis, America gobbled up Swedish bombshell **Anita Ekberg** on the cover of *Life* magazine, replete with peek-a-boo decolletage and references to European glam.

Bespectacled **Henry Fonda,** staying true to his actor's interpretartion of the shy and awkward character Tolstoy had crafted—despite the sometimes screaming denunciations of the film's producer, Dino De Laurentiis.

rate, people without much depth."

Time lauded Audrey Hepburn but noted, "Fonda's leanness at first seems all wrong for the massive, moon-faced, soul-tortured Pierre, but he builds beautifully in his part."

The critic for the *Los Angeles Times* wrote, "Fonda seems like an anti-character in his behavior on the battlefields. He is actually a symbolic figure of peaceful thinking in the story, representing the heroine's lasting romance."

Hollis Alpert, in *The Saturday Review,* found the film adaptation "only intermittently interesting, and that aside from making a sort of pictorial sour-mash of the original work, is not particularly good movie-making."

In the *Encyclopedia of American War Films,* Larry Langman wrote: "The sweep and spectacle of the film cannot compensate for its weaknesses, such as the miscasting of Henry Fonda."

***

Much of *War and Peace* would be shot in Rome. Henry, aboard a plane with Jane and Peter, landed in the city to set up temporary housekeeping. Susan, with baby Amy, flew in several days later.

Upon her arrival, Susan was photographed at the airport. A local tabloid defined her as "a society girl two decades younger than Grandpa Fonda."

Rome might be known as the Eternal City, but "eternal" was not a word that applied to the Fondas. As a family unit, they would not survive Henry's filming in Rome.,

Here's a handsome spin on **Henry Fonda** in *War and Peace*— a cinematic, makeup-enhanced romantic hero in the style of Lord Byron.

In this press photo, he looks the way De Laurentiis wanted him to—without spectacles and without the awkwardness and ugliness Tolstoy had originally associated with the character Fonda had been assigned to portray.

A classic, librarians have said, "is a work of art that transcends the time and space of its setting and relays truth and meaning to new generations of readers, or listeners, or viewers."

Here's a photo of **Leo Tolstoy** three years before his death in 1910, with his long-suffering wife of forty-eight years, **Sofia**, the obedient, once-vivacious daughter of a prominent doctor favored at the time by the Tsarist regime.

During the course of a turbulent marriage marked by his volatile behavior, she copied (by hand) his manuscripts, critiqued his writing, bore him thirteen children (eight of whom survived to adulthood), and managed his sprawling estate (4000 acres with 300 serfs). Later, as a deterrent to his penchant for giving away his assets, she also handled his literary sales and royalties.

In her diary entry from 12 November 1866, she wrote: We were having such a good time in the first three weeks of September that I instinctively repressed all bad thoughts. When I do not open my diary for a long time I always think what a pity it is I do not record the happy times. I now spend most of my time copying out Lyova's (aka "Leo's) novel [**War And Peace**], which I am reading for the first time. It gives me great pleasure. Nothing touches me so deeply as his ideas, his genius. This has only been so recently. Whether it is because I have changed or because this novel is extraordinarily good, I do not know. I write quickly, so I can follow the story and catch the mood, but slowly enough to be able to stop, reflect upon each idea and discuss it with him later. He and I often talk about the novel together, and for some reason he listens to what I have to say (which makes me very proud) and trusts my opinions."

"WAR AND PEACE"
starring
AUDREY HEPBURN · HENRY FONDA · MEL FERRER
A Ponti-DeLaurentiis Production · A Paramount Re-Release · TECHNICOLOR®

R63/55

Cinematic replications of literary classics present daunting challenges to everyone involved.

This became obvious during scenes where the armies of yesteryear's empires strutted and conflicted in ways described by Tolstoy in *War and Peace*.

Here's an aerial press photo of some of the film's soldiers headed off—at astronomical expense—to bloody deaths or mutilation, and, perhaps, to short-term glory.

"HOLLYWOOD ON THE TIBER"

THE FONDAS INVADE ROME
WILL HENRY FALL IN LOVE AGAIN?
WILL PETER OR JANE LOSE THEIR VIRGINITY?

SEEKING A NEW AND MORE VIBRANT LIFE WITH A YOUNGER MAN:
WHY HENRY'S THIRD WIFE,
SUSAN BLANCHARD,
DIVORCED HER "LOUSY HUSBAND"

MORE WAR AND MORE PEACE
ALTHOUGH HENRY DOESN'T SEDUCE HIS LEADING LADY (AUDREY HEPBURN)
HE GETS HOT, HEAVY, AND QUASI-ROMANTIC WITH ONE OF ITS SECONDARY PLAYERS,
ANITA EKBERG, THE SWEDISH BOMBSHELL

AFDERA FRANCHETTI
NAMED AFTER AN ACTIVE "STRATOVOLCANO" IN ETHIOPIA
THIS ITALIAN BARONESS CAPTIVATES HENRY "LIKE EVE DID ADAM"

THE BARONESS FRANCHETTI: WAS SHE TRUMAN CAPOTE'S INSPIRATION FOR HOLLY GOLIGHTLY IN
BREAKFAST AT TIFFANY'S? AND WHY DID EVERYONE CALL HER *MISS DRACULA?*
*Could drinking a quart of pig's blood every day,
as prescribed by her doctor for anemia, have had anything to do with it?*

ALFRED HITCHCOCK'S COURTROOM CLASSIC
THE WRONG MAN
HOW HENRY BEHAVED
*"Henry Fonda made two movie classics—The Wrong Man and 12 Angry Men—
each more appreciated by future generations that present movie-goers."*
—Bosley Crowther in *The New York Times*

HANDSOME, HUNKY, & HORNY
JAMES FRANCISCUS
"I plan to kiss Jane as she's never been kissed before."

How
ANTHONY PERKINS
Co-Starred with Henry (a Seedy Bounty Hunter) in
THE TIN STAR, and how He Became Hitchcock's *PSYCHO* and
Jane's First Leading Man

A "Regional Theater," Omaha-based, Father-Daughter rendition of
The Country Girl

In June of 1955, Henry, with his third wife, Susan Blanchard, attended the graduation of his daughter, Jane, from the Emma Willard School. There had been little, if any, discussion of her career ambitions.

Before Henry and the Fonda family flew to Rome for him to shoot scenes from *War and Peace* (1956), there was a prelude to the trip that has passed largely unnoticed. Herny and Jane made their father-daughter stage debut at the Omaha Playhouse, where Henry's stage career had begun.

In and around the Omaha arts scene, Harriet Peacock, Henry's sister, had assumed many of the official duties once carried out by the mother of Marlon Brando.

Harriet phoned her brother in New York and asked if he could fly to Omaha for five nights of benefit performances, hoping to raise enough money to build a new community theater.

His former co-star from the Omaha of long ago, Dorothy McGuire, had already agreed to appear with him in a reprise of *The Country Girl*, that play by Clifford Odets.

Much of America had already seen the 1954 film version of *The Country Girl*. It had starred Grace Kelly in an unglamourous role, that of a long-suffering wife married to a has-been, dysfunctional singer. Her co-stars had been Bing Crosby (as her embarrassing, drunken husband) and William Holden (as her "rescuer").

Henry and McGuire would play that husband and wife.

He was surprised when Harriet told him that Jane had already agreed to appear in the production as the *ingénue*. "I don't know if she can act or not," he said. "We'll have to audition her."

After his son Peter agreed to work as a stagehand for the production, the three of them flew to Henry's native hometown of Omaha.

On June 24, 1955, *The Country Girl* played before packed audiences for five performances.

Jane's most difficult scene was in the last act, when she has to come onstage shedding real tears. Henry doubted if she could pull it off, but she did. Her secret? She had a stagehand slap her really hard, five times, before making her entrance.

For the most part, the Fondas were praised by local critics, one suggesting that Jane's eyes "were those of a hunted animal."

At the Omaha Playhouse in 1955, shortly after **Jane Fonda's** graduation from the Emma Willard School, she migrated to her father's home town (Omaha) for a small role.

In the lowest photo, she emotes with him on stage.

The middle photo shows father and daughter, rehearsing, with Omaha-born **Dorothy McGuire,** watching from the left.

It was the talk of Omaha, a stage reprise of the *The Country Girl* (1954), the movie where the usually very glamourous Grace Kelly had dared to appear as a repressed frump married to (the wrong) actor.

The top photo shows **Henry Fonda** with **Dorothy McGuire**, also an Omaha native, together on the cover of the production's program.

After that short run, Henry warned his daughter to think seriously before deciding to become a professional actress. "It's a brutal profession, filled with rejection and peopled by bastards who will break your heart."

After Omaha, and after a stopover in New York, the Fondas winged their way to Rome.

***

The "La Dolce Vita" of Postwar Rome

They invaded Rome during the peak years of its celebration as "Hollywood on the Tiber." A slew of flamboyant Tinseltown celebrities were seen coming and going. They were in Rome to make movies or to simply enjoy the city, which had blossomed into a romantic mecca in the decades after World War II.

It was filled with enticing restaurants, elegant hotels, lavish parties, luxurious boutiques, and world-class gossip. The most expensive address was the jeweler, Bulgari, on Via dei Condotti, soon to become a favorite of Elizabeth Taylor.

At night, the Via Veneto was star struck. On any given evening, you might see Tennessee Williams escorting Anna Magnani; or Gregory Peck, Ingrid Bergman, Alain Delon, Rock Hudson, Brigitte Bardot, Frank Sinatra, Orson Welles, or Marcello Mastroianni.

In January of 1949, massive press coverage had been devoted to Henry's friend, Tyrone Power, when he wed Linda Christian, having dumped Lana Turner, at the Santa Francesca Romana church in Rome, near the Colosseum. Surrounded by thousands of guests and hysterical fans, they were later received by Pope Pius XII.

Female sex divas were on the rise in Rome—especially Gina Lollobrigida. Local talent also included "that divine goddess," sultry Sophia Loren, who, as a teenager, had portrayed a (voluptuous) slave girl in *Quo Vadis* (1951), starring Robert Taylor, another friend of Henry's.

In 1953, Audrey Hepburn, now Henry's co-star in *War and Peace,* had shot to stardom playing an *ingénue* princess on the loose opposite Gregory Peck in *Roman Holiday.*

Another major event in Rome in 1953 focused on the arrival of Clare Boothe Luce, the Eisenhower-appointed ambassador to Italy from the United States. Her well-connected husband was Henry Luce, publisher of *Life, Time,* and *Fortune.*

Cinecittà Studios (Studio City) was a vast film production sprawl lying five and a half miles southwest of Rome. This is where Hepburn and Henry would shoot many of the interior scenes of *War and Peace.* The location came to international prominence when Roberto Rossellini filmed his gritty 1945 drama here. Opening to worldwide critical acclaim, it was called *Roma, Città Aperto* (aka "Open City").

Fellini's *La Dolce Vita* (1960) brought even more fame to *Cinecittà* and the fascinating city that housed it. Dolce Vita starred Mastroianni and Anita Ekberg, almost four years after she'd appeared in *War and Peace* with Henry.

***

Susan Says "Andiamo" to Henry and Her Marriage

De Laurentiis had rented, for the Fonda's use, the Villa Uscida off the Via Appia Antica. It was a sprawling property complete with a mineral water pool and gardens growing vegetables. In time, it would be purchased by director Franco Zeffirelli.

Until Jane began to meet people and even find a boyfriend, she was bored. She

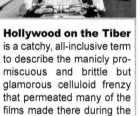

Hollywood on the Tiber is a catchy, all-inclusive term to describe the manicly promiscuous and brittle but glamorous celluloid frenzy that permeated many of the films made there during the 50s and early 60s.

There were many ironies associated with comparisons of "the "Holy City" to the lecheries of America's film capital. But they seemed appropriate for a way of life which had only recently been liberated from its Fascist grip,

And indeed, the visuals of Rome were always intriguing, especially when lots of very beautiful partially undressed people and scads of money got involved.

said, "There was nothing to do at the villa but eat figs and get fat, or else watch our next-door neighbor, Gina Lollobrigida, through binoculars."

At fifteen, Peter was not bored. In the villa's cellar, he discovered a wine cellar that Henry did not know existed. "I consumed two quarts of wine a day, at least two. I did more than that. I lost my virginity."

One afternoon, he was standing on the square overlooking St. Peter's Cathedral when the wife of a U.S. Army officer came up to him and started talking.

"She was young and quite pretty," Peter later claimed. "She told me her husband was currently on duty at the port of Brindisi. She said she was lonely and invited me back to the apartment she'd rented with her soldier boy. That was the afternoon I lost it."

In a memoir, he phrased it more colorfully: "She balled me, and it blew my life out."

From her very first week in Rome, Susan's troubled marriage to Henry entered its final stage. Mostly, its problems were based on a lack of communication.

"He was upset over his movie role," Susan said. "That made him upset about everything, including family problems. He had not visited my bed in a long time. We had problems to talk over, but all I got from him was a deaf ear. If a confrontation arose, he would walk out the door, perhaps to sit idly at one of Rome's cafés, watching life pass him by."

As Henry recalled, "The age difference between Susan and myself began to show its ugly face. She was vibrant, full of life, and wanted to accept the fabulous invitations that poured in daily. I wanted to memorize my lines for tomorrow's shoot and go to bed."

She started going out on the town alone. Often, as Henry was preparing to leave for the studio, she was just coming home from partying.

Henry later wrote, "She wanted the kind of thing a girl of her age wants, and I couldn't manage the work and the social things, too. She was unhappy, so very unhappy, and she let me know that in no uncertain terms. Our marriage had come to that fork in the road. She was heading in one direction, and I was taking a different route."

"I did fall in love with Henry at first," Susan later admitted. "But almost after two months of our marriage, I realized he was the wrong companion for me. Actually, he wasn't much of a companion at all. Since I knew I'd married the wrong man, I found it amazing that I stuck around as long as I did."

"One night, when I could not stand it any more, I confronted him when he came home from another bad day at the studio. He looked so depressed, I didn't want to spring the news on him. But I did anyway. I had to save myself. I told him I was taking Amy to New York with me. Our marriage was over. I'd be pursuing a divorce in Reno."

"He didn't scream or shout, but remained silent, looking at me like a stern father facing an errant daughter. There was a scream inside Hank, but one I feared would never be screamed. There was a laugh in him that would never be laughed. I wanted a new and different type of man for my husband, perhaps one of my own age."

The next morning, since both Susan and Jane were still in their bedrooms, Peter ate breakfast alone.

Susan later came down and joined Peter at table. Wasting no time, she shared her feelings. "I want a husband with whom I can share romantic secrets, one with lots of intimacy. I want to sing and dance the night away, arriving home as the sun is rising. I want to go to parties, meet glamourous people and have fun. I'm twenty-seven years old, and I don't want life to pass me by. That's why I'm returning to New York with Amy. I'll be filing for divorce."

Her parting remarks to Peter were, "I will always love you."

He was devastated and later admitted, "I burst into tears as she left the room. I had only recently learned that my mother, Frances, had cut her throat, committing suicide. My Dad told me she had died of a heart attack. I had to find that out from a tabloid. Susan had been a surrogate mother to me. I had wanted her to stay, but realized that morning that she had to escape to find a life of her own. Suddenly, Rome had lost its gaiety."

FURIOUS FONDA: Like many actors, Henry was affable and charming some of the time, and unpleasant when he was angry or depressed.

During much of his time on location in the strange, sometimes absurd venue called "post-war, *Dolce Vita* Rome," he was more than usually stern, "as unfunny as a tornado in the Dust Bowl," according to some of the people he reluctantly interacted with in Rome,

Jane had not come down from her bedroom upstairs, so Peter climbed the steps to tell her about the upcoming divorce. After a knock on her door, he entered her room, where she had just risen from bed.

She had this glow about her," Peter said. "Far from being unhappy, she was actually radiant. I soon found out why."

The previous night, as she confessed, she'd almost lost her virginity. She didn't name her would-be seducer. It could have been this Italian boy she'd been dating, Romano Gigioli. Don't you love that last name? Sounds like *gigolo*. I didn't want to ruin my sister's afterglow, but I felt I must. I told her what Susan said. She didn't seem shocked at all."

"I knew divorce was inevitable," Jane said. "Susan and Dad are not compatible, so why go on with a sham marriage? Their interests are completely different."

Still in mourning, Peter retreated to the wine cellar for the rest of the day, where the inventories inside were reduced by four quarts.

May of 1956 found Susan in Reno, filing for divorce from Henry, citing the "intense mental pain" he had caused her.

News of their divorce was broadcast around the country and published in major newspapers.

Anthony Quinn, as he appeared in *Zorba the Greek* (1964) with **Eleni Anousaki**, a Greek actress and later, politician.

***

Anthony Quinn's Advice to Henry About Learning a New Language? "Start Fucking a Local"

Anthony Quinn had recently arrived in Rome, and he called Henry for a dinner date, wanting to discuss their doing a movie together. Henry had something else on his mind…his loneliness. "I'd been to the studio to watch him play Pierre," Quinn said. "In private, he looked like Pierre watching Moscow go up in flames in *War and Peace.*"

Over cocktails, he complained to Quinn that he was "having a rough time since he spoke only ten words in Italian. "I can't even convey to my chauffeur where I want to be driven."

Quinn had a solution: "Start regularly fucking a gal who speaks no English, only Italian. You'll learn the language quickly enough, at least some boudoir Italian."

A week later, when Quinn and Henry met again for drinks along the Via Veneto, that hangdog look on Hank's face had disappeared. "Did you take my advice about that Italian gal?"

"Not quite," Henry said. "I found one better, a buxom blonde who speaks both English and Swedish. Anita Ekberg."

"You're having a fling with HER?"

"Indeed, but there are problems. She's just too much woman for me, barking orders about which zone to satisfy. To me, this worldwide sex symbol is completely unsexy."

"Pass her on to me," Quinn said. "My goal is to impregnate every good-looking woman in the world."

In 1955, **Henry** met **Afdera Franchetti.** She was a witty, glamorous multi-lingual socialite from a old Venetian family with an illustrious (some said Fascist) lineage associated with the rise and fall of Mussolini.

In the hedonistic context of the then-prevalent *La Dolce Vita*, he began an affair with her.

Here, they're seen together taking in some of the antiquities of southern Europe. The tabloids followed their relationship carefully, headlining it "Romance Amid the Ruins."

***

Introducing Afdera, the Baroness Franchetti

With his wife Susan far away and back in New York, Henry began to socialize again. Mel Ferrer had finished his work on *War and Peace* and was in France making a film with Ingrid Bergman.

His wife, Audrey Hepburn, asked Henry if he would escort her to a dinner party. The setting was a quaint little palazzo beside the Piazza Lovatelli. It was the home of Lorian Franchetti, married to Count Lollo. Among the guests invited were Afdera Franchetti, Lorian's sister. She was engaged to Augusto Torlonia at the time. He was divorcing the actress, Maria Michi, who had starred in Rossellini's *Rome, Open City*. After his divorce, he planned to marry Afdera.

At the time that Henry was introduced to "this beautiful and enchanting princess," she was in the throes of divorcing Howard Taylor, whom she had wed in 1954.

Afdera's fiancé at the time, Augusto Torlonia, known informally as "Lord of Earth," never went anywhere without being heavily armed. In 1949, as newspapers reported, he had survived an assassination attempt. On one of his estates, he had employed a young man as a shepherd. For some reason, he became embittered and tried to assassinate his boss with a revolver.

Afdera recalled her introduction to Henry, finding "something pure and very sensitive about him. His eyes were very blue, cool and detached. He looked untouched and untouchable, which I found attractive."

Although another guest was seated between them, throughout the dinner, Afdera caught Henry's attention by asking for one item after another from the salt shaker to a basket of bread.

"The first time I looked into her eyes, I felt they were a depository of secrets that dated back to the day when Eve tempted Adam with that apple," Henry said. "As I learned later, her father knew her well when he named her after an active volcano."

[*Afdera* is an isolated stratovolcano in northeastern Ethiopia, at the crossing point of three fault systems. EDITORIAL NOTE: Parts of Ethiopia were invaded and occupied by Italy for about five years (1936-1941) during Italy's Fascist regime of Benito Mussolini.]

At first, Afdera called Henry "Fonda" because "I liked the Italian sound of it. But after two weeks, I nicknamed him, 'Hank.'"

Although she had flirted all evening with him, he left the party with Hepburn and "didn't pick up on any of the signals I sent out."

Three nights later, Afdera hosted a dinner party of her own, inviting, among other guests, her friend, Jean Stein, who arrived, coincidentally, with Henry Fonda. At the time, Jean was the girlfriend of William Faulkner, but he was in America at the time. Stein was the daughter of Jules Stein, the founder of the talent agency Music Corporation of America (MCA).

[*Henry and Jules Stein had been friends from their days in Hollywood, and that is why Jean had invited him to accompany her to Afdera's dinner party. Afdera's apartment was on Via Monte Briano, with a balcony that opened onto a panoramic vista of the Tiber and the Castel Sant'Angelo.*]

In her early 20s at the time, Henry interpreted Afdera as "a striking, sloe-eyes seductress with golden hair and all the enchantment of a Venetian beauty."

He expressed to her his discontent with his role of Pierre in De Laurentiis' *War and Peace*. "It should have gone to Peter Ustinov."

"I must tell him that," she said. "He's close friend of mine."

He phoned her the following night, and in the aftermath of that call, Afdera became Henry's guide to Rome, showing him the sights, both the obvious ones and the secret places known mainly to the Romans themselves.

She revealed her family's lineage: Born in 1931, she defined herself as an Italian "baroness," and revealed that she was descended from an old Jewish family from Venice. It had intermarried with the Rothschilds before eventually converting to Roman Catholicism.

She was the daughter of Baron Raimondo Franchetti, a famous explorer, who had traveled extensively in then-uncharted regions of Africa, especially Ethiopia (which was eventually "conquered" by Italy and maintained, in the late 1930s, with a lot of atrocities and bloodshed, as an overseas "colony."

One writer described Afdera's father, Baron Franchetti, as resembling one of the Nietzschean heroes of his friend and contemporary, the author

Snapped in New York in 1957, near the theater where a crew was filming Henry's then-upcoming movie, *Stage Struck*, this photo circulated widely a few days before the announced nuptials of **Afdera Franchetti** with **Henry Fonda**.

The press release that accompanied it made it a point to mention their ages: 24 and 51, respectively, and that Henry had already been married three times.

Gabriele D'Annunzio. Baron Franchetti had also been a friend of the Italian Fascist and dictator, Benito Mussolini.

The explorer stood six feet, three and renamed his offspring after exotic places he had visited during his "explorations" (some said "colony building"). The baron had been assassinated when a bomb exploded within the plane he was flying from Cairo to Addis Ababa. In her memoir, *Never Before Noon*, Afdera insisted that her father's death had been based on orders from Winston Churchill.

Afdera had been named, as mentioned earlier, after an active volcano in Ethiopia. The name of the baron's oldest daughter, Simba, for example, translated from Swahili as "lion."

Lorian, whom Henry had met on the evening of his first encounter with Afdera, was named after an African swamp where elephants went to die.

The name of Baron Franchetti's only son, Afdera's brother, was Nanuk, meaning "Eskimo." He had been assigned the name after his father's "exploration" of the North Pole.

Nanuk was a close friend of the novelist, Ernest Hemingway, who had hunted with him in the Caorle Lagoon, about thirty-six miles northeast of Venice. Throughout Afdera's courtship of Henry Fonda, Nanuk continuously urged his sister to marry that Italian duke.

One night, Afdera discussed her friendship with Hemingway, claiming that it was she who had inspired his character of the young Italian heroine in his novel, *Across the River and Into the Trees*, published in 1950.

She also claimed that another of her friends, Truman Capote, had used her to mold his character of Holly Golightly in his famous novella, *Breakfast at Tiffany's.*

In Rome, she not only showed Henry the sights, but introduced him to the *glitterati* of *La Dolce Vita's* heyday.

She spoke six languages, all of which Henry could hear her speaking at various parties they eventually attended. Soon, through her, he met scions of the Fiat manufacturing dynasty, the Agnellis, Roman politicians, Florentine artists and socialites, businessmen from Milan, what was left of the French *ancien régime*...even tin magnates from Bolivia.

Henry finally got around to discussing with Anthony Quinn the possibility of making a movie together. It turned out to be *Warlock* for Fox, released in 1959.

He told Quinn about his involvement with Afdera, admitting that so far, their relationship had been platonic, although they were seeing a lot of each other. "I have one great reservation about her. I fear that she might be a cannibal."

"You're joking, of course," Quinn said.

"A container filled with dark red blood, a whole quart of it, arrives daily at her flat. She drinks the whole thing."

[As it turned out, Afdera was suffering from anaemia. Her doctor suggested that she arrange with a local butcher for its delivery every afternoon, after the morning's slaughter. "I think you had better start calling me "Signora Dracula," she had told him.]

Afdera's flamboyant father was the eccentric explorer, Baron **Raimondo Franchetti,** known for his explorations of barely charted regions of Antarctica and Africa, and for his close friendships with high-level Italian Fascists close to Mussolini.

Here, he appears in 1930 in the Afar Triangle, a dessicated, anthropologically important region of East Africa.

At the time, Italian Fascists were strengthening their colonial claims on, among others, Ethiopia. When Franchetti's plane exploded in midair en routh to Addis Ababa from Cairo, lots of people speculated that it had been as a reprisal for his pro-Italian colonial conspiracies in Ethiopia, Djibouti, and Eritrea.

LOVE, ITALIAN STYLE
GETTING TO KNOW THE "VAMPIRE" YOU'VE BEEN DATING

Jokingly, Afdera once noted that she had "bloodthirsty tendencies," raising anxieties, according to Henry, that she might be a vampire.

She was referring to a daily dietary supplement, prescribed by her doctor, for anemia.

From a local butcher, she had arranged for the delivery, every afternoon after the morning's slaughter, of a liter of fresh pig's blood. Then, she drank it throughout the course of the afternoon for what had been diagnosed as a cure for some of her ailments.

Relatively common at the time, this type of "cure" —based on the possiblity of transmission of blood-borne diseases—has, since the days of Afdera Franchetti, fallen into disfavor.

Still keeping the relationship platonic, Henry accepted her invitation to ride the train with her to Venice to visit her Renaissance-era palazzo. She chose to ride the train since she had a fear of flying since her father died from that bomb that exploded inside his plane.

[Henry had another reason for wanting to visit Venice. He had not seen his stepdaughter, Pan, since Frances' suicide. She was enrolled in an art school there.

He arranged to meet her, and, from all reports, their reunion devolved into a horrible argument when she cited him as the motivation for her mother's suicide. Henry would never see her again.]

He visited Afdera's ancestral home, a decaying villa on land outside Venice. Rows of damaged antique garden statues lined the walkway that led up to its entrance.

Henry commented on how badly the statues had deteriorated.

Afdera claimed that after a former *duenna* of the estate had objected to the fact that the statues were nude, Hemingway and her brother, Nanuk, had shot the phalluses and testicles off the male statues and the breasts off the statues of the females.

During the train ride back to Rome, Henry had booked separate compartments for each of them, but on the night of their transit, he visited her compartment, after which their relationship was no longer platonic.

She telephoned her sisters the following day to report on what had happened: "Henry gave me a mink coat and always sees that I have a steady flow of tangerines, which, as you know, is my favorite fruit. Also, and most importantly, he always has a hard-on at his age." *[Henry himself, years later, cited her use of the English-language vernacular, "hard-on" in lieu of an Italian or French equivalent.*

Afdera's relationship with Henry Fonda progressed to the point where she eventually agreed to visit him in New York. But before flying off to America to join him, her brother, Nanuk, gave her a severe beating for breaking off her engagement to Augusto Torlonia.]

***

Wild Jane at Vassar

After their time in Rome, Jane and Peter returned to New York for the beginning of their school terms in September of 1955.

Jane would begin her freshman year at Vassar, and Peter would matriculate to Westminster School, a boarding school at Simsbury, Connecticut.

Vassar was a college for women that had been founded in 1861 at the start of the Civil War. It was a private liberal arts school, lying on the outskirts of Poughkeepsie, New York, seventy miles north of New York City. Unapologetically prestigious, it was a member of the "Seven Sisters" *[Highly selective, and including both Wellesley and Smith, each of them at the time accepted only women, many from upperclass WASP families, in environments designed to parallel the educational savvy of the (traditionally all-male, at least at the time) Ivy League colleges.]*

Jane was pleased that Brooke Hayward, her childhood friend, was enrolled there, too. Jane had nothing but sympathy for her. Her mother, Margaret Sullavan, was having various mental breakdowns, and her siblings, both Bridget and Billy, had been in and out of mental institutions.

Brooke told Jane, "Vassar is where you can prepare for marriage, motherhood, and menopause."

Before they found new boyfriends, her classmates often talked of sweethearts left behind after graduation from high school. In contrast, Jane could speak of film stars she'd met, including Clark Gable, John Wayne, and James Stewart, or else having Bette Davis drop in on a Saturday afternoon.

By the time of her 18th birthday in 1955, Jane had reached her full height of 5 feet, 7 ½ inches. She had lost the chubby look, her baby fat melting away, and she had emerged, as one observer claimed, "slim, lithe, and sexily alluring."

Jane Fonda as she appeared as a student at Vassar.

A fellow classmate, Brooke Hayward, the daughter of Margaret Sullavan and Leland Hayward, said, "Whenever I saw Jane, she'd fill me in on all the intimate details of her dates. I got furious when I learned that she had beat me in the matter of losing our (respective) virginities."

"She said it was to an older man, not a college kid, that he was experienced, knew what he was doing, not fumbling around like some boy. I think she said he was Italian, and much older."

She still liked to eat heartily, but to keep her weight down, she often vomited the contents of a meal.

She also began to date, preferring good-looking young men from Yale. Weekends were often spent in Manhattan.

The future television talk show host, Dick Cavett, recalled his time at Yale: "I used to hear the click of Jane's high heels as she invaded our dorm after hours, heading for the bedroom of one of my classmates."

The novelist, Michael Thomas, the first husband of Brooke Hayward, was quoted as saying, "Jane was beautiful but cold as ice. She was sought after not just for her looks, but because she was the daughter of Henry Fonda. At Vassar, she had a reputation for being very promiscuous. It was rumored that she'd broken a taboo and had once been fucked in the "sacred halls" of Skull & Bones. *[Famous for generations as a secret society for (male) students at Yale,* Skull & Bones *was defined by* The Atlantic, *in their edition of February 25, 2013, as a group that for generations granted a coterie of white, privileged, predominately heterosexual men easier entry into the upper echelons of American society.]*

"As for my Dad, there were long periods where we didn't have any contact." Jane said. "He was too busy playing Henry Fonda."

Peter Fonda as a Preppie

In contrast, a different story was unfolding for Peter at Westminster. He soon discovered that "girls get just as horny as guys. It all began at a school dance when this girl pressed herself tight up against me. I knew she wanted me to slip away with her for some heavy kissing and feeling—and I did. She desired more, but I found we had to get back to the school dance."

"I wasn't interested in girls my own age," Peter said. "When Dad was making *The Wrong Man*, I had the hots for his leading lady, Vera Miles, but she didn't find me suitable, I guess."

Back in New York, Susan, still Henry's wife, was packing up and preparing to vacate the townhouse, with Amy in tow. "Both Jane and I hated to see her go, but Dad was romantically involved with this piece he'd picked up in Rome. She called herself a baroness."

Peter Fonda, as he appeared in *Tammy and the Doctor* (1963), looking clean-cut and preppy.

At Westminster, Peter would have many unfortunate encounters, as he hated the restrictions placed on him. Early in his term, he claimed that "some Nazi brownshirts searched my room, going through all my stuff. One of them found a package of cigarettes in my overcoat. Smoking was against school rules."

"I was sent to the principal's office, where this Goebbels-like geezer gave me thirty whacks with a leather belt. He probably got a hard-on doing that. Alas, my term had begun."

"I felt like I was in Sing Sing. While I was tossing the mattress of one of my classmates out the second-floor window, I got goosed in the ass. I hated that. I punched the jerk in the face. No one gooses my ass."

"In time to come, I would make that clear to officials from the F.B.I. who strip-searched me and also from agents of the U.S. Customs and Treasury. Even perverts from the Army draft board juggle your balls and stick their fingers in your rosebud. Who would take a job like that? Only the sickest of deviates. Imagine the creeps who like to play with the balls of forty or so young men a day, under the pretense of giving them a physical."

***

The Wrong Man

After the "rigors" of on-location filming in Italy, as a means of re-establishing himself in Hollywood, "Comeback Fonda" signed with Alfred Hitchcock to star in a grim drama, *The Wrong Man*. The Paramount release was rushed into production for a nationwide premier three days before Christmas of 1956.

Defined at the time as a "docu-drama *film noir*," it was drawn

HAVE YOU SEEN The Wrong Man --ALFRED HITCHCOCK'S *NEWEST* ADVENTURE INTO TERROR!

HENRY FONDA · VERA MILES ... ALFRED HITCHCOCK'S THE WRONG MAN from a real-life tragedy about an innocent man charged with a crime.

It had originally been configured as a short story by Maxwell Anderson—the playwright, author, poet, journalist, and lyricist—and entitled *The True Story of Christopher Emmanuel Balestero*. It described how he got tangled into a crime he did not commit. He is a down-on-his-luck musician, working for $85 a week at the swanky Stork Club in Manhattan. He needs $300 for dental work for his wife, Rose, and with that intention, applies for a loan at an insurance office but is turned down.

During the time he's inside its premises, the insurance company is held up by an armed bandit, who makes off with $217, all the cash the company has on hand. Eyewitnesses incorrectly identify Emmanuel (aka "Manny") as the culprit, and he is arrested, imprisoned, and put on trial.

He is only freed when the real robber is arrested, convicted, and imprisoned. Meanwhile, the mental stability of his wife, Rose, is destroyed and she is forced to retreat to a sanatorium.

Hitchcock read about the real-life incident in a newspaper and became so intrigued by Maxwell Anderson's story that he bought the film rights.

The works of Anderson had long been sought by Hollywood producers. He had written the screenplay for the classic *All Quiet on the Western Front* (1930). Before that, in 1924, he'd had a Broadway hit in another war story, *What Price Glory?*

Another massively popular screen adaptation was *The Private Lives of Elizabeth and Essex* (1939), starring Bette Davis and an actor she loathed, Errol Flynn.

Yet another Anderson work was incorporated into the 1948 film *Joan of Arc* starring Ingrid Bergman as the misunderstood French saint.

Bergman would soon face disgrace when her affair with Roberto Rossellini, the Italian film director, was exposed. Her Hollywood film career was destroyed, and she moved to Rome, where she divorced her Swedish husband [*Dr. Petter Lindström, whose marriage with her lasted from 1937 to 1950*]; married the Italian director; and for a while, made *avant-garde* films in Europe.

Ingrid Bergman, then the most reviled woman in America, portraying the much-abused saint, *Joan of Arc* (1948), in yet another screen adaptation of a literary work by Maxwell Anderson.

When she persisted in changing some of the dialogue he'd written, he called her "that big, dumb, goddamned Swede."

Hitchcock would hire Anderson again for the screenplay of *Vertigo* (1958), starring James Stewart. "Of all of Jimmy's movies, this was one of my favorites," Henry said.

In *The Wrong Man*, Hitchcock seemed intent on exposing just how unreliable so-called eyewitnesses can be.

In the plot, Manny's attorney, Frank O'Connor (Anthony Quayle), can't find any reliable witnesses to substantiate Manny's alibi.

The Oklahoma-born actress, Vera Miles, was cast as Rose, Manny's wife. At the time, *McCalls* was billing her as "the next Grace Kelly."

When she met Henry, she told him, "I've had a rough start getting launched in Hollywood. I was dropped by every big studio."

Hitchcock developed a fondness for her, and he cast her in *Psycho* (1960), the film horror classic.

When Miles met Henry, she had already co-starred in *Tarzan's Hidden Jungle* (1956). Bodybuilder Gordon Scott played Tarzan. Fans of the jungle hero by the thousands, especially the gay ones, viewed Scott as the most perfect specimen of all the Tarzans who had ever essayed the role.

Miles must have agreed, as she married Scott in a union that lasted from 1956 to 1960.

As Manny's attorney in the film, the English actor, Anthony Quayle, did a superb portrayal. He would go on to star in such classics as *Lawrence of Arabia* (1962) and would also be nominated for a Best Supporting Actor Oscar for his portrayal of Cardinal Wolsey in *Anne of the Thousand Days* (1969).

Hitchcock was so pleased with Miles' performance in *The Wrong Man* that in 1958, he cast her in *Vertigo*, starring James Stewart. Pregnancy forced Miles out of the role, which went to the miscast Kim Novak instead.

Afdera Franchetti flew into New York to resume her affair with Henry, visiting him during the day at various sets in New York, having told him that she was breaking her engagement to the Italian nobleman.

Then she flew back to Europe, having overcome her fear of airplane travel.

Long in advance of its release, she gave her review of *The Wrong Man*: "From what I saw being filmed, it is sad and boring. It also had something to do with Henry's memory of his second wife, the one who committed suicide."

The documentary-style *The Wrong Man,* widely defined as a major departure for Hitchcock, especially as regards pacing and suspense, disappointed many of his fans and most of the critics. *[Although it flopped at the box office, it was later rediscovered by another generation of movie addicts.]*

To Henry, its plot vaguely evoked two of his previous movies from the 1930s, *You Only Live Once* and *Let Us Live.*

The *Los Angeles Times* wrote, "As drama, unhappily, *The Wrong Man* proves again that life can be more interminable than fiction."

The *Washington Post* critic weighed in with: "Having succeeded often in making fiction seem like fact, Hitchcock in *The Wrong Man* now manages to make fact seem like fiction."

The *New Yorker* found the story "not very gripping." That conflicted with the critic for *Variety,* which viewed the picture as "a gripping piece of realism, a grim and absorbing melodrama."

Years later, the movie received much more favorable reviews after screenings by a young set of critics. Roger Ebert stated that the film "May be the least fun of Hitchcock's Hollywood period, but it's as fluently styled a movie as the director ever made."

Richard Brody of *The New Yorker* wrote that "few films play so tightly on the contrast between unimpeachably concrete details and the vertiginous pretenses of reality. Hitchcock's ultimate point evokes cosmic terror: Innocence is merely a trick of paperwork, whereas guilt is the human condition."

***

12 Angry Men

Henry was first introduced to the plot of *12 Angry Men* when he saw a teleplay broadcast in September of 1954 on CBS's *Studio One.* The script was written by Reginald Rose, and its star was Robert Cummings.

The drama takes place mostly in a jury room, where twelve very different male strangers are sequestered to decide the fate of a nineteen-year-old Puerto Rican accused of stabbing his father. If found guilty, he faces the electric chair.

So taken with the teleplay, and believing it would make a first-rate feature film, Henry shopped the script to Fox, MGM, Paramount, Warners, and Columbia. Each studio rejected it, citing it as "too grim" or as "box office poison."

In desperation, he and the scriptwriter, Rose, decided to form their own production company, Orion-Nova Productions, and they set about raising $337,000 for a three-week shoot in Manhattan. To save money, both Rose and Henry took salary deferrals.

Sidney Lumet was tapped as its director, although he'd never helmed a feature film. He became one of the first directors to move from television into feature films. When Henry met him, he was in the process of divorcing actress Rita Gam and planning to marry the heiress, Gloria Vanderbilt.

Lumet was a wise choice on Henry's part, since he would go on to be nominated for a Best Director Academy Award. Other Oscar nominations lay in his future, one which produced "gold" for his direction of *Dog Day Afternoon* (1975) and another for *Network* (1976).

After *12 Angry Men,* Lumet became one of the most prolific directors in Hollywood, helming, among other movies, five starring Sean Connery. The Lumet/Connery films included *Marnie* (1964), *The Hill* (1965), *The Anderson Tapes* (1971), *The Offence* (1972), and *Murder on the Orient Express* (1974).

Lumet and Henry selected a strong supporting cast of well-

The director's blocking of this shot from *12 Angry Men* has been cited as representative of the talent of Sidney Lumet, who never wasted an inch of screen space without "filling it" with items of interest.

In this case, his talent was obvious in the showcasing of a dozen very different and very angry American men, each members of the same jury, and each flexing his muscles. Their collective, misguided fury was cadenced only by **Henry Fonda's** quiet, contemplative, and calming effect on the trial process.

known character actors.

Known for playing arrogant, abrasive, and intimidating roles, Lee J. Cobb was cast as Juror #3, a hot-tempered owner of a courier business. He is estranged from his son and is a passionate advocate of a guilty verdict.

Cobb had starred as Willy Loman in the original Broadway production of Arthur Miller's *Death of a Salesman,* a role rejected by Henry. The play had opened to rave reviews on Broadway in 1949.

Cobb would later be nominated for a Best Supporting Actor Oscar for his performance in *On the Waterfront* (1954), starring Marlon Brando.

Juror #4, E.G. Marshall, was an unflappable and analytical stockbroker who is diligently concerned with the facts of the case.

He, too, had been one of the founders of the Actors Studio alongside Marlon Brando, Montgomery Clift, Kim Stanley, and Julie Harris. Actually, Cobb became best known for his TV roles, especially as Lawrence Preston in *The Defenders* (1961-65).

Ed Begley Sr., as Juror #10, is a pushy, loud-mouthed, and xenophobic garage owner. He would go on to distinguish himself in Tennessee Williams' *Sweet Bird of Youth* (1962), which brought him a Best Supporting Actor Oscar for his role as the mob boss of a redneck Southern town. He also achieved fame when he starred as Debbie Reynolds' father in *The Unsinkable Molly Brown* (1964).

Martin Balsam, playing Juror #1, was designated as the jury's foreman, a calm and methodical assistant high school football coach. Also associated with the Actors Studio, Balsam would go on to play the detective in *Psycho* (1960). In *Breakfast at Tiffany's* (1960), he was Holly Golightly's agent.

After the release of *12 Angry Men*, First Lady **Eleanor Roosevelt**, in her nationally syndicated and very influential newspaper column, "My Day," recommended it.

"The movie points up what it means to serve on a jury when a man's life is at stake. In addition, it makes vivid what 'reasonable doubt' means when a murder trial jury makes up its mind on circumstantial evidence."

Jack Klugman, Juror #5, plays a wisecracking salesman and baseball addict who is sensitive to observations about how he grew up in a violent slum. In the beginning, he loudly asserts that no amount of evidence will change his vision of a guilty verdict.

The film is brilliant in revealing the failures, faults, prejudices, and doubts of the jurors.

The action takes place during a sweltering New York summer in a locked, isolated jury room with a lone table and chairs. At the first vote, eleven jurors want to see the kid burn in the electric chair. The lone juror voting not guilty is Henry's character. From there, the action proceeds as Henry, point by point, challenges the so-called hard-fisted evidence.

In the end, Henry, portraying Juror #8, persuades the eleven other men to vote "not guilty," saving the defendant, cast with John Savoca, from the death penalty.

Henry does that by urging the jurors to look beyond their racism and prejudice.

Hollis Alpert of *Saturday Review* found that Henry's character was close to being "the American symbol of the unbiased, uncorrupted man. He is just about perfect for the role of Juror #8.

A.H. Weiler of *The New York Times* wrote, "Fonda gives his most forceful performance in years as the open-minded juror. In being strikingly emotional, he is both natural and effective."

Mike Massie wrote, "*12 Angry Men* is thought-provoking, continually riveting, and absolutely unforgettable—and surprisingly designed around a very simple, tightly budgeted, special-effects premise. It's an astonishingly profound example of storytelling trumping "spectacle."

Initially, Henry never received a cent for his double-duty as co-producer and star of the film. But as time went by, *12 Angry Men* became a classic, and has often been voted as one of the best courtroom dramas in movie history, rivaled by *To Kill a Mockingbird* (1962), starring Gregory Peck.

As time went by, *12 Angry Men* was shown frequently on television, in small "art theaters," and in school auditoriums.

One afternoon, Henry complained to his accountant, Charles Rentha, "I will never produce another film as long as I live. After all that struggle, not one god-damn dollar."

"You've not been studying your profits and losses over the years," Rentha answered. "*12 Angry Men* has, by now, earned you far more money than any film you ever made."

***

After shooting was wrapped on *12 Angry Men,* Henry wanted to take some time off to be with Peter and Jane, perhaps a visit from his stepdaughter Amy, if Susan would agree to release her.

His sister, Harriet Peacock, flew in from Omaha to help look after the brood.

For two months during the summer of 1956, he rented a big clapboard house next to the Kennedy family's compound in Hyannis Port. During the first week there, both Robert and Ted Kennedy dropped in to pay their respects to Henry, praising the films they had seen. Robert's favorite was *The Grapes of Wrath,* with Teddy preferring *Fort Apache.*

A lot of things were happening at Hyannis Port during the summer that Henry Fonda and his family rented a house near the Kennedy compound.

The photo above shows **John, Robert, and Teddy Kennedy,** with one of their houses in the background, at Hyannis Port in 1948.

John, despite his messed-up shirt, was representing Massachusetts in Congress: Bobby had recently graduated from Harvard and had entered law school; and Teddy, then aged 16, was still in high school.

Their high jinx and shenanigans was keenly followed by their nearby neighbors, (Henry, Jane, and Peter Fonda), and by virtually everyone else in town, too.

Three weeks later, they were invited for a barbecue at the Kennedy compound, where they met John F. Kennedy. A lifelong Democrat, Henry and JFK spent most of their time together, ignoring the rest of the party. Except for two women cooks, the Kennedy women were absent. Henry wanted to ask about Jacqueline, but out of discretion, chose not to.

For Henry, the summer brought back memories—some pleasant, others painful— of 1928, when he had worked at the Dennis Playhouse on Cape Cod.

Although he tried to join in the festivities, he also retired to make frequent phone calls to Afdera, eliciting her promise that she'd fly in for a visit in August, overcoming her fear of air travel.

He had lied about his age, telling her he was 48 when he had passed his 50th birthday.

Jane reported that she'd like to sign on as an apprentice at the Dennis Playhouse, which came as no surprise to Henry, since she'd already appeared in *The Country Girl* with him in Omaha the previous summer.

***

Summer Love on the Cape: Jane and James

On her first day at the Playhouse, she met a blonde, blue-eyed Adonis, the troupe's stage manager. Born in Clayton, Missouri, James Franciscus was three years older than her and unmarried. His father had died during World War II when young James was nine years old. He later studied theater arts at Yale where James graduated *magna cum laude.*

James' nickname was "Goey," which Jane thought was inappropriate. A female student said, "Goey sounds like semen being mopped up after a guy has yanked it out and shot off on a girl's belly."

In spite of the inappropriate nickname, Jane found James Franciscus highly intelligent, witty, and displaying an affection for the theater that appealed to her. His dedication to acting in many ways evoked her father.

From the first day she met him, Jane claimed she was "smitten." Her feelings were reciprocated, and they began to date. Seeing each other every day. Reportedly, they did not "go all the way" that summer. That would happen in the fall, but they were known to indulge in some heavy petting.

Having lost her baby fat, Jane had blossomed into one of the most beautiful eighteen-year-old girls on the Cape. Other young wannabe actors were interested in her, but James had staked his claim. Of course, several members of the Playhouse were gay, and almost every day, he faced propositions.

Young Love: **James Franciscus** with **Jane Fonda** in Provence—an extension and continuation of the friendship they'd previously pursued on Cape Cod.

"James was one male hunk," Jane told one of the young actresses.

When she and James had time off, they explored the Cape in his old red Ford convertible, going all the way to Provincetown.

"When I first took Jane in my arms, I was determined to kiss her as no man had ever kissed her before. I could tell by her response that I accomplished my mission."

[As an actor, James Franciscus, born on the last day of January in 1934 in Clayton, Missouri, never became a bigtime movie star. Yet he was one of the most familiar faces on television, starring in a number of series: Mr. Novak, The Investigators, Longstreet, Doc Elliot, *and* Hunter. *His first major role had been as Detective Jim Halloran in ABC's* Naked City.

In the 1960s and 1970s, he also starred in many feature films, most notably in Youngblood Hawke *(1964), where he played a southern writer who sets New York literary society ablaze. The character was clearly inspired by Thomas Wolfe.*

At the Cape during the summer of 1956, he met both JFK and Jacqueline. Ironically, he would eventually portray the President in The Greek Tycoon *(1978) and in* Jacqueline Bouvier Kennedy *(1981).*

"I should have married Jane," he recalled. "I was in love with her, but in my heart, I felt she was still a teenager and eager to learn a lot more about life before settling down to just one man."

Four years after dating Jane, James would marry Kathleen Wellman, the daughter of the famous director, William A. Wellman, and the couple would have four children. Wellman had directed Henry in The Oxbow Incident, *one of his most memorable films.]*

At Dennis, James was instrumental in getting Jane cast as a maid in a Restoration comedy, which Henry and Peter attended on opening night. She had no lines, but her father was pleased with her self-assurance on stage. More and more, he was wondering if she'd pursue acting as a career. In evaluating her performance of her small role, he used words like "charming" and "delightful."

Henry himself was asked to appear in *The Male Animal* for eight performances beginning on August 20. The play was based on the James Thurber work that Henry had first brought to the screen in 1942 with Olivia de Havilland as his co-star. Jane was cast in the *ingénue* role as Patricia Stanley.

"When Jane appeared, the audience sat up and took notice," Henry claimed. "She had this presence that made her stand out. Although I didn't tell her that night, I knew in my heart that I had fathered an actress."

An even bigger event that summer for Henry was the arrival of Afdera, "who blew in like a *sirocco,*" in Henry's words.

"Hanky wanted me to get acquainted with his *bambini,*" she said. "I knew Susan Blanchard was a tough act to follow, since Jane and Peter reportedly adored her."

"Afdera had a certain hard-sell charm," Jane said. "I didn't trust her from the beginning. Both Peter and I thought she was a phony. She was certainly no Susan, and I didn't respond to her like I did to my previous stepmother. Bringing this so-called Italian noblewoman into my life put more distance between Dad and myself."

In a memoir, Afdera later shared her impression of Peter. "We struck up a lukewarm relationship. It quickly cooled. Peter and I were like a cat and a dog sharing the same sofa. We treated each other with a weary and feigned tolerance. I took an instant dislike to him, for his pus-filled pimples and the beers he drank from the can."

Peter could hardly tolerate her, viewing her as "a flaky bitch, part of that Eurotrash preying on Americans. I felt she was after Dad's money. My, how this mock baroness put on fancy airs. I'm sure she was no more than an international tramp. God only knows how many guys had plowed into that overworked latrine. Just as much as I loved Susan was how much I disliked this Roman baggage who had flown in to bring more disaster to Dad. He should know by now that he is not the marrying kind."

In spite of Jane's indifference and Peter's obvious hostility, Henry moved ahead to fulfill his desire to marry her.

Henry had already failed in three marriages, but he assured his sister Harriet, "This one will work."

Afdera Franchetti with **Henry Fonda:**

"She had a certain hard-sell charm, but I didn't trust her."

—Jane Fonda.

"Brother, dear, marrying her would be like marrying a daughter, not a wife. She's barely out of her diapers."

As the last of the summer winds were blowing across Cape Cod, Henry at twilight walked her to the edge of a pier at Hyannis Port, the same pier where John Kennedy had walked with Jacqueline Bouvier.

There, he took her hand and looked deeply into her eyes, which seemed to have a twilight glow.

"I want you to marry me," he said. "Will you?"

"No, I will not," she said at once.

He grabbed her and kissed her passionately, ignoring her refusal.

When he finally broke away, he told her, "Beginning tomorrow morning, I will start making arrangements for our wedding day and honeymoon."

The sun had gone down when Henry and Afdera returned to his rented home. Whereas she retired to their bedroom, Henry, Jane, and Peter sat together in the living room.

Their vacation would soon be coming to an end, and each of them would be going in different directions. Jane would travel back to Vassar for her sophomore year. Peter would be enrolled at Westminster, that Connecticut boarding school for boys.

Afdera would be flying back to Rome to take care of her affairs, and Henry would return to Hollywood to make a Western with Anthony Perkins as his co-star.

"This time, kids, I've gotten it right. No more cheating whores like Margaret Sullavan. Not another Frances like your mother committing suicide." He deliberately omitted any mention of Susan, since he knew how devoted his children were to her.

***

The Tin Star

Ever since he made *Fort Apache* a decade previously, Henry had experienced no desire to make another Western. "My daughter Jane loves horses. I do not. If I want to go riding, I prefer to do so behind the wheel of an automobile. Frankly, horseback riding leaves me with a sore ass."

However, when director Anthony Mann approached him about starring in a new Western, Henry agreed to do so, but only after discussing it with his friend, James Stewart.

The picture was *The Tin Star*, written by his friend, Dudley Nichols, for a Paramount release in 1957.

Stewart was definitely a reliable source of information, since Mann had become a key player in his career.

Stewart had given his career a blood transfusion when he appeared on Broadway in the play *Harvey* in 1947. He played an eccentric whose best friend is an invisible rabbit as large as a man. He then starred in the successful screen adaptation of *Harvey* in 1950.

That summer, he formed a partnership with Mann to appear in a series of Westerns, often playing a troubled cowboy seeking redemption. The movies that spun off from that original theme included *Bend of the River* (1952), *The Naked Spur* (1953), *The Far Country* (1954), and *The Man from Laramie* (1955).

Stewart urged Henry to accept Mann's offer, and he did, signing to co-star with Anthony Perkins in one of this young New Yorker's first films. Perkins had scored a hit when he starred in *Friendly Persuasion* (1956), which brought him an Oscar nomination for Best Supporting Actor. In it, aging Gary Cooper played his father.

Even before Henry signed on, Mann had chosen a stellar cast of supporting players. The female lead went to actress Betsy Palmer in the role of Nona Mayfield. She is shunned by the rest of the town because she has a "half-breed" son named

Warner Brothers press photo from the set of *The Tin Star!*

Here's **Henry Fonda,** perhaps passing on "grizzled older cowboy" secrets to the then-newcomer, **Tony Perkins.**

Kip (Michel Ray).

She was about to become known to millions of Americans in 1958 when she would replace Faye Emerson in the hit TV program, *I've Got a Secret.*

When Henry worked with her, she was already married to Vincent J. Merendino. Before that, she had a months-long affair with James Dean.

Henry was already well-acquainted with Palmer, since she had played the nurse in the otherwise all-male cast of *Mister Roberts.*

In the plot, Henry is a bounty hunter, Morgan Hickman, who arrives in the sleepy little outpost with a dead body carried across the back of a pack horse. He has come to claim his reward.

Tony Perkins, close to the time he was filming *The Tin Star* with Henry, as he famously appeared as a repentant but homicidal maniac in *Psycho* (1960).

At the sheriff's office, he meets Sheriff Ben Owens, a young and callow greenhorn, who tells him he'll have to stick around a few days to claim his loot.

He is shunned by the people of the town, and even refused a room at the local hotel. That's when he turns to Palmer and her son for shelter and food.

Trouble soon looms for Henry's character when he learns that the corpse is related to Bart Bagardus (played by Neville Brand), the town bully who wants Morgan out of the way…or else.

A highly decorated soldier of World War II, Brand had played a key role in the hit World War II drama, *Stalag 17* (1953), starring William Holden.

Character actor John MacIntire was cast as the ill-fated "Doc" Cord. After delivering a baby son to a remote homesteader, he is later waylaid by Ed McGaffey (Lee Van Cleef). After McCord treats his brother, who is wounded in an attack he was making on a stagecoach, Van Cleef murders Doc to keep him quiet.

McIntire would appear in some 65 movies during the span of his career but became a familiar face on TV beginning in 1960 when he replaced Ward Bond in the series hit, *Wagon Train.*

Henry and Anthony Perkins bonded, and Henry was well aware of the young actor's homosexuality, which he was trying to keep a secret. Coincidentally, within a few years, Perkins would be co-starring with Jane Fonda in her film debut, during which she'd develop a crush on him.

One night, when Perkins talked privately with Henry, he expected him to reveal his struggle with homosexuality. But he got a different story instead. He confessed that his mother, Janet Esselstyn, had sexually abused him. "She would touch me all over, caressing me, even stroking the inside of my thighs right up to my crotch."

The year Perkins co-starred with Jane, he also was hired by Alfred Hitchcock to star in *Psycho,* which would propel him into international fame as the homicidal owner of the Bates Motel. The after-effects of the character he played and its multiple sequels affected the remainder of his career. His greatest love, Tab Hunter, was soon to emerge into his personal life.

The Tin Star became one of the first low-budget Westerns to be Oscar-nominated for Best Screenplay.

Bosley Crowther of *The New York Times* found "Perkins too much of a hayseed; McIntre fine as the old doc; and Brand as a real ornery bully." As for Fonda, "he is the steadiest pair of optics of anyone in the trade."

William K. Zinsser of the *New York Herald Tribune* credited both Fonda and Perkins for bringing an unusual depth to their roles. "Fonda is sincere and appealing. Behind his dirty, unshaven face when he comes to town—and no Western hero can look quite as seedy as Fonda—there obviously lurks a kind and lonely man."

The 93-minute Western garnered $1.4 million at the box office.

Henry himself had little to say about his role in the movie. "Call it my impersonation of Gary Cooper in *High Noon.*"

***

The Love Saga of Jane (Fonda) and James (Franciscus)

After the summer on Cape Cod, Jane came back to Vassar for her sophomore year. She still had not definitely decided that her future would be as an actress. However, she was given the lead in a play by Garcia Lorca where she played a young Spanish girl who sang songs and cuckolded her husband.

"I had not decided to be an actress, but of one thing I was certain: I wanted to get out of Vassar."

She often skipped classes and spent little time with her schoolbooks. Brooke Hayward was reported as saying, "Jane was studying *Boys 101*. With her slim new figure and classic beauty, she was heavily booked by a string of beaux."

Jane was a poor student at Vassar. "I drank too much, got hooked on Dexedrine, and failed most of my exams."

She hoped that she might be expelled. Instead of studying history, she much preferred sneaking off campus with her handsome hunk, the blonde-haired Adonis who later became a well-known movie actor, **James Franciscus.**

"When I discovered boys, and learned how much they liked me, I went wild," Jane said.

A fellow sophomore at Yale, Bud Kinney, called her, "a sex pistol."

In calls to her father, she begged him to let her drop out of Vassar, but he adamantly refused. Looking back at her desperation to leave college, she claimed, "I drank too much and experimented among my passions."

She knew another way she might get kicked out of Vassar. The college had a rule that only single girls could enroll. If a girl got married, she was expelled. "Perhaps" as Jane considered, "she might wed."

The idea was in the back of her mind when she invited James Franciscus, her Cape Cod summer love, for a long weekend at a small, lonely farm in upstate New York.

As she recalled, years later, that was the weekend that she lost her virginity, although there had been previous reports, one from Peter, that she'd lost it in Rome.

As a blizzard whirled outside, the handsome young actor made love to her. From other reports from future girlfriends, he was a skilled lover, concerned as much with a woman's pleasure as his own.

It was perhaps one of the most romantic weekends of her life. There were bubble baths together. James was not shy, and Jane got to observe the male anatomy as never before. She obviously liked the plumbing. As an afterthought, she added, "He also taught me how to make a whiskey sour."

She also experienced the thrill of waking up in bed with a man she loved. However, by the end of their interlude, she decided not to press a marriage proposal from him. "I began to fear I was not ready to settle into the role of a housewife with kids. I feared I'd get mired in a hole from which it would be hard to escape."

Back at Vassar, she noticed that many of her classmates, including her friend, Brooke Hayward, were dropping out to get married.

Her final memory of Vassar involved taking an exam in music history. "I filled my notebook with pictures of women screaming."

When Henry learned of her affair, he told James Stewart, among other friends, "When she was a little girl, we nicknamed her Lady Jane. Now she may not be much of a lady, but she certainly, from what I hear, has become a woman experiencing adult pleasures."

Two press and PR "I'm ready for my close-up" portraits of **Jane Fonda**, *left*, from her early years at Vassar, and *right* from 1963.

TYRONE AND LINDA GET MARRIED

CHAPTER FOURTEEN

HENRY'S FOURTH WIFE, A "SOCIALLY FEROCIOUS" ITALIAN COUNTESS, IS
AFDERA FRANCHETTI

"She looks like she just stepped out of a Botticelli painting"
—Peter Ustinov

"If my Dad's brides get any younger, he'll have to start changing their shitty diapers."
—Jane Fonda

"Henry Fonda is the first to admit he's a lousy husband and an absentee father."
—Afdera Franchetti

THE "ACTORS STUDIO'S FIRST DAUGHTER,"
SUSAN STRASBERG
DURING HER CO-STARRING GIG WITH HENRY IN
STAGE STRUCK
COMPARES HIM, UNFLATTERINGLY AND THOUGHTLESSLY, TO HER THEN-LOVER,
RICHARD BURTON

PLAYTIME ON THE FRENCH RIVIERA

THE FONDAS GET FRIENDLY WITH THE TEMPTATIONS OF THE *CÔTE D'AZUR* POLITICIANS AND BILLIONAIRES (GIANNI AGNELLI! THE KENNEDYS!), & WORLD-CLASS ARTISTS (HEMINGWAY! PICASSO!)

TEDDY, FUTURE "LION OF THE SENATE," EYES JANE

"ME GRETA, YOU JANE!"
HOW **GARBO**, AFTER SEXUAL INTERLUDES WITH JOSEPH P. KENNEDY (FATHER OF JFK) TURNS HER EYES ON THE SCANTILY DRESSED
JANE FONDA

OOOOOOOH- LA LA!
HENRY MEETS the NUDE, VERY DESIRABLE, and VERY FRENCH ACTOR, JEAN MARAIS
[The Widely Acknowledged Lover of the French Arts & Culture Dynamo, Jean Cocteau]
"Jean Marais really is the perfect Male Specimen"
—Henry Fonda

LOVE IN THE AFTERNOON
AS REGARDS 21-YEAR-OLD JANE,
IT'S THE STATED GOAL OF THE HANDSOME AMERICAN ACTOR, **JAMES FRANCISCUS**

TWO FOR THE SEESAW
THE BROADWAY PLAY BRINGS STARDOM TO ANNE BANCROFT

"But it doesn't do a thing for me!"
—Henry Fonda

JFK's INAUGURATION
WHAT, IF ANYTHING, HAPPENED BETWEEN THE PRESIDENT-ELECT AND AFDERA FRANCHETTI ON HIS INAUGURATION NIGHT?

MAKING PASTA WITH MARILYN MONROE
IN HENRY FONDA'S KITCHEN
THE AMERICAN SEX GODDESS GIVES THE ITALIAN SOCIALITE SOME COOKING TIPS:
"Pour Lots of Honey on the Salad Greens!"

WARLOCK
CRITICS SUGGEST THAT HENRY AND ANTHONY QUINN SHARE AN UNDERSTATED HOMOEROTIC DYNAMIC ONSCREEN

THE MAN WHO UNDERSTOOD WOMEN
IT WASN'T HENRY

LOVE: Upscale, Italian-Style, and Burdensomely Chic

On March 10, 1957, 26-year-old Afdera Franchetti flew from Rome to New York to marry Henry Fonda. During the westbound flight, she drank heavily, and—as she admitted—"I was puffy, red-eyed, and jet-lagged. Manhattan appeared to me like I was looking through the wrong end of opera glasses."

The wedding was scheduled for five days after her arrival. She was certain she'd have time to recover an appearance of being "gay, witty, naughty, and outrageous."

As her "dowry," she brought along her maid and her boyfriend from Rome. Soon, they would be added to Henry's payroll. Filalma was an eighteen-year-old who stood four feet ten inches tall. Guiseppe, her beau, was a former grocer who used to deliver food to Afdera's apartment.

They took a taxi to East 74th Street. As they neared the Fonda brownstone, the driver said, "I hear the actor, Henry Fonda, lives on this street. He's been a passenger of mine. He told me he's soon gonna marry this Italian broad."

Afdera had just days to recover and get ready for the wedding. Her reunion with her husband-to-be took place mostly in the bedroom.

During one of his business meetings in an office near Broadway, she explored the house and was appalled by the way it was furnished. She'd have to throw everything out and re-decorate. One salon she wandered into evoked a chamber that Fellini might have used to film an orgy. Another room she interpreted as "sterile, the equivalent of the waiting room of a dentist's office in Omaha, Nebraska."

Soon, overnight guests began to arrive. The first was Peter Fonda, whom Henry had designated as his Best

270

Man. He made it immediately obvious that he was opposed to the wedding.

He announced that he had been given a nickname at school. From that point on, he announced, he wanted to be called "Holden Caulfield" the anti-hero of J.D. Salinger's best-selling novel, *Catcher in the Rye*, which was being read in high schools and on college campuses across the nation. "The kid looked at me as if he had just swallowed a steak from a skunk," Afdera claimed.

Henry soon learned that Peter had socked the headmaster at Westminster in the nose, bloodying it. The superintendent had told him that he felt his father's fourth marriage was "not only un-Christian but disgusting."

Arriving from Vassar, Jane greeted Afdera coldly but politely.

Privately, Peter and Jane joked about their father marrying a woman so young. She said, "If my Dad's brides get any younger, he'll have to start changing their shitty diapers."

In contrast to his rambunctious children, Afdera found Henry quite docile. "He was on his best behavior, catering to me, since he knew how lucky he was for a man of his age to be getting a beautiful young girl to marry him. If I had told him that *la merde* was caviar, he would have devoured it. And I'm sure he would have raved about how good it tasted."

Henry's sister, Harriet Peacock, flew in from Omaha with her husband, Jack. Flying in from Los Angeles at Henry's expense was Stella Sernas, Afdera's oldest friend, who would be the Matron of Honor.

The wedding took place in the Library of the Fonda brownstone, with an elderly Jewish man from New Jersey presiding. He sat on the Supreme Court of New York State.

During the ceremony, when he pronounced the words, "Till death do us part," Afdera let out an audible gasp. "My flesh was crawling with goose bumps," she noted later to her friends.

After the wedding guests departed, Henry and Afdera retired to the upstairs bedroom for a night of lovemaking. She was the first to rise the next morning, and she pulled back the draperies that concealed a view onto the street below. She screamed when she saw the casket of a corpse being removed from the funeral parlor across the street.

Henry woke up and moved toward her side to hold her in his arms and comfort her. She ordered him to have that window permanently blacked out.

He then indulged in his morning ritual of standing on his head for five minutes, followed by yoga exercises.

For their honeymoon, Henry had arranged a flight to Mont Tremblant in Québec. There, they were driving to their honeymoon abode, a cold, drafty, chalet without adequate heat. The weather was near blizzard conditions, and Henry had caught an awful cold. He was coughing violently even before they reached the chalet.

Afdera put him to bed at once and summoned a doctor, but he never came. She didn't want to catch his flu, so although she tended to his needs, she stayed in the guest room.

After two traumatizing days, they flew back to New York, where he was still ill.

There, she heard a false report that her former *fiancé*, Augusto Torlonia, had tried to commit suicide after receiving news of their marriage. *[Actually he'd already found a new girlfriend, a Neapolitan beauty that could have been the younger sister of Sophia Loren.]*

As soon as he recovered, Henry reported to work on his latest film, *Stage Struck*, which was (conveniently) scheduled for shooting

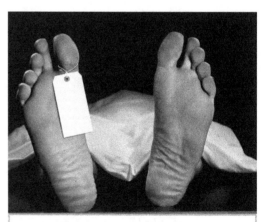

According to Afdera Franchetti:

"After my honeymoon night in bed with my new husband, I woke up the next morning and pulled back the draperies, hoping for a scenic view of Manhattan., What I saw was a casket being moved toward a waiting hearse."

"He lived across from a funeral parlor. I could not tolerate that. All my life, I've had this terror of death. I could not confront it every morning. I told Henry that if he didn't block that view of the death chamber across the street, that I would return to Italy."

271

in Manhattan.

Jane, it had been decided, would return to Vassar. Peter, however, presented another problem. To the rescue came Henry's sister Harriet, who agreed to fly him to Omaha, where he would remain for four years attending the University of Omaha. Henry learned that his son had an "exceptionally gifted" IQ of 160.

The first week had been rough on the Peacocks, as Peter, during his residency in their home, was in withdrawal from heavy drug use. Harriet phoned Henry, assuring him that she would secure psychiatric help for him.

After hearing that, Afdera told her maid, "At last Pimples is out of my hair. Jane told me she wants to leave Vassar and go to Paris. It looks like I'll have both of those monsters somewhere else. Henry will be problem enough for me to tend to without that excess baggage of unwanted teenagers. You may disagree, but I feel some kids should be smothered at birth."

***

Stage Struck (1958)

Henry teamed with director Sidney Lumet once again to film *Stage Struck*, a 1958 release from RKO. "I'm playing second fiddle, Sidney, only because I value you so much as a director."

Even though he would get star billing in his portrayal of a suave Broadway producer, Lewis Eaton, the movie would really belong to Susan Strasberg as the *ingénue* Eva Lovelace, intent on conquering the Broadway stage.

Although many actresses were considered, Lumet had opted for Strasberg, whom he had seen in her breakout role at 18 when she'd starred in *The Diary of Anne Frank* in 1955. That put her on the cover of both *Life* and *Newsweek*.

Only a year younger than Jane Fonda, she was the widely publicized, frequently indulged daughter of Lee Strasberg of the Actors Studio; a ferociously possessive "family friend" of Marilyn Monroe; and a former lover of Richard Burton. Her other lovers included former child star, Bobby Driscoll, Warren Beatty, and the much older bisexual actor, Cary Grant.

"I hear Susan and I may have some kissing scenes," Henry said. "I've met the girl. She's very short. She'll have to stand on platform shoes to reach my lips."

A husband-and-wife writing team, Augustus and Ruth Goetz, had adapted the script for *Stage Struck* from the stage play, *Morning Glory*, by Zoë Atkins.

[A 1933 film adaptation of Atkins' Morning Glory had already brought fame to Katharine Hepburn, who had won her first Oscar for her portrayal of its female protagonist, Eva Lovelace. Atkins was already famous to producers on Broadway for her earlier work. She had won a Pulitzer Prize for her play, The Old Maid in 1935, a dramatization of the Edith Wharton novel. The Old Maid, in 1939, had been adapted into a film with Bette Davis and her arch enemy, Miriam Hopkins.

In 1936, Atkins had written the screenplay for Camille, a movie based on the Alexandre Dumas novel, La dame aux camelias. That movie earned Greta Garbo her third Oscar nomination.]

In *Stage Struck*, Eva Lovelace (portrayed by Susan Strasberg) seems willing to sacrifice anything and anyone in her race for onstage fame and glory. In spite of the differences in their ages, and in spite of the fact that Henry's character, a sophisticated Broadway producer, should have known better, he

Susan Strasberg, perpetual *ingénue*, "first child" of the Lee Strasberg Studios, and poster child for Method acting, emotes here with **Henry Fonda**, a no-nonsense acting pro who had "already seen it all."

That handsome Canadian, **Christopher Plummer**, before he "stiffened" into Captain Georg von Trapp in *The Sound of Music* (1965).

Here, he's emoting gallantly with **Susan Strasberg**, a hysterically ambitious "star of tomorrow" in that Henry Fonda movie about the rancors of Broadway, *Stage Struck*.

falls improbably but desperately in love with her.

Secondary roles were assigned to Herbert Marshall, Joan Greenwood, and Christopher Plummer making his film debut.

Marshall, a Londoner, emerged from retirement to portray a "veteran actor." During World War I, he'd had a leg amputated, but throughout the Golden Age of Hollywood, he maneuvered on a prosthetic leg to woo Greta Garbo, Joan Crawford, Bette Davis, and Marlene Dietrich.

A Canadian, Christopher Plummer portrayed a down-to-earth playwright, Joe Sheridan. Plummer's career would span seven decades and include gigs as Macbeth, Hamlet, the Duke of Wellington, J. Paul Getty, and Captain von Trapp in *The Sound of Music* (1965).

Another Londoner, Joan Greenwood, known for her husky "Tallulah Bankhead" voice, was cast as the "play-within-the-movie's" temperamental leading lady, Rita Vernon. When she storms out, Eva moves in to claim her role and become a star, a familiar refrain in many other tales of Broadway past.

[For years. Greenwood had been starring in such memorable stage roles as Nora in A Doll's House *and as Ophelia in* Hamlet. *In time, hers would become the voice of "The Black Queen" in* Barbarella *starring Jane Fonda.]*

Eventually, *Stage Struck* emerged as a stylish but predictable overview of the ambition and (often failed) striving of the cocktail-soaked *demi-monde* of Broadway. A.H. Weiler of *The New York Times* wrote, "Susan Strasberg is competent as the determined Eva Lovelace. She is petite and fragile and sometimes expressive but strangely pallid in a role that would seem to call for fire, not mere smouldering. Henry Fonda is largely a placid type as the producer, who discovers that his heart can be reached with love as well as the theater."

Variety cited Henry for "playing with his customary quiet authority and a disarming command."

On looking back, Susan said, "I revered Henry as an actor, especially in *Mister Roberts*, but Richard Burton is a better kisser."

***

A "Steeped in Chic" Second Honeymoon for a Fourth Marriage

Although their brief first honeymoon had been a Québec-based disaster, Henry and Afdera's second honeymoon, in Europe during the summer of 1957, morphed into a star-studded, world-class extravaganza.

Almost as a public statement about the tone of their upcoming "celebrity summer," Afdera extended a dinner invitation to the Duke and Duchess of Windsor at the Fonda brownstone in Manhattan. Afdera had met the royal couple in Venice several years before.

At the catered affair, Henry was not impressed with the personal charms of either the Duke or his Duchess. However, he was awed to think that the Duke, who had fitfully reigned for less than eleven months, in 1936, as Britain's King Edward VIII, had once presided, however briefly, over the British Empire "on which the sun never sets."

"The Duchess was an arrogant, snobbish bitch," Henry recalled. "She and my wife spoke the same language. I tried unsuccessfully to engage in a serious talk with the Duke, but mostly, he spoke of new styles in male dress. I had hired five smartly dressed waiters for our dinner, one of whom looked like a more striking version of Tab Hunter."

"I noticed, as the evening went on, the Duke paid more attention to that blonde, blue-eyed Adonis than he did to me. When he had enough drinks in him, His Majesty discreetly slipped the waiter his card. He didn't know I was watching out of the corner of my eye. Not the world, but international society, knew the Duke of Windsor was gay."

Two days after that private dinner in Manhattan, Henry and Afdera flew to Ven-

Edward, the Duke of Windsor with his notorious America-born Duchess, **Wallis Warfield Simpson.**

Although Henry Fonda was unimpressed, h*aute* transatlantic society will never be the same, and the messy memories of wartime divisions within Britain's Royal Family never forgotten.

Scratching her way up from the cornfields of Iowa, **Elsa Maxwell** was the most socially "connected" hostess of the mid-20th century,

Here, for a costume gala in Venice in 1950, she appears accessorized in ways fit for any opera diva or princess.

273

ice, his wife's former stamping ground. There, they checked into the deluxe Hotel Danieli, a *palazzo* on the Grand Canal that had been built by Doge Dandolo in the 14th Century.

They had arrived in Venice at the peak of its fashionable season, when it was top-heavy with a bevy of international celebrities. Presiding over the cream of jet-setters was Elsa Maxwell, the American-born "hostess with the mostest."

A gossip columnist and professional hostess, she had crawled out of Keokuk, Iowa, to become world-renowned for her lavish parties, at some of which she "introduced" bemused and giddy versions of treasure and scavenger hunts.

Although she had never completed grammar school, Maxwell could engage in conversations with the likes of Fanny Brice, Cole Porter, Noël Coward, and Tallulah Bankhead, whom she had known since the 1920s. Maxwell was a virtual pimp for Cole Porter, supplying him with a steady armada of handsome and acquiescent young men.

Her matchmaking achievements included introducing Prince Aly Khan to Rita Hayworth, a successful matchmaking that led to their (disastrous) marriage in 1948. She also introduced opera diva Maria Callas to Aristotle Onassis, who became the most famous lovers in the Greek-speaking world. In the process, Maxwell, a lesbian, fell in love with Callas, who was forty years her junior. The opera star spurned her advances.

Actually, Maxwell had met the love of her life, the Scottish singer, Dorothy Followes Gordon *[a.k.a. "Dickie"]* in 1912. Maxwell was still with her when the hostess finally died in November of 1963, the month of President Kennedy's assassination.

Maxwell almost immediately learned about the arrival in Venice of the Fondas, and phoned them, inviting them to a lavish masked ball she was hosting on the Lido. Henry not only accepted the invitation but spent the next three days in his suite at the Danieli making masks.

This was much to the chagrin of Afdera, who wanted to introduce her new husband to the cream of Venetian society, "Hanky dressed as a faun."

Maxwell's ball came off as spectacular event within the glamourous context of that chic summer in Venice. The very next day, the Fondas flew from Venice to the airport at Nice on the *Côte d'Azur*.

Jane and Peter Fonda would ultimately join them as that summer of 1957 morphed into a Fonda family holiday on the Riviera.

***

From the airport at Nice, the Fondas were transferred by limousine to their rented villa at St.-Jean-Cap-Ferrat, the most chic and ferociously secluded hideaway on the *Côte d'Azur*. *[Cap Ferrat was named in 2012 as the second most expensive residential location in the world after Monaco.]* Three miles away lay the resorts, restaurants, and nightclubs of the more densely populated Villefranche.

The Fondas arrived to spend July and August here, the most desirable (and most expensive) season, when an array of international celebrities flew in, especially during the Cannes Film Festival.

The Fondas were lodged at a large stucco-sided white house perched on the side of a cliff above the Mediterranean. To reach the sea, one had to descend a steep series of stone steps leading to the beach. For the most part, the family preferred their private swimming pool.

Overlooking their rented home from an even higher cliff was the lavish villa of Gianni Agnelli, the major shareholder of the Fiat empire. He was in residence with his wife, Princess Marella Carraciolo de Castagneto, whom he had married in 1953. He never was faithful to her, having affairs ranging from Jacqueline Kennedy to Pamela Harriman.

Henry and Agnelli became friends. Before the end of summer, Agnelli presented him with a specialty Fiat with wicker seats and a red canopy.

Insiders from his home town, Turin, referred to **Gianni Agnelli,** the owner of Fiat, as either *"l'Avvocato"* (the Lawyer) or "The King." During his flamboyant tenure there, Fiat alone once accounted for 5 percent of Italy's GDP.

Relentlessly stylish, and to some degree Italy's "ambassador" to the postwar world at large, he made both dictators and U.S. presidents jealous.

In 1962, while sailing in the Mediterranean aboard Agnelli's yacht, First Lady Jacqueline Kennedy received a telegram from her husband complaining about the tabloid coverage her antics were generating back in the U.S.

"More Caroline," it read. "Less Agnelli."

The Kennedy compound was near the Fonda villa, and Joseph Kennedy was in residence with his sons, Robert and Teddy. John arrived later.

The Kennedy clan's founding father was Joseph Kennedy Sr., the (hugely controversial) former U.S. Ambassador to the Court of Saint James's. That summer, on the *Côte*, he sustained sexual affairs with both Greta Garbo and Marlene Dietrich. When JFK arrived, he, too, inaugurated an affair with Dietrich.

The Kennedy family's youngest brother, Teddy, became smitten with Jane. Although he was a frequent visitor, he apparently did not win her heart that summer. The competition for her affections was too fierce.

Afdera seemed to know nearly all the major celebrities, and she was swamped with invitations to gala events with Henry. Her fellow jet-setters learned that summer that her favorite fashion designer was Valentina.

Although born in Spain, **Pablo Picasso** spent most of his adult life in France, painting and developing a legacy as one of the most influential painters in human history.

Here's how he looked at the time he proposed to Henry Fonda, *père*, that he'd like to paint his late teenaged daughter, Jane, in the "fully nude."

Afdera did not always go over with Jane Fonda's friends. Her new stepmother was introduced to Brooke Hayward, Leland Hayward's daughter. She later shared her impression of Afdera with Jane, calling her "a train wreck, a nightmare, and a complete horror."

As the summer wore on, Afdera claimed, "Our lives seemed ripped from the pages of F. Scott Fitzgerald's *Tender is the Night.*

The Fondas were thrilled to receive an invitation to visit the studio of Pablo Picasso in the medieval village of Vallauris, on the western edge of Antibes. They were allowed to watch him at work on his latest canvas. Afdera later compared that to listening to Yehudi Menuhin playing the violin.

Picasso had seen Jane on the beach, and he asked Henry if he'd let him paint his daughter in the nude. Henry politely rejected the offer, but later regretted it. "I should have let Jane pose. No one would recognize her anyway, because Picasso would probably give her two heads, and if he gave her the painting, and she sold it, she might have collected millions in later years, enough to retire for life."

Picasso was not the only celebrity to entertain the Fondas. Greta Garbo arrived and called on Henry, with whom she had had a brief affair in Brentwood back in the 1930s. [*James Stewart, Henry's roommate at the time, also was rewarded with Garbo's "love nest."*]

Terribly stylish and more than a bit effete, here's Greta Garbo's avowed enemy, fashion designer **Valentina,** with her Russian emigre husband, **George Schlee.**

Although virtually forgotten today, Valentina was once an international icon of chic.

Garbo and Henry spent a long afternoon talking, mostly about yesterday. She was frank in her appraisal of her life: "I have tried everything at various times, but my thoughts and my body have never been satisfied."

Henry expressed the many disappointments of his own life: "I'm ashamed for being married so many times. Four down and maybe more to come in my future. These divorces make me look like a fool and a failure. From Bette Davis to Joan Crawford, from Lucille Ball to Jeanette MacDonald, my affairs led nowhere, only temporary relief from my loneliness."

Garbo must have been impressed with Jane, as she invited her to go swimming, not in the Fonda's pool, but in the Mediterranean below. Both of them descended the winding stone steps that led to the sea. Once there, 20-year-old Jane retained her swimsuit, but Garbo stripped down and entered the waters naked. "I always swim nude in the sea," she told Jane.

[*Throughout her life, Garbo divided her intimacies between men and women, seguéing among affairs with silent screen heartthrob John Gilbert; Maria Huxley (wife of author Aldous Huxley); socialite Mercedes de Acosta; and Leland Hayward.*

Currently, Garbo was having an affair with Henry's neighbor, Joseph P. Kennedy, the former U.S. Ambassador to the Court of St. James's.

Soon, George Schlee, with whom Garbo sustained her longest-running affair, arrived on the Riviera as her guest. Since 1921, he had been married to the fashion designer known only as "Valentina." Formally designated as Valentina]

Nicholaevna Sanina, she had been born in 1899 in Kiev, then part of the Russian Empire.

During the 1920s, she and her husband had entertained luminaries of the Jazz Age: Gloria Swanson, Gertrude Lawrence; Lynn Fontanne, and Katharine Cornell, among many others.

Valentina and Schlee lived together in the same apartment house (on the east side of midtown Manhattan) as Garbo. As such, the two grandes dames *went to some length to avoid running into each other in the lobby and in the building's elevators.*

When Schlee met Henry, he told him, "Being faithful to a wife or husband is strictly for the middle class, not for those of us with artistic souls. You and I must remain free to sample the fruits of the world. I have flown to France with a beautifully created gown designed by Valentina, although Greta usually prefers Valentino gowns. The name of one designer, you know, ends with an "a," the other's with an "o."

"My wife's final words of advice to Afdera are, 'fit the century, not the year.'"]

Two talented, alcoholic, and desperately unhappy crazies: **Ernest Hemingway** and his difficult, often drunk, fourth and final wife, **Mary Walsh Hemingway.**

Like everyone else in Hollywood, Henry was eager to hear "Papa's" points of view about the cinematic adaptation of his novels.

Ernest Hemingway was also a visitor to the French Riviera that summer. Henry met him at a party and concealed his own opinion of the author. Privately, he defined Hemingway as "a big macho fart with a scaly beard. I prefer the novels of John Steinbeck."

Fonda and Hemingway each wanted to talk about the recent (i.e., 1957) film adaptation of his 1926 novel, *The Sun Also Rises,* dealing with the Lost Generation. The Technicolor movie produced by Darryl Zanuck had starred Tyrone Power, Ava Gardner, Mel Ferrer, and Errol Flynn in his declining years.

Fonda told "Papa" that he had originally been offered the role of Robert but had another commitment. The role had subsequently been assigned to Ferrer. Harry King, who had previously directed Henry in *Chad Hanna* (1940), had directed it.

"I'm sorry to hear that," Hemingway said. "I think you would have made a far more believable Robert. Actually, I didn't want Power in the lead. I preferred Gregory Peck, since I was pleased with his performance in *The Snows of Kilimanjaro* (1952). I'm a friend of Ava's, and I had to lobby hard to get her cast as Lady Brett. Zanuck held out for Jennifer Jones."

Henry was shocked when Hemingway delivered his private opinion of the film adaptation of *The Sun Also Rises*: "I walked out of the screening of it after twenty-five minutes. Zanuck had created the Cook's Tour of Europe's Lost Generation—bistros, bullfights, and more bistros. It's pretty disappointing—and that's being generous. Most of my story is set in Pamplona, but Zanuck shot it in Mexico. It was meant to feature Spaniards, but all you see are Mexicans walking about. I guess the best thing about the film was Errol Flynn, and he was drunk every day of the shoot."

The end result of Henry's talk with Papa was to take his family to Pamplona for the annual running of the bulls.

***

Henry and the Haute French Literati

Afdera had known the French writer, Jean Cocteau, in Paris. The poet, playwright, novelist, designer, and filmmaker had arrived on the Côte d'Azur with his lover, Jean Marais, the French actor, writer, director, and sculptor.

The *National Observer* suggested that "during the 20th Century, Cocteau came closest to being a Renaissance man." In addition to being the muse and lover of Cocteau, Marais in his career would star in a hundred feature films, notably *Beauty and the Beast* (1946), written by Cocteau.

Although Afdera had devoured the works of both artists, Henry was unfamiliar with their artistic output. The night before he met them, he read *Les Enfants Terribles,* Cocteau's 1929 novel.

Jean Cocteau shares an intimate (and at the time, dangerous and illegal) moment with his long-time companion and collaborator, **Jean Marais.**

"As writer and actor," Cocteau said, "Marais and I were descended from the Gods."

As it turned out, Afdera was among the lesser of the many celebrities Cocteau knew. His circle of the ferociously prestigious artists he'd cultivated since the early 1920s featured Marcel Proust, André Gide, Maurice Barrès, Vaslav Nijinski, Pablo Picasso, Amedeo Modigliani, Sergei Diaghilev, and the French poet Raymond Radiguet, with whom he'd a long affair.

Cocteau made no attempt to conceal his homosexuality from Henry. He was one of the celebrities who believed that Henry himself had had homosexual relationships, as was widely rumored at the time.

"As far back as I can remember," he told Henry, "I find traces of my love of boys. I have always loved the strong sex that I find legitimate to call the fair sex. My misfortune came from a society that condemns us as a crime and forces us to reform our inclinations."

When Henry first arrived at the Cocteau villa, he found Marais lying nude on the sun terrace. Afdera had remained in another part of the house, talking to Cocteau. When Marais noticed Henry eyeing his nudity, Marais said, "God turned me into the most perfect male specimen currently created in France. Maybe there were greater bodies in centuries past, but the torch had been passed to me, and I see no reason to hide my manly flesh."

"It certainly seems the perfect body for viewing," Henry responded diplomatically.

Over the course of his career, Marais would be awarded the French Legion of Honor for his contribution to the nation's cinematic patrimony.

In the 1950s, after the travails of guiding the UK through the horrors of World War II, an increasingly frail **Sir Winston Churchill** spent more and more of his time as an honored guest in other people's hotels, other people's villas, and aboard other people's yachts.

Here, he's welcomed aboard the *Christina*, the legendary pleasure cruiser of **Aristotle Onassis,** seen standing here on the upper left.

It was into this heady brew of world-class sophisticates, on the French Riviera, that the American movie star, Henry Fonda, led his children, Peter and Jane, in the now halcyon-looking summer of 1957.

Aristotle Onassis, Maria Callas, and Sir Winston Churchill

News of Henry's arrival on the Riviera reached Aristotle Onassis, the Greek billionaire, whose yacht, *Christina O.*, was anchored off the coast of the nearby resort city of Cannes. Henry and Afdera were invited to spend the day with him and his mistress, Maria Callas.

Once onboard, Henry was taken on a tour of the magnificent vessel, which had been named for Onassis' daughter, Christina. Launched in 1943 as the HMCS *(Her Majesty's Canadian Ship)* Stormont, it had been a convoy escort during World War II's Battle of the Atlantic and had been present at the Allied invasion of Normandy in June of 1944.

After the war, and after it had been condemned as "scrap," Onassis shrewdly bought the vessel for only $34,000. Of course, he had to spend $4 million to morph it into the spectacularly upscale vessel it was when Henry, a U.S. Navy veteran with memories of far less luxurious vessels during his own military stint, came aboard.

Henry later ordered drinks at the bar, whose stools were meticulously upholstered with the carefully preserved foreskins of whales.

In time, those barstools would be occupied by the *derrières* (magnificent or otherwise) of Elizabeth Taylor, Richard Burton, Grace Kelly, Prince Rainier, John F. Kennedy, Rudolf Nureyev, Frank Sinatra, Eva Peron, John Wayne, and J. Paul Getty.

Henry was delighted to learn that one of his alltime heroes, Sir Winston Churchill, was on board, having been drinking heavily since 10am that morning.

The World War II hero indulged Henry in long talks about the Battle of Midway.

[In 1976, Henry would star in Midway, *the saga of one of history's greatest naval battles, this one between the naval forces of the United States and those of the Empire of Japan.]*

***

At the start of the Fonda family holiday on the *Côte d'Azur*, Afdera wanted to provide the proper escorts for Jane during the parties and gala events she'd be attending. Her stepmother was proud of Jane's emerging figure and beauty.

For the most part, Jane was not impressed with the sons of Europe's fading aristocracy, nor with the sons of titans of postwar industry, either.

The lone exception was Giovanni Volpi, who was a year younger than she was. He was an Italian-Algerian who had inherited a fortune upon the death of his father, Count Giuseppe Volpi di Misurata, a "sometimes Fascist" politician and financier who'd founded the Venice Film Festival.

During World War II, Giovanni's father had been Benito Mussolini's Minister of Finance and one of his chief advisors. At the end of the war, he'd managed to escape prosecution.

Young Giovanni went on to a carve out a vastly different reputation for himself as an automobile racing manager and *Formula One* team owner.

After he dated Jane, Volpi founded, in 1961, the car-racing team *Scuderia Serenissima*. For it, he commissioned specially designed Ferraris, one of them known as the Ferrari Breadvan.

Giovanni's sister, Countess Maria Cicogna, also made an appearance on the Riviera that summer. *The New York Times* described her as "the first major female Italian film producer and one of the most powerful women in European cinema." Giovanni speculated that his sister might transform Jane into an international film star.

Giovanni found Jane "charming" but their fling was brief. As he was one of the most desirable males on the continent, he soon moved on. He would later marry Dominique Rizzo and retreat to a mansion in Geneva.

After the American actor James Franciscus finished his studies, *magna cum laude*, at Yale alongside Dick Cavett, he was free to fly to the Riviera to join Jane, sharing her bedroom at the Fonda's rented villa by the sea.

Their love affair resumed. She later was quoted as saying that she had come to appreciate the pleasures of "love in the afternoon" as an overhead fan whirled above them. Franciscus became her "Goey" once again.

He later told his friends that he planned to propose marriage to Jane when his life became more stabilized.

Goey's best friend, Jose de Vicuna, a sophisticated Spaniard, soon joined Jane and Goey for their Riviera adventure. Without any evidence, gossips speculated that they were involved in a "love triangle" that summer. Sometimes, they went to the beach, where Goey was not embarrassed to toss off his swimming trunks and swim in the nude like Garbo (and many others along the French Riviera at the time) had done. "If you've got it, flaunt it!" was his motto.

One morning, the three of them headed west towards the emerging little resort of St. Tropez. Director Roger Vadim was credited with having brought the resort into world attention when he shot *And God Created Woman (Et Dieu créa la femme)* starring Brigitte Bardot there in 1956. Vadim had married the blonde, buxom "sex kitten" in 1952, but their union had headed for the divorce courts by 1957.

Actually, St. Tropez had been known to celebrities long before Bardot and Vadim rendered it famous once again. The novelist, Colette, once lived there, as did Signac, Matisse, Bonnard, and Guy de Maupassant.

Jane, her escorts, and thousands of other moviegoers had seen *Et Dieu créa la femme*. In spite of the critical assaults levied against it, and the banning of some of its scenes in the United States, it became an international hit. In America, its greatest success was in Kansas City, where one theater ran it more or less continuously for a full year.

After Franciscus returned to the United States, Jose remained behind. It was widely assumed—assumed, but never proven—that he began a brief fling with his best friend's girl. The young Spaniard was called "well bred and worldly wise."

Although Jane's affair with Franciscus would continue on and off for another year or so, their marriage never happened. Their end had been predicted by Afdera: "James was just too nice and too straightforward for a complicated woman like Jane. I knew their love affair was destined to fail before they did."

***

At the urging of Hemingway, the Fondas set out for the province of Navarre in northern Spain. They arrived in the overcrowded city of Pamplona to celebrate, with thousands of others, the annual Festival of San Fermín.

The highlight of the festival was the famous "Running of the Bulls" as depicted in the pages of *The Sun Also Rises*.

The dangerous running involved hundreds of young men dashing through the medieval city's narrow streets followed by rampaging bulls and six oxen or steers.

During the run to the bullring, some 200 to 300 young men are injured yearly (in some cases, gored to death) in this savage and—some say, iconically primal—spectacle. Before the end of the Festival, many of the bulls would meet their *Death in the Afternoon* as depicted in Hemingway's epic book about bullfighting.

Because of crowded conditions, the Fonda could not stay at the same hotel, but were scattered about in rooms across Pamplona. Jane was there with James Franciscus. Peter and some other young men ended up elsewhere. It was agreed in advance that the Fondas would meet for dinner.

During the first running of the bulls, Henry with the rest of his family searched for Peter, but he was not to be found.

Suddenly, after the run began, to his horror and dismay, Henry spotted his rebellious son, Peter. He was the leader of a pack of young men fleeing from the rampaging bulls, each seemingly intent on goring them to death.

For some men, including the then-teenaged Peter Fonda, **running with the bulls through the streets of Pamplona** is a rite of passage for rebels who were "born to be wild."

For those seriously injured, and in some cases, crippled, it's akin to insanity.

***

Two for the Seesaw

While Henry vacationed with his family in Southern France, three American men were hard at work on a Broadway-bound play called *Two for the Seesaw*. It was a three-act, two-character play written by William Gibson, directed by Arthur Penn, and produced by Fred Coe.

Its protagonist is a character named Jerry Ryan, a recently divorced, middle-aged attorney newly arrived in New York from Omaha, Nebraska, which coincidentally, had been Henry's hometown.

In Manhattan he meets Gittel Mosca, an eccentric native of the Bronx, a free-wheeling dancer with unrealistic dreams of becoming a ballerina.

She struggles with ailments of her stomach. Following a chance meeting, Act One ends with Jerry and Gittel becoming romantically involved, although they make an unlikely pair since their backgrounds are so different.

Act II focuses on Gittel being rushed to the hospital, suffering from a bleeding ulcer. Jerry takes care of her.

By Act III, Jerry is making frequent calls to his estranged wife, Tess, in Omaha. Finally, he reveals to Gittel that he is still in love with Tess and plans to move back to Omaha. At the end, in a wrenching farewell phone call, Jerry and Gittel discuss their brief but meaningful relationship.

Fred Coe had risen from the swampy depths of Alligator, Mississippi, to become a producer, especially in television. He would be mainly known for *The Goodyear Television Playhouse* and *The Philco Television Playhouse* (1948-55), and *Playhouse 90* (1957-1962).

Henry had already worked with Coe before in the 1955 telecast of *The Petrified Forest*, with co-stars Humphrey Bogart and Lauren Bacall.

A native of Philadelphia, Arthur Penn was a leading director of what came to be known as the American New Wave. He was not only a director, but a producer in film, television, and the theater. Penn would go on to helm critically acclaimed

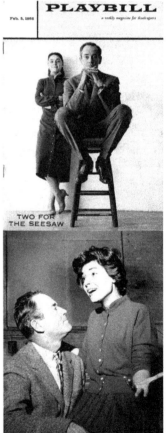

An unexpected pairing that took Broadway by surprise: **Anne Bancroft** with **Henry Fonda.**

The young Italian-American actress pleaded with Henry to get both of them cast in the movie version, but he refused. Their roles went instead to Robert Mitchum and Shirley MacLaine.

films in the 1960s, notably *The Chase* (1966), that starred Jane Fonda with Marlon Brando and Robert Redford. His big hit was a crime film, *Bonnie and Clyde* (1967), that had starred Warren Beatty. Jane Fonda rejected the role of Bonnie, which was subsequently assigned to Faye Dunaway.

While *Two for the Seesaw* was evolving into a hit on Broadway, Gibson would be at work on another huge success for Bancroft. She received a Tony Award for Best Performance by a leading actress in a play teaching the deaf child Helen Keller how to communicate.

Bancroft repeated her role in the play's film adaptation, *The Miracle Worker* (1962), for which she won a Best Actress Oscar.

Bancroft could not fly to Hollywood to receive her award because she had to star in the play, *Mother Courage and Her Children*. In her place, Joan Crawford agreed to accept the Oscar for her. Bancroft thus beat out Bette Davis for her performance in *What Ever Happened to Baby Jane?* which, coincidentally, also starred Crawford.

Henry did not know this at the time, but Gibson did not want him to play opposite Bancroft, as Jerry. His actor of choice was Richard Widmark. He felt that Henry was "too old." For about a week, Gibson also considered Richard Basehart after Widmark rejected it.

Copies of the original script were sent to Barry Nelson, Don Murray, Eli Wallach, Robert Preston, Van Heflin, and Paul Newman. Some of these actors declined immediately. Others considered it before turning it down.

Henry and Gibson battled furiously during rehearsals for *Seesaw*. Later, the playwright called working on the script with Henry "the most odious experience of my life."

Henry wanted the character of Jerry to be stronger. He felt that whereas Gittel was full-bodied as a character, Jerry was one-dimensional.

At times, Henry became violent, even calling Gibson such names as "asshole."

Henry had another reason to be uncomfortable in the presence of Gibson. His wife, Margaret Brenman-Gibson, was a psychotherapist and had worked at the Austin Riggs Center in Stockbridge. Frances, Henry's first wife, had been a patient there before she committed suicide.

Henry's main complaint was that Jerry "is an attractive version of myself. I'm playing straight man for Gittle. She has desires. I have shifting moods."

Gibson worked on the character of Jerry until the night before the play opened. "Even so, he never got it

right," Henry complained. "I finally gave up on him and ordered the jerk out of my dressing room."

The tension, conflicts, and trauma of bringing *Two for the Seesaw* to Broadway was later revealed in a book, *The Seesaw Log* by Gibson. The playwright traces the drama from its inception in 1953 to opening night in January of 1958.

The Seesaw Log voices the playwright's challenges associated with Henry's (the production's main financial backer) many demands. Gibson also revealed the difficulties associated with casting the two leads.

Casting the female lead (Gittel) was difficult. None of the actresses considered

In the photo above, **Anne Bancroft** appears as the seductive Mrs. Robinson in *The Graduate* (1967). Nearby appear views of men she co-starred with before Henry Fonda:

Upper row, *left to right:* **Aldo Ray, Cornel Wilde, Dan Dailey, Farley Granger,** and **Guy Madison.**

In the lower row appear **Audie Murphy** (as the centerpiece of a U.S. postal stamp); **Ricardo Montalban, Scott Brady,** and **Richard Widmark.**

got the Bronx accent right—not Gwen Verdon or Lee Grant. Not Gaby Rodgers, Julie Harris, or Kim Stanley, then hailed as "The Female Marlon Brando."

Only a B picture actress, a refugee from Hollywood, Anne Bancroft, a native of the Bronx, got it right.

When Henry became the first investor in the play, he had total power over casting Gittel. His investment of $20,000 gave him 25% of the production. That brought with it a guarantee of $2,500 a week against 15% of the gross receipts for six months, the term of his contract.

Jane Fonda was quoted as saying, "Bancroft was a Method actress. My dad detested the Method because it required an actor to go plumbing into his depths. Dad hated any probe of his emotions."

Before he would agree to co-star with Bancroft, he ordered the staff to arrange for him to see several of her movies. He had seen her on the screen only once and that was in *Don't Bother to Knock* (1952) with Richard Widmark and Marilyn Monroe.

It is not known which of Bancroft's fourteen films he sat through, but he was not impressed with her performance in any of them.

Cast as the Comtesse de St. Malo, she starred opposite Cornel Wilde in *Treasure of the Golden Condor* (1953). That was followed by *Tonight We Sing* (also 1953), where she played Emma, wife of the celebrated impresario Sol Hurok (David Wayne).

Teamed with Dan Dailey, she co-starred in the baseball comedy-drama, *The Kid from Left Field* (also 1953).

In 1954, Bancroft got lost in *Demetrius and the Gladiators*. Victor Mature in the title role played a Christian slave forced to fight in the Roman arena. Susan Hayward was cast as Messalina, wife of Claudius.

In the Civil War drama, *The Raid* (1954), Bancroft starred opposite Van Heflin.

Her most embarrassing role was in the horror film, *Gorilla at Large* (1954). The costumed gorilla stole the show, even though Cameron Mitchell had the star role.

That horror flick was followed by *A Life in the Balance* (1955), an American-Mexican thriller that pitted Bancroft against Ricardo Montalban and Lee Marvin.

In *New York Confidential,* a 1955 *film noir,* Bancroft faced competition from the blonde bombshell, Marilyn Maxwell. Her co-stars were Broderick Crawford and Richard Conte. Its director, Russell Rouse, had made it clear that he'd have preferred George Raft and Paul Muni as the male leads. "I forgot this film except for one thing," Bancroft said. "Desi Arnaz showed up on a few occasions to screw Maxwell."

That same year, she made *The Naked Street* with Farley Granger and Anthony Quinn. Granger called the movie, "preachy, trite, and pedestrian."

Another Civil War film, *The Last Frontier* (also 1955) had her cast as Corrina Marston waiting at the fort for her missing husband, Robert Preston. Bancroft was later quoted as saying, "I didn't know which of my other co-stars, Victor Mature or Guy Madison, would be the first to seduce me off screen."

Jacques Tourneur, the French director, teamed Bancroft with Aldo Ray in another crime-based *film noir* entitled *Nightfall* (1956). As Marie Gardner, she appears as a model nursing a drink at a bar, with no money to pay for it.

In CinemaScope and Technicolor, *Walk the Proud Land* (1956) teamed Bancroft with Audie Murphy, the most decorated American soldier of World War II. Bancroft was cast as a Native Indian widow, Tianay.

A "B movie mystery," *The Girl in Black Stockings* (1957), pitted Bancroft opposite Lex Barker (the former Tarzan) and a Marilyn Monroe clone, Mamie Van Doren. "No one noticed me," Bancroft complained. "The gays focused on Lex's crotch, the straights on Mamie's tits."

After that, Bancroft wandered into the picture, *The Restless Breed* (1957). A Western, it co-starred Scott Brady. "He wore me out. I almost didn't have enough energy left over to perform after he finished a session with me. In the afterglow, he bragged about the size of his equipment."

After sitting through some of these low-budget movies, Henry was convinced that Bancroft should not be cast. However, after he watched her first rehearsal as Gittel, he changed his mind. "Anne was Gittel in language and movement."

Bancroft, a graduate of the Actors Studio, finally won Henry's approval and was signed for $550 a week.

The play opened on Broadway at the Edwin Booth Theater on January 16, 1958.

Henry avoided going to the cast party, opting to attend a private gathering at his townhouse instead, with Afdera presiding. "As the night wore on, his face grew longer and longer," she said, "and his blue eyes turned to gray."

With her guests, Afdera put up a brave front before the morning papers arrived. When they did, and after she digested them, she announced to the other guests present: "*Seesaw* is going to run for five years, and I want a mink coat."

Henry learned that he'd received only minor praise. Instead, nearly all the reviews focused on the brilliant performance of Bancroft as Gittel. Headlines read:

A NEW STAR SHINES ON BROADWAY
and
ANNE BANCROFT BECOMES BROADWAY'S NEWEST SENSATION.

Fred Coe had been the first to arrive with a copy of *The New York Times*. Brooks Atkinson had written: "Mr. Fonda is a wonderfully straightforward actor who plays at low pressure. As Jerry, he gives his most limpid and moving performance. What he does not say in the dialogue, he says with the silent eloquence of a fine actor."

Fred Aston in the *New York World-Telegram,* wrote: "The lanky Fonda, secure with dry delivery and understated emphasis, could grip any audience on which he might concentrate. In the current instance, he is concentrating for dear life."

Ronald Coleman in *The Daily Mirror* found that "Fonda sets up the laughs for Bancroft to cash in on. He gives an honest portrait of a troubled man in search of his soul."

John McClain in the *New York Journal* said: "Henry Fonda has never given a poor performance within my memory, but this may be one of his best. It is, of course, an exhaustive part, and he takes full advantage of even the most minute pantomime."

At the end of six months, Henry's contract expired. "I escaped like that proverbial bat from hell. My role—playing a son of a bitch—had come to an end. Dana Andrews, my former co-star in *The Ox-Bow Incident*, tried to fill my shoes."

Two for the Seesaw would stay on Broadway for a total of 750 performances.

At awards season, Tony nominations for *Two for the Seesaw* went to Best Play, Best Director (Arthur Penn), and Best Featured Actress in a play (Anne Bancroft), which she won. She was also the recipient of a Theatre World Award for her performance during the 1958 Broadway season.

Elizabeth Taylor wanted to play Gittel in the movie version of *Seesaw*, starring opposite Paul Newman. Previously, they'd scored a big hit together in Tennessee Williams' *Cat on a Hot Tin Roof* (1958).

But after she got sucked into re-runs and re-shootings on the set of *Cleopatra* in Rome, she abandoned the project, and Newman wandered into a pool hall to shoot *The Hustler* (1961).

Eventually, the film roles went to Robert Mitchum and Shirley MacLaine, who began an off-screen love affair. The movie version got mixed reviews and did not generate massive sales at the box office.

In 1973, the play was adapted into a Broadway musical with book by Michael Bennett. It closed after 296 performances.

✳✳✳

A TV Series: The Deputy

Henry returned to Hollywood for only one reason and that involved "the promise of cash on the barrelhead plus residuals in my future." He was offered the lead to star in and be the narrator of a new TV Western series, *The Deputy*, in which he would appear as Chief Marshal Simon Fry in the Arizona territory of the early 1880s.

The series was created in part by Norman Lear, on the dawn of great success in his future with such sitcoms as *All in the Family, Maude, Sanford and Son, One Day at a Time,* and *The Jeffersons.*

Henry narrated nearly every episode and starred as an actor in only six

it was the first of what would become a LOT of Westerns for the Nebraska-born stage actor, **Henry Fonda**. He appears above, in full cowboy drag, waiting for what viewers fear might be an almost certain death, with his co-star in the series, **Allen Case.**

telecasts during the first season, thirteen in the second, which ran for thirty minutes on NBC every Saturday night at 9PM. He narrated almost every episode.

The permanent star was a handsome young actor and singer, Allen Case, who was both a storekeeper and a sheriff's deputy who hated to use a gun.

A son of Dallas, Case appeared with a different co-star each week. His favorite was Vivian Vance, who starred as Ethel Mertz on *I Love Lucy*.

Afdera Franchetti with **Henry Fonda** during their crisis-plagued honeymoon in Canada.

Later in life, as his acting career waned, Case became a designer of fur coats for men made from wolves, Norwegian seals, and muskrat. He sent Henry one made from sheared rabbit.

Wallace Ford was cast as the elderly marshal, Herk Lamson. He had been a star on Broadway in the 1920s and in the 1930s, he became a movie star, launching himself in the film *Possessed* (1931) starring Clark Gable and Joan Crawford.

The Deputy, although profitable, never made it into the bigtime Western TV series circuit like *Wagon Train*, *Bonanza* or *Gunsmoke*.

TV critic John Crosby viewed one episode where bandits hold up a train. "The episode looked straight out of the 1903 *The Great Train Robbery*. I thought the film industry had been set back eighty years. Fonda just walked through his part—that is, if he even appeared at all. I guess he didn't want to work up a sweat."

"Afdera virtually forced me to do the series because she needed more money to buy emeralds and give lavish parties," Henry said. "She detested being referred to as Mrs. Henry Fonda, preferring to be known as Countess Afdera Franchetti. She was no more a countess than my flannel shirt."

She loved meeting legends. Her friend, Douglas Fairbanks Jr. arranged for Henry and her to be presented to Queen Elizabeth at Buckingham Palace.

Afdera was a longtime friend of actor Peter Ustinov, and she and Henry were invited to sail the Greek Island in his 58-foot ketch. Ustinov told Afdera that she looked like she "had stepped out of a Botticelli painting."

Noting that Afdera was a flamboyant social climber, the New Orleans-born, Broadway-based costume designer, Lucinda Ballard Dietz compared her to "an exotic bird from the magazine of natural history."

***

The Affectations of Afdera

When Afdera and Henry were installed in their brownstone in Manhattan, she staged one gala party after another. Director Josh Logan likened her extravagance "to throwing Henry's money out the window by the bushel. "At her parties or dinners, the kings and queens of Hollywood were honored guests. They ranged from Tyrone Power to Olivia de Havilland, from Bette Davis to Joan Crawford. James Stewart and Gloria were regular visitors.

Lucille Ball, Henry's former co-star and lover, turned up one night. "I was amazed. Afdera had turned the downstairs floors into the setting of a Venetian *palazzo*. I glanced over at poor Henry. He looked like he was at the wrong party. He fitted into this setting like a grandfather clock would in a *Louis Quinze* salon."

One night, Cary Grant arrived with Sophia Loren. About the evening, Afdera said, "While I chatted with Grant, my longtime heartthrob, although he was mostly gay, Henry sat on the sofa with Loren. I heard them talking about possibly co-starring in a picture together."

"Loren was a woman of passion, but not for sex…for spaghetti," Afdera continued. "Everybody was hungry, and she asked to take over my kitchen, although we had a hard time finding spaghetti in my pantry. She served us a magnificent pasta dinner. For me, pasta is something you can take or leave. In my case, leave—it's fattening."

In 1959, Henry and Afdera met this "charming couple" (her words), John and Jacqueline Kennedy. "Henry told me Jack was going to be the next president."

"All night, he flirted with me, and I found him enchanting. Jackie was something else entirely. She was the embodiment of *Jaws*, with 200,000 glistening white teeth and two cunning eyes, one on either side of her head.

The distance between those eyes of hers was the exact difference between Denver and San Francisco."

"I never saw both of her eyes at the same time," Afdera continued, "since my eyes are fairly close together. I could focus on only one eye at a time before shifting my focus onto her other eye. She had to have glasses especially made. From that mouth of hers, with its razor-sharp teeth, emerged a voice that sounded like a girl in junior high."

JFK had the strong support of the Fondas during his race for the White House. At his inauguration, an invitation was extended, but Henry could not leave Manhattan. Afdera went instead, and she remembered the occasion as "party, gala, party, gala, all taking place in spite of a severe snowstorm."

After the last party, Afdera, along with a select group of JFK supporters, was invited to the home of columnist Joe Alsop. The newly elected President was the last to arrive.

Alsop appointed Afdera as the person in charge of making a spaghetti dinner, "since you are the only Italian."

"Sophia Loren had not taught me well, and the spaghetti dinner I turned out was a horror, but the men, including Jack, ate it heartily."

What happened in the house before dawn is still controversial. Rumors spread that Afdera and the newly elected "most powerful man in the world" retired as a couple to an upstairs bedroom.

Other reports named as many as eight other women who might have been seduced that night by the POTUS-elect. All that is definitively known is that as the sun rose over a bitterly cold Washington, D.C., JFK and his Secret Service were spotted leaving at dawn. Afdera left later that day, flying back to New York and her husband.

All she had to say was that "I found Jack so normal, so natural, and so alone, so lonely."

***

Henry and Afdera—mainly at her insistence—continued to entertain many Hollywood notables. On a memorable occasion, Marilyn Monroe and Arthur Miller were their guests.

At the time, Monroe was recovering from her landmark comedy *Some Like It Hot* (1959). She was also trying to be a housewife (she was married to Arthur Miller at the time) and failing in that domestic role. She talked with Afdera, not about the lovers in her life, but recipes. Her secret to a good salad dressing, as she relayed to Afdera, was "lots of honey on the greens."

"Monroe was a gentle dove," Afdera claimed. "But that was only a small part of her. Beneath that façade beat the heart of a ruthless woman. She was overcome by the American Dream that had entrapped her. She was not a big star, but an even bigger goal loomed ahead—and that was the need to find herself."

At large parties, Henry and Afdera invariably encountered the society hostess, Elsa Maxwell. "She was ugly, wicked, and amusing," Afdera said, "and she took a fancy to me. A well-known lesbian, she looked like a man and talked like a man. She seduced some of the most famous married ladies in Hollywood, but not this one."

"Liz Taylor was a woman of great desires and passions," Afdera claimed. "She introduced me to Richard Burton, the two of them found each other, although each of them was married at the time. Their love and needs were so powerful I felt it might destroy them."

One evening, David Niven arrived on their doorstep. He was a real gentleman," Afdera said, "but with a naughty twinkle in his eye. He made it clear he wanted to take me to bed, but he restrained himself."

That was the night she also met Kirk Douglas. "He told me he thought I was a pain

The photo above shows then-President **John F. Kennedy** delivering his inaugural address on January 20, 1961.

It was widely rumored that after the parties and balls that followed, he inaugurated a brief "post-inaugural fuck": with Henry Fonda's semi-estranged wife, **Afdera Franchetti.**

It was she who had prepared the spaghetti for that evening's "the party's over" supper for him and his exhausted cronies.

At the urging of his wife, Afdera, Henry Fonda entertained some of the most celebrated and famous couples in the world.

One night, they hosted **Marilyn Monroe** and her then-husband, the respected playwright, **Arthur Miller.**

"MM was unsuccessfully trying to be the housewife of a Jewish husband," Afdera claimed.

In the photo above, the unhappy couple appear in April of 1957 in Manhattan at the April in Paris Ball.

in the ass. He then pinched said ass to test its firmness. He was real sure of himself, a really bizarre man."

"There was nothing feminine about my husband, Henry Fonda," Afdera said. "Yet so many rumors still existed that he was a secret homosexual. He was always getting propositioned, mostly by young actors who wanted him to use his influence to get them cast in a picture. If his heart had ever belonged to anyone, it was to James Stewart. But they weren't seeing a lot of each other anymore."

***

Getting Artsy and Theatrical with Young Peter Fonda

Since his move to Omaha, Peter saw little of Henry. His son's growing interest in the theater was almost unknown to his dad at the time. Peter appeared in several productions at the Omaha Community Playhouse, dancing and singing in the chorus of *Guys and Dolls.*

Henry flew in to see his son portray Elwood P. Dowd in *Harvey,* in which Peter had been cast with an imaginary rabbit. Henry's best friend, James Stewart, had made the role famous on Broadway and in the movies.

"I don't know why I was cast as Dowd, a 78-year-old man," Peter recalled. "At the time, I was only 19 and looked it."

After the curtain went down, Peter received a surprise visitor backstage in his dressing room. It was Henry, who had flown in from Los Angeles. He praised his son's performance, and the cast seemed thrilled to meet a real live movie star in the flesh.

"Appearing in *Harvey* touched my soul," Peter said. "Sometimes, the rabbit and I went off for long walks together to talk over my future. *Harvey* convinced me I was Broadway bound, just like Dear Old Dad. Except Henry was appearing in this dumb Western series called *The Deputy* at the time."

Back in New York, Henry told Afdera, "Peter, like Jane, is going to be an actor. It seems that their lives, like mine, will be a tragedy."

"You're mistaken," Afdera responded. "Your life hardly rises to the level of tragedy. I'd call it more of a soap opera."

***

Warlock

Henry continued to tell reporters how much he disliked working in Hollywood, but admitted that he could always be lured there, "even if I have to play a vampire."

He was referring to that picture he had recently made, *Warlock* (1959), which had been formatted by 20th Century Fox in both CinemaScope and Technicolor.

When the script arrived one afternoon, he found that it wasn't about blood sucking vampires. It was a Western. Its director, Edward Dmytryk, was still basking in the glow of his success with *The Caine Mutiny* (1954), which had been nominated for Best Picture of the Year at Oscar time.

In 1947, he'd become one of the "Hollywood Ten," a group of blacklisted industry professionals who had refused to give testimony before the House Un-American Activities Committee. In 1952, Stanley Kramer had helped restore Dmytryk's career.

The project had been adapted from the novel, *Warlock,* by Oakley Hall, with a screenplay by Robert Alan Aurthur. Henry had been disappointed to learn that he would be second-billed to Richard Widmark, with supporting roles essayed by Anthony Quinn (he and Henry had long talked about appearing in a movie together), Dorothy Malone, Wallace Ford, Tom Drake, and Richard Arlen. A lot of the movie was shot on location in Utah at Dead Horse Point and at Kings Bottom.

Widmark had burst onto the Hollywood scene when he was Oscar-nominated for the villainous Tommy Udo in his debut film, *Kiss of Death* (1947). He later played

Richard Widmark and **Henry Fonda** confront each other in *Warlock*, a movie set in the 1880s, when aging gunmen like the Fonda character had increasingly evolved into outmoded symbols of a bygone era.

"I was told to carry around a melancholy look," Henry said.

285

anti-hero roles in *films noirs*, eventually branching out to appear in more heroic roles in Westerns.

[Ironically, during the final decade of his life, in 1999 (he died in 2008), Widmark would marry Susan Blanchard. She had been Henry's third wife.]

Chicago-born Dorothy Malone had won the Best Supporting Actress Oscar for her performance as heiress to an oil fortune in *Written on the Wind* (1956) opposite Rock Hudson. She had married Jacques Bergerac, the French actor who had divorced Ginger Rogers.

Brooklyn-born Tom Drake was cast as the gang leader of a rowdy bunch of cowpokes. He had achieved fame playing Judy Garland's "Boy Next Door" in *Meet Me in St. Louis* in 1944.

In a minor role, Richard Arlen had been a big star in silent pictures, notably in *Wings* (1927) opposite Clara Bow. By the 1950s, he'd become a familiar face on TV.

Henry had a reunion with Wallace Ford, who had starred in his TV series *The Deputy.* In *Warlock,* Ford played Judge Holloway.

Full of dark psychological twists, the plot had cast Henry as Clay Blaisedell, a freelance marshal with implacable methods for dealing with troublemakers The subplot centered on his club-footed assistant, Tom Morgan (Quinn). Some critics suggested a homoerotic relationship between the two men. Morgan sublimated his homoerotic attraction into a warped devotion to Blaisedell, a renowned gunfighter.

Cowboys worked for Abe McQuown (Tom Drake), who was boss of this colony of villains. They often roared into town, killing on a whim or beating or humiliating any deputy sheriff.

Johnny Gannon (Widmark), one of the cowboys, became sickened with them and stays behind. Tired of his gang's murderous ways, he signed on as Blaisedell's deputy.

Blaisedell's former girlfriend, Lily Dollar (Malone) arrived in town and took an instant shine to Widmark (Johnny).

Blaisedell, who always had that faraway look in his eyes, will eventually leave town as he realizes that the Old West he has known is gone forever.

Bosley Crowther, in *The New York Times,* wrote, "Mr. Fonda, as usual, is excellent—melancholy, laconic, and assured—and Mr. Widmark is properly nervous but full of sincerity and spunk. Mr. Quinn plays it a little heavy, in a slightly pathetic role. Colorful and noisy, *Warlock* should drag Western fans from their TV sets."

***

The Man Who Understood Women

Although continually tempted to abandon Hollywood, Henry stayed around to appear in *The Man Who Understood Women,* a box office flop. For a 1959 release for Fox, it was shot in CinemaScope and was directed, produced, and screen-written by Nunnally Johnson. He and Henry went way back. Johnson had won an Oscar for his screenplay of *The Grapes of Wrath* (1940), adapted from the John Steinbeck bestseller.

For this new venture, Johnson had adapted the screenplay from the Romain Gary novel, *The Colours of the Day.*

A major postwar writer of French literature, Gary, over the course of his career, would pen some thirty novels, some under a pseudonym. From 1962 to 1970, he would be (disastrously) married to the doomed American actress, Jean Seberg.

[When he discovered that she was having an affair with Clint Eastwood, he challenged him to a duel using pistols. Eastwood declined. Some years later, Gary would use that same pistol to commit suicide.]

Perhaps Johnson's worst mistake involved casting Leslie Caron, the French

The Man Who Understood Women had a title that did not apply to **Henry Fonda.** "I never understood women," he confessed to his co-star, the miscast French actress, **Leslie Caron**.

The film mocks the Hollywood rat race.

After seeing a screening, Henry dropped out of that rat race and disappeared from the screen for the next three years.

dancer and singer, as the film's female lead, taking star billing over Henry. Although Caron was an accomplished actress, the role itself was wrong for her. As Johnson later admitted, "She and Henry had no on-screen chemistry at all."

The actress had survived the horror of the Nazi occupation of Paris during World War II. A gifted dancer, she was discovered by Gene Kelly and cast with him in the classic film *An American in Paris* (1951). *[Cyd Charisse had been that film's original star but had to drop out because of pregnancy.]*

Caron would reach her pinnacle in Hollywood when cast in the title role of *Gigi* (1958) with Louis Jourdan and Maurice Chevalier.

On Henry's first day of rehearsal, Johnson suggested how he should play the male lead—a Hollywood producer named Willie Bauche. "Think Orson Welles and Charlie Chaplin, with a little piss and vinegar from Erich von Stroheim."

In the plot, Willie is obsessed with morphing his actress wife Ann (Caron) into the biggest and sexiest star in Hollywood. In his desperation to achieve this lofty goal, he ignores her needs as a woman.

She flees back to her native France, where she meets a handsome aviator, Marco Ranieri (played by Cesare Donova). He lives up to what the title promises as *The Man Who Understood Women*.

Henry learns of his wife's affair and hires assassins to kill his rival in love. However, these supposed killers turn out to be romantics and spare the lives of both Ann and Marco.

When Henry discovers that they did not execute the plan he hired them for, he rushes to France to save his marriage.

There, after falling off a cliff on the French Riviera, he is hospitalized and heavily bandaged. Learning of his near-disaster, Anne rushes to the side of her stricken husband.

Love—this time within the marriage—blooms anew.

During the time Henry was working on this bad movie, his friend, James Stewart, was starring in the infinitely more prestigious and enduring *Vertigo* (1958) and *Anatomy of a Murder* (1959), each a classic directed by Alfred Hitchcock.

***

In *Films in Review*, and in reference to *The Man Who Understood Women*, Henry Hart wrote, "Fonda does well in his none-too-consistent role, in which he mocks the Hollywood rat race of which he is a part. Throw in a touch of Erich von Stroheim. Caron ends up playing Trilby to Henry's Svengali."

The critic for *Variety* wrote: "The pace is fast, the lines are funny, and the overtones of romance promising. What happens after that is something of a mystery. It's as if Nunnally Johnson could not make up his mind in which direction to proceed. The film fusses and fumes, roams between long and dull sketches and then back to exquisitely acted and staged sophistication and humor."

Time magazine weighed in with: "Good heavens, how could Hank had accepted such a role? There on the screen prancing awkwardly in mandarin robes, flamenco suits, a clown costume, a silly goatee, was Henry Fonda in the role of Willie Bauche, the most elaborate phony since the Big Bad Wolf."

In disguise, Henry slipped into a movie house where *The Man Who Understood Women* was having a sneak preview. He left ten minutes before the ending.

Late the following day, he told a reporter from *Variety*, "This is my last motion picture. I'm returning to my first love, the Broadway theater. I will not be back."

OOOH
LA
LA!

LA COTE D'AZUR

During its heyday, which coincided with the Fondas "decampment" on its shores, the coastal resorts of southern France were fun, stylish, and sensual—a celebration of the "body triumphant" after the deprivations and humiliations of its Nazi occupation and the rigors of France's widely loathed and "collaborationist" Vichy regime.

Glam and photo-ops were everwhere, and sightings of celebs clad in everything from nothing at all to *haute couture* were *de rigeur,* but rarely before noon.

The Fondas, guided through the region's social labyrinths by Henry's multilingual new wife, Afdera, were "at home," as were (clockwise from center, top) **the Bouvier sisters (Jacqueline and Lee)**; **Maria Callas** (depicted here in full operatic drag); **Greta Garbo; Brigitte Bardot** on the beach; and the absolutely sensational **Marlene Dietrich**, conducting, at the time, an affair with Joseph P. Kennedy, father of a future president.

CHAPTER FIFTEEN

JANE FONDA

Hey, Moviegoers! Henry's Daughter Sizzles on the Silver Screen!
SLEEPING AROUND PARIS
THANKS FOR THE MEMORIES
As a Twenty-Something Art Student in the City of Light,
Jane Poses Nude for *la Crème de la Crème* until Her (Furious) Father "Grounds Her"

WARREN BEATTY
Jane's Screen Tests and Her Torrid Affair with the Hollywood Casanova

MARGARET SULLAVAN
Commits Suicide in a New Haven Hotel.
A Few Months Later, Her Daughter, Bridget, Does the Same,

TALL STORY
During the Filming of her First Movie,
Although Both Jane and Its Director Fall Madly in Love With
TONY PERKINS,
Tab Hunter Emerges as the "Ultimate Victor"

JANE INHERITS A TRUST FUND & USES IT
1. To Declare Independence from Her Father;
2. To Buy Herself Out Of a "Slave Contract" with Josh Logan;
3. To Strut Her Stuff at the Actors Studio; and
4. to Temporarily "Acquire" a Bisexual, Timmy Everett

EXOTIC MENTORS COME AND EXOTIC MENTORS GO
Moving and Shaking on Broadway with the Flamboyant Greek Expatriate
Andreas Voutsinas

INVITATION TO A MARCH
Jane Conquers Broadway after Maneuvering her Way Around an Only Slightly Crazy
SHELLEY WINTERS

"Jane Fonda is an actress always in search of a script for her life."
—Gail Sheehy, author of *Passages*

"Jane Fonda can quiver like a tuning fork."
—Kenneth Tynan

After that summer vacation on the Côte d'Azur with Henry and Afdera, twenty-one-year-old Jane had no intention of enrolling at Vassar for a third term. Instead, she persuaded Henry to finance her an extended stay in Paris, based on vague goals that she might want to become a painter. Although she enrolled at the *Académie de la Grande-Chaumière [a school devoted to the teaching of sculpture and painting without the strict allegiance to academics at its more rigorous (and prestigious) competitor, the École des Beaux-Arts]*, she attended classes there only three times.

"My French was not very good, and I had no idea what the professors were talking about," she was quoted as saying.

At the time, her former stepmother, Susan Blanchard, was also living in Paris. Although she was caught up in the social whirl of her own life, she devoted what time she could spare to Jane, helping her meet prospective beaux, and occasionally inviting her to parties and nightclubs.

A room for Jane was rented within a respectable private home along the wide, tree-lined Avenue d'Iéna in the prestigious 16th *arrondissement,* but she spent as little time there as possible. Presided over by an aging and "almost destitute" countess, the apartment she occupied reminded Jane of a morgue, as the heavy black draperies of the formal rooms were always closed. "There was always this smell of boiling turnips in the air," she said.

***

Barely Restrained, Stylish, and Underpaid: Jane as an Intern at The Paris Review

During her first days in Paris, she sat alone in such celebrated cafés as *La Closerie des Lilas,* once patronized by Hemingway, Picasso, and Modigliani; and at *La Coupole* in Montparnasse, sometimes reading the latest issue of *Paris Review.*

Perhaps as a means of linking herself socially with its staff, she set up an interview with George Plimpton, its New York-born editor, a Harvard graduate and sportsman known for his patrician demeanor and familiarity with contemporary literature. His father, George Arthur Plimpton, would soon be appointed by JFK as the U.S. deputy ambassador to the United Nations.

No doubt because she was Henry Fonda's daughter, Plimpton hired her as a copy girl. That unpaid job meant she had to run errands for the male staff and bring the editors coffee whenever requested. The young men who worked for the *Paris Review* began to date her.

Her circle of friends and beaux grew rapidly. Mart Martin, in his book *Behind to Doors of 201 Famous Women,* wrote that Jane went out almost every night with "an array of American expatriate intellectuals and *habitués* of Left Bank *boîtes.*"

A New York tabloid writer, Frank Mason, wrote an article in which he claimed, "Henry Fonda's daughter, Jane, is having a high old time hopping from bed to bed in Paris."

For most undergraduates from Vassar in the late 1950s, an internship at the French headquarters of the esoteric and trendy **Paris Review** would have been the crowning gemstone in anyone's glittering tiara.

Jane, however, grew disillusioned with her very limited "eye candy' duties there, and quickly moved on to "Other Voices and Other Rooms" within the Movable Feast of one of that city's greatest eras.

Depicted above, on the right, is the *Paris Review's* flamboyant editor-in-chief,. the "participatory journalist" and member of the Franco-American literary *avant-garde*, **George Plimpton.**

Susan Blanchard often included Jane in her night clubbing and attendance of private parties. At one such party, Jane met the French actor Christian Marquand. *[He was often cast as a "heartthrob" in French movies of the 1950s. For his debut in the film industry, he played a footman in Jean Cocteau's* la Belle et la bête *(Beauty and the Beast; 1946).]*

Jane had seen only one of his films, *And God Created Women (Et Dieu créa la femme).* In it, he starred as Antoine Tardieu, who has a brief fling with Juliette (Brigitte Bardot). In the film, he eventually spurns her by leaving town without her.

One night, Marquand invited Jane to dinner at Maxim's, an upscale *belle époque* monument often filled with international celebrities. Joining the table that night was the young director, Roger Vadim, who had helmed *Et Dieu créa la femme.*

He had divorced Bardot and had found a new mate. Jane remembered him as "a tall, dark, rather intense young man with exotic eyes and an erotic aura. She also was introduced to Annette Stroyberg, who looked as if she were about to give birth to Vadim's baby.

It was obvious that Vadim and Marquand were very, very close. In the late 1940s, they had lived together as lovers. Both of them growing up had had sex without gender preference.

In June of 1949, they'd met Marlon Brando in a café. He had just completed his gig as Stanley Kowalski on Broadway in Tennessee Williams' *A Streetcar Named Desire.*

Vadim had invited him to join their table inside the café. Before midnight, Brando had moved in with the two Frenchmen, the first stages of what became a *ménage à trois.*

Before Vadim married Stroyberg and produced a daughter, Nathalie, he'd previously fathered a boy. He had lived with the then-teenaged Catharine Deneuve. Together, they had produced a boy whom Vadim had named Christian in honor of Marquand.

Ironically, when Brando married the Mexican actress, Motiva Castenada, they, too had a son whom he named Christian, also in honor of Marquand.

Jane, during her marriage (1965-73) to Vadim, would learn a lot more about Deneuve.

At the end of that dinner at Maxim's, Jane was preparing to leave with Marquand when Vadim stepped up to kiss her goodbye. It was not one of those traditional and relatively chaste Gallic kisses on each cheek. He kissed her deeply and directly on her luscious lips, giving her a taste of his tongue. At least that is what he later claimed.

Although Jane had already attended an English-language screening of *And God Created Woman,* she was spotted entering a Left Bank movie house with Christian Marquand and Vadim on each arm, to sit through the French-language version of *Et Dieu… créa la femme.*

One of the reasons Susan Blanchard had given for divorcing Jane's father was that she wanted to go dancing almost every night. One evening, she invited Jane, with a date she'd arranged, to accompany her and her beau to *l'Éléphant,* a nightclub on Paris' Left Bank.

Jane was not particularly intrigued by her date that night: Instead, she was entranced with Blanchard's escort, an Italian count. In reference to their dancing, "Susan and the count were the Astaire and Rogers of the Left Bank that night," Jane said.

The count and Blanchard were not in love, and he later aimed his charm directly at Jane. She was hardly attracted to him, but, perhaps out of boredom, she accepted his invitation to spend a weekend with him at a manor house in the *Île de France.*

It was during the course of that weekend that she agreed to pose, nude, as a model for some of his "art photos."

Apparently, the count couldn't manage to remain discreet and secretive about his photo-session(s) with Jane, and word soon spread along the grapevine, through a friend of Afdera, back to New York. Afdera told Henry, who was furious.

When Jane flew into New York for Christmas of 1959, he wanted her grounded. "No more Paris for you, girl." She later phrased it as, "He chewed my ass off…really good."

Two views of French heartthrob **Christian Marquand.** *Upper photo:* in the throes of love; *lower photo,* with the premier "sex kitten," of the 1950s, **Brigitte Bardot.**

After appearing as Stanley Kowalski on Broadway in *A Streetcar Named Desire,* **Marlon Brando** *(left)* flew to Paris, where he became the lover of **Christian Marquand.**

It evolved into a lifelong relationship.

***

Silent Night, Lonely Night

The widely celebrated playwright, Robert Anderson, had rented a house in Los Angeles. At 5AM one Sunday morning, he heard a loud pounding at his door. He had been sleeping peacefully until this noise woke him up.

Still half asleep, he stumbled toward the door, opening it to find Henry Fonda standing on the stoop, holding a script of his most recent drama, *Silent Night, Lonely Night* in his right hand.

"The role of John Sparrow I am destined to play," Henry said, barging in and heading in the direction of the kitchen to brew a pot of coffee. Their talk lasted through a lunch of sandwiches until Henry finally left at 3PM.

A deal was struck. Phone calls to the two men in charge of the production for the Playwrights Company were delighted that Henry wanted to sign on. They had already assigned the female lead of Katherine to Barbara Bel Geddes.

Rehearsals would begin at the Morosco Theatre in Manhattan for a premiere scheduled for December 3, 1959.

At the time that Henry joined forces with Anderson, he was married to the actress, Teresa Wright, who showed up on several occasions, telling Henry, "Barbara is a good actress, but in *Silent Night, Lonely Night*, the role of Katharine was actually created with me in mind. Alas, I had another engagement."

[Anderson was widely known at the time for his tender screenplay for Tea and Sympathy, *which had opened on Broadway in 1956 starring Deborah Kerr and John Kerr (no relation). Anderson also received an Oscar nomination for Best Writing, Screenplay Based on Material from Another Medium, for his drama,* The Nun's Story *(1959).]*

The distinguished English director, Peter Glenville, was named as its director. However, Henry later claimed that "he lost interest after about two weeks."

Glenville's lifetime partner and lover, the U.S. naval veteran Harry William Smith, virtually took over., Glenville had hooked up with him after World War II, and the two men bonded for life. Often working together as a team, Smith produced and Glenville directed plays for the London stage.

Glenville also directed Tennessee Williams' *Summer and Smoke* (1961) and the 1964 Broadway version of Jean Anouilh's stage drama, *Becket,* starring Laurence Olivier and Anthony Quinn. The Anouilh play had opened in Paris in 1959 and on Broadway in 1961. Three years later, he directed the screen version of *Beckett*, starring Richard Burton and Peter O'Toole.

John Chapman of the *New York Daily News* found the performances of **Henry Fonda** and **Barbara Bel Geddes** splendid, but the play itself a bore.

Bel Geddes had scored a Broadway triumph when she starred as Maggie the Cat in Tennessee Williams' *Cat on a Hot Tin Roof*. Right before working on stage with Henry, she had filmed *Vertigo* (1958) alongside his best friend, James Stewart.

Silent Night, Lonely Night was a sad story of a man (John Sparrow) and a woman, Katharine, each married to other parties, coming together for a reunion on Christmas Eve at an inn in New England. His philandering had driven his wife to a mental institution. Likewise, Katharine was also dealing with problems with her estranged husband.

Their time together, although brief, is meaningful. "On looking back," Henry said, "I think many of my lines were too morbid. Take, for example, when I say, 'I could imagine if we could hear all the stifled cries for help in the world, it would be deafening.'"

On opening night, Henry was in no mood to welcome visitors backstage. However, he made an exception for his old friend, Gary Cooper.

As Cooper remembered it, "Hank was so disappointed with his own performance that at one point, he banged his fists against the wall. I didn't think he was all that bad."

The slow-talking cowboy from Montana, **Gary Cooper**, made the cover of *Time* magazine in 1941, at the peak of his screen career. But when he came to see Henry on opening night, he was on his last legs.

When Henry looked into the face of Cooper, he was horrified at how he'd aged, although the actor tried to conceal it.

"Henry later said, "Coop looked to me like he'd come to the end of the trail."

Indeed, he had. In May of 1961, international media outlets carried the sad news that the legendary star was dead.

After Cooper's backstage visit, reviews for *Silent Night, Lonely Night* started pouring in: "It was a mixed bag,"

Henry said. Brooks Atkinson of *The New York Times* wrote, "Fonda lounges across the stage and talks with a leisurely deliberation that makes everything seem sort of spontaneous and genuine."

Ronald Coleman in the *Daily Mirror* claimed, "Fonda, easy of manner and movement on the surface, suggests admirably the torments of the man."

Richard Watts Jr. of the *New York Post* found that he could not think of "a pair of players who could bring a finer or more sensitive quality to the script."

A lot of brickbats were tossed at Henry and the play itself. Many found the play "too talky," whereas others thought its depiction of loneliness was so grim that they could not imagine patrons standing in line to buy tickets.

Others called the play "a drama too morbid to endure. You'll find yourself squirming in your seat."

The play was so dismal and attendance so poor, it closed after 124 performances., many of them presented to mostly empty seats.

***

Lost and "At Loss" in New York

After her return from Paris, Jane lived with Henry and Afdera at their Manhattan brownstone for six months. She remembered that chapter of her life as "my most miserable period," Not knowing which direction her life should go, she slept twelve to thirteen hours a day. She found the atmosphere at her home toxic. Her father's marriage to his fourth wife seemed all but over.

"Dad and Afdera had drifted so far apart that they went days without speaking," Jane said.

"After nearly four years of marriage," Afdera said, "Henry is still a stranger to me. He no longer introduces me to people as his wife but calls me a social butterfly because I stage four or five parties a week. Otherwise, I was out of the house until late most nights attending parties in Manhattan, going to gala events, patronizing Broadway with friends." She was seen with various male escorts, most of them in her own age bracket.

As time went by, the generation gap between Henry and Afdera became even more pronounced. She claimed, "I was still young, but he wasn't. The 1960s were around the corner, and I wanted to be alive and vital to greet this new decade. If I had taken him as a boyfriend back in the 1920s, our marriage might have worked out. But our age difference formed too wide a gap by the end of the 1950s. At my parties, he always wanted to go to bed, that is, go to bed to sleep and for no other purpose."

Many young men at that time wanted to go to bed with her, but not for sleep.

Many guests who attended Afdera's parties recalled Henry looking desolate and lonely and sitting in a corner. "His face had one expression," Barbara Bel Geddes said, "and it was one of disgust."

Leland Hayward remembered that at one birthday party, guests were served large scoops of vanilla ice cream covered with chocolate sauce.

"It was a wild evening. I couldn't believe what I was seeing. They started throwing all that ice cream and chocolate sauce against the walls of Hank's living room, while he sat silently by, glaring at them."

Jane never felt part of Afdera's social life as she had with Susan Blanchard in Paris. With no real dedication, she signed up for piano lessons at New York City's Mannes School of Music, but soon, decided that the career of a professional pianist wasn't for her.

Once again, she considered the prospect of becoming a painter, and enrolled in the Arts Studio League. "I was no match for the budding Picassos of tomorrow," she claimed.

She worked temporarily in an unpaid job for the *Paris Review*, as she had in Paris. Her job involved answering the phone, typing letters, and soliciting subscriptions for the financially unprofitable magazine, read mostly by the New York literati.

With Henry's marriage crumbling before her eyes, Jane moved in with Susan Stein, living in her three-bedroom apartment on East 76th Street. Stein, the daughter of Jules Stein, the founder of MCA, had been her roommate at Vassar.

An object of envy and fascination for Jane Fonda and virtually every other woman in America, here's **Suzy Parker,** then one of the world's most widely desired models, on the cover of *Harper's Bazaar* edition of January, 1957

Since she needed money to pay for her share of the rent, Jane temporarily pursued a career in modeling.

She went to the office of Eileen and Gerald Ford, who had founded one of the earliest internationally recognized modeling agencies in the world. Jane was inspired by the success of Suzy Parker, who appeared on the covers of dozens of magazines as well as in ads and even in movie roles. Parker became the first model to make $100,000 a year, which in 2022 terms would be close to a million dollars.

Parker was the most in-demand model in New York, with her effigies appearing frequently in *Vogue* hawking products for Revlon and Max Factor.

In July of 1959, a glamourous photograph of Jane Fonda graced the latest issue of *Vogue*. She had posed for it at the studio of Richard Avedon, America's most celebrated photographer. This son of San Antonio was known for more than just his fashion pictures of models. He also shot photographs of political and cultural figures who included Marilyn Monroe, the evangelist, Billy Graham, President Dwight Eisenhower, and George Wallace of Alabama.

At the end of the season, Avedon gave Jane some advice: "Always dress in Chanel or Dior and live life in a *ménage à trois*."

During her short time as a fashion model, Jane dated a lot, the young men coming and going from her life. Occasionally, there would be a notable exception. Alexander Whitelaw, nicknamed Sandy, was introduced to Jane by Afdera. At the time, Jane was unaware that he'd been the lover of her stepmother.

Handsome, crewcut, and "butch," this Harvard graduate was a champ on the tennis courts of Long Island in summer, and a topnotch skier in winter on the slopes of Vermont.

Born to an officer in the Scottish Army, he had lived abroad for most of his youth and was proficient in Spanish, Italian, French, and German. His mother had lived a tragic life, once a prisoner of the Nazis during World War II.

Sandy was employed at the time by the New York office of producer David O. Selznick, who was married to actress Jennifer Jones. They treated Sandy almost like their son.

One night, Selznick invited Jane to their suite at the St. Regis. She recalled having met Selznick before when she was with Brooke Hayward. He didn't seem to think much of Jane back then but predicted major stardom for Brooke. Encountering Jane years later, he had a different appraisal, suggesting that he might put her under contract and morph her into an even bigger star than he had Ingrid Bergman, two decades earlier.

Jane cemented her friendship with Susan Strasberg and made a new friend, Christopher Plummer. Each was laboring at the time to complete the filming of *Stage Struck* (1958), in which Henry played one of the leads.

[She'd already seen the William Holden movie, Picnic *(1955), in which Susan had played Kim Novak's younger sister. Likewise, she had thrilled to Susan's Broadway performance in* The Diary of Anne Frank. *Directed by Garson Kanin, it ran for 717 performances from 1955 to 1957.]*

Jane had also visited Susan backstage when she was performing opposite Richard Burton and Helen Hayes in Jean Anhouilh's Broadway play, *Time, Remembered. [After its opening at the Morosco Theater in November of 1957, it ran for 248 performances. Jane soon learned that young Susan, during its run, began a torrid affair with her much older Welsh co-star.]*

Plummer, the Toronto-born actor, was making his screen debut in *Stage Struck*. He admitted later "From the first, I had the hots for her (Jane), finding her young, boyish, sexy, and fresh-faced."

To Jane, Plummer didn't seem to have the looks, the sex appeal, or the charm to become a leading man for the film industry. To her surprise, Plummer would later shine as Captain Georg von Trapp in the film version of *The Sound of Music* (1965), alongside Julie Andrews.

When Jane met him, Plummer was in the throes of divorcing his first wife, Tammy Grimes.

He later told David Selznick that he had found Jane "delectable." Whether he pursued her or not is not known. He neither confessed nor denied it.

She was stunned to see Plummer evolve into one of the most outstanding actors in Hollywood, with a career spanning seven decades. He could

Left photo: Actress **Jennifer Jones** left her husband, Robert Walker, to marry **David O. Selznick**, producer of *Gone With the Wind*.

Selznick hinted that he might turn Jane into a big star, but didn't follow up on that.

In the *right-hand* photo, **Alexander ("Sandy") Whitelaw**, Selznick's British associate and *protégé*, was passed on to Jane by her stepmother (Afdera Franchetti) after she'd dumped him.

convincingly play historical figures as diverse as Leo Tolstoy, the Duke of Welling-ton, Rudyard Kipling, or J. Paul Getty, and handle multiple Shakespearean venues too: *Hamlet, King Lear, Macbeth*, and Iago in *Othello.*

For a brief period, Jane was seen dating a handsome young French soldier on leave from resisting the guerilla fighters of Algeria's atrocity-soaked War (1954-1962) of Independence.

At one party, Jane met Lillian Ross, a writer for *The New Yorker* magazine. "Everybody keeps urging me to become an actress," Jane confided to Ross. "But I'm afraid of comparisons to my father. After all, he's one of the best actors in America, and I'd be scared shitless if I went up against him."

"Why do that?" Ross said. "You'll not have to compete with him. Your movie roles will be in a very different genre. Besides, comparisons are odious."

***

For six months, Jane continued to live "a miserable existence" at the Manhattan brownstone of Henry and Afdera, "watching their marriage rot away."

"Until I begin to branch out and make friends of my own, I was bored and lonely. I enrolled in a class to learn French. I spoke a bit of French already but was far from fluent. In my near future, I would be speaking more French than English, since I'd moved to Paris."

She still did the occasional modeling job, but hardly aspired to make that her career. "I never saw myself as a mannequin," she claimed.

She began to date a number of beaux, as she found many young men eager to take out the daughter of Henry Fonda. None of them captured her heart, but she became well-informed about contraceptives and an expert on the diaphragm.

Jane never knew when the day would come that Afdera would file for a divorce from her father, but she felt it was imminent. Rather privately, Afdera was going out with other men, and Henry was self-involved in his own career.

Lauren Bacall had expressed an interest in him after her husband, Humphrey Bogart, died in 1957. She had also been dumped by one of her later lovers, Frank Sinatra, so she was available—but Henry showed no interest in her.

News of Henry Fonda's increased estrangement from his temperamental wife, Afdera Franchetti, spread quickly through the Hollywood grapevine.

Lauren Bacall, after the death of her husband, Humphrey Bogart, in 1957, found this very interesting.

Recently widowed, Bacall had already had an affair with Frank Sinatra, but he dumped her. She then decided that she wanted to become the next Mrs. Henry Fonda.

Here's Bacall arriving at the Port of New York aboard the *Ile de France* in 1951 with her son, **Stephen**, and **Humphrey Bogart,** then, arguably, the most famous actor in the world.

The summer of 1958 marked a turning point in Jane's young life. That was the season she committed herself, for the first time, to becoming an actress.

Her decision to go on the stage or screen within a few months became immediately clear to Brooke Hayward. "She was determined to become a serious actress. To achieve that goal, she was willing to work hard, showing total dedication. It was not a game with her like those games we used to play as girls back in California. As an actress, in time, Jane would receive the public applause she never got in private from her father. I don't think I've ever seen such naked ambition as I saw in her."

***

Summer of 1958: The Fondas Move to Santa Monica
Henry Stars in his First TV Series: **The Deputy**

Beginning in the summer of 1958, Henry agreed to host and perform narrations for the TV series, *The Deputy* (it aired from 1959-1961) and to occasionally play the lead as well. As he told Jane, "I'm doing it only for the money."

In his search for accommodations, Henry met with Linda Christian, who had recently divorced his friend, Tyrone Power. In the settlement, she had acquired a spacious beach villa in Santa Monica, which she agreed to rent to Henry. Into it he moved Afdera, Jane, and Peter.

Lee and Paula Strasberg, along with their children, Susan and John, lived six houses away.

That summer was hardly a time of family-related bonding among the Fondas, as each member of the household seemed to be going in separate directions. Sometimes, when Henry was in a downstairs room with Jane and himself, all one heard was "the sound of silence."

Susan Strasberg was getting the kind of reviews Jane, at the time, could only wish for. In the press, Susan was

295

referred to as "the next Katharine Hepburn-type *ingénue*." The young actress was also hailed as "the next competition for Jean Simmons or Audrey Hepburn."

Jane had meant to call on Susan, but kept postponing it. She liked her, but secretly, Jane was also touched with a sense of jealousy.

Brooks Atkinson, in *The New York Times*, wrote, "[Strasberg] is a slender, enchanting young lady with a heart-shaped face, a pair of burning eyes, and the soul of an actress."

Late one morning, Jane was strolling along the beach when she spotted Susan lying on a towel. Susan signaled for her to come over and join her.

At first, Susan could only speak of Richard Burton, her former co-star and lover, who had dumped her after her previous play, *Time Remembered* closed on Broadway. "I will never love anyone the way I loved Richard," Susan confessed. "He's abandoning me and movlng on to his next series of conquests. Regardless of what happens in the future, I will always have this special love for the Welsh bastard."

That was more or less true, as Susan continued to read about Burton's previous and future conquests. On the set of *Ice Palace* (1960), in which he had an affair with his co-star, Roberta Haynes, he boasted: "If there's a dame I can't screw, then my name is not Richard Burton."

Conquests would come and go from Burton's life: Claire Bloom, Zsa Zsa Gabor, Ava Gardner, Sophia Loren, Jean Simmons, Barbra Streisand, Virna Lisi, Rachel Roberts, and, ultimately, Elizabeth Taylor.

As a young actor, he'd "experimented" with homosexuality with such stars as Laurence Olivier and the Welsh playwright Emlyn Williams, "but it didn't take" (his words).

It was under the blaring noonday sun that Susan suggested, that day on the beach at Santa Monica, that Jane study acting with Susan's father at the Actors Studio in Manhattan. "Of course, he'll have to agree to take you on, and he's turned down hundreds of applicants. Right now, my father and my mother, Paula, are helping Marilyn Monroe get through her latest picture. It's a comedy directed by Billy Wilder and starring Tony Curtis and Jack Lemmon, who appear mostly in drag."

Jane had read much about Lee Strasberg and the Actors Studio. In 1931, Lee had co-founded the Group Theater, which had been hailed as America's first true theatrical collective.

Two decades later, he joined Elia Kazan, Harold Clurman, and Cheryl Crawford in founding the Actors Studio in New York City.

An impressive array of future movie stars had already passed through its portals—Montgomery Clift, Marlon Brando, Anne Bancroft, Robert De Niro, Al Pacino, James Dean, Geraldine Page, Eli Wallach, Paul Newman, Julie Harris, Dustin Hoffman, and many others, some of whom would never, of course, make it to stardom.

The Strasbergs, The Actors Studio, and Warren Beatty

Although Lee Strasberg had been heavily influenced by the teachings of Konstantin Stanislavski, he was infusing the techniques being taught at the Actors Studio their own distinctive style.

Tennessee Williams had already commented on Lee's pupils to the press: "They act from the inside out. They communicate emotions they really feel. They give you a sense of life."

[Soon, Jane would be starring as the female lead in one of Williams' plays, A Period of Adjustment.]

To gain access to Lee, Jane had to meet his wife, (Susan's mother), a rather fierce, widely disliked "guardian of the flame" who always dressed in black, perhaps to conceal her fat. She was a staunch protector of both her husband and Marilyn Monroe.

[Henry, incidentally, had already denounced the Strasbergs, asserting that they were just using Monroe to advance their own fame and fortune, and that Method acting was "useless garbage."]

Since Jane was Henry Fonda's daughter, Paula arranged a brief meeting for her with her husband. When that moment came, the acting guru was brief: He immediately asked her, "Is it true that you want to become an actress?"

Her answer seemed to surprise him: "It was either that or become a veterinarian."

"Among current working actresses, which one would you like to emulate?"

Without hesitation, Jane said, "Geraldine Page."

Her interview with Strasberg passed quickly, and she was invited to enroll that autumn in his acting class in Manhattan's Hell's Kitchen, for which he'd charge her $35 a month.

Her meeting with Strasberg changed her life, Jane recalled. Later that summer, she not only became part of Actors Studio, but over a period of time, the director told her that she possessed the rare talent of an actress.

"His praise marked a turning point in my life. I went to bed thinking about acting, dreaming about acting, and waking up determined to be an actress. It was as if the roof had come off my life."

Jane Fonda—beautiful, quick-witted, and relentlessly ambitious, appears here in 1960 as part of a promotional campaign for *Tall Story*.

One afternoon, Susan invited Jane to visit the set where Marilyn Monroe was filming *Some Like It Hot* (1959). Lemmon and Curtis were in drag, as she'd been previously informed. Jane fleetingly knew Lemmon already, since he'd appeared with her father in *Mister Roberts*.

Billy Wilder, *Some Like It Hot's* director, was tangling with Paula Strasberg, who hovered over Monroe like a protective hen, trying to take over the direction of the film herself.

Wilder later had a moment alone with Jane. He looked over at Paula. "I hate that bitch. She's more of a cunt than Gloria Swanson." He was referring to having helmed the former silent screen vamp in *Sunset Blvd.* (1950).

When Monroe finally got through a minor scene that required eight takes, she sauntered over to greet Susan and to meet Jane.

"She spoke to me in a voice that sounded far away," Jane recalled. "She also had a faraway look in her troubled eyes."

"It's such a dumb part," Monroe said. "I'd have to be an idiot not to know that Lemmon and Curtis aren't women, but two men in drag."

She told Jane that she'd seen her father in only one movie, and that was when he appeared in *The Male Animal* (1942) with Olivia de Havilland. "If I'd been born a decade earlier, I could have played Scarlett O'Hara. I'd be good at acting like a Southern bitch. Gotta go."

Jane then watched her saunter toward her dressing room, trailed by Paula.

***

Lee later admitted "I signed Jane for two reasons: One, she's Henry Fonda's daughter. Two, I saw panic in her eyes."

Back in Manhattan, when Henry saw his daughter, who wanted to talk about her experiences at the Actors Studio, he cut off that conversation at once. *"Shut up!* I don't want to hear it. I'm going to bed."

Before heading upstairs, he said, "You don't need all that Method acting shit. Just follow the advice of Spencer Tracy. Learn your lines and don't bump into the furniture."

At the Studio, Jane faced both friendship and jealousy from her fellow students. The first time she tried to perform a scene, Tyrone Guthrie watched it from the audience. An English theatrical director, he was the founder of the Statford Festival in Canada.

After seeing her perform, he asked her, "What else have you done other than be the daughter of Henry Fonda?"

Every day at the Actors Studio, she seemed to meet someone she knew by reputation.

The playwright, Clifford Odets, told her he was hard at work on a Broadway play that would star Marlon Brando as Beethoven.

Shelley Winters was real raunchy, confiding to her that she used to go down on Marilyn Monroe in their early days in Hollywood when they were "roomies." She also told Jane that actor John Ireland "has the biggest dick in

Hollywood. I suggest you try it one night."

The ice blonde, Carroll Baker, related experiences she'd had working on the film *Giant* (1956), with James Dean, Rock Hudson, and Elizabeth Taylor. She also told stories of how it was playing *Baby Doll* (also 1956), based on the Tennessee Williams play. "I had to learn thumb sucking."

Marilyn Monroe showed up one day and sat in front of Jane. At the end of his class, Lee Strasberg ordered her a big ice cream soda topped with a cherry "in memory of how you lost yours years ago when you were far too young."

That same afternoon, Jane met playwright Arthur Miller, who was (dysfunctionally) married to Monroe at the time. He was very candid, telling her, "I detest Lee Strasberg. He is just using Marilyn. And that Paula bitch is a leech."

Jane was also reported to have met Orson Welles one afternoon, as he's been eyeing her seductively. "I could turn you into a big star," he boasted. "Even bigger than my former wife, Rita Hayworth. I already have a title for the first film in which I'd want to cast you: *The Ribbon of Dreams.*"

***

The first movie role Jane was offered came from director Mervyn LeRoy, who had made a star of Lana Turner in the late 1930s. He wanted her to play the daughter of James Stewart in *The FBI Story* (1959), Hollywood's paen to J. Edgar Hoover, Chief of the Federal Bureau of Investigation. Since Jane was already the goddaughter of Stewart (who'd been cast as an FBI Field Officer). LeRoy thought it would be a "hoot" for Jane to play his daughter on the screen.

At first, Henry liked the idea and even drove up to Warners with Jane for a meeting with LeRoy and Stewart. Sometime before that afternoon ended, he decided he didn't want Jane to break into movies through his connection. "It all sounds too clubby, a bit incestuous," he said, unhelpfully, "since Jimmy is my best buddy."

Jane finally agreed with him, and they left the studio heading home. The next morning, they read in *Variety* that Diane Jergens had been cast in the role of the daughter.

***

"Buying Off" Josh Logan; "Screen Teaming" with Warren Beatty

As a Hollywood director, Josh Logan was riding high, having helmed Marlon Brando in *Sayonara* (1957), earning him his second Oscar nomination as Best Director. The following year he'd helmed the movie version of *South Pacific* (1958), after his huge success with the stage version of that show on Broadway.

For Logan's next project, he acquired the screen rights to the novel *Parrish,* written by Mildred Savage. This melodrama was set in the tobacco fields of Connecticut. The romantic male lead was an aggressive young tobacco grower with love complications and the "associated trauma" of his mother's marriage to his most ruthless competitor.

Logan was known for developing crushes on his leading male actors, and for maneuvering them onto sexually compromising positions on their roads to stardom. At this point in considering the lead for *Parrish,* he focused on a then relatively unknown actor, Warren Beatty, the brother of Shirley MacLaine.

When he heard from Henry that Jane was studying at the Actors Studio, he came up with the idea of casting two unknowns as the leads: MacLaine's brother and Henry Fonda's daughter. He thought that that casting combination would generate "tons of publicity before the film was even shot."

Logan didn't stop there. For the film's older couple, he came up with the idea of reteaming Clark Gable with Vivien Leigh.

Logan could envision the headlines: RHETT BUTLER AND SCARLETT O'HARA REUNITED IN LOVE.

But as he later lamented, "Both Rhett and Scarlett turned me down."

He knew there would be hundreds of fading movie stars willing to play the mid-

Even the most frantic marketing efforts of director/producer Joshua Logan couldn't reunite, under any circumstances, **Vivien Leigh** (as Scarlett O'Hara) and **Clark Gable** (as Rhett Butler) into a revised screen team.

Each, by now, was thoroughly exhausted by the romantic illusion they'd successfully crafted during their filming of *Gone With the Wind* (1939).

298

dle-aged couple. More important to Logan, however, was to see if there were any chemistry between Beatty and Jane. He ordered a screen test.

For the test, Logan was more interested in making a star out of Beatty than he was of Jane. Tennessee Williams was already fully aware of the director's obsession with Beatty, referring to Logan as "Warren Beatty's fairy godmother."

Logan decided to engage Jane with Beatty in a kissing scene. Rehearsals took fifteen minutes before the actors were camera ready. Logan later said, "They tongue-kissed. A lot of saliva was exchanged between them before that scene ended. I had called 'cut' three times before they would stop devouring each other's mouths."

As Beatty later described it, "Jane and I kissed until we had practically eaten off each other's heads."

She had a different take on the screen test. "We were thrown together like two lions in a cage."

As it turned out, Beatty wanted more from Jane than a deep-throat kiss. Around the time she started an affair with Beatty, she was still more or less going steady with Sandy Whitelaw.

Beatty had already told Logan, "I don't really like Jane, and I certainly don't understand her. She is too neurotic for me, but I'm madly in love with her, and didn't think I could live without her. I know that doesn't make any sense."

"It makes sense to me," Logan said. "That's how I used to feel about Henry Fonda when we were young."

Sandy got carried away and one night, he broke into her apartment when she was out of town and read her diary. In it, he came across this entry: "I don't love Sandy and I have no intention of marrying him."

"I was seriously pissed off, but I didn't drop her," Sandy said. "She tried to swallow a man whole. She took more than she gave."

His affair with Jane ended on a sour note. He arrived unannounced at the studio, where she was preparing for another screen test with Beatty.

After he knocked on the door of her dressing room, he heard her call out, "Warren?"

"It's Sandy, bitch!" he shouted through the door.

When he got inside, they got into a fierce argument. At one point, in a jealous rage, she broke her dressing room mirror.

After about ten minutes of accusations, Beatty himself arrived on the scene and immediately ascertained what was going on. He'd been present at scenes like this before.

"I know exactly how you feel, fellow," Beatty said to Sandy. "Once, in a hotel room in Philadelphia in a similar setup, I threw a mattress out a seven-story window. I'll go for a walk until you guys settle this crap."

When he returned, Sandy was gone. Nothing else was said about his departure.

After Logan sat through a screening of the Jane Fonda/Warren Beatty screen test, he offered Jane a five-year contract with the guarantee of $10,000 annually. In spite of the very low payments associated with it, she signed.

"She must have been damn eager to get on the screen at that time," Henry said. "Josh was always a tightwad."

Eventually, Logan let his option expire on *Parrish*. Other investors spearheaded by director/screenwriter Delmar Daves took over. His original choice for the younger pair of lovers involved Anthony Perkins and Natalie Wood, each of whom rejected it. Daves then cast Troy Donahue and Connie Stevens. The role of the older tobacco baron went to Karl Malden, with Claudette Colbert emerging from retirement to play his wife. It was the farewell performance of her legendary screen career.

Warren Beatty's affair with Jane survived the screen test for *Parrish*, and they began to date. One memorable night, they dined together at La Scala in Beverly Hills.

At their table, Beatty seemed to be looking at Jane with one eye while scanning the room with his other eye, perhaps hoping to settle on his next conquest.

Here appear a young **Jane Fonda** and her male counterpart, **Warren Beatty** snapped informally in the days after Josh Logan's screentest, but before Beatty left the California starlette for the British flame thrower, Joan Collins.

Warren Beatty: Possibly the sexiest and usually, the most (heterosexually) promiscuous man in Hollywood.

Marlene Dietrich became famous for her cheekbones ("It's all in the genes, dahling"), even if she had to have them surgically altered.

299

Seated a few tables away, he spotted the British sexpot, Joan Collins. Collins was immediately attracted to Beatty and perhaps signaled her interest. Later, she described her first sighting of Jane: "She was quite pretty but a little too full of face."

Of course, Jane by now no longer possessed those "chipmunk cheeks." Even so, an executive at Warners had suggested that Jane "pull a Marlene Dietrich."

[He was referring to the German-born actress who had her jaw surgically broken and reconstructed to place an emphasis on her high cheekbones. It was also recommended that as part of the process and at the same time, she should have her back molars removed.]

Jack Warner had also seen Jane's first screen test, and he wrote to Logan: "She is flat-chested. If one of my directors uses her, he'll have to insist she wear falsies."

Collins' cursory first impression of Jane and her facial structure did not do her justice. The best description of Jane's look at the time was written by Thomas Kiernan:

> *"At twenty-one, Jane was taller than most of her contemporaries. Her thick, dark-gold hair fell to her shoulders when she didn't wear it up in a knot or have it coiffed into the beehive hairdo so popular in 1958. Through constant dieting, she had reduced her weight to about 120 pounds. Her upper cheeks had lost the fullness of her teenaged years, and when her hair was up, her face had a ballerina's gaunt expression. Her steep, broad, rounded forehead was like a smooth palisade above her wideset eyes. The rest of her face was elongated, angling sharply from her prominent cheeks to her long jaw. Its length accentuated by the pouty triangular shape of her mouth. Her teeth were large for her mouth, especially the upper ones. When she smiled, which she did with a suddenness that was unexpected from so stern a mouth, her slightly convex teeth jumped out in a flash of brilliant white."*

In short order, Beatty dumped Jane for Collins, ending up in her bedchamber three nights later. In reference to Beatty, "Dating top female stars and having all those gay playwrights lusting after him was one way to climb the stairs to stardom," said Elia Kazan.

The renowned playwright, William Inge, also had a "mad crush" on Beatty, for whom he'd written a period drama that was later adapted into a film, *Splendour in the Grass* (1961), a tale of two high school sweethearts in Kansas in the 1920s, each navigating sexual repression, love, and heartbreak.

Britain's most durable movie star, **Joan Collins**, as she appeared in 1954.

Known in Hollywood as "the British Open, she said, "I've got a great body. Sometimes it looks terrific, and if it's photographed right, it can look absolutely great."

Lee Strasberg asked its director, his longtime friend, Elia Kazan, to shoot a screen test with Beatty and Jane as the sweethearts. Jane was cast as Deanie Loomis, who takes her mother's advice to resist her desire for her handsome boyfriend, Bud Stamper, cast with Beatty, the son of the town's most prosperous family.

The screen test went far better for Beatty than it did for Jane. Whereas he won the role of Bud, Jane was rejected in favor of Natalie Wood.

On the set that day, watching the screen test, was Daniel Petrie, a Canada-born film, TV, and stage director. He later claimed, "In the test, Jane looked like a female impersonator doing an impression of Henry Fonda."

Beatty may have been AWOL from Jane's bedchamber, but on several occasions, in the future, directors considered them as a possibly dynamic screen team.

In fact, in Jane's first movie, *Tall Story* (1960), Logan debated casting Beatty as a star basketball player opposite Jane in the role of a brainy coed.

Beatty, however, had signed for another role, and the lead in *Tall Story* went to Anthony Perkins.

Beatty was also a candidate as the Texan who gets involved with Jane and the world of prostitution in New Orleans. That role in *Walk on the Wild Side* (1962) eventually went to the English actor, Laurence Harvey.

For the 1967 film comedy, *Barefoot in the Park*, producer Hal B. Wallis considered a Beatty-Fonda team. They would inhabit a fifth floor walkup in Greenwich Village. At the last minute, the young husband-and-wife roles went to Jane with another heartthrob, Robert Redford.

A final, unsuccessful, attempt to team Warren Beatty with Jane Fonda occurred during the casting of *Bonnie and Clyde* (1967). Although Jane was offered the role of

Although Jane Fonda was considered for the bloodthirsty role of Bonnie opposite **Warren Beatty** (left), the female lead of *Bonnie and Clyde* infamously went to **Faye Dunaway** (right) in photo above.

Jane would forever regret turning down the role of Bonnie.

Bonnie, her husband at the time, the French director, Roger Vadim demanded that she reject the role so that she could star, instead, in his upcoming movie, *Barbarella* (1968). Eventually, much to Jane's later regret, the blockbusting role of Bonnie was eventually assigned to Faye Dunaway.

***

The Suicide of Margaret Sullavan

Henry began the first day of 1960 on a sad note: That was the January 1 that a call of anguish came in from Leland Hayward. Both men had been married to Margaret Sullavan, and now a news report revealed that she had committed suicide in New Haven.

As Henry remembered, "I shed no tears on hearing the news, but a deep depression descended over me. It took weeks before I could shake it. Poor, doomed Maggie. In my way, and as painful as it was, I loved her, I guess. Of course, I'm not sure I really know what love is."

She had traveled a long road to her suicide. Some sources claimed that her death was from an accidental overdose of pills, but Henry knew better.

Her troubles had begun years before when she and Hayward were getting a divorce. They had produced three children—Brooke, Bridget, and William, nicknamed Billy.

At the separation, Bridget and Billy wanted to remain with their father, even though she pleaded with them to stay with her. They adamantly refused.

That had led to one of Sullavan's many breakdowns, and temporarily, she was committed to a mental institution. "Perhaps the desertion of my son, Billy, my youngest child, stabbed at my heart more than anything else," Sullavan said.

In her 1977 autobiography, *Haywire*, Brooke wrote, "Maggie humiliated herself by begging her son to remain with her. He wanted to live with his father. Our mother went into a screaming rage."

A friend of the family, Millicent Osborne, came to the house and went to Margaret's bedroom, where she discovered her under her bed, tangled in a fetal position and desperately whimpering.

She spent the next two and a half months in a mental clinic in Connecticut.

In the autumn of 1959, Augustus and Ruth Goetz had approached Sullavan with the script of their most recent play, *Sweet Love Remembered*, the title inspired by a sonnet by Shakespeare.

The main characters were a husband-and-wife writing team. Of course, Sullavan realized that the Goetz couple were writing about themselves and their tribulations.

She phoned the next day, telling them that she approved of the script and relayed her willingness to star in it. *Sweet Love Remembered* went into rehearsals on December 1, 1959 and premiered on Broadway on February 4, 1960 after a "soft opening" in New Haven.

In 1934, then-*ingénue* **Margaret Sullavan** had been on the cover of *Photoplay* (left photo), and in 1935, she'd been applauded, nationwide, as one of the stars of *The Good Fairy* (right photo).

Now, at the dawn of the 1960s, increasingly identified as caustic and unpredictable, she was dead, from suicide, after a decline in both her bookings and her self-esteem.

Actresses throughout Hollywood, many of them as ferociously ambitious as Sullavan and with even fewer kindnesses and compassion, took immediate notice.

Her co-star was the film and stage actor, Kent Smith, who, years before, had been a friend of both Sullavan and Henry Fonda during their summer stock period on Cape Cod.

Harold Clurman, one of the finest directors on Broadway, stepped in to direct *Sweet Time Remembered*.

At the same time, Sullavan's daughter, Brooke, then aged 22, was making her stage debut at the Gate Theater in Manhattan, starring in *The Marching Song* playing a prostitute.

Back in New Haven at the Taft Hotel, although Sullavan was to go on stage that night, she had not answered her phone all day. The producers of the show, Henry Margolos and Martin Gabel, went to the Taft at 5:30PM. Even then, the evening of the New Haven premiere, she would not answer her door. They found it bolted from the inside. The manager, who eventually broke down the door, was summoned to help them gain entrance.

They discovered her alive, lying nude on the bed, but unconscious. Several empty or half-empty bill bottles were on her nightstand. An ambulance was summoned to rush her to the Grace New Haven Hospital. There, shortly after 6PM, she was pronounced dead. One report softened the news, asserting that her death resulted from an accidental overdose of Seconal.

News of her death was flashed across America. It was announced that Arlene Francis would take over her stage role.

At her funeral, many celebrities showed up, including Joan Crawford, who attracted the most attention from the press, along with David O. Selznick and his wife, Jennifer Jones. Sullivan's co-star, Kent Smith, was there, too, seated next to Joseph Mankiewicz.

Sullavan was only fifty years old at the time of her death, and many reporters claimed that she was too young to die. One writer said, "Her life was filled with thunderous applause but at her burial, it had died down to a dim murmur of grief."

Sullavan's death was but a prelude to the suicides of two of her children, Bridget and Billy.

Jane would later speculate about Sullavan and her daughter, Bridget.

"Here were two women who had infinite spirit—a certain kind of brilliance, a crazy brilliance, erratic, difficult, and neurotic—but still unique. I don't think society offers solutions to people like that, especially women. They were never provided with a constructive way of harnessing that kind of energy and brilliance. It turned inward and destroyed them."

***

Otto Preminger, in 1951, had staged a Broadway production of *The Moon is Blue* at the Henry Miller Theatre. It was a hit, running for 1,000 performances, with a cast headed by Barbara Bel Geddes, Barry Nelson, and Donald Cook. It was later adapted into a controversial film starring William Holden, David Niven, and Maggie McNamara in her screen debut.

Initially, the movie drew objections from censors, and some small-town theaters refused to show it. There were many protests to its "light and gay treatment of the subject of illicit sex and seduction."

In the summer of 1959, before Jane was about to make her film debut, she agreed to star in the McNamara role in a summer production of *The Moon Is Blue* at Fort Lee, New Jersey.

"At that time, Jane was talented but had little experience," claimed her agent, Ray Powers. "She had appeared with Henry Fonda on the stage in Omaha in *The Country Girl*—but that was about it."

Local Omaha critics interpreted her performance as "sweet, innocent, and showing promise."

***

Tall Story: Falling Temporarily in Love with Tony Perkins

"I was just good enough to get by," Jane said before leaving for Hollywood to film *Tall Story* (1960), marking her first appearance in a movie after failed attempts to nab the starring roles in both *Parrish* and *Splendour in the Grass*. At the time, Jane was under contract to *Tall Story's* director, Joshua Logan.

The film was cast with Tony Perkins as a basketball star and honor student, Ray Blent.

Jane played June Ryder, who has come to college, it seems, mainly to find a husband. The character she played was the polar opposite of the independent woman Jane later personified. She joined the pom-pom girls, cheering on the basketball stars—especially Blent. A subplot involves him being propositioned by a gambling syndicate to lose a key game to a visiting Russian team.

Set for a 1960 release by Warner Brothers, the movie was based on a 1957 novel, *The Homecoming Game,* by Howard Nemerov. It has been a success on Broadway in 1959, and Jane had gone to see it and didn't like it.

> Neither **Jane** nor **Tony Perkins** had yet been "shoehorned" or "typecast" into the psychologically complicated public images they'd develop in the years immediately following the release of the "high jinx on campus'" context of *Tall Story.*
>
> For the moment, at least, each was interpreted as a wholesome American post-adolescent, saying and doing cute, adorable things.
>
> For the moment, at least, there was 'nary a trace of the political traps into which Jane would fall, nor any of the scary *Psycho* associations that would later plague Tony Perkins.

However, Logan assured her that her role in the upcoming movie would be expanded, and that the screenplay would be by the writing team of Russel Crouse and Howard Lindsay.

By the time Jane started to work on the film, it had been retitled *The Way the Ball Bounces*.

Years later, on looking back at her performance, she called it a "Kafka-*esque* nightmare. I suffered from bulimia, and irrational fears that I was boring, untalented, and plain. I also became a sleepwalker and woke up to find myself nude at night on the sidewalk in front of my house."

There was another complication, too: Both Josh Logan and Jane were in love with Tony Perkins. Perhaps she also heard rumors that Logan had had a long-ago crush on her father when they'd worked together on Cape Cod and lived together in California.

Jane had long admired Perkins on the screen. He was the son of a famous actor, Osgood Perkins, and his ancestors had arrived on American shores aboard the *Mayflower*.

She had seen him at his best in *Friendly Persuasion* (1956), a movie he'd made with Gary Cooper. For that role, he'd been Oscar-nominated as Best Supporting Actor of the Year.

But his greatest role, and the part for which he would be forever remembered, was just months away. That came when Alfred Hitchcock cast him as the homicidal owner of the Bates Motel, where, while dressed in drag, he slashes poor Janet Leigh to death in a shower. That role and its multiple sequels would "haunt me for the rest of my life."

[As a footnote in Hollywood history, the future super star, Robert Redford, is seen in an uncredited role in Tall Story.]

Perkins was paid $125,000 for his performance, Jane taking home only $10,000. After seeing the final cut, Logan lamented, "I should have cast Warren Beatty."

Tall Story generated only $1.7 million at the box office and was critically attacked. *Time* magazine wrote: "Nothing could possibly save the picture, not even the painfully personable Perkins doing his famous awkward act, not even a second-generation Fonda with a smile like her father's and the legs of a chorus girl."

The critic for *Motion Picture* claimed that "*Tall Story* is an old-fashioned tale of a man-mad girl, played by cinematic newcomer Jane Fonda, who is unlikely to follow in her father's distinguished footsteps if *Tall Story* is the type of material she will pursue."

Howard Thompson in *The New York Times* wrote, "On the basketball court, the gangling Mr. Perkins jounces around convincingly enough. Near Miss Fonda, he generally gapes and freezes, and who can blame him? If Fonda seems to be looking a bit askance now and then, you can blame her?"

***

Although he was shy around women, Perkins found Jane extremely supportive when she learned he was a homosexual. Although generally tight-lipped, he felt he could be open with her. She was the extreme opposite of a homophobe.

He was open enough to admit an early childhood drama, claiming that after his father's death, his mother "compulsively eroticized our relationship. She was constantly running her hand all over my body, especially my thighs right up to my crotch. She did this even until I was eighteen years old."

His most public affair was with the blonde-haired Tab Hunter at the time of his top box office appeal, in 1956. Perkins' first affair with a woman was delayed until he turned 39 and seduced actress Victoria Principal.

In 1972, he would marry "Berry" Berenson, the younger sister of actress and model Marisa Berenson. He was still wed to her at the time of his death in 1992 from an AIDS-related illness.

Even after his marriage, he continued to have gay affairs, including with artist

At the time, *Tall Story* seemed like a simple, "girl-maneuvers-boy into a campus romance" flick without a clue about how important social issues would become to movie audiences within a few months after its release.

Left photo, tall and skinny **Tony Perkins** shows some skin. *Right photo*: So does **Jane**, a then 23-year-old who in real life was a LOT more sophisticated than the perky coed she played.

Speculation about **Tony Perkin's** gender preferences plagued him, sometimes famously, throughout the course of his long and troubled career. Hollywood pundits relentlessly described his affairs with Tab Hunter, Timmy Everett, and a half-dozen others. .

Here, in January of 1974, he appears with his understanding and long-standing wife, **Berry (Berinthia) Berenson** on the cover of Andy Warhol's very avant-garde *Interview* magazine..

Christopher Makos, dancer Rudolf Nureyev, composer/lyricist Stephen Sondheim, dancer/choreographer Grover Dale, French songwriter Patrick Loiseau, director René Clement, actor Robert Francis, plus lots of hustlers and an array of tall, thin dancers, a special preference of his.

The author and social gadfly, Truman Capote, knew him quite well. "I don't like blood," he claimed, "but Tony is a sadist. He likes to see blood during the sex act. I mean, he is really Norman Bates."

Andy Warhol, another friend, claimed that Perkins hired male hustlers to climb a ladder leaning against the window of his bedroom, where they would tie him up and rape him.

One day, Timmy Everett appeared on the set of *Tall Story*, and Perkins introduced him to Jane. He had a torrid affair with Everett when he was not seeing Tab Hunter, but by the time Jane met him, Perkins' ardor for the young performer was waning.

The blue-collar son of a Montana couple was two years younger than Jane, having been born in Helena, although he'd

Timmy Everett (left) with one of the major playwrights in America at the time, **William Inge**, whose sponsorship (some say "obsession with') was later defined as essential to the young actor's success.

Everett was not the first actor to fall into (or avail himself of) the male-dominated preferences of William Inge: So did Warren Beatty and Brandon De Wilde.

grown up in North Carolina. He had curly hair and was about two or three inches shorter than Jane. He seemed imbued with a love of the theater, and was an actor, singer, and dancer (aka "a triple threat").

He'd broken into show business lying on the casting couch of playwright William Inge. The older man eventually developed a big crush on him, perhaps not as much as his obsessive-compulsive all-consuming love for Warren Beatty.

Unlike Beatty, Inge found Everett willing to have sex with him any time of the day or night.

As his reward, Everett got cast in Inge's 1957 play, *The Dark at the Top of the Stairs,* set in a small Oklahoma town in the early 1920s. Everett was assigned the role of Sammy Goldenbaum, offering support to the stars Eileen Heckart, Pat Hingle, and Teresa Wright.

Elia Kazan, the director, thought he saw in Everett "the makings of a new James Dean, since we've lost the real one."

His selection of Everett proved on target, as did the play itself, running for 468 performances at the Music Box Theatre in Manhattan.

In 1960, *Dark at the Top of the Stairs* was adapted into a movie, starring Robert Preston and Dorothy McGuire. Shirley Knight earned a Best Supporting Actress nomination. Everett's stage role of Sammy was awarded to actor Lee Kinsolving.

Everett had followed that stage role by getting cast in the 1958 play, *The Cold Wind and the Warm,* again because of Inge's influence.

Written by S.H. Behrman, the play opened at the Morosco in Manhattan, and starred Maureen Stapleton and Eli Wallach, with Everett essaying the role of "the boy," Tobey.

Both Everett and Jane had been enrolled at the Actors Studio, "but she took no notice of me until Tony introduced me to her on the set of *Tall Story,*" the actor said. Still confused about his sexuality, he met her again at a Thanksgiving party one night in Manhattan when she was with another beau. "Fearing rejection, I asked her if she'd worked with me on a scene to present before the Actors Studio. To my surprise, she agreed.

He was living at the time in a dingy little walkup on the Lower East Side of Manhattan. For their first "rehearsal," she invited him to her luxurious apartment on East 76th Street.

He brought along his script from Dylan Thomas' *Adventures in the Skin Trade.*

In the middle of a rehearsal one night, they stopped. As he recalled, "A wave of tenderness and desire swept over me, and I got an erection. She looked back at me like she wanted to swallow me in one gulp."

Within minutes, he was ascending the stairs inside her apartment to her bedroom, "where we remained for the next three days, with meals sent to us. We showered together, and Jane and I did everything. Each day, six or seven times. I lost count."

When Josh Logan heard that, he said, "Surely, Timmy is exaggerating."

Everett and Jane celebrated when Otto Preminger offered him a role in his upcoming film, *Exodus* (1960). But he was bitterly disappointed when the temperamental director withdrew the offer at the last moment, assigning the role instead to Sal Mineo.

Jane, at 22, Inherits a Trust Fund

Jane was no longer dependent on Henry for her financial support. At the age of twenty-two, her trust fund had come in for her, a bequest from her late mother.

"This poor boy that I was found himself in the months ahead showered with presents from Jane," Everett said. "Suits from Brooks Brothers, a gold watch, a pair of alligator shoes, cashmere sweaters, even a pink one."

Everett and Jane, for the most part, lived together for the next eighteen months. He had many questions about his own sexuality, and she had her own anxieties, too. Both of them ended up in therapy.

Here's **TImmy Everett** with **Jane Fonda** in *There Was a Little Girl* (1960)

Tony Perkins claimed, "Jane was attracted to Timmy's theatricality. He was a troubled guy—aggressive, antagonistic, and soulful. At this point in his life, he was bisexual."

***

Jane, on Broadway, in a Story About Rape

Logan approached Jane with another offer, one that involved making her Broadway debut in a play, *There Was a Little Girl*, written by Daniel Taradash. It was a tangled psychological drama in which an upperclass young woman was raped by a hoodlum. Later, she had to face charges that she had invited the assault.

Tall Story had not yet been released, and Jane went for the role, sharing her enthusiasm with Everett. He agreed to rehearse her lines with her.

When Henry heard about the theme that drove its plot, he was adamantly opposed to his daughter taking on such a dismal role., But she was determined and was goaded on by Everett.

Her own agent, Ray Powers, later asserted, "I think Everett has found a new meal ticket. He seemed to be taking over Jane's career as her manager. Logan was his tightwad self, offering Jane only $150 a week to star on Broadway as the rape victim.

Pre-Broadway, the play opened in Boston. Everett emerged as Jane's most enthusiastic critic. He told her, "I saw the future Sarah Bernhardt walk on the stage tonight."

During the play's tryout in Boston, tragedy struck on opening night. Although he missed two or three of his lines, Louis Jean Leydt managed to get through the first act, despite behaving erratically. Backstage in his dressing room, he collapsed and fell to the floor, dead from a heart attack.

William Adler went on in his place for the second act and stayed with the play until the end of its run on Broadway. Jane's other co-stars included Dean Jones and Ruth Matterson.

Its Broadway premiere had been scheduled for February 29, 1960, but it ran for only sixteen performances. Nonetheless, Jane was nominated for a Tony for Best Actress in a Featured Play.

Brooks Atkinson of *The New York Times* claimed that "a future stage actress has found not only a role that suits her, but a life's career, in fact."

Various words were used to describe her performance: "Fragile, febrile, translucent, coltish, virginal."

"My favorite review was one that did not mention that I was the daughter of Henry Fonda," Jane claimed.

Puckishly and provocatively, Logan asked Everett, "Is sex better with Jane or with Tony Perkins?"

"I can't compare them," he answered. "They are completely different experiences."

One night, Jane invited her brother, Peter, to her apartment for dinner. Their talk lasted well into the night. She relinquished her bed to Peter, and moved with Everett onto a fold-away bed in the living room.

At around 3am, Peter was awakened by screams coming from downstairs. He rushed down the steps to find Everett naked in the kitchen. He'd stabbed his hand, near where it connected to his wrist, with a butcher knife, and was bleeding profusely. Jane was on the phone pleading for medical assistance. To this day, circumstances remain unclear, but evidently, they'd had a fight.

"After that night, it was all over between Jane and this boy," Peter said. "He was devastated, but she had moved on to another man…also from the Actors Studio. My sister could be cold as ice when it came to telling a man it was time to go," Peter said.

During her time with Everett, *Look* magazine ran a sexy picture of Jane frolicking in the surf. She was labeled a "sex kitten."

Coincidentally, those were the words most frequently applied to the French actress, Brigitte Bardot. From 1952-1957, she had been married to director Roger Vadim, but they were divorced. *[Vadim would eventually become the hus-*

band of Jane.]

On looking back, Everett said, "If Jane and I could have loved ourselves as much as we loved each other, it might have worked. Alas, that was not to be."

Everett struggled on in his career, but only in minor roles, often hosted either by Ronald Reagan for the *General Electric Theater,* or in the TV series, *Naked City.*

On March 4, 1977, it was reported that he had died in his sleep after a heart attack, He was only 38 years old.

***

Jane's Exotic Mentor, Andreas Voutsinas

Andreas Voutsinas became the new man in Jane's life, replacing Tony Everett. He'd been a kind of Svengali to Anne Bancroft before assuming that role in Jane's life.

When she first encountered Voutsinas at the Actors Studio, she did not find him sexually attractive. She characterized him as "dissipated and serpentine."

She set out to learn what she could about him.

He was born in the summer of 1932 in Khartoum, as a member of that city's Greek community, in the Sudan. His family had immigrated there from the Ionian island of Kefalonia (also known as Cephalonia).

After his parents moved to the Sudan, they became part of the Greek colony there, a subculture that coexisted more or less amicably with a few thousand Egyptians, living there within a "colony" of their own. Voutsinas' father opened a small pasta factory, and later supplied spaghetti to Mussolini's Italian army during the Fascist invasion of neighboring Abyssinia (now Ethiopia).

After World War II, the Voutsinas family emigrated to Athens. While still a teenager, Voutsinas saved enough money for passage to Paris. There, he hustled and became a drag performer at a Left Bank *boîte.* For a while, he designed costumes in the atelier of *couturier* Jacques Fath.

When he eventually returned to Athens, he met and married a young woman, Dinah, even though he was bisexual. They had a son, Marios, but Voutsinas was not suited for married life and fatherhood. He soon escaped, once again, to Paris, leaving his wife and son behind.

From France, he made his way to London, where he studied at the Old Vic Theatre School. He then set out to Canada, where he studied acting and appeared in minor roles in Stratford, Ontario. He big break came when he was cast in *Oedipus Rex,* starring James Mason.

The following year found him in Manhattan, where he had a chance meeting with director Elia Kazan, a fellow Greek. The men bonded and soon Voutsinas was introduced to Lee Strasberg at the Actors Studio.

Within weeks, he had ingratiated himself with Strasberg, becoming his chief assistant. Strasberg was so impressed with his acting technique that he allowed him to coach actors that he did not have time to work with.

Before Jane, Voutsinas was devoted to Anne Bancroft, even interfering in her private life. She was dating comic Lenny Bruce, and Voutsinas broke up that affair.

He did the same when she launched another affair with Norman Mailer, the novelist, who had achieved fame with his World War II novel, *The Naked and the Dead.*

Voutsinas warned Bancroft, "Mailer is a lunatic and violent. If you stay with him, you'll end up with a butcher knife in your heart—all bloody on your kitchen floor."

Voutsinas also developed a powerful crush on actor George Peppard, who was soon to be cast as the hustler alongside Audrey Hepburn in *Breakfast at Tiffany's* (1961).

Peppard wasn't interested, and Voutsinas had to settle his obsession by stealing a pair of the actor's used jockey shorts.

Everett was still on the scene. He met Voutsinas, later telling Jane, "He's too effeminate for you. To make extra money, he dresses in drag and appears at this little dive in

Once a member of the expatriate Greek community living and doing business in the Sudan, **Andreas Voutsinas** was one of the most cosmopolitan people anyone in Jane Fonda's inner circle had ever met.

Cultivating an exotic appearance that some observers likened to a cross between Rasputin and a vampire,, he appears here as a stern taskmaster with the power to intimidate neophytes in the ultra-avant garde theatrical circles in which he thrived....until he didn't.

By almost anyone's standards, Andreas Voutsinas was a "major-league exotic," with a series of cultural references that very few people in the Broadway community really understood.

The object of Voutsinas' unwanted affections was **George Peppard**, pictured here in his most famous role, as the male lead, opposite **Audrey Hepburn** cast as Truman Capote's thinly veiled hooker, Holly Golightly, in *Breakfast at Tiffany's* (1961).

Greenwich Village. Besides, if you get too involved with him, he'll steal all your makeup."

At first, Jane showed up at Actors Studio looking like a model for *Vogue*, which had had been in real life. Everett remembered her wearing a pink Chanel suit with black high heels that added four inches to her height. He advised her to dress more Bohemian, and she did, showing up on occasion in pants and a black turtleneck with flat shoes.

In terms of scene-stealing dress codes, no one attracted more attention that the beret-capped, "a vision in black" Voutsinas himself. Lee Strasberg also appeared in black, but it was Voutsinas who was more theatrical. His clothing was black, his beard and mustache were black, and around his shoulders he draped a flamboyant black cape. Susan Strasberg gave him the nickname "Mephistopheles."

"I was surprised when I learned that Andreas was having an affair with Jane," said Susan. "He had told me he was gay. I thought he was, since he was always propositioning young men at the Actors Studio."

"My father would have taught me a lot about acting, but he chose not to," Jane said. "He never was my mentor, and I needed someone to play that role in my life. I turned to Andreas for guidance. When Henry met him, he despised him, calling him a cheap little hustler—and warned me to drop him."

To *Ms.* magazine many years later, Jane gave her opinion of her relationship with Henry when she was an aspiring actress in her early twenties:

"My only major influence had been my father. He had power. Everything was done around his presence, even when he wasn't there—I became my father's 'son,' a tomboy. I was going to be brave, to make him love me, to be tough and strong. He's so honest. He's just full of good intentions and honesty. I've even learned to love the things that are strange about him, like how he can say things that are extremely warm and intimate to the press about me, but he won't say them to me directly. I really love him but it's just that he won't tell me; he tells the world. On the other hand, when I was twenty-three and flexing my own muscles and trying to become independent of him, my anger came through the press rather than dealing with him directly."

For several months, Jane had been a pupil of Lee Strasberg at Actors Studio, but she had never performed an audition. She turned to Voutsinas for help, and he came up with a scene from the movie *BUtterfield 8* that had brought Elizabeth Taylor a Best Actress Oscar, although she hated the role of a high-priced prostitute. For himself, Voutsinas modestly claimed the Eddie Fisher screen role, not the star part as essayed by Laurence Harvey.

Jane walked out on the same stage where Marilyn Monroe had earlier performed in a scene from *Anna Christie*. For her costume, she appeared in a white satin slip with a casual mink coat slung over her shoulders.

During rehearsals for the audition, Jane had chewed her fingernails to the quick. Voutsinas insisted she wear false ones, but they kept popping off during her actual performance.

Her judges would be formidable: Lee Strasberg, producer Cheryl Crawford, and Elia Kazan.

In the scene, Gloria (Jane) tries to slit her wrists. On stage, during its crescendo, she broke a glass goblet, retaining a shard of glass from it and aiming it at her throat.

This was not what had been rehearsed.

In panic, Voutsinas perceived, incorrectly or not, that Jane was actually going to commit suicide on stage. He darted toward her, removing the glass fragment from her hand.

Then he took her trembling body in his arms and hugged her tightly as an unrehearsed continuation of the same scene. The entire episode had quickly morphed into the pinnacle of emotionally fraught theatricality.

For almost forty seconds, there was silence from the audience until Kazan rose from his seat and led the applause. "Tonight, a star is born," he shouted.

In the wake of that audition, Jane Fonda became a lifelong member of the Actors Studio.

It was midnight before Voutsinas left the Actors Studio for Jane's new apartment, where she had gone earlier to chill the champagne.

No longer would Jane depend on Henry to finance her. With the funds from her mother's inheritance, she bought an elegant cooperative apartment on West 55th Street just off Fifth Avenue. She decorated it herself with paintings and antiques.

She not only wanted to be free from Henry, but from director Josh Logan. She had foolishly signed that "slave contract" with him, which guaranteed her only $10,000 a year. She already had her lawyer working to free her from it. Logan would eventually relent and "liberate" her, but only after his receipt (Jane called it a payoff") of $100,000.

When Voutsinas arrived the night after her triumphant audition at the Actors Studio, "Svengali and Trilby" talked until dawn. The big question now was, "in which direction would her career travel from this day forth?"

***

Based on its racy content, many theaters throughout America had rejected the play, *No Concern of Mine*, although it had run for three months in the West End of London, doing fairly good business.

Andreas Voutsinas thought Jane's audition at Actors Studio had gone so well that she was ready to play the female lead in *No Concern of Mine*, the work of playwright Jeremy Kingston. The comedy/drama had been greenlighted for presentation at the Westport Playhouse in Connecticut.

Its plot centered on Lee and his sister Jacky (Jane's role) who share a basement apartment with Bernard. The trio occupy the same bed.

Lee is thrown out of drama school for being lazy. Later, he attempts suicide, but is rescued by a medical student. Bernard and Jacky realize that they will have to spend the rest of their lives looking after him.

Jane's two male co-stars were Bradford Dillman and Ben Piazza. The son of a San Francisco stockbroker, Dillman, seven years older than Jane, had just co-starred with Orson Welles and Dean Stockwell in the tense drama, *Compulsion* (1959). He would soon be reunited with Welles in the film *Crack in the Mirror* (1960), shot in Paris.

WESTPORT COUNTRY PLAYHOUSE
JULY 11 Thru JULY 16
IN PERSON
JANE FONDA
NO CONCERN OF MINE
A New Play by Jeremy Kingston

No stage director ever avoided putting young **Jane Fonda** on an advertisement for one of her plays, gorgeous famous, and hyper-photogenic as she was.

Here's how she was promoted as the female lead of a play that had been successful on London's West End, and which she had helped reprise on Off-Broadway—in this case, in tony Westport, Connecticut.

The gay actor, Piazza, a son of Little Rock, Arkansas, had just made his Hollywood debut in *The Hanging Tree* (1959).

Actor Geoffrey Horne later reported on the tension during rehearsals. "Egos came forth in the form of our director, Andreas Voutsinas. The bastard must have thought he was Erich von Stroheim. Voutsinas was a diva, throwing his daily tantrum. He went easy on Jane but made the rest of us live through hell."

Ben Piazza, also in the cast, echoed these same sentiments.

The play ran for only a week and garnered fair reviews. The critic from the *Danbury Times* called Jane's performance "graceful and completely captivating."

Dancer Jeanne Fuchs became a "comrade" of Voutsinas. "I just adored him. One night, he invited me to a performance at this gay club where he appeared in a sequined jockstrap. What a hoot! I called him a macho fag."

Timmy Everett showed up in Westport, in part, to visit Jane. As he later told author Thomas Kiernan, "In Jane's dressing room, we were lying around in the nude when Voutsinas entered. He took one look at us and began to remove his own clothes. At this time, I had a lovely body, but his body was really ugly. We hung out for three hours just talking. Then we left for dinner."

"After that," Everett continued, "I slowly faded from Jane's life, but would make a few more appearances. I didn't like Voutsinas, but he touched the sense of rage bubbling beneath the surface in Jane. In other words, he went beyond her goody-goody façade and tapped into her dark side, bringing out that part of her that helped her a lot in those offbeat film roles of her future."

Voutsinas had continued his friendship with Anne Bancroft, and she later met and began dating Mel Brooks, eventually becoming his wife. She introduced Voutsinas to Brooks when he was casting *The Producers*, starring Zero Mostel.

Brooks thought Voutsinas would be ideal cast as the assistant to the character of Roger De Bris, a flamboyant gay director who helms the Broadway show, *Springtime for Hitler*. Voutsinas asked Brooks how he should play the role. Enigmatically, Brooks replied, "Look like Rasputin but act like Marilyn Monroe."

***

JFK, Shelley Winters, and Invitation to a March

Arthur Laurents was a playwright, screenwriter, director, and librettist. He became best known for his work on Broadway in three major musicals—*West Side Story, Gypsy,* and *La Cage aux Folles.*

Because of his leftist leanings during the Joseph McCarthy anti-Communist "Witch Hunt" of the early 1950s, Laurents had been blacklisted, even though he had never officially joined the Communist Party.

Before that, he had written the Alfred Hitchcock screenplay for *Rope* (1948), which had starred James Stewart and Farley Granger. At the time, Granger and Laurents began a love affair.

He and Granger went on an extended trip to Europe. Upon their return, Laurents

Famously gay, famously influential, and famous as collaborators who thrived in the entertainment industry, **Arthur Laurents** (right) and his companion of fifty years, **Tom Hatcher,** were captured in this photogenic pose beside a pool in Los Angeles in 1962.

wrote his most successful drama, *The Time of the Cuckoo* (1952). As the negative effects of the blacklist faded, Laurents wrote screenplays, notably the script for *Anastasia* (1956), which brought Ingrid Bergman an Oscar.

While in Hollywood, Gore Vidal suggested that Laurents visit an upscale men's store to check out a young salesman, Tom Hatcher. Laurents followed Vidal's invitation and he and Hatcher fell in love at first sight, their union lasting for 52 years, until Hatcher's death.

Laurents and Hatcher also worked in summer theater, each of them focusing on their co-authored script for a play entitled *Invitation to the March*.

Word reached them that Jane Fonda had "burst into bloom" as an actress.

As they labored to set up their play's production, Laurents and Hatcher offered Jane the key role of a young college girl whose life is such a bore that she can barely stay awake. She drifts into a trance, becoming a "Sleeping Beauty." Only a handsome prince can bring her alive again.

Actually, that so-called prince was a plumber named Aaron.

James MacArthur, the adopted son of Helen Hayes and playwright Charles MacArthur, was cast into the role of "the prince." He and Jane would talk about the problems faced by the son and daughter of famous stars.

MacArthur would show off his studly physique when he starred with Henry Fonda in *Spencer's Mountain* (1963).

***

When Shelley Winters was first presented with the script of *Invitation to a March*, she found that the play had four strong roles for women, but she had not been told which character Laurents wanted her to play.

Visiting him at his vacation home on Long Island, she was told that the script was not yet complete. When she learned which role he wanted her for, she was disappointed, as her character appears in only three scenes. When confronted, Laurents made a solemn promise that he would beef up her part and even give her star billing above the title.

In the guest bedroom of Laurent's summer house that night, Winters explored a nearby writing table. On it lay the script for a play entitled *High Point Is Built On a Career.* When she saw that it had been written by Tennessee Williams, she read it avidly.

Later, to her astonishment, when she went to see Jane star in Williams' *Period of Adjustment*, she realized that it was the final version of that sketchy draft she'd uncovered at Laurents' home.

There was another coincidence that stemmed from that weekend. During their long, drunken talks, Winters had shared many personal stories about her early life. When she went to see the film version of *The Way We Were* (1973), star-

SHELLEY WINTERS
IN
"INVITATION TO A MARCH"

The 1950s had not been kind to **Shelley Winters**. In 1951, she was at the top of her game, featured on the cover of *Movie Play* magazine, clad in scarlet and mink and with a *décolletage* she'd been famous for.

At the Actors Studio, Jane had first conversed with Winters, who told her that Lee Strasberg was "a guru, shrink, god, and the devil—fucking scary. I love him. He taught me to use myself. He'll do the same for you."

Jane later recalled, "During Shelley's time appearing in *Invitation to a March*, she complained constantly. She hated everything and everybody—especially Arthur Laurents."

ring Barbra Streisand, Winters realized that many stories she'd told to Laurents about her own life had been worked into the film script for Streisand.

In addition to Jane, in *Invitation to a March*, Winters faced stiff competition from two veteran character actresses, each of them quite formidable. The best role seemed reserved for Eileen Heckart.

In a career that would span six decades, Ohio-born Eileen Heckart often played mothers. Specific instances included a performance as Rocky Graziano's mom in *Somebody Up There Likes Me;* and a rendering of the mother of a murdered child in *The Bad Seed*, each released in 1956.

A Canadian actress from Montréal, Madeleine Sherwood was cast as Jane's mother. She would achieve her greatest fame appearing in film adaptations of Tennessee Williams plays. In 1958, she played the mother of those "no-necked monsters" in *Cat on a Hot Tin Roof*, starring Elizabeth Taylor and Paul Newman. In 1962, she also starred in Williams' *Sweet Bird of Youth*, again with Newman. Geraldine Page played the aging film diva who picks up the seductive hustler Chance Wayne, portrayed by Newman.

During rehearsals, Madeleine Sherwood and Jane became friends, often seen holding hands backstage.

309

Sherwood opened up to Jane and relayed horrendous stories about her life in Montréal, where her father, a dentist, had sexually molested her. In an act of sadism, he yanked out all of her lower teeth without an anesthetic. She was later sent to a mental institution but escaped to New York to find work as an actress.

Sherwood was with Jane when news arrived that her friend, Bridget Hayward, daughter of Leland Hayward and Margaret Sullavan, had committed suicide. After hearing the news, Jane sank into a deep depression.

"I offered Jane what comfort I could," Sherwood recalled, "because on three separate occasions, I had also flirted with suicide. For all I knew, Jane herself had contemplated killing herself like her mother did. But Jane and I had a way to escape thoughts of suicide through acting. We used acting like a ladder to escape the depths of depression. It was like a kind of therapy playing someone else. Acting was a way of exorcizing our demons and not feeling guilt about doing so."

During her abortive involvement with *Invitation to a March*, Winters was reveling in a career peak. She had recently won a Best Supporting Actress Oscar for her performance in *The Diary of Anne Frank* (1959).

She would get to know Jane a lot better when they co-starred in the upcoming film *The Chapman Report* (1962).

During rehearsals, Winters and her director, Laurents, had many bitter arguments. She complained that she was merely being used to sell tickets and not for her talent as an actress, and frequently threatened to drop out of the play. In Columbus, Ohio, she was *en route* to the theater when she stumbled into a rally for John F. Kennedy, who was running at the time for President. Teddy Kennedy recognized her and asked her if she'd go to the podium and say a few words in support of JFK. Flattered by the invitation and the attention, she agreed and was warmly welcomed onstage by the future president.

At the end of her endorsement, she realized she was late for the theater. JFK ordered her driven, accompanied by a police escort, to the theater.

There, she encountered an angry producer, Cheryl Crawford, with Laurents "steaming in fury."

Later, in Boston, during a performance, Winters made a rash decision. She simply walked off the stage, grandly abandoning the play, as she had seen so many actresses do in films about Broadway in the 1930s.

Laurents said, "Winters is probably going off on the campaign trail to fuck John F. Kennedy."

He immediately replaced her with Celeste Holm.

[Holm was already very famous as an actress. She had appeared in Elia Kazan's Gentleman's Agreement *(1947) with Gregory Peck. Her performance in 1948 in* The Snake Pit *had earned her renown, and she'd also been applauded for her key role opposite Bette Davis in* All About Eve *(1950).]*

After Holm replaced her, the then-disgraced Winters, wearing a disguise based on the fear that she'd be stopped and interviewed by a reporter, slipped into a theater to see Holm execute the role "that should" according to Winters, "have been mine."]

Without Winters, *Invitation to a March* opened on Broadway on October 29, 1960, where it would run for three and a half months. It was staged at the Music Box Theater in Manhattan, amid stage sets that evoked the South Shore of Long Island in midsummer.   *Newsday* wrote that "Miss Fonda has a glow which almost dims the moonlight."

In the *New Yorker,* Kenneth Tynan claimed, "Jane Fonda can quiver like a tuning fork and her neurotic outbursts are as shocking as the wanton piecemeal destruction of a priceless harpsichord. What's more, she has extraordinary physical resources."

In spite of the praise, Jane was her own harshest critic, referring to her performance as that of a "slick Ginger Rogers *ingénue.*"

Cast as Jane's mother in *Invitation to a March*, **Madeleine Sherwood** became a close ally of Jane.

During a rehearsal, Sherwood kissed Jane on the mouth, but Laurents objected. "That was a lesbian kiss—not a mother-daughter kiss."

"I think you're wrong," Sherwood said. "It was a gentle, loving kiss. If it had been a dyke kiss, we would have slobbered a lot."

CHAPTER SIXTEEN

AFTER A MIDWINTER TRIP TO SWEDEN FOR NEGOTIATIONS WITH INGMAR BERGMAN,

HENRY DIVORCES HIS BARONESS AND MARRIES A BEAUTIFUL, DEEPLY DEVOTED FLIGHT ATTENDANT

DURING THEIR DIVORCE HEARING, WHEN CONFRONTED BY THE JUDGE, AFDERA FRANCHETTI DECLARES THAT HENRY IS NOT IMPOTENT, "IN SPITE OF HIS AGE"

HENRY REPLICATES MARRIAGE, ILLNESS, AND DEATH FROM CANCER IN A WRENCHING STAGE PLAY WITH OLIVIA DE HAVILLAND

JANE FONDA ON BROADWAY, STARS "IN ONE OF THE FIVE WORST PLAYS OF ALL TIME"

WARREN BEATTY LAUNCHES AN AFFAIR WITH HENRY'S EX-WIFE

PETER FONDA IS DEVASTATED WHEN THE LOVE OF HIS LIFE, BRIDGET HAYWARD, COMMITS SUICIDE

EDWARD ALBEE WANTS HENRY TO STAR IN *WHO'S AFRAID OF VIRGINIA WOOLF,* BUT HIS AGENTS REJECT THE OFFER WITHOUT TELLING HIM

"I shall walk the earth and search for something that I shall not find. Henry Fonda always eluded me."
—Edward Albee

WALK ON THE WILD SIDE

JANE FONDA RISES TO CELLULOID FAME IN HER PORTRAYAL OF A TRASHY WHORE IN A NEW ORLEANS BORDELLO

In October of 1960, as autumn leaves were falling in Central Park, Henry summoned his son, Peter, to his townhouse. With a sad, depressed look on his face, after greeting him at the door, Henry said, "Sit down, son. I have some bad news."

Henry was aware that Peter had fallen in love with Bridget Hayward, and now, he had the sad task of informing him that, like her mother, Margaret Sullavan, Bridget had committed suicide. Again and again, Henry said, "Poor Leland, poor Leland," a reference to her father, Leland Hayward.

[Seventeen years later, in 1977, Bridget Hayward's surviving sister, Brooke, published a pain-soaked, best-selling memoir entitled Haywire, *which outlined the spectacularly dysfunctional family life of the glittering "Hollywood success story" spun around the union of Margaret Sullavan (Henry Fonda's first wife) and the entertainment-industry powerhouse she married, Leland Hayward. It was interpreted as a scathing indictment of the false gods of celebrity, fortune, and ambition as "worshipped" near the end of the studio system in Hollywood.]*

According to Peter, "When I heard the news, and as Dad kept ranting about poor Leland, my thoughts were on my love, Bridget. I wanted to jump from a thirteenth-floor window to end my despair. Maybe by the time I splashed my guts all over the sidewalk, I would no longer experience the pain of lost love."

He later shared his grief with his childhood friend, Robert Walker Jr., now a struggling actor, too. His cinematically famous father, Robert Walker Sr., was the doomed movie star noted for his affair with Nancy Davis (later Mrs. Ronald Reagan) and for his disastrous marriage (from 1939 to 1945) to Jennifer Jones, who left him to marry David O. Selznick, the temperamental genius who produced *Gone With the Wind* (1939).

"Bridget looked like her mother, Margaret Sullavan," Peter told Walker, "and physically, I was often compared to my Dad. Whenever I had sex with Bridget, it was like we were re-living the sexual escapades of our parents."

Young Peter had visited Bridget's father, Leland Hayward, on several occasions. The theatrical producer and Broadway agent had even promised Peter that he might pull some strings and get him cast in film roles.

As children, Bridget and Peter had grown up together. As such, he had been kept abreast of the marital difficulties of her very stylish parents—in fact, he was intrigued by them.

Bridget Hayward: Beautiful and rich, but tragically, chronically, almost "chromosomally" unhappy, she was one of three members of a regal Hollywood family who committed suicide.

Daughter of Henry Fonda's first wife, Margaret Sullavan, with Leland Hayward, Bridget's obvious talent and beauty were often overshadowed by demons.

One of her lovers, Peter (later, "*Easy Rider*") Fonda, Henry's son, was deeply distressed by the waste, stupidity, and despair of her passing.

In 1949, two years after his divorce from Sullavan, Hayward had married the American socialite and fashion icon, Nancy ("Slim") Keith (aka "Lady Keith," "Slim Hawkins," and/or "Slim Hawks") after her divorce from director Howard Hawks. Slim had been engaged in a torrid affair with Clark Gable, who had not wanted to marry her.

The Hayward marriage had been frequently strained because of Slim's numerous affairs, including a one-night stand with Frank Sinatra and a long-running romance with Peter Viertel.

Hayward divorced Slim in 1960 to wed Pamela Churchill, the "ferociously social" former wife of Randolph Churchill, the errant son of Sir Winston. At the time he met her, she was the mistress of Elie de Rothschild. Pamela and Hayward were married in Carson City, Nevada, only hours after his divorce from Slim was final.

Pamela and Hayward remained married until his death in 1971. On the day of his funeral, Pamela took off with statesman W. Averell Harriman, 79, whom she married later that year.

"Whatever I do with my life," Peter told Walker, "I don't plan to use Leland as my role model."

***

Peter was said to have never really recovered from the death of Bridget. But in the depths of his grief, his friend, Robert Walker Jr., introduced him to Susan Jane Bremer, a graduate of Sarah Lawrence, and he began dating her.

He turned to her for love and support as he was making his Broadway debut. His sister, Jane, had suggested that he study at the Actors Studio, but, like his father, he held Method acting in contempt. "Do you expect me to go on stage like some faggot and pretend I'm a rock or a tree?"

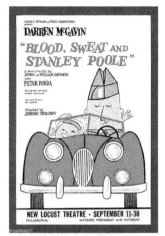

He made his Broadway debut in *Blood, Sweat, and Stanley Poole*, which opened on October 5, 1961 and ran for eighty-four performances. The play was the work of brothers James and William Goldman, who created this comedy about an Army supply sergeant posted in the South. Peter's co-star was Darren McGavin. The future star, James Caan, was cast in a small role. To win the part, Peter had to compete with two-hundred other actors who showed up to audition.

Howard Trauman of *The New York Times* did not like the play, claiming, "Its plot is spaced out mechanically, as if it were to run forever on the home screen."

Peter received praise for his performance, and later won The New York Drama Critics Award for it.

Henry attended opening night and went backstage to embrace his son, which he rarely did. He was not a man for showing emotions. He told Peter, "A true actor, a son of the theater, was born tonight. In time, your achievements will make your old man a distant memory."

Three days after his opening night on Broadway, Peter wed Susan Brewer, the stepdaughter of Noah Dietrich. With an iron hand, that skillful business executive had adroitly ruled the movie-making and oil-industry empire of the eccentric billionaire, Howard Hughes, from 1925 to 1957.

Peter Fonda in *Blood, Sweat, and Stanley Poole.*

After his first audition for the role, he was rejected as "too skinny." Weeks later, he was called back and given the part.

On opening night, critic Walter Kerr wrote, "Even Peter Fonda's eyes looked terrified."

Although to his regret, Henry had another commitment and could not break free to attend his son's wedding in 1961. It was the last time that those siblings and half-siblings, Peter, Jane, Pan (the daughter of Jane Seymour Brokaw, Henry's second wife, from her first marriage), and Amy Fishman (the adopted daughter of Henry and Susan Blanchard, Henry's fourth wife) were in the same room together.

To his wedding, Peter insisted on inviting Susan Blanchard, his former stepmother, as both of them still carried love for each other.

As a wedding present, Jane lent her elegant apartment to the honeymooners.

At the time of his wedding, young Peter was making $290 a week on Broadway. He had wanted to wear his favorite black boots but was talked out of it. He owned one pair of black shoes, and he wore those, although the one for his right foot had a big hole in it.

As his best man, Peter designated his longtime friend, Eugene ("Stormy") McDonald, one of the heirs to the $30 million Zenith electronics fortune.

[Four years later, the life of Peter's best man would end tragically. In 1965, in Tucson, Arizona, he slit his wrists. When he didn't seem to be bleeding quickly enough, he shot himself in the head. A large stash of marijuana was found in his room, and there was an inquest. No foul play was discovered, and Stormy's death was officially defined as a suicide.]

Although Jane had attended her brother's wedding, she later admitted, "Peter and I were not very close. I didn't understand his life, and he felt uncomfortable around my friends."

Waking up after their honeymoon night, Susan learned what her new husband always wanted for breakfast. In an electric blender, he tossed two bananas, three raw eggs, and chocolate milk.

After leaving Manhattan, the newlyweds returned to Hollywood. He drove her to Tigertail Road in Brentwood, where he had grown up. A devastating fire, fueled by the Santa Ana winds, had swept across parts of Bel Air and Brentwood. The only thing that remained of what had been the Fonda home were two stone chimneys. He wanted to buy the land and build anew

Peter Fonda weds **Susan Brewer** in their 1961 wedding as his father, **Henry,** looks on.

Brewer was the stepdaughter of Noah Dietrich, a cloak-and-dagger "make it work at any price" henchman of the demented but legendary aviator, Howard Hughes.

but his funds were too meager.

Peter wanted to find film work but got off to a slow start. He tried out for the role of John F. Kennedy in *PT-109* (1963) but lost it to Cliff Robertson because of lobbying from the then-President himself. *[Previously, JFK had rejected Paul Newman for the role as "he looks too Jewish." In contrast, Jacqueline had lobbied for Warren Beatty.]*

Wed in 1961, Peter's marriage to Susan would last until 1975. During its course, they would produce both a daughter and a son.

His daughter was born on January 27, 1964. Peter named her Bridget in honor of his lost love. Like the other Fondas, she also grew up to become an actor. She got an early start, appearing in *Easy Rider* (1969), her father's film, when she was only four years old. In the movie, Peter and Dennis Hopper visit a hippie commune populated with ragged parents and their children.

It wasn't until 1990 that Bridget got her breakthrough role when she starred in *The Godfather Part III*.

A son named Justin was born to Peter and Susan on July 8, 1966. He, too, grew up to be an actor. Among other parts, he was assigned a small role in the 1965 film, *The Rounders,* that paired his grandfather, Henry Fonda, with Glenn Ford. Unlike the rest of the Fondas, Justin has chosen to keep his private life private.

Henry was not exactly pleased with becoming a grandfather, as he told his longtime friend, James Stewart, "No more romantic leading man roles for me. All my future movies will show me as an old coot with a beard in a Western, a sort of Walter Brennan type. If I hit on a gal, she'll probably look me over and say in astonishment, 'Gramps, can you still get it up?'"

As the years went by, Susan realized she had married a philandering husband. Sometimes, Peter was gone for weeks at a time.

One week, he brought a handsome young screenwriter to live with them for a while. He and Peter were working on a script about an incestuous relationship between a brother and sister. When the script was finished, he planned to offer the sister role to his own sister, Jane. He wondered how they might perform and react in passionate love scenes where both of them were nude and horizontal together.

When Peter had to go away—actually he was with another woman in Palm Springs—he returned to learn that his wife had become involved in a sexual relationship with the young screenwriter. After thirteen years of marriage Susan divorced Peter in 1974.

The following year, he took a second wife, Portia Rebecca Crockett. This union was far more successful, lasting for thirty-six years until they divorced in 2011.

In his 70s, Peter Fonda then took a third wife, Margaret DeVogelaere, in 2011, the union lasting until his death on August 16, 2019. He was 79 years old. The cause of death was respiratory failure caused by lung cancer.

Jane faced the press and said, "I am very sad. He was my sweet-hearted baby brother. The talker of the family. Our father was more the silent type. I had beautiful alone time with him in his last days. He went out laughing."

***

Walk on the Wild Side (1962)

For Jane's second film role, *Walk on the Wild Side,* a drama directed by Edward Dmytryk, all memories of young love on the basketball court (her first movie) were forgotten. This second time around, Jane would be "lurid, tawdry, thieving, and sleazy," playing a prostitute in a Depression-era bordello in the wicked city of New Orleans.

Jane joined an all-star cast that featured Laurence Harvey, Barbara Stanwyck, Capucine, and Anne Baxter.

During pre-production of the film adaptation of then-president JFK's memoir, *PT-109*, armies of press and PR staff wondered who the president (and/or his First Lady, Jacqueline) would finger as the actor who'd portray him as the wartime combat hero he "sort-of" was.

Many actors were considered, including Peter Fonda, who was ultimately rejected, probably because of his close familiarity, and endorsement, of the then-terrifying "sex and drugs and rock-and-roll" counterculture.

The lucky winner in the "Who will portray JFK during combat" was **Cliff Robertson,** seen here dutifully re-reading one of the zillions of adulatory biographies then circulating about the then-POTUS.

This "in her prime" photo of **Bridget Fonda** (granddaughter of Henry Fonda, daughter of Peter Fonda, niece of Jane Fonda) as she appeared in *The Godfather, Part III.*

Featured in dozens of movies as a strong but vulnerable woman that EVERYONE adored, she was living proof that the Fonda family's famous genes are alive and durable and strong. In the aftermath of a shattering car crash in 2003, she took a hiatus from the often unhappy milieu of filmmaking.

Capucine, often cited, between 1960 and the late 1980s, as the most beautiful woman in Europe, was a spectacularly successful model for *haute couture* in Paris.

Hauntingly, she too, committed suicide by jumping to her death from her 8th-floor apartment window in the otherwise spectacularly staid Swiss city of Lausanne.

The script was based on a novel by the controversial Nelson Algren, hailed as "the Bard of the Down and Out." His novels were peopled with pimps, prostitutes, freaks, drug addicts, prize fighters, hoodlums, and corrupt politicians.

His novel, *The Man with the Golden Arm,* had won the 1949 National Book Award. *Walk on the Wild Side* would be Algren's last big commercial success.

Jane had known Barbara Stanwyck since she was a child. When Henry heard his daughter would be working with his former co-star, he said, as he had asserted so many times before, "I've never gotten over my big crush on Babs."

Stanwyck (playing Jo Courtney) is the madam of a whorehouse, combining toughness with a motherly tenderness toward her girls—all except Hallie Gerard (Capucine) with whom she shares a lesbian passion. The lesbianism is subtle, and many of the more innocent members of the audience didn't get it.

It was rumored that during the shoot, Stanwyck and Capucine conducted a lesbian affair of their own. Capucine, too, was bisexual, her affairs ranging from William Holden to her best friend, Audrey Hepburn.

Like so many movie stars, the life of Capucine would also end in suicide.

Jane Fonda in *Walk on the Wild Side.* One critic claimed that in her portrayal of a working prostitute, Jane was "only as naughty as a cornsilk cigarette."

[On March 17, 1990, Capucine, then age 62, once the most beautiful and photogenic model in the world, with a gift for showcasing haute couture *during its heyday, jumped to her death from her eighth-floor apartment in Lausanne, Switzerland.]*

Jane worked smoothly with Laurence Harvey. As the film's male lead, Dove Linhorn, he hooks up with Jane's character of Kitty Twist.

His only criticism of her involved a suggestion that her makeup made her look like "an Abyssinian cat."

Harvey was a Lithuanian-born British actor, known for his clipped, refined accent, his stylish humor, and his debonair screen presence. Jane had recently seen him in two of his finest films: *Room at the Top* (1959), and *BUtterfield 8* (1960), in which Elizabeth Taylor won a Best Actress Oscar for her portrayal of a high-class prostitute.

At the time he worked with Jane, Harvey would also star as the pitiable, brain-washed sergeant in *The Manchurian Candidate* (1962).

The very talented Anne Baxter had a thankless role as Teresina Vidaverri, a local café owner who befriends Dove.

In the movie, Kitty (Jane) starts working at the bordello after Jo (Stanwyck) bails her out of jail, where she has been confined for vagrancy.

Distributed by Columbia Pictures, *Walk on the Wild Side* was made for $2 million and took in $4.5 million at the box office.

Bosley Crowther in *The New York Times* compared Stanwyck to "something out of mothballs. Jane Fonda is elaborately saucy and shrill (a poor exposure of a highly touted talent)." *Variety* said, "Jane Fonda steals the show with her hoydenish behavior."

Paul V. Beckley of the *New York Herald Tribune* wrote: "Jane Fonda is a bouncy, wiggly, bratty little thief and prostitute. She seems more like a Nelson Algren character than anyone else in the movie."

***

The Fun Couple (1962)

As Jane's relationship with Andreas Voutsinas entered the twilight zone, he prevailed upon her to accept the lead in an upcoming Broadway

Laurence Harvey as *The Manchurian Candidate,* with **Angela Lansbury,** portraying the most conniving, destructive mother since Medea.

According to Harvey, "In this picture, I redeemed my reputation as an actor after being called one-dimensional in *Walk on the Wild Side.*"

play which he was directing, *The Fun Couple,* scheduled for a premiere in the autumn of 1962. Her co-star would be Bradford Dillman. Each of them had been cast as newlyweds who do not want to grow up and face adult burdens.

Rounding out the cast was Ben Piazza and a very young Dyan Cannon.

Dillman, the son of a San Francisco stockbroker, had won a Golden Glob for his performance in the melodrama *A Certain Smile* (1958). He'd also scored a success in *Compulsion* (1959) with Dean Stockwell and Orson Welles.

Although over the course of her career, Dyan Cannon would be nominated for three Academy Awards, her greatest coup, it was said, was her marriage, in 1965, to Cary Grant. He was thirty-three years her senior. Together, they produced a daughter, Jennifer, born in 1966.

The third member of *The Fun Couple's* cast was the gay actor from Little Rock, Arkansas, Ben Piazza. Before appearing with Jane, he had made his Hollywood debut in *The Hanging Tree* (1959).

[From 1973 until his death in 1991 from an AIDS-related cancer, Piazza was the lover and long-time companion of Wayne Tripp.]

A rumor spread that the play had been written by a moonlighting dentist, but that was not true. It had been the work of two different men, Jay Julien, who wrote under the *nom de plume* of Neil Jansen, and John Haase, based on a novel he had written.

Julien told Sam Zolotow of *The New York Times* that the plot focused on attractive newlyweds "who create a bright and funny world of their own, then seek to substitute it for the everyday world around them."

[Jay Julien, a New York-based attorney, at least deserves a footnote in theatrical history. After his theatrical disaster with Jane, he would work on such productions as The King of Comedy *(1982),* King of New York *(1990), and* Smile *(2009).*

Through Julien's connections, he often served as a "go-between" with links to the Hollywood film industry and the movie colony in Rome, He was instrumental in helping fading actors in America such as Ben Gazzara and Martin Balsam find roles in European film productions—thereby creating second film careers for many of them.]

According to Dillman, "During rehearsals of *The Fun Couple,* its director, Voutsinas, behaved like a hysterical diva, shouting orders and throwing temper fits. He was hardest on Jane."

Piazza found his direction "murky." Cannon claimed: "Jane and I were two drowned rats."

Lee Strasberg attended a tryout and advised Voutsinas to shut down the production. "Under no circumstances should you open this on Broadway. It isn't even a play."

Ignoring Strasberg's advice, Voutsinas opened *The Fun Couple* on Broadway on October 26, 1962, the week of the Cuban missile crisis.

Many of the seats on opening night had been allocated to members of the Actors Studio. After fifteen minutes, many in the audience began to "hoot and holler." Dozens of people walked out.

Richard Watts in the *New York Post* claimed, "The most incredible thing about the play is that two talented performers, Jane Fonda and Bradford Dillman, were willing to accept these roles. Even the sight of Miss Fonda in a bikini doesn't rescue *The Fun Couple* from being an epic bore."

Walter Kerr, the noted theater critic, labeled *The Fun Couple* as "one of the worst five plays of all time." After its opening, the Schubert Organization had a tense meeting with Voutsinas, telling him that advance ticket sales for the production had totaled only two hundred dollars, and therefore, *The Fun Couple* would be closing.

Before its opening, Jane had announced that *The Fun Couple* would make Voutsinas a director "to be reckoned with" on Broadway.

At its closing, she said, "How can I ever forgive him for making me the laughing stock of Broadway? I feel my life upon the wicked stage has forever ended. I'm fleeing to Hollywood."

***

Critics' Choice (1960)

Although Henry prolonged his self-imposed exile from Hollywood, he never devolved into a forgotten figure of yesterday among its industry insiders. Every month, three or four scripts, sometimes more, arrived for his con-

Awesomely photogenic, and alert to "how to pose" since puberty, young **Jane Fonda**—thanks to bad direction and an opening night that corresponded to a key moment in the Cuban Missile Crisis—was NOT a hit on Broadway in *The Fun Couple.*

Photos of the congenial Hollywood warhorse, **Mildred Natwick**, regardless of her age or the costume she was wearing, are usually instantly recognizable

sideration. An avid reader, he devoured every one of them, and seriously considered pushing some of them through to production. But he was not ready to appear on the screen again.

When Otto Preminger, after completing *Exodus* (1960), phoned, Henry took notice. Preminger had told the press about him, "I just adore the boy." Likewise, Henry was filled with praise for the temperamental director.

The play being considered was *Critic's Choice*, a comedy by Ira Lewin.

As Henry read its script, he realized that the inspiration for the play came from the life of Walter Kerr, the critic for the *Herald Tribune,* and his playwright wife, Jean.

Costumes would be by the then very newsworthy Oleg Cassini, who at the time was busy designing the wardrobe of Jacqueline Kennedy.

THE
PLAYHOUSE
THEATRE
present

Henry Fonda in **"Critic's Choice"**

Henry: "I played the male lead in *Critic's Choice* like it was written. On screen, Bob Hope made a burlesque of it."

Henry would be cast as Parker Ballatine, a theater critic in his early 40s. Gena Rowlands would play his younger wife, Angela.

After only a few days of rehearsal, Preminger realized that Rowlands was wrong for the part. He fired her and hired Georgann Johnson, a very minor actress of no marquee value, instead. Way back in 1953, she had appeared opposite Jack Lemmon in the Broadway revival of *Room Service.*

Character actress Mildred Natwick was cast as Angela's mother. For the sake of his (failing) marriage, she begs Parker to give the play (and her daughter's performance in it) a positive review. Seven years later, Natwick would play the mother of Jane Fonda in *Barefoot in the Park.*

Critic's Choice opened on December 14, 1960, at the Ethel Barrymore Theatre and ran for 189 performances.

Howard Taubman in *The New York Times* wrote, "For Mr. Fonda, his role is like so many he has done in the past, yet he plays it as if it were new."

In the *New York Post,* Richard Watts Jr. said: "Fonda acts so skillfully, with that quiet and seemingly effortless manner of his, that he often creates the illusion that he is appearing in a comedy of some substance."

Preminger was able to sell the rights to *Critic's Choice* to Warners. Gossips more or less accurately mocked it as a "dead on arrival" purchase. The studio then miscast Bob Hope with Lucille Ball in a production released in 1963.

The Gift of Time (1962)

Once again, Henry put off his return to the screen and accepted the lead in a stage play entitled *A Gift of Time.* His co-star would be Olivia de Havilland, with whom he had previously teamed in *The Male Animal* (1942).

A Gift of Time was based on a true story as detailed in Lael Wertenbaker's memoir, *Death of a Man,* which described her husband's death in France from colon cancer.

Wertenbaker had begun her career in Berlin in 1938, writing about Hitler and the Nazi Party during their preparations for World War II. The Nazi propaganda Czar, Josef Goebbels, labeled her "a dangerous woman."

Fleeing Berlin, she arrived in London, where she reported on the activities of European governments in exile. In 1942, she married Charles Wertenbaker, the foreign editor of *Time* magazine.

Later, the couple settled in Paris, where they became friends with Ernest Hemingway. It was in France, in 1956, that Charles learned that he had colon cancer. He had only a year to live, most of it spent in agonizing pain.

Olivia De Havilland and **Henry Fonda** commiserating, musically, in *A Gift of Time.*

According to Henry, "This was the only stage show in which I appeared where the audience didn't applaud at the final curtain. They found the play too painful to accept. Instead, they waited outside to tell me how grateful they were, in hushed voices."

317

In her memoir, Lael wrote about her last words to her husband as she pumped painkillers into his arm while he slashed open his wrists. "I love you. Please die!"

For its stage adaptation, Henry accepted the role of Charles, with De Havilland cast as his wife. The stars had known each other for decades, their friendship dating from the days when his former roommate, James Stewart, had had an affair with her.

During rehearsals out of town, the two stars shared many long talks. She had heard of the strong support Henry had given President Kennedy during his campaign.

"I met Jack during the War," De Havilland said. "He asked me out on a date and was very persistent. I turned him down. How did I know he was going to become President of the United States? Had I known that, I would have turned myself over to him like I did with Howard Hughes and director John Huston."

Henry found himself back on the stage of the Ethel Barrymore Theatre on opening night, February 22, 1962.

After the curtain went down, his first visitor was Paul Newman. He rushed backstage and not only hugged Henry but gave him a wet kiss, too. "That was the God damnedest, greatest performance I've ever seen.," the younger actor said.

The play would run for 92 performances.

Howard Taubman of *The New York Times* wrote, "There are delicate, probing scenes between Mr. Fonda and Olivia de Havilland. They reveal a deep and comprehending love with humor and anguish and, praise be, without a trace of mawkishness."

Walter Kerr of the *New York Herald Tribune,* said, "It would be difficult to offer enough respect to Henry Fonda's plain, unblinking, straightforward and unbelievably controlled performance."

Norman Nadle in *The New York World Telegram* weighed in too: "Every privacy of a dying man is mercilessly invaded. Fonda doesn't spare himself in this—not that he does in anything. He adds depth and clarity to the role of the dying man."

Garson Kanin announced that a film version would be shot in France in the summer of 1962, but the deal fell through.

***

Who's Afraid of Virginia Woolf? (1962)

"I want to write a play for Broadway in which I force theatergoers to face themselves." So said Edward Albee, who had begun work on a play that eventually was named *Who's Afraid of Virginia Woolf?*. For legal reasons, he could not keep its original title, *Who's Afraid of the Big Bad Wolf?*

He discussed casting with his lover of the moment, James Leo Herlihy, who would later write the novel, *Midnight Cowboy.*

"It's a four-character play centering around Martha and George who live on the campus of a New England college," Albee said. "I see her as a strong-willed woman married to a weak husband, a professor. I'm modeling the professor with Henry Fonda in mind."

"My inspiration for Martha is Bette Davis. She is harsh, acerbic, diabolic, sexy, a bit vulgar, and, when she wants to be, hilarious."

That was what Albee revealed in private. Years later, he publicly made a different claim, asserting that Martha and George were based on two of his friends, New York socialites Willard Maas and Marie Menken, who were known for their tempestuous, extravagantly volatile relationship, much of which was embarrassingly played out in public. At one of their intimate gatherings, drinking would begin at 4pm and end up in the wee hours of the following morning, usually with everyone present recuperating from lacerating emotional wounds.

The first draft of *Who's Afraid of Virginia Woolf?* was sent to Henry's agents. *[He had recently switched from MCA to the recently formed CMA.]* Months later, to his horror, he learned that his new agents had rejected the script without even consulting Henry.

An array of other actors was considered, too, including the British actor, Robert Fleming, Arthur Kennedy, Jose Ferrer, Richard Kiley, Gig Young, and Jason

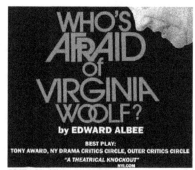

It was the most acerbic, "punch to the gut" play about marital discord anyone had ever seen.

Although the eventual movie roles went to Burton and Taylor (who gained thirty pounds just to emulate the semi-psychotic harridan, Martha, more convincingly), Henry Fonda, for a brief shining moment, almost got the part that was eventually assigned to Richard Burton.

Based on his own multiple marital dischords and failed marriages, he probably would have portrayed the desperately unhappy academic, with quiet gusto, intensity, and brilliance.

Robards Jr.

Finally, Arthur Hill was assigned the role. At the time, he was in London filming *In the Cool of the Night* with Jane Fonda, Angela Lansbury, and Peter Finch.

Hill interpreted it as a terrific role for himself but issued a dire warning: "It won't make a dime on Broadway."

A native son of Saskatchewan, Hill had made his Broadway debut in Thornton Wilder's *The Matchmaker* in 1957.

` From the beginning, it was decided that Uta Hagen—in the event that Bette Davis wasn't available—would be the best choice for the shrewish Martha.

[Born in Germany as the daughter of an opera singer, Thyra A. Leisner, Hagen had emigrated to the United States in 1924. Early in her career, she had appeared on stage with such legends as Eva Le Gallienne, Alfred Lunt, and Lynn Fontanne, in plays by George Bernard Shaw and Ibsen. She later took the Blanche DuBois role in A Streetcar Named Desire for its national tour.]

In 1938, she met and married actor Jose Ferrer, divorcing him in 1948. She later married the acting teacher, Herbert Berghof.

Hagen later became a noteworthy acting teacher herself, her pupils including Robert De Niro, Steve McQueen, Lee Grant, Anne Jackson, Geraldine Page, Jack Lemmon, and Whoopi Goldberg.

In a nutshell, George and his very outspoken wife, Martha are visited by another married couple, young Nick (also a professor at the college) and Honey. Their party devolves into an existential horror evocative of *Walpurgisnacht*.

George Segal was considered for the stage role of Nick but was rejected for being "too Jewish." *[Ironically, four years later, in 1966, he was assigned the same role in the play's film adaptation. In the movie, Sandy Dennis would play the young professor's socially inexperienced and very young wife.]*

At the suggestion of Albee, the role of Honey went first to Lane Bradbury, who was later fired and replaced with Melinda Dillon.

The part of Nick in the stage version was essayed by George Grizzard.

The play became a Broadway hit, and Henry went to see it. He had become enraged after learning that his agents, after receiving a copy of it, had not even transferred the script to him.

One columnist had written, "Arthur Hill is Henry Fonda, without Fonda's name recognition."

After seeing the show, Henry wrote Hill one of his rare fan letters: "You're one lucky fart to have walked off with the role. You were terrific. Surely only I could have done it better."

When Albee sold the movie rights to his play, he was told that the studio wanted to feature Bette Davis and James Mason as George and Martha. That did not happen, since Elizabeth Taylor and Richard Burton, as an acting team opted to commandeer the movie roles. *[This happened despite the fear that Burton was considered too strong a "force" to portray a weak-willed college professor. In contrast, Taylor assured studio bosses, "I know how to play a harridan bitch. Have no fear!"]*

For her portrayal of Martha, Taylor (aka "the most beautiful woman in the world") opted to gain thirty pounds for her portrayal of the frumpy, "fifty-ish" female protagonist. For her efforts, she won the Best Actress Oscar that year.

A belief had long existed in both the theater world and in the film colony that Albee had originally written *Who's Afraid of Virginia Woolf?* as a dramatic vehicle for four men (i.e., two gay male couples). *[Over the course of many years, the playwright adamantly denied that allegation.]*

However, in 1970, Henry conspired with Richard Burton to revive the play on Broadway with themselves and two other (male) actors. Burton jokingly said, "We can cast Warren Beatty and Jon Voight as our wives."

When Albee heard of this, he ordered his lawyers to shut down pre-production before it got off the ground.

"God is Dead," "Hell is others," and themes about existential loneliness were stylish and in vogue when *Who's Afraid of Virginia Woolf?* became wildly fashionable as a blockbusting play, and then as a notorious Burton-Taylor cinematic slugfest.

For a brief shining moment, Henry Fonda was almost assigned the male lead—until, according to Henry—his agent screwed it up.

Players from two troubled marriages include **Elizabeth Taylor** and **Richard Burton** (upper photo) and **George Segal** and **Sandy Dennis**.

***

319

Henry's last trip to Europe with Afdera was to Sweden. Their plane landed in Stockholm, and they were driven by car and then transferred by boat to the island home of the fabled Swedish director, Ingmar Bergman. He wanted to discuss plans with Henry about starring in a future movie to be shot in Sweden.

"I met his two mistresses and a flock of unruly children," Afdera claimed. "When I discovered that there was only one toilet for the entire household, I fled back to Stockholm to buy antiques. Henry stayed on to talk about that film that never was."

By 1960, Henry and Afdera were still married—at least officially. They slept in separate bedrooms. Intimacies and tenderness associated with any semblance of marriage had more or less ended, although on some occasions, its participants maintained a quasi-believable façade.

"My last months with Henry were like two incompatible strangers forced to share a compartment on a fast-moving train," Afdera said.

"At our last Christmas dinner together, he hardly spoke a word. Finally, I rose to my feet and said, 'Do you know we've been married nearly four years?'"

He sat sipping his wine and without looking up, said, "Seems more like seventeen to me."

Afdera claimed that she must have brought up the subject of divorce twenty times before it actually happened. "When I dared to mention divorce, he would get up and walk out of the room. He never wanted to discuss it with me."

Despite their deepening marital problems, Henry Fonda, with his then-wife Afdera Franchetti, visited the famed Swedish film director **Ingmar Bergman**, depicted above with his long-time companion, Norwegian actress **Liv Ullmann**.

Although Afdera was bored to death by the "intensity and stillness" of these Nordic artists, Bergman and Ullmann were deeply sensitized to the nuances of marital pain: He had directed her in the gut-wrenching six-part TV series, *Scenes from a Marriage* (1973), and although they never married, they eventually produced a child together.

When separation seemed inevitable, Henry rented a suite at the Croydon Hotel on Madison Avenue at 86th Street. He let her remain in his townhouse, giving her plenty of time to pack up her belongings and take whatever paintings and antiques she desired. He had already purchased a cooperative apartment for her on Park Avenue.

After she moved out, he inspected his townhouse, finding that she had been very generous to herself in taking the most valuable paintings and antiques.

He was furious at her for taking Jane's canopied antique bed, which was so huge that two windows had to be removed from the townhouse façade so that it could be lowered to the street.

He demanded that she return it to Jane's bedroom, which meant removing and later replacing and restoring once again those two upper windows.

Afdera had decided to apply for her divorce in Juarez, Mexico. On the morning of her scheduled departure for her flight there, he phoned her at 4AM.

"This is your last chance to call it off," he said.

"I've made up my mind," she answered in a soft voice, before putting down the phone.

In Juarez, the judge demanded to know her grounds for divorce. Afdera said there were none.

"There must be grounds," the judge demanded. Then, noting the difference in their ages, he asked if Henry were impotent.

"No, he's a competent lover. I was too young when I married him. I didn't know my own mind. I was immature."

Finally, after consulting with Afdera's lawyer, the judge granted a divorce on the grounds of incompatibility.

When Henry heard the news, he said, "It was stupid to try to hold on. In many ways, the marriage was hopeless from the very beginning."

In a memoir, Henry wrote: "The fights became more frequent. I wasn't the husband for her. She must have realized I wasn't the kind of guy who could lead her kind of life forever. I didn't want the marriage to fall apart. I dreaded another divorce. I thought that if there was any way to compromise, I'd compromise. I was ashamed to get another divorce. But there was no way to avoid the break."

Afdera was quoted as saying, "He slapped me once, but not really hard. I goaded him into that slap. He should have slapped me more. I might have respected him more if he had done that."

When news of his father's divorce reached Peter, he was overjoyed. "She never had any use for me, and I detested the bitch."

On March 16, 1961, news of the Fonda divorce appeared in newspapers and on radio and television stations across the country. Afdera told the press, "The fault is mine. Mr. Fonda is a fine man, but I was too young for marriage.

I was not ready to settle down and become a housewife."

Later, Henry said, "I hold myself in contempt for marrying that woman who called herself a Baroness. What was I thinking?"

In the weeks that followed the divorce, and out of loneliness, Henry phoned Susan Blanchard, who was staying in a vacation villa, at the time, on Fire Island *[a barrier island parallel to the south shore of Long Island, New York]* with her daughter, Amy.

She allowed Henry to visit, but any hope of a reconciliation seemed ill-advised. She had moved on with her life. It seemed that he spent most of the weekend alone with his adopted daughter, Amy, on the beach.

***

In the wake of her divorce from Henry, a new love entered Afdera's life. He just happened to be one of the hottest, sexiest, and most sought-after actors in Hollywood. His name was Warren Beatty, and he had recently enjoyed a torrid affair with Jane, Afdera's former stepdaughter.

As the story goes, Beatty was visiting a private home where, in the hallway, he discovered an oil painting of a beautiful young woman. It was an exaggeration, of course, but wags said, "For Warren, it was like stumbling across the *Mona Lisa* for the first time."

When Beatty had first become entranced with the portrait, he may not have known that the ex-Mrs. Henry Fonda had posed for it. He would, however, soon find out.

He phoned her the next day and asked her out. At the time, thousands of women would probably have responded favorably to his call. *[Recent examples of women who had succumbed to his charms had included Lee Radziwill and Diana Ross.]*

"He fell for me in oils," Afdera said, "but preferred me in the flesh. In a way, he was determined to bring that painting of me alive."

They began to date and sleep together. She found him "young, talented, amusing, and a lot of fun. With him, I was laughing again."

She later described their affair as "just a fling, short and sweet. He smelled of honey, like Lady Chatterley's lover, Warren was the kind of man whose body you wanted to cover with daisy chains. He was a naughty boy, charming, playful, spraying me with soda siphon one minute, talking seriously the next."

Then revered as an "über-horny studmuffin," here's **Warren Beatty** as he famously appeared with **Natalie Wood** in *Splendor in the Grass* (1961), around the time he was pursuing the stylish divorcee, Afdera Franchetti.

"He spent a lot of time in front of the mirror, checking out his face and body," she said. "He thought he was too beautiful and was eager to see the onset of gray hair and wrinkles, or at least that's what I heard. Of course, I didn't believe that for a moment. No actor could desire aging."

"On occasion, he compared his face to that of his sister, Shirley MacLaine, feeling that she has a lot more character," Afdera said. "He felt he was good-looking, but too bland."

Afdera's affair with Warren Beatty soon ended. There were no hard feelings, as they moved on to other affairs. She referred to their time together as "an enjoyable interlude."

As for Beatty, he had dozens of other love goddesses to conquer.

***

Still living in his townhouse in Manhattan, Henry spent no time mourning the loss of his fourth wife, the Baroness Franchetti.

In Manhattan, in the afternoon, he would sometimes be seen walking along Madison Avenue, going in and out of art galleries. One time, he ran into Greta Garbo doing the same thing. They chatted briefly, making no mention of their past relationships. Then she hurried on her way.

From his base within his Manhattan townhouse, Henry took up with two fairly new friends, actor Orson Bean and Sydney Chaplin, the son of "The Little Tramp." The trio began to show up at the overcrowded singles bars of Manhattan. "It wasn't really my thing, but I went along with Orson and Syd. Those two guys were always on the make. We also hung out almost every night at P.J. Clarke's."

[Established in 1884 by an Irish immigrant, the watering hole on East 55th Street attracted visiting celebrities in addition to its regulars. To the arts world, the place was already famous: Johnny Mercer had penned "One for My Baby (and One More for the Road)"—one of the great torch laments of all time—one night at P.J. Clarke's, writing the words on a napkin. On another occasion, Nat King Cole recommended that Henry order its bacon cheeseburger, which the singer defined as, "The Cadillac of

burgers." The bar in Billy Wilder's The Lost Weekend (1945), starring Ray Milland, was based on P.J. Clarke's.]

James Stewart, who lived in Los Angeles, was still Henry's best friend, but the two actors saw little of each other during Henry's residencies in New York. Tiring of Bean and Chaplin and their lifestyles, he found a new best friend, actor George Peppard. For a while, they were seen at P.J. Clarke's almost every night.

Truman Capote, *left*, with the object of his affection, **George Peppard** *(right)*.

One evening, they encountered the novelist Truman Capote. Peppard had just starred as the struggling writer/gigolo, Paul Varjak, in the film adaptation of Capote's *Breakfast at Tiffany's* (1961).

Peppard told Capote that the director, Blake Edwards, didn't want him for the role, preferring at least four other candidates instead. He also confessed that Audrey Hepburn was very indifferent to him, and that Patricia Neal told people that he was cold and conceited.

Capote made a confession of his own, asserting that he had devised his character of Holly Golightly for a screen interpretation by Marilyn Monroe. "In 1955, I was on the town with Marilyn, and took her to P.J. Clarke's. Shortly after entering, she fled. She told me she found the clientele here disgusting."

Both Henry and Capote assured Peppard that he'd rise to the top in Hollywood. In fact, *Variety*, during the previous week, had assured him that he was "Hollywood's next big thing."

Flirtatious and provocative, Capote asked the actor, "What did they mean, "the next big thing?"

"Stick around until I need to take a piss," Peppard answered roughly, "and then follow me to the urinal. That will answer your question."

Henry remained silent. He didn't like that kind of talk.

***

One night at P.J.'s, Henry met a fashion coordinator for a photographer from *Vogue.*

After a brief flirtation, she became his first affair, post-divorce. In his memoirs, he does not give her real name. They lived near each other, on East 74th and East 75th Street, respectively.

Their big night out was when Fox arranged a chauffeur and a limousine to take them to the world premiere of Darryl F. Zanuck's *The Longest Day* (1962), in which Henry had a cameo.

Later, he would recall the night, not for the glamour of its movie premiere, but for his first sighting of his future wife. As he emerged from the studio limousine, and before he reached in to help his date out of their car, he eyed "a tall vision of loveliness" staring at him. Beside her stood her slightly shorter escort.

"The girl's eyes suggested she wanted to devour me," Henry later claimed.

Years later, Shirlee Mae Adams also remembered "the night that changed the rest of my life."

For the premiere, she had spent all her cash on a midnight black, floor-length jersey gown, a rip-off of a Dior first shown at a Paris fashion show.

A casual boyfriend, an out-of-work actor, had invited her to the premiere. He was hoping to meet some director or producer, to whom he would volunteer his services both on and off the stage or screen.

Her boyfriend said, "That's Henry Fonda!"

"I was not an avid movie fan at the time—that would come later," Shirlee said. "All those star names were just something on a marquee. Sure, I could tell one actor from another—Henry Fonda, Kirk Douglas, Alan Ladd, Gregory Peck, John Wayne. I'd seen two movies with Clark Gable, and I now knew who Fonda was. When I first spotted him, I saw that Henry was an older man, but he was god damn handsome."

TILL DEATH DO US PART

AKA,
"THE BRIDE WORE WHITE"

Shirlee Mae Adams marries **Henry Fonda.**

"As a stewardess, as they were called back then, I met a lot of good-looking guys. But I found Henry the most attractive man in the world."

Later in the theater, Shirlee and her actor friend were seated across the aisle from Henry and his date. During the run of this intense war film about the D-Day landings, she cast furtive glances at Fonda. He returned the flirtation, and at one point even winked at her.

"At that wink, I was a goner," Shirlee said, hopelessly in love. "In spite of his age, I knew I had met my Prince Charming. He was old enough to be my father—

maybe grandfather—but I knew the man of my dreams had arrived. The challenge involved how to meet him and how to get rid of that model. I knew I couldn't do everything in one night."

In one of those rare coincidences that happen in life, two days later, Shirlee was in a high-fashion women's clothing shop on Fifth Avenue. She was here to pick up an altered gown that she was to wear in an upcoming fashion show in Los Angeles.

Another well-dressed woman entered the shop, and when she heard Shirlee mention Los Angeles, she said, "I wish I was there. That's where my boyfriend flew to last night."

"Who is your boyfriend?" Shirlee asked.

The woman's answer was unexpected: "Henry Fonda."

Shirlee suddenly recognized her as Henry's date from the premiere of *The Longest Day*.

***

Having recently re-established himself in Los Angeles, Henry was not ready for the party scene there, even though he was showered with invitations. Many older women, whose husbands had divorced them in pursuit of younger women, thought Henry Fonda would be ideal as their next husband. "A big-name star, and a rich one at that—you can't beat it," said Lana Turner.

One night, a press agent called, wanting Henry to emcee a minor awards ceremony. At first, Henry said, "no," but was talked into it. To "sweeten the deal," the agent invited him for dinner with his date. "I've arranged this hottie for you. She's young, well-stacked, and gorgeous. She told me she considered you a dreamboat. She saw you at the premiere of *The Longest Day*."

"Is this gal tall? Henry asked.

"Tall and beautiful," the agent answered.

"I think I remember her. Okay, the date is on, and I'll even emcee that damn awards ceremony. It's about time somebody started awarding ME."

Over dinner, Henry's blue eyes lit up at the sight of Shirlee. Although he listened to the agent, his eyes were focused on her. Under the table, she held his hand.

After dinner, Henry and Shirlee thanked their hosts and disappeared into a joint along the Strip for a nightcap.

He later extended yet another invitation to Shirlee—this one to his home—telling her, "I live alone. The staff doesn't come in until morning."

"I have the weekend off," she said. "And frankly, I can't think of anything I'd like better than spend it with you."

"Don't worry about my age," he said. "I can still cut the mustard."

"I bet you can…and more."

The home Henry took Shirlee to was at 10050 Cielo Drive in Bel Air, a white stucco building surrounded by acres of cultivated foliage, especially fruit trees. Henry also had a large vegetable garden.

Once there on a visit, actor Clifton Webb noted both the beauty of the neighborhood and its aging population. He called it "Forest Lawn for the Living."

Henry's invitation for Shirlee to spend the night was not only accepted but extended until the end of his life. As the years went by, Shirlee continued to sleep in the same bed where Henry had charmed and seduced her on that pivotal night so long ago.

***

As the months went by, Henry learned more and more about Shirlee and her past. He had been born in 1905. She had come into the world on February 11, 1932 in Aurora, Illinois, an hour's drive from Chicago.

At the age of four, her parents divorced, and she was sent to the Mary A. Goddard Juvenile Home. Here, she suffered a rigid, humorless, and rather stern upbringing.

In time, she became an avid church-goer, first as a Presbyterian and later as a Lutheran. Regardless of the denomination, she sang in the choir of whatever church she was associated with.

She never learned to smoke, and alcohol made her sick. According to her teachings, nearly everything she might do was viewed as a "sin," and that included dancing and going to a motion picture theater. That is why she had never seen a movie starring Henry.

She never attended college. The moment she turned eighteen, she bolted from Illinois and enrolled in the American Airlines Stewardess School. "I wanted to fly high in the sky and go from one adventure to another," she said.

As a kid, she had felt unloved and unwanted since her parents abandoned her at the age of four. When she became a flight attendant, she was much appreciated by men of all ages on her flights. Almost no flight went by that didn't involve her getting asked out on a date.

Before Henry, her most serious love interest was Stirling Moss, a racecar-driving Londoner who was only three years older than her.

At the time of his involvement with Shirlee, Moss had separated from his first wife, Katie Molson, the heiress to the Canadian brewer, Molson. The magazine *Private Eye* had surmised that Moss was primarily interested in "cars, women, and sex, in that order."

In a lifetime of car racing, Moss would eventually win 212 of the 529 races he entered. In a seven-year (1955-1961) span, he finished as a champ runner-up four times and in third place the other three times.

When Shirlee started dating Henry, she ended her affair with Moss.

Writer Devin McKinney gave the best description of Shirlee at the time:

"Trim, well-assembled, adroit yet unimposing, Shirlee has the not-yet-formed nose of an adolescent girl, and her smile defines pert. *Of Henry's wives, she is the only one whose manner suggests no hidden agenda or dark inner world. She presents an image of healthy youth, the good life, yet she is concerned with social ills, and works extensively for charities. She is eager for people to get along, proud to be a helper, and her clearest ambition is to serve and support Henry.]*

British racecar champ **Stirling Moss** at the Dutch Grand Prix in 1961, around the time he dated Shirlee.

"Like many movie stars I would meet in my future, many of them were self-centered, conceited bastards," Shirlee said. "Not Henry, who was quite modest. When we went to see a movie, he would stand in line with the other ticket holders, waiting his turn like everybody else. He had a rule, though: 'No Henry Fonda movie.' He told me he hated to see himself on the screen. Many of his future films he did only for the money. At home, he showed me his favorite old movies like *The Grapes of Wrath.* That was not my favorite. I thought he looked his sexiest in *The Lady Eve* with Barbara Stanwyck."

"Henry was often moody, even deeply depressed at times," Shirlee said. "He was grumpy in the morning. Regardless of his mood swings, I was always there for him."

Only once or twice during the years he lived with Shirlee did Henry bring up the subject of marriage. "For me, marriage is out of the question. I've failed at that institution four times, and I don't plan to get married and divorced again. I guess I'm just not the marrying kind."

"Shirlee saved me from the depths of my depression on many a night," Henry said. "She made me feel like a kid again. If such a thing were possible. I wanted to send her a Valentine every day of the year."

His daughter Jane had already warned Henry about getting married again. "Like the others, Shirlee will drop you, perhaps run off with a younger man like your Baroness bride. She'll drop you, break your heart, AGAIN."

"Like hell she will," he protested. "No lover leaves a Fonda unless I want her to."

[*In October of 1965, Henry was back on Broadway, appearing in the play* Generation *at the Morosco Theatre.*

One day, "from out of nowhere" (her words) Henry proposed marriage to Shirlee.

"I almost fainted," she recalled. "Before I could utter the words, 'Sure I will,' he grabbed me and gave me the most passionate kiss of my life."

On December 3, 1965, Henry married Shirlee in the Chambers of Justice Edwin Lynde in Mineola, New York.

Actress Elizabeth Ashley was Maid of Honor, and George Peppard served as Henry's Best Man.

Although Henry's son, Peter, had disapproved of his father's previous marriage (to Afdera), he had a different opinion about his links to Shirlee: "That young girl should be marrying me—not my dad."

In time, Jane seemingly came to approve of her father's marriage to a fifth wife. "This is the kind of union I wish he had had earlier in his life. The two of them represented the best people who rose out of the earth in the heartland of America."

***

Over the years, Henry and James Stewart had maintained their friendship. Back in California, Henry found himself living near his friend once again. They spent long hours with each other, often with their wives, Shirlee and Gloria. Hank and Jim would even co-star in films together.

"Hank was always bringing me vegetables from his garden and lots of fruit," Stewart said. "I appreciated the gesture. But where did he get the idea I liked eggplant? What a disgusting vegetable."

"Hank was also a beekeeper, and on occasion, he brought me a jar marked "Henry Fonda Honey." I really liked his honey. One day, he warned me that you had to be careful because bees sting. Like I needed to be told that."

"I would not have predicted it, but his marital bliss with Shirlee went on and on," Stewart said. "After years of searching, that bastard found what was to become his lifetime companion. She was his nurse through his future illness, always at his side, tending to his every need. As for me, I got it right the first time. Gloria was the gal for me."

The actress Barbara Bel Geddes once visited the Fonda home on a winter's night. When she was ushered into the living room, Shirlee was watching TV near the fireplace, and Henry was on the sofa doing his needlework.

"What a domestic scene of tranquility, contrasting with his previous tempestuous marriages," Bel Geddes said.

Although best friends, Stewart and Fonda had differences on everything from politics to religion. "Jim was conservative, Fonda a liberal. Jim was a Christian, Fonda a non-believer," said George Peppard. "He once told me, "I don't think people were descended from Adam and Eve. We came from apes."

Friends were surprised that Shirlee, throughout the rest of her life, continued to call her husband "Fonda."

The USPS issued this honorary 37-cent postage stamp in 2005.

"I've never told anybody this before," Stewart said one night to Josh Logan. "Hank, you know, fancies himself a painter. One day, he asked me to pose nude for him. He wanted to put on canvas the dick that had seduced at least 250 starlets and some of the grandest dames in Hollywood, from Garbo to Norma Shearer. I turned him down, telling him that if he wanted to paint my dick, he would have to do it from memory. He saw my junk night after night when we lived in that cramped little box in Manhattan during our starvation years."

Horror struck the Fondas and everyone else in their neighborhood on August 9, 1969. Henry was devasted when he heard about the satanic murder of starlet Sharon Tate, the wife of director Roman Polanski.

On that night, members of the Charles Manson gang of sickos broke into the Polanski/Tate home and murdered Tate and four of her guests, including Jay Sebring, Henry's hairdresser.

Tate was eight and a half months pregnant at the time, and she pleaded for the life of her unborn. For that, she was rewarded with knife stabs in her stomach.

Tate and Polanski had became part of a social group in Hollywood that included both Jane and Peter Fonda, Joan Collins, Mia Farrow, and older members of the film colony, both Henry and Yul Brynner, for example, along with Danny Kaye and Kirk Douglas.

Tate and Polanski lived on Cielo Drive, as did Henry and Shirlee. The home had been previously occupied by Candice Bergan and Terry Melcher, the son of Doris Day. Henry and Shirlee had visited the home several times.

On the night of the slaughter, Polanski was in London.

Shock waves went through Hollywood," Henry recalled, "especially from Shirlee and me, because they were our friends. Security guards were flown in from Florida. I put our home under 24-hour guard," Henry said.

Later, he commented on the night of the murders. "It was when the 1960s came to an end."

Many of his friends suggested that Henry should move out of the neighborhood with all its memories of blood and slaughter. But he and Shirlee remained in their hacienda until he died there. She, too, would go on living there, although one investor offered her $20 million for Henry's house.

Shirlee Fonda, loyal to the end.

"I never wanted to leave our home," she said. "It's filled with too many memories. Here I lived with the love of my life. Sometimes at night he visits me, summoning me to come and join him somewhere in time and space. You know, true love does not die, but it can live on through eternity. When the time comes for me to go, I know his hand will be reaching down for me. I will be Fonda's bride for eternity."

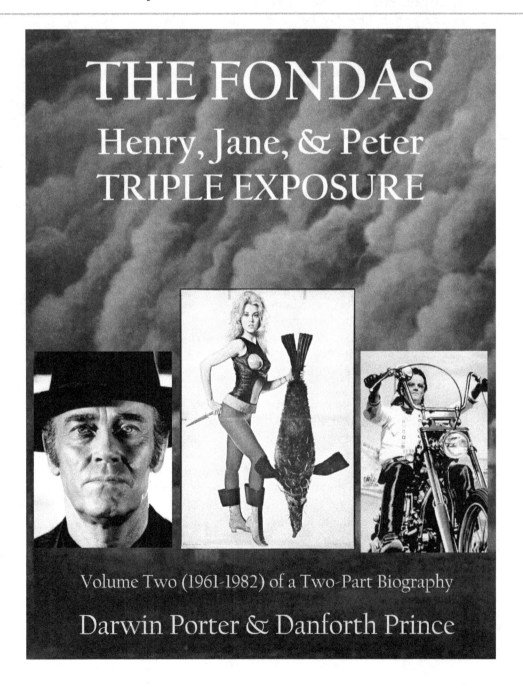

THE FONDAS
Henry, Jane, & Peter
TRIPLE EXPOSURE

Volume Two (1961-1982) of a Two-Part Biography

Darwin Porter & Danforth Prince

DARWIN PORTER

As a precocious nine-year-old, **Darwin Porter** *began meeting entertainers through his mother, Hazel, a charismatic Southern girl whose husband had died in World War II. Migrating from the Depression-ravaged valleys of western North Carolina to Miami Beach during its most ebullient heyday, Hazel became a personal assistant to the vaudeville comedienne* **Sophie Tucker***, the kind-hearted "Last of the Red Hot Mamas."*

Loosely supervised by his mother, Darwin was regularly dazzled by the likes of **Judy Garland, Dinah Shore, Frank Sinatra, Ronald Reagan** *(at the time near the end of his Hollywood gig), and* **Marilyn Monroe***. Each of them made it a point, whenever they were in Miami (either on or off the record), to visit and pay their respects to "Miss Sophie."*

At the University of Miami, Darwin edited the school newspaper, raising its revenues, through advertising and public events, to unheard-of new levels. He met and interviewed **Eleanor Roosevelt** *and later invited her, as part of a sponsored event he crafted, to spend a day ("Eleanor Roosevelt Day") at the university, and to his delight, she accepted. Years later, in Manhattan, during her work as a human rights activist, he escorted her, at her request, to many public functions.*

On another occasion, he invited **Lucille Ball and Desi Arnaz***, then at the pinnacle of their fame and popularity, to the University. On campus, after the photographers and fans departed, Lucille launched a bitter attack on her husband, accusing him of having had sex the previous night with two showgirls. Because of that and other upsets that unfolded that day, Darwin learned early in his life that Lucille Ball and Desi Arnaz were definitely not Ricky and Lucy Ricardo.*

After his graduation, Darwin, in a graceful transition from his work as editor of the University's newspaper and his sponsorship by **Wilson Hicks** *(Photo Editor and then Executive Editor of* Life *magazine) became a Bureau Chief of* The Miami Herald *(the youngest in that publication's history) assigned to its branch in Key West. At the time the island outpost was an avant-garde literary mecca and — thanks to the Cuban missile crisis — a flash point of the Cold War.*

Key West had been the site of Harry S Truman's "Winter White House" and Truman returned a few months before his death for a final visit. He invited young Darwin for "early morning walks" where he used the young emissary of The Miami Herald *to "set the record straight."*

Through Truman, Darwin was introduced and later joined the staff of **Senator George Smathers** *of Florida. Smathers' best friend was a young senator,* **John F. Kennedy***. Through "Gorgeous George," as Smathers was known in the Senate, Darwin got to meet Jack and Jacqueline in Palm Beach. He later wrote two books about them —* The Kennedys, All the Gossip Unfit to Print, *and one of his all-time bestsellers,* Jacqueline Kennedy Onassis—A Life Beyond Her Wildest Dreams. *(A commemorative new edition was released in 2022 as* JKO: Her Tumultuous Life & Her Love Affairs).

Buttressed by his status as The Miami Herald's *Key West Bureau Chief, Darwin met, interviewed, and often befriended* **Tennessee Williams. Ernest Hemingway, Tallulah Bankhead, Gore Vidal, Truman Capote, Carson McCullers,** *and a gaggle of other internationally famous writers and entertainers:* **Cary Grant, Rock Hudson, Marlon Brando, Montgomery Clift, Susan Hayward, Warren Beatty, Christopher Isherwood, Anne Bancroft, Angela Lansbury,** *and* **William Inge.**

Eventually transferred to Manhattan, Darwin worked for a decade in television advertising with the producer and arts-industry socialite **Stanley Mills Haggart***. In addition to some speculative ventures associated with Marilyn Monroe, they also jointly produced TV commercials that included testimonials from* **Joan Crawford** *(then feverishly promoting Pepsi-Cola);* **Ronald Reagan** *(General Electric); and* **Debbie Reynolds** *(Singer sewing machines). Other personalities they promoted, each delivering televised sales pitches, included* **Louis Armstrong, Lena Horne, Rosalind Russell, William Holden***, and* **Arlene Dahl***, each of them hawking a commercial product.*

Beginning in the early 1960s, Darwin joined forces with the then-fledgling **Arthur Frommer** *organization, playing a key role in researching and writing more than 50 titles and defining the style and values that later emerged as the world's leading travel guidebooks,* **The Frommer Guides.** *Darwin's particular journalistic expertise on Europe, New Eng-*

YESTERDAY,
WHEN HE WAS YOUNG

DARWIN PORTER

A social historian fascinated by biographies and the ironies of the American Experience.

land, California, and the Caribbean eventually propelled him into authorship of (depending on the era and whatever crises were brewing at the time), between 70 and 80% of their titles. Even during the research of his travel guides, he continued to interview show-biz celebrities, discussing their triumphs, feuds, and frustrations. At this point in their lives, many were retired and reclusive. Darwin either pursued them (sometimes though local tourist offices) or encountered them randomly as part of his extensive travels. **Ava Gardner, Lana Turner, Hedy Lamarr, Ingrid Bergman, Ethel Merman, Andy Warhol, Elizabeth Taylor, Marlene Dietrich, Bette Davis**, **Judy Garland,** and **Paul Newman** were particularly insightful.

Porter's biographies—at this writing, they number sixty-three— have won thirty first prize or "runner-up to first prize" awards at literary festivals in cities or regions which include New England, New York, Los Angeles, Hollywood, San Francisco, Florida, California, and Paris.

Darwin, also a magazine columnist, can be heard at regular intervals as a radio and podcast commentator, reviewing the ironies of celebrities, tabloid culture, politics, and scandal.

A resident of New York City, where he spent years within the social orbit of the Queen of Off-Broadway (the eccentric and very temperamental philanthropist, **Lucille Lortel),** Darwin is currently at work on a series of books with eyebrow-raising revelations about the dazzling personalities who kept the lights sparkling both On and Off Broadway in the 70s and 80s.

DANFORTH PRINCE

A graduate of Hamilton College and a native of Easton and Bethlehem, Pennsylvania, he's president and founder (in 1983) of the Porter and Prince Corporation, the entity that produced the original texts and updates for dozens of key titles of **THE FROMMER GUIDES**—travel "bibles" for millions of readers during the travel industry's go-go years in the 80s, 90s, and early millennium.

He also founded, in 1996, the Georgia Literary Association, precursor to what morphed, in 2004, into **Blood Moon Productions**, the corporate force behind dozens of political and Hollywood biographies. Its vaguely apocalyptic name was inspired by one of Darwin Porter's popular early novels, **Blood Moon**, a thriller about the false gods of power, wealth, and physical beauty. In 2011, Prince was named "Publisher of the Year" by a consortium of literary critics and marketers spearheaded by the J.M. Northern Media Group.

Prince has electronically documented his stewardship of Blood Moon in at least 50 videotaped documentaries, book trailers, public speeches, and TV or radio interviews. Most of these are available on **YouTube.com** and **Facebook** (keyword: "Danforth Prince"); on **Twitter** (#BloodyandLunar); or by clicking on **BloodMoonProductions.com.**

Hearkening back to his days as a travel writer, Prince is also an innkeeper, maintaining and managing a historic bed & breakfast, **Magnolia House (www.MagnoliaHouseSaintGeorge.com).** Affiliated with AirBnb, and increasingly sought out by filmmakers as an evocative locale for moviemaking, it lies in St. George, at the northern tip of Staten Island, the "sometimes forgotten Outer Borough" of New York City. A landmarked building with a formidable historic and literary pedigree, it lies in a neighborhood closely linked to Henry James, Theodore Dreiser, the Vanderbilts, and key moments in America's colonial history.

Set in a terraced garden with views over New York Harbor and nearby Manhattan, it's been visited by show-biz stars who have included **Tennessee Williams, Gloria Swanson, Joan Blondell, Edward Albee, Jolie Gabor** (mother of Zsa Zsa, Eva, and Magda), soap opera queen **Ruth Warrick,** the Viennese chanteuse **Greta Keller,** and many of the luminaries of Broadway. It lies within a twelve-minute walk from the ferries regularly chugging their way across the harbor to Wall Street and Lower Manhattan.

Publicized as "a reasonably priced celebrity-centric bed & breakfast with links to the book trades," and the beneficiary of rave ("superhost") reviews (including "New York's most fascinating B&B") from hundreds of previous guests, **Magnolia House** is loaded with furniture and memorabilia collected from around the world during his decades as a travel journalist for the Frommer Guides. **Since the onset of the Covid Crisis, social distancing and regular decontamination regimens have been rigorously enforced.** For photographs, testimonials from previous guests, more information, and reservations, click on

www.AirBnb/H/Magnolia-House

In reference to historic Magnolia House's status as a "super-hosted" AirBnb, your handler, concierge, and problem-solver is **Danforth Prince**, who says, "It's more interesting than a cookie-cutter bandbox, and the resident ghosts and spirits will usually be glad to know you're here. Come with your friends and/or family (children and well-behaved dogs are welcome) for the night, and use it as your base for exploring nearby Manhattan."

Even with social distancing, Covid cautiousness, and a lot more 'scrub-a-dub-dubbing,' it's about healing, recuperation, razzmatazz, show-biz, Classic Hollywood, sightseeing, and conversation—if it interests you—in the greatest city in the world.

photo courtesy Frank Lugo

Magnolia House is a proud, architecturally protected landmark within the St. George, Staten Island Historical District.

It's depicted here in a photo snapped by New York City's Department of Finance as part of its 1940 Tax Census.

Some visitors liken Magnolia House to a *grande dame* with a centuries-old knack for nourishing high-functioning eccentrics. Many have lived or been entertained here since New York's State Senator Howard Bayne, a transplanted Southerner, moved in with his wife, the daughter of the Surgeon General of the Confederate States of America, in the aftermath of that bloodiest of wars on North American soil, the War Between the American States.

Since then, dozens of celebrities have whispered their secrets and rehearsed their ambitions within its walls. They've included movie vamps from the silent screen, midnight cowboys, dancers from the dance, *Butterflies in Heat*, a heavyweight boxing champ, writers from every hue, faded film goddesses, playwrights who crafted blockbusters for both Marilyn (Monroe) and Elizabeth (Taylor), *ultra-avant-garde* diarists, every known variety of *prima donna* and *diva*, including some from the world of opera, and a world-class Olympic athlete.

They've also included authors Darwin Porter and Danforth Prince, who spent decades here renovating it and producing, within its walls, a stream of FROMMER TRAVEL GUIDES and award-winning celebrity biographies.

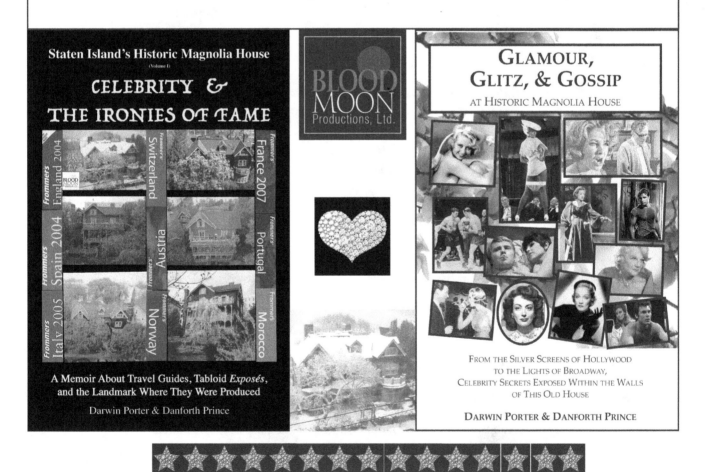

JUDY GARLAND & LIZA MINNELLI

TOO MANY DAMN RAINBOWS

Judy and Liza were the greatest, most colorful, and most tragic mother-daughter saga in show biz history. They live, laugh, and weep again in the tear-soaked pages of this remarkable biography. Darwin Porter and Danforth Prince have compiled a compelling "post-modern" spin.

According to Liza, "My mother—hailed as the world's greatest entertainer—lived eighty lives during her short time with us."

Their memorable stories unfold through eyewitness accounts of the typhoons that engulfed them. They swing across glittery landscapes of euphoria and glory, detailing the betrayals and treachery which the duo encountered almost daily. There were depressions "as deep as the Mariana Trench," suicide attempts, and obsessive identifications on deep psychological levels with roles that include Judy's Vicky Lester in *A Star is Born* (1954) and Liza's Sally Bowles in *Cabaret* (1972).

Lesser known are the jealous actress-to-actress rivalries. Fueled by klieg lights and rivers of negative publicity, they sprouted like malevolent mushrooms on steroids.

As Judy faded into the 1960s, Liza roaringly emerged as a star in her own right. "I did it my way," Liza said. She survived the whirlwinds of her mother's drug addiction with a yen for choosing all the wrong men in patterns that weirdly evoked those of Judy herself.

For millions of fans, Judy will forever remain the cheerful adolescent (Dorothy) skipping along a yellow brick road toward the other side of the rainbow. Liza followed her down that hallucinogenic path, searching for the childhood, the security, and the love that eluded her.

Judy Garland, an icon whose memory is permanently etched into the American psyche, continues to thrive as a cult goddess. Revered by thousands of die-hard fans, she's the most poignant example of both the manic and depressive (some say "schizophrenic") sides of the Hollywood myth.

Deep in her 70s, Liza is still with us, too, nursing memories of her former acclaim and her first visit as a little girl to her parents at MGM, the "Dream Factory," during the Golden Age of Hollywood.

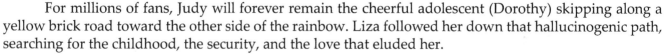

Judy Garland & Liza Minnelli: Too Many Damn Rainbows
Darwin Porter & Danforth Prince
Softcover, 6" x 9", with hundreds of photos. ISBN 9781936003693
Available Everywhere Now

LOVE TRIANGLE

RONALD REAGAN, JANE WYMAN, & NANCY DAVIS

HOW MUCH DO YOU REALLY KNOW ABOUT THE REAGANS?

THIS BOOK TELLS EVERYTHING ABOUT THE SHOW-BIZ SCANDALS THEY DESPERATELY WANTED TO FORGET.

UNIQUE IN THE HISTORY OF PUBLISHING, THIS SCANDALOUS TRIPLE BIOGRAPHY focuses on the Hollywood indiscretions of former U.S. president Ronald Reagan and his two wives. A proud and Presidential addition to Blood Moon's Babylon series, it digs deep into what these three young and attractive movie stars were doing decades before two of them took over the Free World.

As reviewed by Diane Donovan, Senior Reviewer at the California Bookwatch section of the Midwest Book Review: "Love Triangle: Ronald Reagan, Jane Wyman & Nancy Davis may find its way onto many a Republican Reagan fan's reading shelf; but those who expect another Reagan celebration will be surprised: this is lurid Hollywood exposé writing at its best, and outlines the truths surrounding one of the most provocative industry scandals in the world.

"There are already so many biographies of the Reagans on the market that one might expect similar mile-markers from this: be prepared for shock and awe; because Love Triangle doesn't take your ordinary approach to biography and describes a love triangle that eventually bumped a major Hollywood movie star from the possibility of being First Lady and replaced her with a lesser-known Grade B actress (Nancy Davis).

"From politics and betrayal to romance, infidelity, and sordid affairs, Love Triangle is a steamy, eye-opening story that blows the lid off of the Reagan illusion to raise eyebrows on both sides of the big screen.

"Black and white photos liberally pepper an account of the careers of all three and the lasting shock of their stormy relationships in a delightful pursuit especially recommended for any who relish Hollywood gossip."

In 2015, LOVE TRIANGLE, Blood Moon Productions' overview of the early dramas associated with Ronald Reagan's scandal-soaked career in Hollywood, was designated by the Awards Committee of the HOLLYWOOD BOOK FESTIVAL as Runner-Up to Best Biography of the Year.

LOVE TRIANGLE: Ronald Reagan, Jane Wyman, & Nancy Davis
Darwin Porter & Danforth Prince
Softcover, 6" x 9", with hundreds of photos.   ISBN 978-1-936003-41-9

Less than an hour after the discovery of Marilyn Monroe's corpse in Brentwood, a flood of theories, tainted evidence, and conflicting testimonies began pouring out into the public landscape.

Filled with rage, hysteria, and depression, "and fed up with Jack's lies, Bobby's lies," Marilyn sought revenge and mass vindication. Her revelations at an imminent press conference could have toppled political dynasties and destroyed criminal empires. Marilyn had to be stopped…

Into this steamy cauldron of deceit, Marilyn herself emerges as a most unreliable witness during the weeks leading up to her murder. Her own deceptions, vanities, and self-delusion poured toxic accelerants on an already raging fire.

"Darwin Porter is fearless, honest and a great read. He minces no words. If the truth makes you wince and honesty offends your sensibility, stay away. It's been said that he deals in muck because he can't libel the dead. Well, it's about time someone started telling the truth about the dead and being honest about just what happened to get us in the mess in which we're in. If libel is lying, then Porter is so completely innocent as to deserve an award. In all of his works he speaks only to the truth, and although he is a hard teacher and task master, he's one we ignore at our peril. To quote Gore Vidal, power is not a toy we give to someone for being good. If we all don't begin to investigate where power and money really are in the here and now, we deserve what we get. Yes, Porter names names. The reader will come away from the book knowing just who killed Monroe. Porter rather brilliantly points to a number of motives, but leaves it to the reader to surmise exactly what happened at the rainbow's end, just why Marilyn was killed. And, of course, why we should be careful of getting exactly what we want. It's a very long tumble from the top."

—ALAN PETRUCELLI, Examiner.com, May 13, 2012

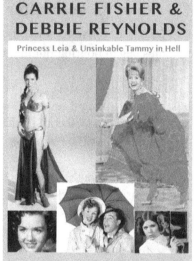

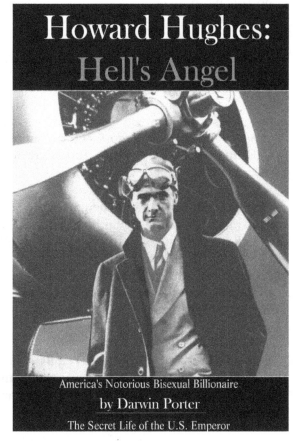

SCARLETT O'HARA,

DESPERATELY IN LOVE WITH HEATHCLIFF,

TOGETHER ON THE ROAD TO HELL

Here, for the first time, is a biography that raises the curtain on the secret lives of **Lord Laurence Olivier**, often cited as the finest actor in the history of England, and **Vivien Leigh**, who immortalized herself with her Oscar-winning portrayals of Scarlett O'Hara in *Gone With the Wind*, and as Blanche DuBois in Tennessee Williams' *A Streetcar Named Desire*.

Dashing and "impossibly handsome," Laurence Olivier was pursued by the most dazzling luminaries, male and female, of the movie and theater worlds.

Lord Olivier's beautiful and brilliant but emotionally disturbed wife (Viv to her lovers) led a tumultuous off-the-record life whose paramours ranged from the A-list celebrities to men she selected randomly off the street. But none of the brilliant roles depicted by Lord and Lady Olivier, on stage or on screen, ever matched the power and drama of personal dramas which wavered between Wagnerian opera and Greek tragedy. Damn You, Scarlett O'Hara is the definitive and most revelatory portrait ever published of the most talented and tormented actor and actress of the 20th century.

Darwin Porter is the principal author of this seminal work.

"The folks over at TMZ would have had a field day tracking Laurence Olivier and Vivien Leigh with flip cameras in hand. Damn You, Scarlett O'Hara can be a dazzling read, the prose unmannered and instantly digestible. The authors' ability to pile scandal atop scandal, seduction after seduction, can be impossible to resist."

—THE WASHINGTON TIMES

DAMN YOU, SCARLETT O'HARA

THE PRIVATE LIFES OF LAURENCE OLIVIER AND VIVIEN LEIGH

Darwin Porter and Roy Moseley

Winner of four distinguished literary awards, this is the best biography of Vivien Leigh and Laurence Olivier ever published, with hundreds of insights into the London Theatre, the role of the Oliviers in the politics of World War II, and the passion, fury, and frustration of their lives together as actors in the West End, on Broadway, and in Hollywood.

ISBN 978-1-936003-15-0   Hardcover, 708 pages, with about a hundred photos.

DONALD TRUMP
WAS THE MAN WHO WOULD BE KING

This is the most famous book about our incendiary ex-President you've probably never heard of.

Winner of three respected literary awards, and released three months before the Presidential elections of 2016, it's an entertainingly packaged, artfully salacious bombshell, a scathingly historic overview of America during its 2016 election cycle, a portrait unlike anything ever published on CANDIDATE DONALD and the climate in which he thrived and massacred his political rivals.

Its volcanic, much-suppressed release during the heat and venom of the 2016 Presidential campaign has already been heralded by the Midwestern Book Review, California Book Watch, the Seattle Gay News, the staunchly right-wing WILS-AM radio, and also by the editors at the most popular Seniors' magazine in Florida, BOOMER TIMES, which designated it as one of their BOOKS OF THE MONTH.

TRUMPOCALYPSE: *"Donald Trump: The Man Who Would Be King* is recommended reading for all sides, no matter what political stance is being adopted: Republican, Democrat, or other.

"One of its driving forces is its ability to synthesize an unbelievable amount of information into a format and presentation which blends lively irony with outrageous observations, entertaining even as it presents eye-opening information in a format accessible to all.

"Politics dovetail with American obsessions and fascinations with trends, figureheads, drama, and sizzling news stories, but blend well with the observations of sociologists, psychologists, politicians, and others in a wide range of fields who lend their expertise and insights to create a much broader review of the Trump phenomena than a more casual book could provide.

"The result is a 'must read' for any American interested in issues of race, freedom, equality, and justice—and for any non-American who wonders just what is going on behind the scenes in this country's latest election debacle."

Diane Donovan, Senior Editor, California Bookwatch

DONALD TRUMP, THE MAN WHO WOULD BE KING
WINNER OF "BEST BIOGRAPHY" AWARDS FROM BOOK FESTIVALS IN
NEW YORK, CALIFORNIA, AND FLORIDA
by Darwin Porter and Danforth Prince
Softcover, with 822 pages and hundreds of photos. ISBN 978-1-936003-51-8.

Available now from Ingram, Amazon.com and other purveyors, worldwide.

LINDA LOVELACE

INSIDE LINDA LOVELACE'S DEEP THROAT
DEGRADATION, PORNO CHIC, AND THE RISE OF FEMINISM

THE MOST COMPREHENSIVE BIOGRAPHY EVER WRITTEN OF AN ADULT ENTERTAINMENT STAR, HER TORMENTED RELATIONSHIP WITH HOLLYWOOD'S UNDERBELLY, AND HOW SHE CHANGED FOREVER THE WORLD'S PERCEPTIONS ABOUT CENSORSHIP, SEXUAL BEHAVIOR PATTERNS, AND PORNOGRAPHY.

Darwin Porter, author of more than thirty critically acclaimed celebrity exposés of behind-the-scenes intrigue in the entertainment industry, was deeply involved in the Linda Lovelace saga as it unfolded in the 70s, interviewing many of the players, and raising money for the legal defense of the film's co-star, Harry Reems.

In this book, emphasizing her role as an unlikely celebrity interacting with other celebrities, he brings inside information and a never-before-published revelation to almost every page.

"This book drew me in..How could it not?"
Coco Papy, Bookslut.

THE BEACH BOOK FESTIVAL'S GRAND PRIZE
WINNER FOR
"BEST SUMMER READING OF 2013"

RUNNER-UP TO "BEST BIOGRAPHY OF 2013" THE LOS ANGELES BOOK FESTIVAL

PINK TRIANGLE

THE FEUDS AND PRIVATE LIVES OF
TENNESSEE WILLIAMS, GORE VIDAL, TRUMAN CAPOTE,
& FAMOUS MEMBERS OF THEIR ENTOURAGES

Darwin Porter & Danforth Prince

This book, the only one of its kind, reveals the backlot intrigues associated with the literary and script-writing *enfants terribles* of America's entertainment community during the mid-20th century.

It exposes their bitchfests, their slugfests, and their relationships with the glitterati—Marilyn Monroe, Brando, the Oliviers, the Paleys, U.S. Presidents, a gaggle of other movie stars, millionaires, and international débauchés.

This is for anyone who's interested in the formerly concealed scandals of Hollywood and Broadway, and the values and pretentions of both the literary community and the entertainment industry.

"A banquet... If PINK TRIANGLE had not been written for us, we would have had to research and type it all up for ourselves…Pink Triangle is nearly seven hundred pages of the most entertaining histrionics ever sliced, spiced, heated, and serviced up to the reading public. Everything that Blood Moon has done before pales in comparison.

Given the fact that the subjects of the book themselves were nearly delusional on the subject of themselves (to say nothing of each other) it is hard to find fault. Add to this the intertwined jungle that was the relationship among Williams, Capote, and Vidal, of the times they vied for things they loved most—especially attention—and the times they enthralled each other and the world, [Pink Triangle is] the perfect antidote to the Polar Vortex."

—Vinton McCabe in the NY JOURNAL OF BOOKS

"Full disclosure: I have been a friend and follower of Blood Moon Productions' tomes for years, and always marveled at the amount of information in their books—it's staggering. The index alone to Pink Triangle runs to 21 pages—and the scale of names in it runs like a Who's Who of American social, cultural and political life through much of the 20th century."

—Perry Brass in THE HUFFINGTON POST

"We Brits are not spared the Porter/Prince silken lash either. PINK TRIANGLE's research is, quite frankly, breathtaking. PINK TRIANGLE will fascinate you for many weeks to come. Once you have made the initial titillating dip, the day will seem dull without it."

—Jeffery Tayor in THE SUNDAY EXPRESS (UK)

PINK TRIANGLE—The Feuds and Private Lives of Tennessee Williams, Gore Vidal, Truman Capote, and Famous Members of their Entourages

Darwin Porter & Danforth Prince
Softcover, 700 pages, with photos   ISBN 978-1-936003-37-2   Also Available for E-Readers

THOSE GLAMOROUS GABORS

BOMBSHELLS FROM BUDAPEST

Zsa Zsa, Eva, and Magda Gabor transferred their glittery dreams and gold-digging ambitions from the twilight of the Austro-Hungarian Empire to Hollywood. There, more effectively than any army, these Bombshells from Budapest broke hearts, amassed fortunes, lovers, and A-list husbands, and amused millions of voyeurs through the medium of television, movies, and the social registers. In this astonishing "triple-play" biography, designated "Best Biography of the Year" by the Hollywood Book Festival, Blood Moon lifts the "mink-and-diamond" curtain on this amazing trio of blood-related sisters, whose complicated intrigues have never been fully explored before.

***

"You will never be Ga-bored...this book gives new meaning to the term compelling. Be warned, Those Glamorous Gabors is both an epic and a pip. Not since Gone With the Wind have so many characters on the printed page been forced to run for their lives for one reason or another. And Scarlett making a dress out of the curtains is nothing compared to what a Gabor will do when she needs to scrap together an outfit for a movie premiere or late-night outing.

"For those not up to speed, Jolie Tilleman came from a family of jewelers and therefore came by her love for the shiny stones honestly, perhaps genetically. She married Vilmos Gabor somewhere around World War 1 (exact dates, especially birth dates, are always somewhat vague in order to establish plausible deniability later on) and they were soon blessed with three daughters: Magda, the oldest, whose hair, sadly, was naturally brown, although it would turn quite red in America; Zsa Zsa (born 'Sari') a natural blond who at a very young age exhibited the desire for fame with none of the talents usually associated with achievement, excepting beauty and a natural wit; and Eva, the youngest and blondest of the girls, who after seeing Grace Moore perform at the National Theater, decided that she wanted to be an actress and that she would one day move to Hollywood to become a star.

"Given that the Gabor family at that time lived in Budapest, Hungary, at the period of time between the World Wars, that Hollywood dream seemed a distant one indeed. The story—the riches to rags to riches to rags to riches again myth of survival against all odds as the four women, because of their Jewish heritage, flee Europe with only the minks on their backs and what jewels they could smuggle along with them in their decolletage, only to have to battle afresh for their places in the vicious Hollywood pecking order—gives new meaning to the term 'compelling.' The reader, as if he were witnessing a particularly gore-drenched traffic accident, is incapable of looking away."

—*New York Review of Books*

ROCK HUDSON

BILL & HILLARY
So This Is That Thing Called Love

CONFUSED ABOUT HOW TO INTERPRET THEIR RAUCOUS PASTS?

THIS UNCENSORED TALE ABOUT A LOVE AFFAIR THAT CHANGED THE COURSE OF POLITICS AND THE PLANET IS OF COMPELLING INTEREST TO ANYONE INVOLVED IN THE SLUGFESTS AND INCENDIARY WARS OF THE CLINTONS.

"This is both a biographical coverage of the Clintons and a political exposé; a detailed, weighty exploration that traces the couple's social and political evolution, from how each entered the political arena to their White House years under Bill Clinton's presidency.

"Containing gossip, scandal, and biographical sketches, it delves deeply into the news and politics of its times, presenting enough historical background to fully explore the underlying controversies affecting the Clinton family and their choices.

"Sidebars of information and black and white photos liberally peppered throughout the account offer visual reinforcement to the exploration, lending it the feel and tone of both a gossip column and political piece - something that probes not just Clinton interactions but the D.C. political milieu as a whole.

"The result may appear weighty, sporting over five hundred pages, but is an absorbing, top recommendation for readers of both biographical and political pieces who will thoroughly enjoy this spirited, lively, and thought-provoking analysis."

—THE MIDWEST BOOK REVIEW

***

Shortly after its release in December of 2015, this book received a literary award (Runner-up to Best Biography of the Year) from the New England Book Festival. As stated by a spokesperson for the Awards, "The New England Book Festival is an annual competition honoring excellence in books, with particular focus on projects that deserve closer attention from the academic community. Congratulations to Blood Moon and its authors, especially Darwin Porter, for his highly entertaining analysis of Clinton's double-barreled presidential regime, and the sometimes hysterical overreaction of their enemies."

BILL & HILLARY—SO THIS IS THAT THING CALLED LOVE
Softcover, with photos. ISBN 978-1-936003-47-1

BURT REYNOLDS
PUT THE PEDAL TO THE METAL
How a Nude Centerfold Sex Symbol Seduced Hollywood

In the 1970s and '80s, Burt Reynolds represented a new breed of movie star.

BURT REYNOLDS

PUT THE PEDAL TO THE METAL:

How a Nude Centerfold Sex Symbol Seduced Hollywood

Leading Ladies & Box Office Smashes from a Good Ol' Boy

Another Outrageous Celebrity Exposé by
Darwin Porter & Danforth Prince

Charming and relentlessly macho, he was a good old Southern boy who made hearts throb and audiences laugh. He was Burt Reynolds, a football hero and a guy you might have shared some jokes with in a redneck bar. After an impressive but tormented career, rivers of negative publicity, a self-admitted history of bad choices, and a spectacular fall from Hollywood grace, he died in Jupiter, Florida, at the age of 82 in September of 2018.

For five years, both in terms of earnings and popularity, he was the number one box office star in the world. *Smokey and the Bandit* (1977) became the biggest-grossing car-chase film of all time. As he put it, perhaps as a means of bolstering his image, "I like nothing better than making love to some of the most beautiful women in the world." Perhaps he was referring to his romantic and sexual involvements with dozens of celebrities from New Hollywood. More unusual dalliances occurred with Marilyn Monroe, whom he once picked up on his way to the Actors Studio in New York City. Love with another VIP came in the form of that "Sweetheart of the G.I.s," Dinah Shore, sparking chatter. "I appreciate older women," he once said in a moment of self-revelation. According to Sally Field, "Burt still lives in my heart." But then she expressed relief that, because of his recent death, he never read what she'd said about him in her memoir.

Men liked him too: He played poker with Frank Sinatra; shared boozy nights with John Wayne; intercepted a "pass" from closeted Spencer Tracy; talked "penis size" with Mark Wahlberg; went "wench-hunting" with Johnny Carson; and threatened to kill Marlon Brando, to whom his appearance was often compared. He also hung out with Bette Davis. ("I always had a thing for her.")

His least happy (some said "most poisonous") marriage—to Loni Anderson—was rife with dramas played out more in the tabloids than in the boudoir. According to Reynolds, "She's vain, she's a rotten mother, she sleeps around, and she spent all my money."

This biography—the first comprehensive overview of the "redneck icon" ever published—reveals the joys and sorrows of a movie star who thrived in, but who was then almost buried by the pressures and insecurities of the New Hollywood. A tribute to "truck stop" America, it's about the accelerated life of a courageous spirit who "Put His Pedal to the Metal" with humor, high jinx, and pizzazz. He predicted his own death: "Soon, I'll be racing a hotrod in Valhalla in my cowboy hat and a pair of aviators." On his tombstone, he wanted it writ: "He was not the best actor in the world, but he was the best Burt Reynolds in the world."

PETER O'TOOLE

HELLRAISER, SEXUAL OUTLAW, IRISH REBEL

When it was published, early in 2015, this book was widely publicized in the *Daily Mail,* the *New York Daily News,* the *New York Post,* the *Midwest Book Review, The Express (London), The Globe,* the *National Enquirer,* and in equivalent publications worldwide

One of the world's most admired (and brilliant) actors, Peter O'Toole wined and wenched his way through a labyrinth of sexual and interpersonal betrayals, sometimes with disastrous results. Away from the stage and screen, where such films as *Becket* and *Lawrence of Arabia,* made film history, his life was filled with drunken, debauched nights and edgy sexual experimentations, most of which were never openly examined in the press. A hellraiser, he shared wild times with his "best blokes" Richard Burton and Richard Harris. Peter Finch, also his close friend, once invited him to join him in sharing the pleasures of his mistress, Vivien Leigh.

"My father, a bookie, moved us to the Mick community of Leeds," O'Toole once told a reporter. "We were very poor, but I was born an Irishman, which accounts for my gift of gab, my unruly behavior, my passionate devotion to women and the bottle, and my loathing of any authority figure."

Author Robert Sellers described O'Toole's boyhood neighborhood. "Three of his playmates went on to be hanged for murder; one strangled a girl in a lovers' quarrel; one killed a man during a robbery; another cut up a warden in South Africa with a pair of shears. It was a heavy bunch."

Peter O'Toole's hell-raising life story has never been told, until now. Hot and uncensored, from a writing team which, even prior to O'Toole's death in 2013, had been collecting under-the-radar info about him for years, this book has everything you ever wanted to know about how THE LION navigated his way through the boudoirs of the Entertainment Industry IN WINTER, Spring, Summer, and a dissipated Autumn as well.

Blood Moon has ripped away the imperial robe, scepter, and crown usually associated with this quixotic problem child of the British Midlands. Provocatively uncensored, this illusion-shattering overview of Peter O'Toole's hell-raising (or at least very naughty) and demented life is unique in the history of publishing.

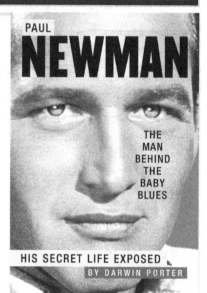

JAMES DEAN
TOMORROW NEVER COMES

HONORING THE 60TH ANNIVERSARY OF HIS VIOLENT AND EARLY DEATH

America's most enduring and legendary symbol of young, enraged rebellion, James Dean continues into the 21st Century to capture the imagination of the world.

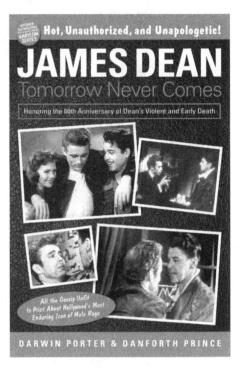

After one of his many flirtations with Death, which caught up with him when he was a celebrity-soaked 24-year-old, he said, "If a man can live after he dies, then maybe he's a great man." Today, bars from Nigeria to Patagonia are named in honor of this international, spectacularly self-destructive movie star icon.

Migrating from the dusty backroads of Indiana to center stage in the most formidable boudoirs of Hollywood, his saga is electrifying.

A strikingly handsome heart-throb, Dean is a study in contrasts: Tough but tender, brutal but remarkably sensitive; he was a reckless hellraiser badass who could revert to a little boy in bed.

A rampant bisexual, he claimed that he didn't want to go through life "with one hand tied behind my back." He demonstrated that during bedroom trysts with Marilyn Monroe, Rock Hudson, Elizabeth Taylor, Paul Newman, Natalie Wood, Shelley Winters, Marlon Brando, Steve McQueen, Ursula Andress, Montgomery Clift, Pier Angeli, Tennessee Williams, Susan Strasberg, Tallulah Bankhead, and FBI director J. Edgar Hoover.

Woolworth heiress Barbara Hutton, one of the richest and most dissipated women of her era, wanted to make him her toy boy.

Tomorrow Never Comes is the most penetrating look at James Dean to have emerged from the wreckage of his Porsche Spyder in 1955.

Before setting out on his last ride, he said, "I feel life too intensely to bear living it." *Tomorrow Never Comes* presents a damaged but beautiful soul.

JAMES DEAN—TOMORROW NEVER COMES
DARWIN PORTER & DANFORTH PRINCE
Softcover, with photos. ISBN 978-1-936003-49-5

Of the many male stars of Golden Age Hollywood, Kirk Douglas became the final survivor, the last icon of a fabled, optimistic era that the world will never see again. When he celebrated his birthday in 2016, a headline read: LEGENDARY HOLLYWOOD HORNDOG TURNS 100.

He was both a charismatic actor and a man of uncommon force and vigor. His restless and volcanic spirit is reflected both in his films and through his many sexual conquests.

Douglas was the son of Russian-Jewish immigrants, his father a collector and seller of rags. After service in the Navy during World War II, he hit Hollywood, oozing masculinity and charm. Conquering Tinseltown and bedding its leading ladies, he became the personification of the American dream, moving from obscurity and (literally) rags to riches and major-league fame.

The *Who's Who* cast of characters roaring through his life included not only a daunting list of Hollywood goddesses, but the town's most colossal male talents and egos, too. They included his kindred hellraiser and best buddy Burt Lancaster, John Wayne, Henry Fonda, Billy Wilder, Laurence Olivier, Rock Hudson, and a future U.S. President, Ronald Reagan, when winning the highest office in the land was virtually unthinkable.

Over the decades, he immortalized himself in film after film, delivering, like a Trojan, one memorable performance after another. He was at home in *film noir*, as a western gunslinger, as an adventurer (in both ancient and modern sagas), as a juggler, as Tennessee Williams' "gentleman caller," as a Greek super-hero from Homer's *Odyssey*, and as roguish sailor in the Jules Verne yarn, exploring the mysteries of the ocean's depths.

En route to his status as a myth and legend, his performances reflected both his personal pain and the brutalization of the characters he played, too. In *Champion* (1949), he was beaten to a fatal bloody pulp. As the sleazy, heartless reporter in *Ace in the Hole* (1951), he was stabbed with a knife in his gut. As Van Gogh in *Lust for Life* (1956), he writhed in emotional agony and unrequited love before slicing off his ear with a razor. His World War I movie, *Paths of Glory* (1957) grows more profound over the years. He lost an eye in *The Vikings* (1958), and, as the Thracian slave leading a revolt against Roman legions in *Spartacus* (1960), he was crucified.

All of this is brought out, with photos, in this remarkable testimonial to the last hero of Hollywood's cinematic and swashbuckling Golden Age, an inspiring testimonial to the values and core beliefs of an America that's Gone With the Wind, yet lovingly remembered as a time when it, in many ways, was truly great.

Hugh Hefner, the most iconic Playboy in human history, was a visionary, an empire-builder, and a pajama-clad pipe-smoker with a pre-coital grin.

In 1953, he published his first edition of *Playboy* with money borrowed from his puritanical, Nebraska-born mother. Marilyn Monroe appeared on the cover, with her nude calendar inside.

Rebelling against his strict upbringing, he lost his virginity at the age of 22.

His magazine, punctuated with nudes and studded with articles by major literary figures, reached its zenith at eight million readers. As a "tasteful pornographer," Hef became a cultural warrior, fighting government censorship all the way to the U.S. Supreme Court. As the years and his notoriety progressed, he became an advocate of abortion, LGBT equality, and the legalization of pot. Eventually, he engaged in "pubic wars" with Bob Guccione, the flamboyant founder of Penthouse, which cut into Hef's sales.

Lauded by millions of avid readers, he was denounced as "the father of sex addiction," "a huckster," "a lecherous low-brow feeder of our vices," "a misogynist," and, near the end of his life, "a symbol of priapic senility."

During his heyday, some of the biggest male stars in Hollywood, including Warren Beatty, Sammy Davis, Jr., Mick Jagger, and Jack Nicholson, came to frolic behind Hef's guarded walls, stripping nude in the hot tub grotto before sampling the rotating beds upstairs. Even a future U.S. president came to call. "Donald Trump had an appreciation of Bunny tail," Hef said.

Hefner's last Viagra-fueled marriage was to a beautiful blonde, Crystal Harris, 60 years his junior. "There's nothing wrong in a man marrying a girl who could be his great-granddaughter," he was famously quoted as saying.

This ground-breaking biography, the latest in Blood Moon's string of outrageously unvarnished myth-busters, was the first published since Hefner's death at the age of 91 in 2017. It's a provocative saga, rich in tantalizing, often shocking detail. Not recommended for the sanctimonious or the faint of heart, and loaded with ironic, little-known details about the trendsetter's epic challenges and the solutions he devised.

PLAYBOY'S HUGH HEFNER
EMPIRE OF SKIN

by Darwin Porter and Danforth Prince
978-1-936003-59-4

Blood Moon Productions proudly announces its compilation of lurid, vintage scandals from the Golden Age of Camelot.

It's in the form of a new edition of Darwin Porter's classic 2014 biography of the most watched, most enigmatic, and most controversial woman of the 20th Century,

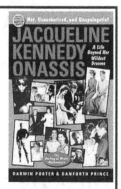

JACQUELINE KENNEDY ONASSIS
HER TUMULTOUS LIFE & HER LOVE AFFAIRS

JACKIE INVADES WASHINGTON BABYLON, EUROPE, and BEYOND

This is a new edition of the most compelling compilation of cash-soaked ambition, sexual indiscretion, and social embarrassment about a former first lady ever published,

Available now from **Ingram** and from **Amazon.com** worldwide, in honor of one of America's favorite Valentines

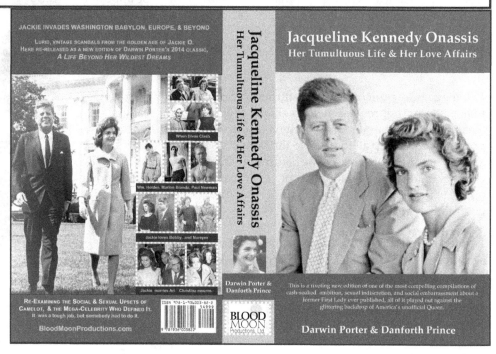

JAQUELINE KENNEDY ONASSIS
HER TUMULTUOUS LIFE & HER LOVE AFFAIRS
ISBN 978-1-936003-82-2   Originally published in 2014 as
A LIFE BEYOND HER WILDEST DREAMS by Darwin Porter & Danforth Prince
700 fascinating pages with hundreds of photos

Conceived in direct and sometimes defiant contrast to the avalanche of more breathlessly respectful testimonials to the life and legacy of "America's Queen," this book is the latest installment in Blood Moon's endlessly irreverent MAGNOLIA HOUSE series.

RE-EXAMINING THE SOCIAL AND SEXUAL UPSETS OF CAMELOT AND THE MEGA-CELEBRITY WHO DEFINED IT.

IT WAS A TOUGH JOB, BUT SOMEBODY HAD TO DO IT.

CPSIA information can be obtained
at www.ICGtesting.com
Printed in the USA
JSHW032331140822
29190JS00005B/53